Cause Lawyering and the State in a Global Era

OXFORD SOCIO-LEGAL STUDIES

General Editor: Keith Hawkins, Reader in Law and Society, and Fellow and Tutor in Law of Oriel College, Oxford.

Editorial Board: John Baldwin, Director of the Institute of Judicial Administration, University of Birmingham; William L. F. Felstiner, Professor of Sociology, University of California–Santa Barbara; Denis Galligan, Professor of Socio-Legal Studies and Director of the Centre for Socio-Legal Studies, Oxford; Sally Lloyd-Bostock, Senior Research Fellow, Centre for Socio-Legal Studies, Oxford; Doreen McBarnet, Senior Research Fellow, Centre for Socio-Legal Studies, Oxford; Simon Roberts, Professor of Law, London School of Economics and Political Science.

International Advisory Board: John Braithwaite, Australian National University; Robert Cooter, University of California–Berkeley; Bryant Garth, American Bar Foundation; Volkmar Gessner, University of Bremen; Vittorio Olgiati, University of Milan; Martin Partington, University of Bristol.

Oxford Socio-Legal Studies is a series of books exploring the role of law in society for both an academic and a wider readership. The series publishes theoretical and empirically informed work by social scientists and lawyers, from the United Kingdom and elsewhere, that advances understanding of the social reality of law and legal processes.

NEW TITLES IN THE SERIES

World Jury Systems
Neil Vidmar

The Justice of Islam: Comparative Perspectives on Islamic Law and Society
Lawrence Rosen

Just Lawyers: Regulation and Access to Justice
Christine Parker

CAUSE LAWYERING AND THE STATE IN A GLOBAL ERA

Edited by

AUSTIN SARAT & STUART SCHEINGOLD

UNIVERSITY PRESS

2001

OXFORD
UNIVERSITY PRESS

Oxford New York
Athens Auckland Bangkok Bogotá Buenos Aires Calcutta
Cape Town Chennai Dar es Salaam Delhi Florence Hong Kong
Istanbul Karachi Kuala Lumpur Madras Madrid Melbourne
Mexico City Mumbai Nairobi Paris São Paulo Shanghai Singapore
Taipei Tokyo Toronto Warsaw

and associated companies in
Berlin Ibadan

Copyright © 2001 by Oxford University Press, Inc.

Published by Oxford University Press, Inc
198 Madison Avenue, New York, New York 10016

Oxford is a registered trademark of Oxford University Press

All rights reserved. No part of this publication may be reproduced,
stored in a retrieval system, or transmitted, in any form or by any means,
electronic, mechanical, photocopying, recording, or otherwise,
without the prior permission of Oxford University Press.

Library of Congress Cataloging-in-Publication Data
Cause lawyering and the state in a global era / edited by Austin Sarat, Stuart Scheingold.
    p. cm.—(Oxford socio-legal studies)
  Includes bibliographical references and index.
  ISBN 0-19-514116-4; ISBN 0-19-514117-2 (pbk)
    1. Public interest law. 2. Lawyers. 3. National state. 4. Globalization. I. Sarat, Austin.
  II. Scheingold, Stuart A. III. Series.
  K118.P82 C38 2001
  340'.115—dc21   00-038593

9 8 7 6 5 4 3 2 1

Printed in the United States of America
on acid-free paper

*In memory of Nellam Tiruchelvam,
who dedicated his life to the
struggle for human rights*

Acknowledgments

This project has been, from its inception, a genuine collaboration, first between the two editors, and then among all of the participants. We are grateful to the extraordinary group of scholars who assembled to pool their efforts to understand cause lawyering for their energy, interest, and insight. We would like to thank Terrence Halliday, formerly chair of the Working Group on the Comparative Study of the Legal Profession, for his continuing encouragement and Michael McCann for his helpful commentary on this volume. Support for this project was provided by a grant from the Program on Law and Social Science of the National Science Foundation (SES-9818366) and from the Rockefeller Foundation. We want to acknowledge the wonderful hospitality provided by the Rockefeller Foundation's Bellagio Study and Conference Center, which hosted a meeting of the cause-lawyering project in June 1999.

Contents

Contributors, xi

1. *State Transformation, Globalization, and the Possibilities of Cause Lawyering:* An Introduction, 3
   AUSTIN SARAT AND STUART A. SCHEINGOLD

I. Global Developments/Local Contests: New Opportunities/New Challenges

2. *Two Worlds of Ghanaian Cause Lawyers,* 35
   LUCIE WHITE

3. *From the Fight for Legal Rights to the Promotion of Human Rights:* Israeli and Palestinian Cause Lawyers in the Trenches of Globalization, 68
   LISA HAJJAR

4. *Taking on Goliath:* Why Personal Injury Litigation May Represent the Future of Transnational Cause Lawyering, 96
   ANNE BLOOM

5. *Cause Lawyering in the Shadow of the State:* A U.S. Immigration Example, 117
   SUSAN BIBLER COUTIN

II. Globalization and State Transformation: Patterns of Conflict and Cooperation between Cause Lawyers and the State

6. *Cause Lawyers in a Cold Climate:* The Impact(s) of Globalization on the United Kingdom, 143
   ANDREW BOON

7. *State Transformation and the Struggle for Symbolic Capital:* Cause Lawyers, the Organized Bar, and Capital Punishment in the United States, 186
   AUSTIN SARAT

8. *Cause Lawyers, Clients, and the State:* Congress as a Forum for Cause Lawyering during the Enactment of the Americans with Disabilities Act, 211
   NETA ZIV

9. *The Global Language of Human Rights:* Patterns of Cooperation between State and Civil Rights Lawyers in Israel, 244
   YOAV DOTAN

10. *Legal Advocacy, Global Engagement:* The Impact of Land Claims Advocacy on the Recognition of Property Rights in the South African Constitution, 264
    HEINZ KLUG

11. *State-Oriented and Community-Oriented Lawyering for a Cause:* A Tale of Two Strategies, 287
    RONEN SHAMIR AND NETA ZIV

III. The Globalization of Cause Lawyering

12. *Latin American Cause-Lawyering Networks,* 307
    STEPHEN MEILI

13. *The Politics of Imported Rights:* Transplantation and Transformation in an Israeli Environmental Cause-Lawyering Organization, 334
    NOGA MORAG-LEVINE

14. *Constructing Law Out of Power:* Investing in Human Rights as an Alternative Political Strategy, 354
    YVES DEZALAY AND BRYANT G. GARTH

15. *Cause Lawyering and Democracy in Transnational Perspective:* A Postscript, 382
    STUART A. SCHEINGOLD

Index, 407

Contributors

ANNE BLOOM is a graduate student in political science at the University of Washington.

ANDREW BOON is Head of the School of Law at the University of Westminster, London.

SUSAN BIBLER COUTIN is Assistant Professor of Criminal Justice at California State University–Los Angeles.

YVES DEZALAY is a Director of the Centre National de la Recherche Scientifique.

YOAV DOTAN is Senior Lecturer at the Faculty of Law at Hebrew University, Jerusalem.

BRYANT G. GARTH is Director of the American Bar Foundation.

LISA HAJJAR is Assistant Professor of Sociology at Morehouse College.

STEPHEN MEILI is Clinical Associate Professor of Law at the University of Wisconsin.

HEINZ KLUG is Assistant Professor of Law at the University of Wisconsin.

NOGA MORAG-LEVINE is Assistant Professor of Political Science at the University of Michigan.

AUSTIN SARAT is William Nelson Cromwell Professor of Jurisprudence and Political Science at Amherst College.

STUART A. SCHEINGOLD is Professor of Political Science at the University of Washington.

RONEN SHAMIR is Professor of Sociology at Tel-Aviv University.

LUCIE WHITE is Louis A. Horvitz Professor of Law at Harvard Law School.

NETA ZIV is a JSD candidate at Stanford Law School and a lecturer at Tel-Aviv University Law Faculty.

Cause Lawyering and the State in a Global Era

CHAPTER 1

State Transformation, Globalization, and the Possibilities of Cause Lawyering
An Introduction

AUSTIN SARAT AND STUART A. SCHEINGOLD

Just as the formation of nation-states was one of the defining characteristics of an earlier era, their rapid and often radical transformation is one of the defining characteristics of ours. Under pressures variously labeled transnationalism and globalization, state forms throughout the world alter and adapt, adding new functions, shedding old ones, refining institutional processes, developing new alliances within and beyond national borders, sometimes increasing democratic tendencies, sometimes weakening them. In response to those pressures and the alterations and adaptations of states, local and subnational forces assert themselves, sometimes challenging the state, sometimes working with and within it. As a result, increasingly scholars in many different fields are examining complex global-local linkages and are attentive to the manifestations of global phenomena at the local level (see, e.g., Kearney, 1995).

All of this is by now something of a familiar story. Yet this is not true for scholars of, or scholarship on, the legal profession. Rarely has research on the legal profession taken the connection of lawyers and the formation and transformation of states as its subject (for an important exception, see Halliday and Karpik, 1997). While state transformation and globalization clearly influence, and are influenced by, law and lawyers, with two notable exceptions (Dezalay and Garth, 1996; Halliday and Karpik, 1997), available research tends to ignore these interdependencies. Instead, as Terrence Halliday (1998a: 3) puts it, most research on lawyers focuses "on the internal organization and behavior of legal professions, overwhelmingly attends to single countries and, within national studies; it is the economic organization and behavior of professions, especially the market for legal services, that has captured most scholarly attention."

Similarly, the literatures on state transformation and globalization, again with a few of important exceptions (Trubek, et al., 1994; Santos, 1995; Keck and Sikkink, 1997), ignore law and lawyers almost entirely and tend to treat the rule of law as something of a taken-for-granted black box.[1] The result is that not only are lawyers neglected but so, too, is the wealth of research that decenters law and documents its pervasive presence and constitutive power as social practice throughout civil society, culture, politics, and the economy (McCann, 1994: 6–9). This volume is intended to respond to the situation by connecting research on one kind of lawyering, what we have elsewhere (Sarat and Scheingold, 1998) labeled cause lawyering, to the analysis of the state and state transformation in a global era.

Our earlier work concentrated on cause lawyering as both an intellectual construct and a social process (Sarat and Scheingold, 1998). In the terms of social science, cause lawyering was the dependent variable—with our search directed primarily at identifying the political and professional circumstances that contributed to and/or inhibited its growth in a variety of sites around the world. By incorporating globalization and state transformation, with a particular emphasis on democratization, into the analysis of cause lawyering, we contribute to an assessment of the significance of that kind of lawyering in terms of two of the defining social and political developments of our era.[2]

In this era state power flows outward *via globalization* to transnational forces and institutions, and it flows inward *via democratization* to subnational institutions and social movements.[3] Both bring new pressures to bear on, and complicate, state action. Both play out in different ways in different nations and in the different arenas of the state. *Cause Lawyering and the State in a Global Era* brings together contextually sensitive, cross-cultural, and comparative research that analyzes the ways in which cause lawyering is influencing, and being influenced by, the disaggregation of state power associated with democratization and globalization.

Independently and in combination with one another, democratization and globalization confront cause lawyers with new issues and new burdens while altering their resources and their tactical and strategic options. As a result, cause lawyering faces a welter of challenges, opportunities, and imperatives that are taken up in this volume. By investigating how cause lawyers respond, this research marks an important advance for cross-cultural and comparative research on the legal profession generally and also contributes to scholarship on state transformation and globalization.

The Disaggregated State

The context for this inquiry into cause lawyering, thus, is defined by two processes, globalization and state transformation/democratization and the way that each in its own way, and in combination with the another, contributes to the redistribution or reconfiguration of state power. In our analysis, we want to honor the analytical distinctions between globalization and state transformation while at the same time recognizing their intense interactions with one another. To an important extent globalization and at least one form of state transformation, namely democratization, work in tandem—encroaching on state power from above (globalization) and from below (democratization), but that is only one part of the story.

Globalization may, in some circumstances, promote democratization but only a rather limited form of democracy. Accordingly, advocates of democratization often find globalization more of a problem than a solution. Additionally, to the extent that globalization does foster democratic transformations of states and greater democratization in already democratic states, it is as an incidental by-product rather than as an intended consequence. This is because globalization, as we will argue below, is driven by, and gives priority to, the economic rationality of corporate capitalism. Despite some convergence, then, democratization and globalization follow different trajectories and are at least as likely to work at cross-purposes as to be mutually reinforcing. They may push cause lawyers in different directions, the one creating opportunities and possibilities as the other poses obstacles and imposes barriers.

Globalization and State Transformation

In the abstract, globalization has many plausible meanings relating to the recent intensification of worldwide social relations which link distant localities in such a way that local happenings are shaped by events occurring many miles away and vice versa (Giddens, 1990:64). Consider culture, for example, where globalization results in the penetration of even the most closed societies by common symbolic forms (Appadurai, 1996). As Susan Silbey (1997: 212) puts it:

> [R]ap music from American urban ghettos is played in the shops in Paris and on the streets in Budapest, portable telephones manufactured in Finland adorn the hips of stock brokers and manual laborers from Santiago to Sidney, from Cancun to Cape Town, and television stations around the globe fill their schedules with the likes of *Melrose Place* while the office workers from Moscow to Buenos Aires munch on Big Macs and Fries.

The driving force behind this diffusion of culture and the hallmark of globalization as it is generally understood is the worldwide spread of corporate capitalism and neoliberal values (Chase-Dunn, 1991). In other words, globalization should not be equated with the construction of an open, apolitical, and beneficent global village (Jameson, 1998). Instead, it is first and foremost a vast project in political economy that is restructuring the global order in ways that maximize its compatibility with the values and interests of multinational corporate enterprise and reorient dominant political ideologies.

The global economic system has been institutionalized in organizations like the World Bank, the International Monetary Fund, the World Trade Organization, and the North American Free Trade Area, to name only a few. These institutions seek to impose the discipline of the market on economies that have been, it is claimed, corrupted by crony capitalism, welfare state social policy, and other autarchic tendencies. Accordingly, the mission of institutional messengers of globalized capitalism is to dismantle barriers to the free flow of populations, commerce, information, and especially capital—all in the service of economic growth and industrial development.

To an extent hardly foreseeable ten or fifteen years ago, this venture has been successful. Thus Edward Luttwak contrasts what he calls "turbo capitalism" with the "strictly controlled capitalism" of the postwar period (1999: 27). Whereas controlled capitalism used regulatory mechanisms to provide social safety nets (Western Europe); to guarantee full employment (Japan); and to protect against "disruptive" competition (United States) (ibid.: 29), the goal of turbo-capitalism is to be "liberated from government regulation, unchecked by effective trade unions, unfettered by sentimental concerns over the fate of employees or communities, unrestrained by customs barriers or investment restrictions and molested as little as possible by taxation" (ibid.: 27). Among the material consequences of thus unleashing the forces of corporate capitalism has been massive expansion of private wealth accompanied by decreasing rates of public investment, intensified patterns of privilege and deprivation, and a growing gap between rich and poor (Sassen, 1998: chap. 7).

These material changes have significant social and political repercussions. Job markets in industrial and industrializing states have become more volatile as a result of corporate downsizing, involuntary underemployment, and shifts from manufacturing to the service sector. In addition, because the service sector tends to be sharply divided between low-wage, unskilled retail jobs and well-paid, high-skill jobs in technology, the job market is increasingly segmented. The result has been a return to a kind of social Darwinism, bringing to the "losers" the pain of downward mobility and to the work force in general the burdens of unstable work environments and career paths.[4] "Perpetual insecurity becomes," as Nikolas Rose puts it, "the normal form of labor" (1999: 158).

The unsettling ups and downs of this brave new world of corporate capitalism have, however, been legitimated by the widespread dissemination of neoliberal values. These values give priority to the aggregation of private wealth and to individualistic conceptions of freedom at the expense of equality and social welfare. Rose characterizes this as a shift from the social state, to advanced liberal, values—leading, in effect, to "a reconstruction of subjectivity":

> National and international competitiveness was recoded, at least in part, in terms of the psychological, dispositional, and aspirational capacities of those who make up the labour force. Thus each individual is solicited as a potential ally of economic success. (Ibid.: 162)

A new emphasis on empowering individuals and on holding them responsible for the choices they make goes hand in hand with the decline of loyalty. "By accelerating structural change," as Luttwak sees it, "turbo-capitalism rewards agility as much as competence" (Luttwak, 1999: 85–86).

In addition, neoliberalism seeks to transform states by introducing market values into public processes. Whereas once laissez-faire meant keeping the state out of the market, today neoliberalism means bringing the market into the state and transforming citizenship into another means for expressing and obtaining preferences. Just as competition is good within the market so too competition within and among state agencies is, in the neoliberal pantheon, something to be encouraged.

In sum, globalization opens up state processes to far-reaching forces and leads to reconfigurations of state power. As these global forces impinge on the state, cause lawyering itself is transformed. Cause lawyers both serve and respond to global forces. They become engaged in new local contests over global economic and political developments. As states take on new forms and new values, new possibilities for working within, as well as against, the state open up (see Shamir, 1998). Moreover, in a global political economy, cause lawyering itself can be and is being globalized. New networks and connections emerge, new resources for sharing information and obtaining advice open up. Lawyering no longer can be contained by or within national boundaries (Halliday, 1998b).

Yet efforts by cause lawyers to take advantage of these changes embroil them in controversies: Are they being co-opted by corporate capitalism? Do the international institutions of globalization serve primarily to advance Western interests and ideas, thus promoting neoimperialism and neocolonialism? In response, can cause lawyers develop new strategies of legitimation? As it engages these questions, the research reported in this volume reveals opportunities and challenges posed by globalization for cause lawyers serving a variety causes in different national contexts.

Democratization and State Transformation

Clearly the globalized political economy is exerting a transformative impact on states. It does so directly through norms established and imposed by the formal institutions of the global order. But globalization also works indirectly through the investment decisions of corporate enterprise—decisions that influence the distribution of power between and among officials and unofficial political actors. States respond in a variety of ways to the pressures of globalization—developing new governing ideologies, increasing some commitments while backing away from others, rearranging institutional forms, etc.

But state transformation is not a one-way street. Each state has its own distinctive character, structure and ideology, and trajectory—all the product of deeply embedded historical, cultural, and material factors. Transformation, for example, proceeds differently in corporatist, as opposed to pluralist, states; in centralized, as opposed to decentralized, states; in one-party authoritarian, as opposed to multi-party, states with electoral accountability; and so on. There are, in short, inertial and idiosyncratic forces at work internally that moderate and shape the impact of globalization.

Nevertheless, throughout the world, one of the most important dimensions of state transformation in a global era is democratization. One indicator of this development is the fact that democracy, at least in the formal, procedural sense, has in recent years been gaining ground in many modernizing states. The so-called third wave (Huntington, 1991) of emergent democratic institutions has been spearheaded first by the collapse of communist regimes in Eastern and Central Europe, with the collateral discrediting of Marxist-Leninist approaches to modernization. More recently, the Asian economic crisis has discredited the authoritarian capitalism of that region. Modernizing states around the world are now, with varying degrees of enthusiasm, pursuing neoliberal paths to economic expansion. In the political realm, this has often but not always meant, as Rueschemeyer and his colleagues have pointed out, the introduction of "free and fair elections of representatives with universal and equal suffrage." It has also often but not always meant transferring "responsibility of the state apparatus to the elected parliament (possibly complemented by direct election of the head of the executive)." Finally, states have acknowledged the importance of "the freedoms of expression and association as well as the protection of individual rights against arbitrary state action" (Rueschemeyer et al., 1992: 45).[5]

This last element of the new politics of modernization moves into the social realm in general and into the development of civil society, in particular. An "organized social life that is voluntary, self-generating, (largely) self-supporting, autonomous from the state [although protected by it], ... [and] bound by a legal order" (Diamond, 1994: 5) and receptive to corporate enterprise are all seen as preconditions to successful democratic development.[6] In short, it is more and more widely recognized and accepted that there are synergies among the needs of capitalism, the rule of law, and at least partial democratization of the political process (Halliday and Karpik, 1997) such that transformative interactions among the global, the national, and local are influencing the course of democratization.

Especially in modernizing states, reform of existing institutional arrangements may occur under the pressure of an overt directive (e.g., conditions for a loan from the I.M.F.) or more subtle forms of adaptive pressure. But in these settings the relations of globalization and democratization are partial and potentially problematic (Robinson, 1995). Rueschemeyer and his colleagues (1992) argue, for example, that the link is contingent and, indeed, that democracy develops as a reaction against, rather than a consequence of, the global spread of capitalism.

> It is not an overall structural correspondence between capitalism and democracy that explains the rise and persistence of democracy.... Rather we conclude capi-

talist development is associated with democracy because it transforms class structure, strengthening the working and middle classes and weakening the landed upper class. It was not the capitalist market nor capitalists as the new dominant force, but rather *the contradictions of capitalism* that advanced the cause of democracy. (Rueschemeyer et al., 1992: 7; italics added)

The scholarly literature on globalization reveals much the same kind of contingent and antagonistic encounters between neoliberal and democratic values in advanced capitalist, as in developing, economies (Greider, 1997; Held, 1995).

Of course, democratization is itself a contested concept. The liberal democratic institutions that are making increasing headway in modernizing states are just one form of democratic ordering. Democratic aspirations often extend well beyond electoral accountability, representative institutions, and legality to more participatory institutions and to the pursuit of social and economic justice. Thus, democratic beachheads in many modernizing states may seem to some to be sufficient, albeit tenuous, realizations of democratic ideals, while others may see them as only timid steps in what may, or may not, be as the right direction. Roughly this same debate characterizes democratic politics in advanced capitalist states, and, for this reason, there are those who see the current emphasis on formal or procedural democracy as leaving space for transformation in an even more democratic direction.

In so-called advanced capitalist societies, basic democratic institutions are well entrenched but coming under increasing pressure. To begin with, a deterioration of civil society is signaled by declining rates of participation in elections and in civic and political associations—all, some would say, indicative of a civil society losing its vigor (Putnam, 1995 and 1996). In addition, the encroachment of the state on civil society is threatening its autonomy (Cohen, 1987; Rose, 1996a and 1996b; Donzelot, 1997). A number of other structural problems are also plaguing advanced capitalist states. The very scale of government seems to overwhelm efforts at democratic management (Habermas, 1986). So, too, do the "contradictions of the welfare state" which pit the preconditions for economic growth against the fiscal resources required for inclusionary forms of social and economic citizenship (Offe, 1984). As a consequence, a certain paralysis of democratic institutions has been detected and with it an inability adequately to confront the complex and divisive problems facing advanced capitalist societies (Garland, 1996; Lowi, 1979).

Put another way, a restricted vision of democracy that is confined to competitive elections, the rule of law, etc., is one thing—clearly compatible with the "advanced liberalism" (Rose, 1999) of "turbo-capitalism" (Luttwak, 1999). On the other hand, a more robust vision of democracy that emphasizes egalitarian values and participatory institutions, and is responsive to grassroots social movements, is quite another. These latter developments are much more threatening to corporate capitalism and thus likely to encounter opposition from entrenched interests in both modernizing and advanced capitalist states.

For cause lawyers, what this means is that globalization and state transformation may be a mixed blessing. In some contexts they may help to provide a political structure wherein minimal rights claims and legal defenses against abuses of state power become meaningful. In other contexts, they may erode support for the kinds of social changes which these lawyers, and the movements with which they are affiliated, seek to advance.

In modernizing societies, where democratic institutions are rudimentary and fragile, the issue becomes whether and how cause lawyering itself plays a role in the process of converting the contradictions of capitalism into opportunities for democratic transformation. In liberal democratic states, cause lawyering is in a much more favorable and secure position than in settings where modernization is still a work-in-progress (Sarat and Scheingold, 1998). Yet even in advanced capitalist societies the position of cause lawyers, in recent decades, has grown more problematic. Long-established social, economic, and legal rights are under pressure (Simon, 1997; Garland, 1996). Cause lawyers face the dual burden of greater need and dwindling resources (Scheingold and Bloom, 1998), which occurs with the triumph of neoliberalism.

In other words, the process of disaggregating and reconfiguring state power leads directly to the question of whose norms and cultural prescriptions will prevail. Whether at the level of supranational institutions or reformed domestic ones, globalization alters competition and contestation over norms, over the content of legal regulations and standards (Cheah, 1997). It opens up the terrain of competition to new forces and rearranges that terrain to favor some interests over others.[7] In sum, while globalization contributes to democratization by way of political accountability, civil society, and the rule of law, there is reason to believe that this contribution is conditional, derivative, and arguably unreliable.

Cause Lawyering and the State in a Global Era is directed at trying to understand how cause lawyers are implicated in, and responding to, these developments. We want to explore the distinctive challenges and opportunities facing cause lawyering in this era of globalization, human rights, and state transformation. As Shamir (1998) notes, most research on cause lawyers posits that their work comes from below and is addressed upward to state institutions. But state institutions, under global economic and human rights pressures, are hardly unitary. In both modernizing and advanced capitalist settings, the looser coupling of the agencies and institutions of fragmenting states that results from both economic and political globalization provides multiple points of access to state officials and, thus, to influencing state policies for cause lawyers. As a result, Shamir (1998) urges us to recognize that cause lawyers work in a professional domain that cuts across the state/society divide.

Human Rights and State Transformation

Paralleling globalization as a factor in the transformation of states, while softening some of its insistent economic imperatives, are newly emergent international and supranational human rights regimes.[8] Today governments everywhere claim to believe in and respect the dignity of their citizens (Teson, 1985; Parekh, 1993). As a result, the *language* of human rights, if not human rights themselves, is nearly universal (Weissbrodt, 1988).[9] "The past few decades," Richard Wilson (1996: 1) notes, "have witnessed the inexorable rise of the application of international human rights law as well as the extension of a wider public discourse on human rights, to the point where human rights could be seen as one of the most globalized political values of our times."[10]

Yet, as the concept of rights has been deployed transnationally, it has expanded from the narrow domain of civil and political rights exercised by the citizen against the power of the state (Merry, 1996). Human rights is increasingly seen as extending to a range of social, economic, and cultural rights such as the right to food and to housing—thus defining much more broadly the obligations of a state to its citizens. At the same time, questions are being raised about the fit between human rights and respect for cultural difference and the integrity of cultural traditions— that is to say, about whether human rights are, in truth, culture specific.

There are today serious disagreements about the meaning of human rights or what they entail (Donnelly, 1982; Kauskin, 1993; Ahmed An-Na'im, 1987).[11] As the foreign minister of Singapore put it in a statement at the Vienna Conference on Human Rights (see Tang, 1995: 243), "the extent and exercise of rights ... varies greatly from one culture or political community to another ... because [rights] are the products of the historical experiences of particular peoples." Moreover, disagreements frequently arise over particular rights claims or the distinctive points of emphasis that shape the way a particular culture interprets the content of rights (Renteln, 1988 and 1990).

Because the contemporary human rights regime represents the diffusion and broad acceptance of notions of the individual and the state from its Euro-American origins (Cheah, 1997), commentators here and elsewhere, many of whom are concerned with the work of cause lawyers, worry that reliance on human rights in political struggles and by political movements creates a situation in which Western ideas and institutions take on an unhealthy prominence. As the "rights industry" flourishes and the export of American ideas of rights grows dramatically, from abroad we hear claims that the spread of human rights is the latest manifestation of Western hegemony,[12] that it reflects a particularly insidious form of cultural imperialism (Peller, 1997).

Moreover, even where there is agreement in principle, human rights are not consistently respected in practice. There are also serious doubts about the effectiveness of human rights in protecting subject populations from abuse (see Shute and Hurley, 1993; also Bell, 1992). However defined, those rights are variably realized; indeed, they are regularly violated by some of the same governments that proclaim their adherence to them.[13]

The situation of human rights is, of course, all the more complicated when we take into account the fact of postcoloniality—the fact that formerly colonized nations are now trying to develop new legal institutions and new forms of state-society relations (Chambers and Curti, 1996). And, in a postcolonial world, human rights claims can, and have been, mobilized by cause lawyers against metropolitan nations. Here the work of cause lawyers is particularly controversial, bringing them face to face with increased corporate power, funding constraints, and ideological resistances and, in part, contributing to increased attacks on lawyers themselves.

Although at times human rights run up against barriers to change, appeals to a realm of transnational legality, on occasion, can transform power relations within states and open up new possibilities for forces seeking social change (Sarat and Kearns, 2001). Human rights can, thus, be both a source of empowerment and protection for persons against the societies in which they live, or they can constrain those same persons (Merry, 1995). Human rights can liberate or limit the imagination of the possible; they can revolutionize or conserve. Like all rights, international human rights both authorize action and undermine authority's claims.

This is all enormously significant for cause lawyers who seek to deploy human rights norms locally to mobilize social movements or to legitimate particular demands (Collier, 2001). The allure of human rights for social movements and for cause lawyers persists, in part, because they can, and do, mean many things at once.[14] The universalistic language of human rights is part of democracy's appeal, providing as it does the basis for connecting local struggles to global interests and for building alliances across national boundaries. That language provides at least a rhetorical counterweight to global capitalist development in areas where the spread of capitalism threatens to exacerbate problems of dignity and equity.

Cause lawyers, with or without recourse to transnational networks, can pursue democratization and the vindication of human rights through confrontations with central institutions of the state. These confrontations may occur by way of test-case litigation—both national and supranational—as well as by way of leveraging the threat of litigation to force political concessions. But cause lawyers also work to exploit the fragmentation of state institutions (Scheingold, 1998; see also Fine and Picciotto, 1992). In short, as the essays in this volume demonstrate, democratization and human rights are produced, in part, by the activities of cause lawyers as they emerge in both national and transnational social movements.

Cause Lawyering

Whatever its relationship to the complex processes of globalization and state transformation that we have been describing, cause lawyering is at one and the same time distinct from, and enmeshed in, conventional lawyering (Rosen, 1999). The objective of the attorneys that we characterize as cause lawyers is to deploy their legal skills to challenge prevailing distributions of political, social, economic, and/or legal values and resources (Sarat and Scheingold, 1998). Cause lawyers choose clients and cases in order to pursue their own ideological and redistributive projects. And they do so, not as a matter of technical competence, but as a matter of personal engagement (see, for example, Sarat, 1998). They have no qualms about embracing the values and goals of those whom they represent. Indeed, they take pride in thus challenging traditional conceptions of professionalism.

At least in principle, then, cause lawyering stands in sharp and self-conscious contrast to traditional conceptions of lawyering, according to which attorneys are expected to provide case-by-case, transaction-by-transaction service to particular clients without reference to either their own or to their clients' values, policy preferences, and political and social commitments. In practice, however, cause and conventional lawyering overlap in a multiplicity of ways (Rosen, 1999). As Shamir, in particular, has repeatedly emphasized, cause lawyering is, itself, something of a moving target (Shamir and Chinsky, 1998). Individual lawyers frequently cross and recross the lines between cause and conventional legal practice. Cause and conventional lawyers may also construct and reconstruct their professional identities and practices as a result of their experiences. Moreover, cause and conventional lawyers work within the broader market for legal services; they engage in many of the same practices and strategies; and may well represent similarly situated clients and interests. Further muddying the waters is the wide variety of ways in which cause lawyers practice and the wide variety of objectives that they pursue.

The fluidity of the boundaries that distinguish cause lawyering from, as well as connect it to, conventional lawyering emerge in a particularly pronounced fashion in the research findings reported in this volume. These cause lawyers are, after all, engaging with state structures and a global order that are in incessant and interdependent flux. States, however, continue to be the primary site of governance and authority, and they vary widely in their receptivity to the tactics and strategies of cause lawyers.

Cause lawyering all over the globe is in constant transition as it seeks to adjust to the changing configurations of state power. These transitions relate to the strategy, tactics, recruitment, reproduction, and organization of cause lawyers—as well as to relationships between cause lawyers and mainstream professionals. Cause lawyers are developing transnational networks to defend their causes against globalization and also to take advantage of the redistributive potential of globalization. New opportunities are matched by new constraints. The already complicated world of cause lawyering is further complicated by the webs of possibilities and barriers associated with contemporary multiplication of legal spaces at both national and transnational levels, with disaggregating, loosely coupled state structures, proliferating networks of activists, lawyers, and nongovernmental organizations, and new ideological configurations.

As a result, even where cause lawyering is well entrenched, it has been necessary to adjust to changing circumstances. In settings where its roots are shallow and its opportunities uncertain, the mission is to put cause lawyering on a firm footing (see Ellmann, 1998; Lev, 1998). In this latter situation there tends not to be an experienced and committed cadre of cause lawyers with a grasp of what to do and how to do it, nor are there established and receptive institutional channels in which to work.

We believe that, in their relationship to cause lawyering, state transformation and democratization must be understood and analyzed as both a condition and a consequence. Generally speaking, there is a natural affinity between cause lawyering and democratization (Sarat and Scheingold, 1998). On the one hand, the record indicates that cause lawyering is much more likely to flourish in democratic settings. On the other hand, in nondemocratic settings, cause lawyering has sometimes proven to be one of the few avenues open to those who are subjected to repression.

The relationship between cause lawyering and globalization is more complex. The association of globalization with corporate capitalism makes for an uneasy fit with cause lawyering, given the emphasis of cause lawyering on human rights, marginalized peoples, and moral activism. Yet cause lawyering and globalization are enmeshed with one another in ways that this volume clearly demonstrates. Globalization decenters national legal orders, bringing them into stark juxtapositions, bringing new forces to bear in contestation over legal rules and practices, bringing new patterns of power as legal life gets rearranged (see Merry, 1996). Thus, globalization creates openings that cause lawyers working within states can exploit for their own purposes.

Human rights norms provide an instructive example. To understand the possibilities for advocacy under conditions of globalization, it is important to analyze how those norms and the new system of legal regulation of which they are a part are mobilized by various local actors both within and outside the Euro-American community (see Keck and Sikkink, 1997). Put another way, the more insistent these pressures toward an outward redistribution of state power whether at the economic, cultural, or political level the more cause lawyering itself has an incentive to go global by mobilizing human rights. Cause lawyers in one country might well be expected to join forces with lawyers in other nations fighting similar local battles. The globalization of cause lawyering could occur with one-way transfers of resources, technologies, ideologies from the West—especially from the United States, outward. But cause lawyers in the West may also draw on strategies and approaches developed elsewhere.[15]

These ambivalent and uncertain implications of globalization and the ways they intersect with state transformation provide a major portion of the vitality for our project. The interactions among globalization, neoliberalism, and cause lawyering could be synergistic and centripetal as well as disruptive and disaggregative. One of the principal objectives of research reported in this volume is to determine whether, to what extent, and under what conditions cause lawyers are contributing to, and benefitting from, transnational networks. Dezalay and Garth (1996) suggest that whether lawyers will choose to work transnationally, that is, invest their presently available social capital (their status and reputation) in the construction of a transnational legal field depends largely on whether that investment figures to somehow increase their social capital. Thus, understanding how and why cause lawyers go global involves assessing the material and symbolic incentives available to them in transnational arenas discounted by the incentives available in the more familiar national legal fields.

As we have already suggested, our focus is on the forces that are impinging on states and facilitating their transformation. Our goal is to determine how cause lawyers are affected by, and implicated in, the dual redistribution of state power associated with globalization and democratization. We seek to understand the varying responses to these developments by cause lawyers working in different countries, associated with different causes, and functioning with varying resources and degrees of legitimacy. In the face of globalization at the economic, cultural, and political level, we examine the ways cause lawyers serving particular causes are mobilizing and what the impact of this mobilization is on the transformation of the state. We also want to call attention to the ways cause lawyers are involved in the construction of new global arrangements.[16]

In the chapters that follow we explore these developments, focusing on different national settings and different types of cause lawyering. In each, we locate cause lawyering in its complex and contingent relations to globalization and state transformation, showing how cause lawyers both shape and are shaped by these crucial turn-of-the-century phenomena.

Overview of the Book

The first section of this book—*Global Developments/Local Contests: New Opportunities/New Challenges*—begins with Lucie White's "Two Worlds of Ghanaian Cause Lawyers." White's essay examines the way that economic globalization and the globalization of human rights concerns play out among different kinds of cause lawyers in an economically underdeveloped African nation. The cause lawyers she studies are involved in economic development policy and advocacy for women's rights. The context for her examination of the different worlds in which those lawyers operate are radical shifts in Ghana's fiscal, economic, and social policies funded and mandated by the United States and other northern nations through international organizations, like the International Monetary Fund.

The first group of cause lawyers, many of whom were trained in elite universities in the United States, seek to graft international mandates into Ghanaian law in the hope of raising the standard of living for all Ghanaians. They are, White suggests, deeply politically and morally committed even though they tend to work within government agencies. Seen from one perspective, they are in positions to wield considerable power, but they see themselves as relatively powerless, enmeshed in global ideological and institutional networks within which they have little influence. They maintain deeper connections to communities outside Ghana than to other Ghanaian cause lawyers who are confronting the consequences of the structural adjustment policies those lawyers are helping to implement.

The second group of cause lawyers are women lawyers in private practice who volunteer and work with nongovernmental organizations to promote an international agenda of basic rights for women. They focus on ending violence against women and opening up economic opportunities for women. However, they, too, are tethered to a global network of groups and institutions, e.g., American foundations, lawyers in other southern nations, etc. White argues that, while these cause lawyers believe that their work makes a difference in the lives of Ghanaian women, their traditional human rights agenda has not yet come to terms with the challenges to women's welfare engendered by the economic development policies being pursued at the national level. Globalization, with its different faces, pulls Ghanaian cause lawyers outward, forging divergent connections and agendas and impeding the development of the kind of indigenous alliances necessary to deal with the most pressing threats to the welfare of Ghanaians.

A similar interest in the way international ties and transnational political developments affect cause lawyering at the local level is seen in Lisa Hajjar's "From the Fight for Legal Rights to Promotion of Human Rights: Israeli and Palestinian Cause Lawyers in the Trenches of Globalization." This chapter takes up global-local linkages in the work of human rights lawyers, in what Hajjar calls "Israel/Palestine." Hajjar describes the evolution of the work of lawyers who concentrated on vindicating the rights of Palestinians living in the occupied territories. For these cause lawyers the globalization of human rights had the effect of providing a unifying, popular political rhetoric that, for a period, helped them overcome their own previously atomized and politically isolated situation.

To understand this phenomenon, Hajjar traces the development of the human rights enterprise in the international arena over a fifty-year period, stressing the importance of the development of new organizations and transnational networks in the 1970s. She argues that the legalistic and principled discourse of human rights has been a powerful force in local struggles for democracy and the rule of law, and that cause lawyers were both principle architects of the globalization of human rights and principle beneficiaries of its success. In the context of Israel/Palestine she notes that globalization is reflected in the careers and work of lawyers in the territories, and she points out how those lawyers worked to exploit the awkwardness of the right to self-determination in a nation where nationalism and state sovereignty do not precisely align.

Hajjar's research demonstrates how cause lawyering can be transformed by macro-political developments on the international stage, in particular the so-called Oslo Accords. Oslo took the steam out of human rights activities by refocusing the Israeli/Palestinian conflict as a matter of territorial separation, not respect for universal rights. Moreover, with the creation of a Palestinian Authority some cause lawyers joined the government, working as agents of an emergent new state. Here the story is one in which success at one level of political transformation comes at the cost of a waning of energy among cause lawyers dedicated to the pursuit of human rights.

The emphasis on tracing the impact of globalization in local contests is also seen in Anne Bloom's essay on workers' rights litigation in Texas. Bloom's research examines the way in which globalization plays out in metropolitan, northern nations, raising new issues, posing new challenges, and the way cause lawyers in those nations come to terms with those issues and challenges. She does so through a case study of a suit against multinational corporations brought in the courts of Texas on behalf of Costa Rican workers seeking monetary damages for injuries allegedly caused by the negligent use of pesticides.

Bloom uses Santos's (1995) theorization to explore the "emancipatory" potential of litigation in one national context on behalf of workers living elsewhere. This emancipatory potential seems to be realizable first in the creation of new alliances, in this case of personal injury lawyers, who brought and funded the suit, with more traditional cause lawyers representing environmental, consumer, and civil rights interests, second in the possibility of bringing greater legal leverage against multinational corporations, and third in the use of extrastate norms to solve intrastate problems. And, indeed, initially it looked like the emancipatory potential would have some real payoff when the Texas Supreme Court affirmed the right of foreign workers to sue in Texas courts.

But, as was the case in Hajjar's study of Israel/Palestine, new political developments, in this case at the intrastate level, namely the growth of the tort reform movement in Texas, overwhelmed and undermined this possibility. In part because of the inherently unstable alliance of personal injury and more traditional cause lawyers, when these political developments manifested themselves in legislative proposals to overrule the Texas Supreme Court decision, the coalition disintegrated, with the personal injury lawyers deserting their new allies to protect their own economic interests. What started out as a victory for workers in the newly emergent global political economy ended up as another chapter in the ongoing debate about the litigation explosion in the United States.

Another of the challenges that globalization poses for nations like the United States arises from the increased movement of persons across national boundaries, sometimes legally, but often outside legal channels. Migration accelerates in response to innovations in communication and transportation as well as growing inequalities of wealth and opportunity between nations. How cause lawyers respond to this movement of persons is the subject of Susan Coutin's chapter. Focusing on organizations serving Salavadorians seeking entry into, or permanent resident status in, the United States, Coutin documents the way cause lawyers simultaneously work with existing legal categories, while in other activities challenging those same categories.

The claims of immigrants, Coutin argues, necessarily decenter law and lawyers' work. Immigrants are situated both within, and yet between, nations. As a result, advocacy on their behalf straddles national and international normative orders. Cause lawyering in the area of immigration is structured by foreign policy considerations over which cause lawyers have little influence, but it is also embedded in transnational solidarity networks. Those networks are crucial in articulating and sustaining their work as critics and advocates for new understandings of state and citizen even as they supply resources to carry on legal battles within the existing national legal framework of the United States.

Coutin describes a wide range of activities in which cause lawyers engage. When they interview clients, and decide whom to represent in court they work within traditional legal categories and traditional professional models. Yet they go beyond both in their efforts to educate the communities which they serve about existing law and in their political work in transnational movements. By examining these varied activities, Coutin shows how cause lawyers may end up serving as both agents and critics of the state in a global era.

As we noted earlier, we live in an era of state transformation, much of which is attributable to the need to accommodate the imperatives of globalization. Cause lawyers are active in promoting such transformations and designing new institutions, and are under pressure to respond and adapt to new circumstances associated especially with the neoliberalism and the disaggregation of the state. These pressures are felt in states with very different kinds of political traditions and institutions. The next section—*Globalization and State Transformation: Patterns of Conflict and Cooperation between Cause Lawyers and the State*—provides case studies of cause lawyers' responses to recent changes in the institutions and ideologies of the state in the United Kingdom, the United States, Israel, and South Africa.

We begin with England, where Andrew Boon argues that the need to cooperate and compete within the new international economic order has promoted the hegemony of neoliberal values under both Conservative and Labor governments. The power of neoliberalism is reflected in a shrinking of the public sector, limitations of public spending, and a propaganda war against dependency on the state. The commitment of Thatcher and her successors was, and has been, to destabilize expectations of entitlements under social democracy, one of which is the expectation of government-supported legal services under Legal Aid.

Neoliberalism, Boon contends, threatens to move lawyers from the center to the periphery of the state. Lawyers resist by seeking to reinvest their activities with legitimacy. One way they do so is by trying to appropriate the symbolic capital associated with cause lawyering. Governmental-funded legal aid, in the United Kingdom, traditionally has been the major vehicle for cause lawyering devoted to meeting the legal needs of the poor. Under Thatcher, Legal Aid was, however, very vulnerable to attack because its greatly escalating costs gave credence to the criticism that its work was largely a response to lawyer-induced demands. This criticism fit in well with the neoliberal targeting of professionalism and professional prerogatives. Neoliberals argued that the former was simply a mask for an inefficient monopoly, and dramatically cut legal aid.

In this situation the nature of cause lawyering in the United Kingdom itself has changed. Boon highlights the significance of two of those changes. The first is the blurring of the line between cause lawyering and traditional contingent fee lawyers in the personal injury area. Here litigation concerning tobacco is particularly instructive. The other change is the growth of *pro bono* provided by large firms. This has filled the gap in cause lawyering associated with cuts in Legal Aid and, at the same time, has helped supply a response to neoliberal critiques of professionalism. *Pro bono* allows, he argues, mainstream lawyers to capture the legitimating values associated with cause lawyering and also to accommodate themselves to neoliberalism's twin emphasis on market solutions and volunteerism. While some large firms devote their *pro bono* work to one cause, making their work recognizable within the traditional conception of cause lawyering, Boon urges a reconsideration of the conceptual boundaries of cause lawyering appropriate to the accommodations made necessary by neoliberalism.

Sarat's chapter, "State Transformation and the Struggle for Symbolic Capital: Cause Lawyers, the Organized Bar, and Capital Punishment in the United States," also examines the responses of cause lawyering to neoliberal values, focusing on the more conventional kind of cause lawyering associated with advocacy against the death penalty. Sarat notes that, in addition to emphasis on markets and the hegemony of market values which they promote, neoliberal governments reorient themselves and their governing ideologies toward law and order and crime control. In the United States this can be seen not only in a dramatic escalation in prison populations and public expenditures supporting incarceration of criminals, but in an attack on due process and procedural protections for criminal defendants.

For those accused of capital offenses, or sentenced to die, this attack has resulted in a rapid retreat from the commitment to providing "super due process" that formerly was mandated in capital cases. This retreat resulted in the recent defunding of governmentally supported organizations designed to secure adequate legal representation at trial and on appeal as well as the passage of the so-called Anti-Terrorism and Effective Death Penalty Act, which contained dramatic curtailments of *habeas corpus* protections for those who receive death sentences. These changes in policy mark a dramatic shift in the pattern of state investment of its "symbolic capital," one result of which, Sarat argues, has been the creation of an alliance, however unstable, between the organized bar and death penalty lawyers.

The bar is investing its own symbolic capital to defend both the abolitionist cause and the lawyers who take up that cause. This was most vividly exemplified by the passage in February 1997 of a resolution by the American Bar Association calling for a nationwide moratorium on capital punishment. Here, unlike in Boon's account of the English situation, mainstream lawyers respond to the rise of the neoliberal agenda by legitimating the work of cause lawyers. They are doing so in the name of protecting the rule of law which they believe is threatened by the neoliberal state's law-and-order campaign. They help sustain a type of legal practice in which cause lawyers challenge state policy and defend individual rights.

But conflict between cause lawyers and the state is by no means the only possible kind of relationship under contemporary conditions. That this is the case is demonstrated in the next three chapters. The first, by Neta Ziv, focuses on what she calls legislative cause lawyering in the United States. This kind of cause lawyering, she contends, does not conform to the conventional individual-state paradigms through which cause lawyering is commonly understood. Under this framework cause lawyers use their expert knowledge to protect underrepresented individuals or groups against the state. In the conventional conception two things stand out: first, the assumption that client interests are determinate, and second, that the state can be treated as a unified institution whose interests are uniformly opposed to those of the client group.

Ziv seeks to revise this conception, taking as her example the lawyering on behalf of persons with disabilities which culminated in the passage of the Americans with Disabilities Act. She deploys what she calls a "relational view of democracy" to emphasize the process through which the interests of citizens are formed in and through their political articulation. In this process cause lawyers working in the legislative arena must keep in mind not only the rights of those they represent, but also the political interests of those they seek to persuade, creating mutuality of interest wherever possible. Cause lawyering of this kind, Ziv contends, "transgresses common divisions between clients, lawyers, and the state" of the kind exemplified in Sarat's discussion of death penalty lawyers. Causes, Ziv notes, break "down into a series of dialogues, negotiations, and deliberations." Each of these events creates different configurations of relations, some conflictual, but many of which are cooperative.

Passage of the ADA seems like a classic civil rights victory, but it is one which calls attention to the contingent relations between cause lawyers and state actors, relations which alter as state forms themselves alter. These relations are responsive to differences in the issues and the institutions of the state in which cause lawyers ply their trade. Pursuing legislative victory requires different strategies and orientations from the pursuit of victory in a class-action lawsuit, though no less commitment to a cause. While it may appear that conflict with the state insures that cause lawyers are not co-opted, Ziv suggests that, if we look below the surface, cooptation risks are no greater where cooperative relations predominate. Over time many kinds of cause lawyering have a dynamic relationship with state actors in which conflict sometimes predominates and in which cooperation is at other times the operative mode.

Yoav Dotan's "The Global Language of Human Rights: Patterns of Cooperation between State and Civil Rights Lawyers in Israel" provides another example of the way cooperative relations between cause lawyers and particular state actors emerge in specific issue domains, this time in the context of litigation before the Israeli Supreme Court over the rights of Palestinians in the Occupied Territories. Like Ziv, Dotan argues for a conception of cause lawyering that accommodates such relations instead of seeing cause lawyers and state actors as unalterable ideological opponents. Such a conception must be historically and culturally sensitive enough to recognize that, at particular times and in particular places, lawyers may share a cause even while arguing different sides of a case.

In the context of the litigation he studied, Dotan labels the cause shared by the ostensible adversaries as "the rule of law." In Israel, a democratic state constantly feeling the pressure of national security and military necessity, commitment to the rule of law may unite human rights advocates and government lawyers against other state actors responsible for maintaining security under occupation. The lawyers for the Palestinians whom Dotan studied litigate on behalf of the Association for Civil Rights in Israel. They are all Jews who do not criticize the concerns for national security that are so prevalent in Israel; rather, they seek to insure that those concerns are met within a framework of adherence to law. In this sense they are well within the mainstream of Israeli society. Lawyers on the other side, who work in the Office of the High Court of Justice of the Attorney General's Office, seek a similar accommodation.

While these two sets of lawyers may differ over particular facts or whether those facts merit particular legal conclusion, they both see themselves as cause lawyers. Their professional commitments are political and ideological. They define their cause such that there is something more important to them than an absolute and unflinching identity with any set of partisan interests. As a result, they are able over the course of their careers to switch sides, moving from civil rights work to the government side and vice versa.

Finally, reminiscent of White's discussion of Ghanaian cause lawyering, Dotan notes that some kinds of cause lawyering may exist within the state. Indeed, he argues that globalization itself, especially the development of a global ethos of human rights, may fuel not only advocacy within and on behalf of nongovernmental organizations, but also the work of lawyers seeking to democratize their governments from within.

This emphasis on the importance of forces external to, and not contained within, the nation-state in shaping the work of cause lawyers is found in Klug's "Legal Advocacy, Global Engagement: The Impact of Land Claims Advocacy on the Recognition of Property Rights in the South African Constitution." Focusing on cause lawyering before, during, and after the end of the apartheid regime, and in particular lawyering concerning property rights for South Africa's black majority population, Klug calls attention to the fact that the resolution of "the property question was framed by international options." Anti-apartheid coalitions outside South Africa played a large role in fortifying the work of cause lawyers in the country. But they were also aided in their struggles by unusual allies, including the World Bank.

Yet within the frame of these supernational influences, Klug describes the movement of cause lawyering from conflict to cooperation, from a posture of opposition to an authoritarian and repressive regime to leadership in a democratic one. His is a story of how the transformation of the apartheid government transformed cause lawyering itself. He examines the strategies of cause lawyering in full opposition and its role during complex negotiations leading to the inclusion of a provision in the new constitution ensuring restitution of illegally seized land and ensuring land reform. Moreover, he shows how after the transition some of the same cause lawyers who helped bring down the former regime became leading figures in the new government. Nonetheless, Klug argues, their goals and relations to their clients remained unchanged. What did change was that instead of speaking to power they now could exercise it. Operating from within the state in a global era presents new opportunities but imposes new constraints and responsibilities on cause lawyers.

Like Klug, the last chapter in this section draws attention to the importance of forces external to, and not contained within, the nation-state in shaping the work of cause lawyers. Here Shamir and Ziv criticize cause-lawyering scholars for focusing almost exclusively on the political action of the state and quasi-state agents. This top-down view, they contend, misses the growing importance of what they call "subpolitics" as a locus for cause lawyering. Drawing on Ulrich Beck's (Beck, 1997; Beck, Giddens, and Lash, 1994) work, they define subpolitics as "political action from below, carried out through agents situated outside conventional political structures, and who nonetheless actively take part in policy shaping, in the distribution of social power and in setting the political agenda." Examination of subpolitics focuses on "citizens' initiative groups, issue related organizations, and voluntary associations."

In their chapter, Shamir and Ziv analyze two different styles of cause lawyering, one of the traditional state-centered variety and one that exemplifies subpolitical activity in the context of a dispute arising from the attempt to prevent Arab citizens of Israel from living in a community called Katsir. The traditional state-centered cause lawyering that emerged to fight this ethnic discrimination was strictly legal. It was centered on the development of a petition to the Supreme Court of Israel.

The other, which they see as more effective, took the form of a behind-the-scenes effort by a lawyer and a voluntary organization to orchestrate a change in the facts on the ground by helping an Arab family buy land and build a home in

Katsir through the mediation of a Jewish person who did not disclose the fact that the land was intended for an Arab family. This form of activism "employed a form of resistance that coincided with postmodern conceptions of personal empowerment and subversion." Moreover, it put the majority group in a defensive position by requiring them to appeal to the state for protection from a minority and to justify their discriminatory policies. Shamir and Ziv see the latter kind of work as exemplifying the "relative erosion in the centrality of the state" in Israel and the emergence of community-centered rather than state-centered forms of political activism in which cause lawyers continue to play a role in the struggle for social change.

They urge those interested in cause lawyering to look beyond and outside the state. They draw our attention to the simultaneous development of suprastate politics associated with globalization and subpolitics that erodes state centrality from below. The former involves the development of new legal regimes or networks across national boundaries. The latter involves "community or market-oriented legal action which bypasses, avoids or simply moves politics away from state arenas."

One of the effects of the kinds of changes that Shamir and Ziv describe involves the globalization of cause lawyering itself, its decentering from the nation-state as its primary locus of organization, and the increase of technology transfers among cause lawyering organizations as well as the development of new relationships among cause lawyers across national boundaries. We have already seen the importance of such transfers and relationships in the context of human rights work in Israel/Palestine and immigration work in the United States. The first essay in the last section of this book—"The Globalization of Cause Lawyering"—focuses on this same kind of impact among Latin American cause lawyers.

Steve Meili's research examines when, why, and how Latin American cause lawyers create or participate in transnational cause-lawyering networks. He asks how, if at all, do those networks alter the forces that cause lawyers can bring to bear in their work at the national level? Meili argues that there has been a proliferation of transnational networks among cause lawyers, some amounting to little more than an occasional informal contact, but some quite formal and institutionalized. Following Keck and Sikkink (1997), he notes that transnational networks emerge when channels between state actors and cause lawyers are blocked. In such situations cause lawyers seek allies and resources outside their country in order to bring new leverage to bear at the state level. At the same time, networking among Latin American cause lawyers is inhibited by resource shortages. Given the choice between working on a case and going to an international conference or seminar, cause lawyers typically choose the former.

Latin American cause lawyers pursue one of two general strategies, a traditional legal-rights strategy, focusing on protection of individuals from abuses of state power, or a social-rights strategy, focusing on positive rights to housing, health care, etc. Meili finds that transnational networks among lawyers who focus on legal rights are more formal and tend to be initiated and funded from outside the region. Paradoxically, however, with the success of transitions to democracy in several Latin American nations, this kind of cause lawyering and the networks that support it tend to decline. Social-rights cause lawyering tends to be organized more informally and yet it remains as relevant after democratization as before.

Another way in which globalization impacts cause lawyering is through the exportation of models of and approaches to that practice from one national context, generally from the United States, to others. As Meili points out, cause lawyering expands beyond the boundaries of already established liberal regimes, but in so doing it enters arenas with neither respect for rights nor long traditions of support for civil association and social movement activity. Thus the question becomes whether or not cause lawyering can survive and prosper in these new contexts.

Noga Morag-Levine's "The Politics of Imported Rights: Transplantation and Transformation in an Israeli Environmental Cause-Lawyering Organization" provides one response, again examining the globalization of cause lawyering from the perspective of what might be called a "recipient" society. Morag-Levine's chapter argues that the IUED, which was patterned after the American Natural Resources Defense Council, initially attempted to use strategies and tactics appropriate for a society with liberal, pluralist traditions of governance in what she calls a "corporatist" context. Initially, Morag-Levine argues, this cause lawyering organization was "bifocal," working in Israel but dependent for resources as well as its orientation on the United States.

Analyzing three cases in which the IUED sought to stop what it regarded as an environmentally unsound practice, this chapter describes the difficulties of IUED's adaptation to the Israeli context. Built from scratch, the IUED had to recruit lawyers with no particular commitment to environmental issues, lawyers who converted to the cause while on the job. Moreover, facing defeat in its litigation efforts, the IUED has had to come to terms with the distinct dynamics of Israeli politics. Over time, as it has encountered difficulty and defeat, this cause-lawyering organization has looked beyond narrowly legal efforts to try to build coalitions and a base of support among the Israeli population, the results of which are not yet clear. It has, in essence, had to shift its attention away from maintaining global linkages and increasingly toward developing an indigenous constituency.

The next chapter in this book illustrates, with great vividness, the complex relationships between cause lawyering and the state in a global era. Taking as their focus what they call the "field of international human rights," Yves Dezalay and Bryant Garth describe the cross-border linkages, patterns of exportation, and continuing connection among cause lawyers in the United States and Latin America as well as how, in both the north and the south, cause lawyering influences, and is influenced by, transformations in state policy, politics, and regime form. They argue that human rights organizations and human rights lawyers, funded and supported by philanthropic foundations in the United States, mobilized the international community in efforts to stop local human rights abuses and, as a result, were in the forefront in challenging authoritarian regimes in Latin America and helping democratize those societies.

Dezalay and Garth also focus on the careers and professional opportunities available for such lawyers both in Latin America and the United States. In each of these places, they argue, cause lawyering is inseparable from the "palace wars" that mark its national politics. Thus, in the United States, Dezalay and Garth suggest that the growth of support for human rights organizations occurred with what they call the "shattering of the Cold War consensus" and that changes in human rights organizations and strategies have been, and are, closely linked to political changes within as well as between nations.

In Latin America, as Meili also notes, with the spread of democracy has come the decline of human rights cause lawyering. Cause lawyers who, under authoritarian regimes, were leaders in challenging those regimes have today returned to more traditional careers as "power lawyers," often occupying positions inside the government. And because Latin American societies lack a tradition of "moral investment" in law, new generations have not emerged to take their place.

This analysis calls attention to the sociological and biographical, as well as political, configuration of a movement of human rights lawyering from north to south. Like the argument of Norag-Levine, it emphasizes the key roles of American foundations as well as the media. Dezalay and Garth remind us that, while throughout the last three decades, the agenda of human rights lawyering in the south has been inseparable from the agendas of state, law, and media in the north, the dynamic of American influence cannot sustain it.

In the postscript, Stuart Scheingold tries to identify recurrent themes and findings in cause lawyering research and to raise issues for subsequent work on cause lawyering. What emerges most insistently from this inquiry is the complex, contingent, and mutually constitutive relationship between cause lawyering and democracy. The relationship is complex because democracy is, itself, complex, and the research reveals that cause lawyering most readily contributes to, and draws sustenance from, liberal pluralist iterations of democracy. But cause lawyering is often driven by more expansive visions of social and economic democracy and, more specific, by egalitarian values and redistributive objectives. These aspirations are, however, only occasionally compatible with the resources cause lawyers have at their disposal, and this essay addresses how, when, and why convergence between cause lawyering and robust versions of democracy occurs.

The two kinds of strategic choice confronting all cause lawyers emerge as another continuing theme in the research, as summarized by Scheingold. To begin with, all cause lawyers must negotiate the Hobson's choice between working in close proximity to the state or distancing themselves from it. By choosing to work in proximity to the state, cause lawyers are likely to maximize their influence but in so doing tend to confine themselves to accommodation and complicity with the state project. The stakes of a second choice, between political and legal strategies, turn out to be more professional than political. That is, insofar as cause lawyers deploy litigation and other forms of accepted legal action, they are more likely to enlist the support of the organized legal profession—support that is put at risk by the politicization of cause lawyering.

Finally, Scheingold assesses the ambivalent impact of globalization on cause lawyering. Evidence indicates that cause lawyers draw significant discursive and institutional sustenance from globalization but only insofar as they pursue liberal pluralist objectives and privilege legal over political strategies. The neoliberal values driving globalization both strengthen and destabilize state structures and the social orders in which they are embedded. The globalization of corporate capital and its privileged political position presents cause lawyers with both formidable adversaries and with discursive ammunition for mobilizing resistance. At the same time, the globalization of corporate capital is also regularly linked to the introduction and/ or the strengthening of rule of law institutions. These institutions provide opportunities for cause lawyers to pursue liberal democratic reforms but are neither receptive to, nor supportive of, economic and social democracy.

Taken together, the essays collected in this volume illustrate the multiple involvements of cause lawyers in the process of the globalization and transformation of states as well as the implications of those phenomena for cause lawyers. In so doing, they reveal ways in which cause lawyering emerges from and yet is able to transcend distinct national traditions and ways in which it responds to developments beyond the nation-state while playing itself out in state institutions. In sum, they highlight new possibilities and new constraints which both globalization and transformations in the state make available to, and impose upon, this distinctive type of lawyering.

Notes

1. And when they do not do so, law is equated almost entirely with courts. This way of thinking has been vigorously articulated as juridical democracy. See Lowi, 1979: 295–313.

2. Lawyering can, of course, encompass the whole range of relationships between lawyers and political causes, including lawyering for both progressive and conservative causes. However, in this volume we have concentrated on the former rather than the latter. Future research might profitably examine right-wing cause lawyering and its contribution to state transformation in a global era.

3. While the outward/inward distinction does capture an important aspect of what is happening, we hasten to add that these processes are not discrete from, nor are they necessarily in opposition to, one another. Indeed, both the synergies and antagonisms that link the disaggregative impact of democratization and globalization on the state will be considered below.

4. There are, however, exceptions. Corporate executives, Luttwak observes, are rewarded for their successes but may be well insulated from their failures and, thus, from the

vicissitudes of the market. "Lawrence Coss, the chief executive officer of Green Tree financial, concurrently appeared on two different 1997 *Business Week* rankings of US corporate chiefs: one for the highest earners of 1996—he was number one at $102,449,000, or $280,682 per day including weekends and vacations—and one for the least effective in raising shareholder value" (Luttwak, 1999: 1–2).

5. Note that globalization is also associated with technocratic rather than democratic decision making by, for example, the so-called Eurocrats in the European Union and non-elected officials in the International Monetary Fund, the World Bank, and other such bodies.

6. In this formulation what distinguishes "civil society" from " 'society' in general" is that civil society "involves citizens acting collectively in a public sphere" (Diamond, 1994: 5).

7. There is, moreover, reason to believe that the association of neoliberal values with market-driven economies and lower barriers to the flow of people, products, and values across national borders may, from time to time and in different places, precipitate a neo-populist xenophobic political backlash. This sort of backlash could well pit democratic forces, including cause lawyers, in modernizing and advanced capitalist societies against one another.

8. As we see them, international and supranational human rights are not themselves necessary consequences of economic globalization. Given their institutional trajectories and their ideological foundations, we believe it is important to see such globalization and human rights regimes as separate and distinct from one another. While there are affinities and even alliances, they march to very different drummers: globalization to the requisite of worldwide capitalism and human rights to moral principle.

9. For a different perspective see Howard, 1992: 80. Howard argues that "most known human societies did not and do not have conceptions of human rights." See also Alford, 1992.

10. With the fall of communism and the spread of democratization in Africa, Asia, and Latin America, the idea of rights has taken on new salience in political struggles in places where rights talk was formerly avoided or denigrated (Elster, 1991). As Posner (1994–95: 137–38) notes,

> Many of the Asian governments, like those of China and Singapore, that are most critical of U.S. human rights policy and seek to characterize it as Western-based and culturally biased are among the declining number of regimes that absolutely prevent any independent human rights group from operating. Their claims of cultural relativism can only be sustained if they continue to prevent their own people from raising human rights issues. But they are fighting a losing battle. Recent experience in countries as diverse as Chile, Kuwait, Nigeria, South Africa, and Sri Lanka leaves no doubt that where people are allowed to organize and advocate their own human rights, they will do so. The common denominators in this area are much stronger than the cultural divisions.

11. Pheng Cheah (1997: 8–9) claims that "existing human rights practices can be divided into three voices: what I will call the first voice is the position of governments in constitutional democracies in the economically hegemonic North or West. The second voice refers to the position of Asian governments. The third voice refers to the position of human rights NGOs in the South."

12. The debate at the Conference on International Human Rights in the summer of 1993 highlighted this critique. This debate illustrated the dialectic of nationalism and globalization in which national boundaries and traditions both are vehemently defended and, at the same time, give way to culture contact and the widespread circulation of images and ideas. In such an environment, does rights talk provide a global vocabulary which can respect

local variation, or does the fact of globalization lose meaning if rights are adapted to the particular, the contingent, and the varied?

13. As Ahmed An-Na'im (1992: 1) puts it, "More than forty years after the adoption of the Universal Declaration of Human Rights in 1948, persistent and gross violations of fundamental human rights continue to occur in most parts of the world."

14. As Cheah (1997: 10) argues, "the open-ended nature of the human rights enterprise is expressed in the exhortative nature of the *Declaration* (The Universal Declaration of Human Rights) which involves a pledge by all signing nations to achieve a nonexhaustive common standard." Put another way, human rights are, by definition, mandatory claims, yet they are fecund with interpretive possibilities (Minow, 1987).

15. See, for example, the impact of the alternative law movement in Latin America on critical lawyering in the United States. Trubek and Kransberger, 1998.

16. As Halliday (1998: 6) reminds us, lawyers must also be understood as institutional designers, creating and constructing national, regional, and global markets, enabling and limiting state powers, constituting civil society and the public sphere.

References

Ahmed An-Na'im, Abdullahi (1987). "Islamic Law, International Relations, and Human Rights: Challenge and Response," 20 *Cornell International Law Journal*, 335.

——— (1992). "Introduction," in *Human Rights in Cross-Cultural Perspectives: A Quest for Consensus*, Abdullahi Ahmed An-Na'im, ed. Philadelphia: University of Pennsylvania Press.

Alford, William (1992). "Making a Goddess of Democracy from Loose Sand: Thoughts on Human Rights in the People's Republic of China," in *Human Rights in Cross-Cultural Perspectives: A Quest for Consensus*, Abdullahi Ahmed An-Na'im, ed. Philadelphia: University of Pennsylvania Press.

Appadurai, Arjun (1996). *Modernity at Large: Cultural Dimensions of Globalization*. Minneapolis: University of Minnesota Press.

Beck, Ulrich (1997). *The Reinvention of Politics: Rethinking Modernity in the Global Social Order*. Mark Ritter, trans. Cambridge, Eng.: Polity Press.

Beck, Ulrich, Anthony Giddens, and Scott Lash (1994). *Reflexive Modernization: Politics, Tradition, and Aesthetics in the Modern Social Order*. Cambridge, Eng.: Polity Press.

Bell, Diane (1992). "Considering Gender: Are Human Rights for Women, Too? An Australian Case," in *Human Rights in Cross-Cultural Perspectives: A Quest for Consensus*, Abdullahi Ahmed An-Na'im, ed. Philadelphia: University of Pennsylvania Press.

Chambers, Ian, and Lidia Curti, eds. (1996). *The Post-Colonial Question: Common Skies, Divided Horizons*. London: Routledge, 1996.

Chase-Dunn, Christopher (1991). *Globalization: Structures of the World Economy*. Cambridge, Eng.: Polity Press.

Cheah, Pheng (1997). "Posit(ion)ing Human Rights in the Current Global Conjecture," 9 *Public Culture*, 8.

Cohen, Stanley (1987). *Visions of Social Control*. Cambridge, Eng.: Polity Press.

Collier, Jane (2001). "Durkheim Revisited Human Rights as the Moral Discourse for the Post-Colonial Post-Cold-War World," in *Human Rights: Concepts, Contests, Contingencies*, Austin Sarat and Thomas R. Kearns, eds. Ann Arbor: University of Michigan Press.

Dezalay, Yves, and Bryant G. Garth (1996). *Dealing in Virtue: International Commercial Ar-*

bitration and the Construction of a Transnational Legal Order. Chicago: University of Chicago Press.
Diamond, Larry (1994). "Rethinking Civil Society: Towards Democratic Consolidation," 5 *Journal of Democracy* (July), 4–17.
Donnelly, Jack (1982). "Human Rights and Human Dignity: An Analytic Critique of Non-Western Conceptions of Human Rights," 76 *American Political Science Review*, 303.
Donzelot, Jacques (1987). *The Policing of Families*. Baltimore: Johns Hopkins University Press.
Ellmann, Stephen (1998). "Cause Lawyering in the Third World," in Austin Sarat and Stuart Scheingold, eds., *Cause Lawyering: Political Commitments and Professional Responsibilities*. New York: Oxford University Press.
Elster, Jon (1991). "Constitutionalism in Eastern Europe," 58 *University of Chicago Law Review*, 447.
Fine, Robert, and Sol Picciotto (1992), "On Marxist Critiques of Law," in *The Critical Lawyers' Handbook*, Ian Grigg-Spall and Paddy Ireland, eds. London: Pluto Press.
Garland, David (1996). "The Limits of the Sovereign State: Strategies of Crime Control in Contemporary Society," 36 *British Journal of Criminology* (4), 445–71.
Giddens, Anthony (1990). *The Consequences of Modernity*. Stanford, Calif.: Stanford University Press.
Greider, William (1997). *One World, Ready or Not: The Manic Logic of Global Capitalism*. New York: Simon & Schuster.
Habermas, Jurgen (1986). "The New Obscurity: The Crisis of the Welfare State and the Exhaustion of Utopian Energies," 11 *Philosophy and Social Criticism* (Winter), 1–18.
Halliday, Terrence (1998a). "Lawyers as Institution-Builders: Constructing Markets, States, Civil Society and Community," in *Crossing Boundaries: Traditions and Transformations in Law and Society Research*, Austin Sarat, et, al., eds. Evanston, Ill.: Northwestern University Press.
——— (1998b). "Cause Lawyering and Transnational Networks: Pitfalls and Possibilities." Paper presented at the 1998 Law & Society Association Meeting.
Halliday, Terrence, and Lucien Karpik (1997). *Lawyers and the Rise of Western Political Liberalism*. New York: Oxford University Press.
Held, David (1995). *Democracy and the Global Order: From Modern State to Cosmopolitan Governance*. Cambridge, Eng.: Polity Press.
Howard, Rhoda (1992). "Dignity, Community, and Human Rights," in *Human Rights in Cross-Cultural Perspectives: A Quest for Consensus*, Abdullahi Ahmed An-Na'im, ed. Philadelphia: University of Pennsylvania Press.
Huntington, Samuel P. (1991). *The Third Wave: Democratization in the Late Twentieth Century*. Norman: University of Oklahoma Press.
Jameson, Fredric (1998). "Notes on Globalization as a Philosophical Issue," in *The Cultures of Globalization*. Durham, N.C.: Duke University Press.
Kausikan, Bilhari (1993). "Asia's Different Standard," 92 *Foreign Policy*, 24.
Kearney, Michael (1995), "The Local and the Global: The Anthropology of Globalization and Transnationalism," 24 *Annual Review of Anthropology*, 547.
Keck, Margaret, and Kathryn Sikkink (1997), *Activists Beyond Borders: Transnational Advocacy Networks in International Politics*. Ithaca, N.Y.: Cornell University Press.
Lev, Daniel (1998). "Lawyers' Causes in Indonesia and Malaysia," in *Cause Lawyering: Political Commitments and Professional Responsibilities*, Austin Sarat and Stuart Scheingold, eds. New York: Oxford University Press.
Lowi, Theodore J. (1979). *The End of Liberalism: The Second Republic of the United States*. New York: Norton.

Luttwak, Edward (1999). *Turbo Capitalism: Winners and Losers in the Global Economy.* New York: HarperCollins.
Offe, Claus (1984). *Contradictions of the Welfare State.* London: Hutchinson.
McCann, Michael W. (1994). *Rights at Work: Pay Equity Reform and the Politics of Legal Mobilization.* Chicago: University of Chicago Press.
Meili, Stephen (1998). "Cause Lawyering and Social Movements: A Comparative Perspective on Democratic Change in Argentina and Brazil," in *Cause Lawyering: Political Commitments and Professional Responsibilities*, Austin Sarat and Stuart Scheingold, eds. New York: Oxford University Press.
Merry, Sally Engle (1995). "Wife Battering and the Ambiguities of Rights," in *Identities, Politics, and Rights*, Austin Sarat and Thomas R. Kearns, eds. Ann Arbor: University of Michigan Press.
Merry, Sally (1996). "Legal Pluralism and Transnational Culture: The *Ka Ho' okolokolonui Kanaka Maoli* Tribunal, Hawaii, 1993," in *Human Rights, Culture and Context: Anthropological Perspectives.* Richard Wilson, ed. London: Pluto Press.
Minow, Martha (1987). "Interpreting Rights: An Essay for Robert Cover," 96 *Yale Law Journal*, 1884.
Parekh, Bhirkhu (1993). "The Cultural Particularity of Liberal Democracy," in *Prospects for Democracy*, David Held, ed. Stanford, Calif.: Stanford University Press.
Peller, Gary (1997). "Cultural Imperialism, White Anxiety, and the Ideological Realignment of *Brown*," in *Race, Law, and Culture: Reflections on Brown v. Board of Education*, Austin Sarat, ed. New York: Oxford University Press.
Posner, Michael (1994–95). "Rally Round Human Rights," 97 *Foreign Policy*, 137.
Putnam, Robert (1995). "Bowling Alone," 6 *Journal of Democracy*, 65–78.
——— (1996). "The Strange Disappearance of Civic America," 24 *American Prospect* (Winter), 34–48.
Renteln, Alison Dundes (1988). "Relativism and the Search for Human Rights," 90 *American Anthropologist*, 64.
——— (1990). *International Human Rights: Universalism versus Relativism.* London: Sage.
Robinson, Ian (1995). "Democratic Critiques of the Institutions and Processes of Neoliberal Economic Integration: An Assessment," 24 *Cahiers de Recherche Sociologique*, 161–83.
Rose, Nikolas (1999). *Powers of Freedom: Reframing Political Thought.* Cambridge: Cambridge University Press.
——— (1996a). "The Death of the Social? Re-Figuring the Territory of Government," 25 *Economy and Society* (August), 327–56.
——— (1996b). "Expertise and the Government of Conduct," 14 *Studies in Law, Politics, and Society*, 359–97.
Rosen, Robert (2000). "On the Social Significance of Critical Lawyering," 3 *Legal Ethics.* (forthcoming).
Rueschemeyer, Dietrich, Evelyne Huber Stephens, and John D. Stephens (1992). *Capitalist Development and Democracy.* Chicago: University of Chicago Press.
Santos, Boaventura de Sousa (1995). *Toward a New Common Sense: Law, Science, and Politics in the Paradigmatic Transition.* New York: Routledge.
Sarat, Austin (1998). "Between (the Presence of) Violence and (the Possibility of) Justice: Lawyering Against Capital Punishment," in *Cause Lawyering: Political Commitments and Professional Responsibilities*, Austin Sarat and Stuart Scheingold, eds. New York: Oxford University Press.
Sarat, Austin, and Thomas R. Kearns (2001). "The Unsettled Status of Human Rights: An

Introduction," in *Human Rights: Concepts, Contests, Contingencies*, Austin Sarat and Thomas R. Kearns, eds. Ann Arbor: University of Michigan Press.

Sarat, Austin, and Stuart Scheingold (1998). "Cause Lawyering and the Reproduction of Professional Authority: An Introduction," in *Cause Lawyering: Political Commitments and Professional Responsibilities*, Austin Sarat and Stuart Scheingold, eds. New York: Oxford University Press.

Sassen, Saskia (1998). *Globalization and Its Discontents: Essays on the New Mobility of People and Money*. New York: The New Press.

Scheingold, Stuart A. (1998). "The Struggle to Politicize Legal Practice: Left-Activist Lawyering in Seattle," in *Cause Lawyering: Political Commitments and Professional Responsibilities*, Austin Sarat and Stuart Scheingold, eds. New York: Oxford University Press.

Shamir, Ronen (1998). "De-centering of State and Cause," Paper presented at the 1998 Law & Society Association Meeting.

Shamir, Ronen, and Sara Chinsky (1998). "Destruction of Houses and Construction of a Cause: Lawyers and Bedouins in Israeli Courts," in *Cause Lawyering: Political Commitments and Professional Responsibilities*, Austin Sarat and Stuart Scheingold, eds. New York: Oxford University Press.

Shute, Stephen, and Susan Hurley (1993). "Introduction," in *On Human Rights: The Oxford Amnesty Lectures 1993*, Stephen Shute and Susan Hurley, eds. New York: Basic Books.

Silbey, Susan (1997). " 'Let Them Eat Cake': Globalization, Postmodern Colonialism, and the Possibilities of Justice," 31 *Law & Society Review*, 212–35.

Simon, Jonathan (1997). "Governing Through Crime," in *The Crime Conundrum: Essays in Criminal Justice*, Lawrence M. Friedman and George Fisher, eds. Boulder, Colo.: Westview Press.

Tang, James, ed. (1995). *Human Rights and International Relations, in the Asia Pacific*. London: Pinter.

Teson, Fernando (1985). "International Human Rights and Cultural Relativism," 25 *Virginia Journal of International Law* (1985), 869.

Trubek, David M., Yves Dezalay, Ruth Buchanan, and John R. Davis (1994). "Global Restructuring and the Law: Studies of the Internationalization of Legal Fields and the Creation of Transnational Arenas," 44 *Case Western Reserve Law Review*, 407–98.

Trubek, Louise, and M. Elizabeth Kransberger (1998). "Critical Lawyers: Social Justice and the Structures of Private Practice," in *Cause Lawyering: Political Commitments and Professional Responsibilities*, Austin Sarat and Stuart Scheingold, eds. New York: Oxford University Press.

Weissbrodt, David (1998). "Human Rights: An Historical Perspective," in *Human Rights*, P. Davies, ed. London: Routledge.

Wilson, Richard (1996). "Human Rights, Culture and Context: An Introduction," in *Human Rights, Culture and Context*, Richard Wilson, ed. London: Pluto Press.

PART I

Global Developments/ Local Contests

New Opportunities/
New Challenges

CHAPTER 2

Two Worlds of Ghanaian Cause Lawyers

LUCIE WHITE

This chapter is a case study of two worlds of cause lawyers in Ghana. I seek to evoke those worlds from a distance, on the basis of interviews with Ghanaian lawyers in March of 1999, which I did as part of a larger project on the interplay of gender, Ghana's legal cultures, and the U.S. government's emerging economic agenda for sub-Saharan Africa. In these interviews, I sought out rank-and-file lawyers, rather than the most elite members of the Ghanaian legal profession. Thus, unlike Yves Dezalay and Bryant Garth, for instance, whose research is reported in the final chapter of this volume, I did not interview distinguished barristers, legal academics, or law-trained political leaders. Instead, I spoke with young men with Ghanaian law degrees and U.S. connections who work as midlevel civil servants in Ghanaian state agencies that regulate domestic trade and development policies. I also spoke with middle-aged Ghanaian women with British law degrees, teenaged children, and jobs in small law firms, who volunteer at nonprofit, internationally funded women's law organizations. In these interviews, I sought to understand the moral worlds that these lawyers seek through their practice. I also sought to map out the real worlds, of colonial legacies, human needs, and global pressures, in which those practices are embedded.

In the chapter I suggest that the two groups of cause lawyers that I study are deeply concerned about the course of Ghana's development. Each group seeks to promote economic development policies that respond to the needs and aspirations of Ghana's common people. As political pragmatists, both groups recognize that their nation's development policies must answer to the demands of cosmopolitan elites. They are well aware that even though they are lawyers, they have little real power, either individually or as a profession, to resist external pressures in ways that create new options for their country's development. This gap between these lawyers' cause, on the one hand, and their real capacity to further it, on the other, does not result from the blunt tools of state or private-sector terror that so often obstructs the work of "third world" cause lawyers. This chapter does not tell a story of how the state stymies the work of Ghanaian cause lawyers by throwing them in jail. Nor does it tell a story of how wealthy elites have enticed Ghana's cause lawyers to sell out their professional autonomy for private gain. Rather, the chapter suggests that the moral vision of these lawyers is confounded through more subtle, more insidious, historically embedded forces—political, cultural, psychological—which are woven into the texture of these lawyers' works and lives.

For one thing, the cause lawyers that are the subject of this chapter work in institutional niches that confine the scope of what they can do. Some of the lawyers that I interviewed work as civil servants inside the state bureaucracy. The limitations that are imposed on a lawyer's "room to maneuver" by such a job should be fairly obvious. Other lawyers work for nongovernmental organizations established by Ghanaians to further women's rights. The limitations that their work setting imposes on these lawyers are more subtle. These lawyers are obviously constrained by their funders' explicit objectives. But they are also constrained by the implicit cultural values of those funders, who are mostly from foreign governments, multilateral aid organizations, and large, first-world charitable foundations.

But beyond these obvious constraints that their job situations impose on what these lawyers can do, the lawyers also seemed to be constrained by their own deeply embedded notions about the lawyer's proper role and the natural course of their country's economic and political development. In the chapter, I suggest that one analytical lens which can help to reveal these lawyers' deeply embedded values and beliefs is gender. I was struck, as I interviewed these Ghanaian lawyers, by the critical differences—in these lawyers' job positions, career paths, professional relationships, and in their ways of talking about what mattered the most to them, like their country's development and their own vocations—that gender seemed to make. This difference led me to pose gender as one of the core questions of this chapter. In framing this question, I understand gender as a verb rather than a noun. That is, I think of gender as a historically constituted social dynamic, rather than a fixed category of sociological analysis. To borrow Saskia Sassen's turn of phrase, I view gender as a question, a mathematical puzzle for which a solution, though possible, has not yet been found (Sassen, 1998).

The chapter poses the gender question in three ways. The first is most familiar. It asks how issues of obvious and pressing concern to Ghanaian women have been discounted, both in the Ghanaian state's economic development policies of the last two decades, and in the priorities and practices of both economic development practitioners and women's rights lawyers. I am particularly interested here in the ways that the material needs of Ghanaian women, particularly non-elites, have all but escaped notice, both in the nation's official economic policies and in the practice-worlds of Ghanaian cause lawyers. These needs have escaped notice in the fast-paced world of globally oriented economic development bureaucrats. But they have also escaped notice in the supposedly more gender-attuned world of women's rights advocates. Simple, everyday questions, like access to water that doesn't kill babies and access to emergency health care for childbirth complications that does not require prepayment in cash—the most basic of *women's* questions—are not at the center of anyone's attention in either of these lawyering worlds.

The second way that the chapter poses the gender question is by asking about the less obvious gendered effects of development policies and lawyering practices. How do apparently gender-neutral development strategies, strategies that lawyers in both worlds take for granted, exacerbate preexisting gender troubles? For instance, how has the recent retrenchment on public spending for rural health interacted with the rapid expansion of urban economies, to push impoverished, unschooled, and culturally dislocated rural women into Ghana's coastal region in search of work? How does this surging population of destitute young women affect employment practices in coastal enterprises? And how do the new cash wages that women workers can earn in such jobs, the abuses that they suffer, the new social networks that they enter, and the new political consciousness that they develop all have gendered significance?

Finally, I ask how gender influences the professional identities and lawyering practices of both economic development practitioners and women's rights lawyers. Gender is not the only ideological force that shapes the roles and relationships of these lawyers, but it is a critically important one. The ground-level, economic development lawyers I talked with drafted statutes and regulations for the government. Yet they did not consider themselves to have much power. Indeed, they expressed the view that the only way any actor could exercise agency in the economic policy context was by making astute moves in a complex strategic game. They considered the most elite actors in the world of economic development—like high Ghanaian political leaders, international philanthropists, U.S. government officials, and finance capitalists—to have a good deal of strategic power. In contrast, they saw themselves as bit players on a big game board, and dismissed the fact with an ironic shrug of the shoulders.

The women's rights lawyers with whom I spoke had a very different sense of their own situation. Unlike the economic development lawyers, they believed that they had the power to make a big difference in women's lives. Indeed, they believed that their work enacted their values directly, irrespective of its measurable consequences. Thus, when one of the women lawyers talked with me about counseling a divorce client, she explained that by taking the time to explain the law to this woman, she was enacting her commitment to women's empowerment, regardless of whether or not her client felt or acted any differently as a result of her work. And when she talked about the public speaking that she had begun to do about women's human rights, she explained that by raising her voice she was manifesting the equal citizenship of women, whether or not her words made any impact on changing public policies that undermined women's power.

Such gendered influences on the professional identities of these two groups of lawyers may help to explain why there is not more informal connection between them, at least to the degree that their job roles would allow it. Becoming more self-conscious about the subtle ways that their gender socialization helps to shape their moral values and professional styles might enable such lawyers to see new opportunities for strategic linkage. In the chapter's conclusion I suggest that denser ties between these two groups of lawyers might give both groups a little more leverage for charting meaningful alternatives to prevailing agendas for Ghana's development.

The chapter has two parts. The first part, "Nine Short Pieces," is a mosaic of short vignettes on the current scene in Ghana. These pieces address themes from Ghana's colonial history, socioeconomic landscape, global-policy environment, and cause-lawyering worlds. The second part, "Notes and Questions," considers the two worlds of Ghanaian cause lawyering in somewhat more detail. It then raises questions about the social-justice implications of the practices and ideologies that those worlds presume.

Part One: Nine Short Pieces[1]

Histories

"AM I THAT NAME?" (*RILEY, 1988*)

> The ancient slave stockades do not seem ever to have vanished; they appear more to have expanded....
>
> (*Soyinka, 1999*)

I met Wilhelmina on the dining patio of a government-owned resort about a mile west of Cape Coast in the Republic of Ghana. Until 1957, Cape Coast was the whitewashed colonial capital of the Gold Coast colony of the British Crown.

Today, the city's former villas are home to dogs and chickens and extended families of fishermen and market women and computer technicians and hotel workers and university teachers. There are also many children. The older children cluster around the crumbling villas in their dark brown European-style school uniforms, shorts and knee socks for the boys and short pleated skirts for the girls. The toddlers, some sporting freshly changed Pampers, mill around the villas' former gardens with the elders and dogs. Kwado Opoku-Agyemang, a Ghanaian American poet who went to school in Cape Coast in the 1950s, describes it as a city of "irrational streets . . . and night-mud houses / Their eyes half-shut"—

> An aged town
> It stands on the one good foot
> Shaking and forgetful
> What matters
> Is not just the ruins
> Or the years devouring one another

But the veins
That still escape with the blood.

(Opokyu-Agyemang, 1996)

The Ghanaian government had just expanded the resort where Wilhelmina works to accommodate the recent surge of foreign tourists. Over the last decade, as privately held wealth in industrialized countries has grown, tourists have come to Ghana in increasing numbers. They come to tour the necklace of forts and castles that the Dutch built along the coast to promote the region's first major export-oriented industry, the sale of slaves to the Americas.

Wilhelmina's body is slight and strong like a runner's, but her eyes are like water and her fingers quaver like grass. Even her starched blue uniform—straight skirt, double-breasted jacket, white shirt—cannot entirely contain her movement. Her nametag describes her as a "Trainee." She tells me that she has two children, both girls, a baby and a four-year-old who is about to start school. They stay with her mother near a rival resort, the Shangra La, while she works down the beach at the government-owned hotel. The Shangra La is the private venture of an American computer baron. Except for the skin color of its wait staff and maids, the Shangra La could be on the Kona Coast of Hawaii's Big Island. Wilhelmina's workplace feels very different. It was constructed before "the great decline" of the mid-1970s, when the Ghanaian state still endorsed Kwame Nkrumah's grand vision of African Nationhood. In spite of its extensive high-end, first-world tourist market–oriented renovations, the resort still looks like it belongs somewhere along the Black Sea.

When I visited the slave fort a mile down the beach from Wilhelmina's workplace, my tour group was guided by a teenaged boy in a black tee shirt with the slave fort's multicolored logo stamped across its back. Our guide led us down into the holding room where men and women were inspected and branded before the healthy ones were ushered through a four-by-four-foot opening into the boats that would shuttle them out to the ships that would take them to the New World.

Then we were led up to an enclosed courtyard, where the women were stripped and hosed down with water before they were guided down to the holding room. A small balcony hung out over the courtyard wall. Our guide told us this was where the Dutch governors would select their nightly sleeping partners from among the naked women slaves. As he told us the story of this nightly event, he started to cry.

The Dutch governors, who were in charge of this coastal shipping operation, risked "getting themselves into trouble with the slavers" if too many of the cargo gave birth to fair-skinned babies during the Middle Passage. So, during the inspection, any woman who "looked pregnant" was pulled out of the group to be sold as a wife to one of the Dutch men who lived in the Cape Coast colony. If she turned out not to be carrying the governor's child, she would be sent back to the slave fort for export to America. Otherwise, her child would take her new husband's name. And thus, three centuries later, my trainee waitress at the Ghanaian government's newly renovated coastal resort was named Wilhelmina.

A LONELY PLANET

In their introduction to *The Lonely Planet*'s volume on West Africa—subtitled a "travel survival kit" for "independent travellers"—the authors opine that the region "has a power of attraction which, despite its sometimes primitive conditions, continues to entice Westerners to spend time and even careers there" (Newton and Else, 1997). For each nation that they cover in the volume, including Ghana, they begin with a couple of paragraphs on its main attractions—the greatest health risks, the highest waterfalls, the most impoverished regions (they should be avoided), the best photo opportunities for aspiring journalists, and the best values for lonely, independent bargain hunters, who have ventured far beyond their local shopping malls. The section on Ghana begins with a praise-song to its "people":

> If an award were given for the country with the friendliest people in West Africa, Ghana would probably win. One of the best educated peoples in Black Africa at independence, Ghanaians are a proud, open people and they like to do things their way. Accra may not be the most beautiful city in Africa, but it's their city—not a city catering to tourists or Western expatriates. And they like to have fun. (Newton and Else, 1997: at 361)

Over the next several pages, the authors set out what their readers need to know about the country's history. In 1482, the Portuguese built a fort along the coast to facilitate the export of gold. "The real wealth, however, turned out to be in slaves." They constructed and fortified a chain of "forts and castles" to enable this commerce, some seventy-six in all. These forts and castles were traded among the Portuguese, the Dutch, and the British for more than three centuries, until finally, in the early nineteenth century, the British decided that it was in their interest to end the trade. A half century later they finally subdued the Ashanti kingdom in the battle of Kumasi, made the region one of their crown colonies, and called it the Gold Coast.

The account then moves into the twentieth century. "The British set out to make the Gold Coast a showcase. It was to be an African country, not dominated by outsiders." In keeping with this program, the British "allowed few Europeans to settle or even be employed there." They established boarding schools for the local chiefs' children. Until 1948, when they established a university within the country modeled on Oxford, they sent the most promising Ghanaian students to Oxford and the United States for advanced study. One of these students, Kwame Nkrumah, spent the years 1935 to 1945 at Lincoln University, in Pennsylvania, reading W. E. B. Du Bois and Karl Marx. In 1957, when the British decided to grant the Gold Coast independence, they asked him to become the head of state (Newton and Else, 1997: 361–64).

To people all over Africa, Nkrumah remains a hero: "handsome, charismatic, and articulate, he espoused the cause of African unity on every occasion." Yet the guidebook reports that for Ghanaians, Nkrumah's tenure was "an economic nightmare." He "borrowed heavily to finance grandiose schemes." Many of these projects were "wasteful," notably a "grandiose" project to dam the mouth of the great Volta River to electrify the countryside. His policies alienated many sectors: the business community, by "turning over a large portion of the economy to state-run enterprises, very few of which became profitable"; his army "by setting up a private army answerable to him alone"; the West, "by his never ending denunciation of imperialism and neocolonialism." Even the people, who liked the social services and infrastructure that his grassroots socialist priorities ensured, "became disillusioned by conspicuous corruption among the party's leaders." By 1966, "it was all too much": while visiting Hanoi, he was ousted by his generals and exiled to Guinea, where he died.

In the fifteen years that followed, which the guidebook calls, in boldface, "The Great Decline," the country was not an appropriate destination for independent travellers: "[U]nless they changed money on the black market, [they] had to pay the equivalent of US$1 for an orange. Little wonder they began to avoid Ghana" (Newton and Else, 1997: 365). The production of cocoa, the country's main agricultural export, fell by half. Staple goods like milk and detergent became unavailable. Roads and school buildings crumbled. Elites sent their children and their money outside of the country, before leaving themselves. Though the country never reached a state of widespread famine, people starved. Finally, in 1978, military officer Jerry Rawlings seized power. After a period of trial and error with anti-Western rhetoric and extreme measures for arresting the country's economic decline, Rawlings, in the early 1980s, came up with a plan. He clamped down on public-sector corruption and civil-sector liberties, setting himself up as the president of a one-party state. In this political setting, he instituted an Economic Recovery Programme—a package of what were called "fiscal reforms" and "structural adjustments," but might more precisely be called amendments to domestic legislation to alter the relationship between state power and economic activity.

These reforms included the devaluation of the currency, the downsizing of the civil service by tens of thousands, the removal of price controls and government subsidies on most nonessential goods and services, and the divestiture of state-owned enterprises. The reform package endorsed the familiar goal of "balancing" the state's budget without skipping any interest payments on the huge foreign debt that had accrued in the first two decades after independence. This agenda required a good deal of "austerity" in public spending for other needs. According to the *Lonely Planet*'s authors, this package happened to be "exactly what the IMF and the World Bank told [President Rawlings] that he should do." It also seemed to send the right signal to people with money. Investors, both public and private, who had fled the country during the Great Decline, began to return with their money.

For a while, the economy thrived. The annual "growth rate" climbed to the 5 percent level. Inflation declined. Earnings from exports increased, and the percentage of GDP attributable to manufacturing began to climb. Yet these structural adjustments were not enough to trigger a "take off," in the South East Asian style. By 1991, for reasons that have sparked intense debate among the economists who initially prescribed them, structural adjustment policies stopped working their magic. The conventional indicators of economic growth began to tell a confusing story: the only thing that was clear was that "growth" had slowed down.

Interventions

FIGURING HUMAN DEVELOPMENT

In its 1997 report on Ghanaian Human Development, the United Nations Development Program sets out a report card on how official development policies have affected the health, educational, employment, and high poverty sectors of the society (1997). The report begins by listing the "positive features" of each of these sectors and then moves on to highlight the areas of greatest concern. Overall, the report does not paint a simple picture of the state of human development in the society. Nor does it promote a simple response to the IMF-endorsed reforms. Yet the report does surface the patterns of hidden cost that the structural adjustment agenda had imposed.

The pattern in the health sector gives a good window into wider trends. By 1997, the life expectancy of the "average" Ghanaian had risen to fifty-seven years, which was substantially higher than the figure for other sub-Saharan nations. This figure signaled that some groups of Ghanaians could expect to live as long as elites in industrial nations. Trade liberalization had improved the flow of prescription drugs and medical supplies into the country, for those who could pay. And yet, especially in rural areas, infant, maternal, and child mortality remained very high. Most important, over the 1990s, the *gaps* in these mortality figures—between higher and lower income groups and more and less developed geographical districts—had steadily grown. Thus, in 1992–93, the aggregate maternal death rate for the entire country was just over two hundred dead women for every one hundred thousand live births. Yet in the Kasena Nankana district in the northeast, that figure was four times higher. That means that one out of every eighteen pregnant woman in that district could expect to die in childbirth. Almost half of these deaths, from unchecked bleeding or infection, were of a kind that was easily preventable with access to the most basic health care.

Yet by 1994, more than 40 percent of Ghanaians had no access at all to modern health services (UNDP, 1997: 29). Women in rural areas like Kasena Nankana were the most likely to have no access to emergency care because in the laissez-faire economy, doctors and clinics had become increasingly concentrated in rapidly urbanizing coastal cities. Furthermore, several features of structural adjustment policies interacted to worsen the problem, superimposing a new *wealth-linked* gap in access to basic health services like maternal care upon a widening *geographic* one. Four features of the structural adjustment program can be noted in particular.

First, the priority on limiting government spending for social needs in order to meet interest payments on foreign debt without either raising taxes or accruing new debt has led to a decline in public spending on the health sector. Thus, the share of central government spending on health dropped from 10 percent in 1989 to just under 5 percent in 1994 (UNDP, 1997: 29, Table 3.5, citing to Ghana Statistical Services, Quarterly Digest of Statistics [multiple years]). In the same year, 27 percent of the central government's budget went into interest payments on the public debt. By 1997, the interest figure had climbed to more than 35 percent of the central government's total budget, which was the highest single budget item. The total percentage of the government's budget for *all* governmental goods and services, including health care, education, and infrastructure, was just over 14 percent.

Second, the policy of divestiture of state-owned enterprises was translated into law, within the health sector, as a new regime of user fees for health facilities and per-item charges for drugs and medical supplies, implemented by regulation in 1985. These measures, known as the "cash and carry" system, were immediately successful in generating a new stream of revenue for the health sector: the new program generated 8.5 percent of the health sector's total budget in its first year. Yet in that same year, outpatient attendance at primary health facilities in impoverished rural areas like Kasena Nankana dropped by 50 percent (UNDP, 1997: 30, Box 3.2, citing to the Hospital Fee Regulations, 1985 [L.I. 1313]; the Report of the Cash and Carry Review Committee, 1995; and other sources). Qualitative studies suggest that this abrupt interruption of access to modern health services that the cash-and-carry system imposed "especially among the disadvantaged, amplified recourse to use of other facilities" (UNDP, 1997: 28, 31, citing Korboe, *Extended Poverty Study: Access to and Utilization of Basic Social Services by the Poor in Ghana*, 1995).

By 1997, the twelfth year of the cash-and-carry system, 40 percent of rural deliveries were not attended by any trained health-care personnel, and 30 percent of rural women did not seek out any prenatal care, even though, according to the UN's report, "existing modern maternity facilities remain under-utilized." The report attributes this "anomalous situation" to a complex interplay of "cultural and material conditions," including women's difficulty performing cultural rituals in modern maternity settings, "the unsympathetic and disrespectful attitude of health personnel," and finally, "the cost burden" imposed by cash-and-carry medical services in what was still a largely exchange-based rural subsistence economy (UNDP, 1997: 28).

Third, in the interest of "transparent governance," the structural reform agenda encouraged the devolution of governmental authority from the central government to provincial and district authorities. Devolution of governmental functions to state and local levels is structural adjustment's prescription for rooting out the corruption and inefficiencies that are said to plague large bureaucratic governmental operations, especially in poor countries. The strategy behind the devolution solution is simple: one dismantles what is said to be the root cause of the problem, the infrastructure of the national state. At the same time, devolution seeks to promote "good governance" by giving civic institutions and individual consumer-citizens the opportunity to engage directly in the oversight of government operations, close to their homes. In the health and education sectors, this high-flown idea has translated into the shifting of *fiscal*, as well as managerial authority for primary health and educational facilities from the central government to district and local authorities. This move passes the buck for big infrastructure expenditures onto the strata of government with the least capacity to raise revenues.

This is a familiar, and widely criticized, backdoor tactic for cost-savings in developed countries. Yet it is much more disruptive to basic public services in developing nations like Ghana, where in only the most affluent enclaves is there the kind of economy that would permit capital funds to be borrowed against future revenues. Thus, decentralization in the name of good governance places the poorest rural areas, with the greatest need for a public health-care infrastructure, in the very worst position to provide it. This policy virtually guarantees that what has remained of the rural health-care infrastructure put in place during the Nkrumah era would erode even further, and that the geographical poverty gap would widen. Structural adjustment policies that require cuts in social spending for public goods that support the health sector, like transportation, utility infrastructures, and post-secondary education, compound this crisis in public funding for health-care facilities (UNDP, 1997: 29).

Finally, structural adjustment policies in sectors unrelated to health-care have increased background health risks across the society, and therefore also increased the demand for health services. Thus, policies that draw government attention away from basic needs like clean water, sanitation, and food security in high poverty urban areas have the effect of increasing the incidence of infectious diseases, and the *need* for basic health services. And the HIV epidemic is placing catastrophical levels of increased demand on health services, even in sub-Saharan nations like Ghana, where the epidemic has still not spun out of control.

If we step back from the primary health-care example, we see a complex moving picture. Structural adjustment policies have affected each sector of the social landscape—health care, education, employment, and so forth—differently. Within each of these sectors, the structural adjustment imperative has been translated into an array of domestic legal and regulatory policies, like cash-and-carry health-care financing, the devolution of hospital-building maintenance from central to local government, and the like. Each of these measures, in turn, has had multiple, interacting effects, within each domain and across sectors. These effects produce a dynamic field, with different effects on differently situated groups of social actors. The poorest women in Kasena Nankana will be affected *differently* than female law professors, for instance, by the array of legal policies, all triggered by structural adjustment, that are reshaping Ghanaian maternal health-care policy. The reliable generalizations that can be made about Ghana's regime of structural adjustment are that it eroded the social infrastructures that had been put in place in the Nkrumah era and increased the risk that the wealth gap would widen over time.

Yet these broad effects must be viewed in historical context before they can be fully evaluated. The fact that poor women in rural Ghana face an increasing risk of bleeding to death in childbirth while maternal health facilities are underutilized and deteriorating, is not, ipso facto, a signal of social wrong. It may be, as some would surely argue, that the array of policies in question makes moral sense. They may be the best policies that human moral logic can muster for moving the country away from the Great Decline of the recent past and maneuvering it around the black hole of civil disorder. Women needlessly dying in childbirth are not, after all, the only risk to human flourishing that postcolonial sub-Saharan Africa has been called on to endure. For residents of the United States, the rhetoric of structural adjustment may evoke negative memories of the domestic platform of Ronald Reagan. And there is no doubt that in Ghana, structural adjustment has been translated into odd social policies like "cash-and-carry" health care for landless, pregnant women. Yet the world is complex and the history of past wrongs carries a heavy shadow. It may just be that in the long run, this trickle-down approach to African development, as its proponents insist, is the best way to give a future to the most promising of Ghana's children (Shklar, 1990).

"EMERGING AFRICA"

> The slave trade... imposed a rupture in the organic economic systems of much of the [African] continent. It is a distortion that—partially at least, and compounded later by the imposition of colonial priorities in raw materials for Europe's industrial needs and the advent of multinational conglomerates—must surely account today for the intractable economic problems of that continent... We know that strategies for the transformation of society often demand a measure of pragmatism or, to put it crudely, deals.... (Soyinka, 1999: 26, 39)

> "If you subject an egg and a stone to the same external environment," says Kwesi Botchwey, "after a while, under the heat of the sun, a chicken will break out of

the egg, but not out of the stone." The folkloric metaphor at first sounds odd, coming from an accomplished economic bureaucrat like Botchwey, who was finance minister in Ghana for 13 years before coming to Cambridge in 1995, where he now directs a new research program on development in Africa.

[T]he occasion for Nelson Mandela's historic visit to the University last September was the launching of Botchwey's "Emerging Africa" program, an ambitious effort to rethink—and improve—the course of economic development in the continent below the Sahara.

East Asia and Africa were not that significantly different through the 1960s," Botchwey says, but they began to diverge in the early 1970s, and the gap widened into a chasm in the following decade. (O'Keefe, 1999)

According to the UNDP's 1997 Ghana report, the frequent comparisons between the development paths of Ghana and the "Tigers" of Asia fail to take account of significant differences among these nations' development indicators at the time of Ghana's independence. Although their aggregate GDP's were similar, in such key areas as adult literacy, primary and secondary school enrollment, life expectancy, and infant mortality, Ghana lagged significantly behind the Tigers. Indeed, while the infant mortality rate in Ghana in 1960 was 132 per thousand births, the rate in Singapore was only 36 (UNDP, 1997: 14, Box 1 [citing previous UNDP Human Development Reports]).

The "macroeconomic stabilization" measures [Botchwey] applied in Ghana—letting the market determine the currency's foreign-exchange rate, attacking inflation, collecting tax revenues, and balancing the budget . . . weren't and aren't sufficient to encourage sustained growth. "We had taxied to the end of the runway," Botchwey says of Ghana's experience, "but we weren't taking off." And so, "emotionally and intellectually drained," . . . Botchwey decided to head for the academy. . . .

At Harvard, Botchwey and economist Jeffrey Sachs, head of Harvard's Institute for International Development, launched a new joint venture, called Emerging Africa, which is "focused on pioneering new approaches to beginning, and sustaining, economic growth."

Now the man who would save Africa, [Sachs] has previously been the man who would save Bolivia, Poland, and Russia. . . . In Bolivia, he slashed hyperinflation. In Poland, he converted a socialist economy into a market economy. In Russia, he tried to do both, and people still argue about whether the failure was his. His prescriptions for Africa contain elements of all these prior experiences. . . . [in] an HIID paper, "A New Partnership for Growth in Africa," which subsequently transmogrified into the African trade bill. (U.S. House of Representatives, 1999a; Scmitt, 1998; Global Trade Watch, 1999)

Sachs and Botchwey's development approach would supplement IMF-style fiscal reforms with institutional reforms and infrastructure development oriented to attracting the sort of foreign investment that could stimulate rapid, sustained growth in industrial output. The institutional reforms would focus on eliminating governmental corruption, streamlining cumbersome statist procedures and strengthening the state's obligation to protect the assets of commercial investors, domestic and especially foreign. The idea, in the words of one HIID adviser, would be to change Ghana's infrastructure of domestic laws in a way that would convince investors that they "could put their money there without a politician who doesn't like you coming and seizing it."

The infrastructure reforms would be aimed toward attracting investment in labor-intensive export-oriented processing. Thus, the infrastructure investments might include transportation and communications facilities, such as deep-water harbors, coastal rail links and highways, and the like. They might include the infrastructures necessary to service investors and entrepreneurs, such as legal, accounting, and business consulting services, world-class hotels and restaurants, high-end residential and retail infrastructure, and state-of-the-art policing and crime control. Finally, they might include the infrastructures required to deliver a high-quality, low-cost manufacturing workforce, like educational and health services, and other social infrastructures conducive to a labor supply that is healthy, adequately educated, reliable, and quiescent. The point to these infrastructure expenditures would not be to improve the quality of life for the population in a direct way. Rather, the expenditures would be calculated to create a climate that would attract the kind of foreign capital investment that would generate a quick rise in the export of manufactured goods.

To jump-start the process of attracting this kind of foreign investment, the Sachs-Botchwey plan would encourage African states to follow the lead of Asian and Latin American countries, establishing free-trade zones "to exploit their own competitive advantages, based, for example, on the availability of local cotton crops and inexpensive labor." They cite Mauritius as the African prototype for this policy. That island nation has used a free-zone policy to attract an enclave of export-oriented textile manufacturing firms. This policy is credited with helping the nation sustain an annual growth rate of 6 percent over three decades. The deep-water commercial harbor that was built for the export-processing zone industries has doubled as a key infrastructure for the tourist industry. According to Botchwey, Mauritius, just like the Asian Tigers, has taken off.

A FREE ZONE

On August 31, 1995, the Parliament of the Republic of Ghana enacted the Free Zone Act (Kufor, 1997).[2] Its stated purpose was "to enable the establishment of free zones in Ghana for the promotion of economic development; to provide for the regulation of activities in free zones and for related purposes (Parliament of the Republic of Ghana, 1995: Preamble)."

The law gives the national president the power to declare segments of land within the national boundaries as "free zones." Such zones are to be made available to corporate developers to operate enterprises for the production of "any type of goods and services for export," so long as they are not "environmentally hazardous." The law places on free-zone developers the responsibility to construct and maintain all infrastructure necessary for their own activities, to fence and secure the zone, and to contribute to the costs of any on-site customs services that the Ghanaian Customs Services sees fit to require. Free-zone enterprises must be licensed by the Free Zone Board; the board has the discretion to "attach to a license such conditions as it thinks appropriate concerning employment skills, job opportunities, and the degree of export orientation." The act exempts most goods that are either imported into or exported from free zones from the country's regular trade laws, taxes, and duties. However, if the enterprise gains the board's approval for selling its products inside of Ghana—up to 30 percent of its total production—those goods are taxed as imports.

Part VI of the act sets out a list of "Incentives" to entice investors to set up free trade zones. The first of these incentives excuses free-zone enterprises entirely from the payment of Ghanaian income taxes on their profits for the first ten years of their operations and freezes their tax rate at a maximum of 8 percent thereafter. The second allows foreign investors to own up to 100 percent of any free-zone enterprise. The next incentives enable free-zone enterprises the right of unconditional transfer of all dividends, profits, and proceeds of the enterprise outside of the country, "in free convertible currency." Further incentives protect free-zone enterprises from government takeover, "except in the national interest or for a public purpose," after the payment of fair compensation, the observation of statutory procedural safeguards, and High Court review. The next incentive, sandwiched between "investment guarantees" and "operation of foreign currency accounts," provides that all disputes between free-zone enterprises and the Ghanaian government, "in respect of any activities of the free zone," shall be settled by "mutual discussion," or, that failing, through the "rules of procedure for arbitration" that have been established "for the settlement of investment disputes" by international trade agreements. Whenever there is "disagreement between the licensee and the Government as to the method of dispute settlement to be adopted," the law announces, "the choice of the licensee shall prevail."

Only near the bottom of the free-zone law's litany of "Incentives" does it reach the topic of "employment." The incentive here is simple:

> Free zone developers and enterprises shall be free to negotiate and establish contracts of employment with employees that include wage scales, minimum working hours, employee suspension and dismissal, settlement of disputes ... and other such terms of employment as shall be consistent with I.L.O. Conventions on workers' rights and conditions of service.

Thus, the country's old-fashioned labor laws, throwbacks to the Nkrumah era, will not be hung round the necks of investors who dare to reenter the Gold Coast after the decades of Decline. No such thing will be put in the way as a new generation of cyber-wired, flexibly specialized developers—world citizens—sense their way into that elusive niche for real growth that a renascent Africa can offer to the world. According to the free-zone law's ninth Incentive, Ghanaian labor rights do not reach to the people who cross over the law-mandated "fencing and enclosures" to work inside the zones.

But the law is not all incentives. The regulations enacted in 1996 to implement the law require that "free zone employers shall pay to their employees wages which shall not be below the recommended minimum wages prevailing in the country at any given time." These regulations interpret the statute to require free-zone employers to comply with Ghanaian legislation that peripherally addresses labor rights, i.e., "social security and pensions, workmen's compensation, [and] public holidays." Investors must comply with most of Ghana's health, safety, and environmental regulations, including the Factory, Offices, and Shops Act of 1970, which regulates occupational health and safety. Free-zone industries must open their doors to inspectors from the nation's environmental protection agency, factory inspectorate department, and town, metropolitan, and district governments. And finally, each developer must contribute "at least an additional 1 percent of their total wage and salary bill . . . toward the training of their employees from the country."

HOPE FOR AFRICA

The countries of sub-Saharan Africa form a region of tremendous human creativity . . .

Despite this enormous potential, Africa has the largest number of the poorest countries in the world. . . . Indeed, 40 percent [of Africans] live on less than $1 per day. In addition, 40 percent of Africans suffer from malnutrition and hunger, while 1 in 5 children in Africa die before the age of 5. . . . The per capital income for sub-Saharan Africa . . . fell from $752 in 1980, when the neo-liberal development model was initially imposed on numerous African countries, to $613 in 1988 (in constant 1980 US dollars).

The International Monetary Fund . . . and other international financial institutions and aid agencies have required African nations to adhere to "structural adjustment programs" which have imposed enormous preventable suffering on African people.

These programs orient economies toward export production, placing downward pressure on wages, encouraging unsustainable resource exploitation, and undermining food security.

These programs lead to major reductions in government spending, including in the crucial areas of education, healthcare, and environmental protection, and they particularly harm women, who are most severely hurt by the elimination of the social safety net and the policy's neglect of small and domestically oriented farmers. . . .

Structural adjustment programs force recessionary policies that most seriously victimize the poor, and these programs tend to exacerbate income and wealth inequalities and undermine basic well-being, as measured by access to food, shelter, medical services, and a sustainable livelihood, even when traditional economic indicators show economic growth. (U.S. Congress, 1999b)

The HOPE for Africa Bill was Jesse Jackson Jr.'s response to a Clinton Administration bill, the African Growth and Opportunity Act (U.S. Congress, 1999a). The Clinton bill called for North-South political and economic partnership to promote fair opportunity for African nations to trade their wares on the global market. It encouraged African nations to change their domestic laws to stimulate growth in the sectors, like labor intensive manufacturing, that might be particularly attractive to foreign investors, and might produce goods or components, like garments, shoes, and electronics, that are particularly in demand by global consumers. Jackson's HOPE bill takes a fundamentally different approach to the African development question.

The centerpiece of the HOPE bill is the forgiveness of most of the African nations' foreign debt. The bill would then place the United States behind development strategies that are democratically negotiated by each African nation. In order to promote each nation's political capacity to make such decisions, the bill explicitly requires that a fixed percentage of the revenues that would otherwise have gone to debt service must be used to fund the human capacities, social fabric, civic institutions, and local governance processes that a vigorous, participatory democracy requires. Thus, the bill would use U.S. domestic law to create leverage for the continued investment in social needs and human service infrastructures by the Ghanaian government.

Jesse Jackson Jr. appears to have read the work of David Held and Robert Putnam. Although he uses the language of African nationalism, he seems to recognize the risk that is posed to democracy when the social fabric in any nation is allowed to fray (Held, 1995; Putnam, 1995).

Conversations

A POOL-SIDE BEER

In a late-night meeting over Club Beers on the pool deck of the Atlantic Breeze Hotel, two graduating classmates at the Ghana School of Law talked with me about their visions of the future. It was the end of March. The first, who was ranked near the top of his law school's class, had just been accepted into an elite U.S. law school's masters' degree program for the following fall. The second planned to work for a year at a local business-law firm and to apply to U.S. law schools for the following year. Both young men described themselves to me as "neo-Nkrumah" democrats. In several hours of impassioned conversation, they gave hints of their vision for their country in the new millennium. It was a fluid vision, one that had little relation to the platitudinous renditions of postcolonial aspiration that any of the competing versions of the "Africa Growth and Opportunity Act" suggested. But neither, for that matter, did their late-night musings seem to have all that much relation to the run-down pool deck on which we were sitting, the chaotic city around us, or their own employment plans.

Aesthetically, theirs was a Frank Gehry vision, of a chrome-and-concrete built environment, jutting out at you from everywhere, at unexpected angles, climate-controlled without refrigeration, cyber-linked without the wires. This was a designed space, but one that seemed to *subsume* the chaos of the older order without even purporting to contain it. Economically, theirs was a postindustrial fantasy of laissez-faire gone good. The traditional markets had gone on-line without passing through any central data base. Entrepreneurs, venture capitalists, and investors were linked in an open system, through which they could sense emerging market opportunities with the exquisite sensitivity of a cat's feet, and then curl into them like fog. Politically, the democratic fabric was elastic, but certainly not "experimental": that would evoke the pretensions of a scientific faith that was long-since passé. And culturally, it was hybrid, rather than plural: infused with an endless desire for other voices, but defiant toward the schoolmarm who would work too hard to hear them.

When their words were spent, the first young man told me that he wasn't all that interested in studying critical or cultural theories of law when he was in the States. With only a year to spend in America, he needed to learn the black-letter doctrine of U.S. administrative law, banking law, and commercial transactions so he could come back to do his part to clean up corruption in the civil service, and make it a little easier for foreign companies to get free-zone licenses.

At the same time he would do this kind of work by day, he planned to continue working with his friend on a project that they had started at the law school earlier that year, after doing an internship at a U.S.-funded public interest law firm in South Africa. In the project, they had organized fellow law students to do a weekly "advice center" in a church in the largest and poorest informal settlement in the Accra region. Because the students were not permitted to represent clients in court, they were limited to giving their clients advice on the informal settlement of their legal problems. This project kept them "in touch with the people at the grassroots," they told me.

They talked about this weekly trek to the urban advice center as work that could shift the political meaning of the daytime lawyer's work that they envisioned doing for pay. These treks to the squatter settlement would make their day jobs, of helping to purge the government of the last traces of Nkrumah-era socialist red tape and nationalist cronyism, into political action. They could not say exactly *how* or *why* this night work with the poor should be understood to have so substantial a political consequence, and I did not press them. Perhaps I did not want to push them to admit how tenuously they believed the assertion themselves.

A CONFERENCE WITH MR. A—

Mr. A— had graduated in the early 1990s from the Ghana School of Law. We met in a conference room just behind one of the main lecture halls of the law school. He was typical of many idealistic young Ghanaian men who were a few years out of law school. He was employed by the Ministry of Trade and Industry in the division that administered the free-zone law. He had played a minor role in drafting the law and was heavily involved in the day-to-day bureaucratic tasks of governmental oversight of free-zone licensing, zone supervision, and conflict resolution. The work of his ministry overlapped that of the "Gateway" Secretariat, where several of his law school colleagues had found jobs. The Gateway is the governmental division that has oversight of large public works projects, funded in large part by foreign donors, that are charged to develop the infrastructures—a deep-water harbor, coastal access roads, communication channels, etc.—that will link the Ghanaian economy to the outside world.

The first part of our meeting was formal. Mr. A— began by giving me a firm handshake and my own copy of the glossy, four-color folder that the Ghanaian government distributes to potential foreign investors. My folder contained the full text of the Free Zone Act and regulations, a pamphlet setting out the free-zone Incentives in bullet-point format, and a two-page flow chart that walks applicants through the ten regulatory steps they have to take to set up shop in a free-trade zone. Then he gave me a minilecture about the miracle of Mauritius; I had already read that story in the *Harvard Magazine.*

Then Mr. A— told me that the Ghanaian trade unions had made a presentation to the Ghanaian legislature before the Free Zone Act was passed. He told me that the leadership of the Ghanaian Trade Union Congress had initially opposed the act because its member unions, the miners, the textile workers, and the civil servants, feared that their power would be undercut if individual workers had the option of nonunionized free-zone jobs, and if employers could move into the zones in order to bust their unions. Eventually, as a result of this trade union intervention, the Ghanaian free-trade zone statute incorporated more explicit protections of workers' rights than the free-trade zone laws in many other nations. For one thing, the Ghanaian statute makes clear that the minimal labor standards of the International Labor Organization, including the right of workers to organize unions, can be enforced against free-zone enterprises by the Ghanaian state.

In response to a question, Mr A— told me that the "sweatshop" issue was a problem with free-zone development that all of the players in the Ghanaian debate were aware of, but none considered it a reason to question the policy's underlying wisdom. He said that the Ghanaian unions viewed the question of free-zone employees' working conditions as a question of transnational labor-union politics. The Ghanaian unions were concerned that non-union manufacturing firms in the free zones would significantly weaken their power in Ghanaian domestic politics, yet at the same time they were suspicious that the strident campaign by the U.S. labor movement to write first-world labor standards into third-world free-zone statutes was "retro-imperialism": it was a flailing effort by first-world workers to protect their vanishing colonial privilege, at least inside their own borders.

When I asked Mr. A— what he thought about the situation of the young women who worked in the Mauritian free zone, he evaded my question. He told me that the unions had assumed that most of the free-zone jobs, like most jobs in Ghana's domestic manufacturing sector, would go to skilled male workers who were part of the well-entrenched, elite, urban industrial labor force. I said that the workforce in free zones in Asia and the Americas is overwhelmingly female, and that many free-zone policy analysts have concluded that the costs and benefits of free-zone employment, at least to the first generation of workers, cannot be assessed without taking account of gender. Mr. A— seemed perplexed, but not disinterested, and assumed a less formal demeanor. The conversation continued.

We talked about incentives. He told me that the country needed foreign capital in order to develop. Ghanaians and their families needed cash, any way they could get it, in order to survive. He reminded me that about 12 percent of Ghanaian kids, some living very close to the city's plush coastal hotels, have severe nutritional deficiencies. He asked if I had seen any of these kids yet, with their huge bellies and reddish hair. He reminded me that Ghana had been spared the worst of the HIV epidemic, at least so far, but there was no guarantee that this luck would continue. AIDS would be harder for Ghanaian families to deal with than child malnutrition. He then said that the main resource the free-zone policy was seeking to capitalize on was the North-South differential in the standard of living. This was the one hidden jewel that the era of colonial expropriation had left behind. He said that "we" had no business getting in the way as his government tried to sell off this wealth to spark a new era of Ghanaian prosperity. Surely they had suffered enough to claim that meager property right. I said that I doubted the wage differential would sell, even with the added sweeteners of tax forgiveness and labor deregulation, unless the infrastructure support was super, the "public health" and "environmental quality" problems were under control, at least in the areas where foreign investors would come to do business, and the workforce was sufficiently healthy, educated, and reliable.

I was starting to sound like a salesgirl for the Emerging Africa initiative. I prayed that the despairing logic behind my flip calculation was flawed. Indeed, I realized on reflection, the greatest draw of the zones might be for Asian textile producers to set up shop in the zones in order to add just enough of an African finish on their own export products to circumvent the industrial countries' import quotas. But the shenanigans of international trade weren't my field, so the conversation moved on.

We focused on how export-processing platforms might jump-start a course of development that would be good for Ghanaians, at least in the long run. What features of their free-zone law ensured that these firms would have the desired wider impact on Ghanaian development? And what might that impact be? The circulation of more wages in Ghana's consumer economy? Technology transfer, including the transfer of industrial work-discipline and specific job skills to a new cohort of workers and their families? The educative effects of the free-zone industries on the wider practices and culture of Ghanaian business? The spill-over benefits of the new public infrastructure investments like improved coastal roads? I was on a roll; I could go on. I could also trot out the typical counterarguments from free-zone skeptics: that the deal was a ripoff for Ghana because the rents taken by the free-zone developers were excessively high; that very little technology would be transferred; that the cultural effects would be minimal because the free-zone firms would keep themselves isolated from the much less "developed" Ghanaian mainstream; that the obvious idea behind the policy—of offering up human bodies as the disposable instruments of a cheap-labor-based development strategy—was all too familiar, and still just as bad, both morally and pragmatically. Seeing any person in such terms, even if it was purportedly for their nation's longer-term benefit, was no way to make a better world.

At the end of this internal point-counterpoint, I posed my next question.

What likelihood do you see, I asked my host, that the concessions that were written into the law for labor—the ILO's minimum labor standards, for instance, or the 1 percent tax on firms' annual profits for the education and training of workers—would actually be enforced? After asking this question, I reminded Mr. A— that the law's dispute-resolution provisions seemed blatantly skewed to favor investors: the statute provided no private right of action for the enforcement of its terms. Mr. A— dropped any remaining pretense of distance and did not hesitate to answer my question. The ministry cannot afford to press these issues, he told me. Enforcing these provisions would give Ghana a bad reputation in the global competition, among developing countries, for free-zone business. After he told me this, he looked distracted.

I told him about a radio report I had recently heard. Anti-sweatshop protesters in the United States had picketed their local Disney Stores to vent their outrage about low wages and exploitive working conditions in a Haitian toy factory. The factory employed several hundred people and was one of the only sources of cash in a region where people were starving. According to the story, the protesters did not try to confer with Haiti-based nongovernmental organizations or workers before launching their campaign. To show its respect for the moral scruples of its first-world consumers, Disney responded to their protest by moving the plant to Honduras.

Once I get into storytelling mode, one tale leads to another. The next one I told Mr. A— was about the "Buffalo Hunt" in North Carolina, where I had been raised. After our textile factories moved to Mexico and Singapore to find cheaper labor, many states and municipalities in southern states enacted free-zone laws to attract high-tech industries like electronics to replace the shops that had run away. Ultimately, the strategy got mixed reviews. Industrial development took off in most of the states in the region. And yet many of the communities that had built extensive infrastructure or compromised their tax laws to attract particular industries became impoverished by the effort. Large public debts were incurred to fund infrastructure needs of particular firms or industries, with no planning for how those projects would help to sustain good development, over the longer term. The firms that had been lured to the region in search of cheap labor were the kind that could pick up and leave without much problem; that is why we had caught them in the first place. They had no reason to transfer technology to potential competitors in the local community, or to foot the bill for any worker training that was not absolutely necessary to their own operations. And as soon as they could operate more cheaply elsewhere, which, for most, was the mid-1970s, they moved away.

I told Mr. A— that in the two decades "after the buffalos had disappeared," some of the common folks in these communities, impoverished by the trade-zone phase of industrialization, had been working together to rethink the whole idea of development in varying shades of green. Mr. A— seemed to get the point of my story. He told me he wanted to find policies for Ghanaian development that would be good for all of his people and that would keep working over the long run, but he could not do very much about that idea from his position in the Trade Ministry.

THE GOOD WOMAN FROM FIDA

When I went to visit the good woman who worked at FIDA, she was preoccupied by many things. First, a blue-ribbon committee of management consultants, brought together by the Ghanaian government's council of state, was in the conference room next to her office, meeting with her and her board of directors. They had been meeting all morning to hammer out a long-term strategic plan for the organization, complete with benchmarks and performance standards. As part of its good governance initiative, and with the encouragement and support of the U.S. government, the Ghanaian council of state had decided to include FIDA in a new initiative to promote "transparency and good governance" in the administrative agencies of the central government. Through this initiative, a team of private-sector management consultants would meet with each agency to develop and carry out a long-term strategic plan, focused on institutional reforms that would increase the agency's capacity to deliver on their goals.

The council had decided to include one nongovernmental organization in the initiative. In part because one of FIDA's long-time members had recently been appointed to a seat on the council, FIDA was chosen. The choice was not entirely arbitrary, however, because a major feature of the government's larger good governance initiative is to promote the "rule of law" throughout the country. One aspect of this project is to popularize the idea of citizen access both to civil courts and to lawyers, in order to ensure the widespread enforcement of the rapidly expanding array of private property rights. The strategic plan that the consultants were working out with FIDA's board envisioned that over the next decade FIDA would become a nationwide network of legal-service offices, staffed by full-time lawyers and providing direct representation in civil cases to clients who could not afford a private lawyer. The plan called for FIDA to continue to restrict its services to women clients with cases in such areas as domestic law, inheritance and property rights, and gender discrimination. Yet the FIDA plan was of interest to the government because FIDA offices throughout the country would help to promote the new idea of legal representation as a private good, a consumer service, to be purchased by individuals on a free market and subsidized only in circumstances where an individual's indigence required it. This new liberal idea of a rule of law that gave each person in Ghana her own bundle of formal equal rights, including the right to hire a lawyer to enforce them—this new idea of law was a critical complement to the new economic order that had been ordained by structural adjustment policies.

FIDA itself—the Federacion Internacional de Abogadas—began in the Southern hemisphere, in 1944, when women from five Latin American countries came together to found a new international organization "to promote and enhance the status of women and children in society." The organization now has more than fifty chapters, worldwide. The Ghanaian chapter was launched in 1974, and since then has provided advice, research, networking, and legal literacy programs on "laws and traditional practices which negate the development and aspirations of women and children in the civil, educational, and business fields." FIDA established the first legal-aid program in Ghana in 1985, in Accra. This program employs one staff lawyer. She interviews clients in FIDA's main office on the third floor of a walk-up office building in central Accra. She then refers clients who might benefit from formal legal representation to a network of FIDA members, who take cases on a rotating basis, free of charge. When I visited FIDA in March of 1999, my host was the staff attorney. A solicitor on a leave of absence from a small business-law firm, she was in her late forties, with two children in college in the United States.

The current FIDA brochure boasts that "[t]he informal atmosphere prevailing affords the best opportunity for interaction of Legal Aid officers with aid applicants for better ascertainment of their problems and difficulties" (FIDA-Ghana, n.d.). Yet my host at FIDA explained that one of the main priorities of the organization's new strategic plan was to professionalize its systems and services—hiring staff lawyers to replace the network of volunteers, computerize the offices, systematize its intake and case files, and the like. Indeed, it was the "informality" of the office's operations, along with the gathering of dignitaries in the next room, that were the greatest sources of her immediate preoccupation.

As we talked about the history of FIDA and its current activities, she and the program's only other employee, a clerical assistant, were rummaging through a huge pile of case files. They said they were searching for a letter from the United States Information Agency awarding the organization a small grant to do a series of legal literacy workshops in the northern districts of the country. The workshops would focus on FIDA's priority issues: administration of estates, children and maintenance, wills, intestate succession, and divorce. The grant was one of several that the U.S. government had awarded to help build "democratic institutions" in the country. Another had gone to the legal advice center that the young law graduate I had shared a beer with had set up through the Ghana Law School. Since FIDA's founding, these legal literacy classes had been the organization's second service priority, after their storefront legal clinic. My host, the FIDA staff attorney, gave me a set of densely worded pamphlets that the "FIDA–Ghana Legal Literacy Project" had produced for grassroots women in each of its priority areas of law.

After she found the USIA grant letter and settled the dignitaries down to a lunch of fried fish, rice, and vegetable stew, she returned to her office to talk. She announced that the organization had just represented its first sexual harassment plaintiff before an administrative labor board: an office worker in a downtown Accra business. She reiterated that FIDA's goal for the next decade would be to expand its legal clinic coverage, so that women all over the country could get access to free legal aid. When I asked about FIDA's service priorities over the next decade, she said that the organization's goal was to represent Ghanaian women on the same issues that are of urgent concern to women all over the world: domestic violence, sexual harassment, girls' education, women's rights to abortion and divorce, and their right to secure their property after divorce and pass it along to their children.

She said that Ghanaian women were far better off than many, because of the matrifocal traditions among the Ashanti and other tribal groups. Yet she told me not to be deceived. The problems that Ghanaian women face in securing their own safety, and property, were not all that different, really, from the problems that women face in every part of the world. She said it was rewarding for women who had been trained as lawyers to help other women with these problems. Then we talked about North Carolina, where she would be going the following week to attend the graduation of her daughter from college.

Part Two: Notes and Questions

Two Worlds of Cause Lawyers

The conversations that I had with these four young lawyers drew me into two different worlds of Ghanaian cause lawyers. The world of the men I interviewed is one of economic development bureaucrats; the world of FIDA lawyers is one of women's rights activists. In this section, I want to draw on these conversations as well as others to offer a few more impressions of those two different worlds.

In the world of economic development practice, the actors who have some power tend to be established members of the Ghanaian legal profession, business, or political elites. These men have strong personal ties to equally powerful actors in government, universities, major corporations, and large foundations in the United States or other industrial nations. These key actors are surrounded by less powerful professional agents: academics, development consultants, computer wizards, financial advisers, entrepreneurs, and government bureaucrats, some of whom are also lawyers. When these actors make speeches about the nation's future, they talk of an African renaissance. They talk about how open-door trade policies, secure property, transparent governance, equality of opportunity, a thriving civil society, and full-scale political democracy can come together to ensure that sub-Saharan development will finally take off.

In another institutional domain, young civil servants like Mr. A— do the everyday work of rewriting the country's tax codes and tariff schedules, stripping down labor and environmental regulations, and beefing up private property protections so as to bring that renaissance about. These young lawyers often have iconoclastic views about what is wrong with current development policy and strong feelings about the kind of world that they ultimately want development to achieve. But they do not perceive themselves to have very much power to influence the course that Ghanaian development is actually taking. These young lawyer-bureaucrats tend to be recent graduates of Ghana's law school. Some have advanced degrees from U.S. universities and others would like to. Most, but not all, are men. They work side by side with non-law-trained civil servants. Together with these nonlawyers, they do the everyday tasks of weaving externally imposed development conditions into the fabric of Ghana's domestic laws.

In the world of women's rights activists, the people who tend to hold power are academics, philanthropists, and political leaders in the United States and other industrial countries, as well as a small circle of Ghanaian academics and activists with whom they regularly do business. When the elites in this world of women's rights speak publicly about the future, they talk about a world in which all girls and women are free from violence—in the fields and marketplaces, the sweatshops and schoolrooms, the inner offices of the loftiest international tribunals, and their own homes. It is a world in which the girls in rural villages as well as elite suburbs stay in school, just like the boys, and then grow up free to choose any line of work that is open to men. It is a world where their bosses respect their minds, rather than gaze on their bodies, and pay them the same wages as men. In this world of the future, girls don't have to get circumcised or married unless they want to. They can get divorces and abortions on demand when they are young, and pensions when they are old. They can buy their own homes and then leave them to their children. In this world of empowered modern women, the tangled underbrush of Ghanaian "custom" has been artfully pruned, but not entirely uprooted, and the rising tide of transnational fundamentalism has gone back out to sea.

FIDA lawyers are in regular contact with the women in these circles: this is the world to which they must appeal to get money, legitimacy, and protection. Yet rank-and-file FIDA women do not have a voice in this world. Rather, they do the everyday work of bringing the global "women's rights" agenda inside the institutions of civil and customary law in their own country. Rank-and-file FIDA women are in private law practice in small firms that serve the country's urban middle class. Many have close personal ties in northern nations: some received advanced law degrees in British or U.S. universities; others send their children abroad to school. Even though they do not have much power in elite circles, these are modern, independently minded women: they stay in touch with each other by cell phone, get annual mammograms, and read their e-mail in the privacy of their own homes. Many are married to lawyers who do the work of economic development, but they like to keep their work lives separate from their private affairs.

But Are They Really Cause Lawyers?

I refer to the rank-and-file lawyers in these two professional worlds as "cause lawyers." The concept, as set forth in Sarat and Scheingold's first *Cause Lawyering* volume, centers on lawyers who self-consciously represent political or moral agendas in traditional litigation contexts (Sarat and Scheingold, 1998). Ghanaian women's rights lawyers fit easily within this conception. Civil servants like Mr. A—, or prospective ones like the two young man I talked with by the pool do not. They do not litigate on behalf of individual clients whose claims correlate with their own political values or social visions. Rather, they work for the party *against* whom cause litigators typically file their lawsuits: the state. And worse yet, they do not litigate on behalf of their client. Instead, they do the detail work required to reframe the legal rules through which the state configures economic activity. What could I possibly be thinking to call such functionaries "cause lawyers"?

For one thing, the cause-lawyer label signals that, notwithstanding the differences, these civil servants are engaged in the same kind of vocational project as traditional cause lawyers, in several important respects. Just like public interest litigators, lawyers like Mr. A— are motivated by their own moral visions and political values as well as the legal profession's generic practice standards. Just like traditional cause lawyers, they do what they can to promote those commitments from within the constraints that their jobs impose. And even though they do not litigate, they deploy other traditional lawyering skills to advance their "causes." They draft statutes, administrative regulations, and the like; they negotiate on behalf of the government with representatives of private enterprise; they investigate these actors' conduct to ensure their compliance with legal rules.

More to the point, though, applying the cause-lawyer label to these civil servants draws our attention to features of the traditional conception that warrant further attention, particularly as we expand the cause lawyering project into the global field. All of the essays in this volume focus on lawyers who work for love, as well as money, in settings where localized social fabrics, national legal orders, international norm-setting institutions, and cross-national political forces conflict, intermingle, and converge. It is an understatement to say that this is a complex, multilayered, and dynamic power field. The points at which the Ghanaian civil servants' practice most emphatically *diverges* from the taken-for-granted picture of domestic cause lawyering may be the very points at which the concept itself needs to be rethought to provide a useful map of the cause-oriented lawyering practices that are emerging in this field. What, then, are the most striking divergences between the vocational world of these civil servants and the world of the traditional cause-oriented public-interest litigator?

First, although Mr. A— uses recognized legal skills, many of his coworkers do not have formal legal training or certification. Unlike litigating, the work of designing legal systems and practices, which is one of the most highly demanded forms of legal expertise in the transnational field (Sassen, 1998), has not yet, and is not likely to be, monopolized by the legal profession. Thus, a reworked conception of "cause lawyering" in the global arena may need to be broad enough to encompass the other professionals—accountants, information systems experts, organizational consultants, and the like—who are increasingly collaborating to do this legal design work in the global era.

Second, many of Mr. A—'s coworkers, both lawyers and nonlawyers, do not share his sense of mission. Rather, they simply do the work that they are given. Some are motivated by a sense of craft; others simply work to get paid. At the core of the traditional conception, cause lawyers work in practice settings—typically nonprofit law firms that were founded to further a specific political mission—that have been constituted as new *institutions* precisely to promote the cause. Will this convergence of the cause lawyer's vocational purpose with his law firm's institutional mission be as likely among cause lawyers in the global field?

Third, Mr. A— does not believe that the kinds of action that his role allows will produce much leverage to further his cause. Unlike a litigator in a well-funded public-interest law firm, who has great freedom to fashion test cases that he can believe will "make a difference," Mr. A— is under no illusion that the work he can do as a lawyer might make a profound difference to his cause. He is under no illusion that the subtle power he can wield as he distributes the burdens in an administrative-oversight procedure or targets a firm for an occupational safety inspection, for instance, will do very much to protect the common people of Ghana against the hegemony of foreign capital. The scope of Mr. A—'s power to promote his cause within his institutional role is not all that different from that of the government litigators described in Yoav Dotan's essay in this volume, "The Global Language of Human Rights: Patterns of Cooperation between State and Civil Rights Lawyers in Israel." Are global cause lawyers more likely than their domestic predecessors to occupy institutional roles, as lawyers, that constrain them to promote their causes in oblique rather than direct ways?

Finally, Mr. A—does not think of his cause in person-like terms. He does not think of himself as speaking *for* his cause in the same way that he might advocate for an individual client in a legal or political contest. Rather, Mr. A—sees his role in the Ghanaian central government's bureaucracy to be more like that of an artisan, or a mole. His challenge is to rework the web of legal ground rules that constitute state power so that the texture of his cause becomes a little more prominent in that fabric. Mr. A— presumes a postmodernist conception of the state as he works as a lawyer to challenge and redirect its power. Mr. A—'s beliefs about both the state and his cause, as revealed through his actual lawyering practices, thus leave him with a less audacious understanding of his own political agency than the "traditional" cause lawyer presumes (Halliday, 1998; Santos, 1995; Sassen, 1998; and Shamir, 1997, on postmodernist conceptions of law and lawyering). This "downsizing" of Mr. A—'s self-concept *as* a legal actor is worth further reflection as we work out our theories and practices of global cause lawyering. Is such a postmodernist sense of their own vocational and political agency a widespread feeling among "global" cause lawyers? Is this self-concept more likely to emerge among some types of causes, or in some practice settings? Are lawyers who identify themselves with the cause of international human rights, for instance, less likely than Mr. A— to have such a downsized conception of their own efficacy? Are human-rights lawyers likely to rework their understanding of their own political agency as they move from the easily "readable" domain of formal civil and political rights, and into the much more challenging domains of economic and social rights or multiethnic constitutionalism, for instance? Does a postmodern conception of their own agency give such lawyers more adequate existential and vocational grounding for doing the hard, uncertain work of pursuing justice in those murky domains?

Separate Lawyering Worlds

The radical shifts in Ghana's fiscal and economic policies that have occurred in the 1980s and 1990s have been conditioned by extraterritorial political forces like the U.S. government, the International Monetary Fund, the World Bank, and the major philanthropic foundations. These policy shifts have been worked into the fabric of Ghana's domestic laws by Ghanaian civil servants. Some, like Mr. A—, are politically committed lawyers who have done their best to position themselves to be of some use to their cause on a complex power field. The effects of structural adjustment conditionalities on the common people of Ghana have yet to be mapped out on the ground with any precision. Yet we already know that the domestic policies that have been enacted in response to external pressures are having multiple interacting effects on different sectors of Ghana's population.

Some of the effects of externally conditioned Ghanaian policy changes are dramatic, like the precipitous drop, in the 1980s, in the country's inflation rates, or the equally precipitous rise, in the early 1990s, in the number of children, most of them teenaged migrants from the fiscally neglected northern districts, living on Accra's streets (Catholic Action for Street Children, 1999, n.d.).[3] Other effects, like the multiple impacts of changes in Ghanaian health financing on maternal and child well-being in the northern district, are harder, but not impossible, to trace. Other effects are more elusive. Our tools of policy analysis are too crude to assess the impact of externally conditioned economic development policies on the life-worlds of Wilhemina and her two children. And it is hard to assess the value of the social infrastructures that will *not* be provided because international donors, according to Mr. A—, are considering multimillion dollar commitments for building the roads and deepening the harbors that will make Ghana's coastal corridor, yet again, the Gateway through which African goods can be shipped to the world. Even in these hard cases, however, we can intuit that externally conditioned domestic policy changes are likely to impact on the least powerful of Ghana's common people, particularly non-elite, geographically dispersed women and children, in particularly harmful ways.

What is striking about this picture is the distance between the world of the lawyers who write these new global ideologies into Ghana's laws and that of the lawyers who seek to protect women's rights. The economic development lawyers have come to terms with their marginal power to reshape Ghana's laws to conform with external conditionalities without harming common people. They use the game-talk of the market to describe the limited scope of their political agency. At the same time, perhaps to make peace with their predicament, some of these lawyers moonlight in Accra's most impoverished quarters, providing random acts of charitable legal service for the poor. They rationalize these good works with the implausible claim that their efforts might reawaken the masses to Nkrumah's dream that strong democracy can protect them from the power of the dollar. At the same time that they spin out such explanations for their face-to-face human service however, they do not talk about its imminent, rather than instrumental, value.

Meanwhile, in a separate professional sphere, the women's rights lawyers do not grapple with the consequences of structural adjustment policies for Ghanaian women. These issues are not within the global priorities that their overseas funders, or the transnational circles of elite women who define global women's rights agendas, have laid out for them. Instead of grappling with the impact of structural adjustment policies on the migration and subsistence of destitute rural women and girls, for instance, the women's rights lawyers focus on the sexual harassment of elite women in Accra's office towers. More recently, as part of their campaign for "good governance" in African nations, foreign funders have encouraged the women's rights lawyers to put aside substantive priorities altogether, and take up the formal proceduralist agenda of providing "access to legal services" for all Ghanaian women. Like access to health care, this service might be offered on a "cash and carry" basis, so long as access is even-handed for those who can pay.

In spite of the pressures to pursue such agendas, Ghanaian women's law organizations like FIDA are continuing to do the face-to-face work of legal representation and community legal education. This work keeps them in touch with the ways that new economic policies are affecting real Ghanaian women. Because they understand their moral agency in humanist, rather than strategic terms, they believe these acts of witness to have great, indeed, incommensurable significance. This faith in the value of their work is what sustains them; it provides its own rewards. Yet it also sustains a sense of resignation, or even complacency, about the scope of their political responsibility in the face of globally conditioned economic policies that are disproportionately hurting the least powerful Ghanaian women.

But Are They Really Separate?

I have described the worlds of the economic development civil servants and women's rights advocates as contemporaneous but separated. Is this a fair description, or do both worlds actually promote a single, overarching normative agenda? The lawyers in each of these worlds put forth, through their practice, distinctive understandings of underdevelopment: how it came to be, why it is a problem, what should be done about it. In the world of the economic development civil servants, underdevelopment is shown through the nation's low per-capita income and GDP. It can be cured by luring foreign capital to fund a new labor-intensive manufacturing sector that will give skills and cash to Ghanaian workers, thus drawing them into the global consumer economy. The economic development lawyers seek to further this vision of development without doing unnecessary harm to Ghana's common people. But they do not challenge its basic premises or implications.

In the world of women's rights lawyers, underdevelopment is shown through the nation's high rates of infant mortality and gender violence and low rates of girls' school attendance. It can be cured by increasing and effectively targeting health and educational spending, thus shoring up the capacities of impoverished Ghanaian women and girls for economic and political agency in the modern world. Like the economic development lawyers, the women's rights lawyers want these interventions to do minimal harm to Ghanaian women. And like the economic development lawyers, the women's rights lawyers define underdevelopment in relation to U.S. norms: underdevelopment is signaled by *not as much* cash in individual Ghanaians' bank accounts or *not as many* years in their lives. Neither group of lawyers worries over *how* or *why* raising the individual income, lifespan, or "capacity," for that matter, of the "average" Ghanaian individual will produce good development outcomes.

These two accounts of underdevelopment might seem at first glance to be opposed to one another. Yet when viewed side by side, the congruence in their assumptions and implications is striking. Both accounts promote the same basic concepts of human agency, the national economy, and the state in a modern, "developed" world. Both accounts call for more linkages between Ghanaian and multilateral or U.S.-based institutions in order to pursue development. Neither account incorporates particularities of Ghanaian history, culture, or institutions into its visions or practices of development in a sustained or searching way. Nor does either account infuse its conception of development policy with a pervasive sensitivity to historically rooted power differentials. Thus, both accounts fit quite well within an overarching vision of development in which the absorption of the "rest" into a worldwide regime of consumer capitalism and liberal, representative democracy is taken for granted.

In view of the way that the Ghanaian legal landscape is embedded in wider global dynamics, it should not be surprising that these two groups of Ghanian cause lawyers function as unknowing agents of this global agenda. But it may not be inevitable. The ground-level actors in both worlds, though constrained, have some room to maneuver around this fate. For a start, each world of Ghanaian cause lawyers might do more to link up with the other. Such horizontal linkage, once begun, might take on its own momentum. As linkages strengthen, their force might enable these Ghanaian lawyers to come up with some new ways of thinking about their country's welfare. More linkage between these two spheres might embolden these lawyers to listen more closely to the experience of the least advantaged Ghanaians in the present economic order. More linkage might give these lawyers new strategies for confronting the foreign actors that seek to dictate local priorities, and more leverage to negotiate with them. It might give these lawyers more energy to support sister social movements in other countries. It might open up a little space for what Boaventura de Sousa Santos has called globalization's *counter*hegemonic potential (Santos, 1995).

At present, however, there is little interaction across these two professional worlds. Because the actors do not understand themselves to be engaged in related projects, they do not see any reason to collaborate. This disconnection seems "natural" because the kinds of work that they perceive themselves to be doing are very different. The economic development civil servants draft the legal rules that govern the economy. The women's rights lawyers represent aggrieved women in litigation or other dispute resolution procedures. The professional self-conceptions of the two groups of lawyers are also very different. They have different visions of good practice. They measure success in different ways. They do not share a common language of vocational aspiration through which to seek out opportunities for collaboration.

These professional self-conceptions are not merely different. They are also, quite strikingly, gendered. Thus, the project of creating linkages across these two professional worlds in order to open up new options for Ghanaian development is also the project of critiquing and reworking the gender norms that keep these two worlds apart.

Conclusion

I suspect that the picture I have drawn of Ghana is not unusual in developing countries. Many peripheral nations, in Asia and Latin America as well as Africa, have, over the last several decades, been influenced by international women's rights networks, on the one hand, and structural adjustment conditionalities, on the other. I suspect that in many of these other nations, as well, two gender-inflected worlds of cause lawyering arose in the last several decades, and, since then, have been drifting, or driven, farther apart. I will end on a theme that I have touched on several times in the chapter, though I will not develop it at length. This is the theme of enhancing the linkage across these two different worlds *within* every such peripheral nation.

A key task that women's law groups need to undertake in order to respond to the gendered meaning of structural adjustment policies is to create nuanced maps of the impact of specific development policies within their own nations and to develop plausible strategic responses to those policies. Such maps can best by drawn by connecting with like-minded actors *inside* the world of economic development policy administration *within* their own national borders. The joint effort to produce detailed analyses of specific development policies could, in turn, build relationships that would create the potential for new analytical and strategic projects.

One fascinating example of such an approach in action is the Women's Budget Initiative in South Africa (Budlender, 1998; Hurt and Budlender, 1998). In this project, a group comprised of lawyers and policy analysts inside and outside of government prepares an annual report on several domains of domestic legislative policy that do not explicitly involve women and yet have significant gender impacts. These analyses are then made available to women's rights and sector-specific cause-lawyering groups. They are also translated into community education materials. This project both draws upon and strengthens relationships between women's rights advocates and like-minded government officials. By doing so, it creates materials that give women's rights and economic development lawyers a set of common priorities to debate and respond to. In the Ghanaian experience, we saw how lawyers sought to reclaim some political agency through random acts of charity, on the one hand, and the promotion of generic women's rights agendas, on the other. The Women's Budget project is the sort of approach that might yield action strategies to join these two worlds of cause lawyers, strategies that are solidly grounded in local circumstances and astutely responsive to global forces at the same time.

Notes

1. These sketches are based on my fieldnotes from research I conducted in Ghana in March of 1999. Many of the place names, proper names, descriptions, biographical details, and accounts of specific events and conversations have been fictionalized in order to preserve

confidentiality. Any resemblance between the persons or events depicted in these sketches and actual events or individuals is coincidental.

2. There is an extensive body of literature on free trade zone legislation in other developing countries, as well as similar investment incentive policies, such as enterprise zones, in the United States. In general, this literature draws attention to the difficulty of shaping such schemes in ways that target the first-order benefits, such as increasing the transferable skill levels of zone employees, in predictable or rational ways. The question of whether such schemes can have more holistic effects on the dynamic of an entire economic system or subsystem is harder to answer, because such longer-term processes are much more difficult to model, and these wider-scale effects are much more difficult to evaluate.

3. Catholic Action for Street Children, a Ghanaian nongovernmental organization founded in 1993, maintains a registry of street children in Accra and has done fieldwork tracing their origins. According to CAS's tabulation, the population of street children in Accra increased from 10,000 to 15,000 in the three-year period between 1996 and 1999. CAS is affiliated with Street Girls Aid, a nongovernmental organization that serves the growing population of adolescent girls on Accra's streets. Street Girls Aid maintains a daycare center in central Accra for about two hundred infants and toddlers of the young girls it serves.

References

Budlender, Debbie, ed. (1998). *The Third Women's Budget*. Cape Town, South Africa: Idasa.
Catholic Action for Street Children (1999). <http://www.BFinternet.com/~CAS>, updated March 1999.
Catholic Action for Street Children (n.d.). "Catholic Action for Street Children," unpublished pamphlet on file with the author.
FIDA-Ghana (nd). "The International Federation of Women Lawyers," Accra, Ghana: Fida-Ghana (Xeroxed pamphlet on file with the author).
Global Trade Watch (1999). "Side-by-Side comparison: Hope for Africa (H.R. 77) and Africa "Growth and Opportunity Act (H.R. 434)" (updated March 3, 1999), <http://citizen.org/pctrade/Africa/HOPE/comparison.htm>.
Halliday, Terrence (1998), "Lawyers as Institution-Builders: Constructing Markets, States, Civil Society and Community," in Austin Sarat, et al., *Crossing Boundaries: Traditions and Transformations in Law and Society Research*. Evanston, Ill.: Northwestern University Press.
Held, David (1995). *Democracy and the Global Order: From the Modern State to Cosmopolitan Governance*. Stanford, Calif.: Stanford University Press.
Hurt, Karen, and Debbie Budlender, eds. (1998). *Money Matters: Women and the Government Budget*. Cape Town, South Africa: Idasa.
Kufor, Kofi Oteng (1997). "The Ghana Free Trade Zone Act," 10 *Transnational Law Journal*, 245–263.
Newton, Alex, and David Else (1997), *West Africa: A Lonely Planet Survival Kit*, Oakland, CA: Lonely Planet Publications, 13, 361–440.
O'Keefe, Matt (1999). "Emerging Africa: Coming to Terms with an Overlooked Continent," *Harvard Magazine* (Feb.-Mar.), <http://www.harvard-magazine.com/ma99/africa.ssi., 1>.
Opokyu-Agyemang, Kwado (1996), "Cape Coast Town," in *Cape Coast Castle: A Collection of Poems*. Accra, Ghana: Afram Publications (Ghana) Ltd., 33.
Parliament of the Republic of Ghana (1995), Act 504, Free Zone Act (Date of Assent, August 31, 1995).

Putnam, Robert (1996). "Bowling Alone," 6 *Journal of Democracy*, 65–78.
Riley, Denise (1988), *"Am I That Name?" Feminism and the Category of "Women" in History*. Minneapolis: University of Minnesota Press.
Santos, Boaventura de Sousa (1995), *Toward a New Common Sense: Law, Science, and Politics in the Paradigmatic Transition*. New York: Routledge.
Sarat, Austin, and Stuart Scheingold (1998), "Cause Lawyering and the Reproduction of Professional Authority: An Introduction," in *Cause Lawyering: Political Commitments and Professional Responsibilities*, Austin Sarat and Stuart Scheingold, eds. New York: Oxford University Press.
Sassen, Saskia (1998), *Globalization and Its Discontents: Essays on the New Mobility of People and Money*. New York: The New Press.
Scmitt, Eric (1998), "Bill to Push Africa Trade Is Approved," *New York Times*, March 16, 1998, A-9.
Shamir, Ronen (1998), "De-centering of State and Cause," Paper presented at the 1998 Law & Society Association Meeting.
Shklar, Judith (1990), *The Faces of Injustice*. New Haven, Conn.: Yale University Press.
Soyinka, Wole (1999), *The Burden of Memory, The Muse of Forgiveness*. New York: Oxford University Press, 19.
United Nations Development Programme (1997), Ghana Human Development Report 1997. Accra, Ghana: United Nations Development Programme.
United States Congress (1999b). HOPE for Africa Act. H. R. 772, 106th Cong. §3.
United States Congress (1999a). Africa Growth and Opportunity Act, H.R. 434, 106th Cong.

CHAPTER 3

From the Fight for Legal Rights to the Promotion of Human Rights
Israeli and Palestinian Cause Lawyers in the Trenches of Globalization

LISA HAJJAR

The subject of "cause lawyering" represents a departure from the concerns that tend to guide inquiries into the legal profession. Rather than emphasizing the role of lawyers in society as conflict arbitrators, consensus builders, or proponents of regulation, the study of cause lawyering probes the transformative and destabilizing potentials of legal work. Rather than focusing on the norms and standard practices of lawyers as members of a corporate group, or individual exemplars of their profession, the study of cause lawyering focuses on those who transgress (or reject) professional conventions. What distinguishes cause lawyers from "conventional lawyers" is that the former apply their professional skills in the service of a cause other than—or greater than—the interests of the client in order to transform some aspect of the status quo, whereas the latter tailor their practices to accommodate or benefit the client within the prevailing arrangements of power.

The kinds of activities that constitute cause lawyering have a long and varied history, many examples of which have commanded significant scholarly attention (e.g., lawyers' participation in independence, civil rights, and opposition movements). But the development of cause lawyering as a distinct sociolegal subfield reflects a desire to place politically motivated legal practitioners *at the center of analysis* of political causes. The very notion of "cause" implies agency and consciousness, social identifications, political relations, and goals. Cause also implies mobilization, and the creation or exploitation of opportunities for intervention within a given field of hegemonic relations. Thus, to study cause lawyering is to explore how lawyers contribute professionally (i.e., legally) to causes to which they subscribe, and how the politics of the cause at issue affects and is affected by lawyers' work.

Human rights is one of the most prominent and common causes to which politically motivated lawyers around the world have aligned themselves. Indeed, many examples of cause lawyering are tantamount to human rights work, and human rights "works" in large part through the efforts and activities of lawyers. As Stanley Cohen (1995:5) notes, "Lawyers are the dominant profession to claim ownership of the human rights problem and have succeeded in establishing a virtual monopoly of knowledge (how the subject is framed) and power (what strategies of intervention are used)." This monopoly reflects the fact that human rights are legal rights. But placing cause lawyers at the center of analysis can illuminate the transformation of human rights into an *international movement*, and the development of the movement into a more influential force in the international arena.

Consider the impact on the international human rights movement as a result of the activities of several Spanish legal professionals who propelled forward an indictment against former Chilean dictator Augusto Pinochet. Taking their activities and commitments as the analytical point of departure would direct our attention to questions about what made such an initiative possible at this juncture, and what effects the indictment has had on the larger context, in this case the international order itself. Juan Garces and Balthusar Garzón, working in concert with sectors of the international human rights movement, have helped to put the very meaning of state sovereignty up for political debate and legal reinterpretation by successfully targeting Pinochet personally for the gross violations perpetrated during his regime. These lawyers, championing the enforcement of international law, have expanded the possibilities of cause lawyering on a global scale, and made human rights violators everywhere more vulnerable to the prospect of prosecution that had previously existed only on the level of imagination. The Pinochet case exemplifies the ways in which cause lawyers contribute to the integration and interpenetration of "global" and "local" arenas, relations and institutions that characterize the human rights enterprise.

In this chapter, I focus on the contributions of Israeli and Palestinian cause lawyers to the creation and development of a human rights movement in Israel, the West Bank and Gaza (Israel/Palestine). I contend that it was their work *as cause lawyers* that spurred their interest in and mobilization around the cause of human rights. I also contend that the history of human rights activism in Israel/Palestine is an integral, if contextually specific, part of the history of the international human rights movement.

Although there are many examples and avenues of cause lawyering in Israel/ Palestine, I focus on those who have been professionally and politically engaged in matters relating to the rights of Palestinian residents of the territories occupied by

Israel in 1967, particularly those who have worked in the Israeli military court system. This focus on military court lawyers is not arbitrary; the history of human rights as a form of politico-legal activism in Israel/Palestine begins with them.

In the early years of the Israeli occupation of the West Bank and Gaza, a few politically motivated lawyers began representing Palestinians in the Israeli military courts. Others followed suit, drawn into this system out of a conscious desire to traffic in the charged fray of the Israeli-Palestinian conflict, whether they conceived their cause as opposition to the Israeli occupation, support for the Palestinian struggle for self-determination, and/or a sense of duty to intervene against Israeli policies and practices that contravened the rule of law (see Hajjar, 1997). Yet until the end of the 1970s, the professional practices of military court lawyers remained an atomized struggle for the legal rights of their clients.

In 1979, a transformation in cause lawyering was initiated through the adoption of a human rights approach to the struggle for Palestinians' rights. That year, several Palestinian lawyers founded the first human rights organization in the occupied territories. Within a few years, several other human rights organizations were established. As a result, cause lawyering took on a more collective, proactive, and internationalist cast. The impetus behind these developments was a desire to utilize international law more effectively as a counterbalance to the military and emergency laws used by the Israeli state to govern Palestinians in the territories. Among the effects of these mobilizations were the generation of increasingly sophisticated critiques of the legality of Israeli policies, and the construction of a counternarrative about the nature of the conflict as, foremost, a problem of government. This constituted a critique and an alternative to reductionist (but prevalent) interpretations of the conflict as a problem of terrorism, security, or land. Lawyers were crucial agents in the process of translating the conditions on the ground into a framework of international human rights.

In the late 1980s, the Palestinian population in the territories mounted a collective uprising against the occupation, which was met with fierce reprisals by the Israeli military to quell the unrest. The existing human rights organizations were well positioned to document and report on the resultant rights violations, and many new human rights organizations were established in Israel and the territories during this period. Although there were certainly tensions, rivalries, and disputes among the various organizations, their common mandate of promoting enforcement and adherence to international law facilitated cooperation and collaborations. The creation of a "transnational" Israeli-Palestinian human rights movement was one of the (few) positive consequences of the uprising.

The crisis of the uprising drew unprecedented international attention to the situation in the occupied territories. Local human rights organizations were propelled into the international limelight because of their ability to provide both data about violence and analysis about violations of human rights. They, in turn, relied heavily on military court lawyers for information, since the latter had access to prisoners, strong connections with members of the Palestinian community, and daily contact with members of the Israeli military. The more prominent cause lawyers were in heavy demand as informants for representatives of international human rights organizations, who were coming to Israel/Palestine in droves to monitor and report on conditions in the courts, prisons, and streets.

By the early 1990s, however, the human rights movement in Israel/Palestine lost some of this momentum. The political changes wrought by the signing in 1993 of an Israeli-Palestinian Declaration of Principles and the establishment in 1994 of a Palestinian Authority (PA) providing limited "self-government" for Palestinians in parts of the territories contributed to a dissipation of the collective mission that had inspired Israeli-Palestinian collaboration around a politics of human rights during the uprising. The high profile that human rights organizations had previously enjoyed was eclipsed as international attention shifted to the negotiating process and the changing political arrangements in the West Bank and Gaza. These developments also affected the practices and commitments of military court lawyers. The court system was "downsized" when the Israeli military redeployed and the PA assumed some of the responsibilities for control and security. While a few lawyers have continued to work in the Israeli military courts, others shifted their political and legal activities to struggles for democratization either within Israel or in the Palestinian self-governing areas. And many abandoned cause lawyering entirely to pursue conventional legal practices or other types of careers.

As I elaborate on this history below, two distinct but interrelated sets of issues inform the discussion. One is the dialectic between "lawyering" and "cause," which in this context pertains to the politics of the Israeli-Palestinian conflict. The other is the dialectical relationship between a local and an international human rights movement. The possibilities for activism and the obstacles confronting activists and organizations are informed by shifting constellations of power on an international scale. Yet what happens locally is never a mere reflection of global forces. Israeli and Palestinian lawyers' adoption of human rights as a cause, which contributed to the establishment of a local human rights movement, was certainly inspired, influenced and bolstered by the growing popularization human rights elsewhere around the world. But it emanated from local initiatives rather than being imposed or directed from "outside." What this demonstrates is that mobilization around the cause of human rights is not an *effect* of globalization but one of its *manifestations*.

Cause Lawyering and Human Rights

To understand the role that cause lawyers played in the development of a human rights movement in Israel/Palestine, and the linkages between local and international human rights organizations, it is necessary to consider briefly the transformation of human rights as a politico-legal cause. Human rights were "created" in the decades following World War II through the promulgation of a plethora of new international laws and conventions. This process internationalized the rights of human beings by establishing norms of government and standards of treatment that apply to all people. Initially, human rights discourse was concerned principally with civil and political rights ("first generation rights"), which center on the obligations and restrictions on states vis-a-vis their subjects. But the potential impact of these new rights was undermined by the lack of effective enforcement mechanisms capable of holding states accountable. It was also undermined by the international political climate, namely Cold War polarizations, the often violent and always difficult process of decolonization, and the challenges of postcolonial statebuilding. Moreover, in the first few decades, the human rights enterprise tended to be monopolized by elite legal and political professionals, and thus bore little popular influence or wider appeal.

By the 1970s, a shift occurred as human rights started becoming globalized. This was evident in the mushrooming of human rights organizations around the world, and the strengthening of transnational networks through which human rights information was being circulated and used (see Keck and Sikkink, 1998). Among the effects of this shift was the diminishment of the elite bias characterizing the earlier period. In countries throughout the Third World where national independence had replaced colonial rule, human rights discourse contributed to the shaping of democratic expectations and postcolonial struggles for "good government"—representative in nature and law abiding in practice. This appeal was particularly evident in countries where authoritarian or military regimes were perpetrating violations on domestic populations, or where states were discriminating or tolerating discrimination against certain sectors. Human rights discourse also appealed to social movements seeking to redress gross economic and social inequalities ("second generation rights"). International solidarity in the 1970s and 1980s (e.g., the U.N. Decade of Women, the struggle against apartheid in South Africa) was thoroughly infused by the discourse and politics of human rights, notwithstanding vigorous debates over the meaning and legitimacy of "universalism." The debates themselves exemplified this process of globalization as people appropriated the language and extended—or rejected—the ideas of international human rights in relation to local needs, expectations, and circumstances. Cause lawyers were crucial agents in this globalizing process as they made increasing uses and references to international laws to leverage their struggles for rights, justice, and legality.

By the 1990s, demands for accountability obtained increasing force within the international movement. In a number of societies having undergone major political transitions, the provisions and protections enshrined in international law informed efforts to judge the recent past against human rights standards, by means such as lustration or truth commissions. The most profound manifestation of this shift is the adoption of more expressly legalistic strategies to enforce international laws by prosecuting violators. This is exemplified in the establishment of international tribunals to try those charged with war crimes and crimes against humanity in Rwanda and the former Yugoslavia, the passing of a new treaty to establish a permanent International Criminal Court, and the arrest of Pinochet.

The creation, popularization, and enforcement of human rights, and the social, legal, and political forces behind these changes indicate the ways in which law influences people's consciousness about themselves and the world, and stimulates politically significant action and interaction. The globalization of human rights devolves on the legitimation and direction that international laws provide for movements seeking to challenge local hierarchies of privilege, subordination and discrimination on the basis of race, nationality, ethnicity, gender, sexuality, etc. According to Jack Donnelly (1985: 21), "[T]he primary use of human rights will be to change existing institutions." These institutions encompass *government*—in the broad sense of structures, relations, and processes that constitute order, rule, and rights (see Gordon, 1991).

When movements mobilize to challenge the denial or violation of people's rights, the legal terrain provides a crucial site of struggle, and politically committed legal professionals provide vital skills and services. What links disparate struggles for rights around the world into an international human rights movement is a common commitment to change government in conformity with international legal standards.

The politics of the international human rights movement encompasses a diverse range of activities and strategies (monitoring, reporting, advocacy, litigation) to promote and enforce adherence to international laws. While human rights *standards* are international, bringing those standards to bear involves efforts to institutionalize and enforce them locally. However, the process of extending international standards into the fields of national legal regimes often is stymied when those standards conflict with or challenge the political interests of states and ruling elites. As Richard Falk (1985: 60) explains:

> [T]he cause of human rights in the present world system is overwhelmingly dependent on the normative orientation of the governing process at the state level. Some pressure can be brought on this process from outside, as by impartial transnational organizations ... especially where the leadership in the target polity seeks to avoid having an international reputation as repressive and the abuse can be corrected without seeming to erode the quality of governmental control. Yet this pressure can only be marginal.... [T]he governing orientation of states is primarily shaped by internal factors....

States represent the main (albeit not the exclusive) focus of human rights movements because they bear primary responsibility for adopting and enforcing international law locally. This responsibility translates as the obligation on states to bring their own practices into conformity with international legal standards, and to ensure that these standards obtain in practices and relations of all sorts (public and private) in areas within their political and geographical control. As Abdullahi An-Na'im (1994: 167) argues:

> States are responsible for bringing their domestic law and practice into conformity with their obligations under international law to protect and promote human rights.... This responsibility is fully consistent with the principle of state sovereignty in international law, since it does not purport to force any state to assume legal obligations against its will. It simply seeks to ensure that states effectively fulfill legal obligations they have already assumed under international law.

Of course, states often fail or resist fulfilling their responsibility to adhere to and enforce international human rights standards. As evident in the first few decades after World War II, without popular, public pressure, human rights remained an abstract set of principles. But gradually, movements mobilized to try to close the gap between local conditions and international standards. The ideas and principles of human rights enshrined in international laws have provided people, whose rights are not being secured and protected through domestic legal institutions, with a countervailing source of authority to challenge prevailing arrangements of power and opportunity. Drawing upon human rights to resist or transform the status quo entails strategic uses of legalism to orient and legitimize counter-hegemonic struggles. Rhonda Copelon (1998: 218) addresses this dynamic:

> It may seem ironic or naive even to suggest that something so fragile or abstract as international human rights could be a counterweight to [destructive and dangerous] local and global trends. Human rights "law" bears little resemblance to the formalities that we associate with law.... For the most part, enforcement depends on states' voluntary responses to public scrutiny and shaming. Indeed, the insight that law is inseparable from politics is nowhere more fitting than in the sphere of human rights. Nor does the universality of human rights make them less indeterminate or susceptible to manipulation than domestic rights. The substance and potential of international human rights depends ultimately on the courage, persistence and vision of human rights movements.

Over the last thirty years, the international human rights movement has had an increasingly influential, if uneven, impact on the international order by challenging or stimulating challenges to the sovereign prerogatives of states. Human rights activism and networking have come to fulfill a panoptic function of international surveillance which feeds other types of efforts (military, diplomatic, economic, and legal) to regulate the policies and activities of states to ensure that human rights gain local legal recognition and enforceability. Because of the institutional weaknesses of enforcement mechanisms at the interstate level, human rights activists, including cause lawyers, have found—and created—opportunities to operate in the breach, bringing their interpretations of international law to bear on behalf of their cause. Contestations over the interpretation and applicability of international laws have been an obstacle to enforcement, but they have also been productive: They have fueled discursive, political, and legal interventions that serve, albeit in limited and inconsistent ways, to operationalize an international jurisdiction of law.

Human Rights in Israel/Palestine

Against this background, we can consider why human rights came to influence and inform cause lawyering in Israel/Palestine, and how this stimulated the creation of a local human rights movement. On one level, the situation in Israel/Palestine and the issues that have perpetuated the Israeli-Palestinian conflict lend themselves readily to a human rights approach. First, since Israel is a sovereign state, it is subject to the regulations and restrictions enumerated in international human rights laws. Second, since the right to self-determination is basic, inalienable and universal, and prominently enshrined in numerous international laws and conventions, Palestinian demands for self-determination can be articulated as legal claims.

Yet on another level, the political arrangements and dynamics in Israel/Palestine complicate the application of a human rights approach. Human rights laws tend to assume a postcolonial order in which sovereignty and self-determination are complimentary, whereas the order in Israel/Palestine is quasicolonial; although Israel has been the ruling state throughout since 1967, its relationship to the Palestinian people in the West Bank and Gaza is that of a foreign administrator. In this regard, the situation in Israel/Palestine illuminates a fundamental paradox of international law: the (potential) contradiction between states' rights and human rights. Sovereignty is a form of states' rights, legitimizing their authority to rule. Domestically, legitimation is contingent on the state's capacity to represent the people living within its domain. Internationally, sovereignty is a principle that governs relations among states by recognizing states' rights to autonomy and noninterference based on respect for boundaries. Self-determination is a form of peoples' rights; the national "self" is a demographic collectivity. The need for complimentarity between sovereignty and self-determination has become a globalized norm of "good government." However, even under the best circumstances, the paradox remains: Self-determination is inherently particularistic (although the nature of the national "self" varies significantly). It devolves on the notion that all people can be divided (territorially and demographically) into mutually exclusive nations, each of which deserves its "own" sovereign state. Sovereignty, on the other hand, is the modern universal, the pillar of political authority around the world and upon which the international order is built. While international law recognizes self-determination as a universal right, it also recognizes states' rights to rule, including the right to counter and punish those who challenge or rebel against governing authorities. Such prerogatives are fundamental to the politico-legal constitution of sovereignty. Thus, international law not only lacks clear capacity to reconcile the contradictions between self-determination and sovereignty; it makes the interpretation of law part of the conflict in contexts were the boundaries of state and nation do not harmonize.

Israel/Palestine is a case-study example of a context in which the boundaries of state and nation do not harmonize. Israeli rule over the West Bank and Gaza is the result of conquest through war. Military occupations are "exceptional" political arrangements. Technically, they constitute a cease-fire in an ongoing state of war, and therefore are both temporary in principle and clearly contrary to the normal/normative international standards of government. Under any military occupation, there is no formal political reciprocity between governors and governed. Indeed, the Israeli state has never claimed or sought the right to *represent* the Palestinians in the territories, only the right to *rule* them as long as the occupation continues.

Military occupations are governed by international humanitarian laws, foremost the Fourth Geneva Convention (1949), which accord occupiers the legal status as de facto sovereigns. The rights of the occupying state include the prerogative to institute measures deemed necessary to ensure stability and security. Because occupations preclude political reciprocity, occupiers' powers are unilateral. But international humanitarian laws establish certain rights and protections for occupied civilian populations, although the right to self-determination is not among them, since this right would be "deferred" until the conflict that sustains the occupation is resolved.

However, what materialized in the West Bank and Gaza was a sharp departure from the international legal guidelines governing military occupation. Rather than conceiving the status of the West Bank and Gaza as foreign territory and its own status as a temporary occupant, the Israeli state claimed that the status of the territories was disputed and its own status was that of "administrator" (see Shamgar, 1971, 1982). The purpose of asserting such a position was to leave open the possibility of a future claim on (some or all of) the captured lands. On the basis of this legal rationale, Israel has rejected the *de jure* applicability of the Fourth Geneva Convention to its rule over the West Bank and Gaza. Rather, Israeli officials forged an original interpretation of the state's rights and duties in the territories, which tended to prioritize Israeli national interests (see Hofnung, 1996; O'Brien, 1991; Playfair, 1988, 1992; Zamir, 1988, 1989).

A crucial aspect of Israel's interpretation of its own rights in and claims to the territories is the way in which Palestinian statelessness has been made *legally significant* in Israeli policymaking. By interpreting international humanitarian laws as pertaining exclusively to the rights and duties of sovereign states ("High Contracting Parties") in their relations and conflicts with one another, it was possible to argue that stateless peoples are not their intended beneficiaries. Since there has never been an independent state of "Palestine," Israeli officials have argued that the Palestinian people could not be the rightful sovereigns of the West Bank and Gaza because there is nothing in international law that prescribes the recognition of sovereignty to a non-state, nor anything that demands the creation of a heretofore nonexistent state in territories seized in war.

Israeli rule over Palestinians in the territories was exercised through a military administration. The Palestinian population was regarded and treated as "foreign enemy civilians." Most attempts on their part to mobilize around a collective national identity or to assert their rights to self-determination were deemed threatening to Israeli security and thus classified as criminal violations. Punishable crimes have included not only acts of violence and open rebellion against the occupying authorities but any expression of Palestinian nationalism and a range of nonviolent activities related to public life. Moreover, Israel related its control of territory (e.g., use and distribution of resources; travel and mobility; land ownership) to the security needs and interests of the state. While Palestinians were not dispossessed wholesale, their possessive rights *to the land* were made individual and tenuous, and their rights *in the land* were sorely circumscribed through policies such as deportation, confiscation, and Jewish settlement. However, it is crucial to understand that while these policies violated both the letter and the spirit of the Fourth Geneva Convention, they were not undertaken extralegally; rather, Israel constructed an elaborate legal order to rationalize, authorize and legitimize the ways in which it governed the West Bank and Gaza.

The official Israeli position on the inapplicability of the Fourth Geneva Convention, and the policies that have ensued on that basis, have been strongly criticized by the international community. There is an enduring international consensus that the territories are occupied and the Convention is applicable in its entirety. However, since there is no effective international mechanism capable of enforcing the Convention, Israel faced little *legal* resistance, at least initially, to its contravention or disregard for the restrictions and limitations enshrined in it or in other international laws. Gradually, however, this gap between international law and local rule sparked a response in the form of a mobilization around the cause of human rights.

The conflict over the West Bank and Gaza, which has gradually become the nexus of the larger Israeli-Palestinian conflict, has manifested itself as a struggle over rights, pitting the rights and prerogatives of the Israeli state against the human rights of the Palestinian population (i.e., to self-determination, legal protections, civil liberties). What makes this situation such a challenge—and such an opportunity—for adapting a human rights approach is the fact that the Israeli state places great stock in the importance of law and legality. Here, as elsewhere, the state has utilized law to legitimize its authority, while at the same time law offers, however minimally, certain avenues of resistance and formal protections for subjects of state power.

Legal resistance to the occupation began in the military court system, and was initiated by Israeli and Palestinian cause lawyers. It started as a struggle for the legal rights of Palestinians being charged and tried for security violations. Despite official Israeli claims that the military administration in the territories abides by rule of law standards, the military court system is rife with problems that seriously compromise even minimum standards of due-process protections. These problems—some of which are openly and officially acknowledged, although justified as necessary for Israeli security and the fight against Palestinian terrorism—include the use of soldiers in a policing capacity, the prevalent use of coercive interrogation tactics, prolonged periods of incommunicado detention, routinized obstruction of defense lawyers' right to meet with clients in prisons, the use of third-party confessions that are extremely difficult to challenge, the use of "secret evidence" by prosecutors, and a strong judicial preference for the testimony of prosecution witnesses (especially soldiers).

Cause lawyers working in the Israeli military court system have used the legal terrain as a site of resistance to reform or transform the way the state exercises its power. Their sense of cause *as lawyers* developed out of—and changed as a result of—their actual experiences of representing Palestinians in this system. One of the most significant changes was the adoption of a human rights approach in their work, which entailed increasing reference to international law to challenge the legality of Israeli rule in the territories. To understand *how* a human rights approach came to be adopted in this context, it is necessary to place cause lawyers at the center of analysis.

The Early Years

We could begin this account of cause lawyering in Israel/Palestine with a bloody shirt. A single bloody shirt probably would not even appear on the radar screen if the center of analysis was the larger conflict or international law or indeed anything other than cause lawyers. But for a lawyer, such a detail could be quite significant if the blood is that of a client. The nature and substance of lawyers' work is the welfare and status of their clients, and this applies even to cause lawyers who might regard their clients *politically* in more collective terms.

Felicia Langer, a Jewish Israeli lawyer, begins her autobiographical book, *With My Own Eyes* (1975), with an account of a meeting in January 1968 with a Palestinian man who came to her office in West Jerusalem seeking her services. He had chosen Langer because of her reputation as a politically engaged lawyer and active member of the Israeli communist party. He presented her with a bloody shirt belonging to his son, who had been arrested by the Israeli authorities. It alerted her to the possibility that torture might be going on in Israeli prisons. The son became Langer's first Palestinian client from the occupied territories. This detail has a cascading significance: it set Langer's career on a new course, representing Palestinians in the Israeli military court system. Langer was the first—and for a brief period the only—*cause* lawyer working in the military courts. As other Israeli and Palestinian lawyers gradually joined Langer in such work, the military court system became the institutional nexus of the legal struggle for rights of Palestinians living under Israeli occupation.

In 1968, when Langer began working in the military courts, Israelis were still reeling from the lightening victory over the surrounding Arab states and the conquest of the West Bank and Gaza. Popular notions in Jewish Israeli society that the Israel Defense Forces (IDF) represented a "purity of arms" helped to legitimize military rule over the 1.3 million Palestinians living in the occupied territories. Most Jewish Israelis accepted the occupation as a necessity on military, political, and even moral grounds, and acceded to the IDF's discretion in maintaining order and security. For Langer, however, who became intimately familiar with the conditions of life for Palestinians through her work, the military's rule was harsh and repressive. She became a vocal critic of the occupation, challenging official assertions that it was being managed in "benign" and "enlightened" ways.

Langer literally invented a cause for herself: She sought to break what she referred to as a "conspiracy of silence" among Jewish Israelis about what was happening across the 1949 armistice boundary (Green Line) by seeking publicity for her work. She believed that the way to change the situation on the ground was to help foment public pressure on the government, and the means of doing this was by informing Israelis about the kinds of policies being undertaken in their name. In order to enhance her legitimacy among her target audience—the Jewish public—and make her critiques credible, she drew lines around what she considered defensible, refusing to take cases of people charged with violent crimes. She did not, then, align herself squarely with the Palestinian National Movement (which, at the time, made no distinctions between nonviolent and armed acts of resistance), although she was politically sympathetic to the Palestinian struggle for self-determination. The way she conceived of her cause at that time could be compared to the mandate of Amnesty International, an organization then in its relative infancy, which distinguished between "prisoners of conscience," whom the organization was established to support, and those who advocated or used violence, who did not merit support (except for the right not to be tortured).

Langer never succeeded in stimulating a Jewish Israeli critique of the occupation. On the contrary, she earned a reputation as a "self-hating Jew," and a "terrorist sympathizer." By representing Palestinian clients, Langer had crossed not only a geographic boundary but a political line that was, at the time, quite clearly demarcated. Although the rule of law accords people accused of crimes a right to defense counsel, defense lawyers often earn the unsavory reputation of "helping criminals." In this context, where crime was politicized and conflated with national conflict, and where the very survival of the Israeli state was deemed to be at stake, the prosecution of "terrorists" was valorized, and the defense of Palestinians derided. Langer was positioned in an adversarial relationship not only with military prosecutors, but seemingly with the Jewish nation that the IDF was acting to defend. Rather than earning praise (or even acceptance) for her legal role, her professional activities condemned her politically in the eyes of the Jewish Israeli mainstream, including those in the legal profession. For example, Moshe Landau, when he was deputy president of the Israeli High Court, commented on Langer's *With My Own Eyes*:

> This book glorifies the views of the terrorist organizations seeking to undermine the existence of the State of Israel by various kinds of violence. It is a sort of record of the author's activities as a defence lawyer, especially in the military courts, and she instantly turns every allegation said by her clients to have been received from their interrogators into irrefutable truth, claiming that the rejection of these accusations by the courts would be a miscarriage of justice. The book does, indeed, contain passages which extol the cause of the Palestinian Arabs, but these passages grate on one's ears considering the known aim of the terrorist organizations, to which the book is, both in spirit and in its formulation, openly sympathetic. (Quoted in Shefi, 1982: 322–23)

Although Langer failed to foment protest among the Jewish Israeli public against repressive policies of the military administration, she succeeded in paving the way and serving as a role model for a younger generation of Jewish and Arab Israeli cause lawyers who would follow her into the military courts. In 1971, Leah Tsemel, also Jewish Israeli, became an estagière (apprentice) in Langer's office. Tsemel had become politically radicalized while studying law at Hebrew University. When she decided to practice in the occupied territories, Langer was the logical mentor.

Langer and Tsemel often are compared to one another because of the overlap in their career paths and their positioning on the far left of the Israeli political spectrum. But there are some significant differences in their work as lawyers and the nature of the cause to which they have aligned themselves that are instructive to understanding the history of cause lawyering in Israel/Palestine. Before 1967, when the Israeli state had utilized a military administration to govern Palestinians living within Israel, Langer had represented many Arab clients charged with security violations. Her decision to represent clients from the occupied territories constituted a geographic extension of an existing legal practice. For Langer's generation, the communist party was the chief vehicle for leftist politics in Israel, and provided the only forum for Jewish-Arab alliance. Her political views were in keeping with the communist party line, which advocated an end to Israeli occupation and a two-state solution to the conflict. This was, at the time, a radical position, since the idea of an independent Palestinian state was rejected by most Jewish Israelis (and the idea of recognizing Israel and forfeiting claims to those areas was rejected by most Palestinians). But it afforded Langer a means of maintaining an image of *herself* as acting in what she regarded as the Israeli "national interest."

Tsemel, on the other hand, was part of a "post-'67" generation of leftists, for whom alliances were more fluid and whose views of the political establishment were more critical. Tsemel was active with a small Trotskyist group of Jews and Arabs, Matzpen, which was committed to "internationalist" principles, not Jewish or Palestinian ethnonational exclusivity. In this context, where national issues and differences completely dominate the political terrain, her "antinational" views branded her a traitor to "her people." She actively contributed to this image by working out of an office in a Palestinian neighborhood of East Jerusalem, and cultivating not only professional but social connections with Palestinians throughout the West Bank and Gaza. Because Tsemel (and Matzpen more generally) regarded Israel as a colonial state on both sides of the Green Line, not only in the occupied territories (the position of the communist party), she quickly earned a reputation as even farther from the mainstream pale than Langer.

The two women also differed in their understandings of their mission as lawyers. Unlike Langer, Tsemel made no distinctions about the kinds of cases she would handle. For her, a defense lawyer's duty was to provide the best possible legal services to anyone who was arrested. She adopted a nondiscriminating attitude about clients. While Langer regarded and treated her legal work as a political reflection of herself, Tsemel was doggedly committed to the interests and rights of her clients, whoever they might be or whatever crimes they might be charged with. Tsemel embraced a "universalist" ideology of rights and law that would eventually become the cornerstone of an Israeli-Palestinian human rights movement, although in the early 1970s there was virtually no public elaboration, by Tsemel or anyone else, of an explicit commitment to international human rights.

A third difference between them was in their regard for the utility of publicity in bringing about change. Langer sought the limelight, hoping to generate attention to herself that would reflect on the problems of occupation. Tsemel did not shun publicity, but neither did she put much stock in the idea that political change would come about by trying to move the mainstream Jewish Israeli public to sympathize with Palestinians' suffering at the hands of the IDF. Rather, she emphasized the importance of political organization, and cultivated alliances with other lawyers and nonlegal activists who shared her principles and concerns. Thus, while Langer personalized cause lawyering by making her own society the focus and herself the subject, Tsemel helped to politicize the legal profession by linking lawyering to a broader movement mobilized in a struggle for rights and justice. In reflecting on the cause that has motivated her, Tsemel said, "I have done no favors and deserve no thanks. I am simply trying to make the place where I live free of occupation, oppression, exploitation and racism."

Langer also mentored the handful of first-generation Arab Israeli military court lawyers, who started out as estagières in her office. Her public persona had enlightened them to the possibilities of such work, and her membership in the communist party was a legitimizing factor, since this was the party with which many Arab citizens of Israel politically identified. Most Arab Israelis viewed the occupation over the remainder of historic Palestine as another chapter in the national tragedy.

But it also provided new opportunities for them to reconnect with Palestinians living across the Green Line. This spurred a "rediscovery" of their identity as Palestinians, which the state had suppressed since 1948 (see Rouhana, 1997). This also entailed, especially among the younger generation, a growing identification with Palestinian nationalist politics. As a result of the defeat and discrediting of the Arab regimes in 1967, the leadership of the Palestine Liberation Organization (PLO) was taken over in 1968 by militant factions. The "new" PLO became an increasingly popular symbol of national solidarity and a vehicle of national struggle, especially after it gained international recognition as the sole legitimate representative of the Palestinian people in 1974.

The young Arab lawyers who decided to work in the military courts did so, in part, as a political gesture of support for the Palestinian national struggle. It also provided a direct means of cultivating ties with their conationals, Palestinians living under occupation. One Arab Israeli, Walid Fahum, who had started his military court career in Langer's office, described his sense of cause:

> Felicia [Langer] works for other people. I work for my people. Felicia is an Israeli [i.e., Jewish]. She does this work because she is a communist and she has done great work. But when I defend a Palestinian, I am in a sense defending myself, because the Palestinian struggle is my struggle.

But there were also more personal issues involved in Arab Israeli lawyers' decisions to work across the Green Line. The military courts provided a career opportunity that did not really exist for them inside Israel; structural-institutional discrimination against Arabs ("non-Jews") marginalized them in the domestic legal market. Consequently, Arab lawyers sought—and found—opportunities in the military courts to put their education and first-hand knowledge of Israeli society to use in ways that would benefit themselves personally and professionally, and the Palestinian struggle politically and legally.

In the first years of the occupation, very few Palestinian lawyers from the territories took up military court work. The entire legal profession in the West Bank went on strike, refusing to work in any Israeli institution as a protest against the occupation (see Bisharat, 1989). In Gaza, there were only ten lawyers in 1967, four of whom began working in the military courts because their services were requested by families of people being arrested. The Israeli military also encouraged—and needed—their services because of the large number of people being charged with serious crimes. Gaza was, for several years after the war, a site of open and armed resistance. Palestinian lawyers were actually escorted to and from the courts in Israeli military vehicles until Gaza was "pacified" in 1971.

By the mid-1970s, a few West Bank lawyers had begun breaking the strike to work in the military courts, largely in response to community pressure to represent those who had been arrested. Their numbers grew over time, leading to a sharp division in the legal profession in the region over the matter of cause, whether the principled position was to support the strike and refuse to practice or to break the strike to provide needed legal services. In general, Palestinian lawyers from Gaza and the West Bank have defined their cause in terms of "national duty."

Reframing Problems

Throughout the 1970s, although lawyers tended to regard their decision to work in the military courts as political, their practices were confined largely to the immediate needs of their clients, and most of their work entailed arranging plea bargains. Dealing is an individualizing process where the particulars of a case largely determine defense-prosecution negotiations over the outcome. It undermines lawyers' abilities to use the legal process itself for political ends, and tends to keep lawyers atomized from one another.

Under the prevailing conditions, struggling for even minimum legal rights of their clients was an uphill battle for a number of reasons: The Israeli military laws promulgated for the territories were labyrinthine, convoluted, and constantly changing; the courts themselves did not regard any decision as having precedential status, thereby causing vast discrepancies in outcomes of similar cases; and the advantages enjoyed by the prosecution made conviction a virtual inevitability for most of those who were charged. But perhaps the most deleterious factor in lawyers' struggle for the legal rights of their clients was the military administration's refusal to adhere to the Fourth Geneva Convention. This position was reinforced by Israeli High Court decisions and accepted by the military courts (see Pach, 1977).

In contrast to the original and elaborate legal arguments advanced by Israeli officials and state supporters to project an image of Israeli rule as benevolent and law-abiding, matters of law barely figured in critiques of the occupation throughout the 1970s. While some Israeli legal academics intervened with criticisms or interventions about specific policies of the military administration (see Dinstein, 1972, 1978), there was little concerted effort to challenge the state's position on international law or to assess the legality of the laws in force in the territories in terms of international legal norms and standards. Nor did an attention to law or legalism significantly inform the strategies of political movements, the rhetoric of Palestinian national interests, or scholarly writing on the Palestinian struggle for self-determination. This was a period of Palestinian militancy, and the discourse of rights tended to be formulated in political-national rather than legal terms.

This lacunae had negative effects on lawyers working in the military courts, and the first efforts to redress the problems were undertaken by lawyers themselves. The results were twofold: the establishment of the first local human rights organizations with mandates pertaining directly to conditions in the West Bank and Gaza, and the elaboration of legal critiques of the occupation which took international law as their point of reference. This process began in 1979 with the establishment of Law in the Service of Man (LSM, later renamed Al-Haq). Two of the organization's founders, Raja Shehadeh and Jonathan Kuttab, were lawyers who worked regularly in the military courts. LSM, the first Palestinian human rights organization, was a West Bank affiliate of the International Commission of Jurists (ICJ). Its creation provided a new opportunity and means to channel criticism about the violation of Palestinians' rights into an international framework. By adopting an explicit rule of law mandate (in keeping with that of the ICJ), LSM eschewed nationalist militancy and promoted itself as nonpolitical and legal.

The kinds of strategies pursued by LSM (monitoring, reporting, and advocacy) were undertaken to challenge to the Israeli state's narrative of legitimacy by documenting how the military administration routinely failed to adhere to rule of law standards. But from the outset, as Mouin Rabbani (1994: 29) notes, the organization faced three problems: being a Palestinian organization under Israeli occupation; seeking to address grievances in a context in which Palestinians "were generally held to be incapable of dispassionate investigation of anything concerning Israel"; and intervening on matters in a context in which Israel was, at the time, internationally perceived as "not a serious offender" of human rights compared to other Middle Eastern regimes. LSM responded to this predicament by denying the relevance of politics to human rights and referring exclusively to the universal standard of international law in its appraisal of Israeli conduct.

In 1980, Shehadeh and Kuttab published *The West Bank and the Rule of Law*. This book, describing changes in the West Bank legal system since the onset of occupation, was the first effort to compile a comprehensive account of Israel's use of military orders and emergency laws. It was, in part, a response to their own and their colleagues' needs as practicing lawyers to understand and evaluate the environment in which they were working. The publication of this book served both to extend the critique of the occupation into the legal terrain and to set in motion what would come to characterize the production of knowledge about the legality of Israeli rule: a cycle of criticism and rejoinder. This discourse took on a distinctly polemical tone, since criticisms of the occupation (or any aspect thereof) were *read* by officials and supporters of the state as "pro-Palestinian" attacks on "Israel," and were responded to in kind.

A rejoinder to Shehadeh and Kuttab's book was published in 1981 under the title *The Rule of Law in the Territories Administered by Israel*. Although not an official report, it was authored by Israeli government lawyers. In the foreword, Haim Cohen, an Israeli High Court justice, describes the former as a *tracatus politicus*, contrasting it to the present book which he refers to as "a sober statement of law and fact" (Cohen, 1981:xii). Cohen writes:

> While the study of Messrs. Shehadeh and Kuttab can in no way be accepted as a correct statement of either the facts or the law, it is a welcome challenge to state both fact and law as they really are—not unlike a legal pleading whose *ratio vivendi* is to stand until authoritatively corrected. (Ibid., viii–ix)

In 1985, Shehadeh published another book, *Occupier's Law*, in part as a rejoinder to *The Rule of Law*. He wrote (1988 [2d ed.]: 3–4):

> Lawyers in the military administration of the West Bank ... attempted to justify Israel's activities by referring to international law to prove the consistency of these actions with the law of occupation.... This declared policy is irreconcilable with the facts which seem to indicate that the Israeli goal is gradually to drive out the local Palestinian population and to annex the territory. Israel has been astute in the way it has tried and still tries to present all it is doing in terms of international law of occupation.

By the mid-1980s, a mounting body of literature was being produced that formulated increasingly elaborate arguments about Israel's violations of international law in the territories (see Kretzmer, 1984; Sommer, 1986; Tsemel, 1984). As a result, issues that had previously been treated as political problems were being reframed as legal violations, and this was serving to politicize law itself.

LSM, now renamed Al-Haq, was a center for this activity, engaging in human rights monitoring and reporting, and in the production of human rights scholarship (aimed primarily at an international audience) and educational materials (aimed primarily at local Palestinians). A number of foreign cause lawyers and human rights activists came to the West Bank to lend their services to the organization. According to Joost Hiltermann (2000: 43), one of the organization's foreign volunteers:

> [Al-Haq] began to provide an ever-growing audience [i.e., its local constituency] with a new vocabulary and a concrete methodology to challenge specific actions of the governing authority. These were presented in the form of the "Know Your Rights" series, one of al-Haq's most important undertakings during its first decade. These booklets inculcated in those who read them the crucial notion that not only did they—Palestinians, victims, fighters, people—have fundamental rights, but they had a right to assert these rights, and the booklets showed how they might begin to do so.

Several other Palestinian human rights organizations were established in the early 1980s, including a Gaza affiliate of the ICJ. The director of the Gaza Center for Rights and Law, Raji Sourani, and a number of the organization's employees were military court lawyers who were motivated by their own experiences and those of their clients to translate their activities into a human rights framework. On the other side of the Green Line, through the mid-1980s, the only Israeli organization that had significant dealings with Palestinian rights issues was the Association for Civil Rights in Israel (ACRI). Modeled on the American Civil Liberties Union, ACRI's mandate pertains to civil, political, and legal rights of individuals. Consequently, while ACRI was critical of some of the Israeli state's practices in the territories, the organization never pursued a role of challenging the occupation, promoting the cause of Palestinian national/collective rights, or asserting a position independent of the state's on the applicability of the Fourth Geneva Convention (see ACRI, 1985).

Although only a handful of lawyers working in the military courts affiliated themselves directly with the new organizations, many contributed to the development of a local human rights movement by providing crucial information about what was occurring in the courts and prisons. Conversely, the growing attention to human rights served to legitimize their work and to help them articulate a clearer and more collective sense of cause. As human rights was developing gradually into an institutionally important realm of political action, lawyers' profiles and contributions were increasingly recognized as a form of political capital. Their struggle was becoming less atomized.

The growing appeal of human rights was a response to conditions on the ground. Because of the patently unrepresentative nature of occupation and the unilateral ways in which the military administration was exercising its prerogatives as the de facto sovereign, people had no choice but to look "upward" to international law to orient their aspirations and legitimize their demands. In this context, human rights activism was not functioning as a rejection of nationalist politics, since it was being drawn upon to advance national goals and secure national rights (foremost Palestinian self-determination). But it was coming to constitute an alternative to "official" politics dominated by leaders, parties, and regimes. Moreover, efforts to reframe struggles against the occupation in human rights terms was serving to internationalize the conflict in new ways by inviting—and even demanding—the attention and involvement of the international community.

The Uprising

In December 1987, a collective Palestinian uprising (*intifada*) against the occupation began. The factors that contributed to this explosion of unrest included Israel's invasion of Lebanon in 1982 and the subsequent defeat and expulsion of the PLO to Tunisia, and the 1985 institution of increasingly harsh governing policies in the territories (referred to officially as the "Iron Fist"). The uprising transformed the human rights scene on both sides of the Green Line. Between 1988 and the early 1990s, existing organizations expanded their activities and many new Israeli and Palestinian organizations were established.

Among the factors that spurred mobilization under the mantle of human rights was the publication of an official Israeli investigation into interrogation practices of the General Security Services (GSS) (Landau, 1987). The Landau Commission report confirmed what had long been alleged by Palestinian detainees and their Palestinian and Israeli lawyers: that GSS agents had routinely used violent interrogation methods since at least 1971, and that they had routinely lied about such practices in court when confessions were challenged on the basis that they had been coerced. Rather than condemning such practices, the Landau Commission recommended that the government sanction them as necessary and legal in the fight against "hostile terrorist activity," which, in the view of the report's authors, encompassed virtually all activities of nationalist-minded Palestinians. The Landau Commission's recommendations were adopted by the government, thereby making Israel the first (and to date the only) state in the world to officially sanction the use of interrogation methods that constitute torture according to international law. Thus, the Landau Commission report decisively transformed the *discourse* of Israeli interrogation while preserving the *practices*. But the report also transformed human rights discourse and practices by providing lawyers and activists with a now-public focus for their criticisms and efforts to stop torture (see Cohen and Golan, 1991, 1992; Kremnitzer, 1989). For example, Tsemel and other Jewish Israeli cause lawyers and activists formed the Public Committee against Torture in Israel to challenge (through both publicity and litigation) the state's sanctioned use of violent and coercive interrogation tactics (see Hajjar, 2000; Pacheco, 1999a, 1999b).

The coincidental timing of the Landau Commission report's publication and the outbreak of the uprising directed increasingly critical attention to the military court system. Such attention derived, on the one hand, from the obvious relationship among interrogation, confessions, and convictions, and, on the other hand, from the dramatic rise in the number of people being arrested, interrogated, and tried as part of the military administration's strategy to end the uprising. Virtually every local human rights organization, and many international organizations began investigating and reporting on the operations of the military courts (see Al-Haq, 1988, 1990; Amnesty International, 1991; Golan [for B'Tselem], 1989; Human Rights Watch/Middle East, 1994; Lawyers Committee for Human Rights, 1992, 1993; Paust et al. [for the ICJ], 1989). Such organizational activities and discursive outpourings indicated that the local human rights movement had become firmly linked to a global effort to promote international legal standards and enforce international law. Holly Burkhalter, who was then Washington director of Human Rights Watch, held up Al-Haq's work during the uprising for special praise:

> There weren't at that time many groups in the [global] South that were doing highly sophisticated human rights investigations. To have *that* kind of quality of documentation, especially from Palestinians, was very important in dispelling the prejudice that existed. In the United States, "Palestinian" was an adjective modifying the noun "terrorist." Al-Haq's work was essential in getting out the truth not only about human rights violations in the occupied territories, but about Palestinians themselves. (Cited in Hiltermann, 2000: 44)

Human rights was being popularized at the local level through the activities associated with *doing human rights*: taking affidavits from victims, reporting and publicizing violations, organizing conferences, hosting foreign monitors from international organizations, and so on. Human rights work also contributed directly to a heightened international awareness about conditions on the ground, which, in turn, increased the international community's concern about the conflict and the rights of Palestinians. (An important factor during this period was the establishment of internet links, making it easier and faster to disseminate information to activists and organizations abroad.) As in the earlier period, while few lawyers were directly affiliated with human rights organizations, they were integral to such activities, especially through their role in providing information about the treatment of Palestinians to which they were privy through their work. According to Jawad Boulos, an Arab Israeli military court lawyer:

> [I]t took the efforts of many lawyers to bring international attention to what is going on. A few years ago, no organization dared to challenge or criticize Israel. ... But by exposing the facts about the occupation, now organizations and people not only can criticize Israel but must do so because the evidence is growing. Even the US State Department criticizes Israel for its policies in the territories. This is an achievement for Palestinians.

Thus, while the situation on the ground was worsening and violations of all sorts were escalating, lawyers and activists were buoyed by the degree of international attention and criticisms that their activities were helping to generate.

During the period of the uprising, the popularization of "human rights consciousness" was evident in the ways increasing numbers of Palestinians and Israelis were expressing their critiques of the current situation and aspirations for peace. The universalist language of human rights and the internationalist nature of organizing and networking promoted the rule of law and the principle of rights. This posed an explicit challenge to the discourse and politics of Israeli national security that anything could be justified in the fight against terrorism. But it also challenged the discourse of Palestinian nationalist militancy that anything could be justified in the fight for liberation. Israeli and Palestinian human rights activists were not taking their cues from their respective national leaders, but rather were pressuring those leaders through the criticisms and recommendations being generated by their work. Israeli officials strove to counter criticisms of the state's human rights record by attacking the legitimacy or information of critics (see Office of the Military Advocate General, 1992; Straschnov, 1994; Yahav, 1993). The PLO, while seeking to reap benefits from human rights criticisms of Israel, was not inclined to embrace or promote a movement whose modus operandi is to subject official authority to scrutiny. In effect, during this period conventional nationalist politics was being challenged by the politics of human rights.

Things Fall Apart

The uprising did not bring about an end to the occupation. But it did make clear that the status quo ante was untenable, and this was a major factor leading to the start of direct Israeli-Palestinian negotiations in 1991. Ironically, the breakthrough in the negotiations which led to the signing of a Declaration of Principles in 1993 resulted in a serious blow to the human rights movement. There are several reasons for this. First, Israeli and Palestinian leaders pressured their respective constituencies to curb criticisms in order to enable the talks to proceed. Second, international attention was redirected to the negotiations where select Israeli and Palestinian representatives were deciding the fate of their nations. And third, because many people were initially optimistic that invigorated negotiations would resolve the conflict, their own commitment to human rights waned. As a result, the struggle for rights was shifted to the negotiating table, effectively delinking legalistic and popular strategies of resistance from the politics of ending the occupation. Raja Shehadeh, who was serving as a legal adviser to the Palestinian negotiating team, quit in disgust when it became clear that neither Israel nor the PLO had any interest in using international law as a guiding framework for the agreements. His early warnings that human rights would suffer as a result of such disregard proved prescient.

The local human rights movement suffered a further blow with the establishment of the Palestinian Authority in 1994. The structure and agenda of the PA was oriented (by negotiated agreement) to provide security for the Israeli state by controlling (repressing if need be) Palestinians in the territories (see Usher, 1997). As the lines of governmental authority became blurred by these new institutional arrangements, it became harder for activists to determine how to monitor adherence to international legal standards and whom to hold accountable for violations.

These developments affected the practices of many of the military court lawyers, including undermining a collective sense of cause that had animated their work during the *intifada*. Jewish Israeli liberals, for whom cause had been primarily the legal behavior of their own state, abandoned the military courts on the belief that the establishment of a PA and the Israeli military redeployment from Palestinian population centers made their concerns moot. For Arab Israelis, the negotiations effectively reinforced their political separation from Palestinians in the territories. While a few Arab Israeli lawyers who had relocated to East Jerusalem have continued doing military court work, others abandoned the territories to practice in Israel. Jewish Israeli leftist lawyers have continued doing military court work, in part because they are almost alone in *being able* to do such work these days. Most Palestinian lawyers from the territories have been effectively barred from working in the military courts because of tightened Israeli travel and permit restrictions that have "closed" the Palestinian areas in response to a number of attacks by militants opposed to the Israeli-Palestinian agreements.

But the biggest blow of all for the human rights movement was related to the direction the negotiations were taking, namely the emphasis on security and territory rather than rights. To the extent that human rights activism had helped to promote the centrality of rights to understanding and resolving the conflict, the negotiations fortified an interpretation of the conflict and its resolution as a matter of geography, namely where a permanent separation of some sort could be instituted. Consequently, human rights activism has been constrained by the separation agendas of Israeli and Palestinian national elites, making it increasingly difficult to formulate mandates and coordinate strategies among organizations. Those activists who have continued to monitor and report on violations, whether perpetrated by the Israeli state or the PA, have been criticized for being "anti-peace."

The individual lawyers who had contributed to the rise and expansion of a local human rights movement were strongly affected by these turns of events, although they have responded in differing ways. Felicia Langer, whose legacy was so important to the development of cause lawyering in Israel/Palestine, emigrated to Germany in 1991. She had become disgusted by the idea that she was lending legitimacy to oppression, and discouraged that lawyers could do nothing positive for their clients or their cause. She felt that publicizing her reasons for quitting was the last honorable gesture she could make.

Raja Shehadeh gave up cause lawyering, and has become a conventional lawyer, although he continues to publish critical scholarship. His Ramallah firm represents many foreign companies that have begun investing in the PA areas. Jonathan Kuttab now divides his time between the Israeli military courts and Palestinian civil courts, the latter work representing conventional lawyering.

Leah Tsemel, who remains one of the most active and visible cause lawyers in Israel/Palestine, has been most frustrated by the diminishment of international attention to continuing human rights violations. In a 1997 interview, she said,

> During the 1980s, I was very optimistic about all these international human rights people who were coming to join the struggle. But I became cynical about them too because, after they did their reports, they moved on, and I never heard from many of them again. Human rights is just an industry, not a political cause.

She also has been very critical of those Palestinian colleagues who have turned a blind eye to violations by the PA. To her, this indicates that their commitment to human rights was merely tactical.

Some Palestinian lawyers who had worked in the military courts have joined the PA. Freih Abu Middein, former head of the Gaza Bar Association and onetime champion of prisoners' rights, is now the PA minister of justice. Ironically, he has become one of the staunchest and most vocal critics of human rights organizations and activists (see Hammami, Hilal, and Tamari, 1999). Other lawyers have tried to influence without directly challenging the PA, struggling to construct an effective legal order where people's rights will be respected and protected. Ahmed Sayyad, head of the Mandela Institute for Political Prisoners (established during the uprising), has tried to strike a balance between Palestinian national interests and human rights concerns by offering training courses to PA security agents:

The PA must be dealt with differently than the occupation authorities; they are part of our own people. Most of the human rights organizations deal with the PA like they dealt with the Israelis—like they are [sic] the enemy. This makes our work harder and more dangerous. We should get close to the PA and help them learn what it means to respect the rule of law. Human rights shouldn't be used to undermine PA legitimacy. Our goal should be to end PA violations, not destroy the PA.

Those Palestinian lawyers who are most critical of the direction and results of the negotiations have remained firmly committed to human rights activism. Raji Sourani formed a new organization, the Palestine Center for Human Rights (PCHR), after the PA took over the Gaza Center for Rights and Law and turned it into an official mouthpiece. He has strived to maintain an international focus on local problems, for example by organizing conferences that bring foreign legal experts and activists to Palestine. Sourani cultivates a high profile for himself and his organization because it is a means not only of getting his criticisms into broader circulation but also serves a protective function against the possibilities of PA repression. The current strategies of the PCHR are clearly influenced by recent trends in the international human rights movement: The organization has been active, along with human rights groups from many other countries, in an international campaign for improved implementation and enforcement of the Fourth Geneva Convention, shedding a comparative light on the situations in Israel/Palestine, Bosnia, Kosovo, East Timor, and other trouble spots. This campaign embraces the goal of enforcement through the prosecution of violators, with the Pinochet case serving as a prospective model for extraterritorial legal activism.

Conclusion

As this account reveals, individual cause lawyers have played a crucial and groundbreaking role in introducing and institutionalizing a human rights approach into the politics of the Israeli-Palestinian conflict. But, as it also reveals, the results have been quite mixed and even contradictory.

Although the lawyers who worked in the military courts rarely achieved the form of professional success that comes from helping their clients "win," let alone success for the political cause that brought them into the courts in the first place, the negative experiences of such work created a sense of community-in-adversity. From this emerged efforts to analyze the problems they were confronting in light of international legal standards, and to publicize those problems through the establishment of local human rights organizations working in alliance with an international human rights movement. The results of these activities served to generate a compelling counternarrative of the conflict as a struggle over rights, rather than a problem of land, security, or terrorism. Unfortunately, the Israeli-Palestinian negotiations undermined a collective sense of cause by derailing the social and political forces that had embraced and adopted this counternarrative. People in Israel/Palestine have been pushed politically back into the confines of their respective national communities and ideologically encouraged to view the world through the parochial lens of national interests.

Yet the legacy of human rights activism and the universal principles that undergird it remain evident in Israel/Palestine. We can see this in the new directions that cause lawyers have been moving. For example, some of the Arab Israeli military court lawyers have been active in a burgeoning civil rights movement in Israel, drawing on international law and appealing to the international human rights movement in their struggle to promote democracy and equality, to transform Israel into a state of and for all its citizens. Some of the Palestinian military court lawyers are working with Palestinian nongovernmental organizations to democratize PA rule and resist authoritarianism and repression. And Jewish Israeli leftist cause lawyers who continue to represent Palestinian clients have been active in challenging the Israeli state's use of torture in interrogation. In 1999, their long struggle netted a significant victory when the Israeli High Court finally rendered a decision prohibiting the routine use of "moderate physical pressure." In a widely circulated (and then published) "open letter," Tsemel (1999: 2) wrote about the lawyers' reactions: "We sat there incredulous in the Supreme Court.... To my ears, the decision was exquisite music.... Every argument we had researched, every claim we had brought over the years, fell naturally into place with this decision."

Although the human rights movement in Israel/Palestine has lost some of its momentum, the achievements have been notable: the language of human rights has come to permeate discourse about the conflict, and the standards of international law are sure to figure heavily in future evaluations of the past. Moreover, despite changing political arrangements, governing relations in Israel/Palestine continue to entail institutionalized discrimination and rights-violating practices. This sustains opportunities—and needs—to continue to look "upward" to international law and "outward" to the international human rights movement and the international community to support local struggles for rights. This maintains the relevance of human rights to the challenges facing cause lawyers in their continuing work for political and legal justice.

References

ACRI (1985). *The Legal and Administrative System*. Jerusalem: Association for Civil Rights in Israel.

Al-Haq (1988). *Punishing a Nation: Human Rights Violations during the Palestinian Uprising*. Ramallah, West Bank: Al-Haq.

——— (1990). *Nation under Siege*. Ramallah, West Bank: Al-Haq.

Amnesty International (1991). *Israel and the Occupied Territories: The Military Justice System in the Occupied Territories: Detention, Interrogation, and Trial Procedures.* New York: Amnesty International USA.

An-Na'im, Abdullahi (1994). "State Responsibility under International Human Rights Law to Change Religious and Customary Laws," in *Human Rights of Women: National and International Perspectives,* Rebecca Cook, ed. Philadelphia: University of Pennsylvania Press.

Bisharat, George (1989). *Palestinian Lawyers and Israeli Rule: Law and Disorder in the West Bank.* Austin: University of Texas Press.

Cohen, Haim (1981). "Foreword," in *The Rule of Law in the Areas Administered by Israel.* Tel Aviv: Israel National Section of the International Commission of Jurists [sic].

Cohen, Stanley (1995). *Denial and Acknowledgment: The Impact of Information about Human Rights Violations.* Jerusalem: Center for Human Rights, Hebrew University.

Cohen, Stanley, and Daphna Golan (1991). *The Interrogation of Palestinians during the Intifada: Ill-Treatment, "Moderate Physical Pressure" or Torture?* Jerusalem: B'Tselem.

——— (1992). *The Interrogation of Palestinians during the Intifada: Follow-up to March 1991 B'Tselem Report.* Jerusalem: B'Tselem.

Copelon, Rhonda (1998). "The Indivisible Framework of International Human Rights: Bringing It Home," in *The Politics of Law: A Progressive Critique,* 3rd ed., David Kairys, ed. New York: Basic Books.

Dinstein, Yoram (1972). "Legislative Authority in the Administered Territories," 3 *Iyunei Mishpat* [Hebrew] 330–335.

——— (1978). "The International Law of Belligerent Occupation and Human Rights," 8 *Israel Yearbook on Human Rights* 104–143.

Donnelly, Jack (1985). *The Concept of Human Rights.* New York: St. Martin's Press.

Falk, Richard (1985). *Human Rights and State Sovereignty.* New York: Holmes & Meier Publishers.

Golan, Daphna (1989). *The Military Judicial System in the West Bank.* Jerusalem: B'Tselem.

Gordon, Colin (1991). "Governmental Rationality: An Introduction," in *The Foucault Effect: Studies in Governmentality,* Graham Burchell, Colin Gordon, and Peter Miller, eds. Chicago: University of Chicago Press.

Hajjar, Lisa (1997). "Cause Lawyering in Transnational Perspective: National Conflict and Human Rights in Israel/Palestine," 31 *Law and Society Review* 473–504.

——— (2000). "Sovereign Bodies, Sovereign States and the Problem of Torture," 21 *Studies in Law, Politics and Society* 101–134.

Hammami, Rema, Jamil Hilal, and Salim Tamari (1999). "Civil Society in Palestine." N.p.

Hiltermann, Joost (2000). "Al-Haq—The First Twenty Years," 214 *Middle East Report* 42–44.

Hofnung, Menachem (1996). *Democracy, Law and National Security in Israel.* Hanover, N.H.: Dartmouth Publishing Co.

Human Rights Watch/Middle East (1994). *Israel—Torture and Ill-Treatment: Israel's Interrogation of Palestinians from the Occupied Territories.* New York: Human Rights Watch.

Keck, Margaret, and Kathryn Sikkink (1998). *Activists beyond Borders: Advocacy Networks in International Politics.* Ithaca, N.Y.: Cornell University Press.

Kremnitzer, Mordechai (1989). "The Landau Commission Report—Was the Security Service Subordinated to the Law, or the Law to the 'Needs' of the Security Service?" 23 *Israel Law Review* 216–279.

Kretzmer, David (1984). *Israel and the West Bank: Legal Issues.* Jerusalem: West Bank Data Base Project.

Landau, Moshe, et al. (1987). *Commission of Inquiry into the Methods of Investigation of the General Security Service Regarding Hostile Terrorist Activity.* Jerusalem: Government Press Office.

Langer, Felicia (1975). *With My Own Eyes: Israel and the Occupied Territories, 1967–1973.* London: Ithaca Press.

Lawyers Committee for Human Rights (1992). *Lawyers and the Military Justice System of the Israeli-Occupied Territories.* New York: Lawyers Committee.

——— (1993). *A Continuing Cause for Concern: The Military Justice System of the Israeli-Occupied Territories.* New York: Lawyers Committee.

O'Brien, William (1991). *Law and Morality in Israel's War with the PLO.* New York: Routledge.

Office of the [Israeli] Military Advocate General (1992). *Response of the IDF Military Advocate General's Unit to Amnesty International Report on the Justice System in the Administered Areas.* Tel Aviv: Office of the [Israeli] Military Advocate General.

Pach, Arie (1977). "Human Rights in West Bank Military Courts," 7 *Israel Yearbook on Human Rights* 221–252.

Pacheco, Allegra (1999a). "Proving Torture: No Longer Necessary in Israel." N.p.

———, ed. (1999b). *The Case against Torture in Israel: A Compilation of Petitions, Briefs and Other Documents Submitted to the Israeli High Court of Justice.* Jerusalem: Public Committee against Torture in Israel.

Paust, Jordan, Gerhard Von Glahn, and Gunter Woratsch (1989). *Inquiry into the Military Court System in the Occupied West Bank and Gaza.* Geneva: International Commission of Jurists.

Playfair, Emma (1988). "Israel's Security Needs in the West Bank, Real and Contrived," 10 *Arab Studies Quarterly* 406–423.

———, ed. (1992). *International Law and the Administration of Occupied Territories: Two Decades of Israeli Occupation of the West Bank and Gaza Strip.* New York: Oxford University Press, Clarendon Press.

Rabbani, Mouin (1994). "Palestinian Human Rights Activism under Israeli Occupation: The Case of Al-Haq," 16 *Arab Studies Quarterly* 27–52.

Rouhana, Nadim (1997). *Palestinian Citizens in an Ethnic Jewish State: Identities in Conflict.* New Haven, Conn.: Yale University Press.

Shamgar, Meir (1982). "Legal Concepts and Problems of the Israeli Military Government— The Initial Stage," in *Military Government in the Territories Administered by Israel, 1967–1980: The Legal Aspects*, Meir Shamgar, ed. Jerusalem: Harry Sacher Institute for Legislative Research and Comparative Law, Hebrew University.

——— (1971). "The Observance of International Law in the Administered Territories," 1 *Israel Yearbook on Human Rights* 719–732.

Shefi, Dov (1982). "The Reports of the U.N. Special Committees on Israeli Practices in the Territories: A Survey and Evaluation," in *Military Government in the Territories Administered by Israel, 1967–1980: The Legal Aspects*, Meir Shamgar, ed. Jerusalem: Harry Sacher Institute for Legislative Research and Comparative Law, Hebrew University.

Shehadeh, Raja (1988). *Occupier's Law: Israel and the West Bank.* Washington, D.C.: Institute for Palestine Studies.

Shehadeh, Raja, and Jonathan Kuttab (1980). *The West Bank and the Rule of Law: A Study.* Geneva: International Commission of Jurists.

Sommer, Hillel (1986). "The Application of the Fourth Geneva Convention in Israeli Law," 11 *Iyunei Mishpat* [Hebrew] 214–228.

Straschnov, Amnon (1994). *Justice under Fire: The Legal System during the Intifada.* Tel Aviv: Yediot Aharanot [Hebrew].

Tsemel, Leah (1984). "Applicability of Geneva Conventions," 1 *Palestine Yearbook of International Law* 37–68.
——— (1999). "An Open Letter to Abu Jerry," 213 *Middle East Report* 2–3.
Usher, Graham (1997). *Palestine in Crisis: The Struggle for Peace and Political Independence after Oslo*, 2nd ed. London: Pluto Press, in association with the Transnational Institute and the Middle East Research & Information Project.
Yahav, David, ed. (1993). *Israel, the "Intifada" and the Rule of Law*. Tel Aviv: Israeli Ministry of Defense Publications.
Zamir, Itzhak (1989). "Human Rights and National Security," 23 *Israel Law Review* 375–406.
——— (1988). "Rule of Law and Control of Terrorism," 8 *Tel Aviv University Studies in Law* 81–93.

CHAPTER 4

Taking on Goliath
Why Personal Injury Litigation May Represent the Future of Transnational Cause Lawyering

ANNE BLOOM

In a world where the largest multinational corporations are richer than the vast majority of countries and governments (Gray 1999), who polices the corporations? This essay explores an instance in which a Texas personal injury firm attempted to police the misconduct of a group of multinationals operating in Costa Rica by filing a lawsuit in Texas state courts. According to the allegations in the lawsuit, a group of Costa Rican farm-workers had been left sterile after being exposed to a pesticide while working for an American-owned plantation in Costa Rica. Although the pesticide had allegedly been manufactured in the United States, and the plantation grew bananas for shipment back to the United States, the defendants in the lawsuit argued that the lawsuit should not be heard in Texas. In a precedent shattering ruling that sent shockwaves across the international business community, the Texas Supreme Court disagreed.

Declaring that the Costa Rican workers in *Alfaro* had an "absolute right" to sue for their injuries in Texas courts, the court announced that Texas courts could not refuse to hear cases that arose on foreign soil when wrongdoing by Texas-based multinationals was alleged (*Dow Chemical v. Castro Alfaro* [1990]). Although the Texas legislature ultimately overturned the ruling, the *Alfaro* litigation—and the Texas Supreme Court's ruling in the case—remains significant in several respects. First, the ruling of the Texas Supreme Court was unprecedented in that it extended U.S. legal protection to workers who were not U.S. citizens and who were injured while working outside of the United States. Never before had U.S. courts been willing to hold multinationals accountable in the United States for their conduct overseas. Second, when the Texas Supreme Court held that the Costa Rican workers had an "absolute right" to sue multinationals in the United States, it effectively opened up a whole new space for litigation in a transnational context.

Among other things, this new space for litigation allows for the possibility of legal strategies that seek to hold multinational corporations accountable through the transnational application of U.S. law. Thus, *Alfaro* is suggestive of new possibilities for cause lawyering in the transnational context. Finally, *Alfaro* is of interest because the lawyers who brought the litigation were personal injury lawyers whose status as "cause lawyers" is a matter of some debate (Menkel-Meadow, 1998). As I explain below, because of the unique tools that personal injury lawyers bring to cause lawyering against multinationals, their involvement in transnational cause lawyering deserves greater attention. At the same time, the experience in *Alfaro* also suggests that personal injury lawyers may experience more difficulty than traditional cause lawyers with keeping "cause" at the center of their efforts.

The research for this essay is based primarily upon litigation documents, media reports, and transcripts of the legislative hearings on *Alfaro*. I also conducted interviews of the lawyers, activists, and reporters who were involved in the litigation and legislative proceedings. My findings and analysis are presented in three parts. Part I describes the litigation and the legislative reversal of *Alfaro* in more detail. Part II focuses on the involvement of personal injury lawyers in the *Alfaro* litigation. Finally, in Part III, I draw some tentative conclusions about the potential advantages and drawbacks of personal injury lawyers becoming involved in transnational workers' rights litigation.

Dow Chemical Company and Shell Oil Company v. Domingo Castro Alfaro et al.

The Lawsuit

The *Alfaro* litigation began with a phone call from a Costa Rican scientist to a colleague in the United States. Roberto Chavez, a forensic pathologist, learned about the plight of the Costa Rican farm workers as part of his work for the Costa Rican judiciary. In 1982, he traveled to Rio Frio, a rural Costa Rican community, to interview the workers. What he found disturbed him. The workers in Rio Frio had been employed on a banana plantation owned by a U.S. company at wages of approximately one dollar an hour. As part of their job, they were exposed to the pesticide dibromochoropropane ("DBCP") which they alleged had left them sterile. Upon further investigation, Chavez learned that the pesticide had been banned in the United States after studies linked exposure to the pesticide to sterility in U.S. workers. Outraged that the pesticide had been shipped to Costa Rican for use after it had been banned, and concerned that the Costa Rican legal system provided the workers with little redress against the U.S.-based companies, Chavez called a toxicologist he knew in Houston and asked him to help. The Houston toxicologist, in turn, placed the workers in contact with a well-known Texas personal injury lawyer.

Knowing that the litigation would face an uphill battle, the personal injury lawyers who took on the case searched for an appropriate forum for the litigation. After three unsuccessful attempts to bring the lawsuit in Florida and California, the lawyers turned to their home courts in Texas and met with success. In a case that was entitled *Dow v. Castro Alfaro*, the lawyers alleged that the manufacturers of DBCP, defendants Dow Chemical Corporation and Shell Oil Company, were liable for the injuries of some eighty-two Costa Rican banana workers, under Texas common law theories of product liability, strict liability, and breach of warranty. Although the lawyers believed that the employer of the banana workers, the Standard Fruit Company, was also partially responsible for the workers' injuries, they left the employer out of the lawsuit because of fears of retaliation against family members and workers who still worked on the plantation (Hosmer, 1990: 12). A Texas trial court initially dismissed the case, but an intermediate court of appeals and the Texas Supreme Court eventually affirmed what they called "the absolute right" of the Costa Ricans to sue in Texas courts (*Alfaro*, 786 S.W. 2d at 674).

The Ruling of the Texas Supreme Court

Prior to the rulings of the Texas appellate courts in *Alfaro*, virtually every court in the country had refused to hear similar cases on the ground of *forum non conveniens*, a legal doctrine that enables most of the courts in the United States to decline to exercise jurisdiction over a case when it determines that justice would be better served in a more "convenient" forum. Although the doctrine has been around for centuries, until the 1970s it had rarely been applied in the United States. With the explosion in transnational business, however, U.S. courts began to face more and more requests from citizens from other countries to hear litigation that stemmed from conduct that took place overseas. Looking for a way of dismissing the cases, federal judges and many state courts turned to the doctrine of *forum non conveniens*. What was precedent-setting about *Alfaro* is that, despite complaints from the multinationals that Texas was an inconvenient forum for adjudicating the case, the Texas Supreme Court allowed the litigation to proceed.

The court's reasoning relied on a 1913 statute that required Texas courts to hear the cases of foreign plaintiffs when the home country of the plaintiffs extended similar rights to U.S. citizens. Although the language of the statute seemed to clearly support the court's holding, the Texas Supreme Court was bitterly divided over the case, and, in the end, nine justices on the court issued seven different opinions on how the case should be decided. Ultimately, by a 5–4 vote, the Texas Supreme Court found that the Texas legislature had statutorily abolished the doctrine of *forum non conveniens*. The lead opinion for the majority relied upon the 1913 statute as controlling legal authority and did not discuss the policy implications of its holding. One of the justices in the majority, however, wrote an extensive concurring opinion which made clear that, in his view, the ruling of the majority was necessary to ensure that corporations would be "held responsible" for their conduct in other countries in the increasingly global economy (*Alfaro*, 786 S.W. 2d at 680).

Written by Justice Lloyd Doggett, a well-known friend of personal injury lawyers and a left-wing sympathizer, the opinion emphasized the increasing threat of corporate misconduct in a global economy. Because of "the absence of meaningful tort liability" in other countries, he argued, multinationals were operating "without adequate regard" for the social "costs of their actions" (ibid., at 674). In his view, the majority's holding in *Alfaro* was necessary because only U.S. courts could provide an "effective" restraint on the misconduct of multinationals that were relocating to countries with less developed legal systems (ibid., at 689). Doggett also argued that changing socioeconomic conditions had rendered the doctrine of *forum non conveniens* meaningless. "The doctrine of *forum non conveniens* is obsolete in a world in which markets are global," he wrote. "[It] ignore[s] the reality that actions of our corporations affecting those abroad will also affect Texans" (*ibid.*). Along similar lines, Doggett rejected the arguments of the defendants that it was unfair to allow them to be sued in Texas, noting that "[a]dvances in transportation and communications technology" rendered the doctrine of *forum non conveniens* a "legal fiction" when applied to multinationals (ibid., at 684).

The dissenting justices, in contrast, emphasized that the events giving rise to the *Alfaro* litigation had "little or no connection to Texas"(Gonzalez dissent, ibid., at 690). As one dissenter put it: "what . . . is Texas' interest in adjudicating a foreign claim by foreign plaintiffs?" (Cook dissent, ibid., at 701). More important, several dissenters argued that allowing the litigation to proceed would have adverse public policy consequences because the litigation would add to "already crowded dockets, forcing [Texas] residents to wait in the corridors of [the] courthouses while foreign causes of action are tried" (Gonzalez dissent, ibid., at 690). Other justices in the minority suggested that, in order for Texas multinationals to remain competitive in the world economy, they needed to be provided with immunity for their actions abroad. As one of the minority justices put it, it seemed "plain" to him that Texas "would want to protect the citizens of this state, its constituents, from greater exposure to liability than they would face in the country in which the alleged wrong was committed" (ibid., at 706). Finally, in the most widely quoted excerpt from the dissenting opinions, one justice implied that Texans would suffer economically as the state became the "courthouse of the world":

> Do Texas taxpayers want to pay extra for judges and clerks and courthouses and personnel to handle foreign litigation? If they do not mind the expense, do they not care that these foreign cases will delay their own cases being heard? As the courthouse for the world, will Texas entice employers to move here, or people to do business here, or even anyone to visit? (Hecht dissent, ibid., at 707)

In his concurring opinion, Doggett took great pains to respond to these charges and, in particular, to the claim that allowing the Costa Ricans to sue would harm the legal rights of Texans. An expert affidavit that was provided to the court had provided extensive empirical evidence that the abolition of *forum non conveniens* in other jurisdictions like Louisiana had not resulted in courthouses that were uniquely overcrowded and, moreover, that states which had adopted *forum non conveniens* had not experienced a significant drop in the number of filings. Drawing upon this affidavit, Doggett argued that the defendants' insinuations about the effects of the court's ruling on the accessibility of the courts for Texans were "misleading and false" (ibid., at 686). Doggett also noted that a logical extension of the defendants' argument meant that the next step would be to strip Texans of *their* legal rights: "If we begin to refuse to hear lawsuits properly filed in Texas because they are sure to require time [and resources], we set a precedent that can be employed to deny Texans access to these same courts" (ibid).

What is curious about this exchange is that, even as the two sides fiercely debated the proper outcome of the litigation, the justices were in fundamental agreement about what was at stake. For both Doggett and the minority, the assumption was that Texas jobs and legal rights *were already threatened* by changing socioeconomic conditions. The only question raised by the litigation was whether the legal rights enjoyed by Texans should be extended to Costa Ricans, in light of those threats. For Doggett, expanding access to people outside of the United States was viewed as critical for policing corporate misconduct in a global economy and ensuring that the legal rights of Texans retained some meaning. For the minority of the Texas Supreme Court and the Texas legislature, however, denying access to people outside the United States was deemed necessary to protect the rights of Texans who were facing "already crowded" courthouses and a loss of jobs to the South. Importantly, the views of the minority justices were bolstered by the submission of some thirty *amicus* briefs from organizations representing the interests of business which argued that the case should be dismissed. Thus, when the majority ruled in favor of expanding access to Texas courts to citizens of other countries, they did so in the face of extreme pressure from the multinational business community. This pressure was intensified by media reports on the litigation, which echoed the sense of alarm that was conjured up in the dissenting opinions.

Media Coverage of the Lawsuit

A Lexis search turned up nearly seventy articles on the *Alfaro* litigation. The vast majority of these articles focused on the dissent's complaint that the *Alfaro* ruling would result in Texas becoming "the courthouse of the world," raising the specter of workers from all over the world responding to *Alfaro* by clogging Texas courts with their claims against Texas-based multinationals. Many of these articles also expressed fear that *Alfaro* would prompt multinationals to flee Texas for countries or states that shielded them from liability. As in the dissenting opinions of the Texas Supreme Court, in the media articles on the litigation, these concerns were linked closely with complaints about the Texas tort system and the threat that personal injury litigation in general posed to the competitiveness of the Texas economy. As more than one commentator acknowledged, the problem with the *Alfaro* ruling was not really that Costa Ricans were permitted to sue in the United States but rather the dangers of personal injury litigation generally. A good example of this appears in an oped piece entitled "Milking the Cash Cow":

> [T]he problem preceded Alfaro.... Great numbers of trial lawyers—fortunately, not all!—perceive the court system as a cash cow to be milked by the man with the fastest fingers and quickest wits.... We could do with a whole new way of thinking about these things.... (Murchison, 1992)

In a similar way, article after article about *Alfaro* conveyed arguments for tort reform. Ultimately, this linkage was so strong that an extraordinary number of news articles about *Alfaro* included coverage of "other" tort reform issues, such as caps on punitive damage awards. With the help of the media, by the time the Texas legislature considered legislation to overturn *Alfaro*, the litigation had become so closely associated with the tort reform movement that one labor activist told me he first heard of this path-breaking transnational rights case as part of his usual monitoring of tort reform legislation.

The Legislative Reversal

Knowing that they did not have the votes to stop the ruling in *Alfaro*, the dissenting justices (and one member of the majority) called upon the Texas legislature to overturn the ruling. Dire consequences for Texans were predicted if the legislature failed to act. In light of this plea and the subsequent media coverage on the case, it is hardly surprising that the debate over *Alfaro* led to action by the Texas legislature. Indeed, according to the lead lawyer for the *Alfaro* plaintiffs, it was "clear" even while the case was still pending before the Texas Supreme Court that the debate over the litigation would move to the legislature: "Even then we were hearing ... if we won there would be immediate attempts to pass the statute that would undo [the Court's ruling]." As predicted, not long after the ruling in *Alfaro*, the multinational defendants in the case and other business interests approached the Texas legislature and asked them to overturn the holding in *Alfaro*. The first attempt to overturn *Alfaro*, however, failed. At the time, the personal injury bar still had a fair amount of influence with the Texas legislature and they were able to kill the bill in committee. By the next session of the legislature, however, the political tides had changed. With the help of the lieutenant governor, negotiations on an "agreed" bill to overturn *Alfaro* began in earnest.

Under ordinary circumstances, an "agreed" bill in the Texas legislature is one that is drafted after extensive negotiations among an array of interested parties. As one local commentator on court politics explained to me, in Texas, this is a common practice because it is a biennial legislature and the legislators are not "full time." To get everything done in a relatively short time, the legislature uses "agreed bills" as a means of avoiding "bloody floor fights." In something of a departure from the usual practice, however, the "agreed bill" to overturn *Alfaro* was crafted in secret and only eight negotiators were invited to participate. Among these eight negotiators were representatives of multinationals, a legal scholar who had argued for adoption of *forum non conveniens* in Texas, the personal injury lawyers who represented the plaintiffs in *Alfaro*, and lobbyists for the Texas Trial Lawyers Association (TTLA) who represent the interests of personal injury lawyers in Texas. Although labor, consumer, and environmental groups had voiced opposition to overturning *Alfaro*, they were not invited to participate in the negotiations. Instead, the only organization invited to participate in the negotiations that had an interest in opposing reversal of the Texas Supreme Court's decision was the TTLA.[1]

In the course of the negotiations, and without consulting with any of the activist groups who were not represented in the negotiations, the TTLA and the personal injury lawyers who represented the *Alfaro* plaintiffs struck a compromise with the business groups, which overturned the most precedent-setting aspects of the *Alfaro* ruling. Under the terms of the compromise, nonresidents of Texas—including foreign nationals—would effectively be precluded from suing in Texas courts, with exceptions carved out for cases brought on behalf of citizens from other states in the United States with claims involving asbestos, airplane crashes, and railroad accidents. In other words, the personal injury lawyers forfeited their interest in representing foreign workers in Texas courts in exchange for being allowed to continue to handle out-of-state asbestos (and other) cases in Texas. As one labor activist later commented, "the TTLA really left us" in the *Alfaro* negotiations.

In subsequent hearings on the agreed bill, activist groups opposed both the process by which the bill was drafted and the substantive impact of the legislation on the rights of foreign plaintiffs to sue in Texas courts. The proposed legislation also drew the ire of other personal injury lawyers, including noted breast implant litigator John O'Quinn, who complained that the bill would preclude breast implant victims from other states from suing breast implant manufacturers in Texas for their injuries (1993). Unlike the testimony of the activists, O'Quinn's testimony focused mainly on how the legislation would impact domestic personal injury practice and paid little attention to how the legislation would affect the rights of people outside of the United States. In an interesting moment, however, O'Quinn pointed out to the legislators how much easier it was to deny the rights of people in the United States, when the rights of people from other countries to sue had been denied first:

> The bill, which is right here, I have it in my hands, says guess what? After discrimination in Section A against nonAmericans... Then in Section B, we decide

to start discriminating against Americans. We're not happy enough that we're gonna discriminate against the non-Americans. Let's start discriminating against the Americans. (O'Quinn, 1993)

Although he did not pursue the point further, O'Quinn's comments echoed the argument of Texas Supreme Court Justice Doggett that Texans could not refuse to extend legal rights to the Costa Ricans, without experiencing a downward pressure on the legal protections that are provided to Texans. Doggett had pointed out, for example, that the argument that corporations needed to be exempt from liability to increase their competitiveness in world markets could just as easily be invoked to deny Texans the right to hold corporations accountable as people from outside of Texas (see *Alfaro*: 686). In other words, by noting how quickly the legislation turned from discriminating against "non-Americans" to discriminating against "Americans," O'Quinn essentially repeated Doggett's warning that the rights of the Costa Rican farm workers and the rights of Texans were linked in such a way that it would not be possible to deny access to Texas courts to the Costa Rican farm workers without also having the effect of making it easier to curtail the rights of Texans.

Despite these protestations, in 1993, a little more than two years after the ruling in *Alfaro*, the Texas legislature passed the "agreed bill" to overturn *Alfaro* and statutorily abolished the right of injured people from other countries to sue multinationals in Texas courts. Meanwhile, the Costa Rican workers settled their litigation quietly for a substantial amount of money that was said to be well into the "eight figures" (Elliott, 1992).[2]

Aftermath

Despite the passage of the anti-*Alfaro* legislation, transnational litigation against multinationals for injuries stemming from their conduct in other countries has continued to be filed in Texas courts. The bringing of this litigation has been possible, in part, because of the nature of the *forum non conveniens* doctrine, which gives judges great discretion to decide whether or not to hear the case. Under the doctrine, courts must consider a number of factors in determining whether it would be more convenient for the case to be heard in a different forum. These factors include a consideration of whether the suing party has an alternative forum in which to litigate the case and whether there is a public interest in hearing the case in the United States. Because there are no clear guidelines on how to assess these factors, however, a judge has tremendous discretion in deciding whether to allow the litigation to proceed. In the typical case, the exercise of this discretion usually results in the case being dismissed because judges in overcrowded courts are anxious to clear their dockets of any cases that they do not absolutely have to hear. But this extensive discretion also creates an opening for sympathetic judges to allow cases by foreign nationals to proceed in their courts and, in recent years, Texas courts appear to be increasingly willing to do so.

Two cases that have received a significant amount of attention are *Mendoza v. Contico* (1997) and *Rodriguez-Olvera v. Salant Corporation* (1999). In *Mendoza*, a personal injury lawyer in a Texas border town filed a case on behalf of a Mexican maquiladora worker who was murdered while delivering the payroll for her U.S.-based employer in Mexico. Although the defendant argued that the case should be dismissed on the ground of *forum non conveniens*, the judge allowed the litigation to proceed in Texas. Ultimately, the case ultimately settled for approximately $2 million in damages and a change in the company's practices.[3] More recent, in *Rodriguez-Olvera v. Salant Corporation* (1999), a prominent Texas personal injury lawyer sued a U.S.-based apparel maker in Texas state court for injuries that occurred to a group of Mexicans employed by the U.S. company's subsidiary in Mexico. According to the complaint, fourteen Mexican workers were killed and several others were injured when a company bus with faulty brakes crashed into a sewage ditch. Although the accident and the injuries occurred in Mexico, Texas courts rejected the U.S. company's attempts to have the case dismissed, without comment. Shortly before trial, the case settled for $30 million.

Thus, with the help of the trial courts, Texas personal injury lawyers are continuing to bring and settle lawsuits on behalf of foreign nationals against multinationals based in Texas, despite the legislative action to overturn *Alfaro*. In the meantime, however, it has become more difficult for residents of other states in the United States to sue in Texas courts. In 1997, four years after the compromise to overturn *Alfaro*, the Texas legislature passed legislation that effectively closed the loophole for out-of-state asbestos, airplane, and railroad accident cases that the lawyers for the *Alfaro* plaintiffs and the TTLA had won in exchange for forfeiting the rights of foreign nationals during the secret negotiations over the *Alfaro* legislation (Elliott, 1997).

Personal Injury Lawyers as Cause Lawyers

As I noted at the outset, one of the more interesting aspects of *Alfaro* is that the litigation was brought by personal injury lawyers. Moreover, it is now clear that *Alfaro* is not an aberration. As the recently settled *Mendoza* and *Rodriguez-Olvera* reveal, Texas personal injury lawyers continue to be attracted to transnational workers' rights cases, despite the fact that the Texas legislature attempted to shut the door on such cases when it passed the legislation to overturn *Alfaro*. While these lawyers are undoubtedly drawn into the litigation by the lure of a potentially large fee, their involvement nevertheless suggests the possibility that it is appropriate to characterize these personal injury lawyers as cause lawyers (cf. Menkel-Meadow, 1998).

In contrast to other lawyers, cause lawyers are typically distinguished by their willingness to elevate the interests of the cause over the immediate demands of a client (Scheingold and Bloom, 1998). While some have argued that private, fee-for-service lawyers may have a higher level of commitment to both the client and the cause (Shamir and Chinski, 1998), the prevailing view is that personal injury lawyers are less committed to the "cause" than traditional cause lawyers, because of their pecuniary interest in the litigation. In *Alfaro*, these concerns were realized when the financial interests of the personal injury lawyers representing the Costa Rican workers came into conflict with the broader cause of the rights of the Costa Ricans workers and others to sue. To dismiss personal injury lawyers as cause lawyers on this basis of the outcome in *Alfaro*, however, may be unfair. While the *Alfaro* lawyers may have abandoned the cause when they negotiated the reversal of the *Alfaro* ruling with the Texas legislature, other personal injury lawyers eventually returned to the cause when they brought new transnational litigation after the legislature attempted to extinguish the issue.

Moreover, as I explain below, for the lead lawyer in the *Alfaro* litigation, representing the Costa Rican workers was something of a transformative experience. After the compromise was reached in the Texas legislature to overturn the *Alfaro* ruling, this lawyer left the *Alfaro* firm and eventually set up his own transnational practice, which he has found to be substantially less remunerative but considerably more "satisfying." Thus, *Alfaro* appears to provide some evidence for the proposition that personal injury lawyers will, in the process of litigating these transnational workers' rights cases, begin to realize the "possibility of becoming or functioning as a lawyer for a cause" (Shamir and Chinski, 1998).

From Personal Injury Litigator to Cause Lawyer

The lead lawyer for the *Alfaro* litigation, Charles Siegel, describes his initial involvement in the case as almost accidental. As he tells it, he was sitting in the law library when a senior partner in the firm asked for help in researching cases on *forum non conveniens*. At the time, Siegel was a summer law clerk and the research project was his first assignment. When he later joined the firm as a first-year associate, Siegel says, he "sort of just became the lead lawyer" on the case. But, despite the somewhat haphazard way in which he became involved in the case, Siegel quickly developed a high degree of commitment to both the clients in the case and the broader issues at stake. According to Siegel, this was in part a result of his first trip to meet the clients in Costa Rica, which he described as having a "very galvanizing" effect.

Siegel characterizes the trip to Costa Rica as "galvanizing" for two reasons. The first reason was that he found his Costa Rican clients to be less "cynical" and more "deserving" than the personal injury victims his firm represented in the

United States. In his words, the *Alfaro* plaintiffs were "absolutely and totally innocent. . . . they [were] not cynical about lawyers, they [were] not cynical about the legal system, the way a lot of American, personal injury plaintiffs are. . . . I mean every single one of them was a young man, you know, who was sterile." The second reason his visit to the plantation was so electrifying was that he became convinced that his clients did not "have a prayer of a shot or a hope of any kind of remedy in Costa Rica." As he put it, the trip made him more sensitive to the "political dimension" of the case and, in particular, to how "utterly ridiculous" it was for multinational defendants to "claim that it is more to convenient to litigate thousands of miles from home than it is to litigate at home."

Thus, in the course of meeting his clients and otherwise litigating the case, Siegel began—like many cause lawyers—to feel a relatively higher degree of commitment to both the clients and the cause at stake in the *Alfaro* litigation. And, like more traditional cause lawyers, Siegel was intrigued by the novelty of the legal issues at stake in the case: "Even then, as a first year lawyer, I could tell . . . [it was] cutting edge stuff and interesting." For all of these reasons, Siegel found the *Alfaro* litigation much more "interesting" and "satisfying" than other cases.

But what of the firm's pecuniary interest in the litigation and the willingness to cut a deal with the Texas legislature that attempted to foreclose the possibility of similar litigation in the future? Significantly, Siegel was not involved in the negotiations over the anti-*Alfaro* bill. According to him, the negotiations for the firm were handled by a senior partner and some lobbyists. It is also clear that Siegel was unhappy with the compromise. When asked about it, he says simply that he "can't defend" the deal "on any grounds" except for the fact that the firm was worried about losing the rest of its practice. Ultimately, his unhappiness about the deal, together with the fact that the firm had decided to no longer handle transnational litigation after settling *Alfaro*, prompted him to leave the firm.

Despite all this, Siegel is sympathetic to the perspective of his old firm and, in particular, to their decision to no longer handle transnational litigation. As he explained to me, when the firm took the case "they never imagined the procedural quagmire that it would become and . . . they never imagined how tenaciously it would be resisted on *forum non conveniens* grounds." Moreover, the firm "had a big practice to run," and the transnational cases were "draining a lot of resources" that could more profitably be put into U.S.-based personal injury litigation. To the extent that the firm was trying to run a profitable business, it simply did not make good economic sense to continue handling these cases.

Siegel, in contrast, viewed himself as "thinking much more idealistically" at the time, and as a result he had a strong "desire to continue" handling transnational litigation, despite the financial risks involved. While Siegel was certainly not averse to the idea of obtaining a large fee for doing transnational workers' rights cases, his interest in the clients and his broader interest in holding U.S.-based multinationals accountable for their misconduct in other countries had begun to outweigh the question of whether the litigation would be profitable and, at any rate, he believed he could "make [the cases] work."

Today, more than a decade after the *Alfaro* ruling, Siegel is in practice for himself, and a very high percentage of his case load is transnational. Although the transnational cases do not earn him enough to sustain his practice, he continues to handle them because they are "more interesting" and the cases "really deserve to be brought." But he also acknowledges that his motivation for taking these cases is at least in some small part pecuniary. As he put it, the cases are "seductive, in that there's sort of the shimmering mirage out there of a potential large fee."

In sum, Siegel's experience as the lead lawyer for the *Alfaro* plaintiffs seems to provide additional evidence to support the contention of Shamir and Chinski (1998) that "lawyers for a cause are not necessarily those who consciously and deliberately orient their professional lives toward promoting that cause." Instead, "[i]t is in the course of engaging" in the acts of lawyering "that the possibility of becoming or functioning as a lawyer for a cause is realized." Although he stumbled into the case by "accident," Siegel's experience of litigating and especially meeting and seeing the living conditions of his clients "galvanized" him to the point where he eventually left his firm and attempted to pursue transnational cause litigation full time. Although the *Alfaro* litigation did not turn Siegel into a cause lawyer in the traditional sense of the term, it is fair to say that "in the course of engaging in the acts of lawyering" on behalf of the *Alfaro* plaintiffs, he began to realize "the possibility of becoming or functioning as a lawyer for a cause" (Shamir and Chinski, 1998).

The Politics of Cause Lawyering

Siegel's motivations aside, a number of aspects of the *Alfaro* litigation suggest that, even when personal injury lawyers come to identify closely with both their clients and the cause at stake, they may be slower than traditional cause lawyers to recognize the political dimensions of the case. As a result, they may be less willing or able to link the litigation with the broader aims of a political movement. Since some scholars have attempted to measure the political utility of cause lawyering in terms of how closely the efforts of cause lawyers are linked to a broader political strategy (see, e.g., McCann, 1994; Scheingold and Bloom, 1998), whether this is in fact the case has important implications for the cause-lawyering enterprise.

In *Alfaro*, the lead lawyer for the plaintiffs told me that both he and the firm's leadership were aware of the political dimension of the *Alfaro* litigation fairly early on. He also told me that by the time the case was before the Texas Supreme Court, they knew that they "had to win this not only in the court but in the legislature." Despite this recognition, the firm made virtually no attempt to generate support for their clients' position among local activists. As a practical matter, this meant that, when the case was before the Texas Supreme Court, not a single *amicus* brief was filed by a Texas or Costa Rican organization in support of the *Alfaro* plaintiffs, even as business interests filed some thirty *amicus* briefs against them. When I asked why this was, the lead lawyer for the *Alfaro* plaintiffs told me that it didn't "really click in his mind to seek" *amicus* support for his clients.

Similarly, although this lawyer later devised a media strategy in connection with developing his own transnational practice, neither he nor the firm made any attempt to formulate a media strategy in connection with *Alfaro*. And, in contrast to traditional cause lawyers (see McCann, 1994), the attorney for the *Alfaro* plaintiffs reported that, even though he knew the battle would eventually reach the Texas legislature, this knowledge had little or no effect on his arguments in court. Although, in retrospect, it is impossible to say whether any of this had any effect on the ultimate outcome in the case, past research suggests that, in order for cause litigation to be politically efficacious, it must be linked closely with political organizing efforts. Moreover, although the *Alfaro* lawyers obtained the ruling they wanted from the Texas Supreme Court without any assistance from Texas political activists, their failure to generate broader support for the litigation probably meant that the political aims of the *Alfaro* litigation were much more vulnerable when the lawyers entered into the negotiations with the Texas legislature. As a local civil rights lawyer explained to me, Texas activists were not notified about the litigation until the *Alfaro* ruling was already under assault in the Texas legislature. And by that time, "everything moved so fast, we didn't have the time to solidify."

It is possible, however, that greater involvement by local activists in the litigation would have made little difference. As both the dissenting opinions in *Alfaro* and the subsequent media coverage demonstrate, the *Alfaro* litigation was brought in a political climate that was highly favorable to tort reform. And, while the attack on lawyers that has characterized tort reform has placed pressure on all cause lawyers (Engel 1994), personal injury lawyers are particularly vulnerable to these pressures. Notably, one of the key supporters of personal injury lawyers at this time was the Texas Supreme Court. As one activist reported, the "conventional wisdom" was that the *Alfaro* court was "bought and paid for" by the personal injury bar. Certainly Justice Lloyd Doggett, who wrote the most widely cited opinion in support of the ruling, was well known as a friend of the personal injury bar. Whether and how much the relationship between the personal injury bar and the Texas Supreme Court influenced the strategies of the plaintiffs' lawyers is difficult to say. The lead attorney for the *Alfaro* plaintiffs, however, did tell me that, despite the widespread perception of the Texas Supreme Court at that time, he thought that they "were going to lose" and was "somewhat surprised" when they won.

At any rate, between 1990, when the Texas Supreme Court decided *Alfaro*, and 1993, when the legislature passed the bill to overturn *Alfaro*, Texas began to undergo a political transformation. According to studies of the Texas Supreme Court by Texas Citizen Action, at the time that *Alfaro* was decided, the Texas Supreme Court was splitting "about evenly" between rulings for plaintiffs and rulings for defendants. By 1996, however, more than two-thirds of the civil rulings of the Texas Supreme Court held in favor of defendants (Press Release of Texas Citizen Action, July 23, 1998). In the meantime, the Texas legislature was also becoming more Republican and pro–tort reform. As one political observer commented, when the legislative battle over *Alfaro* was fought, Texas was effectively in the midst of "a transition to becoming a Republican state".

According to the lead lawyer for the Costa Rican farm workers, an awareness of this changing political situation was one factor that prompted the lawyers for the *Alfaro* plaintiffs and the TTLA to agree to the legislation to overturn *Alfaro*. The firm's senior partner, who gave the go-ahead for the deal to overturn *Alfaro*, "believed that the political tide was turning," and, as a result, he had "clearly legitimate" concerns about the potential threat that these political changes posed for the firm's bread-and-butter asbestos practice. For all of these reasons, the TTLA and the firm that represented the Costa Rican workers had a powerful incentive to walk away from the cause during the legislative negotiations, regardless of whether doing so would damage its ties with local activists.

In the end, both the willingness of the lawyers who brought the *Alfaro* litigation to abandon the cause in favor of a compromise that served the pecuniary interests of the rest of their practice and the seeming reluctance of these lawyers to consider (or even contemplate) political organizing and media strategies in connection with the litigation raises serious questions about whether the involvement of personal injury lawyers in transnational cause litigation may do more harm than good. What seems clear from *Alfaro* is that personal injury lawyers will be both slower to recognize the political dimensions of the case and less willing or able to link the litigation with the broader aims of a political movement than traditional cause lawyers. Under these circumstances, their effectiveness as cause lawyers may be significantly compromised.

What the Personal Injury Bar Offers to Cause Lawyering

So far in this essay, I have emphasized the limitations of having personal injury lawyers involved in transnational cause litigation and, to some extent, the possibilities for such litigation to have a cause-orienting effect on personal injury lawyers. But *Alfaro* also teaches that personal injury lawyers have much to offer the cause-lawyering enterprise. Indeed, it is quite likely that, without the involvement of personal injury lawyers, transnational workers' rights litigation like *Alfaro* might never have been brought in Texas. This is true for three reasons.

The first reason is that transnational litigation is extremely expensive to prosecute. Because of this, as the lead lawyer for the *Alfaro* plaintiffs commented, "it takes lawyers who've got the money to litigate them." The added expense of transnational litigation is due largely to the fact that the litigation involves extraordinary logistical challenges. In *Alfaro*, for example, the Costa Rican farm-workers that they represented live in rural communities where telephones and even paved roads are scarce. To communicate with their clients, the *Alfaro* lawyers had to, among other things, hire local interpreters to make radio broadcasts. And, in order to win case, the lawyers needed the means to hire paid experts on both the causation issues in the case and on Costa Rican law.

Because of the availability of the contingency fee arrangement, and because of other resource advantages, personal injury lawyers are both more willing and able than traditional cause lawyers to litigate successfully under these conditions. Unlike personal injury lawyers, traditional cause lawyers typically have much fewer resources at their disposal and are usually unable to enter into contingency fee arrangements with their clients because of the tax code restrictions on the not-for-profit organizations with which they are affiliated. In short, in light of the extraordinary expense of bringing transnational litigation, it is unlikely that *Alfaro* would have been litigated at all, had personal injury lawyers not be been willing to advance the costs.

A second reason why personal injury lawyers may be key to bringing transnational workers' rights litigation has to do with their unique areas of expertise. Cases like *Alfaro* involve difficult issues of causation and are, in the words of the lead lawyer for the *Alfaro* plaintiffs, "tenaciously defended" by the multinational defendants. As compared to traditional cause lawyers, personal injury lawyers are much more likely to have expertise in developing and proving difficult issues of causation and they are also much more experienced in litigating against multinationals. For all of these reasons, personal injury lawyers bring a wealth of resources and expertise to transnational cause litigation against multinationals that is otherwise unavailable within the cause-lawyering bar.

A final reason why personal injury lawyers may have an important contribution to make to transnational cause lawyering has to do with what Shamir and Chinksi (1998) have referred to as the ability of private lawyers to "survive longer in the field." In their study of lawyers representing the cause of Bedouins in Israel, Shamir and Chinksi (1998) found that fee-for-service lawyers tended to display greater resilience and stamina for the litigation than the more traditional cause lawyers who started out with a greater level of commitment to the cause. Similarly, the experience in Texas after the legislative reversal of the *Alfaro* ruling indicates that personal injury lawyers may have a higher degree of resilience in battling the multinationals in transnational litigation than traditional cause lawyers in Texas.

As I noted above, personal injury lawyers are continuing to bring transnational rights cases, even after the Texas legislature tried to shut the door. Traditional cause lawyers in Texas, on the other hand, reported to me that they have concluded that the anti-*Alfaro* legislation has made transnational litigation too difficult to pursue in Texas. Significantly, cause lawyers in Texas continued to reach this conclusion even after the *Mendoza* case—which obtained relief for the maquiladora worker murdered in Mexico after the legislative reversal of *Alfaro*—was successfully litigated. In my interviews with local activists, I learned that the lawyers for the *Mendoza* plaintiffs made a presentation on the case to a group of Texas cause lawyers during a regional meeting of the National Lawyers Guild. After the presentation, the cause lawyers discussed "at length" whether there was some way that they could become involved in future litigation of this type. According to one cause lawyer who attended this meeting, however, the traditional cause lawyers simply "drew a blank" when it came to thinking about transnational legal strategies.

Although it is too soon to draw conclusions about the relative roles of personal injury lawyers and traditional cause lawyers in the development of transnational cause litigation in Texas, it is clear that personal injury lawyers are currently in the vanguard of this legal movement. It is also clear that, despite their pecuniary interests in the litigation, they have much to offer the cause-lawyering enterprise. Among other things, the contingent fee arrangements that are typical of personal injury practice may provide an important means of expanding opportunities for cause lawyering, particularly as funding for legal services and other cause-lawyering activities is increasingly limited (Scheingold and Bloom, 1998). At the same time, it is important to recognize that personal injury lawyers face some of the same economic pressures as legal services lawyers and other traditional cause lawyers (ibid., 1998). In *Alfaro*, this pressure was exacerbated by a political climate that was especially hostile to personal injury lawyers and that, ultimately, appears to have prompted them to abandon the cause in order to preserve their own economic interests.

In sum, despite the ultimate outcome, the involvement of personal injury attorneys in the *Alfaro* litigation and the continuing involvement of personal injury lawyers in transnational workers' rights litigation holds a great deal of promise for the cause-lawyering enterprise, particularly in light of the challenges to cause lawyering that are posed by the increasingly global economy. As multinationals grow in power and dominant states are under increasing pressure to cut funding for legal services (see Sarat, this volume), some have argued that cause lawyers may never have the resources or the numbers they need to successfully challenge the "battalions" of corporate lawyers in transnational practice (Trubek, et al., 1994: 426, n. 22). The involvement of personal injury lawyers in the *Alfaro* litigation, however, suggests one way in which the cause-lawyering enterprise may reshape itself so as to better combat the growing influence of multinationals.

Conclusions

It is difficult to draw conclusions from a single case study. What we can say from the experience of *Alfaro* and its aftermath, however, is that personal injury lawyers may play a critical role in transnational cause lawyering against multinationals. Despite the fact that the personal injury lawyers representing the *Alfaro* plaintiffs ultimately abandoned the cause, their involvement in the litigation was crucial to the early success of the litigation. Moreover, the involvement of personal injury lawyers in subsequent transnational workers' rights litigation suggests that they will continue to play an important role in transnational cause litigation in the future. Whether and how this involvement of personal injury lawyers in transnational cause litigation influences the possibilities for cause lawyering is not entirely clear. On the one hand, the experience of the lead lawyer for the *Alfaro* plaintiffs suggests that when personal injury lawyers become involved in transnational rights litigation, they may be prompted to act more like "lawyers for a cause" (Shamir and Chinksi, 1998). On the other hand, *Alfaro* also suggests that personal injury lawyers are also more likely to privilege their own pecuniary interests over concern for the cause. How these two, somewhat paradoxical, possibilities will play out in future transnational workers' rights litigation by personal injury lawyers remains to be seen.

One interesting question that is raised (but not answered) by *Alfaro* is what role local courts may play in influencing these developments. Past research indicates that states have "few incentives to cooperate" in recognizing transnational legal rights (Keck and Sikkink, 1998: 203). In *Alfaro*, however, the conduct of the local courts suggests that, for at least some institutions, this is not always the case. Why is it that, even after the Texas legislature passed legislation to overturn *Alfaro*, some Texas courts have been willing to hear the transnational claims of foreign workers? Although there are many potential reasons why a court may choose to disobey the will of its local legislature, one explanation for the willingness of Texas courts to allow these cases to go forward may lie in the increasingly threatened position of local courts in the global economy.

As several scholars have noted, the neoliberal characteristics of the increasingly global, free-market economy are placing pressure on legal rights, particularly in economically dominant countries like the United States (Sarat this volume; Greider, 1997; Held, 1995). Because of this pressure, liberal, democratic states are said to be experiencing a "crisis of legitimacy" (*see* Sarat this volume; *see also* Garland, 1996). The state's inability to regulate multinational conduct overseas, at least arguably, exacerbates this crisis because it exposes the state as unable, or unwilling, to hold multinational corporations accountable under law. As the protectors of rights in liberal societies (if only in myth) and the institutions responsible for holding all equally accountable under the law, the courts—at least arguably—have the most to lose if the crisis is not addressed.

In *Alfaro*, the opinions of the court reveal that justices on both sides of the debate were concerned about the legitimacy of the courts in the increasingly global economy. As I noted above in my description of the court's opinion, the *Alfaro* justices were in agreement that, more than anything else, what was at stake in *Alfaro* was whether Texas courts would be able to continue to provide access to legal rights for *Texans*. For the minority justices, *Alfaro* posed a threat to access for Texans because they feared that allowing foreign nationals to sue would lead to further delays in courts that were perceived by many Texas citizens to be *already overcrowded*. For Doggett, on the other hand, Texas could not refuse to extend legal rights to the Costa Ricans without experiencing a downward pressure on the legal protections that are provided to them. Thus, for both sides of the debate, the continuing ability of Texas courts to provide legal protection—and the closely related question of the legitimacy of Texas courts—appears to have been very much at issue.

One way for courts to respond to concerns about legitimacy is to expand access to legal rights (Keck and Sikkink, 1998). As others have noted in the domestic context, in doing so, courts substantiate the claim of the state that all are treated equally under the law (Halliday and Karpik, 1999). When the crisis in legitimacy stems in part from a perception that multinationals are beyond the law, however, another way to respond might be to increase the capacity of the state to regulate the conduct of multinationals operating outside their borders. *Alfaro* presented the Texas Supreme Court with an opportunity to pursue both of these legitimating strategies at once. And, in Justice Doggett's opinion, there is substantial evidence that these considerations were, at least in part, driving the court's reasoning. Recall, for example, Doggett's argument that Texans could not deny Costa Ricans the right to sue, without experiencing a downward pressure on their own legal rights. This argument clearly links expanding legal access to the continuing capacity of local courts to provide legal protection for Texans and, as a result, ties the court's legitimacy to the expansion of the legal rights to Costa Ricans. Similarly, the *Alfaro* court's decision to expand its jurisdiction extraterritorially to cover multinational conduct in other countries, Doggett argued, was necessary to ensure that the right to sue them in Texas was not rendered meaningless.

This last argument is of particular significance because it goes to the question of the continuing relevance of local courts in a global economy. As I noted at the beginning of this essay, the Texas Supreme Court's ruling in *Alfaro* sent shockwaves across the multinational business community. While perhaps overdramatized in the media reports on the litigation, the fear, quite literally, was that Texas had just declared itself "the courthouse of the world." As a result, for a moment at least, Texas courts became major players in the global regulatory arena. Thus, whether intentional or not, one effect of decisions like *Alfaro*, which recognize a transnational right to sue on the part of the foreign nationals in Texas, is to significantly increase the global stature of Texas courts.

In sum, *Alfaro* suggests that, to the extent that the neoliberal pressures of globalization are prompting dominant states to experience a "crisis in legitimacy," local courts in those states may be motivated to expand access to local legal systems for two reasons. First, local courts—like Justice Doggett—may perceive the litigation as a means of bolstering perceptions of the court's legitimacy at home by, among other things, demonstrating that the courts are still capable of holding even powerful, multinational corporations accountable to its legal norms. Second, and less obviously, by expanding their jurisdiction in this way, local courts may help to ensure that they will continue to play a regulatory role in the global arena. For both of these reasons, Texas courts—at least arguably—had an incentive to work with the cause lawyers to obtain broader institutional support for the expansion of transnational legal rights.

This development, in turn, may have important implications for the cause-lawyering enterprise. According to some observers, the political utility of cause lawyering may depend in part upon the extent to which the cause lawyers maintain something of a "dissident" relationship with state institutions (Menkel-Meadow, 1998; but cf. Michalowski, 1998). Under the circumstances presented in *Alfaro*, however, cause lawyers operate less in opposition to state institutions and more like double-agents. On the one hand, they oppose the state, insofar as they push the state to make good on its liberal claims by expanding the parameters of who has access to the courts. On the other hand, in the transnational context, this expansion of access increases the stature and regulatory power of the state—and local courts, in particular—at a time when both are increasingly in question. In *Alfaro*, the double-agent role of the cause lawyers was compounded by the fact that the litigation was handled by personal injury lawyers who, particularly at the time the *Alfaro* litigation was brought, were in an extremely vulnerable position vis-à-vis local institutions because of the changing political climate within the state. As one activist pointed out to me, the hostile political climate clearly had an important effect on the political strategies of personal injury lawyers:

> The new legislation and the new judges on the courts, the Republicans on the courts, have severely diminished trial lawyer power.... You see a lot of trial lawyers now actually supporting the Republican judges as a way of trying to cut their losses. They understand that the Republican judges are going to win and so they want to be on the winning side ... so they'll be supporting the Republicans.

Thus, given the relative "outsider" status of personal injury lawyers in Texas politics at the time, one wonders if the willingness of the *Alfaro* lawyers and the TTLA to compromise in the legislative negotiations was motivated, in part, by the desire to position themselves as legislative "insiders" in a hostile political climate. From the comments of the lead lawyer for the *Alfaro* plaintiffs, we do know that concern about the changing political tide was an important factor that affected the negotiations and the willingness of his firm to continue to handle transnational litigation. Whether this translated into active desire on the part of the firm to attempt to seek a more cooperative relationship with the state is a question that cannot be answered by this case study. What is clear, however, is that the "outsider" status of personal injury lawyers may have made it more difficult for the *Alfaro* lawyers to keep "cause" at the center of the their efforts.

Perhaps more than anything else, however, the experience in *Alfaro* suggests that the line between cause lawyering and traditional lawyering is not particularly clear or stable (Shamir and Chinksy, 1998). As noted in the introduction to this volume, in practice, "[i]ndividual lawyers frequently cross and re-cross the lines between traditional and cause lawyering" (Sarat and Scheingold). While the *Alfaro* lawyers may have stepped out of their cause-lawyering role when they negotiated the reversal of the *Alfaro* ruling with the Texas legislature, they had good reasons for doing so, and, at any rate, other personal injury lawyers eventually "re-crossed" the line when they opposed the legislation to overturn *Alfaro* and, later, when they brought new litigation to expand access to Texas courts transnationally after the legislature attempted to extinguish the issue. Finally, because traditional cause lawyers have neither the resources nor the ability to enter into the contingency fee arrangements that may be key to allowing such litigation to go forward, and because of the financial incentives presented by transnational litigation, the involvement of personal injury lawyers in transnational workers' rights litigation is probably both necessary and inevitable. The challenge for cause lawyering will be to find ways of helping these lawyers to keep "cause" at the center of their efforts.

Notes

1. As one of the participants later acknowledged, the process by which the legislation to overturn *Alfaro* was drafted "raises significant issues concerning the democratic process" (Weintraub, 1994: 344).

2. It is somewhat misleading to refer to the *Alfaro* litigation as is if it were a single case. In fact, numerous cases with similar factual circumstances were filed and settled by the firm at this time. *Alfaro* was simply the name of the lead case that was argued before the Texas Supreme Court.

3. In an odd twist of circumstances, the legal scholar who is credited as the author of the legislation to overturn *Alfaro* (and who helped to represent one of the *Alfaro* defendants before the Texas Supreme Court) switched sides in the *Mendoza* litigation and argued to the court that the Mexican plaintiffs' case should be heard in the United States. When I asked this lawyer what prompted him to do this, he cited what he considered to be the relatively more egregious conduct of the *Mendoza* defendants as influential.

References

Elliott, Janet (1992). "Arguments Sidestep Alfaro: Reviving Forum Non Conveniens May Depend on Legislators," *Texas Lawyer* (October 12), 1.
Elliott, Jane (1997). "Tort Reform's Last Hurrah?" *Texas Lawyer* (June 9).
Engel, David M. (1994). "The Oven Bird's Song: Insiders, Outsiders, and Personal Injuries in an American Community." In *Law and Community in Three American Towns*, Carol J. Greenhouse, Barbara Yngvesson, and David M. Engel, 27–53. Ithaca N.Y.: Cornell University Press.

Garland, David, (1996). "The Limits of the Sovereign State," 36:4 *British Journal of Criminology (Autumn)*, 445–71.
Gray, Charles (1999). "Corporate Goliaths: Sizing Up Corporations and Governments," *Multinational Monitor* (June), 26–27.
Greenhouse, Carol J., Barbara Yngvesson, and David M. Engel (1994). *Law and Community in Three American Towns*. Ithaca, N.Y.: Cornell University Press.
Greider, William (1997). *One World, Ready or Not*. New York: Simon & Schuster.
Halliday, Terrence C., and Lucien Karpik (1997). *Lawyers and the Rise of Western Political Liberalism*. Oxford: Clarendon Press.
Handler, Joel (1978). *Social Movements and the Legal System: A Theory of Law Reform and Social Change*. New York: Academic Press.
Held, David (1995). *Democracy and Global Order: From the Modern State to Cosmopolitan Governance*. Stanford, Calif.: Stanford University Press.
Hosmer, Ellen (1990). "First World Justice: Costa Rican Farmworkers in Texas State Courts," *Texas Observer* (July 13), 10–13.
Keck, Margaret, and Kathryn Sikkink (1998). *Activists Beyond Borders: Transnational Advocacy Networks in International Politics*. Ithaca, N.Y.: Cornell University Press.
Menkel-Meadow, Carrie (1998). "The Causes of Cause Lawyering: Toward an Understanding of the Motivation and Commitment of Social Justice Lawyers." In *Cause Lawyering: Political Commitments and Professional Responsibilities*, Austin Sarat and Stuart Scheingold, eds., 31–68. New York: Oxford University Press.
Michalowski, Raymond (1998). "All or Nothing: An Inquiry into the (Im)Possibility of Cause Lawyering under Cuban Socialism," In *Cause Lawyering: Political Commitments and Professional Responsibilities*, Austin Sarat and Stuart Scheingold, eds., 523–45. New York: Oxford University Press.
Murchison, William (1992). "Milking the Cash Cow," *Texas Lawyer* (August 17).
O'Quinn, John (1993). Testimony before the House State Affairs Committee of the Texas Legislature (February 15).
Santos, Boaventura de Sousa (1995). *Toward a New Common Sense: Law, Science, and Politics in the Paradigmatic Transition*. New York: Routledge.
Scheingold, Stuart, and Anne Bloom (1998). "Transgressive Cause Lawyering: Practice Sites and the Politicization of the Professional," 5:2/3 *International Journal of the Legal Profession*, 209–53.
Siegel, Barry (1991). "Going an Extra Mile for Justice," *Los Angeles Times* (March 23).
Trubek, David M., Yves Dezalay, Ruth Buchanan, and John R. Davis (1994). "Global Restructuring and the Law: Studies of the Internationalization of Legal Fields and the Creation of Transnational Arenas," 44 *Case Western Reserve Law Review*, 407–98.
Weintraub, Russell J. (1994). "International Litigation and Forum Non Conveniens," 29 *Texas International Law Journal*, 321–52.

Cases

Dow Chemical Co. v. Castro Alfaro, 786 S.W. 2d 674 (1990).
Mendoza v. Contico (1997, Dist. Ct., El Paso Co., Texas, No. 3).
Rodriguez-Olvera v. Salant Corp., No. 97-07-14605 (1999, Dist. Ct., Maverick Co., Texas).

CHAPTER 5

Cause Lawyering in the Shadow of the State
A U.S. Immigration Example

SUSAN BIBLER COUTIN

Immigration has been taken as one of the hallmarks of, yet contradictions within, globalization. Globalization is thought to entail the increased mobility of people, capital, goods, and information across national borders. Studies of globalization often attend to migration, immigration, displaced populations, deterritorialized nation-states, and diasporic communities (see, e.g., Appadurai, 1991; Basch, Schiller, and Blanc, 1994; Gupta, 1992; Kearney, 1991, 1995). At the same time, globalization scholars note that there is a contradiction between the mobility of capital and the forced immobility of people (Schiller, Basch and Blanc, 1995). The North American Free Trade Agreement (NAFTA), for example, removed trade barriers between the United States and Mexico, even as the budget for U.S. border enforcement personnel and technology increased. The nations that facilitate the relocation of production facilities are less willing to permit the foreign workers employed by those companies to immigrate—legally, at least (Sassen, 1989, 1996). This simultaneous mobility-yet-immobility of people complicates debates over the nature and effects of globalization. Increased (illegal) migration seems to erode national sovereignty, yet dispersed citizenries also become national resources for their countries of origin. National membership is not particularly significant if people are members of transnational communities (Soysal, 1994), yet it is more significant than ever if states make legal residency a prerequisite for receiving rights and services (Cornelius, Martin, and Hollifield, 1994; Hammar, 1990). Like many facets of globalization, immigration seems to reinforce yet challenge the state and its categories of personhood.

The complex relationship between people who move and states that allocate membership affects attorneys who advocate on behalf of immigrants. Law is in many ways tied to the nation-state, yet immigrants who claim legal rights are situated both within and between nations. Attorneys who seek justice for these immigrants may find that national laws give them few options. Changing national laws may require forging alliances with foreign governments, mobilizing extra- and/or transnational networks, and creating local constituencies. Seeking rights for unauthorized immigrants can be construed as rewarding law breakers—a cause that is unlikely to be popular. Law defines not only national borders, but also spaces of existence within national territories (Coutin, 2000, forthcoming[a]). Thus unauthorized immigrants are imagined to exist within "the shadows," a place where workers are paid under the table, presences are unregistered, movements are clandestine, and people are undocumented. Providing legal representation to unauthorized immigrants requires addressing these realities in a legal context in which they are difficult to articulate. As a result, lawyering on behalf of immigrants occurs in the shadows of both law and the state.

Legal advocacy regarding immigrants' rights is further complicated by the fact that globalization takes both "legitimate" and "illegitimate" forms (Coutin, Maurer, and Yngvesson, 1999). Globalization occurs not only "above" the level of the state, through the formation of suprastate entities and transnational corporate practices. Globalization also occurs "below" the state, as individuals whose lives or livelihoods are not secure in their countries of origin move elsewhere. Such movements establish transnational linkages within families, communities, organizations, and other groupings (Hagan, 1994; Hamilton and Chinchilla, 1991; Hondagneu-Sotelo, 1994; Kearney, 1995; Miller, 1991; Schiller, Basch and Blanc, 1995; Smith 1996). In contrast to international governance structures and transnational corporate financial practices, immigrants' movements and linkages are frequently criminalized, delegitimized, and problematized. Thus, immigrants who enter the United States without the permission of the U.S. government become "illegal aliens," who travel clandestinely, work illicitly, and transact opaquely. The questionable legitimacy of such actions can affect immigrants' attorneys as well. Attorneys who seem to encourage individuals to remain in the United States without legal status risk legal sanctions.[1]

To shed light on the ways that immigration cause lawyers are situated vis-à-vis states, I analyze the work of Los Angeles–based attorneys and paralegals who advocate on behalf of Central American immigrants. The complicated politics surrounding these immigrants' legal status makes legal advocates' work critical to not only their clients but also national economies and international relations. During the 1980s, the political violence and economic devastation of the Salvadoran civil war led unprecedented numbers of Salvadorans to enter the United States, often without legal authorization. At the time, cold war politics and foreign policy considerations prevented the United States from granting refugee status to these migrants. The U.S. Salvadoran population nonetheless grew, with some Salvadorans acquiring temporary or permanent legal status while others lived and worked in this country illicitly. By the 1990s, when peace accords put an end to the Salvadoran civil war, remittances sent by Salvadoran immigrants to family members in El Salvador had become a mainstay of the Salvadoran economy (Menjívar et al., 1998).

Fearing that mass deportations would create an economic crisis, the Salvadoran government joined Salvadoran community activists in advocating a blanket grant of permanent legal residency to Salvadorans living in the United States. In fact, in 1997, the Salvadoran official in charge of monitoring human rights violations made the rights of Salvadorans living in the United States a focus of her work. In essence, Salvadoran immigrants have become a national "resource" for El Salvador,[2] even as the United States made immigration laws more restrictive.[3] Cause lawyers who represent individual immigrants and who advocate on behalf of Central Americans as a group have the opportunity to shape the criteria according to which these competing strategies are legitimized.

My analysis begins by describing the context in which cause lawyering on behalf of Central American immigrants occurs. Section 1 describes the senses in which immigration cause lawyering occurs in the "shadows" of state legalities. The next three sections discuss the particularities of immigration cause lawyering. Section 2 analyzes attorney-client interviews, section 3 discusses legal service providers' efforts to educate Central Americans about U.S. immigration law, and section 4 describes cause lawyers' political advocacy work. I conclude by noting ways that immigration cause lawyering reproduces yet subverts powerful notions of the state, national membership, and legal legitimacy.

In the Shadows

There are several senses in which immigration cause lawyering occurs in the "shadows" or on the margins of law. First, immigration cause lawyers work for nonprofit groups that stand outside of dominant legal institutions and call for these to act justly. In that they critique and seek to get around certain aspects of immigration law, immigration cause lawyering explores and exposes the limits of law as a constraining force and a malleable resource. Second, the clients of immigration cause lawyers include undocumented immigrants whose very presence is considered to violate the law. Economically, these clients are also marginalized in that they live below the poverty level, work long hours, and lack babysitters and good transportation. These clients not only have a hard time paying for legal services; in addition, it is difficult for them to even meet with their attorneys. Third, immigration involves shady legal practices. It is not uncommon for undocumented immigrants to use fraudulent identity documents, file poorly prepared immigration forms, and entrust their legal cases to individuals (such as pastors or notaries) who are not authorized to practice law. Immigration cause lawyers have to devote considerable effort to fixing cases that have been complicated by such practices. Finally, immigration cause lawyers, like other attorneys, make extensive use of paralegals and support staff. In the case of Central American community organizations in Los Angeles, these legal staffmembers include community activists who may once have been undocumented immigrants themselves, and who have been members of political movements in El Salvador and Guatemala. These activists' political commitments and networks influence the legal strategies that are devised by attorneys who advocate on behalf of Central Americans. Thus, not only attorneys but also paralegals engage in practices that could be termed cause lawyering.

Between 1995 and 1997, I followed the activities of Los Angeles–based cause lawyers who advocate on behalf of Central American immigrants. My research entailed attending hearings in immigration court, observing the legal services programs of three Central American community organizations, and interviewing ninety legal service providers, community activists, and legalization applicants.[4] Throughout this project, I was struck by the ways that the formal immigration system tolerates (and, some might argue, relies on) an industry of individuals who provide shoddy services to immigrants. For instance, during interviews with asylum officials, applicants who wished to testify in a language other than English had to provide their own interpreters. Would-be interpreters whose English may or may not have been adequate to the task "lurked" (to quote one asylum applicant) around the asylum unit, in wait for unprepared interviewees. Though these interpreters were not certified by the U.S. government, asylum applicants were held accountable for their interpreters' translation skills. Similarly, to arrive at the immigration court in Los Angeles, immigrants had to pass through a gamut of "immigration consultants" who hawked their services. Many of these "consultants" were notary publics who took advantage of the fact that in many Latin American countries *notarios* are authorized to provide legal services, much like attorneys in the United States. Immigrants who obtained legal representation were not necessarily much better off than those who do not.[5] Regarding the skill of the attorneys that she usually dealt with, one judge joked with a CARECEN attorney, "What? You have expertise? Is that a requirement? Can you *read*? Can you make objections? If so, you're in the top flight!" In short, immigrants acted in a particularly sleazy legal context.

My own cause-lawyering research focused on the legal services programs of three Central American community organizations in Los Angeles. Two of these groups—El Rescate (Spanish for "the rescue") and CARECEN (Central American Resource Center)—were founded during the early 1980s by activists who supported political movements in Central America. The Frente Farabundo Martí para la Liberación Nacional (Farabundo Martí National Liberation Front) (FMLN) was made up of five organizations, each of which had its own history and membership.[6] When members of these organizations went into exile in the late 1970s and early 1980s, they launched a movement in solidarity with political struggles in Central America. To address the legal and social needs of this community, political committees around the United States founded refugee centers, including El Rescate and CARECEN. Though the political committees that founded them have either dissolved or regrouped since the signing of peace accords in 1992, El Rescate and CARECEN have continued to advocate on behalf of Central American immigrants in Los Angeles. The Association of Salvadorans in Los Angeles (ASOSAL), the third community organization whose activities I observed, was founded more recently, in 1991, as part of the effort to extend the temporary protected status that was awarded to Salvadorans through the 1990 Immigration Act (see Coutin, 1998). Originally a subcommittee of CARECEN, ASOSAL became an independent organization in 1991 so that its members could focus exclusively on the legal, civic, and cultural needs of Salvadorans, rather than on the broader range of issues addressed by CARECEN.

Central American immigrants' legal needs changed over the course of these organizations' histories. Both El Rescate and CARECEN were founded when Central Americans' primary legal need was to avoid being deported to life-threatening conditions. Their legal programs therefore initially focused on preparing asylum applications for individuals who were at risk of persecution and who had been apprehended by the U.S. Immigration and Naturalization Service (INS) and placed in deportation proceedings.[7] An attorney who worked at El Rescate during this period recalled, "There was just an overwhelming need [for clients] to avoid deportation. And we knew that those who were deported could be killed, so that gave an urgency to our work. This was a cause!" By 1995, when I began to work with community organizations in Los Angeles, a sizable segment of the Central American immigrant population had obtained bona fide but precarious legal status through TPS and/or a pending asylum application.[8] Specifically, a legal settlement reached in *American Baptist Churches v. Thornburgh* (ABC, a lawsuit charging the INS with discriminating against Salvadoran and Guatemalan asylum seekers) permitted Salvadorans and Guatemalans to apply for de novo asylum hearings. The 1986 amnesty program[9] had also enabled Central Americans who immigrated before January 1, 1982, to become legal permanent residents and eventually citizens. The legal services that El Rescate, CARECEN, and ASOSAL provided in the mid-1990s reflected these changed circumstances. In addition to trying to save the lives of desperate asylum seekers, staff filled out family visa petition forms, completed naturalization applications, represented individuals who were applying for suspension of deportation,[10] defended aliens who were being deported due to criminal convictions, assisted victims of domestic violence in applying for residency, filled out work-permit renewal application forms, and filed requests for immigration files through the Freedom of Information Act. The urgency of this work which one El Rescate attorney characterized as "trying to keep a family together, or to help someone keep what they've acquired here in the U.S."—came less from a sense that refugees would be killed if they were to be deported and more from an awareness of the devastating effects that U.S. immigration policies could have on individuals, families, and communities.

Although ASOSAL, CARECEN, and El Rescate provided legal services to and advocated on behalf of Central American immigrants, it would not be accurate to call these groups cause-lawyering organizations. Each of these agencies was involved in a variety of projects. El Rescate provided social services—including a shelter, a food bank, clothing distribution, and bus tokens—to local residents. El Rescate also offered ESL classes to immigrants, sponsored cultural and political events, supported the work of Salvadoran hometown associations, worked with a sister organization in El Salvador to monitor the implementation of the Salvadoran peace accords, organized delegations to El Salvador, and launched a credit union intended to promote economic development both locally and in El Salvador. CARECEN organized youth programs, a public market, international student exchanges, leadership training, earthquake-preparedness training, conferences, and cultural events. ASOSAL sponsored a folkloric dance group, organized community events and fund-raisers (such as dances and picnics), helped to plan the annual Central American Independence Day parade in Los Angeles, promoted citizenship and voter registration, and supported Salvadoran hometown associations. Legal services were nonetheless a critical component of these organizations' work.

El Rescate, ASOSAL, and CARECEN faced continual dilemmas about how to balance legal services with advocacy work, provide quality legal services to large numbers of immigrants, and prioritize competing humanitarian, political, and legal goals. Resource constraints were a problem for each organization. Though their size and structure changed several times during my fieldwork,[11] CARECEN and El Rescate usually had two staff attorneys, several paralegals, and a fluctuating number of volunteers and student interns. ASOSAL had no staff attorney and therefore could not provide legal representation. ASOSAL worked in consultation with attorneys, however, and therefore could assist clients in applying for political asylum, naturalization, family visa petitions, and work-permit renewals. Funding for these activities derived from private institutions, fund-raising events (such as banquets or dances), and the fees that clients paid for brief legal services. Because their funds were scarce, organizations limited their most labor-intensive legal services—namely, legal representation in immigration proceedings—to the clients with the most compelling cases. Organizations also held regular charlas or public talks, through which they sought to educate immigrants about their legal rights, their chances of legalizing, and the workings of U.S. immigration law. In addition to direct services and public education, organizations worked to make U.S. immigration law more just. Such advocacy included participating in class action suits, lobbying Congress regarding immigration legislation, issuing human rights reports, holding press conferences, negotiating with INS officials regarding asylum and other procedures, and joining in political campaigns to shape immigration policies. Through attorney-client interviews, public education campaigns, and political advocacy, legal service providers engaged, negotiated, and sometimes reinforced state categories of membership.

Assessing Cases

Immigration advocates' initial consultations with actual or potential clients shed light on advocates' understandings of their mission, immigration law, institutional constraints, and viable legal strategies. During initial consultations, organizations screened out less deserving clients, while clients attempted to obtain free or low-cost legal representation. Each of the three organizations where I did fieldwork scheduled such consultations. At CARECEN and El Rescate, initial consultations were used to dispense legal advice, provide brief services, and elicit information that would allow legal staff to decide whether or not to represent the client in court. Because legal representation was time consuming and unremunerated (CARECEN and El Rescate did not charge for this service),[12] organizations only represented those clients deemed the most legally, politically, and economically deserving. As the time of my research, ASOSAL did not provide legal representation, so initial consultations were used to give advice, identify services that ASOSAL could provide, and refer clients to other attorneys or organizations. Consultations positioned legal service providers in complex ways regarding their clients. On the one hand, service providers helped clients devise strategies through which they could oppose deportation. On the other hand, out of economic necessity, service providers resisted most clients' efforts to obtain free legal representation. Similarly, as these interviews elicited and juxtaposed competing representations of clients' "deservingness," initial consultations aligned legal practitioners with and against state agencies. For practical, political, and humanitarian reasons, practitioners expressed sympathy with the analyses that clients proffered. At the same time, the need to decide which cases were most compelling led attorneys and paralegals to view cases skeptically. Given the shortage of qualified and affordable immigration attorneys, advocates' decisions to grant or deny legal representation affected clients' chances of achieving legal residency.

Instead of attempting a composite picture of clients' consultations with cause lawyers, I describe one such interview that I observed in February 1996. The client in this case was Juana Martinez Arévalo,[13] a thirty-three-year-old undocumented Salvadoran immigrant who was in deportation proceedings. Before obtaining this appointment, Juana had attended the organization's charla on U.S. immigration law. For Juana, the consultation was an opportunity to secure legal assistance that might prevent her from being deported. The interview was conducted by Oscar Navarro, a Central American paralegal who was also involved in political advocacy on behalf of Salvadoran and Guatemalan immigrants. For Oscar, the purpose of the consultation was to assess the strengths and weaknesses of Juana's case, give Juana legal advice, and consider whether his organization could provide her with legal assistance. Juana's two small children, one of whom sat on her lap, were also present, and I observed the interview from the doorway of Oscar's cramped office. The interview was conducted in Spanish. Like others that I observed, this consultation demonstrates how cause lawyers—in this case, a cause paralegal—and their clients negotiate state-based categories of membership.

After eliciting some descriptive information (e.g., number of household members, income, years of schooling) needed for statistical purposes, Oscar asked Juana how long she had been in the United States. This question was important, I knew, because individuals who had seven years of continuous presence in the United States were eligible to have their deportation suspended, if they also could prove good moral character and that deportation would be an extreme hardship. Juana answered that she had arrived in March 1991, which made her ineligible for this remedy.

Oscar then explored the procedural status of her case. He asked, "So you have an appointment with the court? When is it?" Juana answered that her court appointment was in mid-March, two weeks hence. "It's for asylum?" he asked, and Juana said that it was. "Do you have a copy of what they submitted for you?" he asked. By "they," he meant whoever had completed her prior asylum application. His question implied that Juana was not the "agent" of her own legal filings. Juana pulled out a tattered copy of an asylum application, and Oscar began reading it. Oscar asked, "When you went to see the person who submitted this, did you know what you were applying for asylum? What did you tell him that you wanted to do?" When I heard this question, I realized that Oscar recognized the application as typical of the fraudulent claims prepared by notaries. Juana answered, "I told him that I wanted to apply for a work permit." "Just like that?" Oscar asked, "you didn't say anything about asylum?" "No," Juana answered, "I assumed that he knew what it was that I had to submit." "So you didn't know what you were applying for?" he asked. "No," she agreed. Apparently, the individual whom Juana had approached for legal assistance had placed her in proceedings without verifying that she was eligible for a remedy.

Oscar continued reading the form. "Is the information here true?" he asked. "Some of it is and some of it isn't," Juana replied. Oscar began asking specific questions based on what was written in the application. "It says here that you fear forced recruitment by the guerrillas. Is that true?" "Yes," Juana said. "Did they ever try to recruit you?" Oscar asked. "Well," she said, "they try to recruit everyone." "It says that they wanted you to go with them to wash their clothes. Is that true?" "Yes," she said. "Did they try to recruit you sometime?" "I used to hide on my way to school so that they wouldn't," she said. "It says here that you supported the government a great deal. Is that true?" "Yes," Juana said.

It was already clear to me that Juana had what legal staff would consider a "weak" case. The fear that she described—which could indeed have been real—was something that anyone coming from El Salvador could have. She had not been singled out, which is a requirement for winning an asylum case. Oscar nonetheless continued to seek an experience that might qualify as a basis for asylum. "What do you think would happen to you if you returned to El Salvador?" he asked, posing a question that is on the asylum application form. "The same thing," Juana answered vaguely. "What is 'the same thing'?" Oscar queried. "Well, the same thing that happened when I was there," Juana repeated. After further questioning, Juana indicated that she feared the guerrillas. "Peace Accords have been signed in El Salvador," Oscar pointed out, "so supposedly there's peace. The guerrillas have disbanded, and there's no more forced recruitment going on. What do you fear? Do you fear the general situation in El Salvador, or do you fear a specific individual?" Juana said that she feared the general situation, that she didn't want her daughter to see what she'd seen. "And what have you seen?" Oscar pressed. Juana's answer was once again vague: "The terrible things that I saw when I lived in El Salvador, the fear that one has."

"So you fear the general situation?" Oscar concluded. Juana said that she did. "And whom do you fear? Forget about your daughter for the moment, what is *your* fear? And whom do you fear, if the guerrillas are not there anymore?" She said that she feared the political situation, the economic situation, and crime. "I'm afraid of the *cholos*," she commented, referring to the gangs that have cropped up in El Salvador.

Oscar then delivered his first assessment of her case: "I don't think that you have a strong asylum case. Asylum is based on having a fear of political persecution based on race, religion, nationality, and this is not what you fear. You can go to court and you can present your case, but you will have a difficult time winning."

Juana agreed, "Right, I need to have proof. For example, my cousin was killed a couple of months ago. I need proof of this to take to the court." Oscar asked her who her cousin was. She said that he was in the police force, but that she didn't remember exactly. Oscar told her that his death didn't help her case, because it was a distant relationship. She again agreed, saying, "That's right, at the *charla* the attorney explained that the fear has to be based on something that happened to me, not to another person."

Oscar explained to her that what was written on her asylum application was fairly general, and that, even with proof, she might not get asylum. Then, even though Juana lacked the requisite seven years of continuous presence, he began asking questions related to suspension of deportation. "Have you been working?" She hadn't. "Have you taken assistance?" Juana said that she'd been receiving welfare for the past three years, since her daughter was born.

Oscar then delivered a second assessment of her case. He told her that there was no way for her to become legal. With asylum, he said, one's case had to be stronger in order to win. He also advised her not to go to another notary to submit another application of some sort, because it would just be a waste of her money. He explained what was going to happen in court:

> You've already had an appointment with an immigration official to discuss your case, and your case was denied. That means that you are now in deportation

proceedings, and your case has been sent to a judge. If you can convince the judge that you fear political persecution in El Salvador, then you will receive your green card. If you can't, then you will be ordered deported. There are two ways that a person can be deported. One is that the government pays for your flight, and you are allowed a minimal amount of luggage. The other way is that you are allowed to leave voluntarily, and that the judge will give you a certain amount of time to do so. The disadvantage of this is that you have to pay for the flight yourself, but you can bring everything with you, your T.V., your VCR, your car. You just have to do so at your own expense.... It's very important to go to the hearings in court, even if they deport you, because it is a way to keep your record clean. They won't take you into detention there, you'll have time to get things together before you go. Now, if the government pays for your flight, then that means that you are deported, and that you cannot seek legal status for another five years. So if your mother became a [U.S.] resident, she would not be able to ask for you. On the other hand, if you leave on your own, then your record remains clean. So that's what we recommend.

As Oscar described the differences between deportation and voluntary departure, Juana began to cry. Seemingly, until that point she had hoped for a solution to her case.

Oscar continued explaining Juana's legal predicament: "Now, there is a way to stop the deportation. This is called suspension of deportation. But in order to qualify, one must have been here for at least seven years."

Juana was crying obviously by now. She asked, "And my daughter? Can I take her with me?" She hugged the girl protectively. The girl seemed unaffected by this conversation. She was about three years old, and concentrated on fighting with her brother. Oscar said that this was Juana's decision; her daughter certainly could go back to El Salvador with her. He added that her daughter—who was born in the United States—was a U.S. citizen, entitled to enter and leave the United States as she pleased, and that when the girl turned twenty-one, she would be able to petition for Juana to immigrate. Juana's expression seemed to indicate that she found this idea ridiculous, given that her daughter was only three.

Oscar told Juana that he did not like saying the things that he was saying, but that he had to be honest. He told her that she could go elsewhere to get another opinion about her case, but that he thought it would be the same as his. This would be valuable, he said, for her to learn whether or not what he was telling her was true. But, he repeated, don't go to a notary: "A notary can't represent you in court."

Although he had already assessed her case, Oscar questioned Juana further regarding her suspension claim. "What do you have to show that you've been here since '91?" he asked. She said that she had her high school diploma, because she completed high school here. "And your I.D.?" he asked, "Did you get that in '91?" She said that she had. "Do you have income taxes?" No, she said, because she hadn't submitted these. "And you haven't been working," he mused. "What about rent receipts?" "These are in my mother's name," she said. "And do you have the records from the birth of your daughter?" he asked. "Yes," she said, "I have all of the hospital records. "How long have you been on welfare?" "Three years," she repeated, "since my daughter was born." "Do you have any relatives who are U.S. citizens or legal permanent residents?" Oscar asked, and Juana said that she didn't. "What about the father of the children?" She said that he was also undocumented.

"Well," Oscar concluded, "the only thing that will work for you is to marry a U.S. citizen." Oscar was not actually advocating marriage fraud. Rather, he advised her to seek voluntary departure. It seemed to me that Juana started to cry harder when she heard this. That probably seemed impossible, and she was probably already involved in a relationship with the father of her children. Oscar again recommended that Juana request voluntary departure, so that her record would be clean.

With that, Juana left, and Oscar commented, "She's in trouble." Oscar then explained that if individuals had good suspension cases and were close to the seven years, then it was sometimes possible to delay the deportation long enough for them to become suspension eligible.[14] Attorneys could only file appeals if there were legal grounds to do so, but individuals were not subject to such restrictions. If individuals were taught how to do their own appeals, then they could delay their deportation long enough to become eligible for a different status. In Juana's case, Oscar pointed out, there was no reason to pursue this strategy. She was still on welfare, she wasn't working, and her only U.S. citizen relative was three years old, presumably young enough to adapt to life in another country. She was unlikely to win even if she had been continuously present for seven years.

Juana's consultation with Oscar illustrates the political complexity of immigration cause lawyering. Although Oscar expressed sympathy with Juana's plight, he also used official legal criteria to evaluate Juana's case and to decide whether she was a candidate for his organization's assistance. U.S. immigration law limits asylum to individuals who have been denied basic human rights in their country of citizenship. To win, such individuals must have been singled out for actual persecution by identifiable persecutors (Anker, 1992; Coutin, forthcoming [b]). Only persecution that is linked to race, religion, national origin, political opinion, or social group membership counts as grounds for asylum. The threat of persecution must be real. Juana's theory of her asylum claim articulated different criteria. She claimed to have an on-going fear due to having witnessed terrible events. She feared the political and economic situation, as well as rising criminal activity. Her fear was not only for herself, but also for her child. In concluding that Juana's case was not strong enough to merit legal representation by his organization, Oscar prioritized official asylum criteria over Juana's theory. Similarly, plausible hardship theories in suspension of deportation cases include that the applicant has developed strong community ties, is progressing economically and educationally, has family members who would suffer if the applicant were deported, and has acculturated to life in the United States. The hardship theory that Juana articulated during the interview was that she did not want to return to a place where she had suffered, face economic difficulties, or expose herself or her child to crime and violence. This theory did not distinguish Juana from other Salvadoran immigrants who faced deportation, and therefore did not depict her hardship as unusual or extreme. Again, Oscar prioritized "official" criteria (work, family ties, welfare) over Juana's theory. Although his assessment of Juana's case used official criteria, Oscar also used the consultation to empower Juana legally. He tried to reduce her vulnerability to *notario* fraud, he educated her regarding legal proceedings, and he pointed out all possible legalization avenues. Moreover, our conversation following the intake interview indicated that Oscar and his organization were aware of strategies that would enable clients such as Juana to use law to their advantage. Such legal empowerment and strategizing were also pursued during community organizations' public presentations on U.S. immigration law.

Charlas

Public talks, known as "charlas," were critical components of Central American community groups' legal advocacy. Through charlas, legal staff sought to educate immigrants about their rights, enable immigrants to devise viable legalization strategies, dispell popular misconceptions about immigration law, and help immigrants to recast their own experiences in legal terms. Charlas were an attempt to serve at least some of the immigrants to whom organizations could not provide direct services. Organizations sometimes made charla attendance a prerequisite for receiving services from the organization. This prerequisite was deemed a means of ensuring that clients were making informed decisions regarding the services that they requested. Organizations varied in whether charlas were given exclusively by the organizations' own legal staff, by volunteer private attorneys, or by a combination of the two. For private attorneys, charlas were both a public service and a means of obtaining clients. Individuals who attended charlas usually had a particular question or concern in mind, and seemed to view the charla as a means of obtaining a brief but free consultation with an attorney (as appointments for scheduled consultations were limited in number). Many audience members left as soon as their question had been answered. The attorneys and paralegals who gave charlas had different styles. Some focused on establishing rapport with their audience, others sought primarily to convey information; some gave "lectures," others simply answered questions. Though their styles differed and their thinking was not uniform, the legal service providers who gave charlas were generally critical of restrictive U.S. immigration policies and openly sympathized with immigrants and their situations.

Here, I describe a charla that I attended at one community organization in August 1996. The speaker was a private attorney whose name appeared on this organization's referral list. Because he did not speak Spanish, he had brought a bilingual paralegal who translated both his presentation and audience members' comments and questions. As the speaker continually paused while his statements were being translated, I was able to take almost verbatim notes. This particular charla was not a prerequisite for legal assistance from the organization, so charla attendees had come with individual questions or concerns rather than simply as a prerequisite for obtaining services. There were approximately forty people in attendance, most of whom spoke or understood Spanish. As I learned from audience members' questions, some charla attendees had pending legalization cases, others were hoping to naturalize, and still others had never applied for legal status. At the time of this charla, anxiety over U.S. immigration policies was widespread within immigrant communities in Los Angeles. The U.S. government was considering (and eventually passed) legislation that dramatically curtailed the rights of both legal and undocumented immigrants. There were no empty seats in the room.

The attorney began by introducing himself and explaining the format of the charla:

> Welcome, I am an attorney and am an immigrant myself. I am going to be giving the talk. . . . I only have one hour tonight, and then I will have to leave, so I am going to try to give you information. You have lots of information already, from newspapers, friends, and from notaries. . . . I have worked in immigration law for fifteen years. I have found that information is important, because, without this, you can't make the appropriate choices. I will try to answer all of your questions, but please only ask one question, so that everyone gets a turn. And, I will give you an overview of immigration law. Are most of you from Central America?

Lots of audience members raised their hands. "No one from Mexico? No one from Latin America?" Directing himself to an individual in the front row, the attorney asked, "Where are you from?" "Guatemala," the listener replied. "And you?" the attorney continued. "Nicaragua," came the answer.

"Okay, all of you are from Central America," the attorney resumed, "and most of you are refugees. . . . So tonight, I will try to teach you what to do, the game through which you can secure your residency."

As the attorney described immigration law and proceedings, he also attempted to shape listeners' legal consciousness. For instance, he depicted judges as biased, saying, "You will have a hearing before a judge who works for Immigration. This judge is supposed to be independant and impartial, but that is an illusion. The judge is not impartial at all." The attorney attributed this lack of impartiality to a "war": "The war on immigration that we are all experiencing right now began last year, and it built up due to the elections coming up in November [1996]. Just to give you a sense of what this war has consisted of, from 1982 to 1995, there were only eight immigration judges here in Los Angeles. Now there are twenty-two of these judges." To illustrate the nature of this "war," the attorney explained that the

Antiterrorism and Effective Death Penalty Act,[15] which had been approved in April 1996, made individuals who had entered the United States without immigration documents (as contrasted with those who entered with a visa but remained beyond the expiration date) ineligible for suspension of deportation. Turning to an audience member, he asked, "How old are you?" "I'm twenty-six," the woman replied. "And what was your age when you came to the United States?" "Fifteen."

Using this woman as an example, the attorney explained suspension law. The charla thus *deconstructed* immigration categories. In other words, the speaker explained the assumptions that underlie suspension law, and depicted these assumptions as arbitrary, rather than as reflective of social realities (emphases added):

> This is what the judge wants to see in a suspension case. This woman came at a young age, she graduated from a U.S. high school, and she can speak English. This is not a matter of racism on the part of the Immigration judge. They want to know whether or not, *as they define these things,* they should deport her. They want to know if she has taken classes in English. Are you a member of a church? No? Then join one. The judge is looking for this, so it could be important to your case. The judge will want to know what you do for your community, which is not just your family. For instance, have you been on the PTA? Are you involved in the YMCA? Are you involved in your church? What do you give to the community?
>
> Another thing that can help you in your case is to talk about the opportunities that you would have in your country. If you work cleaning houses or cleaning cars, or you're a cook, *they will say* that these jobs exist in your country and that it would not be a hardship for you to return. Have you gone to college? Have you obtained some higher education? Have you paid your income taxes? Do you have white Americans[16] who can speak on your behalf in the courtroom? *The courts here are racist.* What will save this lady is to show that she is Americanized. She has to celebrate the Fourth of July, Thanksgiving. She has to show that she has become acclimated to the United States.
>
> The hardest part of the case is to show that it will cause hardship if you are deported. Everyone can say that they have good moral character—that they haven't committed crimes, that is—and that they've been here the seven years. I'll give you an example. Suppose that she—and again, I don't know anything of her case, so I'm just using this as an example. Say that she can speak Spanish and she can understand Spanish, but she can't write in Spanish. That could be hardship. That would mean that they can't deport her *and have her merge with society there.* You have to look at her and at her family members, her brothers, sisters, grandparents, uncles, any of her close relatives who are residents or citizens. This is what suspension is. *You must be creative* and well informed.

The speakers' recommendations regarding suspension law suggested that immigrants' best strategy was to depict themselves as clearly and inextricably rooted on the U.S. side of national boundaries. Thus, having relatives with legal status in the United States, being more skilled in English than in Spanish, bringing white Americans to court, celebrating U.S. holidays, taking advantage of educational and career opportunities in the United States, and participating in such classic American voluntary associations as church, the PTA, and the YMCA would be viewed by immigration officials as "roots" that should not be pulled up. Moreover, the speaker suggested, immigrants must be creative in depicting their own lives as fitting these criteria. Such comments portrayed law not as a meaningful, rational means of arriving at an empirical truth (in this case, the amount of hardship that a deportation would impose), but rather as ideologically biased, bureaucratically motivated, and arbitrary. In contrast to lofty images of judicial fairness, the speaker attributed judges' decisions to more mundane and unreasonable goals:

> What does the judge want? The judge wants to clear his calendar, that's the most important thing. So the judge will accept any excuse to deport you. Their favorite excuse is that you arrive late to the courtroom. You may have had a flat tire on the way to court. They don't care. So get there on time, because they only accept exceptional excuses, which for them, are a death in the family or being hospitalized.

This negative portrayal of INS personnel extended to less adversarial proceedings: "At the [asylum] interview what will happen is that they will interrogate you. It is a police proceeding. And if they think that you're lying, they will tell the judge. This can be considered adverse information regarding their assessment of your character, which is something that can affect all of your [immigration] benefits in the future."

The speaker also attempted to instruct his audience in ways to "work" the system to their advantage. One strategy, he suggested, was to use the appeals process to delay deportation and to bypass biased immigration judges:

> [I]n the BIA [Board of Immigration Appeals], your case will be heard by three other judges. It takes them two years to decide your case. If you lose with them, you can appeal again. But the important thing to bear in mind is that whenever you're appealing, the appeal stops your deportation. Eventually, you must appeal to the 9th circuit, which is a very high court. There your case will be heard by the best judges in the United States. These are judges who have been listening to the cases since the 1970s, they weren't appointed by Reagan or by Bush, and they understand these cases.

Another possible strategy, the attorney suggested, was for immigrants to certify themselves as laborers with skills that are scarce in the United States:

> So, how can you get legal status . . . ? The answer is labor certification. . . . The only thing stopping you from applying is imagination and the work of the person who will help you fill out all of these forms. For example, a cook. Suppose you cook for your family, and you make Salvadoran food, you make *pupusas*. [Audience members chuckled.] So you're a cook. . . . These visas are closed for [some countries] . . . , but there's no line for Central Americans. And Congress wants to change this law. They see that they've created a loophole. They're thinking, "We thought that doctors and lawyers would come, and instead we're getting Indian cooks."

Like Oscar's idea that as nonattorneys, immigrants might face fewer legal restrictions in filing their own appeals, this attorney attempted to manipulate and reformulate legal proceedings to immigrants' advantages.

The charla concluded with a short question-and-answer period. Audience members wanted to know how to appeal deportation orders, whether letters from their employers had to be certified, whether an apartment manager could qualify for labor certification, whether a parent's naturalization conferred immigration benefits on an adult child, what would happen at an upcoming court appointment, whether a person who was married to a U.S. citizen but who also had a criminal record could immigrate, whether a marriage to a U.S. citizen would obviate a prior deportation order, whether a work permit conferred a right to political asylum, how to change one's address with Immigration, what to do if the INS had lost one's immigration file, how to apply for suspension of deportation, and what the chances were of winning a suspension case. As he answered these questions, the attorney urged immigrants to use their rights, to keep their spirits high, and to withstand the alienating affects of immigration bureaucracy. He advised one man that going to immigration court was "like science fiction, because they don't care about your name, they go by your number." The attorney's parting comment implied that legalization was almost a matter of life and death. Suggesting that a particular audience member ought to try his chances in court, the attorney said, "It's like a battle with cancer. If someone gives you a 50 percent chance, do you take it?" "You take it," the audience member agreed.

Cause lawyers' advocacy work was not limited to helping immigrants discover ways to use U.S. immigration law to win in court. In addition, these attorneys and their organizations attempted to change the law itself. Such efforts required mobilizing transnational constituencies around Central Americans' claims to national membership in the United States.

Political Advocacy

To advocate on behalf of Central Americans, cause lawyers argued that the networks and transactions that Central American immigrants had constructed in the "shadow of the law" (Mnookin and Kornhauser, 1979) warranted legitimation through the conferral of residency on these immigrants. Political advocacy took several forms. Attorneys from Central American community organizations met with INS officials and with liaisons to President Clinton in order to discuss administrative solutions to Central American immigrants' legal predicament. Possible administrative solutions included a presidential declaration that Salvadorans and Guatemalans deserved legal residency, authorizing the INS asylum units to consider the suspension cases of Salvadorans and Guatemalans who were benefiaries of the ABC settlement,[17] and stipulating that ABC class members would face "extreme hardship" if they were deported. Advocates succeeded in that the INS agreed to assess class members' suspension cases during asylum interviews and to grant ABC class members a "presumption" of extreme hardship. Attorneys, paralegals, and other advocates also organized delegations to Washington, D.C., to meet with congressional liaisons, particularly members of the Hispanic caucus. These meetings led advocates to conclude that Congress was unlikely to pass legislation that granted residency to ABC class members. Instead, advocates pursued legislation that would exempt ABC class members from certain provisions of the 1996 Illegal Immigration Reform and Immigrant Responsibility Act (IIRIRA). IIRIRA eliminated suspension of deportation, the remedy on which many immigrants' hopes were pinned. Advocates' legislative efforts resulted in the passage of the Nicaraguan Adjustment and Central American Relief Act (NACARA) in 1997. NACARA created an "amnesty" for certain Nicaraguans and permitted some 300,000 Salvadorans and Guatemalans with pending asylum applications to apply for suspension of deportation under pre-IIRIRA terms.

Like interviews with undocumented clients and charlas with legalization applicants, cause lawyers' political advocacy acknowledged transnational realities. This work required cause lawyers to participate in broad-based movements that sought justice for Central American immigrants. These movements were transnational in character, drew on both official and clandestine networks, and promoted multiple models of statehood, membership, and legitimacy. Attorneys sometimes participated in these movements directly. In addition, as members of organizations that were involved in political advocacy, attorneys were implicitly supporting this work. As participants in these movements, cause lawyers met with Salvadoran and U.S. officials, joined national coalitions, devised political and legal strategies, and negotiated the terms and interpretation of legislation. One attorney, for example, was invited to El Salvador to give presentations on U.S. immigration law to relatives and neighbors of individuals who had emigrated to the United States. This attorney confided to me somewhat jokingly that he had finally realized his dream of giving a "preimmigration charla."

Political campaigns on behalf of Salvadoran immigrants promoted international responsibility as well as national autonomy. Advocates who were involved in the campaign for residency for Salvadoran and Guatemalan asylum seekers argued that Central Americans' claims to membership in the United States were justified by their experiences in their homelands. Reminding listeners of the bombings, torture, massacres, and other abuses that pervaded El Salvador during the civil war, advocates asserted that Central Americans would have been entitled to asylum during the 1980s, had their claims been adjudicated in an unbiased fashion. "I think we already suffered hardship, don't you?" a Salvadoran paralegal asked his audience rhetorically during a political rally in November 1997. Linking the suffering that is grounds for political asylum to the hardship that is a basis for suspension of deportation, this comment suggested that the past hardship that caused one to immigrate is as relevant to legalization as the future hardship that deportation would pose. Activists also argued that the United States had a moral responsibility to accept Central Americans as residents, given its involvement in the civil wars (see also Sassen, 1989). As one activist stated, "We are a product of a government['s] military aid to El Salvador['s] government, that forced us to leave."

Campaigns for residency also emphasized the remittances that Salvadorans who came to the United States without the permission of the U.S. government send to their home communities. Noting that remittances fuel the Salvadoran economy, advocates defined the expatriate Salvadoran community as critical to the future of El Salvador. Some activists depicted remittances as a substitute for both U.S. foreign aid to El Salvador and for expenditures by the Salvadoran government. One activist explained, "After the peace accords were signed, less money came to the [Salvadoran] government through foreign aid. So now the aid that it receives comes in the form of remittances that private citizens send to their relatives, and that therefore enters the economy. These remittances enable people to buy things, which keeps the economy afloat, plus the [Salvadoran] government gets taxes." According to this argument, expatriate Salvadorans, regardless of their organizational status or political affiliations, perform quasi-governmental functions simply through their transnational, extra-statal social networks.

Efforts to obtain political asylum, residency, and citizenship for Salvadorans have both manipulated and reinforced existing models of citizenship. Advocates' affirmation of substantive citizenship—working, paying taxes, obeying the law—as a basis for membership invokes suspension criteria, but deemphasizes the temporal component. In fact, one Salvadoran paralegal criticized the seven-year requirement, pointing out to me, "Why should someone have to be here seven years in order to prove that they are established? Someone could be here for two weeks and already have established himself, if the person came to rejoin relatives." This notion of substantive citizenship seeks to activate an implicit contract between residents and a government that tacitly tolerates their presence, grants them temporary and limited legality, issues them work permits, and collects both fees and taxes. This argument, if legitimized, would have helped Juana immigrate. Salvadorans' invocation of their children's birthrights as U.S. citizens reinforces *jus soli* as a basis for citizenship, but also seeks to transmit minor children's citizenship to their undocumented parents. Such a transmission is not as yet possible within the family visa process (though adult children can petition for their parents), but is recognized in suspension of deportation cases in that having U.S. citizen children strengthens a parent's suspension claim. The argument that the violence of the Salvadoran civil war and the pervasiveness of human rights violations entitle Salvadorans to asylum seeks to broaden the definition of persecution to include the daily terror occasioned by repressive practices and even the economic deprivation caused by civil war—the legal theory that Juana articulated during her interview with Oscar. Finally, the notion that the United States has some responsibility for the victims of the Salvadoran civil war manipulates the foreign policy implications of political asylum, but directs these not toward the current Salvadoran state, but rather to its populace. In other words, activists argue that by supporting a state whose human rights violations rendered it illegitimate, the United States incurred a particular responsibility for the people whose lives were disrupted or destroyed by that state.

In addition to manipulating existing models of citizenship, struggles over Central Americans' legal status have produced alternative modes of being. These include the absence of citizenship, dual citizenship, and acting as citizens of something other than a state. Clandestinity, of both the political and the immigration variety, is produced by the denial of citizenship. People whose existence is denied for political or legal reasons must nonetheless live, work, and interact with others. Such activities create a variety of surprisingly similar illicit relationships and practices, such as working without authorization, transferring funds and goods through unauthorized channels, smuggling people across borders of various sorts, falsifying documents and identities, and locating family members in multiple national spaces. Such clandestine networks and practices create an extrastatal order, sort of a "phantom state" (see Thrift, 1996) that is the inverse of the known, explicit, official (but contested) state. Cause lawyers' advocacy on behalf of Central Americans entails interacting with those who participate in these structures and practices. In addition, to negotiate Salvadorans' legal status in the United States, Salvadorans who were once undocumented have met with U.S. legislators and Department of Justice officials, traveled to El Salvador to petition Salvadoran legislators for a resolution in support of their cause, and asked the Central American presidents to intervene with the U.S. government on their behalf. Such practices, more than formal dual citizenship, redefine citizenship itself in a transnational context.

Conclusion

Immigration cause lawyering in Los Angeles manipulates, reinforces, and reinterprets state-based categories of membership. The clients of the immigration cause lawyers whose activities I studied were, for the most part, outside of these membership categories—at least from the point of view of the United States. Salvadorans and Guatemalans who immigrated to the United States during the 1980s and early 1990s usually did so without the permission of the U.S. government. They therefore became "illegal aliens," beings who lacked legal legitimacy, whose claims to membership were unvalidated, and whose presence, movements, and labor were illicit. To claim membership, they had to meet state-based legal criteria. To obtain political asylum, they had to demonstrate that they had been persecuted in their country of citizenship, making it impossible for them to enjoy the civil protections to which citizens are entitled, and requiring them to seek protection internationally instead of from their own government. To win a suspension of deportation case, they had to show that, although they were not allowed to do so, they had become so "rooted" in the United States that they could no longer "merge" (to quote the charla speaker) with society in their country of citizenship. When immigration cause lawyers limited their legal representation to clients who met these criteria, advocates allowed state-based definitions of membership to shape their own work.

At the same time, advocates also deemed their clients' situations to be legitimate, and sought to reinterpret U.S. immigration laws in ways that would allow clients to prevail in court. During charlas and consultations, some legal service providers deconstructed immigration law, depicting legal categories as arbitrary and legal proceedings as a "game." Advocates suggested that judges might not be impartial, that INS officials would view immigrants' lives differently than do immigrants themselves, and that immigrants could be "creative" and "imaginative" in explaining how their own lives met state-based legal criteria. Advocates pointed out that immigrants could sometimes delay legal proceedings in order to complete required periods of eligibility,[18] define themselves as skilled laborers, or deliberately produce records that would document their ties in the United States. For instance, joining a church, doing volunteer work, learning English, or going to school would produce church attendance records, letters of appreciation, and school transcripts. These documents could strengthen a suspension claim. Thus, advocates suggested, immigrants had some room to maneuver within the U.S. immigration system.

In addition to using and manipulating U.S. immigration categories, cause lawyers also sought legal recognition of their clients' realities. Undocumented immigrants often work without authorization, participate in transnational kin groups, and practice biculturalism. Salvadorans who reside in the United States and send remittances to family members have become a mainstay of the Salvadoran economy. To exempt Salvadorans from certain provisions of IIRIRA, cause lawyers joined Salvadoran officials, activists, and immigrants themselves in arguing that El Salvador's economy would be destabilized if Salvadoran immigrants were deported and remittances were discontinued. Moreover, advocates pointed out, Salvadorans fled devastating economic and political conditions and have since reconstructed their lives in the United States. These arguments suggested that so-called illegitimate forms of globalization—illegal immigration, working without authorization, and forming transnational household economies—were in fact valid. The passage of NACARA in 1997 attests to the potency of such "illegitimate" actions. Perhaps the mobility-yet-immobility of people is not a paradox at all. Some have argued that legal immobility—i.e., restrictive immigration policies—produces mobility by making undocumented workers more exploitable and therefore more desirable to employers (Bach, 1978; Calavita, 1994; Jenkins, 1978). Be that as it may, attorneys' role in negotiating the criteria through which membership is allocated makes immigration cause lawyering critical to individual lives, national economies, and transnational futures.

Acknowledgments

I would like to thank Stuart Scheingold and Austin Sarat for organizing the cause lawyering conference in Bellagio, Italy. My analysis benefited from the astute comments of Michael McCann, Terry Halliday, and all of the conference participants. The research for this paper was funded by the Law and Social Science Program of the National Science Foundation (SBR-9423023). I am grateful to all of the individuals who agreed to participate in interviews. I would also like to thank the following organizations for their assistance: ASOSAL, CAR-ECEN, CHIRLA, the Coalición Centroamericana, and El Rescate. Unless otherwise noted, translations of Spanish quotations or interview material are mine. I have used pseudonymns for all research participants. Finally, I would like particularly to acknowledge Robert Foss, who taught me a great deal about both causes and lawyering.

Notes

1. After giving a public presentation on U.S. immigration law, one Los Angeles–based cause lawyer asked me whether I thought she had advocated that illegal immigrants remain in the United States. She worried that the INS could have sent undercover informers to hear her presentation, and that she might risk legal sanctions.

2. Salvadorans who live in the United States are not necessarily happy about being viewed in this way. Material distributed by Salvadoran organizers at a 1999 conference stated, "The objective of the conference is to foster ideas that permit improvement in relations between El Salvador and the Salvadorans in the United States, especially the image that the government of El Salvador and Salvadoran society have of us either as 'distant brothers' or as producers of foreign currency instead of viewing us as countrymen and human beings" (ASOSAL, 1999: 3).

3. The United States adopted the Illegal Immigration Reform and Immigrant Responsibility Act [IIRIRA—P.L. 104–208 (H.R. 3610)] on September 30, 1996. This law makes legalization more difficult for undocument immigrants. The Nicaraguan and Central American Relief Act [NACARA—P.L. 105–100 (H.R. 2607), Nov. 19, 1997] exempted certain Central Americans from some provisions of IIRIRA.

4. I use the term legalization applicant for convenience. In fact, immigrants were not applying directly for legalization, but rather for political asylum, suspension of deportation, a family-based visa, and so forth.

5. Immigration cause lawyers, who offer quality legal services for low or no fees, are a part of a spectrum of individuals who provide legal services in Los Angeles. At one end of this spectrum are law firms that handle immigration cases along with many other legal matters. Only corporations and affluent individuals can afford their services, which are typically of high quality. At the other end of this spectrum are the notary publics who advertise themselves as immigration specialists and who probably handle the majority of immigration cases. Notaries charge high fees, submit fraudulent applications, mislead clients, refuse to give clients copies of their paperwork, and disappear into the woodwork overnight (Mahler, 1995). To be fair, there are probably some notaries who provide decent immigration services for low cost, but I have encountered few, if any, accounts of such individuals. Private attorneys who practice immigration law range across the spectrum. There are highly skilled, conscientious attorneys (some of whom formerly worked for community organizations) who specialize in immigration law, as well as shadier, what some might refer to as incompetent, attorneys who work with notaries (Hagan, 1994). Both are relatively expensive, but the latter

advertise more aggressively. The final component of this spectrum is made up of nonprofit organizations that handle immigration cases. Nonprofits include advocacy groups such as Legal Aid, as well as organizations that serve particular immigrant communities (e.g., Armenians, Russians, Asians, Central Americans). Clients of community organizations are typically indigent or low-income individuals, sometimes of a particular ethnic or national origin, who have legally compelling immigration cases.

6. These five organizations include the Fuerzas Populares de Liberación (FPL—Popular Forces of Liberation), the Resistencia Nacional (RN—National Resistance), the Partido de la Revolución Salvadoreña (PRS—Party of the Salvadorean Revolution), the Partido Comunista de El Salvador (PCS—Communisty Party of El Salvador), and the Partido Revolucionario de los Trabajadores Centroamericanos (PRTC—Revolutionary Party of Central American Workers) (Montgomery, 1995; see Gordon, 1989, for an account of the formation of the FMLN). For reasons of confidentiality, I cannot identify the political roots of Los Angeles–based organizations.

7. Although the INS was denying 98 percent of the asylum applications filed by Salvadorans and Guatemalans (U.S.C.R., 1986), such "defensive" asylum applications could delay deportation, especially if denials were appealed, and could thus buy the applicant more time in the United States during which conditions in El Salvador would hopefully improve. In addition to defending Central Americans who were in deportation proceedings, El Rescate and CARECEN raised bail funds for immigrants who were in detention, represented detainees in bond reduction hearings, created legal guardianships for detained minors so that undocumented parents did not have to turn themselves in to free their children, and filed "affirmative" (i.e., nondefensive) asylum applications for individuals who had particularly strong cases.

8. The 1990 Immigration Act (P.L. 101–649, 104 Stat. 4978, Nov. 19, 1990) had given Salvadorans who had been in the United States since September 19, 1990, the right to apply for eighteen months of "Temporary Protected Status," or "TPS." When the eighteen months expired, TPS recipients were permitted to register for "Deferred Enforced Departure" status, or "DED." And when DED expired, both DED and TPS recipients were eligible to apply for asylum under the legal settlement reached in *American Baptist Churches v. Thornburgh* [(ABC—1991, 760 F.Supp. 796 (N.D.Cal)]. Guatemalans, who never received TPS status, were also beneficiaries of the ABC settlement. Approximately 80,000 Guatemalans and 180,000 Salvadorans applied for asylum under the terms of the ABC agreement.

9. Immigration Reform and Control Act (P.L. 99–603, 100 Stat. 3359).

10. To qualify for suspension of deportation, an immigrant must demonstrate seven years of continuous presence in the United States, good moral character, and that deportation would be a hardship on the applicant or a close relative of the applicant.

11. For example, extra staff were hired at each of these organizations when Salvadoran ABC class members were applying for political asylum.

12. All three organizations did charge clients for brief services, such as filling out a work-permit renewal form, completing a skeletal asylum application under the terms of the ABC settlement, or applying for naturalization.

13. I have used pseudonyms for all research subjects.

14. This strategy was eliminated by the passage of IIRIRA in 1996. According to IIRIRA, the issuance of a notice to appear in court stops the clock on an individuals' accumulation of time for residency purposes.

15. P.L. 104–132 (110 Stat. 1214).

16. The interpreter translated this as "gringos," and the attorney corrected him, saying that he should say "Americanos blancos," not gringos.

17. The settlement agreement in *American Baptist Churches v. Thornburgh* gave Salvadorans who had been in the United States prior to September 19, 1990, and Guatemalans who had been in the United States prior October 1, 1990, the right to de novo asylum hearings. See note 8, above.

18. Note that IIRIRA made this strategy less viable.

References

Anker, Deborah E. (1992). "Determining Asylum Claims in the United States: A Case Study on the Implementation of Legal Norms in an Unstructured Adjudicatory Environment," 19 (3) *New York University Review of Law and Social Change*, 433–528.

Appadurai, Arjun (1991). "Global Ethnoscapes: Notes and Queries for a Transnational Anthropology." In *Recapturing Anthropology: Working in the Present*, Richard G. Fox, ed. pp. 191–210. Santa Fe: School of American Research Press.

ASOSAL (Association of Salvadorans of Los Angeles) (1999). "El Salvador y los Salvadoreños en Estados Unidos: Dos culturas y un país/Two Cultures and One Country." Conference Program. California State University, Northridge, September 11.

Bach, Robert L. (1978). "Mexican Immigration and the American State," 12 (4) *International Migration Review*, 536–58.

Basch, Linda, Nina Glick Schiller, and Cristina Szanton Blanc (1994) *Nations Unbound: Transnational Projects, Postcolonial Predicaments, and Deterritorialized Nation-states*. Langhorne, Pa.: Gordon and Breach.

Calavita, Kitty (1994). "U.S. Immigration and Policy Responses: The Limits of Legislation," in *Controlling Immigration: A Global Perspective*, Wayne A. Cornelius, Philip L. Martin, and James F. Hollifield, eds., pp. 55–82. Stanford, Calif.: Stanford University Press.

Cornelius, Wayne A., Philip L. Martin, and James F. Hollifield, eds. (1994). *Controlling Immigration: a Global Perspective*. Stanford, Calif.: Stanford University Press.

Coutin, Susan Bibler (1998). "From Refugees to Immigrants: The Legalization Strategies of Salvadoran Immigrants and Activists," 32 (4) *International Migration Review*, 901–25.

——— (2000). *Legalizing Moves: Salvadoran Immigrants' Struggle for U.S. Residency*. Ann Arbor: University of Michigan Press.

——— (Forthcoming [a]). "Borderlands, Illegality, and the Space of Nonexistence," in *Globalization and Governmentalities*. Bill Maurer and Richard Perry, eds., Under review at University of Minnesota Press.

——— (Forthcoming [b]). "The Oppressed, the Suspect, and the Citizen: Subjectivity in Competing Accounts of Political Violence." *Law and Social Inquiry*.

Coutin, Susan Bibler, Bill Maurer, and Barbara Yngvesson (1999) "In the Mirror: The Legitimation Work of Globalization." Unpublished paper.

Gordon, Sara (1989). *Crisis política y guerra en El Salvador*. Distrito Federal (México): Siglo veintiuno.

Gupta, Akhil (1992). "The Song of the Nonaligned World: Transnational Identities and the Reinscription of Space in Late Capitalism," 7 (1) *Cultural Anthropology*, 63–79.

Hagan, Jacqueline Maria (1994). *Deciding to Be Legal: A Maya Community in Houston*. Philadelphia: Temple University Press.

Hamilton, Nora, and Norma Stoltz Chinchilla (1991). "Central American Migration: A Framework for Analysis," 26 (1) *Latin American Research Review*, 75–110.

Hammar, Tomas (1990). *Democracy and the Nation State: Aliens, Denizens and Citizens in a World of International Migration*. Aldershot, England: Avebury.

Hondagneu-Sotelo, Pierrette (1994). *Gendered Transitions: Mexican Experiences of Immigration.* Berkeley: University of California Press.

Jenkins, J. Craig (1978). "The Demand for Immigrant Workers: Labor Scarcity or Social Control?" 12 (4) *International Migration Review* 514–35.

Kearney, Michael (1991). "Borders and Boundaries of State and Self at the End of Empire," 4 (1) *Journal of Historical Sociology*, 52–74.

——— (1995). "The Effects of Transnational Culture, Economy, and Migration on Mixtec Identity in Oaxacalifornia," in *The Bubbling Cauldron: Race, Ethnicity, and the Urban Crisis*, Michael Peter Smith and Joe R. Feagin, eds., pp. 226–43. Minneapolis: University of Minnesota Press.

Mahler, Sarah J. (1995) *American Dreaming: Immigrant Life on the Margins.* Princeton, N.J.: Princeton University Press.

Menjívar, Cecilia, Julie DaVanzo, Lisa Greenwell, and R. Burciaga Valdez (1998) "Remittance Behavior among Salvadoran and Filipino Immigrants in Los Angeles," 32 (1) *International Migration Review*, 97–126.

Miller, Mark J. (1981). *Foreign Workers in Western Europe: An Emerging Political Force.* New York: Praeger.

Mnookin, Robert H., and Lewis Kornhauser (1979). "Bargaining in the Shadow of the Law: The Case of Divorce," 88 *Yale Law Journal*, 950–97.

Montgomery, Tommie Sue (1995). *Revolution in El Salvador: From Civil Strife to Civil Peace*, 2d ed. Boulder, Colo.: Westview Press.

Sassen, Saskia (1989). "America's Immigration 'Problem': The Real Causes," 6 (4) *World Policy Journal*, 811–31.

———(1996). *Losing Control? Sovereignty in an Age of Globalization.* New York: Columbia University Press.

Schiller, Nina Glick, Linda Basch, and Cristina Szanton Blanc (1995). "From Immigrant to Transmigrant: Theorizing Transnational Migration," 68 (1) *Anthropological Quarterly*, 48–63.

Smith, Christian (1996). *Resisting Reagan: The U.S. Central America Peace Movement.* Chicago: University of Chicago Press.

Soysal, Yasemin Nuhoglu (1994). *Limits of Citizenship: Migrants and Postnational Membership in Europe.* Chicago: University of Chicago Press.

Thrift, Nigel (1996). *Spatial Formations.* Thousand Oaks, Calif.: Sage Publications.

U.S.C.R. (U.S. Committee for Refugees) (1986). *Despite a Generous Spirit: Denying Asylum in the United States.* Washington, D.C.: American Council for Nationalities Service.

PART II

Globalization and State Transformation

Patterns of Conflict and Cooperation between Cause Lawyers and the State

CHAPTER 6

Cause Lawyers in a Cold Climate
The Impact(s) of Globalization on the United Kingdom

ANDREW BOON

What is the impact of globalization on cause lawyering in the liberal democracies? In the United Kingdom globalization is fundamentally changing the relationship between government and lawyers in general and cause lawyers in particular. In the United Kingdom, cause lawyering as traditionally conceived may cease to exist. This view is based on the fact that, since the Second World War, cause lawyering blossomed under legal aid. This allowed cause lawyering to become a mainstream activity of the private legal profession and the values of cause lawyering to penetrate deep into professional structures and professional ideology. The decline of legal aid not only strikes hardest at the practice sites most likely to harbor cause lawyers; it strikes at the institutionalized values of cause lawyering that lie at the heart of the ideology of independent legal professions. Growing numbers of lawyers will be employed by the state. Others may seek to become larger or more commercial, thus diluting or compromising their distinctive cause commitments. New sites and different forms of cause lawyering will appear, intensifying professional differentiation and stratification. Meanwhile, elite firms will provide a space for autonomous action no longer found in high street and legal aid firms. Links between these developments and globalization arise in both the economic and normative spheres.

The most obvious thematic connections are economic. In the 1960s the organized capitalism that dominated the early to mid-twentieth century gave way to disorganized capitalism (Santos, 1995). The unpredictable force of the global economy opened up institutions to competition. In the United Kingdom this finally ruptured the settlement between the lawyers and government. The legal profession, in the case of the bar the prototype professional organization, suffered a deluge of criticism, declining jurisdiction in key areas of work and increasing levels of external regulation. Legal aid was not an immediate casualty of revised spending priorities, but declining eligibility levels created a crisis of legitimacy over the state's commitment to access to justice. This stimulated exploration of alternative means of delivering legal services in terms of both methods and personnel. These measures suggest the disinvestment by the state in the symbolic capital of legalism (see also Sarat, this volume). Its result, the increasing marginalization of the legal profession, symbolizes growing doubt regarding the institutionalization of expertise within the state (Johnson, 1993).

Not all sections of the legal profession were adversely affected by economic globalization. City firms remained relatively unscathed by jurisdictional wars and even benefited from them (Boon and Flood, 2000). Although they greatly increased their size, strength, and global reach, they retained the British lawyers' customary suspicion of government. They observed the ideological skirmishes accompanying reform of professional jurisdiction. As the mantra of competition gave way to the touchstone of access, they became aware of the declining ability of legal aid lawyers to legitimate traditional visions of lawyers' roles (Sarat and Scheingold, 1998: 3). Yet their powerful client base does not support the ideological platform on which lawyers' privileges are traditionally based: the promise to protect the individual from the state. At the same time as social models of legal practice declined, therefore, elite commercial firms, particularly in the City of London, expanded the reach of their pro bono programs. The vulnerability of the values of cause lawyering to appropriation by corporate lawyers produces a situation in which some causes will be pursued by those with the greatest investment in the symbolic capital of legal professionalism: elite lawyers. Yet, while popular causes receive enthusiastic support from elite lawyers, there is a risk that marginal and unpopular causes will struggle to find champions in the new political economy of legal services.

The broad theme addressed here justifies this controversial view of the future of cause lawyering in the United Kingdom. The data assembled is diverse. Documentary sources range from the theoretical to the journalistic, the latter giving both a wide source of often disparate information and a sense of the rapid pace of change. Other fieldwork includes interviews with a range of lawyers, politicians and lobbyists conducted for studies of *pro bono publico* described in more detail elsewhere (Boon and Abbey, 1997; Boon and Whyte, 2000). Before considering these data, however, it is necessary to explore the nature of cause lawyering in the United Kingdom through existing definitions, and particularly the key concept of transgressiveness. This will assist in clarifying apparent contradictions in the operations of cause lawyers in the liberal democracies (Halliday, 1999) and provide a bridge between descriptions of cause lawyers in general and specific examples. The reshaping of professional boundaries and expectations brought about by globalization is then explored through consideration of globalization's impact on legal services policy and cause lawyering.

Cause Lawyering in the United Kingdom

Cause Lawyers

The values typically associated with cause lawyers are weakly expressed in the ethos of legal practice in the United Kingdom (Sterrett, 1998). Lawyers subscribe to the ethical principle of neutrality, which dictates that they accept any client (Luban, 1988; Scheingold, 1994). The pervasive strength of this view intensifies the difficulty of distinguishing cause lawyers from other lawyers. Self-identification and identification by others is apt to confuse personal politics and practice (Scheingold, 1988). Even the association of a lawyer with a cause is not conclusive. The clarity forced on lawyers by resistance to oppressive regimes, the defining risks of imprisonment, exile, or death, are absent in liberal states. In extremis, their deviant lawyers may suffer public condemnation or ostracism by professional communities. They may be forced to occupy the margins of the profession with low status groups. But this is not inevitable. There is a space in the liberal system for defenders of the oppressed. Lawyers who fill this role are as likely to be revered as they are reviled. Are they lawyers for a cause or just lawyers exploiting a niche in the market? (Shamir and Chinski, 1998)[1].

Cause lawyering resists tidy categorizations (Halliday, 1999). This explains why most of the research in the area explores either the motivation of cause lawyers or the effectiveness of cause lawyering (Scheingold and Bloom, 1998). In the liberal state the defining characteristics of cause lawyers, pursuit of the goal of social transformation, advocacy and representation for causes and full-time commitment to transformative agendas, is a mainstream activity. Its radical potential is masked by its commitment to pursue the rights of individual clients rather than to use clients to pursue a cause (Sterret, 1998). The difference between cause and other lawyers is therefore relatively weakly expressed. Distinctions might be made by examining their clients, institutional affiliations, and targets in litigation. But this may be inconclusive. The diffusion of their effort across broad categories of cause, their adherence to professional roles and ethics, forces us to define their "cause" at a high level of abstraction. It is to hold powerful institutions, including the state, to account, both for their actions and to their promises. These lawyers attempt to counteract the distortions of justice caused by the unequal deployment of resources. They support individuals through a trial of will in which opponents are willing to crush "causes" by ruining or buying off individuals. In this "cause lawyers" should be, and often are, in the rhetoric of both groups, indistinguishable from other lawyers.

Scheingold and Bloom suggest, on the basis of an empirical study conducted in Seattle, that 'transgressiveness' distinguishes cause lawyering from more conventional kinds of lawyering. Transgressiveness is the degree to which a lawyer is willing to abrogate conventional modes of representation, particularly the principle of neutrality, to stand shoulder to shoulder with clients representative of unpopular causes (Scheingold and Bloom, 1998: 212). At the conservative end of a continuum of transgressive cause lawyering is the pursuit of 'causes,' including meeting unmet legal need, through conventional private practice. Clients are served as individuals, and the conventional social, political, and professional status quo are accepted as a legitimate framework. This embraces the representation of controversial or political causes and a commitment to supporting legal aid and public service legal programs (Scheingold and Sarat, 1998: 4, 7).

The opposite pole, radical cause lawyering, is characterized by full-time employment in pursuit of political goals. Radical cause lawyering subordinates the wishes of individual clients to the goal of social and political transformations for a wider group. The use of law to establish rights is only one of the tactics used to pursue that goal (Scheingold and Sarat, 1998: 7). Between conventional cause lawyering and radical cause lawyering, different modes or loci of practice are more likely to exhibit trangressiveness. From lawyers concerned with unmet needs, the continuum proceeds through lawyers concerned with civil liberties, civil rights, and public policy. Civil liberties and civil rights lawyers tend to be less trangressive because they use litigation as a means of asserting the rights that exemplify their commitment to a cause. Public policy cause lawyers are often transgressive because they are more concerned with legislative policy change than with litigation aimed at remedying individual grievances or asserting rights.

At the radical end of the continuum are radical and critical lawyers. Radical cause lawyers form alliances with social movements committed to changing the basic structures of society. Critical cause lawyers are less concerned with such large-scale transformations and more concerned with the rejection of hierarchy and the primacy of expertise. They aim to "mount small, de-centered small scale struggles at micro-sites of power: the workplace, the family, the community and, indeed, the lawyer-client relationship" (Scheingold and Bloom, 1998: 216). In terms of practice site, Scheingold and Bloom suggest that transgressiveness is least likely to be found in the cause lawyering of corporate lawyers in their pro bono programs, more likely to be found in small firms, and most likely to be found in salaried practice (Scheingold and Bloom, 217). The degree of transgressiveness is therefore affected by the variables of personal, workplace, and societal values (Scheingold and Bloom, 1998: 219). The main reason why small-firm lawyers are transgressive is that, unlike corporate lawyers, cause lawyering is their main reason for practicing law; their practice and work is structured around it (Scheingold and Bloom, 1998: 237).

The Structures of Cause Lawyering in the United Kingdom

The legal profession of the United Kingdom is split between two branches, solicitors and barristers, and 3 jurisdictions, England and Wales, Scotland, and Northern Ireland. At the risk of massive generalization, the legal profession in the United Kingdom is conservative. Pue suggests that this was not always so. Alligned with radical causes and protected by the principle of neutrality, barristers in the eighteenth and nineteenth centuries used court cases as a platform for political views (Pue, 1997: 186). They proceeded from the courts directly into politics, transforming radical liberal notions of the role of the state, and of legal professionals. In the nineteenth century, however, the Inns of Court excluded barristers whose liberal politics or whose actions offended the status quo (Pue, 1997: 192, 199). Both branches of the profession settled into quiet conservatism.

A higher-education boom from the late 1960s onward broadened entry to the profession. This offered opportunities to pose alternatives to conventional professionalism but, Scheingold suggests, there was a failure of will among progressive lawyers. Government sponsorship through legal aid, a natural conservatism, reinforced by a conservative judiciary, status consciousness, social homogeneity, intense socialization and a stifling legal culture, neutralized radicalism (Scheingold, 1993, 1994; Sterret, 1998). English lawyers continued to perceive the legal system as a beneficent social institution and this tended to place cause lawyers in the United Kingdom at the conventional end of the cause-lawyering spectrum. Scheingold's research identified some core characteristics of these lawyers:

> a professional commitment to the have-nots of society; a tendency to think in terms of the class struggle; membership in or sympathy with the Haldane Society of Socialist Lawyers; and acceptance of a relatively modest level of income from a practice financed by legal aid—or through redistribution of the returns of lucrative commercial law to "social conscience" work. (Scheingold, 1988: 123)

Scheingold also states, however, that the failure of lawyers to attack race, gender, and class cleavages in the workplace also suggested a failure to operationalize the goals of critical lawyering (Scheingold, 1994: 265). Before examining this critique of cause lawyers in the United Kingdom it is necessary to outline the structures in which the main activity takes place.

Following the Second World War, the restructuring of British society put legal services at the center of the welfare state. For the first time, legal aid, which spanned the civil and criminal spheres, allowed ordinary people access to lawyers funded to fight cases on terms previously enjoyed only by the rich and powerful (Moorhead, 1998). At the same time a tribunal system was established to deal with immigration, welfare benefits, and employment. Legal costs were not awarded in tribunals, and the use of lawyers was therefore discouraged. The failure to ban lawyers outright, the use of lawyers by institutional defendants, and the juridification of tribunal procedures led to encroachment by lawyers. They were typically instructed by institutional respondents or by wealthier applicants, trade unions, or other institutions. During the 1970s a growing advice sector, Citizens' Advice Bureaux and Law Centres, began to specialize in welfare and tribunal work.

During the 1970s the "not for profit sector" also experimented with representation and advocacy. Private practitioners were connected to the advice bureau and

Law Centres through pro bono services delivered on site or through the Free Representation Unit (FRU) established by bar students in 1972 to provide pro bono tribunal advocacy. Despite the profession's anxiety about the possibility of touting (Zander, 1968), the relationship between advice services and many local lawyers became even closer. Today, some centers employ lawyers,[2] and cases eligible for legal aid are referred by the agencies to local solicitors with complimentary expertise. It is difficult to discern cause lawyering in this patchwork of provision, a problem exacerbated by increasing levels of specialization in private practice since the war. It is often unclear whether the existence of a homogenous client base, coalescing around a type of case or issue, is the result of specialization or evidence of client selection and, hence, indicative of cause lawyering.

The Sites of Cause Lawyering

The not-for-profit sector provided a haven for lawyers who felt that, in private practice, they were too often on the "wrong side" (Verkaik, 1999). Their numbers have always been small, currently around 300–400 in the 3,000 "advice outlets" across the country,[3] relative to more than 60,000 solicitors and 4,000 barristers in England and Wales in private practice. Similarly, legal aid firms, those who sustained a practice largely from legal aid fees, provided a natural home for radical lawyers. An incidental consequence of the legal aid scheme was that lawyers could decide which clients to represent. The growth of the profession, and the wide availability of legal aid, permitted specialization and diversity in practice and encouraged concentrations of expertise to achieve social and political change. Within the population of legal aid firms there are a number that might be considered "political" firms. In criminal defense, for example, these firms are committed to particular groups of clients and the use of law to highlight injustice and bring about political change through disputes with the state, corporations, or employers (McConville et al, 1994).

In the civil field, legal aid firms are identifiable as cause lawyers, although they would be unhappy with the label. These firms span many fields of work, including immigration and family, but their work is usually not exclusively in these fields. There are also a very large number of small firms, and a large number of sole practitioners, in the United Kingdom.[4] On the basis of Bloom and Scheingold's research, we might speculate that they house numbers of "transgressive" cause lawyers. Estimating how large a proportion of the general population of cause lawyers they represent would necessarily require speculation. Numbers would also vary depending on the definition "employed." The focus here, therefore, is on mainstream and well-known practices with clear commitments to causes and groups typically represented on legal aid: Bindman and Partners in civil liberties and Leigh Day and Co. in personal injury litigation (Tsang, 1999). Both firms operate to alleviate legal need and achieve justice for individuals and groups disadvantaged by the civil justice system. Although it would be inappropriate to suggest that either firm is predisposed to "transgressive" cause lawyering, there are aspects of both firms' commitment, described in more detail below, that is radical.

Sites of radical lawyering are not, even in private practice, limited to legal aid firms. Larger institutions of resistance, themselves representating a cause, for example the British labor movement (Scheingold and Bloom, 1998: 233), are aligned with firms that do not rely on legal aid to support their main business. Thus, large specialist personal injury firms, like Thompsons or Russell Jones and Walker, which operate trade union personal injury schemes, might be considered cause lawyers. They help individual trade union members to counter the power of employers and insurance companies. They are simultaneously identified with the cause of injured plaintiffs and with the political project of trade unions (Boon, 1995).

Neutrality and Political Action

The view that the legal profession in the United Kingdom has avoided a radical engagement with cause lawyering must be qualified. Lawyers in advanced capitalist countries have not to be seen as transgressive for three reasons. First, the diversity of legal aid work, and the principle of neutrality, weakens or dilutes engagement in, or identification with, particular causes. Second, they use law, rather than political action, as a mechanism of social change. Third, their involvement in political action may be through groups that are not seen predominantly as "lawyers' groups" although, as will be demonstrated, they are dominated by lawyers. These dimensions of cause lawyering in the United Kingdom are now considered in more detail using Bindman and Partners and Leigh Day and Co. as examples of legal aid firms, and the Legal Action Group as an example of a nongovernmental agency with an operational and policy role in the field of civil justice.

These three organizations are all identified with the provision of quality legal services through the adequate provision of legal aid. Bindman and Partners operates across a number of welfare fields and in civil liberties work, in which area it is the top firm.[5] Bindman himself is described as "the star of the civil liberties legal world" (Gupta, 1998). In the personal injury field, Leigh Day and Co. is a firm that is identified with pioneering personal injury litigation arising from disasters and environmental abuse, including those resulting from "exposure to pollution, (radiation, chemicals, pesticides, sewage in the sea)" (Gupta, 1997).[6] Legal Action Group (LAG) is one of the best-known nongovernmental agencies committed to reform of the legal system in the United Kingdom. Set up in 1971 in order to promote equal access to justice for those socially, economically, or otherwise disadvantaged and unable to access legal services, it is financially independent and employs many lawyers in-house.[7] In its early years it was linked with experimentation in alternative legal services, the green-form scheme for legal advice, and the first wave of law centers. The former director of policy, Vicki Chapman, was initially a solicitor in private practice, worked on legal services policy for the National Association of Citizens' Advice Bureaux and then as a solicitor for Child Poverty Action Group.[8]

In the next section, three key propositions emerging in relation to cause lawyering in the United Kingdom are explored using these exemplars: First, the idea that cause lawyers are transgressive because they place the cause above their clients' best interests. Second, that cause lawyers select clients that further the cause, thus denying the principle of neutrality. Third, that lawyers in the United Kingdom are neither political nor radical. In relation to each, it is argued that lawyers maintain cause affiliations while deliberately not parading them. In doing so, they maintain a vision of professionalism that flows from the embedding of legal professions in the liberal state.

PRIORITIZING THE CAUSE

It is suggested that cause lawyering is institutionalized in advanced capitalist countries. Lawyers need not affiliate with individual causes because their overarching "cause," which needs no justification or defense, is holding large corporations to account for the harm they do to individuals and groups. In striving for this goal they hold the liberal state to its promise of justice for all. Below the surface of this broad commitment, lawyers in the various sites of practice hold different institutions to account and manifest their commitment in different ways. Different degrees of commitment are required. Indeed, the death of lawyers strongly identified with the nationalist cause in Northern Ireland reminds us that cause lawyering in advanced capitalist countries is not necessarily a risk-free activity.[9] Indeed, only 20 of Ulster's 1,400 solicitors routinely defend clients in "politically sensitive" cases (Gibb, 1999a). But even in more mundane areas of practice, cause commitments do influence the way in which lawyers behave. The trade union firms see personal injury litigation engage in a running battle between isolated victims and powerful lobbies, the medical unions, employers, large corporations, and insurers. They are identified with aggressive litigation strategies that mirror their institutional client's battle with employers (Genn, 1982; Boon, 1996).

Clearly, lawyers do not qualify as cause lawyers by being personal injury specialists per se. Indeed, when personal injury work is well paid, there is no need to search for a deeper motive. But there seems little doubt that personal injury work provides examples of cause lawyering: personal injury arising from environmental abuse or exploitation of employees are clear examples (Bloom, this collection). Firms like Leigh Day and Co., however, occasionally manifest transgressive behavior. For example, Leigh Day and Irwin Mitchell, another London-based firm, were recently forced to withdraw cases for 47 of 53 litigants with personal injury claims for tobacco-related illnesses. Leigh Day and Co. advertised in order to coordinate action by claimants. The firm was heavily criticized by the trial judge for their "advertised willingness" to litigate (Robins, 1999). In the wake of the collapse of the majority of cases, and the undertakings given by the firms not to be involved in further actions, calls went out to other firms to pick up the baton of tobacco litigation. These examples suggest that lawyers are not neutral in selecting either their clients or the targets of litigation.

If mainstream lawyers in mainstream areas of work manifest attributes of cause lawyers, what of the cause lawyer's propensity to put the cause before the client? British lawyers are intolerant of the idea that this could ever be acceptable behavior for a lawyer. For example, on withdrawing their clients' tobacco related claims, Leigh Day and Co. and Irwin Mitchell obtained an undertaking by the defendants, Imperial Tobacco and Gallaher, not to seek costs from the plaintiffs. In return, the firms agreed not to launch fresh cases related to tobacco for five years and against the defendants for ten years. The lead partner for one of the firms explained that the costs could have bankrupted several of the plaintiffs and that their primary duty was to the clients (Robins, 1999).

British lawyers are wary of the label "cause lawyer" because they refuse to accept that certain kinds of "trangressiveness" are also consistent with being a lawyer. Thus, the senior partner of Bindman and Co., Geoffrey Bindman, is content to be labeled "political" but rejects the notion that a lawyer could ever subordinate a client's interests to the pursuit of a cause:

> I think it's terribly important that the client, whoever it is, is not made the plaything of some political objective or agenda. The nature of the solicitor's work is to be the voice of the client, to provide the client with the skills and ability to pursue a case which the client doesn't have the know how to do. This is coupled with advice based on experience, helping the client to pursue their aims. . . . The cause lawyering stops in a sense when the client enters an office. I have had many cases where somebody comes along, and you think it looks like a fascinating case, and the client says, "all I want is to get my money back."

This view raises the question of whether lawyers who place the cause before the client are acting as lawyers at all. In the liberal state, willingness to place a cause above a client is what distinguishes a cause advocate, including lawyers acting in that role, from lawyers acting in a representative capacity. There is really no other moral basis on which lawyers, acting as lawyers, can accept mutual responsibility with clients for the purposes of representation (Sarat and Scheingold, 1998). Unless clients' interests are paramount, cause lawyers have no moral basis on which to contradict the "crude instrumentalism" of conventional legal practice and "reconnect law and morality" by demonstrating that professional commitment to clients are more than merely technical (Sarat and Scheingold, 1998). This higher moral component in cause-lawyering is inconsistent with the subjugation of clients to causes. This suggests that we need to look more closely at cause lawyering activity before attempting to categorize it or place it in a hierarchy. There may be several indicators of the presence of cause lawyering, from the nature of the cause to the behavior of the individual when dealing with that kind of case.

NEUTRALITY AND TRANSGRESSIVENESS

Lawyer neutrality suggests a panoply of obligations, including accepting any client and maintaining an emotional detachment from clients. The first of these is more easily observed, but, in the United Kingdom at least, the propensity to choose and refuse clients is not a reliable indicator of transgressiveness. Only barristers are formally subject to the principle of neutrality, exemplified in the "cab rank rule," which requires barristers to take cases in the order that instructions are presented. But barristers become so identified with particular types of case that they do not receive briefs on behalf of causes with which they are not identified. If clients seeks out an unsympathetic barrister *because* they are identified with a cause, there are opportunities to evade the brief (Boon and Levin, 1999: 350). Indeed, barristers, because of their high profile as advocates, are likely to appear in cases of a similar type. In England and Wales lawyers achieving iconic status as cause lawyers are often barristers.[10]

Solicitors are not formally bound by the principle of neutrality. Moreover, many solicitors' firms, through specialization, also act only in certain fields. But further, within their specialized fields they tend to act for only one side of a dispute, for example, criminal defense, and not prosecution. Because they are not required to observe formal neutrality in accepting clients, they can refuse clients or even categories of case. While the reasons offered are usually technical, an underlying suspicion is that a refusal to act is based on cause identification.[11] But evasive measures are seldom necessary. Because of their ready identification with causes, lawyers in sophisticated markets occupy a niche whereby cause identification achieves client selection. As Bindman observes, "Choice of client, reputation, the sort of clients that approach you, your areas of specialisation would tend to be consistent with promoting a cause, or having an agenda." If Bindman did not want to take a client, he would feel no professional obligation to do so. In relation to the Pinochet case, for example, he said:

> I wouldn't want to represent anybody whom I found politically or morally uncongenial. To give you an example, I've been involved with the Pinochet case, representing Amnesty International. The solicitors who were representing Pinochet ... I would never in a million years dream of acting for General Pinochet. I couldn't possibly provide a service to him, not because we don't have the capacity to do it, but to go into court, to try and help him to avoid trial: I couldn't think of anything more objectionable. I'm not saying Kingsley Napsley shouldn't have done it. That's a matter for them and somebody should do it; he's entitled to representation.

Therefore, often despite ethical commitments to neutrality, the values represented by cause lawyers are deeply embedded. In advanced capitalist states, far from representing a deviant strain of legal professionalism (Scheingold and Sarat, 1998), cause lawyers represent dominant strains of the professional ethos. This is because liberalism, however defined,[12] is distinguished by the importance of individual civil and political rights. The lawyer in a liberal state ostensibly pursues the same ends as the state itself: liberty and equality of opportunity. But lawyers hold the state to its promises (Dotan, this volume).

Those lawyers who are seen to have the skill and the commitment to champion the causes that exemplify the commitments of the liberal state swim in the mainstream of professional life. This is evidenced by their acceptance, and the integration of their values, in professional structures, political dialogue, and the popular imagination. Michael Mansfield Q.C., for example, is *The Lawyer's* barrister of the year for his work in the Lawrence enquiry,[13] a high-profile public inquiry into the racially motivated murder of a black teenager, which identified institutional racism in the Metropolitan Police. Martin Day, senior partner in Leigh Day and Co., and a key figure in the tobacco litigation discussed above, is a key figure in the Association of Personal Injury Lawyers; his firm was the winner of *The Lawyer's* Law Firm of the Year award in 1996. Geoffrey Bindman was a member of the Law Society's Working Party on *Pro Bono Publico* and the originator of a proposal, subsequently adopted by politicians, that large firms contribute to a pro bono fund that could be used to supplement legal aid.

While some radical lawyers are imbricated in the legal establishment, others occupy a more ambiguous position. Imran Khan, for example, was the solicitor who briefed Mansfield in the Lawrence Inquiry. Khan shares with many liberal lawyers the view that the law should be used as an instrument to change society for the good (Burrell, 1999) and was himself *The Lawyers'* "Legal Personality of the Year.".Nevertheless, he also attracts criticism, notably for his "politically motivated" campaign to keep the Lawrence case in the public eye for six years until a public inquiry was granted. As a first-generation immigrant, educated at a low status university and working for a small firm in London's unfashionable East End, Khan may have been seen as a lawyer who might be intimidated by or marginalized with such allegations. But Khan also felt that he was the target of criticism from professional colleagues. In one case at least he was accused of overstepping the boundaries of the professional normative consensus. The importance of this is clearly illustrated by considering separate allegations made against Mansfield and Khan in the controversy surrounding the Lawrence Inquiry.

Mansfield's remorseless questioning of police witnesses in the Lawrence Inquiry drew sharp protests from police lobby groups. Mansfield is, however, well known for his willingness to tackle police witnesses head on and his style is professionally mandated, even seen as praiseworthy. Khan, in contrast, was accused of pressurizing a barrister's chambers to abrogate the sacred "cab rank rule" by demanding that they refuse a brief to defend the alleged perpetrator of bomb attacks on minority communities (Tendler and Gibb, 1999). This, if true, clearly contravenes professional norms regarding relations between solicitors and barristers. It is an example of behavior that, taken together with Khan's strong associations with anti-racist organizations, is easy to construct as transgressive. It courts the condemnation of professional colleagues because it risks the lawyer's privileged position above the fray, a position from which they can convert technical to moral authority (Halliday, 1999: 1058). Khan's reaction to the allegation, something less than a full denial, suggests that he appreciated the distinction and was not prepared to defend the professional propriety of such behavior. These examples illustrate why most lawyers keep their professional activities within the bounds of role and seek other vehicles for their political commitments. These are typically nongovernmental organizations, often dominated by lawyers but able to avoid overidentification with lawyers in their professional roles.

POLITICAL ACTION

While the performance of organizations such as the Haldane Society may call into question the radical commitments of lawyers in the United Kingdom (Scheingold, 1988), there are other organizations to which lawyers are affiliated and through which they exercise political influence. Take LAG, for example. In addition to fulfilling a broadly educational role for those concerned with welfare law, LAG has a campaigning and lobbying role. It works closely with organizations like Liberty and Justice, sometimes overlapping and sometimes pursuing separate agendas. It has close links with the National Association of Citizens' Advice Bureaux, the Federation of Independent Advice Centres, the Law Centre Federation, the Advice Services Alliance, and the National Consumer Council.

LAG also has close relations with lawyers and their professional bodies, particularly the Law Society, and to a lesser extent with the Bar Council. Chapman's work with the Law Society relates to legal aid policy, where there is common interest in maintaining levels of spending. Their joint activities include writing letters for the press and holding lobbies. Outside the lawyers' professional bodies, LAG works with the Legal Aid Practitioner's Group. Indeed, Chapman identifies the organization's connections as:

> mainly with the legal aid practitioners.... they teach on our courses, they write for our magazine, they write our books and our products are aimed at the needs of the legal aid practitioner and the advice sector, particularly the specialist advice centre. [But] you might draw a distinction between us and the Legal Aid Practitioners' Group, which is that we are not their mouth-piece; they are not our constituency. Our concern is for poor people getting access to the justice system. Those lawyers, and advice centres, its their concern as well but it's a shared concern and they are facilitating that in the sense that they are providing the services to

the people that we're concerned about. [But] we are not concerned about the protection of the profession.

Legal aid lawyers and the not-for-profit legal sector are the main supporters of LAG in its pursuit of better legal services for disadvantaged sectors of the community. Sometimes interests coincide and sometimes not. LAG has offered strong resistance to the idea of capping legal aid budgets. On the other hand, it has supported proposals, like creating new groups of lawyers employed by the state, that cut across the interests of private practitoners. Because of LAG's independent financing, status, and mission, it enjoys good relationships with radical lawyers and with both the present and previous governments. It is able to act as a lobbyist and a bridge between opposed groups and views. Through organizations like LAG, lawyers are able to be effective advocates for clients and causes and to delegate their political activism. Because they are only indirectly linked with radical agendas, they are able to retain credibility as independent professionals and maintain a wide sphere of influence (Halliday, 1987 chap. 2). This is possible precisely because cause identification is weakened by the principle of neutrality.

Globalization, the State, and the Market for Legal Services

Two dimensions of globalization are of primary concern, the economic and the normative. Both have an impact on cause lawyering in the United Kingdom. Economic globalization has affected the market for legal services and therefore indirectly affected cause lawyering by reducing and redirecting the resources available for this activity (Scheingold and Bloom, 219). In the normative sphere, globalization is a more contested phenomenon. Writ large, it may be taken to imply the convergence of visions of the good society. This is not suggested here, although there is a notable increase in government's willingness to seek out tried-and-tested solutions to global problems. This is reflected in a marked propensity to examine the legal services market in overseas jurisdictions, particularly the United States. Pressure groups, including the legal profession, use counterarguments, insights gleaned from other jurisdictions, and ways of framing problems that have been successful elsewhere. These processes are facilitated by transnational networks of nongovernmental agencies. The debates and processes rarely focus on cause lawyers but, rather, on the profession as a whole. Cause lawyers are merely the unintended victims of measures to curtail the power of lawyers in general. In this way they are subject to global currents that are impinging on relations between a range of interest groups and the state.

Lawyers and the State

In advanced capitalist countries, and especially in the United Kingdom, the boundaries of the state are imprecisely drawn. The state is not a synonym for the government, which acts on behalf of the state, although it can be identified with specific institutions including the judicial branch (Miliband, 1973). At a more abstract level the state is defined, variously, as an entity possessing mechanisms for changing rules or norms and for identifying who will have that power (Giddens, 1986), by monopolies over taxation and money supply and the use of violence (Scott, 1979) or, latterly, as an ensemble of trust strategies (Johnson, 1993). The legal system is a key institution in each of these conceptions of the state, the judiciary its essential personnel. Legal professions, particularly in the common law tradition, are a key institution in the liberal state for changing rules and norms, for resisting the use of legalized violence on individuals, and for encouraging trust in the system. Lawyers legitimize the activities of the state by operationalizing checks on the abuse of state power.

Introducing measures to curtail lawyers is a sensitive step for government in the United Kingdom because the profession has a historic claim to a constitutional position. This is rooted in the Glorious Revolution of 1688 in the case of the barristers (Burrage, 1997) and the mid-nineteenth-century reliance by government on the Law Society's legislative advice in the case of the solicitors (Sugarman, 1996, Burrage, 1996). The central role of the profession in the state was cemented when the Law Society accepted a central role in administering criminal and civil legal aid. Nevertheless, both branches of the legal profession harbor deep suspicion of government. This is reflected in a professional ideology that sees individual rights and the rule of law as fragile and at risk and an independent legal profession as their best defense (Boon and Levin, 1999). Confident of their alliance with the judiciary, the profession was unaware of the tidal wave of change that would soon engulf it.

The Market for Legal Services

In the twentieth century the legal profession grew with the economy and, after the Second World War, with a rapid expansion of the welfare budget (Scott, 1979: 147).[14] The system was thrown into crisis during the 1960s when unpredictable global economic forces constrained the commitment to welfare programes. New Right politicians, President Reagan in the United States and Prime Minister Thatcher in the United Kingdom, perceived the state's capacity to respond to the global economic crisis as a crisis of state authority. The British Conservative governments of the 1980s, for example, blamed the postwar accommodation between labor and capital for systemic inflation, unemployment, and the uncontrolled growth of public expenditure.

The return to classical laissez faire economic policies asserted the superiority of markets and individual choice in allocating resources. Increased governmental authority was demanded so as to guarantee the effectiveness of markets (Gamble, 1994; Soros, 1998).

> If the state makes the protection of the institutions of the free economy its priority then it creates the basis for its own legitimacy. Once all illegitimate functions and responsibilities are stripped from it the state is no longer the weak state of social democracy, overburdened by ever-widening responsibilities and infested by special interests, which seek to use the political process to portray their sectional interest as the public interest. It can concentrate on defending what is the public interest—upholding impartially the rules of the market order. (Gamble, 1994: 39)

Conservative political domination during the 1980s and 1990s brought about a shift in British politics and in attitudes. The idea of a small but authoritative state policing a competitive market, with a shrunken public sector, and limited public spending, was sold through a relentless propaganda war against public expenditure, welfarism (Gamble, 115: 155–57), and corporatism, the delegation of governmental authority. This was accompanied by a search for new ways of delivering public sector services (Gamble, 137). Trials of strength with entrenched lobbies were welcomed because they provided opportunities to assert the authority of the state (ibid., 41).

The legal profession came into the government's sights almost by accident. The ending of the monopoly over domestic house transfers, "conveyancing," began a process by which the profitability of law firms was undermined. Conveyancing was the bedrock work of many "high street practices," and its decline undermined firms' ability to cross-subsidize other kinds of work, including litigation. The radical 1989 green papers of the Lord Chancellor, Lord Mackay of Clashfern, attacked professional restrictive practices (Zander, 1990: 757). The proposals were met by a hostile response from the bar, the judges and, eventually, the Law Society (Zander, 1990). The judges were particularly outspoken. Leading figures, including the former Lord Chancellor, Lord Hailsham, criticized everything from the process of consultation to the proposals themselves. It was suggested that fundamental reform of the profession may be unconstitutional (Zander, 1990: 767). The Consumer Association was virtually alone in supporting the proposals, urging Lord Mackay to stand firm against the professional lobby (Zander, 1990: 771). The profession was relieved that the provisions contained in the Courts and Legal Services Act were a considerable compromise on the green paper proposals, yet the act still contained mechanisms for submitting litigation and advocacy to competition.

The main cause for concern, however, the cost of legal aid, was beyond the scope of the proposals. It was the only uncapped welfare budget. Escalating cost during the 1980s and 1990s, led to progressively restrictive eligibility thresholds and increasing numbers of litigants in person.[15] Plans to restrict legal aid services, first through franchising and then through block contracts, sought to control demand for legal aid and reduce cost. Other cost-saving measures involved replacing legal aid with conditional fee agreements for a limited range of cases, accompanied by the introduction of "after the event" insurance policies that allowed a client with a conditional fee agreement to insure against the risk of losing and being liable for the other side's costs.[16]

The Labour government elected in May 1997 accepted the fact that global markets created a political and fiscal straightjacket. There could be no return to more generous social welfare provision following the massive restructuring of the national economy (Gray, 1998: 18). Instead, Labour proposed a compromise between liberalism, "individual liberty in the market economy," and democratic socialism, the promotion of social justice by the state (Blair, 1998). Labour adhered to the economic disciplines of the Conservatives, accepting the need to cooperate and compete in an international economic order, and to modernize the economy (Gamble, 1994: 44). An early decision to cede control of interest rates to the Bank of England reduced room for political manouevre. The government resolved not "to throw money at every problem," to control tax and ensure that all public spending offered "money for results and reform" (Blair, 1998: 15). It sought new ways to mitigate the social impact of "market fundamentalism," the threat posed to "open society" by social polarization, rising crime, failing education, and low productivity and growth (Soros, 1998).

On the lawyer question, the attitudes of politicians appeared to have hardened. Whereas the Conservatives' touchstone, competition, employed the rhetoric of access to legal services, their measures did not make it central. Labour, however, took more seriously the suggestion that the legitimacy of the justice system was undermined by inaccessibility and cost. The government's actions could therefore be seen as the reflection of a decision to privilege cheap and accessible legal services over proceduralism. Therefore, the legislative and ideological attacks of the 1980s and early 1990s, implemented by the Conservative Lord Chancellor, Lord Mackay, did not abate with the election of a Labour government in 1996. Indeed, Lord Mackay's successor, Lord Irvine, although from the "fat-cat end of the Bar" (Phillips, 1999), showed every determination to tackle the lawyers.[17]

Lord Irvine's strategy was in no sense predetermined. In a speech to a conference of the bar in 1996, for example, he said that he found cost-capping legal aid "unattractive in principle, because legal aid would cease to be a benefit to which a qualifying individual is entitled." Within a year of election he had come to regard legal aid as "a leviathan with a ferocious appetite" (Irvine, 1997: 2). Lord Irvine's 1998 consultation paper noted:

> Legal aid expenditure has been rising at an unacceptable rate. Over the past seven years, the cost of civil and family legal aid has tripled to £671 million, the average cost for proceedings which received full legal aid in 1990/1 was £1,442. If those costs had grown with inflation that would represent £1,760 at 1997 prices. The actual average cost in 1996/7 was £2,684. This represents an increase of 53% above

inflation or an average of 8% per year. While the cost of civil and family legal aid continued to rise last year, the number of acts of help it funded fell by about 39,000. We are spending more and more public money helping fewer and fewer people. (Lord Chancellor's Department, 1998a: 3.3)

Controlling legal aid was one of two quests. The other was fixing "a machine with many faults," the civil justice system (Irvine, 1997: 2). Lord Irvine's program for meeting his twin challenges was bold. He resolved to abolish the Lord Chancellor's Advisory Committee on Education and Conduct, which advised on occupations permitted to conduct litigation and advocacy, because they institutionalized resistance to change and slowed down the process. He implemented the wideranging changes in the court system, proposed by Lord Woolf at Lord Mackay's instigation, that significantly increased judicial control of litigation and introduced controls on legal costs. Finally, he vowed to control legal aid by introducing contracting for services in both civil and criminal cases, by requiring a 75 percent chance of success in any supported case and by replacing legal aid with conditional fees as the main means of funding whole categories of cases (Irvine, 1997).

These promises were made good with the passage of the Access to Justice Act (HMSO, 1999)[18]. Additionally, the act established a Legal Services Commission directly answerable to the Lord Chancellor, and charged it with establishing a Community Legal Service and a Criminal Defence Service. A Community Legal Service Fund replaces legal aid and it has been suggested, used in a way that reflects, first, priorities set by the Lord Chancellor and, second, the commission's duty to secure the best possible value for money. In creating the Community Legal Service, the commission will develop plans to make the best use of available resources in a comprehensive referral network of legal service providers of assured quality. It aims to encompass the "not for profit" advice sector, solicitors in private practice and lawyers' pro bono efforts (HMSO, 1999). It will consider a range of alternatives to traditional delivery, including telephone and mobile advice services and the strategic use of second tier agencies[19] (Steele and Seargeant, 1999).

Henceforth, legal aid is guaranteed only for family, immigration, mental health, and civil disputes arising against the police or from abuses of prisoners' rights. Other areas will be supported only if there is perceived to be a need. These restrictions, combined with franchising and block contracting, threatened to squeeze further legal aid lawyers who had not seen an increase in legal aid rates for six years. In the House of Lords debate on the new methods of funding, Lord Phillips said that the government's claim that quality would be improved by block tendering was the "most incredible of all their claims.... Quality follows remuneration. I should be very surprised if the noble and learned Lord the Lord Chancellor shopped around for a cheap surgeon if he ever needed one, as we devoutly hope he will not" (Hansard, 1999).

The Lord Chancellor promised that proper representation and better value for money would be achieved by replacing the legal aid budget with a Criminal Defence

Service. The House of Lords, however, was dismayed that it was proposed to take into account the sums expended on criminal defense in determining the budget of the Community Legal Service (Hansard, 1999a: 373), in effect a double capping of the civil budget. The Lord Chancellor responded that, while civil and criminal budgets were notionally separate, in the real world he had little scope to exceed fixed spending targets. But he countered, "the only people who could possibly be attracted to a ring-fenced budget for criminal cases would be lawyers." He would contain the demands of the criminal budget he claimed "through monitoring and controlling the contracts." By this means he would "bring downward pressure on excessive fees" (Hansard, 1999a: 381).

Lord Irvine also enacted a range of measures relevant to the profession (HMSO, 1999: part 3). In principle, all lawyers would, henceforth, have full rights of audience before any court subject to reasonable training requirements. This opened up advocacy to the lawyers in the Crown Prosecution and Criminal Defence Services and posed a particular threat to the bar. The proposal was rejected in the House of Lords but reinstated in the House of Commons. In the House of Lords debate, Baroness Mallalieu Q.C. suggested that

> The state which makes the accusation and conducts the prosecution must neither control the defence nor appear to do so. The independent defender is the main safeguard which ensures that this does not happen. The public is rightly concerned about miscarriages of justice.... Many of us worry whether the salaried defender will be permitted to devote the time of his employers to pursuing what were sometimes wrongly seen by others as lost causes. (Hansard, 1999)

The Lord Chancellor continued to insist that the independent bar would continue to perform most defense advocacy (Gibb, 1999b). Others, however, including the shadow attorney general, fear that Lord Irvine's proposals undermine the independent profession and hence the independence of judges, the quality of justice, and the confidence of the public (Garnier, 1999). Concerns regarding the introduction of the Community Legal Service have been more muted; mainly because its final shape is unclear. Although its main thrust is the need to achieve greater coordination and a tightening of administrative controls, the position of lawyers in private practice in relation to the Community Legal Service remains unclear. There is a possibility that small private firms will be squeezed out by franchising and contracting requirements and their expertise replaced, in the longer term, by lawyers employed directly by the Community Legal Service.

The Normative Sphere

Globalization as a process of cultural and normative convergence is a contested concept particularly when one looks beyond the core countries of the global economic order, the United States, Western Europe, and Japan (Soros, 1998; Santos,

1995). Within these countries it is given credence by the dominance of liberal democracy under the rule of law, as a dominant form of government. Normative convergence is facilitated by the disembedding and generalization of experience (Giddens, 1991), the ascendancy of the "sovereign consumer" (Johnson, 1993: 149), and improved communications technology. The social problems generated by economic globalization are also generalized; through the 1980s and 1990s social problems in the United States were also more obvious in the United Kingdom. Global competition fueled local competition and caused wider discrepancies in wealth. Less mitigated by welfare, this created an underclass, economically disadvantaged and threatening. The political and intellectual climate favored the creation of a more competitive and self-reliant society (Gamble, 1994: 7), but the electorate were anxious about, and wanted the state to retain responsibility for, medical care, schooling, and protection from crime (Gray, 1998: 34).

In many areas formerly the province of welfare—for example, pensions—people were encouraged to make personal provision. But this did not address the problems of those who were not in a position to provide for themselves. The United Kingdom had a weak tradition of community involvement and civic responsibility (Theobold, 1993: 13). The task of encouraging social integration through self, community, and private sector solutions[20] forced the state more explicitly into the normative sphere (Habermas, 1973). Denying that state power was "an end in itself," Labour committed itself to "working with the private and voluntary sector; sharing responsibility and devolving power" to form a "strong civil society enshrining rights and responsibilities, where the government is a partner to strong communities" (Blair, 1998: 6). In achieving this, it promised to "revitalise the ethic of public service" and to stimulate "volunteering" as "the cement" of public-private partnerships (Blair, 1998: 14). Global echoes of this are found in President Bush's post-Reagan inaugural address, which also pledged to build on volunteer activity.

In both the United States and the United Kingdom the decline of the social welfare system shifted responsibility for welfare burdens onto the private sector. But while Labour anticipated "engaging business in new partnerships" (Blair, 1998), attitudes that justified individualism and materialism as ends in themselves were even more deeply embedded in the business community. It did not accept civic responsibility or obligation (Gray, 1998: 111). Campaigns were initiated in order to stimulate community activity, including by the Home Office, charities, and governmental agencies. The thrust of these campaigns had already been tested on the lawyers. In 1994, Labour's shadow spokesman on legal affairs, Paul Boateng, warned the profession that legal aid would continue to decline under a future Labour government and demanded greater commitments to *pro bono publico* (Mcleod, 1994). At one point he threatened that a future Labour government would impose statutory pro bono obligations (Gazette, 1996).

The demands placed on the professional elite for pro bono activity is a significant example of globalization or, perhaps more accurate, of the importance of the United States to the process of normative convergence in the core countries. The demand for large firm *pro bono publico* was trailed in the United States by the American Bar Association in 1989 (Boon and Levin, 1999: 237). It is a move consistent with the state's demand for fealty from the social elite and particularly from the business community. The extraordinary power, and undemocratic access to government, enjoyed by transnational corporations has grown significantly since the 1960s (Scott, 1979). The power and leverage of business, exaggerated by globalization, offends the notion of social justice promoted by the liberal state. "Employee volunteering" is a symbol of corporate social responsibility (Theobold, 1993). It perhaps assuages the sense of outrage when any group abuses privilege, as, for example, when directors of privatized utilities reaped massive financial dividends (Wintour, 1999). Professions are important reference points for this kind of activity. They are privileged on the grounds that they promote social cohesion, in part by their commitment to resist the profit motive.

It is noticeable that small and legal aid firms were never really a target of Boateng's efforts to urge *pro bono publico* on the legal profession.[21] During the run up to Labour's election victory in 1997 he specifically targeted the large law firms in the City. He called for a levy on the richest to supplement the £1.6 billion legal aid bill and accused them of failing to honor their moral obligation to ensure "the proper and equitable administration of justice" (The Lawyer, 1994a). Even when Labour came to power, and the issue appeared to slip off the agenda, there were hints of a continued desire for a 'public-private partnership' with lawyers to meet legal and social need.[22] Subsequently, the passage of legal aid and other reforms of the legal services market was accompanied by a government campaign on the issue. During the period leading up to Labour's reform of legal aid, Lord Irvine repeatedly cited the fees, some as much as £1 million per annum, earned by barristers from legal aid (Boon and Levin, 1999; Boon and Whyte, 2000). Labour back-bench MPs argued that pro bono work should be a factor in appointing Queen's Counsel or a commitment to providing pro bono services a condition of taking silk (Hansard, 1999). In January 2000 it was announced that the performance of pro bono work would be a factor in government service promotion. The top government legal officers were to meet to discuss a program to increase levels of pro bono service (Jordan, 2000).

These pressures had little impact on the professional bodies. Large firms' pro bono work was directly influenced by ideas for employee volunteering imported from the United States and disseminated by Business in the Community, which was formed in 1981.[23] The pitch to lawyers was made through its Professional Firms Group, formed in 1989 (Boon and Whyte, 2000). The influence, however, was not just persuasive. During the 1990s large firms were under pressure from business clients, who complained about fees and demanded a public service commitment. In March 1999 British Aerospace threatened to drop firms without pro bono programs from its panel of lawyers arguing that 'their' law firms should be aligned to their values and share a similar culture (*The Lawyer*, 1999b), and in October 1999 it was announced that Zurich Financial Services had followed suit (Jordan, 1999). Other major corporations were also reviewing firms' pro bono commitments in tenders for legal work. Experience in the United States continues to be cited as an example to aspire to and as evidence of the failure of public-spiritedness in English law firms (Egan, 2000).

Pro bono publico was also a useful propaganda tool in the hands of government. The determination to ensure that public servants "generate greater public value from public assets" (Blair, 1998: 17) was apposite in relation to legal aid. Legal aid lawyers were not public servants but it was clearly thought that legal aid should generate more benefit. The strategy of redirecting government money from the pockets of lawyers to the provision of more legal services forced the government into debate with the profession over issues of quality. A campaign suggesting that lawyers could not be trusted to operate the existing system began. The principal idea, again imported from the United States, was that the increasing cost of legal services was caused by "supplier," that is "lawyer," induced demand, rather than of public need (Bevan, 1996; Wall, 1996; Zuckerman, 1996; Moorhead, 1998; 377). Lawyers were accused of maintaining legal aid income by invading the social welfare field, impinging on the work of the "not for profit" sector, of making bogus claims against the fund and of "overworking" legal aid cases.

Undermining the lawyers' ideology of public service, previously unquestioned, was a precursor to directing legal aid resources into the Community Legal Service and to increasing external regulation and control of lawyers. Thus, the relationship between the government and the legal profession is full of ambiguity and contradiction. Of the proposals to make block contractors act as fund holders, responsible for making funding decisions, Vicki Chapman says:

> there are two ways that the government looks at lawyers. On the one hand they can't be trusted and its all about the money; on the other hand they are constantly devolving more and more down to the lawyers and saying we trust you to decide and spend this money sensibly. It's a bit like that with conditional fees, on the one hand they say lawyers should be greatly in favour of conditional fees because they will make more money, on the other hand when lawyers throw up objections to the arrangements for conditional fees, they say this is just about you trying to get more money out of the legal aid fund. Actually, as a lawyer, if you had the choice between running a good case on legal aid or on conditional fee, of course you'd prefer it on conditional fee because you'd get more money.

The role of LAG in the process of policy formation illustrates the influence of nongovernmental agencies on the state. It also demonstrates their potential as conduits in global normative reordering. Although Santos refers to LAG's mode of operation as cosmopolitanism,[24] and Keck and Sikkink refer to it as the use of advocacy networks (Keck and Sikkink, 1998), it is an example of the globalizing process at work within extragovernmental networks between the core countries and, sometimes, beyond. Their primary aim is to achieve normative changes in the way that issues are perceived and dealt with. Their tactics include shaping or reframing issues, using symbols and individual stories, co-opting influential players to campaigns, and holding up to scrutiny the failed commitments of powerful actors, including governments (ibid.:16, 24). Because of their independent status, the testimony of pressure groups may claim greater legitimacy (ibid.: 21). Further, although the effectiveness of networks is difficult to evaluate, it is clear that the character and effectiveness of advocacy often depends on key relationships between campaigners and powerful actors, for example, in government (ibid.: 103, 205).

LAG encapsulates the features of transnational advocacy. It has strong links with countries sharing a common law heritage and similar problems in the realm of civil justice, i.e., Canada, America, Australia, New Zealand, South Africa, and India. Links with European organizations have been less strong because of differences in justice systems, but these are developing with Holland and Denmark. Many contacts were built up by a former director, Roger Smith. Lobbying on issues of concern to LAG is facilitated by information about experience in other jurisdictions. Illustrating these aims and strategies in play, Vicki Chapman suggests that LAG was able to feed into recent parliamentary debates on the Access to Justice Bill and the proposed office of public defender. She feels that the received wisdom in the House of Lords was based on the impression that lawyers employed by the state generally offered incompetent services. She used information obtained by LAG in the United States to argue the contrary:

> that public defenders in America are seen as awful, that's a perception that people have, that it doesn't work, but it's actually not true; there are some good programs where you can have a good public defender, it's often in a mixed model and there are key things you have to have like case-load maximums and overflow arrangements so that you don't get people with 300 cases that can't cope and do a terrible job. We can learn lessons from those jurisdictions on things that we are thinking of doing and an organisation like LAG has those links.

Nongovernmental groups do not monopolize the strategies Keck and Sikkink associate with them. The professional bodies also learned from the tactics of groups like LAG. The Law Society deserted its traditional apolitical stance and openly criticised the plans, including through a £600,000 advertising campaign against the Access to Justice Bill (Mathews, 1999).[25] Just as nongovernmental organizations create and sustain links with nongovernmental organizations overseas to formulate demands for change, the professional bodies formalized their international links, presumably with a view to responding to attacks on monopoly and demands for civic responsibility (Boon and Flood, 1999).[26] Similarly, individual lawyers looked to lawyers in other jurisdictions for support in common causes.[27] At every level, the provision of legal services is a global issue.

The New Political Economy of Lawyering
Legal Aid, Conditional Fees and the "Not for Profit" Sector

The voluntary, or advice, sector will receive a large part of the budget formerly allocated to legal aid. This will supplement support received from a variety of sources, including local authorities[28] and payments made under franchise and contracting arrangements in some agencies.[29] The recognition of these agencies as recipients of franchises will reduce the hold of private practitioners on access to law and, in the longer term, create an ambivalent relationship between the employees of such agencies and the government. An expanding advice sector will pull more lawyers into it and, indirectly, into government control. Expectations of the sector will increase significantly. The outcome of this shift in the strategy for legal services is difficult to predict, and the specific impact on cause lawyers in private practice is a matter for speculation. One noted civil liberties lawyer, Benedict Birnberg, called the Community Legal Service a 'ludicrous sham' and called for the creation of a National Legal Service (Schofield, 2000).

In relation to these debates, LAG holds a neutral position, balancing allegiances to advice agencies and legal aid practitioners. It would like to see generous legal aid provision but believes that the not-for-profit sector can provide many legal services, particularly to those most in need, as effectively as private practitioners. Chapman sees the development of the Community Legal Service as, potentially, a fundamental advance in achieving LAG's mission. Her enthusiasm for the idea is tempered by concern over two issues: the assessment of need and the detail of the plans to satisfy that need. The Access to Justice Act leaves much to directions and regulation. Chapman notes that the advice movement is more positive about the idea of assuming greater responsibility for legal services than in the 1980s when a proposal to transfer all advice work to CABx was rejected by the grassroots. Today there is a stronger feeling that the movement should be involved in delivering services in areas where the legal profession has traditionally been lukewarm. Yet, although a few CABx are engaged in franchising with the Legal Aid Board, many are not geared up for full-service provision including tribunal representation, even in welfare law areas where the advice sector has traditionally been strong.

The increasing scope of conditional fee agreements will introduce personal financial considerations into lawyers' decisions about which clients to represent and on what terms. When conditional fee agreements were introduced for personal injury cases, they were not warmly welcomed. Legal aid continued to be available for those eligible and, in the run up to the Access to Justice Act, it was estimated that 75 percent of cases continued to be funded by legal aid (O'Sullivan and Smith, 1999). Under the Access to Justice Act, legal aid was retained for personal injury cases only where "exceptionally high investigative costs or overall costs are likely to be necessary, or issues of wider public interest are involved" (Lord Chancellor's Department, 1998b: para. 3.7, Legal Aid Board, 1999: 3.3.4).

The government has not specified what types of action, or what relationship between costs, damages, and public benefit, would remain within the scope of legal aid. Take the case, for example, of a miner who recovered £25,000 damages for 70 percent damage to his lungs caused by coal dust. This had disproportionately heavy investigation costs and was in court for 102 days, but the damages recovered were relatively small and the cause of action not novel (O'Sullivan and Smith, 1999). Where legal aid is not available, actions may only be viable under conditional fee agreements in which the plaintiff can be insured against the risk of losing, and paying costs to the defendant. By far the most convenient arrangement for lawyers is one whereby an insurer agrees to insure all their personal injury cases. Very quickly, however, it was rumored that firms with success rates averaging less than 95 percent would have cover withdrawn. Indeed, it is rumored that some companies were insisting on a success rate of 98 percent.

The way in which the absence of legal aid affects cause lawyers was well illustrated by the tobacco litigation. Had the claims been legally aided from the start, Leigh Day and Co. and Irwin Mitchell would have recovered most of the expense they incurred in the cases, notwithstanding their collapse. Under the conditional fee system, not being covered by insurance, they lost £2.5 million in profit costs. Given these risks, there was widespread concern that some causes would become too expensive for all but those with the deepest pockets. (*The Lawyer*, 1999c). For, whereas United States lawyers build up personal injury fighting funds under the contingency fee system, conditional fees are not so generous. Supplanting legal aid with conditional fee agreements therefore poses threats in relation to novel claims where the prospects of success are unclear (Pleasence, 1998: 178). It is predicted that low-value and high-risk personal injury cases[30] or those involving heavy investigation costs are unlikely to be supported by solicitors (Pleasence, 1998: 118; O'Sullivan and Smith, 1999; Day and Patterson, 1999).

The Access to Justice Bill had considerable support, including from some lawyers who accepted the allegation that legal aid was often abused (Greer, 1999). In relation to civil liberties work, legal aid solicitors were more confident that most public interest cases, a large number of which fall within the definition of civil liberties cases, would be funded by legal aid following the passage of the Access to Justice Bill. Again, however, there was uncertainty. Unlike the areas guaranteed civil legal aid, civil liberties cases were likely to be funded if they were "likely to produce real benefits for a significant number of people or which raises an important new legal issue." The government gave an assurance that human rights cases and challenges to the state would be a high priority and possibly involve less stringent cost/benefit ratios and prospects of success requirement. There was some anxiety that identification with public law actions might prejudice legal aid contract claims. Further, cases within the guaranteed area of civil liberties, actions against the police, would not necessarily qualify for legal aid. A Legal Aid Board official thought it likely that an assault by police would be regarded as a public interest case (Bindman, 1999c).

The Marginalization of Cause Lawyering

The impact of these various changes is somewhat unpredictable. The future looks bleak for practice sites most likely to harbor transgressive cause lawyers: salaried practice in public and private agencies and small firms with cause-lawyering objectives (Scheingold and Bloom, 1998: 210). The small firms are most at risk in the new political economy of legal services. The government suggests that some 2,900 solicitors' firms have franchises in one or more of the 10 subject categories in which they are awarded. Over 3,100 further applications are pending (HMSO, 1999). By 2001 it is intended that, of the 11,000 firms that perform legal aid work, about 3,000 firms will be given block contracts and about 6,000 will not. A further 2,000 are in a "zone of indeterminancy" (White, 1999). Most firms built on legal aid should gain contracts because only 5,000 firms perform 92 percent of legal aid work. The smallest firms, however, find it difficult to meet franchising requirements.[31] Some fear that firms that are less "compliant" in terms of meeting franchising objectives may not get a contract (White, 1999; Smith, 1998).

A further threat to cause lawyering is the government's determination to stop lawyers determining the scope of the causes supported. Steve Orchard, the chief executive of the Legal Aid Board, said, "The old system whereby solicitors chose where they would practise and what services they would offer is being swept aside. In the future we will show solicitors where there is a market. It will then be up to them to develop and manage it" (Clarke, 1999). Block contracting will impose on firms an obligation to allocate the budget to categories of cases defined by or through government (Lyon, 1998). Where firms are identified with causes they will be obliged to be even-handed in allocating resources between "cause" and welfare claimants.[32] Although the government proposes making a special case of cases of public importance in the legal aid scheme, the details of how this might work are sketchy and the budget undefined. The imposition of direct responsibility to a funding body further undermines professional relationships between lawyer and client (Abrams, Boon, and O'Brien, 1998) and, in the case of political firms, the unique and exclusive commitment to clients identified with a cause.

Geoffrey Bindman is less concerned with what civil liberties actions are likely to be legally aided than the level at which they are funded. He says that, even at present, his firm remains a legal aid practice "with difficulty."[33] He believes that, in expanding conditional fees, the government was unduly impressed by routinized claim handling by firms like the large personal injury firm Thompsons, which has volumes of clients under institutional schemes. The volume, similarity of case, and backing they enjoy allows these firms to use conditional fees to expand their profits and their base. Where cases are more sporadic and more varied, Fordist assumptions are not valid. Indeed, the commitment to a vision of practice based on legal aid means that Bindman and Partners do not have conveyancing, probate, or wills to subsidize the firm's legal aid work. Bindman is also committed to maintaining standards of legal service by retaining the classical model of firm organization (McConville et al., 1994). Partners take their own cases rather than overseeing cheaper staff, and they do mainly legal aid work.

Bindman sees the major problems of franchising and block contracting as the downward pressure on quality that goes to the heart of the lawyer and client relationship. In order to provide a check on the activities of rich and powerful organizations, it is necessary to compete with their lawyers on approximately equal terms. Legal aid provided that opportunity. The risks of routinization, delegation, and inattention to detail undermine the capacity of lawyers to be partisan or to give individual attention to clients. This will undermine the ability to support clients through situations where they are subjected to financial pressure by the opposition's oppressive use of the litigation process.

The other choice forced on firms like Bindman is to make them more commercially minded, to sponsor cause lawyering with the profit from other kinds of work. Bindman himself already acts in libel cases[34] and does small amounts of commercial work for clients who are "very sympathetic to what we do" and who are "totally supportive of causes we pursue!" He says he was recently asked by a friend to act in a commercial dispute for his company: "It's something that I'm quite happy to deal with. Obviously it's well paid; a City-type case where the reason I've taken it on is because I was asked to, and it's something I can cope with doing, and it's going to help the finances of the firm and I don't feel any moral objection to it. It's a dispute with no political overtones." Bindman is concerned that in order to sustain cause commitments, the firm's commercial portfolio will need expanding. The obvious risk is that, while commercial clients "lift the weight" of anxiety suffered by lawyers who build a practice around cause lawyering, embracing corporate work can bring about a shift in culture. An aspect of this will be a move to less transgressive modes of practice (Scheingold and Bloom, 1998: 243).

Large-Firm Pro Bono Publico

The tradition of *pro bono publico* is not strong in England and Wales. There are no ethical requirements and, until recently, few pro bono programs (Abbey and Boon, 1995; Boon and Levin, 1999: chap. 9). Local solicitors and barristers participating in advice sessions at Citizens' Advice Bureaux and Law Centres were small in number and from high street or legal aid firms (Hiscock and Cole, 1989). The Bar responded to the government's campaign for more *pro bono publico* from the profession by extending support to the Free Representation Unit and, in 1992, establishing a Pro Bono Unit.[35] The Law Society, reluctant to weaken its defense of legal aid, did nothing. It had established a Pro Bono Working Party which, in 1994, made seven recomendations to increase solicitors' pro bono commitments, but the Law Society did not endorse the idea of *pro bono publico* until 1998 (Abbey and Boon, 1995; Boon and Whyte, forthcoming).[36] Large firms of solicitors, including some of the City of London giants, became increasingly committed to *pro bono publico*.

Pressure on large firms to provide legal services *pro bono publico* appear to have an impact. Surveys of the large corporate and commercial firms in the early 1990s suggested a small but growing commitment among some firms (Galanter and Palay, 1995 201; Boon and Abbey, 1997). As the Law Society's reluctance to act on the issue became clearer, Andrew Phillips, a member of the Law Society's Pro Bono Working Party convened an open meeting in 1996. This led to the creation of a small full-time unit, funded by City firms (Bradbury, 1996; *The Lawyer*, 1996), to establish and promote links with local law societies, umbrella organizations, and others interested in the field. A Solicitors' Pro Bono group was formed and developed a strategy of obtaining commitment from large firms (Swallow, 1999). By 1999 the group had a membership of 130 firms, including 40 percent of the top fifty law firms. Five of the largest firms had appointed a full-time pro bono officer (Hoult, 1998: 5). Some firms put very significant levels of time and expertise into cases.[37] Although, with the exception of the formation of the Solicitors' Pro Bono Group, the key initiatives were in place before Boateng began his campaign, activity may have been stepped up. But to what extent can large firm pro bono replace traditional cause lawyering?

It has been suggested that legal services providing *pro bono publico* are distinct from cause lawyering (Sarat and Scheingold, 1998: 5) or, alternatively, that corporate pro bono lawyers are significantly less likely to be transgressive in pursuing causes than are lawyers in other practice sites (Scheingold and Bloom, 1998: 217). Some of the large firm pro bono schemes that have grown up in recent years—for example, advice-center advice sessions staffed by trainees—support this analysis. There is often a lack of engagement in the causes that might underlie the surface of the mundane problems that are typically presented (Boon and Whyte, 2000). Two initiatives supported entirely by free legal services provided by large firm lawyers contradict the notion that corporate cause lawyering is confined to the conventional end of a cause-lawyering continuum: the London Panel, which handles death penalty appeals,[38] and the Liberty Panel.

The London Panel of solicitors deals with death penalty appeals to the Judicial Committee of the Privy Council from the former Caribbean colonies.[39] It was formed in the late 1980s by Bernard Simons, of Simons Muirhead and Burton, who had himself begun working on cases in the early years of the decade. In 1987 Simons approached friends in large city firms for assistance and the Panel was formed. The Liberty Pro Bono Panel was formed in 1993, again before government pro bono campaigns began. Before Simons instigated the panel, the firms willing to act for those on death row in the Caribbean were left-wing or progressive firms. There is no doubt, however, that the colonization of the work by large firms greatly changed, even politicized, the nature of the work.

Before the London Panel was formed, there was little coordination and communication between the firms handling the work. By 1996 there were about 40 firms on the London Panel, many of them City firms, representing around 300 prisoners of which 100 were on death row in the Caribbean. Strong links were developed with the Jamaican Council for Human Rights, and the panel became much more strategic in its approach to death penalty appeals (Huntley, 1995). The governments of Jamaica and Trinidad, the main local jurisdictions, were discomfited by the change in tactics from a "case by case" approach to a campaign calculated to tie the program of executions up in legal and political problems. A large firm lawyer who chaired the panel said:

> a case allocated to a firm is usually done by a solicitor with the help of trainees. You're basically gathering information from Jamaica, which can be difficult. Communications with the prisoner are not always good. You are relying on the Jamaica Council team to write a lot and it is having funding problems at present. We are trying to find ways round that. The authorities have been very slow in the past getting the cases together ... now [they] have started to follow the decision in *Pratt v. The Attorney General for Jamaica*,[40] where the Judicial Committee held that someone who had been on death row for five years should have their sentence commuted ... there has not been an execution for eight to ten years now ... there is great concern that executions will now recommence for people under the five-year threshold.[41]

In *Pratt* the appellants were arrested in 1977, sentenced to death in 1979, and had their appeal to the Jamaican Court of Appeal dismissed in 1980. The Court of Appeal gave reasons in 1984 when an appeal to the Judicial Committee was mooted. The matter eventually came before the Judicial Committee of the Privy Council in 1993, at which time the appellants had spent fourteen years on death row. The Judicial Committee reversed its decision of 1983 so as to hold that execution after such a long period amounted to cruel and unusual punishment. The judgment effectively secured a moratorium on executions until Trinidad executed a man while his appeal was under consideration by the Privy Council.

The execution to some extent reflected the success of the panel's strategy, which was causing political problems. The local population of Trinidad was massively in favor of the death penalty because of problems with drug gangs. In Trinidad there was reported to be a loss of faith in the justice system (Dyer, 1999: 14). Lord Browne-Wilkinson, the senior Law Lord, criticized city firms for providing a quarter of the Law Lords' work through capital appeals and thus 'clogging up the machinery of justice'. He was reported as saying:

> The only reason we are completely laden with Caribbean cases is because City firms are ensuring the cases are well-presented and finding a great deal there that

would otherwise not be observed.... [Consequently] we are extremely unpopular. ... there is great political pressure to hang the murderers and we are saying this is contrary to the constitution. (Mendick, 1999)

In May 1999 three death sentences imposed in Trinidad were quashed following pro bono representation by lawyers from Clifford Chance and Collyer-Bristow and a team of barristers including a Q.C. and two juniors. In June 1999 a triple hanging in Trinidad signaled the government's sensitivity and fueled speculation that a regional supreme court would replace the Privy Council jurisdiction (Haraksingh, 1999, Lehrfreund, 1999, Dyer, 1999).

The Liberty Pro Bono Panel has a very similar history to the London Panel in terms of connections with large firms. Established in 1993 to test human rights issues before the courts, it has both a civil and a criminal arm.[42] The civil panel was established in 1993–34, and almost the first step was to approach City firms. The organizer of the Civil Panel explained his thinking:

> Firms like Bindman's and Birnbergs already do a lot of work in these areas. But we thought some of the City firms aren't doing that sort of work. We had an eye on the States where there is a culture of corporate firms doing pro bono work... these cases wouldn't be taken if it weren't for these firms because we are small and with limited resources... we now have eight firms on the panel and we have referred 25 cases so far.[43]

Liberty required firms to undertake to put the same level of skills and resources into their pro bono work as they did their fee-paying work. Two were sufficiently important to be reported. A peace protester recovered damages from Hampshire police and the Ministry of Defence for having been detained in an underground pit. In the notable "McLibel case"[44] in 1994 two litigants in person had their appeal to the Court of Appeal prepared by Richards Butler. Some cases were litigated through the European Court in Strasbourg, including the Earnest Saunders and right-to-silence cases.[45] These cases were prepared by large solicitors' firms but barristers were enlisted to present them: "We find that barristers are very happy to work on Liberty cases and will work pro bono. Obviously when we can get legal aid we will get legal aid but we have done lots of cases, particularly tribunals, where there is no legal aid, where barristers do lots and lots of work which is not well paid."[46]

Some of the pro bono work of large firm lawyers contradicts assumptions made about this kind of cause lawyering. Death penalty work, for example, is not a full-time commitment of the lawyers described here, but it does absorb massive amounts of time and represents the essential activity of cause lawyering.[47] It often begins with a simple request for assistance, a fact that calls motivation into question (Menkel-Meadow, 1998: 39). But any kind of commitment is not purely neutral. Certain firms, for example, refused to join the Liberty panel on the grounds that Liberty is "a bit too political for us.... some of the issues may lead us into conflict with our clients."[48] Other firms expressly exclude from their pro bono programs work "dedicated to a strong religious, political or sectarian view which would alienate any of our clients and staff."[49] In the case of the London Panel, the lawyers' actions clearly mirror forms of engagement and strategies typical of those of radical cause lawyers. The amount of high-level legal expertise invested in cases is often more than cause lawyers at the radical end of the cause-lawyering continuum could command. There is typically little or no direct contact with the clients, and the lawyers act as if they are motivated by an abolitionist commitment. Specifically, the use of legal process to delay executions is similar to the tactics used by full-time death penalty lawyers and highly transgressive in terms of professional norms (Sarat, 1998).

There is some ways to go before it could be argued that large firm lawyers are responding to the challenge to be cause lawyers. Both death penalty appeals and work for Liberty may be thought relatively safe options for large firm lawyers acting *pro bono publico*. They are insulated by professional neutrality and pursue causes that are held in high public esteem, or in relation to which the public are at least neutral. They may lack the formative, underlying reasons which determine many cause lawyers commitments, for example, the racism Imran Khan experienced at school (Burrell, 1999). This exposes the central weaknesses of large firm cause lawyering. The needs that are not met by patchworks of part-time *pro bono publico* are minority and unpopular causes and commitment is subject to commercial and economic pressures. This was well illustrated when, in January 1999, the *Gazette* carried an article that warned against the dangers of solicitors being identified with the organizations they represented. The main example cited was that of Makbool Javaid, head of the discrimination law unit at City firm Dibb Lupton Alsop, and his connection with a Muslim group, Al Muhajiroun. Following the group's condonation of the bombing of U.S. embassies in Kenya and Tanzania, Mr. Javaid was described as a "terror supporter," "prominent member," "leader," "spokesman," and "co-founder" of the group by the press.[50] He asserted publicly that he had merely acted for the group. He advised other lawyers to cover themselves with written agreements setting out the limits of what could be done for clients connected with unpopular causes (Bawdon, 1999). Large-firm lawyers must be especially sensitive to association with unpopular causes because of the degree of association with such causes that their firms will tolerate.

Lawyers and the State

In the United Kingdom the conditions of cause lawyering have been determined by the relationship between the profession and the state. Professions, by making realms of expertise governable, are a key resource in governing the liberal democratic state (Johnson, 1993: 151). Indeed, Halliday argues that this role may increase with globalization, that "confronted with a surfeit of expectations and an incapacity to resolve them internally," the state will delegate functions to nonstate bodies, including professions (Halliday, 1987: 28). Globalization creates optimal conditions for multipartite negotiation between legal professions, states, and supranational organizations of states (Johnson, 1972; Halliday and Karpik, 1997). At the same time, states within supranational organizations, such as the European Community, cannot cope with levels of regulation (Santos, 1990: 286). New measures, such as the Human Rights Act (1998), threaten considerable legal and administrative burdens on public authorities (Feldman, 1999).

Economic globalization demands a massive reorganization of the state as it is forced to withdraw its protection of national markets (Santos, 1995: 256, 259). This limits the scope for collective political decision-making (Soros, 1998) and exacerbates a crisis of legitimacy that cannot be resolved by democracy, equality, and participation (Habermas, 1973; Giddens, 1991: 212; Santos, 1995). Further, the demand for formal justice, which becomes more insistent, is hampered by the structural limitations of the legal system, its inaccessibility, and expense and its lack of flexibility and speed. The state, as "an ensemble of trust strategies" (Johnson, 1993) must address the systemic failings of legal systems that undermine trust (Santos, 1995 101–4). The state is able to redirect its attention to sectors not controlled by capital, because here its capacity for action is strong (Santos, 1995: 279, 376). The result is often a disinvestment by the state of "its symbolic capital in certain understandings of legality," including the simplification of procedure and the removal of sponsorship for litigants (Sarat, this collection, and see Centre for Legal Process, 1998: 53). This is rationalized by arguing that legal aid is "a subsidy to redress the complexity and inaccessibility of law created by the profession itself" (Moorhead, 377). But the problem is only partly about the cost of legal services.[51] Rather, it is about defining arenas of professional neutrality and autonomy; who identifies consumer needs and the way they are met? (Johnson, 1993).

The Conservative government's unsuccessful attack on the restrictive practices of the legal profession revealed a degree of ambivalence regarding professionalism as a means of occupational control (Zander, 1990 Burrage, 1997; Halliday and Karpik 1997: 34). At the same time as it sought to curtail professional power, the government created a new professional group, insolvency practitioners, in an area of technical complexity (Haliday and Carruthers, 1998).[52] But professionalism was no longer thought necessary to govern routine, state-sponsored legal services. Thus, the failures of the 1989 Green papers, and the refusal to address the position of those unable to afford legal services (Zander, 1990: 774), will be addressed by proposals to increase alternative dispute resolution and a Community Legal Service. This will create different sites for cause lawyers while either subjecting to external regulation or marginalizing those found in legal aid law firms and small firms in private practice. The results are somewhat unpredictable. On the one hand, the removal of pressure to make a living may enhance public lawyers' capacity to be cause lawyers (Bloom and Scheingold, 1988). On the other, their commitment to the disadvantaged will be more closely circumscribed.

The international and corporate law firms are relatively untouched by changes in the legal services market. It remains to be seen whether they will continue to expand their pro bono commitment to cause lawyering as the state withdraws its support. Thus far they have confined their activities to areas, like the death penalty appeals, that do not undermine arguments for legal aid and do not threaten the collegiality of the profession. Yet the widening status gap between these firms, other lawyers, and "proliferating agencies of public advice" (Johnson, 1993), confirms that "the idea of a unified and homogenous solicitors' profession is past its sell by date" (Hanlon, 822). Pressure from corporations committed to "employee volunteering," including clients in the United States (Laferla, 1999), must also chime with recognition that legal services for the poor legitimize the product lawyers sell (Goriely, 242). If the numbers of legal aid and high street firms are reduced, or a formal division appears within the solicitors' branch, different groups of lawyers will gather their symbolic capital in order to negotiate new roles in the state.

Pro bono publico, incongruous in the 1960s (Hoggart, 1995), was anachronistic in the materialistic 1980s, when Margaret Thatcher declared that "there is no such thing as society," and that "no one would remember the Good Samaritan if he'd only had good intentions. He had money as well" (Partington, 1996). By the 1990s the climate had changed. In 1997, a Law Society survey revealed that the vast majority of firms thought that pro bono work enabled them to contribute to the public good, enhanced the reputation of the firm, and was good for business (Law Society, 1997). Those in the traditional sites of cause lawyering resented or mistrusted the attempted hijacking of cause lawyering by large firms.[53] But the City lawyers dismissed suggestions that they could not turn their hands to welfare law or that they should simply pay legal aid firms to perform welfare and cause work. Increasingly aware of the distance their own work was taking them from their traditional roots, and claims to legitimacy, *pro bono publico* offered opportunites to corporate lawyers to reclaim the symbolic capital of "real" lawyers; nobody would remember the Good Samaritan if he had given money but not stopped to help.

Conclusion

The dilemma of public policy presented by economic globalization is the accommodation of deregulated markets and human needs (Gray, 1998: 32). In the postwar period legal aid created a space in which some lawyers built firms with a political commitment. A tripartite system public funding through legal aid, a network of advice agencies and *pro bono publico* legal services provided a patchwork of provision to meet legal need. Successive governments expressed dissatisfaction with the inability of the system to respond to priorities. Finally, a restructuring of legal services was initiated by the Conservative government and continued, even accelerated, after Labour's election victory in 1997. The major players in this structural and normative reshaping of the legal services market participate in a global information exchange, seeking arguments, examples, and models consistent with their aims.

The imperative of providing cheaper access to justice imperils the dominant position of lawyers in the legal services market. Cause lawyers with practices built on legal aid, or in small firms, are particularly vulnerable in this new environment. The funneling of government funding to new practice sites and tighter controls over legal aid spending undermine those sites where cause lawyering is most likely to be found. Legal aid firms may diversify, into the corporate sphere if they can, and balance cause work with more profitable transaction work. Cause lawyering, which flourished as a result of a high degree of professional autonomy in selecting cases, will change. While conditional fees may ease the strain on the public purse, justice is not necessarily made more accessible. Claims that do not involve money are unsuitable for conditional fees and expensive litigation may be too risky for insurance. Many cases will depend on complying with unformed criteria of public importance. The purity of many public interest lawyers' engagement with causes may be difficult to sustain and some causes may be left without their traditional champions.

The performance of *pro bono publico* may make good the deficit in these areas. In the hands of well-resourced large firms, significant action can be taken and rights gained for individuals and groups. There is potential to reconcile the economic imperatives of states trapped between the forces of globalization and the demand for more legal services, and the interests of lawyers in legitimacy and, thus, economic security. Such action will be precipitated by the separation of elite lawyers from sectors of the profession that formerly provided that legitimacy. By ensuring that the liberal state upholds the individualistic, egalitarian, and democratic values that are its central justifications, large firm lawyers respond to the state's demand for the conscientious administration of trust (Theobold, 1993). They also respond to their clients' demands to participate in legitimizing the new socio-economic order. In the process they recapture the public service ethic. The fact that they are able to do so, however, results from the fact that cause lawyers in the United Kingdom have stayed well within the ethical lines provided for professional practice. This raises the hitherto unthinkable possibility that corporate *pro bono publico* is the new face of cause lawyering.

Acknowledgments

My thanks to Avis Whyte and Ching Fang-Weeden for research assistance, to all the participants in the project for comments at the meeting in Bellagio, particularly Terry Halliday and Mike McCann, and to John Flood and Julian Webb for comments on an earlier draft.

Notes

1. Shamir and Chinski suggest that "one lawyer may discover herself as a lawyer for a cause, while another may be vaguely aware of being so, and yet another, in contrast, may carefully construct a distinct identity and standing in the legal field by using an asserted cause as a professional resource."

2. It is not known how many qualified solicitors have full-time employment in the advice sector (but see Verkaik, 1999 below).

3. There are 700 main Citizens' Advice Bureaux with and additional 1,759 outlets, more than 800 independent advice centers, and 53 law centers (Verkaik, 1999).

4. There are 3,745 sole practices and 3,671 with 2–4 partners (Cole, 1997: 33).

5. Founded in 1974 as a legal aid, social welfare, civil liberties and human rights practice, it currently claims specific expertise in defamation and media law, administrative law, employment, crime, housing, matrimonial, children, medical negligence, and immigration. It currently has 13 partners, 8 assistants, and 10 other fee earners (Chambers, 1998).

6. The firm has 10 partners, 14 assistant solicitors, and 11 other fee earners (Gupta, 1997).

7. Begun with a three-year grant from the Nuffield Foundation, all the group's income is self-generated through publications (including its flagship *Legal Action* magazine) and training (it is an educational charitable trust). It now has twelve staff, many of whom are either qualified as lawyers or have completed a law degree.

8. The material in this section is based on an interview with Vicki Chapman on Friday, July 16, 1999.

9. Rosemary Nelson was killed by a car bomb in March 1999. She was identified, not only with high-profile Republican defendants, but also with political activity on behalf of the minority Nationalist community and her willingness to take issues into the public arena. The "loyalist" Red Hand Defenders claimed responsibility, but the Nationalist community alleged that various factors implicated the Royal Ulster Constabulary (RUC)of which she was an outspoken critic. Her death occurred ten years after the death of a prominent Catholic solicitor, Pat Finucane, in 1989 (Burns, Brown, and Wolffe, 1999; Fletcher, 1999; McKittrick, 1999). British Irish Rights Watch alleges that the RUC are incapable of accepting that solicitor are just doing their jobs when representing their clients but identify them with the alleged crimes of their clients (Winters, 2000).

10. Michael Mansfield Q.C. is a case in point. He appeared for the defense in cases arising out of the miners' strike and trials of alleged terrorists and is an outspoken critic of the police, the legal system, and wider society. Mansfield also has a successful practice, much of his work being paid for by criminal legal aid.

11. This was illustrated by a case in 1990 when two firms of London solicitors, both well known in the field of criminal defense, refused to accept as a client a man accused of raping his girlfriend. The reasons given, in the case of one firm that they did not specialize in rape cases and in the other that they did not act where the defense was consent, was seen as an abrogation of the obligation of neutrality (Latham, 1990). This was on the grounds that "consent" defenses generally involved attacking the reputation and character of the alleged victim and because the firm may, as a result of links with women's organizations, have been exposed to accusations of a conflict of interest (Boon and Levin, 1999).

12. A "liberal" is apt to be identified with the defense of welfarism in the United States and with the defense of the free market in Europe.

13. Sir William Macpherson's report made seventy recomendations and could inspire a

fundamental review of the police and criminal justice system. (For details of the awards see *The Lawyer Fifth Annual Awards: Book of the Night,* 1999).

14. In Britain, state expenditure on welfare had grown at a steady rate, from between 25 percent and 30 percent of GNP in the 1920s to 50 percent in the late 1960s.

15. Legal aid certificates for civil claims grew from 9,648 in 1986–87 to 23,194 in 1992–93, yet a working party chaired by Lord Justice Otton in July 1995 found that, in March 1995 alone, there were 4,258 litigants in person involved in actions in the High Court, representing an increase from one in ten cases in 1989–90 to one in three. They absorbed large amounts of court time, and that of court staff, and were less successful than represented parties (*The Times,* 1995; Ames, 1995).

16. Conditional fee agreements allow lawyers to agree with clients that no costs will be paid if the case is lost, but an uplift on the usual fee will be paid if it is won. In July 1995 conditional fees were permitted in personal injury insolvency cases and cases before the European Commission of Human Rights. The uplift and insurance premium are taken from the damages. The maximum uplift was 100 percent of the normal fee, but the Law Society recomended that a maximum of 25 percent of damages be taken where this produced a sum lower than the 100 percent uplift (see further Yarrow, 1997).

17. Lord Mackay's willingness to challenge the legal establishment was attributed to the fact that, as a Scottish lawyer, he was outside the English legal establishment. Despite being hailed as the most reforming Lord Chancellor for over a hundred years, he suggests that he feared "competition without rules" in the market for legal services (Interview with Lord Mackay, May 1998).

18. The act received Royal Assent on July 27, 1999.

19. I.e., consultancy and referral agencies for providers with direct contact with the public (first-tier agencies).

20. The 1996 Social Attitudes Survey revealed widespread rejection of the idea that the voluntary sector should do more to augment or supplant services formerly provided by the public sector. Indeed, more than half the respondents believed that society relies too heavily on volunteers. Only 10 percent agreed that government should do less for the needy by encouraging charities to do more, and over 75 percent disagreed (Farquarson, 1999).

21. Presumably it was accepted that they could not afford free work. Martin Mears, then the Law Society's president, claimed that 25 percent of solicitor earned less than £10,000 a year (*The Times,* 1995).

22. On appointment as special adviser to the Lord Chancellor, Garry Hart, a former partner in Herbert Smith and Co., one of the largest solicitors' firm in the country, urged that senior lawyers should spend more time on pro bono work (*The Lawyer,* March 1, 1999a).

23. Business in the Community was formed following an Anglo-American business conference in 1980, and employee volunteering was an idea based explicitly on experience in the United States. Indeed, Business in the Community published a pamphlet on employee volunteering subtitled "Lessons from America" (Theobold, 1993: 7).

24. "Cosmopolitanism is nothing more than the networking of local progressive struggles with the objective of maximising their emancipatory potential *in locu* through translocal/local connections. It occurs at the margins of the capitalist world system on behalf of the oppressed or those acting in their name and or in their interest, typically through Non-governmental agencies including relief and welfare agencies" (Santos, 1995: 264).

25. It commissioned a poll which showed wide support for retaining legal aid for personal injury claims where there was no affordable conditional fee insurance and that two-thirds of back-bench Labour MPs thought that the act would restrict access to justice (Bindman, 1999a). Several voluntary groups, Refuge, Radar and the National Housing Fed-

eration, and Doreen and Neville Lawrence, allowed their names to be used in the Law Society's campaign (Bindman, 1999b). The Lord Chancellor responded angrily, threatening legislation to restrict the use of funds raised by fees for practicing certificates to education and regulatory activities (Legal Action, 1999).

26. For example, the bar has signed a compact with representatives of other international jurisdictions, the International Consortium on Access to Law, to share knowledge on expanding access to justice (*The Lawyer*, 1994).

27. Martin Day, for example, collaborated with personal injury lawyers in the United States who had a treasure chest for tobacco litigation built up through successful asbestos claims (Robins, 1999).

28. Currently £150 million (Verkaik, 1999).

29. A pilot scheme was established in 1994 for "not for profit" agencies providing legal advice and assistance to the same standard as solicitors' firms. In October 1996 a second stage of the pilot was established to develop systems for contracting for advice and assistance work.

30. Some firms required a 70 percent prospect of success before entering a conditional fee agreement, and some insurers required an 85 percent chance of success before insuring the plaintiff against the risk of paying costs to the defendant (Pleasence, 1998).

31. A deadline of March 31, 1999, for legal aid franchise applications was met by 5,000 solicitors out of a population of about 11,000 firms then providing a legal aid service (Clarke, 1999).

32. See Middleton, 1997: para. 3.29, providing an outline of a merits test to be applied by lawyers involving the prospects of success, cost-benefit, and the importance of the issue to the reasonable person in those circumstances (and see comment by Moorhead, supra, at 383).

33. Interview, January 26, 1996.

34. Bindman concedes that it is not an area typical of "progressive firms," although he sees cases he acts in as tending to "bring the media to account."

35. This Pro Bono Unit was a private initiative by the then chairman of the Bar, Peter Goldsmith Q.C. In 1997 the unit received a £50,000 grant from the Bar Council and commitment from 720 barristers, including 120 Q.C.'s, to provide at least three days a year to *pro bono publico* work.

36. The recommendations included: the publication of a policy statement encouraging solicitors to conduct more pro bono work; a free representation advice agency and the establishment of a Trust Fund to receive voluntary funds to support *pro bono* activities.

37. Lovell, White, Durrant represented the Independent Manchester United Supporters Association in the successful effort to have the Monopolies and Mergers Commission deny media empire BSkyB's takeover of one of the world's largest football clubs. City firm Stephen's Innocent and two barristers, one a Q.C., provided £250,000 of free advice and representation over a six-year period so that a pensioner could gain a decision that the pension funds of electricity workers had been misapplied in making redundancy payments (Verkaik, 1999).

38. The London Panel is not the only route to involvement in death row appeals (see Robins, 2000, Townsend, 2000, regarding appeals conducted by British lawyers in the United States), but it is the best organized.

39. The Privy Council jurisdiction had its origins in the Norman Conquest but its modern role developed with the empire (Privy Council Office, 1999). Today it hears appeals from both dependent and independent territories in both civil and criminal matters. In criminal matters it must grant special leave to appeal against the death sentence, which leave

it reserves for cases of great general importance or where there has been a grave miscarriage of justice. It heard 85 petitions for special leave in 1998 and granted 32 (Lord Chancellor's Department, 1999c).

40. [1994] 2 A.C. 1.

41. Interview with Paula Hodges, Herbert Smith and Co., February 12, 1996.

42. The Criminal Justice Network established a network of approximately 100 solicitors to examine alleged miscarriages of justice. It initially received 40–50 inquiries a month which, by 1996, had dwindled to 5. If there appears to be a case, the solicitor applies for legal aid.

43. In 1996 Liberty was receiving 120 general inquiries a week, of which a small proportion were litigated (Interview with Philip Leach and Penny Sergeant, January 31, 1996).

44. Helen Steel and David Morris v. McDonald's Corpn. and McDonald's Restaurants (1999) (Lawtel 19/4/99, doc. c8 000991).

45. In 1996 legal aid was available for such cases, though it was meager (£250).

46. Interview, January 31, 1996.

47. Although it should be noted that in accounts of radical cause lawyering, pro bono representation is often an obscure but necessary component (Coutin, this collection).

48. Interview, February 14, 1996.

49. Taken from the website of Clifford Chance: http://www.cliffordchance.com/firm/practice/pro bono.

50. Coincidentally Mr. Javaid, formerly a lawyer at Bindman's, was represented by Geoffrey Bindman. Bindman suggests that Javaid had gone to observe a number of demonstrations involving Muslim youths because of suggestions that police used oppressive tactics on these occasions. Following a meeting in a hall, the licensor had refused to return a deposit. Javaid was asked by a member of the group to secure its return, which he did. He denies any other connection with the group. Bindman and partners issued three writs against national newspapers in connection with the story. At time of writing, two of these actions have been settled.

51. Growth in legal aid expenditure is explicable in terms of the growth in claims consciousness in the 1980s, albeit fueled by professional advertising (Dyer, 1998, and see Lyon, 1998).

52. The Insolvency Act of 1986 sought to achieve competition between accountants and lawyers while imposing common threshold standards of competence and ethics.

53. Martin Mears, who used his presidency of the Law Society to speak out for high street firms, claimed that the pro bono work of big City firms has "far less value for ordinary people than pro bono work by High Street practices which are geared up for everyday problems."

References

Abbey, Robert, and Boon, Andy (1995). "The Provision of Free Legal Services by Solicitors: A Review of the Report of the Law Society's Pro Bono Working Party," 2 vol. *International Journal of the Legal Profession*, 261.

Abbott, Andrew (1986). "Jurisdictional Conflicts: A New Approach to the Development of Legal Professions" 2 vol. *American Bar Foundation Research Journal*, 187.

Abel, Richard L. (1986) "The Decline of Professionalism?" 49 *Modern Law Review* 1.

——— (1989). "Between Market and State: The Legal Profession in Turmoil," 52 *Modern Law Review*, 285.

Abel-Smith, Brian, and Robert Stevens (1967). "Legal Services for the Poor," in *Lawyers and* the Courts: A Sociological Study of the English Legal System, 1750–1965. London: Heinemann.

Abrams, Pamela, Andrew Boon, and Derek O'Brien (1998). "Access to Justice: The Collision of Funding and Ethics," 3 *Contemporary Issues in Law*, 59.

Ames, Jonathon (1993). "Public interest" *Gazette* (September 8), 11.

———. (1995). "Rescuing DIY Litigants," *Law Society's Gazette* pp. 14 (July 26).

Bawdon, Fiona (1999). "I'm a Lawyer, Not a Raver," *Gazette* p 22 (January 13).

Bevan, G. (1996). "Has There Been Supplier-Induced Demand for Legal Aid?" 15 *Civil Justice Quarterly*, 99.

Bindman, Dan (1999a). "Battle over Legal Aid Goes Public" *Gazette* 1 (April 28).

——— (1999b). "Who's in Step?" *Gazette* 16 (April 28).

Blair, Tony (1998). *The Third Way: New Politics for the New Century* London: The Fabian Society.

Boon, Andy (1995). "Client Decision Making under Personal Injury Schemes," 23 *International Journal of the Sociology of Law*, 253.

——— (1995). "Ethics and Strategy in Personal Injury Litigation," 22 *Journal of Law and Society*, 353.

Boon, Andy, and Robert Abbey, (1997). "Moral Agendas: *Pro Bono Publico* in Large Law Firms in the United Kingdom," 60 *Modern Law Review*, 630.

Boon, Andy, and John Flood (1999). "The Globalisation of Ethics: The Significance of International Codes of Conduct," 2 *Legal Ethics* 29.

Boon, Andrew, and Jennifer Levin (1999). *The Ethics and Conduct of Lawyers in England and Wales*. Oxford and Portland, Ore.: Hart Publishing.

Boon, Andrew, and Avis Whyte (2000). "Charity and Beating Begins at Home": The Aetiology of the New Culture of *Pro Bono Publico*,' 2 *Legal Ethics* 169.

Bradbury, A. (1996), "Solicitors Rally for UK Pro Bono Scheme," *The Lawyer* (October 15), pp 1.

Burns, Jimmy, John Murray Brown, and Richard Wolffe (1999). "Northern Ireland Car Bomb Killing Deals Blow to Peace Process," *Financial Times* (March 16), 20.

Burrage, Michael (1996). "From a Gentleman's to a Public Profession: Status and Politics in the History of English Solicitors," 3 *International Journal of the Legal Profession*, 45.

——— (1997). "Mrs. Thatcher Against the 'Little Republics,' " in *Lawyers and the Rise of Western Political Liberalism*, Terrence C. and Halliday Lucien Karpick, eds. Oxford: Clarendon Press.

Burrell, Ian (1999) "They said I was a dirty lawyer." *The Independent* June 29 p 14

Centre for Legal Process (1998). *Future Directions for Pro Bono Legal Services in New South Wales*. Sydney: Law Foundation of New South Wales.

Clarke, Alison (1999). "Crunch Time" *Gazette* (April 14), 22.

Cole, Bill (1997). *Trends in the Solicitors' Profession: Annual Statistical Report*. London: The Law Society.

Day, M., and F. Patterson (1999). "Deal That Could Spell the End of Legal Aid," *The Times* (April 20), 41.

Dyer, Clare (1997). "On the Lawyers Who Work for Free," *The Guardian* (July 15) Section 2 pp 17.

——— (1998). "Once It Was Bad Luck, Now It's Get a Lawyer and Sue," *The Guardian* pp 6 (October 17).

——— (1999). "Trinidad Sends Three to the Gallows," *The Guardian* (June 5) 14.

Edwards, Harry T. (1990). "A Lawyers Duty to Serve the Public Good," 65 *New York University Law Review*, 1148.

Egan, Dominic (2000). "Can Pro Bono Be Saved from Death Row?" *The Lawyer* (February 7), 16.
Farquarson, Andy (1999). "Give and Take," *The Guardian* p. 39 (July 28).
Feldman, David (1999). "The Human Rights Act 1998 and Constitutional Principles," 19 *Legal Studies*, 165.
Fletcher, Martin (1999). "Nationalist's Heroine Had Dangerous Foes," *The Times* (March 16). p. 2.
Galanter, Marc (1983). "Mega-Law and Mega-Lawyering in the Contemporary United States," in *The Sociology of the Professions: Doctors, Lawyers and Others*, R. Dingwall and, P. Lewis eds. New York: Macmillan, 166.
Galanter, Marc, and Thomas Palay (1995). "Large Law Firms and Professional Responsibility" in *Legal Ethics and Professional Responsibility*, Ross Cranston, ed. Oxford: Clarendon Press, 189.
Gamble, Anthony (1994). *The Free Economy and the Strong State: The Politics of Thatcherism*, 2d ed. Basingstoke and London: Macmillan.
Garnier, Edward (1999). "Lawyers Must Keep Independence," *The Lawyer* (August 2), 15.
Gazette (1996). "Pro Bono Wrangle" (December 13). pp. .6
Genn, Hazel (1982). *Meeting Legal Need? An Evaluation of a Scheme for Personal Injury Victims*. Oxford: Centre for Socio-Legal Studies.
Gibb, Frances (1999a). The risk that faces frontline lawyers *The Times* March 23, 41.
Gibb, Frances (1999b). "Retire? There Is Nothing I Like More than Work" *The Times* (September 7), 12.
Giddens, Anthony (1985). *A Contemporary Critique of Historical Materialism*, Vol. 2: *The Nation State and Violence*. London: Polity.
——— (1991). *Modernity and Self-Identity: Self and Society in the Late Modern Age*. Cambridge: Polity Press.
Glasser, Cyril (1990). "The Legal Profession in the 1990s—Images of Change," 10 *Legal Studies*, 1.
Goriely, Tamara (1996). "Law for the Poor"—The Relationship Between Advice Agencies and Solicitors in the Development of Poverty Law,' *International Journal of the Legal Profession*, 215.
Gray, John (1998). *False Dawn: The Delusions of Global Capitalism*. London: Granta.
Greenebaum, Edwin H. (1996). "Development of Law Firm Training Programs: Coping with a Turbulent Environment, 3:(3) *International Journal of the Legal Profession*, 315.
Greer, Darryl (1999). "The Legal aid gravy train" 149 *New Law Journal* February 12, 221.
Gupta, Reena Sen, ed. (1997). *Chambers and Partners: A Guide to the Legal Profession, 1997–98*, 8th ed. London: Chambers and Partners.
Habermas, Jurgen (1973). *Legitimation Crisis*, T. McCarthy, trans. Boston: Beacon Press.
Halliday, Terence C. (1987). *Beyond Monopoly: Lawyers, State Crises, and Professional Empowerment*. Chicago and London: University of Chicago Press.
Halliday, Terence C., and Lucien Karpik, (1997). "Postscript: Lawyers, Political Liberalism, and Globalization," in *Lawyers and the Rise of Western Political Liberalism*, Halliday and Karpik, eds. Oxford: Clarendon Press.
Halliday, Terence C., and Bruce G. Carruthers, (1998). *Rescuing Business: The Making of Corporate Bankruptcy Law in England and the United States*. Oxford: Clarendon Press.
Halliday, Terence C. (1999). "Politics and Civic Professionalism: Legal Elites and Cause Lawyers" 24 *Law and Social Inquiry* 1013.
Hanlon, Gerard (1997). "A Profession in Transition?—Lawyers, the Market and Significant Others" 60 *Modern Law Review*, 798.

Hansard (1999a). *Parliamentary Debates: House of Lords Official Report*, ser. 35, Vol. 597, p. 196.
——— (1999b). *House of Commons Written Answers for 11th March* (questions 75785 to 75787).
Haraksingh, Kusha (1999) "Context and Dominion: The Law in Independent Trinidad and Tobago" in McQueen, Rob and Pue, W. Wesley (Eds) *Misplaced Traditions: British Lawyers, Colonial Peoples* Leichhardt, New South Wales: Federation Press. (Special edition (1999) 16 *Law in Context* 151).
Heinz, John P., and Edward, O. Laumann, (1982). *Chicago Lawyers: The Social Structure of the Bar*. Evanston, Ill.: Northwestern University Press.
Hiscock, Lynda, and Godfrey Cole (1990). "The Motivation, Use and Future of Volunteer Lawyers in Law Centres," 6 *Journal of Social Welfare Law*, 404.
HMSO (Her Majesty's Stationery Office) (1999). *Explanatory Notes to Access to Justice Act*.
Hoggart, Richard (1995). *The Way We Live Now*. London: Chatto and Windus.
Hoult, P. (1998). "Allen and Overy Appoints Full-time Pro Bono Co-ordinator," *The Lawyer* (November 3). pp. 5.
Huntley, Graham (1995). "The Panel," in *Caribbean Commonwealth: A Review of the Appeals Process for Death Row Inmates*. London: Deathwatch.
Irvine of Lairg, Lord (1996). "Keynote Address to the Bar Conference" (September 28), 6.
——— (1997). "Keynote Address to the Solicitors" Annual Conference' (October 18).
Johnson, Terence J. (1972). *Professions and Power*. London and Basingstoke: Macmillan.
——— (1993). "Expertise and the State," in *Foucault's New Domains*, Michael Gane and Terry Johnson, eds. London and New York: Routledge.
Jordan, Dearbail (1999). "Zurich In-House Demands Firms Commit to Pro Bono," *The Lawyer* (December 4), 5, 5.
——— (2000). "Attorney General Joins Pro Bono Push," *The Lawyer* (January 17). pp. 8.
Keck, Margaret E., and Kathryn, Sikkink. (1998). *Activists Beyond Borders: Advocacy Networks in International Politics*. Ithaca, N.Y, and London: Cornell University Press.
Laferla, Alison (1999). "The Pro Bono Myth Laid Bare," *The Lawyer* (March 15) 12.
Latham, D. (1990). "Solicitors and the Cab Rank Rule," *New Law Journal* (March 2), 286.
Law Society, Research and Policy Planning Unit (1997). *Panel Study of Solicitors' Firms*. London: The Law Society.
The Lawyer (1994a). "Labour Suggests Levy to Support Legal Assistance" (September 27) 3.
——— (1994b). "Labour Eyes US Pro Bono Model" (November 8). pp. 2.
——— (1996). "Solicitors Vote for Boost to *Pro Bono*" (November 12), 1.
The Lawyer (1999a), March 1, 5.
——— (1999b). March 22, 7.
The Lawyer. (1999c) MPs back the Lawyer over Access to Justice campaign May 10, 3.
Legal Action (1999). "Law Society's Union Role under Threat" (June), p. 5.
Legal Aid Board (1999). *The Funding Code: Decision Making Guidance (Draft for Consultation)*.
Lehrfreund, Saul. (1999) "The Death Penalty and the Continuing Role of the Privy Council," 149 *New Law Journal*, August 20, 1299.
Lord Chancellor's Department (1998a). *Access to Justice with Conditional Fees: A consultation paper*.
——— (1998b). *Modernising Justice: The Government's Plans for Reforming Legal Services and the Courts* (Cm. 4155).
——— (1999). *Judicial Statistics: England and Wales for the Year 1998* (CM4371).

Luban, David (1988). *Lawyers and Justice: An Ethical Study*. Princeton, N.J.: Princeton University Press.
Lyon, A. (1998). "Changes to the Legal Aid System and Increasing Access to Justice: Were the Conservative Government's Proposals for Changes to the Legal Aid Scheme Either Necessary or Constructive?," *Contemporary Issues in Law*, 30.
Mathews, Michael (1999). "Taking the Gloves Off." *Gazette*, May 12, 18.
Mcleod, J. (1994). "Justice Agenda," *Law Society Gazette* (March 16). pp. 12.
McConville, Michael, John Hodgson, Lee Bridges, and Anna Pavlovic (1994). *Standing Accused: The Organisation and Practices of Criminal Defence Lawyers in Britain*. Oxford: Clarendon Press, chap. 2.
McKittrick, David (1999). "Solicitor Risked Safety to Speak Out," *The Independent* (March 16), p. 2.
Mendick, R. (1999). "Browne-Wilkinson Slams City lawyers," *The Lawyer* (May 17), p. 1.
Menkel-Meadow, Carrie (1998). "The Causes of Cause Lawyering: Toward an Understanding of the Motivation and Commitment of Social Justice Lawyers" in *Cause Lawyering: Political Commitments and Professional Responsibilities*, A. Sarat and S. Scheingold, eds. New York and Oxford: Oxford University Press, 31.
Middleton, Sir Peter (1997). *Review of Civil Justice and Legal Aid: Report to the Lord Chancellor*.
Miliband, Ralph (1973). *The State in Capitalist Society: The Analysis of the Western System of Power*. London: Quartet Books.
Moorhead, Richard (1998). "Legal Aid in the Eye of a Storm: Rationing, Contracting, and a New Institutionalism," 25 *Journal of Law and Society*, 365.
O'Sullivan, T., and C. Smith (1999). "Without Legal Aid, This Air Is All This Man Would Have," *The Lawyer* (April 19), p. 20.
Partington, Angela, ed. (1996). *The Oxford Dictionary of Quotations*, rev. 4th ed. Oxford: Oxford University Press.
Paterson, Alan A. (1996). "Professionalism and the Legal Services Market," 3 *International Journal of the Legal Profession*, 137.
Phillips, Andrew (1999). "A Want of Experience," *Gazette* (April 28), p. 4.
Pound, Roscoe (1953). *The Lawyer from Antiquity to Modern Times: With Particular Reference to the Development of Bar Associations in the United States*. St. Paul, Minn.: West Publishing.
Powell, Walter W. (1996). "Fields of Practice: Connections between Law and Organisations," 21 *Law and Social Inquiry*, 959–66.
Prest, Wifred R. (1986) *The Rise of the Barristers: A Social History of the Bar, 1590–1640*. Oxford: Clarendon Press.
Privy Council Office (1999). *The Judicial Committee of the Privy Council*. London: Privy Council Office.
Pue, Wesley W. (1997). "Lawyers and Political Liberalism in Eighteenth- and Nineteenth-Century England" in *Lawyers and the Rise of Western Political Liberalism*, T. C. Halliday and L. Karpik, eds. Oxford: Clarendon Press, 167.
Robins, Jon (1999). "Out of Puff," *Gazette* (March 10), 9.
——— (2000). "Penalty Clause." *Gazette*, Feb. 10, 26.
Santos, Boaventura de Sousa (1995). *Towards a New Common Sense: Law, Science and Politics in the Paradigmatic Transition*. London and New York: Routledge.
Sarat, Austin (1998). "Between (the Presence of) Violence and (the Possibility of) Justice: Lawyering against Capital Punishment," in *Cause Lawyering: Political Commitments and*

Professional Responsibilities, A. Sarat and S. Scheingold, eds. New York and Oxford: Oxford University Press.

Sarat, Austin, and Stuart Scheingold (1998). "Cause Lawyering and the Reproduction of Professional Authority: An Introduction," in *Cause Lawyering: Political Commitments and Professional Responsibilities*, A. Sarat and S. Scheingold, eds. New York and Oxford: Oxford University Press.

Schofield, James (2000). "It's War Going to Work: I Accuse," *The Legal Executive Journal*, May, 8.

Scheingold, Stuart (1988) "Radical Lawyers and Socialist Ideals," 15 *Journal of Law and Society*, 122.

——— (1994). "The Contradictions of Radical Law Practice," in *Lawyers' Work: Translation and Transgression*, M. Cain and C. Harrington, eds. New York: New York University Press.

Scheingold, Stuart, and Anne Bloom (1998). "Transgressive Cause Lawyering: Practice Sites and the Politicization of the Professional," 5 *International Journal of the Legal Profession*, 209.

Scott, John (1979). *Corporations, Classes and Capitalism*. London: Hutchinson & Co.

Shamir, Ronen, and Sara, Chinski (1998). "Destruction of Houses and Construction of a Cause: Lawyers and Bedouins in the Israeli Courts," in *Cause Lawyering: Political Commitments and Professional Responsibilities*, A. Sarat and S. Scheingold, eds. New York and Oxford: Oxford University Press.

Smerin, J. (1995). "For Love Not Money," 92(38) *Law Society's Gazette*, 1.

Smith, Roger (1998). *Legal Aid Contracting: Lessons from America*. London: LAG.

Soros, George (1998). *The Crisis of Global Capitalism: Open Society Endangered* London: Little, Brown and Co.

Stanley, Chris (1991). "Enterprising Lawyers: Changes in the Market for Legal Services," 25 *Law Teacher*, 1.

Steele, Jane, and John Seargeant, (1999). *Access to Legal Services: The Contribution of Alternative Approaches*. London: Policy Studies Institute.

Sterrett, Susan (1998). "Caring about Individual Cases: Immigration Lawyering in Britain," in *Cause Lawyering: Political Commitments and Professional Responsibilities*, A. Sarat and S. Scheingold, eds. New York and Oxford: Oxford University Press, 293.

Sugarman, David (1996). "Bourgeois Collectivism, Professional Power and the Boundaries of the State: The Private and Public Life of the Law Society, 1825 to 1914," 3 *International Journal of the Legal Profession*, 81.

Swallow, Matheu (1999). "Who Is behind Pro Bono?" *The Lawyer* (September 27), p. 14.

Tendler, Stewart and Frances Gibb (1999). "Lawrence Lawyer in intrusion row" *The Times*, November 10 p. 1.

Theobold, Robin (1993). *Business and the "Community": Some Observations on the Development of Corporate Sponsored Volunteering in Britain*. London: University of Westminster Press.

The Times (1995). July 7.

The Times (1995). "Hard Labour?" (November 7). pp. 35.

Townsend, Abigail (2000). "Profile," *The Lawyer* (January 17).

Tsang, Linda (1999). "Day of the public is here" *The Independent*, Jan. 21, 12

Verkaik, Robert (1999). "Law Without Glamour," *Gazette* (January 13). p. 18.

——— (1999). "Lawyers Put in £250K for Free as Pensioners Triumph in Key Claim," *Gazette* (February 17) p. 9.

Wall, David (1996). "Legal Aid, Social Policy, and the Architecture of Criminal Justice: The Supplier Induced Inflation Thesis and Legal Aid Policy," 23 *Journal of Law and Society*, 549.

Webley, Lisa (1999). *Trainee Solicitors / Young Solicitors Group Pro Bono Survey*. London: Institute of Advanced Legal Studies.

White, Richard (1999). "Restricting Access to Justice Bill," *New Law Journal* (February 19). p. 246.

Winter, Jane (2000). "Who Murdered Rosemary Nelson?" *Legal Action* March, 8.

Wintour, Patrick (1999). "War on 'Fat Cat' Bosses," *The Observor* (July 11), 1.

Yarrow, Stella (1997). *The Price of Success*. London: Policy Studies Institute.

Zander, Michael (1968). "Restrictions on Lawyers Working for the Poor," in *Lawyers and the Public Interest: A Study of Restrictive Practices*, London Weidenfeld and Nicolson, 238.

––––– (1990). "The Thatcher Government's Onslaught on the Lawyers: Who Won?" 24 *The International Lawyer*, 753.

Zuckerman, Adrian S. (1996). "Lord Woolf's Access to Justice: Plus Ca Change," 59 *Modern Law Review*, 773.

CHAPTER 7

State Transformation and the Struggle for Symbolic Capital
Cause Lawyers, the Organized Bar, and Capital Punishment in the United States

AUSTIN SARAT

Cause lawyering exists in an unstable equilibrium in relation to liberal states and the organized legal profession (Sarat and Scheingold, 1998: 3; also Minow, 1996), While cause lawyers often work at cross purposes from state actors, defending rights against intrusion or pushing for social change, sometimes their work is supported, even funded, by the state. And while cause lawyers push the boundaries of conventional lawyering, they occasionally forge strategic alliances with the organized bar. Such support and such alliances are possible because cause lawyering, even as it challenges dominant understandings of lawyering and state policy, performs an important legitimation function for both the bar and the state. Indeed, challenge and legitimation go together (Williams, 1980); without such challenges cause lawyering would not be able to legitimate liberal legality. Yet because legitimation depends on challenge, both the state and the organized bar have an ambivalent relationship to cause lawyering, tolerating, encouraging, and sometimes supporting it and then attacking it, reigning it in, and withdrawing state funding (see Boon, 1999).

From the perspective of the bar, cause lawyers, because they commit themselves and their legal skills to furthering a vision of the good society, put a humane face on lawyering, and when they seek help for their work they may regard the bar as an important ally. Yet this potential alliance is never without significant costs for both sides. For the bar it may involve giving support on terms that diminish its own authority, an authority based in claims to technical expertise rather than political commitment (see Halliday, 1987), and for cause lawyers allying with the mainstream of the profession may raise questions about the depth of their political commitment; increased effectiveness is purchased at the cost of the purity of their cause (Sarat and Scheingold, 1998: 3).

Turning from the bar to the state, whether state officials tolerate, encourage, or even fund cause lawyering depends in part on how and where they wish to invest their "symbolic capital," namely "wealth... accumulated-not in the form of money..., but in symbolic form" (Terdiman, 1987: 812). Symbolic capital is one of the resources available in any social field, and authority, knowledge, prestige, and reputation are some of its forms (Bourdieu,1977:171). Other forms of symbolic capital include the repertoire of images, commitments, and rhetorics which are available to, and used by, state actors to identify themselves with particular values (see Bourdieu, 1991: 72). Like any resources, the state's symbolic capital is potent yet at best only partially controllable. This is because it works at both the conscious and unconscious levels to create associations that suggest what the state stands for, what ideas it will defend, what causes it will promote (see Edelman, 1964, 1971).

While the prevailing ideology constitutes and constrains the consciousness of state actors (Gordon, 1984), it leaves room for maneuver as they look for ways to produce and maintain the state's legitimacy. Legitimacy can, of course, be obtained if the state performs well in providing physical security or in providing effective economic management. But legitimacy can also be obtained through prudent investment in symbols. Here, as is widely recognized (Hay, 1975; Scheingold, 1974), law/legality plays a key role. "Law," as Bourdieu (1987: 838) explains, "consecrates the established order by consecrating the vision of that order which is held by the State." What this means for cause lawyers is that the state may support their work as a way of displaying a prominent investment in legality and the rule of law.

However, state investments in symbolic capital are not stable. Various social and political groups compete to influence the state's investment in symbolic capital in ways that are quite similar to the ways they compete to effect the distribution of the state's financial largesse (Edelman, 1988). They work with their allies in state institutions forming coalitions against other groups and their official supporters.[1] The nature and results of this competition, while patterned, are often quite idiosyncratic.

In addition, shifting political, social, and economic conditions lead to changes in investment strategies. This is as true today as it has ever been as liberal states adjust to what Halliday (1987: 343; see also Habermas, 1986; Boyer and Drache, 1996; Offe, 1996) has called their "crisis of capacity." As Halliday (1987: 343) writes,

> All branches of government have come under increasing pressure from the revolution in rising expectations of state intervention. As demands on government have increased in volume and variety, so also have they become more often contradictory and mutually exclusive... It is... a growing incapacity of government to

fulfill the functions expected of it—that results in the ultimate condition in which the overburdened state may find itself—a crisis of effectiveness and legitimacy. The chief task, then, of the state under strain will be to find expedients by which to adapt its functions and structures to the new circumstances impinging on it.

During the 1980s and 1990s, governments in the United States and Western Europe responded to this crisis of effectiveness and legitimacy by slowing the growth of their investment in economic security and regulation and reorienting their governing ideologies to embrace free market policies and market symbols (Offe, 1996). At the same time, as any American who lived through these decades knows, the politics of law and order took center stage. From George Wallace's "law and order" rhetoric in the late 1960s and early 1970s to Bill Clinton's pledge to represent people who "work hard and play by the rules," crime has become such an important issue that some now argue we are being "governed through crime" (Simon, 1997). With a rise in the crime rate, investment in a "tough on crime" rhetoric increased, and the prior emphasis on criminal rights and extended due process declined (Beckett, 1997; also Scheingold, 1998).

In this effort to show toughness on crime, the symbolism of investing in capital punishment has been very important (Steiner, Bowers, and Sarat, 1999). It has also played a central role in the processes of demonizing young, black males and using them to replace the "evil empire" in the pantheon of public enemies (Tonry, 1995). Today no American politician wants to be caught on the wrong side of the death penalty debate.[2]

The politics of capital punishment is crucial in an era of neoliberal withdrawal from other kinds of state intervention. It helps to shift the symbolic capital of the state to an area where, whatever one's doubts about the capacity of government to govern effectively, there can be demonstrable results (Connolly, 1998). As Aladjem (1992: 8) puts it, "It is significant that just when there is doubt as to whether rational democratic institutions can generate a public sense of justice, there has been a resurgence of pre-democratic retributivism and a renewed insistence that it is a 'rational' response to an increase in violent crime." This helps explain the energy behind recently successful efforts to limit habeas corpus and speed up the time from death sentences to state killings (see Yackle, 1996, 1998). A state unable to execute those it condemns to die would seem too impotent to carry out almost any policy whatsoever.[3]

Yet it is precisely this hydraulic political pressure to show that one is tough on crime by turning death sentences into executions that has led to a shift in the state's investment in symbolic capital away from an expanded notion of due process and equal protection (Amsterdam, 1998). To take but one particularly striking example, the much publicized execution of Robert Alton Harris is a telling reminder of the pressure on law to compromise its highest values and aspirations (see Reinhardt, 1992; and Camiker and Chemerinsky, 1992). During the twelve-hour period immediately preceding Harris's execution, no less than four separate stays were issued by the Ninth Circuit Court of Appeals.[4] Ultimately, in an exasperated and unusually dramatic expression of Justice Rehnquist's aphoristic response to the seemingly endless appeals in capital cases—"Let's get on with it"—the Supreme Court took the virtually unprecedented, and seemingly illegal, step of ordering that "no further stays shall be entered... except upon order of this court."[5] With this order, the court stopped the talk and took upon itself the responsibility for Harris's execution.

The court's action in the Harris case was symptomatic of the growing disinvestment in certain notions of legality. It showed how, in an era of neoliberalism, the act of responding to the crime could, in Foucault's words (1979: 9), be rightly "suspected of being in some undesirable way linked with it. It was as if the punishment was thought to equal, if not exceed, in savagery the crime itself... to make the executioner resemble a criminal, judges murderers." Impatience to facilitate state killing arouses anxiety and fear (Dumm, 1990);[6] it suggests that law's violence bears substantial traces of the violence it is designed to deter and punish. The bloodletting the state seems so eager to let loose strains against and ultimately disrupts all efforts to normalize or routinize state killing as just another legally justifiable and legally controlled act. It may be that law is controlled by, rather than in control of, the imperatives of the killing state (Sarat, 1999).

This paper explores the unstable relationships among cause lawyering, the organized bar, and the state in one domain, lawyering against the death penalty in the United States. My hope is to use this case study to highlight the symbolic capital cause lawyers provide to both the state and the organized bar and to explore the marketing of that symbolic capital and its varied success. Thus to study cause lawyering is, in my view, to have an opportunity to explore the fault lines and contradictions of law/state relations in liberal polities (Sarat and Scheingold, 1998).

I have chosen the death penalty in the United States as a domain of inquiry because, in this area, the law has, at least until recently, demanded heightened standards of reliability and fairness before anyone can be put to death. And, the role of lawyers has been seen to be central in insuring that those standards are met (see Steiker and Steiker, 1994). The law demands zealous advocacy on behalf of persons accused of capital crimes and those sentenced to death, but state actors recoil when that advocacy seems too zealous or when it crosses the line between representing individual clients and lawyering against the death penalty itself. Policing this line is crucial in explaining why the state funds, defunds, and refunds lawyering on behalf of disadvantaged populations. Because the bar focuses on the long-term legitimation of the liberal state and the role of law and lawyers in that project (Halliday, 1987), its response to these efforts is often, though not always, one of resistance; the case study of death penalty lawyers in the United States is but one example of this dynamic at work.

Shifting Symbolic Capital: From Legality to Efficacy in the Politics of the Death Penalty

In the mid-1980s, responding to the earlier reinstatement of the death penalty and the growing population of persons on death row, the Congress of the United States authorized the creation of capital defense resource centers to be operated by the Administrative Office of the courts. Similar operations were approved and funded by a few state legislatures (see O'Brien, 1990; Ruthenbeck, 1989; Lacayo, 1992). One purpose of these centers was to help identify and train private lawyers to handle the appellate and postconviction stages of capital litigation for persons under a sentence of death and, where it was impossible to do so, to provide direct representation themselves. By the end of the 1980s resource centers were operating in thirteen of the more than thirty states that used death as a punishment.

Over the next several years those centers played a key role in the death penalty bar (Sarat, 1998a). Because the lawyers who worked in them were better paid than anti–death penalty lawyers in public interest settings and because they had more resources at their disposal, they quickly became critically important in the network of anti-death penalty lawyering around the country, providing advice, information, and even personnel to battle individual death sentences and to develop strategy in the ongoing fight against capital punishment. And, over time, while they made little headway against the death penalty itself, they were very successful in delaying executions, so much so that it seemed for a time as if capital punishment in the United States would exist at the level of a judicially imposed sentence rather than an actually implemented punishment (Gross, 1993).

By the early 1990s, however, the political tide had swung ever more vehemently to the right on criminal justice issues, and the political fervor to see that death sentences were carried out intensified. When the Republicans took control of the Congress in January 1995, one of their first targets was federal funding for capital defense resource centers (Berkman, 1995). The centers were criticized for engaging in guerrilla warfare on behalf of death row inmates and for moving beyond legal representation into politics, for moving from client to cause lawyering (Amsterdam, 1998). Despite a spirited defense of the resource centers by the American Bar Association, in the spring of 1995 Congress refused to reauthorize or refund the resource centers as of October 1, 1996.

The reaction of the American Bar Association to this decision is a key indicator of the unstable equilibrium in which cause lawyers exist, and it provides an important vehicle for exploring the legitimation politics of cause lawyering in the liberal state. It also exemplifies the intense competition to influence the state's investment in symbolic capital in a neoliberal era. Key to understanding the ABA's reaction and its strategy in this competition was the passage of a resolution by the ABA in February of 1997 (American Bar Association, 1997) calling for a moratorium on the carrying out of the death penalty in the United States. This resolution is an instance of what I call "abolitionism as legal conservatism" (Sarat, 1998b) and an indication of the way the bar both needs and defends, while seeking to domesticate, cause lawyering.

To understand the meaning of the bar's response to the defunding of death penalty defense lawyering, one first needs to go back to February 1994 when Justice Harry Blackmun of the U.S. Supreme Court used a dissent from a denial of certiorari to announce that "From this day forward I no longer shall tinker with the machinery of death" (*Callins v. Collins*, 1994: 1141). This dramatic proclamation capped his evolution from long-time supporter of the death penalty to tinkerer with various procedural schemes and devices designed to rationalize death sentences to outright abolitionist. Twenty-two years before his abolitionist announcement, he dissented in *Furman v. Georgia* (1972), refusing to join the majority of his colleagues in what he labeled the "legislative" act of finding execution, as then administered, cruel and unusual punishment. Four years after *Furman* (1972), he joined the majority in *Gregg v. Georgia* (1976), deciding to reinstate the death penalty in the United States. However, by the time he underwent his abolitionist conversion, Blackmun had left a trail of judicial opinions moving gradually, but inexorably, away from this early embrace of death as a constitutionally legitimate punishment. As a result, the denunciation of capital punishment that he offered in 1994 was as categorical as it was vivid. It was most significant as a moment in the transformation of abolitionist politics and as an example of the kind of "abolition as legal conservatism" that the bar would embrace two years later.

In the United States opposition to the death penalty traditionally has been expressed in several guises. Some have opposed the death penalty in the name of the sanctity of life. Even the most heinous criminals, so this argument goes, are entitled to be treated with dignity. In this view, there is nothing that anyone can do to forfeit the "right to have rights" (Bedau, 1992, 1998). Others have emphasized the moral horror, the "evil," of the state willfully taking the lives of any of its citizens (Kateb, 1992:191–92). Still others believe that death as a punishment is always cruel and, as such, is incompatible with the 8th Amendment prohibition of cruel and unusual punishment (see Justice Brennan, *Furman*, 1972).

Each of these arguments has been associated with, and is an expression of, humanist liberalism or political radicalism. Each represents a frontal assault on the simple and appealing retributivist rationale for capital punishment. Each has put the opponents of the death penalty on the side of society's most despised and notorious criminals; to be against the death penalty one has had to defend the life of John Gacey or Timothy McVeigh, of cop killers and child murderers. Thus it is not surprising that while traditional abolitionist arguments have been raised repeatedly in philosophical commentary, political debate and legal cases, none of them has ever carried the day in the debate about capital punishment in the United States (Zimring and Hawkins, 1986). By the time Blackmun wrote his opinion in *Callins v. Collins* (1994), it looked like none ever would.

Blackmun's abolitionism found its locus in neither liberal humanism nor radicalism, nor even in the defense of the most indefensible among us. It was, instead, firmly rooted in mainstream legal values of due process and equal protection. Blackmun did not reject the death penalty because of its violence, argue against its appropriateness as a response to heinous criminals, or criticize its futility as a tool in the war against crime. Instead, he shifted the rhetorical grounds. Harkening back to *Furman* (1972), as if rewriting his opinion in that case, he focused on the procedures through which death sentences were decided. "[D]espite the efforts of the States and the courts," Blackmun noted (1994: 1144), "to devise legal formulas and procedural rules..., the death penalty remains fraught with arbitrariness, discrimination, caprice, and mistake.... Experience has taught us that the constitutional goal of eliminating arbitrariness and discrimination from the administration of death... can never be achieved without compromising an equally essential component of fundamental fairness—individualized sentencing."

Two things stand out in Blackmun's argument. First he acknowledges law's effort to purge death sentences of any taint of procedural irregularity. As he sees it, the main implication of *Furman* (1972) is that a death penalty is constitutional only if it *can be* administered in a manner compatible with the guarantees of due process and equal protection. Here Blackmun moves the debate away from the question of whether capital punishment is cruel or whether it can be reconciled with society's evolving standards of decency. Second, Blackmun identified a constitutional conundrum in which consistency and individualization—the twin commands of the Supreme Court's post-*Furman* death penalty jurisprudence—could not be achieved simultaneously. As a result, Blackmun (1994: 1157) concluded that "the death penalty cannot be administered in accord with our Constitution." The language that Blackmun uses is unequivocal; after more than twenty years of effort, Blackmun says, in essence, "enough is enough."

The new abolitionism that Blackmun championed presents itself as a reluctant abolitionism, one rooted in acceptance of the damage that capital punishment does to central legal values and to the legitimacy of the law itself. It finds its home in an embrace, not a critique, of those values. Those who love the law, in Blackmun's view, must hate the death penalty for the damage that it does to the object of that love. "Rather than continue to coddle the Court's delusion that the desired level of fairness has been achieved," Blackmun (1994: 1145) stated, "I feel morally and intellectually obligated simply to concede that the death penalty experiment has failed. It is virtually self-evident to me now that no combination of procedural rules or substantive regulations ever can save the death penalty from its inherent constitutional deficiencies." In this admonition we again see Blackmun's categorical conclusion that nothing can "save" capital punishment, a conclusion spoken both from within history, as a report of the result of an "experiment," and from an Archimedean point in which the failure of the death penalty is "self-evident" and permanent.

Blackmun's brand of abolitionism opened an important new avenue for engagement in the political struggle against capital punishment and in the competition over symbolic capital, providing abolitionists a position of political respectability while simultaneously allowing them to change the subject from the legitimacy of execution to the imperatives of due process (Sarat, 1998b). It is this position that some in the death penalty bar eagerly embraced and that the ABA would embrace in its defense of the capital defense resource centers and in its reaction to their being defunded (American Bar Association, 1997). It is this position that is central to the politics of legitimation that surrounds the controversy over state funding of this kind of cause lawyering in the United States.

The rhetoric that Blackmun made available to opponents of capital punishment enabled them not to respond to the overwhelming political consensus in favor of death as a punishment; they no longer had to take on that consensus frontally. Instead, anti–death penalty lawyers could say that the most important issue in the debate about capital punishment is one of fairness, not one of sympathy for murderers; they could position themselves as defenders of law itself, as legal conservatives.[7] One could, these cause lawyers now were able to concede, believe in the retributive or deterrence-based rationalizations for the death penalty and yet still be an abolitionist; one could be as tough on crime as the next person yet still reject capital punishment (Sarat, 1998b). All that was required to generate opposition to execution was a commitment to the view that law's violence should be different than violence outside the law as well as a belief that that difference could/should be rooted in the fairness and rationality of the violence that law does.

Yet, despite the new rhetorical and strategic terrain that Blackmun opened up for lawyers opposed to capital punishment, abolition has by no means prevailed. Quite to the contrary. Proponents of capital punishment have responded with a mean-spirited constitutional revisionism (Amsterdam, 1998). They have contested the state's investment of its symbolic capital in extended, super due process and seem to have prevailed in that contest (Zimring, 1998). The neoliberal state, while backing away from previous commitments to provide protections from the ravages of the free market, has, at the same time, shifted its investment to the symbolic capital provided by a strident anticrime rhetoric (Beckett, 1998). In the process, even those procedural guarantees that Blackmun found inadequate to secure fairness and reliability in capital sentencing have been openly and enthusiastically jettisoned. American society seems even more impatient with the procedural niceties and delays attendant to what many now see as excessive scrupulousness in the handling of capital cases (Amsterdam, 1998).

What good is having the death penalty, so the refrain goes, if there are so few executions? Blood must be let; lives must be turned into corpses; the charade of repeated appeals prolonging the lives of those on death row must be brought to an end. In response, not only did Congress defund the resource centers,[8] it also enacted Title I of the Anti-Terrorism and Effective Death Penalty Act (1996), which severely limited the reach of federal habeas corpus protections for those on death row (Yackle, 1996).⁹ Moreover, numerous recent decisions of the Supreme Court have eroded, not enhanced, the procedural integrity of the death sentencing process (Amsterdam, 1998).

Defending Legality: The American Bar Association and the Death Penalty Bar

Yet just at the moment when one might be prepared to consign Blackmun's new abolitionism to the same fate as other forms of abolitionist politics, and, in so doing, to accept that the demand for death now knows no constitutional scrupulousness, an important new voice has entered the fray. Just three years to the month after Blackmun's dissent in *Callins* (1994), the American Bar Association issued a call for a moratorium on executions in the United States (American Bar Association, 1997). Taking us back to *Furman's* (1972) condemnation of the death penalty as "then administered," the ABA proclaimed that the death penalty as "currently administered" is not compatible with central values of our Constitution. Since *Furman* (1972) the effort to produce a constitutionally acceptable death penalty has, in the view of the ABA, been to no avail. Thus the American Bar Association (1997: 1)

> calls upon each jurisdiction that imposes capital punishment not to carry out the death penalty until the jurisdiction implements policies and procedures... intended to (1) ensure that death penalty cases are administered fairly and impartially, in accordance with due process, and (2) minimize the risk that innocent people may be executed.

The language of the A.B.A. resolution (ibid.), unlike Blackmun in *Callins* (1994), is conditional and contingent in its condemnation of death as a punishment. Even as it calls for a cessation of executions, it seems to hold out hope for a process of reform in which the death penalty can be brought within constitutionally acceptable norms.[10] Central to this reform would be refunding capital defense resource centers.

On second glance, the A.B.A.'s recommendation does the work of Blackmun's new abolition without his overt and categorical renunciation. If one takes seriously the conclusions of the report accompanying the A.B.A.'s recommendation, then the largest, most established association of lawyers in the country is asking Americans to save further damage to the law by ending the death penalty.[11] As Bilionis (1998: 36) puts it,

> Like Justice Blackmun's "experience-based reevaluation" of the death penalty..., the ABA's call for a moratorium is one more example of how greater familiarity

with capital punishment breeds, if not contempt, at least greater skepticism. It is thus one more step in what Anthony Amsterdam once described as the "slow but absolutely certain progress of maturing civilization that will bring an inevitable end to punishment by death."

However one reads the A.B.A.'s resolution in terms of the issue of abolition, it represents the culmination of a twenty-year history of A.B.A. activism on death penalty issues. The bar has adopted policies, issued guidelines, passed resolutions, and even established a Death Penalty Post-Conviction Center (Coleman, 1998). Nonetheless, by passing a resolution calling for a moratorium, the A.B.A. dramatically escalated its involvement in the debate about capital punishment. "The organized bar," Bilionis claims (1998: 39), "having perceived the realities of death penalty administration..., comes forward to bear witness to ongoing indecencies—arbitrariness, capriciousness, discrimination, unfairness and tragic errors against the innocent—that the public does not see and the bench and legislature, in a weakness of nerve, fail to admit and address."

The report accompanying and explaining the February 1997 resolution provides three reasons for its call for a moratorium on executions, each of which parallels arguments made by cause lawyers opposed to capital punishment. First is the failure of most states to guarantee competent counsel in capital cases (American Bar Association, 1997: 5; also Bright, 1994). Because most states have no regular public defender systems, indigent capital defendants frequently are assigned a lawyer with no interest, or experience, in capital litigation. The result is often incompetent defense lawyering (Bright, 1994), lawyering that has become all the more damaging in light of new rules requiring that defenses cannot be raised on appeal or in habeas proceedings if they are not raised, or if they are waived, at trial.

The A.B.A. (1997: 5) itself calls for the appointment of "two experienced attorneys at each stage of a capital case." This call highlights the importance of the resource centers that provided competent counsel on appeal and in postconviction procedures. While, in theory, individual states could provide competent counsel in death cases and refund the resource centers, and while there is ample evidence to suggest the value of skilled lawyers in preventing the imposition of death sentences, given the political climate in the United States as it touches on the crime problem, there is, in fact, little prospect for a widespread embrace of the A.B.A.'s call for competent counsel.

The second basis for the A.B.A.'s recommended moratorium is the recent erosion in postconviction protections for capital defendants (Amsterdam, 1998; Yackle, 1998). While the A.B.A. (1997: 11) notes that "the federal courts should consider claims that were not properly raised in state court if the reason for the default was counsel's ignorance or neglect and that a prisoner should be permitted to file a second or successive federal petition if it raises a new claim that undermines confidence in his or her guilt or the appropriateness of the death sentence," the direction of legal change is, as I already have noted, in the opposite direction. Today courts in the United States are prepared to accept that some innocent people, or some defendants who do not deserve death, will be executed. As Justice Rehnquist observed in *Herrera v. Collins* (1993: 395), " 'due process does not require that every conceivable step be taken, at whatever cost, to eliminate the possibility of convicting an innocent person.' "

And, for Rehnquist, what is true in the general run of criminal cases is also true in death cases. If a few errors are made, a few innocent lives taken, that is simply the price of a system which is able to execute anyone at all. In Rehnquist's view, finality in capital cases is more important than an extended, and extremely frustrating, quest for justice. For him, and others like him, the apparent impotence of law, its inability to turn death sentences into executions, is more threatening to its legitimacy than a few erroneous, undeserved deaths at the hands of the state.

Here again, what the A.B.A. (1997: 11) asks for, namely a restoration of some of the previously available habeas remedies, is theoretically conceivable. Yet, like efforts to improve the quality of defense counsel in capital cases, it is hardly a likely or near-term possibility.

The third reason for the A.B.A.'s call for a moratorium is found in the "long-standing patterns of racial discrimination ... in courts around the country" (1997: 12). The A.B.A. report (1997: 13) cites research showing that defendants are more likely to receive a death sentence if their victim is white rather than black, and that in some jurisdictions African Americans tend to receive the death penalty more than white defendants do. The report (1997: 14) calls for the development of "effective mechanisms" to eliminate racial prejudice in capital cases, yet does not identify what such mechanisms would be. Indeed, it is not clear that there are any such mechanisms.[12]

In its 1997 call for a moratorium on executions, the A.B.A. sought to defend the state's investment in legality as a form of symbolic capital. It contested the state's apparent disinvestment in law as symbol as well as the substantive changes in the law governing the death penalty. The A.B.A. sought to advance and defend a particular conception of the relation of law and the state in which cause lawyering plays a key part. As significant sectors of the American state moved to reorient their investment in law, to redefine the legal guarantees and protections afforded capital defendants, the organized bar's generic interest in due process and equal protection intersected with the political commitments of lawyers working to end capital punishment.[13] As a result, it allied itself, however temporarily, with those cause lawyers who dedicate themselves to the abolition of capital punishment.

In an effort to understand the origins and politics of the alliance of the A.B.A. and the death penalty bar against the state and the implications of the alliance with the A.B.A. for cause lawyers, I conducted interviews with fifteen of the people who played key roles in the process which eventuated in the 1997 call for a moratorium and with ten death penalty lawyers.[14] I asked each of those interviewed to tell me about the origins and history of the moratorium resolution, to explain their role in the process, to talk about why in their view the A.B.A. took the position it did, and to assess its costs and benefits for both cause lawyers and the A.B.A.

Origins

The initiative for the moratorium resolution came from the A.B.A.'s Section on Individual Rights and Responsibilities and its committee on the death penalty, a group within the organized bar noted for its political liberalism and long-time activism on death penalty issues (Coleman, 1998: 1). Explaining the process within this section that led to the proposal for a moratorium, one former member of that committee told me,

> The death penalty committee originated the idea for this resolution. We ultimately obtained co-sponsorship from other entities within the A.B.A., including the litigation section which I think is the single largest section. At the point we brought this up, our committee had for many years been involved along with other parts of the individual rights section and other sections of the ABA, in working on a variety of death penalty related issues. Our section created the death penalty representation project as a result of which many lawyers and firms have provided pro bono representation of death row inmates. We were very active in trying to preserve and protect the writ of habeas corpus. We were very active in lobbying against the Anti-Terrorism bill. And, we have been vigilant about the need for competent counsel in death penalty cases. The A.B.A. death penalty representation project was initially instrumental in helping to persuade the Administrative Office of the Courts and Congress to create death penalty resource centers which were providing representation for people in post-conviction and habeas proceedings.

Another member of the Section on Individual Rights and Responsibilities, discussing why that section began to think about a resolution calling for a moratorium on capital punishment, pointed to the significance of

> two things that happened almost simultaneously in 1996. One was the so called Anti-Terrorism and Effective Death Penalty Act. This legislation badly undercuts the effectiveness of habeas corpus. It enshrined some of the worst Supreme Court decisions that prevent people who have meritorious constitutional claims, from getting anybody to rule on the merits. Many lawyers representing people on death row had been warning about the consequences of those decisions and suddenly they looked like prophets rather than prophets of doom. Instead of adopting the policies proposed by the A.B.A. to make sure that everyone has a good shot at having their claims heard, they were going in totally the opposite direction. And, if that were not enough the Republicans pushed through a defunding of the resource centers. So that led us, after those two things happened, to begin considering a moratorium on executions until and unless all the specified A.B.A. policies are carried out.

As another early proponent of the resolution said,

> There was this terrible sense that things were going backwards, you know, this sense that we were losing an enormous amount of ground with the curtailment of habeas and the loss of the resource centers. The number of executions was increasing and you didn't have to be a particularly ardent opponent of capital punishment to see that a lot was at stake. The conservatives were willing to trash what seemed to many of us to be minimum guarantees of due process just to get on with the business of executing people.

These respondents make clear that the A.B.A. acted in response to a shift in state policies. The A.B.A. responded in a defensive manner to what some of its members saw as a dramatic disinvestment in the minimum requirements of legality. Particularly important in this regard were the ending of federal funds for the so called Post-Conviction Defender Organizations, which "not only provided post-conviction representation in capital cases, but also recruited, trained, and supported volunteer lawyers in such cases" (Coleman, 1998: 3). Second was the passage of the Anti-Terrorism and Effective Death Penalty Act that "makes it extremely difficult to obtain review of even meritorious claims in successive or successor petitions and purports to bar federal courts from correcting certain erroneous constitutional rulings by state courts" (Coleman, 1998: 3–4).

What some perceived as the suddenness and radicalness of the shift in the state's symbolic capital away from law embodied in these two acts precipitated an alliance between the organized bar and anti–death penalty lawyers in which cause lawyers could assume the position of legal conservatives rather than political radicals. And, in fact, some of those responsible for proposing the moratorium resolution noted that leaders of the death penalty bar had played a key role in devising both the idea for the moratorium and the strategy for advancing it within the A.B.A. As one person put it,

> We worked pretty closely with the key people whose day to day work involves representing people on death row. That shouldn't be surprising. They have the greatest working knowledge of what the real problems are. I think many people in the A.B.A. would never have thought that they would be in a political alliance with the Steve Brights, Bryan Stevensons, and George Kendalls, but, as they say, politics makes strange bedfellows. In comparison with what the Republicans in Congress and the conservatives on the Supreme Court were doing, those guys looked positively reasonable.

Reactions within the Death Penalty Bar

Yet within the death penalty bar itself the A.B.A. resolution proved to be quite controversial, dividing lawyers between those who, on the one hand, were looking for some short-term vindication and certification of respectability and, on the other, those with a more politically radical and socially transformative vision of their work. As one in the first camp noted,

> The A.B.A. has done a lot on the death penalty. The moratorium seemed like a natural extension of that work in the face of changing political realities. While some people see it as a mixed blessing, I think that there is no real down side. What do we have to lose when a group like the A.B.A. agrees with things we have been saying for years? Sure, we could still be rattling the cage about how capital punishment is cruel and unusual, but nobody has paid any attention to that talk for a long time. But realistically the A.B.A. gave us a bit of political cover which is pretty hard to come by in this line of work.

Other death penalty lawyers felt that the A.B.A. resolution was an important complement to their own effort to speak to history by recording present injustices in the administration of capital punishment (Sarat, 1998a). As one former resource center lawyer put it, again stressing the theme of vindication,

> I told you the last time we talked that what sustains many of us is the belief that our work is speaking to the future, that we are making a record for history, telling stories about poverty, abuse, and injustice. The moratorium resolution helps in a sense to certify that record. It is as if a semi-official body read the stories that we have been telling and said "Sure, we get it. Executing juveniles, the retarded, blacks, denying them lawyers, and cutting back on habeas, this is an America that we do not want. It is not the best in us." And, those of us on the front-line doing this work, well, that's our message. So maybe what the A.B.A. did will help tell the story.

However, others in the death penalty bar were more dubious about the benefit of the A.B.A.'s support, more concerned about the costs of this alliance. One expressed her doubt by pointing to social stratification among death penalty lawyers, differentiating the reactions of the more prominent, politically well-connected members from those involved solely in the day-to-day tasks of representing people on death row.

> Well, I guess if you have been around a while, and if you spend some of your time appearing on television or testifying before Congress, what the A.B.A. thinks or what it says might matter. But from where I sit, no TV cameras and no Congressmen, just trying to save lives and stop the killing, that all seems like a big distraction. I mean who cares. It is sort of like the Pope issuing declarations telling people what he thinks good Catholics ought to do. Well, people just do what they are going to do whatever the Pope says. Who cares about the A.B.A? They been saying stuff about the death penalty for years and no one pays attention. I guess it makes them feel good to come out in favor of justice and maybe there is some grand strategy here, but I don't see it.

Still others believe that the A.B.A. resolution might actually be counterproductive, that it might serve to sustain the death penalty by laying out the terms on which execution could be reformed rather than ended.

> I wish they had said nothing. What did they do exactly? They didn't call for an end to the death penalty. They didn't say that it was cruel and unusual punishment. They didn't point out that we are a laughing stock, that no other so called 'civilized' country still kills its own citizens. They did nothing of the sort. What they said may just keep the illusion alive that we can reform the death penalty. Like Clinton said about affirmative action, 'Mend it don't end it.' So I just don't see what all the hoopla is all about. Call me when the A.B.A. says that the death penalty has to be ended, because it and this society is about racism, poverty, class, abuse. I don't want to be talking petty legalisms. I want to be talking about changing this country.

Several of those with whom I spoke, both inside the A.B.A. and within the death penalty bar, saw the resolution as part of a struggle in which what the A.B.A. was trying to do was to change the subject from the death penalty, with its hotly contested political overtones, to the rule of law, a matter on which lawyers might claim a particular expertise, from the rights of murderers to the defense of due process and equal protection of the law. The particular target audience in this effort was the media and through the media legislators and judges. The hope was that the A.B.A.'s action, because it would seem unexpected, would be newsworthy. "The struggle was for the symbolic high ground," a leader in the effort to call for a moratorium argued.

> The reason that we choose to do it this way (pass a moratorium resolution) was that we were quite frankly furious at the reportage or rater the lack of reportage. When the resource centers were de-funded and even more when habeas was under attack, the little reporting that there was portrayed all that as a way of eliminating frivolous appeals in death penalty cases. It was as if the only thing at stake was the rights of a few of America's most despicable people. When in reality there was no need to do anything about the so called frivolous appeals. What was being done was preventing people from getting relief on what were non-frivolous appeals. Getting executions seemed more important than respecting the law. That is what would get people re-elected, showing how tough they were. We wanted to put the spotlight on what was actually happening and to remind people that everyone has a stake in the rule of law. We wanted to say that whatever one may think about the death penalty, we should all agree that the kind of system that is actually being carried out is unacceptable. I am convinced that if that was gotten across to the American people, they would say one of two things. Either correct these problems so we have a death penalty that comports with due process or let's not have it. The people would see that the attack on the resource centers and on habeas was an attack on law. If they could get away with it in the context of the death penalty, then maybe they would think they could get away with it elsewhere. Our

goal was to do something that would catch the press's attention and that would be reported.

The A.B.A. acted to try to shift the terrain of engagement, to move the public discourse into a domain in which the state's disinvestment in legality in the context of the death penalty might become a rallying point for a coalition of people united, despite differences over the morality of capital punishment, in defense of the rule of law.

Some of the cause lawyers fighting the death penalty were only too happy to support this strategy (Sarat, 1998b); others were not. For the former, the effort to end capital punishment meant taking on different issues. It could succeed, in their view, only if abolitionists could make politicians and the public believe that continuing to execute people would do damage to things in which the American mainstream was already deeply invested. For the latter, the rule of law was not the issue. For them lawyering against the death penalty was a type of political and social, as much as legal, activism. They worried that the A.B.A. resolution ignored the underlying political and social issues of which capital punishment was simply a symptom.

Politics versus Professional Expertise

And indeed it was this separation of legal reform and political and social activism that was critical in the struggle within the A.B.A. over the moratorium resolution. Leaders of the moratorium effort believed that in order to have any chance of successfully participating in the struggle for symbolic capital, the organized bar would have to show that its interests were professional, not partisan. In passing the resolution, the A.B.A. was acknowledging that "many of its former proposed reforms have been rejected directly or resisted actively by the courts, state legislatures, or Congress, but the A.B.A. means to denounce that opposition" (Bilionis, 1998: 42). In so doing the bar would have to marshal its own symbolic capital while avoiding the perception that it was acting out of ordinary political motives.

This effort was complicated by the fact that the Section on Individual Rights and Responsibilities is itself widely known within the bar for its leftish political views and for its activism on death penalty issues. As a result, some within the A.B.A. initially regarded the proposed resolution with suspicion. One leader of another section of the A.B.A. explained that:

> The resolution came out of the Section on Individual Rights and Responsibilities. It was a political resolution reflecting the fact that IRR Is filled with people who are anti-death penalty activists. They're nuts over there. I mean they are all insane. The most conservative one over there would make Al Sharpton look like a moderate liberal. They are all known as flame throwers over there. And I am sure that

people in IRR worked hand-in-hand with abolitionist lawyers to figure out a way to put the A.B.A. on the record as favoring abolition. It would have been a major coup for them, but it would have been an absolute disaster for the Association.

Or, as a member of the Section on Individual Rights and Responsibilities put it,

> It shouldn't be surprising that we took the lead on this [the resolution]. For a long time our section has taken a leadership role on death penalty issues. As a result, we knew that some folks would look twice when we floated the idea for a moratorium. They would think, "Here we go again, first abortion, now the death penalty. Next they'll ask us to retroactively endorse McGovern for President."

For most of the leaders of the A.B.A. with whom I spoke, support for the moratorium resolution depended precisely on their ability to maintain a distinction between what they saw as political activity and what they saw as their distinctive professional expertise. As one explained,

> The resolution came out of IRR as a political resolution. We said that we wouldn't support anything like that. We were willing to support it as a professional resolution, which was simply to say that we the A.B.A. having set down what we think are fair and important procedures that ought to be in place before the death penalty is carried out want to see those procedures respected.

Another told me,

> I know that it is hard to separate politics from this, but what we are talking about are legal procedures to ensure that before the ultimate penalty is exacted somebody is treated fairly. And that's something which I don't think a professional organization can walk away from. Now, you know, it may be that others won't understand, but I think it is most appropriate that a professional organization that deals with legal procedures and having established what it thought fair procedures were, we had to take a stand.

Still another said,

> I cannot imagine an issue on which the A.B.A. could have better standing. Who is it other than lawyers who are dealing with the legal system all the time, who is more qualified to talk about legal procedures? We were moving from a position of strength in an area where we have great expertise and ought to have great credibility.

A fourth differentiated the death penalty moratorium resolution from the A.B.A.'s prior stand in favor of abortion.

> Some people tried to say that this resolution was just like the resolution on abortion. But I think that they were wrong. The moratorium was germane to the concerns of an organization of lawyers in a way that the abortion resolution was not. It spoke directly to issues of jurisprudence and some very technical matters

having to do with the delivery of legal services and rights to appeal. Abortion, sure it's about the constitution, but with the moratorium we are dealing with matters in which lawyers have special professional expertise.

Not surprisingly, those who opposed the resolution did so by claiming that its purpose was political and that the A.B.A. had no distinctive expertise to offer on the issue of capital punishment.

> The issue here was that, try as they might, they couldn't disguise the partisan, political motivation of the moratorium. Even the word "moratorium" has a sixtyish, left ring to it. It was a kind of back door abolitionism. That is what it was about. What business is it of the A.B.A. as an organization to be taking stands on the most contentious issues in the political debate. And, it was sure to backfire, damaging further our credibility on a whole range of issues. If the A.B.A. as an organization is in favor of abortion and against the death penalty why should anyone listen when we claim to have nonpartisan expertise on judicial appointments or legal services for the poor.

Or, as the then president of the A.B.A., Lee Cooper, put it in his remarks to the A.B.A.'s House of Delegates,

> I rise to speak in opposition..., What you really have here is a vote up or down on the death penalty. Folks, bring it in the front door, don't try to get in the back door. Come on in and put it up or down, death penalty, no death penalty. I support constitutional rights,... But what we're really doing here is voting up or down on the death penalty,... The department of Justice thinks it's a bad idea. The White House thinks it's a bad idea. In my opinion our membership would think it's a bad idea,... It is a wolf in sheep's clothing. The wolf is total opposition to the death penalty. The sheep's clothing is couched in constitutional rights.... We should not get out of step with the White House, the Justice Department, the nation, and our membership.

Despite President Cooper's opposition, the House of Delegates voted 270 to 119 in favor of the resolution calling for a moratorium on executions in the United States.

Whatever their differences about the merits of the moratorium resolution, both proponents and opponents of the moratorium resolution agreed that the possibility and propriety of the A.B.A's intervention in the struggle to influence where the state invested its symbolic capital depended on the A.B.A. using its own symbolic capital wisely. That the A.B.A. intervened as it did, that it allied itself with a small group of cause lawyers adamantly opposed to capital punishment, resulted from the conjunction of two things, first the apparent decision by the Congress of the United States, certain justices of the Supreme Court, and certain members of the political class at both the state and federal level to disinvest in policies and symbols which in their view were associated with a growing crisis of capacity and legitimacy, and, second, the ability of abolitionists and their allies in the A.B.A. to cast the vote on the moratorium resolution in the language of what Halliday (1987: 368) calls "civic professionalism."[15]

Civic professionalism refers to the ability of an established profession to "mobilize its ... expertise and bring its associational influence not at the individual but at the *collective* level to the service of state power"[16] (Halliday 1987: 368), In the domain of civic professionalism, Halliday (1987: 356) correctly observes that "lawyers have a distinctive relation to the state because at once they stand astride the public-private boundary of the state and have a normative epistemology. Taken alone, each attribute offers considerable leverage; taken together, the mandate for influence is unparalleled among professions in scope if not intensity."

Through its moratorium resolution, the A.B.A. tried to use its leverage to persuade officials in the Congress, the courts, and the states that they had made a large mistake in throwing away the symbolic capital provided by the resource centers and the lawyers who defended persons on death row, a mistake that is, for the foreseeable future, irreparable. Taking its recommendation and report seriously reminds us that the post-*Furman* effort to rationalize death sentences has utterly failed; it has been replaced by a policy that favors execution while trimming away procedural protection for capital defendants. This legal situation only exacerbates the incompatibility of capital punishment and legality. While the neoliberal state invests in free markets and in a tough-on-crime politics that links economic progress to personal security, the A.B.A., following Justice Blackmun, has embraced abolition as a form of legal conservatism, eschewing a direct address to the violence of law and relying instead on an indirect, though nonetheless, devastating critique.

Conclusion

That the organized bar took up the defense of cause lawyers exemplifies the commitment of lawyers in the United States to a particular vision of the liberal state. Central to this vision is the separation of law from politics, the commitment not to sacrifice essential legal values for political ends (Halliday and Karpik, 1997). Yet the passage of a moratorium resolution concerning capital punishment could not help but push the A.B.A. to, if not beyond, the limits of its claim to both technical and moral authority. Here is one instance in which "technical issues become political issues. [And] professionals become public moralists" (Halliday, 1987: 39). When this occurs, when the symbolic capital of the organized bar is most in question, the leverage of civic professionalism in the struggle over the state's deployment of its symbolic capital would seem to be most attenuated.[17] Thus the alliance of the A.B.A. and cause lawyers fighting the death penalty would itself seem to be a fragile and unstable one, beneficial to the latter in shoring up its morale and providing some important political resources, beneficial to the former in asserting the political claims of professional authority.

But, despite these benefits, this alliance was not without its potential costs. From the perspective of the A.B.A. the most significant of those costs might be a further diminution of its claims to authority based solely on technical expertise; from the perspective of the death penalty bar, the cost of its alliance with the A.B.A. is a possible erosion in its commitment to political and social transformation as well as a deepening of fissures among its members.

The A.B.A.'s embrace of the cause of cause lawyering in the context of capital punishment reveals the role that cause lawyers may play in legitimating liberal legality precisely by vigorously challenging particular state policies. In this embrace, and in others like it, the organized bar seeks to extend and alter the time horizon of the state beyond the immediate push to satisfy politically noisy constituencies, to redirect it to attend to the continuing need to live up to, or at least to appear to live up to, the central promises of liberal legalism (see Sarat, 1998a). The A.B.A.'s response to the defunding of death penalty resource centers and the attack on habeas corpus reveals a persistent, unallieviated anxiety about the uses and disposition not only of its own symbolic capital, but also that of the state, an anxious insistence that law, though it comes into the world born of physical violence, or the violent disruptions of the existing order of things, transcend the violence of its origins. For the A.B.A., the rejection of the death penalty takes the form of an effort to prevent the erosion of the boundaries between law's violence and its extralegal counterpart. Fairness, due process, equal protection, values vigorously defended by the anti–death penalty bar, help solidify that boundary. Attacking lawyers serving persons on death row, the A.B.A. seemed to say, may look good in the short run but will, over time, be counterproductive by introducing new questions about the difference between law's violence and violence outside the law.

Thus, the organized bar's defense of cause lawyers is, in this instance, equated with a defense of law itself.[18] When pressures in the political process are such that the forms of legal procedure and legal representation cannot contain and control any particular form of legal violence, that particular violence must be rejected so that law itself can survive. When pressures in the political process are such that the state seems to be disinvesting its symbolic capital in certain understandings of legality, the bar may use its symbolic capital in ways that support cause lawyers and cause lawyering, even when those lawyers work for causes as politically unpopular as the abolition of the death penalty is in the United States. Cause lawyering is, as the A.B.A. sees it, essential both in the struggle over where and how the neoliberal state's symbolic capital will be invested and in the reproduction of liberal legality itself.

Acknowledgments

I am grateful to the participants in the conference on Cause Lawyering and the State in a Global Era, Bellagio, Italy, June 21–25, 1999, for their helpful comments on an earlier version of this paper.

Notes

1. Among the groups engaged in this competition are the learned professions. While professions are created by states, the state needs professions for the expertise they provide and for their ideological commitments to disinterested service (Halliday, 1987). Thus professions, including the legal profession, have important leverage in the struggle for the state's symbolic capital.

2. Thus in the 1992 campaign Bill Clinton showed he was a different kind of Democrat through his visible support of the death penalty and his use of it while governor of Arkansas (Frady, 1993).

3. Connolly (1998: 198) argues that "the globalization of economic life compromises the nation-state as the highest site of citizen sovereignty.... The globalization of economic life deflates the experience of a sovereign, democratic state by imposing a variety of visible effects upon it that the state is compelled to adjust to.... Perhaps the state will restore its image as a site of effective accountability if it displays awesome power in the single domain everyone cedes to it as its own: criminal punishment."

4. Beneath the headline "After Night of Court Battles, a California Execution" the April 22, 1992, edition of the *New York Times* reported the tangled maze of last-minute legal maneuvers that immediately preceded the death in California's gas chamber of Robert Alton Harris, the 169th person to be executed since the Supreme Court restored capital punishment in 1976. As in many previous executions, the hope for clemency or the possibility of a stay of execution was in Harris's case pursued until the last minute.

5. The court scolded Harris's lawyers for "abusive delay which has been compounded by last minute attempts to manipulate the judicial process" (*New York Times*, April 22, 1992, p. 22). In so doing, it displaced Harris as the soon-to-be victim of law, and portrayed law itself as the victim of Harris and his manipulative lawyers. To defend the virtue of law required an assertion of the court's supremacy against both the vexatious sympathies of other courts and the efforts of Harris and his lawyers to keep alive a dialogue about death.

6. As Dumm (1990: 54) puts it, "In the face of the law that makes people persons, people need to fear. Yet people also need law to protect them.... Hence fear is a political value that is valuable because it is critical of value, a way of establishing difference that enables uncertainty in the face of danger."

7. For a description of the attitudes of the death penalty bar toward the new abolitionism, see Sarat, 1998b.

8. See Pub. L. No. 104–134, 110 Stat. 1321, 1321–34 (1996).

9. See Pub. L. No. 104–132, §§101–108, 110 Stat. 1214, 1217–26 (codified at 28 U.S.C. §§2244–2266 Supp. II 1996).

10. As Bilionois (1998: 30–31) notes, "Hard-and-fast moral opponents of capital punishment might well bristle at some of the particulars of the ABA resolution. By bracketing the question of the death penalty's general propriety, and by intimating that it is possible to run a fair and just death penalty system provided that enough good lawyers and process are thrown at the problem, the ABA evidences an agnosticism that can frustrate those who find state-imposed premeditated killing reprehensible."

11. It is responding to a deeply felt anxiety about the capacity of the state to differentiate its violence from extralegal violence. This anxiety arises because violence, as both a linguistic and physical phenomenon, as fact and metaphor, is integral to the constitution of modern law. As Cover (1986:1602) argues, "[L]egal interpretation is a practice incomplete without violence...." Modern law is built on representations of aggression, force, and disruption lurking just beyond law's boundaries. In large measure, law seeks to authorize and legitimate its bloodletting as a lesser or necessary evil and as a response to our inability to live a truly free life without external discipline and restraint. Yet the proximity of law to, and its dependence on, violence raises a nagging question and a persistent doubt about whether law can ever be more than violence or whether law's violence is truly different from, and superior to, what lurks beyond its boundaries.

12. The pernicious effects of race in capital sentencing are a function of the pervasiveness of racial prejudice throughout the society combined with the wide degree of discretion necessary to afford individualized justice in capital prosecutions and capital trials. Prosecutors with limited resources may be inclined to allocate resources to cases that attract the greatest public attention, which often will mean cases where the victim was white and his/her assailant black. Participants in the legal system—whether white or black—may demonize young black males, seeing them as more deserving of death as a punishment because of their perceived dangerousness. These cultural effects clearly are not remediable. As Blackmun noted in *Callins* (1994: 1157), "[W]e may not be capable of devising procedural or substantive rules to prevent the more subtle and often unconscious forms of racism from creeping into the system.... [D]iscrimination and arbitrariness could not be purged from the administration of capital punishment without sacrificing the equally essential component of fairness-individualized sentencing."

13. Moreover, these concerns for fairness and for equality provide an opening wedge for the globalization of the struggle against capital punishment in the United States. They connect the struggles of the anti–death penalty bar to the broader agenda of human rights and lay the basis for the development of a postcolonial turn in human rights politics, in which arguments deployed by metropolitan nations against the periphery are increasing applied to the metropolitan nations themselves.

14. Each interview was conducted by phone. They lasted on average ninety minutes. Respondents in the A.B.A. were identified by using a snowball sampling technique. Respondents among the death penalty bar were drawn from an earlier sample (see Sarat, 1998a).

15. Halliday's (1987: 368) "civic professionalism" bears a close relationship to Bordieu's (1977) "symbolic capital." It provides a crucial resource for lawyers to use as they engage in political struggles or efforts to build or reform political and legal institutions.

16. Elsewhere Halliday (1999: 18) has defined civic professionalism as the "ability to exercise moral authority in the name of expertise."

17. Halliday (1999: 19) identifies "three contingencies for lawyers' capacity to translate technical expertise into moral authority[:] (1) issues themselves must *not* be highly politicized.... (2) the profession itself must be able to present a relatively unified voice.... And (3), the exercise of moral authority in the name of expert, technical advice works best when it is out of the public glare." In the context of the A.B.A.'s moratorium resolution, the first and third of those conditions would appear not to be satisfied.

18. For a similar discussion in another context, see Shamir, 1995.

References

Aladjem, Terry (1992). "Vengeance and Democratic Justice: American Culture and the Limits of Punishment," unpublished manuscript.

American Bar Association (1997). "Resolution of the House of Delegates" and "Report Accompanying Resolution" (February 3).
Amsterdam, Anthony (1998). "Selling a Quick Fix for Boot Hill: The Myth of Justice Delayed in Death Cases," in *The Killing State: Capital Punishment in Law, Politics, and Culture*, Austin Sarat, ed. New York: Oxford University Press.
Anti-Terrorism and Effective Death Penalty Act (1996). Pub. L. No. 104–132, 110 Stat. 1214.
Beckett, Katherine (1997). *Making Crime Pay: Law and Order in Contemporary American Politics*. New York: Oxford University Press.
Bedau, Hugo Adam (1992). "The Eighth Amendment, Human Dignity, and the Death Penalty," in *The Constitution of Rights: Human Dignity and American Values*, Michael Meyer and William Parent, eds. Ithaca, N.Y.: Cornell University Press.
———(1998). "Abolishing the Death Penalty Even for the Worst Murderers," in *The Killing State: Capital Punishment in Law, Politics, and Culture*, Austin Sarat, ed. New York: Oxford University Press.
Berkman, Harvey (1995). "Costs Mount for Indigent Defense,' *National Law Journal* (August 7), A18.
Bilionis, Louis (1998). "Eighth Amendment Meanings from the ABA's Moratorium Resolution," 61 *Law and Contemporary Problems*, 29.
Boon, Andrew (1999). "Pro-Bono and the Crisis of the Neo-Liberal State: A European Perspective," unpublished essay.
Bourdieu, Pierre (1977). *Outline of a Theory of Practice*. Cambridge: Cambridge University Press.
———(1987). "The Force of Law: Toward a Sociology of the Juridical Field," 38 *Hastings Law Journal*, 805.
——— (1991). *Language and Symbolic Power*. London. Polity Press.
Boyer, Robert, and Daniel Drache, eds. (1996). *States Against Markets: The Limits of Globalization*. London and New York: Routledge, 1996.
Bright, Stephen (1995). "Counsel for the Poor; The Death Sentence Not for the Worst Criminal but for the Worst Lawyer," 103 *Yale Law Journal*, 1832.
Camiker, Evan, and Erwin Chemerinsky, (1992). "The Lawless Execution of Robert Alton Harris," 102 *Yale Law Journal*, 2225.
Coleman, James (1998). "Forward: The ABA's Proposed Moratorium on the Death Penalty," 61 *Law and Contemporary Problems*, 1.
Connolly, William (1998). "The Will, Capital Punishment, and Culture Wars," in *The Killing State: Capital Punishment in Law, Politics, and Culture*, Austin Sarat, ed. New York: Oxford University Press.
Cover, Robert (1986). "Violence and the Word," *Yale Law Journal*, 1601.
Dumm, Thomas (1990). "Fear of Law," 10 *Studies in Law, Politics and Society*, 29.
Edelman, Murray (1964). *The Symbolic Uses of Politics*. Urbana: University of Illinois Press.
———(1971). *Politics as Symbolic Action: Mass Arousal and Quiescence*. Chicago: Markham Publishing.
———(1988). *Constructing the Political Spectacle*. Chicago: University of Chicago Press.
Foucault, Michel (1979). *Discipline and Punish: The Birth of the Prison*. Alan Sheridan, trans. New York: Vintage Books.
Frady, Marshall (1993). "Death in Arkansas," *The New Yorker* (February 22, 1993), 105.
Furman v. Georgia (1972). 408 U.S. 238.
Gordon, Robert (1984). "Critical Legal Histories," 36 *Stanford Law Review*, 57.
Gregg v. Georgia (1976). 428 U.S. 238.
Gross, Samuel (1993). "The Romance of Revenge: Capital Punishment in America," 13 *Studies in Law, Politics and Society*, 71.

Habermas, Jurgen (1986). "The New Obscurity: The Crisis of the Welfare State and the Exhaustion of Utopian Energies," 11 *Philosophy and Social Criticism*, 1.

Halliday, Terrence (1987). *Beyond Monopoly: Lawyers, State Crises, and Professional Empowerment*. Chicago: University of Chicago Press.

———(1999). "Politics and Civic Professionalism: Legal Elites and Cause Lawyers," 24 *Law and Social Inquiry*, 1013.

Halliday, Terrence, and Lucien Karpik (1997). "Politics Matter: A Comparative Theory of Lawyers in the Making of Political Liberalism," in *Lawyers and the Rise of Western Political Liberalism: Europe and North America from the Eighteenth to Twentieth Centuries*, Terence Halliday and Lucien Karpik, eds. Oxford: Clarendon Press.

Hay, Douglas (1975). "Property, Authority, and the Criminal Law," in *Albion's Fatal Tree: Crime and Society in Eighteenth-Century England*. Douglas Hay, et al., eds. New York: Pantheon.

Herrera v. Collins (1993). 506 US 390.

Kateb, George (1992). *The Inner Ocean: Individualism and Democratic Culture*. Ithaca: Cornell University Press.

Lacayo, Richard (1992). "You Don't Always Get Perry Mason," *Time*, June 1, 38.

Minow, Martha (1996). "Political Lawyering: An Introduction," 31 *Harvard Civil Rights-Civil Liberties Law Review*, 287.

O'Brien, Sean (1990). "A Step Toward Fairness in Capital Litigation: Missouri Resource Center," 16 *William Mitchell Law Review*, 633.

Offe, Claus (1996). *Modernity and the State: East, West*. Cambridge, Mass.: MIT Press, 1996.

Reinhardt, Stephen (1992). "The Supreme Court, The Death Penalty, and the *Harris* Case," 102 *Yale Law Journal*, 205.

Ruthenbeck, Arthur (1989). "Dueling with Death in Federal Courts," 3 *Criminal Justice*, 3.

Sarat, Austin (1998a). "Between (the Presence of) Violence and (the Possibility of) Justice: Lawyering Against Capital Punishment," in *Cause Lawyering: Political Commitments and Professional Responsibilities*. New York: Oxford University Press.

———(1998b). "Recapturing the Spirit of *Furman*:The American Bar Association and the New Abolitionist Politics," 61 *Law and Contemporary Problems* (1998), 5.

———(1999). "Killing Me Softly: On the Technologies for Taking Life," in *Death and Dying*, Derek Manderson, ed. London: Pluto Press.

Sarat, Austin, and Stuart Scheingold (1998). "Cause Lawyering and the Reproduction of Professional Authority: An Introduction," in *Cause Lawyering: Political Commitments and Professional Responsibilities*. New York: Oxford University Press.

Scheingold, Stuart (1974). *The Politics of Rights: Lawyers, Public Policy, and Political Change*. New Haven, Conn.: Yale University Press.

——— (1998). "Criminology and the Politicization of Crime and Punishment," in *Politics, Crime Control, and Culture*, Gerald Mars and David Nelken, eds. Aldershot, Eng: Dartmouth/Ashgate.

Shamir, Ronen (1995). *Managing Legal Uncertainty: Elite Lawyers in the New Deal*. Durham, N.C.: Duke University Press.

Simon, Jonatan (1997). "Governing Through Crime," in *The Crime Conundrum: Essays on Criminal Justice*. Lawrence Friedman and George Fisher, eds. Boulder, Co.: Westview Press.

Steiner, Benjamin, William Bowers, and Austin Sarat (1999). "Folk Knowledge as Legal Action: Death Penalty Judgments and the Tenet of Early Release in a Culture of Mistrust and Punitiveness, 33 *Law & Society Review*, 461.

Steiker, Carol, and Jordan Steiker (1994). "Sober Second Thoughts: Reflection on Two De-

cades of Constitutional Regulation of Capital Punishment," 109 *Harvard Law Review*, 305.
Teague v. Lane (1989). 489 US 288.
Terdiman, Richard (1987). "Translator's Introduction for 'The Force of Law: Toward a Sociology of the Juridical Field,'" 38 *Hastings Law Journal*, 805.
Tonry, Michael (1995). *Malign Neglect: Race, Crime, and Punishment in America*. New York: Oxford University Press.
Williams, Raymond (1980). *Problems in Materialism and Culture: Selected Essays*. London: NLB.
Yackle, Larry (1996). "A Primer on the New Habeas Corpus Statute," 44 *Buffalo Law Review*, 381.
——— (1998). "The American Bar Association and Federal Habeas Corpus," 61 *Law and Contemporary Problems*, 171.
Zimring, Franklin (1998). "The Executioner's Dissonant Song: On Capital Punishment and American Values," in *The Killing State: Capital Punishment in Law, Politics, and Culture*, Austin Sarat, ed. New York: Oxford University Press.
Zimring, Franklin, and Gordon Hawkins (1986). *Capital Punishment and the American Agenda*. Cambridge: Cambridge University Press.

CHAPTER 8

Cause Lawyers, Clients, and the State
Congress as a Forum for Cause Lawyering during the Enactment of the Americans with Disabilities Act

NETA ZIV

Hanging on the wall in her office is a picture of attorney Chai Feldblum and Congressman Steny Hoyer, dedicated by Hoyer: "To Chai, my lawyer." Make no mistake. Feldblum had not been working for Congress at the time this picture was taken. She was the leading attorney representing the 29 million persons with disabilities in the United States during the congressional negotiations over the Americans with Disabilities Act of 1990. Still, as this legislative campaign ended with the successful enactment of one of America's most comprehensive civil rights laws, a member of the legislature felt comfortable enough to address the leading lawyer for the disability community, in a public gesture, as "his lawyer." This is not fortuitous. As I will suggest in this paper, legislative cause lawyering does not conform to the conventional individual-state paradigms to which cause lawyering is commonly ascribed. Lawyering on behalf of a socially and politically disadvantaged group within the legislature thus entails reexamining some of the basic relationships between lawyers and others who take part in the process in which politics emerge into law.

This essay focuses on cause lawyering in Congress. Its subject is the group of the lawyers who advocated on behalf of the disability community during the legislative proceedings of the Americans with Disabilities Act (ADA) between 1988 and 1990. Examination of the attributes of cause lawyering within a political institution—namely, Congress—offers an opportunity to reconsider established understandings about legal professionalism and the state. As depicted in this essay, lawyering for legislative reform on behalf of a politically and socially disempowered group does not adhere to the conventional model of client-lawyer-state that seems dominant in cause-lawyering research. Under this dominant framework, lawyers, and particularly cause lawyers, utilize their expert knowledge to protect underrepresented individuals or groups against state abuse or neglect. The interests of the client appear determinable, and the state is treated as a unified institution whose interests are also more or less identifiable. The role of the lawyers is to mediate between the citizenry and the state.

Lobbying and lawyering for legislative reform on behalf of socially and politically disadvantaged groups—a growing phenomenon in the last decade (Aron, 1989: 87–90)—can offer a different view of state politics. We can no longer understand politics as being formed exclusively within the domain of classic political institutions. Rather, as stated by Beck, change occurs as politics from below—social movements, environmental groups, local communities, citizens' interest associations—mobilize to create new forces that in and of themselves are novel forms of politics (Beck, 1994 M: 22–23). These organisms of 'sub-politics' interact with the traditional political institutions, such as the legislature. The space within which such interaction takes place, with its variety of players, is the field of this paper's inquiry.

Congress, as a legislative body, is a central symbol of liberal democracy. Under the theory of liberal democracy, Congress is the institutional site where the aggregate wills and interests of citizens compete with other interests and are transformed into operative laws. Legislative lobbying, under this approach, is a mediating process in which the previously determined interests of the citizens are conveyed into the political domain and contend with other lobbying efforts for the most appropriate outcome. Liberal democratic theory thus assumes that citizens' interests are formulated and fixed before entering the political process and that Congress is a unified site of power in which these interests struggle to achieve recognition.

In this essay I try to fuse new ways of considering cause lawyering and new ways of thinking about politics with the relational model of democratic institutions. Instead of a narrow view of the institutional role of Congress, a relational view of democracy emphasizes the process under which interests of citizens are formed and constructed, both before and during legislative reform. According to this view, individual and group interests are not predetermined prior to their entry into the political course. Rather, they are formulated as the legislative initiative proceeds, through the constant interaction with other codeliberators who partake in this process. Within the institutional domain, the legislative process is thus reflexive: it affects and is affected by the constitution of dialogue and exchange of information between its participants. Political reflexivity occurs not only between individuals and groups that gain access to a political institution. It also takes place between the citizenry and those who make them up, such as members of Congress, their influential staff and aides, and people within the administration. In that sense, will configuration is an indeterminate and evolving process of all those involved in the formation of a policy and its translation into a binding law.

A political cause, the subject matter of a particular legislative campaign, also assumes a less definitive meaning. The "interest"—an abstract idea that leads groups to initiate a political move—breaks down into a series of dialogues, negotiations, and deliberations. Each one proceeds through the legislative process through the formation of diverse alliances and relations—within the social group acting for legislative reform, between the group and its representatives, between those representatives and key players in the state apparatus, and vice versa. This process decenters and redistributes political power. Political power shifts within state institutions—Congress for the purpose of this paper—and between Congress and citizenry, including the representatives that act on behalf of a particular group. Power, Handler explains, "then is not a 'thing,' rather it is 'a property of relations.' Networks of interests are constituted and reproduced through both conscious strategies and unwitting practices." Thus when we study [political] power we should look at the way "agents constitute interests, how they attempt to enroll others to their strategies" (Handler, 1996: 120).

Lawyering for a cause at the legislature can illustrate this understanding of distribution of political power. Cause lawyering overtly aims to change power disparities between social groups; public interest lawyers have been described as lawyers "whose work is directed at altering some aspect of the social, economic and/or political status quo" (Trubeck, 1996: 415, n.2). I suggest, moreover, that within the legislature cause lawyering underscores the indeterminate and relational aspects of political interests and of political choices. Within a legislative campaign, these shift constantly and are modified through the formation of contingent political, personal, and ad hoc alliances between the clients, their legal representatives, and those holding official elected positions within Congress, together with their political, legal, and administrative staff.

Forming alliances and relations between lawyers and the state is not only a matter of tactics or convenience, but it also extends to the essence of the legal professional act. In order to "come out ahead," legislative cause lawyers "must become embroiled in controversial issues of politics and public policy" (Sarat and Scheingold, 1998: 8). Lawyers' assertion that their clients hold "a right" to receive a certain benefit or gain will not suffice. If lawyers wish to enlist the support of members of Congress to a certain cause they must bear in mind the political considerations of those politicians. These oftentimes include the political worthiness of a specific legislative initiative for a particular member as well as the barriers the member is likely to encounter during the course of transforming a social interest into law. Lawyering for a cause under these circumstances frequently entails considering and suggesting possible financial resources to cover the costs of a new law or accepting trade-offs due to financial constraints. As long as lawyers and members of Congress carry a mutual interest to pass a law, lawyers cannot discount these aspects of legislative reform. This is not to say that lawyers are to provide solutions to questions of financing, but that in the course of negotiation they are expected to incorporate such political or economic considerations into their professional decision-making responsibilities. These have to be reconciled with their duties to continue and act "with zeal" (to use the term of conventional lawyering) on behalf of their client group and constituency.

In sum, cause lawyering in Congress transgresses common divisions between clients, lawyers, and the state. Legislative cause lawyering stands in contrast to the archetypal cause-lawyering model in which the state is the central source of abuse against individuals. It calls for a redefinition of "the clients" represented, blurs the division between the interests of the state and the citizen, and requires more complex relations with adversaries.

The study of cause lawyering has been conducted through two main avenues. The first inquired about the relationship between lawyers and their clients. Scholars were concerned with lawyers' excess control over social movements.[1] Public interest lawyers were challenged to develop less hierarchic relations with clients (Lopez, 1992 and 1996), to adopt a client-centered approach (Polikoff, 1996), and to share knowledge and power with them. Doubts were simultaneously raised whether such power sharing is indeed feasible, or at all desired (Simon, 1994). Public interest lawyers themselves have grown aware of the need to address more adequately existing controversies among client groups about the goals and means of a social-legal struggle (Rubenstein, 1997). A second area of research was devoted to the limitations of particular legal strategies, mainly litigation and rights discourse to bring about social change (Rosenberg, 1991; McCann, 1986). In this context lawyers were urged either to diversify their means beyond litigation or to adopt more radical styles of lawyering in an attempt to alter the legal system as it was being utilized (Gabel and Harris, 1983; Trubeck, 1996). However, only limited attention has been given to the "political work in law: relations with power holders" (Bellow, 1996). Establishing and maintaining relations with power holders, notes Gary Bellow—within the state as well as with adversaries—constitutes a central portion of cause lawyers' work and raises the most complex tensions (ibid.).

By examining the characteristics of cause lawyering during the ADA legislative proceedings, I wish to contribute to the study of this important style of legal professionalism in two ways. First, to expand the inquiry about the relationship between lawyers and clients into the legislative sphere, in particular representation of a diffuse and loose constituency, with attenuated accountability of the lawyers. Second, to explore how conflict and cooperation between lawyers and the state play out in cause lawyering for legislative reform. Situated amidst their client-constituencies and members of Congress, lawyers continuously manage the interplay between these parties.

The ADA Case Study

The ADA represents one possible model to portray the relations between cause lawyers, a disadvantaged social group, and the state. In some ways the dynamics of the ADA's legislation were distinct. The subject matter of the law—disability—is a cross-party issue, and it had generally enjoyed support from otherwise political opponents. In the ADA case, Democratic and Republican members of Congress and the Bush administration endorsed the bill. Even though traditional conservative-liberal cleavages do not always correspond with contemporary political struggles that often cut across accepted social and political divisions, minority-majority congressional politics still play an important role in the work of cause lawyers (Beck, 1994: 21). Enlisting the support of a Republican administration and Republican members of Congress placed the ADA advocates at a notable advantage. At the same time, the ADA was structured and portrayed by its advocates as a civil rights law aimed at extending principles already recognized in existing civil rights legislation to persons with disabilities. The 'civil rights nature' of the ADA tended to divide members of Congress along party lines. Indeed, when the business community had concerns over the bill's impact on its operations and costs, its representatives channeled them either through Republican members of Congress or the White House. Nonetheless, given the commitment of the Bush administration to the passage of the ADA and the general support from many Republicans in Congress, such divisions were often ad hoc and issue limited, and did not carry through the final voting on the bill.

The ADA was also unique in that its advocates managed to create an impressive structure that effectively mobilized numerous disability groups around the country when political necessity arose. Concomitantly the disability community maintained a strong lobbying and legal team in Washington, which lobbied Congress zealously for the bill's enactment. In fact, since the enactment of the ADA, it has been difficult to reproduce such an effective campaign on behalf of persons with disabilities.

Notwithstanding these particular qualities, the ADA legislative campaign can provide a useful paradigm to study the practice of cause lawyering. To begin with, it reaffirms the contextual and contingent nature of cause lawyering (as any other type of lawyering). Professional stances depend on the combination and interplay between variables such as the subject matter in question, the political and social circumstances in which lawyering occurs, its structural setting, the identity of the lawyers, and other key figures—that together form and shape this professional activity. Second, it exemplifies the flexible and indeterminate boundaries between clients, lawyers, and official agents of the state, and the relative powers vested in each. And finally, it illustrates how cause lawyers, as representatives of disadvantaged social groups and movements, can develop mechanisms that ameliorate imbalances between disadvantaged and privileged segments of society through mainstream political institutions.

One can remain skeptic about the potential of legislation to bring about actual progress in the lives of persons with disabilities. However, access to political institutions remains an essential course to obtain many desired policy changes. Private and corporate interests aided by their "power lawyers" have long been utilizing these channels to gain prevalence over powerless groups in influential juncture points.[2] Lawyers who represent politically disempowered groups are therefore utilizing similar strategies to rectify injustice on behalf of previously underrepresented people. In this respect, the ADA cause lawyers merged between the dynamics of social movements and the politics of the state. The path they paved through their professional activity—together with others—opened an opportunity for constant flow, input, and feedback of information, knowledge, and understanding between the disability community and Congress.

Legislative Cause Lawyering and Principles of Professionalism Role Morality, Partisanship, and Nonaccountability

The "Dominant View" of lawyering is based upon principles of role morality, partisanship and nonaccountability.[3] Oftentimes lawyering for the public interest does not adhere to these basic concepts and cause lawyering within the legislature even more so. In this section I will explicate the underlying reasons for this incoherence.

Cause Lawyering and the Theory of Role Morality, Partisanship, and Nonaccountability

The theory of role morality draws upon the distinction between common-universal morals and task morals attached to a person's role. In other words, a moral stand, which might not be acceptable in regular circumstances, can be justified because of the particular role one assumes. Accordingly, lawyers are allowed to ascertain a different set of moral obligations because their central duty is to represent other persons, and not their personal ideals or interests (Pepper, 1986; Fried, 1997). Since lawyers do not necessarily identify with the goals of their clients they are not held accountable to the outcome of their representation, and the principle of nonaccountability is considered a prevailing element of conventional legal professionalism. In order to maximize their role, lawyers are also expected to be partisan and act with ultimate professional zeal on behalf of their clients. The requirement of zealous representation is justified by the "adversary excuse" which assumes that the truth will be revealed if each party will assert its claims, and a neutral third party, usually a judge, will decide among the competing arguments.

Role morality, zeal, and nonaccountability are interconnected—the more detached the lawyer is from the ends of representation, the easier it is to justify partisan, zeal and role differentiation. Put differently, if a lawyer is *not* expected to maintain a detached and differentiated moral stand from her client, and if she does not perceive her role only to voice her client's interest (leaving the opponent's lawyer to do the same for her client), partisanship and nonaccountability become harder to justify. If this is so, a lawyer that takes into account other considerations that play a part in the total environment she works in does not act in a way that constitutes a threat to her professional identity. These "other" concerns may well be relationships that need to be maintained with power holders, or even some legitimate concerns of adversaries. Accordingly, identifying with the goals of representation and holding themselves accountable to its ends, a position carried by many public interest lawyers, can offer lawyers an alternative perspective of their professional duties.

The ADA advocates operated as lawyers in the basic sense that they represented an interest other than their own. But underlying this representative role and coloring its nature was the notion that is often (though not always) absent in conventional lawyer-client relationships—a personal commitment to the cause they were advocating for and responsibility for its end results. All ADA lawyers entered the legislative domain with a strong personal conviction toward the social and political ends of their representation and considered themselves personal stakeholders in its outcome. The inadequacies of the conventional paradigms of legal practice are exacerbated even more when we consider the attributes of cause lawyering for legislative reform in Congress.

The Legislative Process: Implications on Legal Ethics and Professionalism

Some of the basic concepts of conventional lawyering do not capture the nature of legislative lawyers.[4] The idea of *a client* to whom the lawyer owes her basic loyalty is prevalent in contemporary legal thought—the client usually presumed to be a person or an organization.[5] But many of the public interest lawyers who represented the disability community during the ADA proceedings had neither a person nor an organization as their client. It is questionable if they had a client at all.

Numerous ethical rules assume that lawyers operate in adversarial conditions or in settings that may become adversarial. Representing the interests of a group or constituency in the legislature often involves conflictual situations or adversarial positions, but by and large the legislature lacks the basic components of an adversarial system. The legislature has no mechanism to ensure the fairness of the proceedings, and there is no requirement that the participants observe certain rules designed to prevent an unjust advantage of one party over another. The process under which negotiation, lobbying, and decision making is conducted is not revealed to the public, including "the client." The official public hearings of committees and the plenary are of course well documented, publicized, and can be monitored, but often they are the outcome of lengthy back-and-forth negotiation, which occurs behind the scenes in an "ex-parte" mode. These discussions, informal meetings, and information dissemination cannot be monitored by the clients and are usually hidden from the public eye.

Legislative proceedings do not have the basic element of adjudication—an impartial figure who oversees the process vested with power to decide among competing arguments of facts and law. The legislative process is a political one, involving political parties and political representatives who are influenced by various considerations that seem irrelevant to the merits of the issue under debate. It is common and acknowledged that the "legal" argument will not necessarily form one's position, but rather political realities, and mainly their constraints. In contrast to adjudication, where the basic theoretical assumption is that if each party will assert its arguments zealously the process will yield the most just result (or the truth), this is not the legitimizing basis underlying the legislative political process. In this setting the "best" law is the consequence of the consideration and accommodation of competing interests, procured through negotiation and compromise. Legislation is not about adjudication of rights but primarily aims to alter policy, and the "truth" thus assumes a different meaning.

Passage of a law entails obtaining the sponsorship and continuous support of members of Congress. To begin with, lobbying for a bill requires one to enlist members of Congress to introduce it. As deliberations over the bill evolve, members who had taken the lead on a bill's passage constitute the connection between the legislature and the citizenry. Under these circumstances lawyers provide legal services not only to their clients and group constituencies, but also to "their members," who recurrently collaborate with the lawyers (and their clients) on the need to refute certain challenges that emanate against the bill. Due to this blend of personal convictions, long-and short-term political calculations, the lawyers, lobbyists, and members of Congress conduct back-and-forth polemic and discussions about topics that arise during the proceedings. But at the end of the day—or the session—it is up to the members of Congress to determine how far they are willing to carry on the struggle on a particular topic. For lawyers, accepting (and at times even empathizing with) the political limitations of a bill's sponsors is as necessary a professional virtue as the ability to provide legal analysis of the current state of the law.

Lawyering in Congress entails working with other public and private figures. To mention only a few, lawyers need to cooperate with lobbyists, interact with grassroots representatives, and operate with media personnel. Lobbyists, for example, play a vital role in the passage of a law. They gather, distribute, and hold information that is closely tied to a bill. Most of them are not lawyers and are not bound by any ethical rules that govern their professional conduct. At times the lawyers depend on the lobbyists for information, they share confidential sources with them, and their activity occasionally overlaps. But the boundaries between these two groups—one that acts within a tradition of professionalism and ethical rules and the other exempt from such constraints—are not clear at all.

To illustrate some of the differences between adjudication and litigation in the context of client representation, it is useful to compare a specific litigation strategy used for institutional reform—class action—to "institutional reform legislation" such as the ADA. Class action suits instigated under various civil rights laws (and under the U.S. Constitution) and group reform legislation raise similar dilemmas relating to intergroup conflicts. In both cases there is a diffuse and unidentifiable client group, and it is necessary to find a mechanism to voice dissenting views. In impact litigation and even more so in legislative reform, people may agree upon a common problem, but remedies may include complex forms of solutions, with a possible trade-off between subgroups within the broader constituency. In both cases the legitimacy of the process and the fact that future generations will be affected by a decision or law requires the input of as many points of view as possible along the way. In both procedures a few people are speaking on behalf of others: named plaintiffs and their lawyers in litigation, and grassroots representatives, lobbyists, and lawyers in legislation. The problems of addressing internal class conflicts in class action have been dealt with thoroughly (Rhode, 1982), and it seems that the existing procedures in class action litigation are not sufficient or not sufficiently used to meet them. Nonetheless, even the basic procedures that do exist in class action suits are lacking in legislation. No one inquires if the representatives that lobby for a law represent groups that have questions of law that are "common" to others not present during legislation, if their claims are "typical" of those not present in Congress and if they would "fairly and adequately protect the interests of the class", basic requirements in class certification.[6] The important juncture points of class certification, subclassification, or the right of notice afforded to class members before approving some settlements are absent from legislation. No figure fulfills the role of a judge who, though limited in many ways, has an important function in assuring that class members' interests are taken into account during the process. Members of Congress cannot be expected to assume this role, and adversaries are not positioned to do so, either. It will be highly unlikely that a dissenting member of a certain disability group will feel comfortable approaching the business community to protect her interests vis-à-vis the majority within disability groups.

Not only the procedural rules, but also the existing ethical rules do not reflect the reality of the legislative lawyer's work. The preamble of the Model Rules recognizes the important role lawyers maintain in "the preservation of society" and their special duties toward the legal system. The rules also acknowledges the possibility of lawyers' contribution to "reform of the law" through employment of legal knowledge, but they mention this duty in passing only, as part of the lawyer's role as "a public citizen."[7] As mentioned above, the basic theme of the Model Rules assumes the existence of an identifiable client and the establishment of a lawyer-client relationship: "Most of the duties flowing from the client-lawyer relationship attach only after the client has requested the lawyer to render legal services and the lawyer has agreed to do so."[8] As much as an organizational client is considered an exception to the rule, so is lawyering in nonadjudicative settings. There is one reference to these circumstances, the rule relating to "Advocacy in Non-adjudicative Proceedings,"[9] and it carries only general guidance regarding the required conduct of the lawyer. The rule obligates the lawyer to inform the tribunal of her representative capacity and to follow basic behavioral modes such as the duty to be truthful to the tribunal and fair to the opposing party. The rules do not relate to the complex functions of lawyers as drafters, negotiators, and representatives of broad nondefinable interests.

As will be presented ahead in detail, the function of many of the legislative public interest lawyers who represented the disability community during the ADA proceedings reached beyond this conventional notion expressed in the existing ethical rules. I will now turn to describe basic components of the ADA, and lay out the structure and setting in which the ADA lawyers operated.

The Americans with Disabilities Act and Its Lawyers

The Americans with Disabilities Act of 1990 is considered one of the most comprehensive pieces of civil rights legislation enacted in the last decade.[10] The ADA outlaws discrimination against persons with disabilities in private as well as public entities, and discrimination is defined in a broad way. For example, an employer's failure to provide reasonable accommodation for an employee's disability or a public service provider's failure to establish reasonable modification of his services may be deemed discrimination. The ADA requires private entities to bear the costs of such modifications, and the unknown future costs of the ADA were a major concern of the business community during its enactment. From its inception the ADA was introduced and treated as a civil rights law that aimed to secure equality, inclusion, and participation of persons with disabilities in all major life spheres. Both the structural and conceptual aspects of the ADA were derived from two existing civil rights laws—the Civil Rights Act of 1964 and Section 504 of the Rehabilitation Act of 1973. The ADA was portrayed as an extension of the existing protections already guaranteed to racial minorities and women, to persons with disabilities.

It would not have been possible to enact the ADA in such a relatively short period of time if not for the successful grassroots disability organizations' lobbying activities before and during the legislative proceedings.[11] Indeed, the social movement that supported the legislation was admirable and managed to unite, for the duration of the campaign, numerous groups of persons with disabilities around a clearly defined goal.[12]

Public interest lawyers played an important role in the enactment of the ADA. Most lawyers had been working on disability issues long before the ADA came into being and entered the legislative process with acquired expertise about the current needs and state of rights of persons with disabilities. The lawyers were all strongly committed to the goal contained in the bill: to achieve full integration and inclusion of persons with all disabilities in mainstream society.[13]

The ADA public interest lawyers operated in a setting that vested much authority in them and offered them an opportunity to use their professional discretion broadly. As I will portray ahead, this resulted from the unclear identity of the client, the nature of the relationship between the lawyers and their constituency, the few rules of procedure in the legislature, and the relation between the lawyers and the state, i.e., the need to align with members of Congress and maintain fiduciary relationships with these decision makers and their aides/staff. At the same time, the lawyers were constantly under the supervision, at times control, of the main lobbyist-strategist responsible for the coordination of the campaign activities. Occasionally this relationship limited their professional discretion compared to domains in which lawyers enjoy exclusive professional jurisdiction (such as adjudication).

Representing Persons with Disabilities during the ADA Campaign

Structuring Decision Making

One of the underlying notions of the ADA had been its non-disability-specific character: the law targeted persons with all types of disabilities. This meant that a common ground that would unite persons with mental, learning, physical, or sensory disabilities needed to be established. The law also applied to many areas of life, and naturally some areas were of greater importance to a certain disability group. The substantial basic principle underlying the bill was easy to agree upon, but the details in each regulated area needed to be worked out and resolved as the legislative process proceeded.

From its inception the disability rights movement in the United States did not operate as a united social movement, and the history of disability struggles was characterized by tensions regarding priorities as "each group tended to see its issues in relation to its specific disability" (Shapiro, 1993). Even though some cross-disability lobbying had been conducted during the decade preceding the ADA, it was necessary to create a structure that would minimize potential conflict within the disability community and that would enable the community to present as unified a position as possible vis-à-vis Congress, the administration, and the bill's opponents.

In Congress the disability community was represented by a coalition of disability organizations' lobbyists called the *Consortium of Citizens with Disabilities* (CCD).[14] A smaller group—the *civil rights task force*—was made up of six to ten members. The task force included representatives of civil rights organizations and occasionally representatives of service providers and professionals and had hands-on connection to the everyday process. CCD held meetings every Monday, during which the strategist and the lawyers briefed, brought up for discussion, and updated the members on the recent legislative developments. Thirty to seventy people, depending on the topic and stage of the legislation, attended CCD's meetings.

In addition to these representatives, a grassroots organizer kept in touch with local disability groups across the country. Through a network of regional contacts the grassroots level was informed about legislative developments and was asked from time to time to send letters or make phone calls to congressional members and to voice their position on specific issues, as guided by the team in Washington.

Throughout the legislative process a group of lobbyists that represented numerous disability groups sustained continuous communication with members of Congress and their staff and ensured that important information flowed back and forth from Congress to the lawyers. The lobbyists were responsible that members of Congress indeed voted when the official voting sessions took place.

A group of lawyers—three permanent members and several others who joined them according to the subject matter under deliberation (mental health, communications, transportation, etc.)—provided the legal resources to these groups and maintained contact with members of Congress and their staff. Each one of the lawyers had been working for a public interest organization, which decided to assign its lawyer to work on the ADA. The lawyers kept in contact with disability "litigation lawyers" from different regions, researched the legal topics under debate, and participated in the negotiations and in the drafting of the law.[15]

All groups were led by a strategist who was the top coordinator of all these activities relating to the ADA.[16]

The grassroots organizers, the lobbyists, and the lawyers engaged in a coordinated effort to pass the law. Their strength was the concerted message forwarded by the disability community, and thus a central goal was to maintain an appearance of a unified position on behalf of this constituency. They wanted to avoid a situation in which one disability group, satisfied with achievements obtained for its members, would give up the fight for other groups in fear of losing its secured accomplishments. Tension of this sort can arise in two main situations. The first is the unpopularity of some disabilities compared to others. It is renowned that among the various disabilities some carry more stigma and prejudice than others. The concern was that persons with physical disabilities, for example, would not firmly resist exclusion of persons with mental illness from the bill's protection if and when the latter group's interests were endangered (as indeed happened in numerous occasions along the legislative process). The second source of tension was the fact that accommodating some disabilities was deemed to be more costly than others. Private employers, private transit companies, and service providers were trying to avoid having costs imposed on them and objected to those parts of the ADA that they anticipated would be too expensive. In this context the concern was that some groups would be willing to give up the struggle for those services that were of less relevance to them.

Another type of intragroup tension related to substantial positions within the bill, in relation to the preferred manner to provide services for persons with disabilities. The debate over special or universal services arose in a mild version in the transportation area. Some groups among the disability organizations preferred paratransit/door-to-door transit services to mainstream bus and train accessibility, and it was important that their opinion be heard as well, despite its relative minor rank.

According to the leading lobbyists and lawyers of the task force, minimizing the potential for dispute and conflicts became a primary objective as the negotiations on the bill proceeded.[17] For this purpose, explained the main strategist for the ADA, P. Wright, two principles were assumed by all groups. The first was the "one for all—all for one" principle, under which all groups agreed *ahead of time* to fight for the rights of others. The second principle verified that when difficulties regarding costs became a real obstacle, the disability community would agree to deferred and flexible timeframes during which the requirements would apply rather then insist on their immediate implementation. These assumptions were meant to reduce the risk of losing substantial gains as well as lessening the potential for intragroup conflicts.

The consent to operate on the basis of these two basic principles was reached, according to Wright, at the initial stage of the legislative process and was discussed in the broadest forum of the disability community involved in the legislation—CCD.[18] At the same time, these underlying understandings provided much leeway and discretion to the lawyers (and the lobbyists) at later stages to decide which issues to bring before the full forum, which to present and share as decisions that have already been resolved, and which to debate and vote upon in full.

The ADA Lawyers and the Disability Community: Identifying the Client

Within the triangle of client-lawyer-state it is worthwhile to discuss some possible configurations of connections between the ADA lawyers and persons with disabilities. I will begin by portraying the notions expressed by the lawyers themselves regarding the identity of their client, and continue with a description of other variables that affected the question of representation.

Most of the ADA lawyers described their clients as "all people with disabilities in the U.S.," or "all people with mental disabilities in the U.S.," or versions of the kind. Even though all lawyers had worked at the time for public interest organizations, they usually did not see their paying organization as their client, in the sense that they owed their ultimate loyalty to that entity.[19] The lead advocate of the disability lawyers, Chai Feldblum, had somewhat of a mixed view about the identity of her client and indeed referred both to "people with disabilities" and to their representatives on Capitol Hill (CCD) as deserving her professional loyalty. The lawyers interviewed did not feel uncomfortable with the notion that they were representing the interest of a diffused and unidentifiable group of people, a constituency practically impossible to communicate with. The professional experience they all had acquired through past representation of this group made them feel that they were connected to their constituency, aware of the issues the law needed to address and their best solutions. They did not regard the lack of a specific and tangible client as a barrier inhibiting adequate fulfillment of their professional tasks.

Some of the basic professional and ethical duties of a lawyer presume the existence of an identifiable client. For example, Model Rule 1.2 states that "[a] lawyer shall be abided by a client's decisions concerning the objectives of representation, and shall consult with the client as to the means by which they are to be pursued."[20] Accordingly, the lawyer is required to communicate with the client and to "keep a client reasonably informed about the status of a matter...."[21] If the client is not communicable, it is not clear how the lawyer is expected to fulfill these basic obligations. Indeed, in situations in which lawyers represent the general interest of a diffuse group, the notion of lawyer-client relationship is essentially undermined.

There existed no apparent mechanism to ascertain the opinions of 29 million people with disabilities on any given topic, except through CCD and in reliance on the lawyers' assumption of their best interest. Under these circumstances, and with CCD not considered by most lawyers to possess a "client status," the lawyers undertook broad discretion to decide about the means to accomplish the legislative objectives and to a certain extent about its goals.

Due to the lack of a typical lawyer-client relationship between the disability lawyers and their constituencies, the presence of other representatives of the disability groups on the legislative scene was of significant importance. It had the potential to involve genuine representatives of the disability community in the evolving legislative developments and to compensate, at least partially, for the lack of a relationship with a client.

In reality, however, this presence played in two different directions. On the one hand, there was no clear procedure to determine when to involve the full membership of CCD in significant legislative developments. The lawyers (usually together with the strategist), decided what would be brought before CCD according to their discretion, if they believed it was necessary or worthwhile to do so. At times they conveyed to CCD decisions that had already been formed, some issues were presented with a recommendation for a preferred position, and others were introduced for open discussion. This process left the lawyers with broad discretion to decide on the extent of involvement of CCD in the negotiations.

On the other hand, the lawyers did not enjoy exclusive professional authority to decide upon numerous issues. Since the overall responsibility for the campaign lay with the lobbyist-strategist, the lawyers were often under the authority of a nonlegal professional who influenced their relationship with members of Congress as well as with CCD. The main lobbyist could request, for example, that information revealed to the lawyers during their deliberations would remain confidential and not be disclosed to CCD, and could also direct what issues would be presented to CCD, when, and in what manner.

The ADA Lawyers and the State: Legislators and the Administration

Describing the association between the disability lawyers, lobbyists, members of Congress and their staff, the two leading attorneys for the ADA used the term 'team' to characterize this relationship.[22] Reflecting on their experiences they both depicted a sense of affinity, which emanated from a common goal striven for, between the small group of lawyers who represented the disability community and those members of Congress, with their staff, who took the lead on the bill and sided with them during the ADA campaign. Obviously, politicians that are involved in promoting a law occupy diverse motives for supporting a particular bill. Such impetus evidently results from a mixture of political calculations and genuine personal convictions. The members of Congress who took the lead on the ADA apparently wanted to help persons with disabilities, they desired political recognition for endorsing this cause, and they hoped for a good and workable law in this area. My purpose is not to identify or explain these motives; I do not believe they can easily be detected, nor are they crucial in understanding the overall relations that developed between the ADA lawyers and official state representatives. Rather, in the next section I will examine the extent and the nature of this entanglement between duly authorized agents of the state and those who are, structurally speaking, outsiders.

Like many other laws that address civil rights issues, the ADA originated from the community the bill aimed to benefit—persons with disabilities. Since the legislative initiative originated from disability activists, the disability community felt it "owned" the bill, bestowing it in the hands of legislators who were supportive and sympathetic. The ADA legislative process began with preliminary deliberations within a number of disability organizations concerning the law they believed ought to be enacted, and an attorney from the National Council on the Handicapped provided the first draft of the bill.[23] The proposal was forwarded to members of Congress, which was a familiar occurrence, describes Feldblum: "... proposals drafted by advocates are simply items that are proffered to interest members of Congress who may consider using the material as the basis for legislation. In the case of the ADA, there were a number of Congressional Members who were interested in using the model bill drafted by the advocates to press forward with a law to prohibit discrimination on the basis of disability."[24] Draft proposals may indeed be "simply" recommendations provided to Congress; however, both the basic concept underlying the ADA and much of its language originated with lawyers who had been active on behalf of persons with disabilities, who drafted them, and who continued to work with congressional staff attorneys throughout the legislative process.

The second version of the ADA (which was eventually enacted) was introduced in the Senate by Senators Harkin, Kennedy, and thirty-two other sponsors in May 1989.[25] The two senators aided by their staff had taken the lead on the development and passage of the ADA.[26] In the House of Representatives the bill was presented by Congressman S. Hoyer and forty-five cosponsors.[27] From then on, the ADA advocates maintained close and continual contact with the sponsors and their staff. Ultimately, whether an amendment to the bill was enacted or not depended on the willingness of the sponsors to support it.

To be effective the ADA lawyers needed to sustain access to sources of information in Congress; this is one of the most important assets of legislative lawyering (Macdougall, 1991). Sometimes relevant information was conveyed to the lobbyists and lawyers in a confidential manner and could not be revealed to CCD. It was vital not to break the ground rules that prevailed in Congress: one is either "in" or "out" of the informed circles. Much of the lawyers' advantage was conditioned upon maintaining the trust of members of Congress and their staff, creating allies and acting according to accepted norms of political behavior.[28] Questioned about a conceivable clash between loyalty to their client and the need to maintain an effective working relationship with members of Congress, most of the lawyers interviewed for this essay did not perceive this tension as imposing a substantial ethical difficulty. They regarded this situation not as a necessary exception to prevailing ethical obligations (due to the special conditions of legislative lawyering) but rather as a means to achieve the best outcome for 'all persons with disabilities'—whom they viewed as their true clients.

Furthermore, special relations between the lawyers and state officials were created because members of Congress needed to receive updated information, legal sustenance, substantive positions, and constituent legitimization from the disability community. Confronted by arguments from adversaries, members of Congress needed "counter-ammunition" to refute them and often turned to the disability advocates to obtain factual and legal retort. If objections to the bill were merited, the disability lawyers were occasionally asked by a member of Congress or the staff person to formulate a compromise that the disability community could accept. When political objection was too strong, the disability lawyers and lobbyists were informed that a particular issue would not be contended.

Under this general framework there is a direct correlation between the two sets of relationships the ADA lawyers were embodied in—the disability community on the one hand and official representatives of the state on the other. Since the lawyers were expected to settle or conciliate to a political demand (with or without merit) at the request of politicians, they needed to relate back to the representatives of the disability community and to share such developments with them. However, full revelation of information, thorough discussions, and orderly resolutions were often hampered because of various factors. As will be illustrated ahead, these included time constraints (some decisions needed to be made on the spot), technical complexities, a notion that explaining the pros and cons of a compromise (or a decision not to compromise) was not the proper procedure, and the inability to convey information that was received in confidence. All these had an impact on the way the lawyers managed their simultaneous relationship with their clients and congressional members.

Decision Making along the ADA Legislative Process.

I have laid out some of my general observations regarding the relations between the ADA lawyers and the disability community as well as between the lawyers and representatives of the legislature. In this section I will demonstrate in more detail how these affiliations played out during the ADA campaign. I will thus provide some stories that explicate or serve as the background to words and sentences that now appear in the law. Each of these episodes tells us about how "law" is actually made, it depicts the limitations and opportunities of lawyering in a political setting, and it illustrates how lawyers construct the cause they represent and, accordingly, the clients to whom they owe loyalty. They demonstrate the complex process of division and redistribution of authority and power that occurred as the ADA, step by step, was crystallized into a binding law. The following examples will be portrayed, as much as possible, differentiating between lawyer-client relations and connections with the Congress and the administration. Some of them, nonetheless, shed light on both.

The ADA Lawyers and Their Clients

The following examples focus mainly on the relations of the ADA lawyers and their clients.

- Paratransit services: Historically, the disability community was divided over the preferred solutions to the reality of marginalization and discrimination of persons with disabilities. The most significant debate of this sort related to deinstitutionalization—whether to demand the closure of large institutions, or to try to improve conditions within them. This controversy peaked during class action litigation on behalf of residents at Pennsylvania's Pennhurst facility for persons with mental disabilities.[29] Additional controversies arose during the litigation of the disability transit cases in the 1970s, over the desirable mode of accessible transportation: special services (door-to-door or on-demand services) or regularly scheduled, accessible buses (Olson, 1984).

These controversies reflect the classic group-equality dilemma of special versus universal treatment, but during the ADA legislative proceedings they did not surface in a significant way. It seems that over time the disability community has opted for the universal-equal-integrative approach. Special services have been associated with segregation, and one of the main objectives of the ADA was to do away with segregation. Moreover, as described by an ADA lobbyist, the ADA was enacted for future generations, and her anticipation was that the next generation would prefer greater independence, without reliance on special services, however comfortable they might seem. Mainstream transportation was therefore the official and clear demand of the ADA advocates.[30]

Behind the scenes, however, there had been some disagreement among various disability groups over the extent to which "special" paratransit services ought to be recognized in the ADA. The major organizations representing persons with physical disabilities (mainly the assertive group ADAPT) advocated accessible buses, but there was also a rather silent minority who had a stake in paratransit services and at the time might have preferred this service. These people included persons with developmental disabilities or older people who could not have been redirected to use buses, people who lived in areas with harsh weather conditions and found it hard to use public transportation,[31] and other individuals who were not part of the organized groups. The dilemma on this issue was not trivial. The ADA was a civil rights bill, mandating full inclusion and integration of persons with disabilities to universal and mainstream facilities. Any exception to this principle might reinforce prejudices against the true abilities of this group and render the transit providers with an excuse not to fulfill their obligations. Nonetheless, there had always been people who genuinely preferred specialized services, for valid and good reasons.

How were these "whispers in the background"[32] supposed to be heard? There was no apparent mechanism to assure these dissenting voices would be noticed, and they depended on their representatives to address their needs in the bill. According to one of the lawyers who worked on transportation issues, CCD held a discussion regarding the extent to which paratransit services ought to be available, during which some 'dissenters' were persuaded that only a narrow exception for paratransit eligibility was justified. With this solution people would be eligible to receive paratransit services depending on their individual (in)ability to use public transportation and not according to a broad category they belonged to (such as blind people).[33] According to another attorney, he considered it his duty to represent persons with disabilities who could fully use accessible buses and those who could not. Both lawyers considered it their professional obligation to make sure that each point of view was addressed during the legislative discussions, despite strong advocacy against specialized services. Consequently the solution adopted took account of these trends by mandating accessibility as the rule, but acknowledging some narrow exceptions.[34]

- Mental disabilities. Persons with mental disabilities (especially mental illness) were constantly under the threat of being excluded from ADA protection. There exists a long history of prejudice and unfounded fear concerning this group, and advocacy on their behalf was necessary at many stages of the legislation. At one stage, playing upon this prejudice, the business community tried to distribute a flyer that conveyed a message that the ADA would compel employers to hire people with mental illness who would then become a life-threatening danger in the workplace. It was not necessary for the lawyers (or lobbyists) to bring this issue up for full discussion within CCD prior to any reaction to this maneuver, since it was obvious that the position taken by the disability community would be to debunk such prejudices.³⁵ The same was true for an attempt to exclude persons with mental illness from coverage regarding their right to ride Amtrak.³⁶ These were clear examples in which the first principle—one for all, all for one—was invoked.

- Medical examinations. The discussions about the scope of permissible medical examinations by employers offers a different rationale for lawyers' decision to presume authority over the arrangement adopted on this topic.³⁷ The ADA lawyers wanted to restrict the testing of employment candidates during the application process and to limit the use of medical examinations by employers subsequent to employment. This issue turned out to be a major concern for the business community, who feared it would be completely restricted from administering tests to their employees. Negotiations on this point were highly technical in their nature, and the language in the bill was altered numerous times before final agreement was reached.³⁸ Despite its centrality, the issue was not debated in depth during the CCD meetings. It was mentioned in one of the memos, and people were given an opportunity to ask questions about it, but no one did. The lawyers were thus entrusted to proceed on this point at their discretion.³⁹

- Food handlers amendment(I): An unexpected amendment to the ADA was raised in the House of Representatives (introduced by Representative Chapman, thereby known as the Chapman Amendment) in an attempt to restrict the rights of persons with HIV. The amendment was presented at the last stages of legislation (after much legislative ground has been achieved). The restaurant owners' lobby wanted to exclude persons with HIV from working in positions where food was handled, thus excluding them from the prohibition against employment discrimination. An amendment of this sort runs against the spirit of the ADA—not to allow prejudice and unfounded fears to determine the rights of persons with disabilities. The "legal reasoning" and the merited rationale to object to the amendment was thus clear, but not sufficient, and it was necessary to use political leverage in order to defeat it. The lawyers needed to pass two stages in order to do so. First, they needed to obtain a definite and unified stand from CCD, which they would present as the disability community's position on the proposed amendment. Second, they needed to enlist enough votes to oppose it.

As for CCD's position, it was not clear to the lobbyists and lawyers if the full forum would actually risk losing what they had already gained in the legislative process to secure the rights of a relatively unpopular group—HIV-infected persons. This explicit question—would the disability community insist on its objection to the amendment, even for the price of losing the bill—was not polled within CCD. The issue was discussed in a general manner before the position of the disability community was made public and presented by the lobbyist-strategist clearly: either the amendment was withdrawn, or the disability community would walk away from the ADA.⁴⁰ However, neither CCD, and obviously not a broader representative group of persons with disabilities, were actually asked if they were willing to risk such a loss. It was assumed, mainly by the lobbyists, that it was legitimate to present such a position on behalf of the disability community, based on the general principle agreed upon in the beginning of the process.[41] It also seems, however, that if CCD had had the status of a client, it would have probably been unethical for a lawyer to do so without obtaining its express consent. Nonetheless, given the lack of such formal constraints and with the lobbyist at the top of the decision-making echelon, it was feasible to do so.

This matter illustrates both the strengths and weaknesses of the setting in which the lobbyists and the lawyers operated. On the one hand, the task force members had broad discretion to speak on behalf of all disability groups, and to apply political leverage where legal arguments were not sufficient. This authority was not limited, however, through formal "checks and balances" derived from client instructions or a clear client mandate.

There is no apparent decision-making process in such circumstances. Putting aside practical difficulties to obtain the position of additional interested people or organizations, it is not clear who should be allowed to have a say on such a question, and if everyone's position ought to carry equal weight. Should persons with AIDS have a stronger voice on this point? Should all persons with disabilities who are affected by the law, but not necessarily by this section, have an equal say on this topic? The pros and cons of a democratic participatory process are well known, and relevant in this context.[42] Potential participants are usually uninformed, as well as unresponsive, to the range of concerns that should be taken into account in such issues (Rhode, 1982: 1232–42). A majoritarian process that would try to reach as many persons with disabilities as possible (if at all practical in a legislative setting) is inappropriate for this type of institutional-principle decision.

According to the grassroots coordinator for the ADA, the existing networking mechanism established to maintain contact with the regional and local disability organizations was not utilized in policy decisions of this sort, because it was impractical to make strategic and substantial judgments through a broad participatory process.[43] Can the same be said, however, about CCD representatives? Could they not have been persuaded of the importance of supporting persons with HIV, as an implementation of the first principle agreed upon? Polling all CCD representatives—a more democratic approach than the one applied—may not have guaranteed the desired response, but there were probably better chances of having the representatives agree on this issue than having all persons with disabilities come to this conclusion. On the other hand it can be argued that, after a decision regarding a certain basic principle had been reached, *these would be exactly the circumstances* in which it was appropriate to assume proxy for the entire disability community, without having the specific decision approved.[44] Under this analysis, the entire disability community is defined as "the client," a definition that grants the lawyers (and lobbyists) discretion to speak on their behalf.

In sum, on a day-to-day basis, the lawyers and the lobbyists decided the issues they would present before CCD for open discussion, which topics they would submit with a strong recommendation for a certain position and which topics CCD would be briefed on and informed of after substantive decisions had already been made. As aforementioned, at the beginning of the negotiations, agreement was obtained that all disability groups would fight for others. But the implementation of this principle left much latitude with the groups' leaders. The more substantive the lawyers and lobbyists perceived an issue to be, the more likely it was to be brought before CCD for discussion and voting. But, as one of the lobbyists stated, ultimately this decision was left to lawyers' and lobbyists' discretion—if it was "necessary" or perhaps "too risky" to do so.[45] The necessity was determined by the nature of the issue—substantial, technical, or minor. Risky meant one of two things: either the position the lawyers/lobbyists wanted to present as the disability community's position may not have survived a democratic vote, or CCD could not be trusted to abide by the rules of the political realm. Additional considerations, such as time constraints and the dynamics of the legislative process, also determined the extent which the lawyers used their mandate to make final decisions on behalf of their client constituency.

The aggregate of these qualifications resulted in a level of discretion and power vested in the ADA lawyers, which deviates from common understandings about lawyers' relationships with their clients. Professional-ethical rules not only aim to explain or justify certain professional behavior, but they also impose numerous restrictions on members of a profession and require adherence to certain behavioral standards. As discussed in section 2 above, the legislature is a setting in which the connection between the fundamental theoretical basis of the legal profession and the actual working environment is weakened to begin with. Collective public interest lawyering renders additional aberrations from the conventional client-lawyer relationship. This situation leaves legislative cause lawyers with less guidance on the way to manage their practice vis-à-vis the group they are representing and in turn creates power imbalances between them. More so, precisely such concerns for abuse of power underlie much of the criticism against public interests lawyers on blurring between their own and their clients' agendas.

The ADA Lawyers and Congress

The following examples focus primarily on the relationship with members of Congress:

- The food handlers amendment (II). This episode, described above, provides insight on the dynamics between lawyers, lobbyists, and members of Congress, in addition to clients. When the vote for this amendment approached,[46] the lobbyists realized they did not have enough supporting votes to defeat it. The lead lobbyist on AIDS-related issues decided to approach one of the Republican House representatives and try to convince him to vote against the amendment.[47] The lobbyist attested before that member that there were no merited public health concerns underlying the amendment but only undue pressure from the

Restaurant Owners Association who were driven by a baseless prejudice and fear of persons with HIV. Following this lobbying effort the required votes to defeat the motion were obtained, conditioned by a certain compromise (to allow the Center for Disease Control to determine which infectious diseases would be restricted from protection in the food-handling business). This compromise was obtained after a verification of the actual premise for the proposed amendment (political calculations rather than public health concerns). During this process, the tasks of getting the votes and engaging in the negotiations were left to the disability lobbyists. When the voting time approached, and was a matter of hours away, the legislative lawyers drafted the required compromise on the spot, and it was voted upon immediately, according to their script.[48] This example sheds light on our common understanding of the identity of a legislator—an official organ of the state. The circumstances under which the language for the compromise was drafted blur the lines between official and unofficial law making. The task of obtaining enough votes to refute the amendment was left in the hands of the disability lobbyists; the ADA lawyer provided the final wording of the law. Lawyering under these circumstances allowed for direct participation and input by handing over official state tasks to representatives of the citizenry.

- The remedy debate: The debate over the remedies that ought to be available to victims of discrimination under the ADA demonstrates the leeway in which lawyers operated as a medium between the disability community and congressional members. This issue was one of the topics negotiated between representatives of the administration and members of Congress Harkins and Kennedy in the early stages of the proceedings. The ADA lawyers wanted to broaden the definition of the term "public accommodations" proposed in the bill, since they believed it was too restrictive in the disability context.[49] Therefore, in exchange for a broader coverage of public accommodations in the ADA, they agreed to limit the remedies available to victims of discrimination under the ADA to those afforded by the Civil Rights Act at the time, which did not include compensatory and punitive damages.

A substantial compromise of this sort needed to be "signed off" by CCD.[50] The lawyers, who supported the compromise, indeed "lobbied" heavily within CCD for its acceptance since the pros and cons of such a trade off were not a matter of common sense.[51] The lawyers strongly endorsed the trade off as a commendable position, after its merit had already been discussed among them at length. CCD agreed to this trade off in principle. At this stage, after CCD had formed its position on this issue, the congressional members who led the negotiations with the White House were given "the green light," so to speak, to present it as an acceptable position by the disability community during negotiations with the White House.[52] The lawyers thus maneuvered between CCD and "their" members, generating a process in which instructions were given to, from, and through the lawyers both to their clients and to representatives of the legislature.

- Parent/local enterprise debate: Working closely with members of Congress during the negotiations and drafting of the law entailed receiving instructions and directions from them regularly. For example: a key term within the ADA was "undue hardship." One of the principles articulated in the bill was that an employer would not be required to provide a reasonable accommodation for a person with a disability if the accommodation entailed undue hardship on his behalf. The business community expressed its concerns about the vagueness of this term and requested that in determining whether a certain expense would be considered undue hardship, the circumstances and resources of the local facility would be taken into account, rather than the parent company. The concern of the National Federation of Independent Businesses was that in small and rural localities stores and facilities would be shut down and services would not be provided if the "hardship" would only be determined by calculating the resources available to the parent enterprise. An amendment was introduced to express this position, and shortly before the vote in the Judiciary Committee, Senator Hoyer directed one of the ADA lawyers to "find a solution" to the concerns of those behind the amendment. Since there was no time to conduct a meeting with CCD, the lawyers debated and drafted the compromise—to take account of the resources available to both parent and local enterprises—in one of the back rooms on site. When negotiations between members of Congress and their staff regarding this amendment resumed, the disability lawyer was expected to leave the room and "return" it to the use of the official representatives. The compromise suggested was ultimately agreed upon.[53]

- Exclusion of specific disorders from the ADA. Members of Congress who sponsor a bill expect that lobbying for a certain position will not take place outside the circle of sponsors. This limits the ability of a lawyer to pursue all possible arguments on behalf of her client or the interest she is representing. From the initial legislative stages it was clear, for example, that the ADA would not apply to private insurance companies, and it was useless to try to fight this political position.[54] Similarly, at a relatively early stage religious entities were excluded from the ADA's requirements.[55] The exclusion of selected disorders from coverage of the ADA illustrates well this type of limitation in advocacy.

The definition of a disabled person in the ADA is quite broad, and follows the definition under the Rehabilitation Act. A person with a disability is: (a.) a person with a physical or mental impairment that substantially limits that person in some major life activity. (b.) a person with a record of such a physical or mental impairment. (c.) a person who is regarded as having such an impairment.[56] During the last stages of the ADA discussions in the Senate, an amendment was introduced to exclude some specific disorders from its coverage. A few of the suggested exclusions (such as manic depression and schizophrenia) provoked response from the sponsoring senators and were overcome; others did not, and section 511 of the bill was eventually passed, excluding from coverage inter-alia, transvestitism and transsexualism, kleptomania, pyromania, and some gender-identity disorders.[57] The amendment was adopted despite the fact that "these exclusions seem wholly inconsistent with the overall tenor of the Americans with Disabilities Act, which encourages participation and decision making based upon individualized determinations of actual ability and not preconceived assumptions and stereotypes. (Burgdorf, 1991: 452)." These limitations were nonetheless added to the bill "with the agreement of the bill's sponsors in the name of compromise (Ibid)." There was not much the lawyers could do for, perhaps, the most unpopular group of all persons with disabilities, which deserved the most assertive representation. Dependence on the sponsors of the bill, in turn, constrained the lawyers' ability to ultimately advocate in zeal on behalf of their clients.

- Testing of police candidates. A typical model of cooperation between lawyers and congressional members is illustrated by the following case: Employer testing has been used grossly to discriminate against persons with disabilities, and the disability lawyers wanted to limit this practice as much as possible. After considerable negotiations a compromise was reached, which banned pre-offer testing of candidates but allowed under certain circumstances testing of employees who had been offered an employment position. However, the chief of police requested an exemption from the prohibition on psychological testing of police candidates, stating that the police force was a special kind of employer that justified a different testing standard. Senator Hoyer, confronted by the amendment proposed by another member on behalf of the police, requested a retort from the lawyers. After consultation with activists and lawyers involved with civil rights advocacy vis-à-vis the police, this request was refuted, and the amendment dismissed accordingly.[58]

- Access to renovated buildings: Not only can relations with the state alter during legislative negotiations but also with adversaries to the bill. In fact, a law has better chances to fulfill its goal "in action" if it adequately addresses concerns of adverse and often opposing parties. A good legislative lawyer may therefore not be performing her role best by articulating her clients' interests *only*. Rather, she will try to understand, to take into account, and to reflect—without compromising the principal interests of her client—those adverse concerns during the negotiations and drafting of a law. The negotiations conducted with the American Institute of Architects on accessibility requirements of renovated buildings illustrate this point. The ADA requires that if a public accommodation chooses to renovate a building, it must ensure that the renovated area is fully accessible. However, there are various qualifications to this duty. If the renovated area serves as a "primary function" area of a public accommodation (such as a dining hall in a restaurant), the accessibility requirements are higher than if the renovation is done in a nonprimary function area (such as storage rooms or kitchen). The path of travel to the primary function area should be fully accessible, unless the costs of making it accessible are disproportionate to the costs of the renovation itself.[59] These qualified obligations imposed upon public accommodation providers were the result of negotiations between the ADA lawyers and the architects, and many of the initial concerns of the builders' representatives were met and incorporated into the law.[60]

In the episodes described above, lawyers did more than represent the interests of their clients. To begin with, representation entailed that the lawyers define the object of their representation, and this definition depended on the manner in which they constructed the cause they believed they were forwarding. It was almost inevitable that even the lawyers who worked together during the ADA proceedings defined their causes and respectively, their clients, differently. Also, these definitions were contingent and often changed over time, as some topics required redefining the interests to which the lawyers owed their allegiance. This flexibility, in turn, enabled the lawyers to develop and maintain relationships, understandings, and working patterns with those who, strictly speaking, were not their clients, such as state officials and adversaries.

Not only "clients" but also Congress cannot be conceived as a fixed and unified entity. Within Congress the lawyers carried general alliances to the members who supported the ADA in principle but not on all specific issues and deeper commitments to the bill's sponsors who were themselves limited by their political constraints. The sponsors also developed an expectation that the ADA lawyers furnish them with legal advice, including negotiation and drafting services—expectations that were often in the immediate interest of the lawyers. Members of Congress also depended on the lawyers to provide them with the legitimacy of CCD, the closest representative of their constituency, and relied on this backing as political leverage during controversial deliberations.

Conflict, Cooperation, Co-optation, and Legitimation during a Struggle for Social Change

Traditionally, the political aspirations of cause lawyers have been to alter the social or political status quo through confrontation and trumping of state institutions. Lawyers and their clients—however we define them or manage their diversities—were situated vis-à-vis the state, the ultimate representative of power. At first blush, this essay offers an alternative paradigm for comprehending a cause-lawyering experience: cooperation and power sharing rather than direct confrontation. If indeed legislative cause lawyering entails working together with official state institutions, the question of its price—institutional legitimation—readily appears. The drawbacks of institutional legitimization that accompany liberal law reform are well known, and public interest lawyers have wrestled with the dilemmas entailed in the legitimizing effects of their work for decades. To what extent do lawyers who work in conjunction with and from within political and legal institutions reify the categories through which a social conflict is defined and reinforce the power disparities in their society? These lawyers have met the criticism that channeling social and political conflicts into "law" hinders substantial structural change (Gabel and Harris, 1983; Ellman, 1992).

However, "co-optation risks" of this sort do not necessarily correlate with the conflict-cooperation dichotomy. The criticism of public interest lawyers was targeted for the most part at litigation practices, which rest on the traditional conflict model. In other words, co-optation dilemmas arise in both kinds of practices. The question remains, nevertheless, if the risk of co-optation is not exacerbated in situations of cooperative lawyering, in which maintaining "good relations" with state officials is an inherent characteristic of the work.

Underlying the rationale of co-optation, however, is a presumption of an established "co-opting" entity with a definite configuration and predetermined interests. "Outsiders" enter its field, and in order to utilize it they must abide by its rules to the point where they find themselves stranded in its power structures, rhetoric, and procedures, which cannot be altered significantly. This insider/outsider analysis does not always capture the more complex realities of transformative legal work. The ADA lawyers themselves were simultaneously insiders and outsiders at the legislature. Their professional activity was continuously constituted and shaped by the special conditions that existed in Congress, and those, in turn, altered the practices, patterns of cooperation, and collaborations within Congress. It is in this meaning that we can talk about muddling the lines between state and citizenry.

The legislature, too—in some ways even more than the court—does not neatly correspond with the insider-outsider cleavage. Contrary to judges, members of Congress do not have pretense to be independent or impartial, and they are explicitly more open to the influences of politics "from below." Interests, rather than rights, must be acknowledged and negotiated. As illustrated in this essay, this essential quality of Congress created a dynamics of legislative lawyering that led to incremental restructuring, redistribution, and alteration of relations, power, and authority. Thus, even though it may appear that the risks of co-optation are more likely to occur in cooperative lawyering because of the need to sustain continuous working relationships with congressional members and staff, these same restraints offer the opportunities to gain political influence and share political power. To be sure, to a certain extent legislative cause lawyering reinforces and strengthens existing institutional arrangements along with the societal inequalities they are built upon. But legitimization and change are not mutually exclusive. If we acknowledge that social transformations occur in "microsites of power," one can think of no better place from which to generate them than a liberal political institution such as Congress.

Second, during a legislative campaign legislative lawyers need to cooperate with "non lawyers"—lobbyists, community organizers, service providers. This reliance mitigates some of the flaws of overdependence on lawyers-as-experts commonly associated with public interest litigation. Under this critique, lawyers lure social movements into law as the preferred avenue for change on account of broader and more comprehensive transformative venues (Scheingold, 1974; Handler, 1978; Rosenberg, 1991; McCann 1986). Clients' reliance on the expertise of professional lawyers results in a passive disposition, depletes the dynamics of "bottom up" activism, and in the long run weakens social movements altogether. Legislative lawyering offers an opportunity to avoid some of these drawbacks and to create mechanisms that are relatively democratic and participatory. As described in this essay, during the ADA legislative campaign the latitudinal structure that was created involved individuals with disabilities and grassroots disability organizations throughout the political process, originating a united disability front that proved essential to the passage of this law.

Third, conflict and co-operation, co-optation and defiance, in the context of lawyering for social change ought to be assessed over time. The organizational network established during the ADA followed at least three decades of grassroots activity, consciousness raising, and the utilization of an amalgam of strategies that placed disability in the realm of the civil rights agenda (see Shapiro, 1993; Mayersone, 1993: 17). Since the ADA's enactment, lawyers have launched thousands of lawsuits to enforce the rights recognized in the law. Subsequent legislative activity, such as amendments to the Individuals with Disabilities Educational Act, has proven less successful. As to the effectiveness of the ADA in improving the overall quality of life of persons with disabilities, the views on this point are nuanced as well. On the one hand, disability activists voice frustration over poor gains in the area of employment, and some assert that over reliance on post-ADA litigation has in fact undermined grassroots activity. At the same time, a recent poll released by the National Organization on Disability shows high awareness, support, and change of attitudes in the general public toward persons with disabilities and the ADA in particular.[61] Thus the period of two and a half years during which the ADA lawyers engaged in cooperative efforts to pass the law is one element in a long and complex project that involves disability cause lawyers and other activists. In this respect legislative cause lawyering differs from other types of lawyering in Congress, and should be evaluated against a long-term social change agenda, as one link in a chain that utilizes various strategies in an ever-changing social and political situation.

Conclusion

Disability cause lawyering carries an ambitious objective—to overturn attitudes and structural barriers to participation of persons with disabilities in society. When cause lawyers engage in the enactment of a law as part of this project, they build upon residues and achievements of past social struggles that have also been "coded in laws." At the same time, enacting a law is a process that "concocts empowering and enabling narratives" and that, together with other acts, "constitute[s] the kind of society in which we live and how people resist and try to transform it" (West, 1998). Legislative cause lawyering offers representatives of disempowered groups an additional venue to lawyer on behalf of disadvantaged people. It entails being partly a community organizer, a legal analyst, a drafter, a lobbyist, and a statesperson and bears the potential to build better alliances between lay people, experts, and officials inside and outside formal state institutions. Given these qualities, legislative cause lawyering underscores the indeterminacy of legal professionalism, and challenges strict definitions of the political, legal and professional as self-contained spheres.

Acknowledgments

I thank Deborah L. Rhode from Stanford University Law School for support and comments on earlier drafts of this article. I appreciate the time and helpful comments of Arlene Mayerson, Patricia White, and David Capozzi. Special and many thanks to Chai Feldblum, who took special interest in the article and provided useful information and comments along the way.

Notes

1. See, for example, Handler, (1978); Gabel and Harris, 1983); and Ellman, (1992).
2. For a vivid and critical description of the abusive use of access to political power by "power lawyers" on behalf of their corporate clients, see Nader and Smith (1998).
3. For a thorough review of the basis of the Dominant View and its refutation, see Simon (1998). I borrow the term "Dominant View" from this book. See also Luban (1988): xix–xxii; Review Essay Symposium (1999).
4. On government lawyering in Congress, see Yoo (1998); Glennon (1998); and Klark (1998).
5. Model Rules of Professional Conduct (1995 ed.), Rule 1.13: Organization as Client. Deborah L. Rhode, *Class Conflicts in Class Actions*, 34 Stan. L. Rev 1183 (1982).
6. *See* Fed. R. Civ. P. 23(a).
7. Model Rules of Professional Conduct (1995 ed.), Preamble, Scope and Terminology, section 5.
8. Ibid., Scope of Representation.
9. Rule 3.9 (ibid). imposes on the lawyers the duties included in Rules 3.3 (Candor toward the tribunal), 3.4 (Fairness to opposing party and council), and 3.5 (Impartiality and decorum of the tribunal).
10. Pub. L. No. 101–336, 104 Stat. 327 (1990) codified at 42 U.S.C. ss 12101–12213 and 47 U.S.C. ss 225, 611.
11. The first bill was introduced in the 100th Congress in 1988 (S. 2345, 100th Cong. 2d. Sess. 134 *Cong. Rec.* H2757), and the ADA was passed during the 101st Congress in 1990.
12. For a chronological description of the social forces and people involved in the campaign, see Shapiro (1993).
13. In addition to reviewing documents related to the enactment of the ADA, this paper is based on telephone interviews conducted in the months November 1996 through January 1997, and in October 1997 and April 1998, with: Chai Feldblum, the leading attorney for the ADA, at the time with the American Civil Liberties Union; Arlene Mayerson, a leading attorney for the ADA from DREDF (Disability Research Education and Defense Fund); attorney James Weisman from Eastern Paralyzed Veterans of America, attorney David Capozzi, at the time with Paralyzed Veterans of America, attorney Bonnie Millstein, at the time with the Mental Health Law Project; the main strategist and lobbyist responsible for the overall coordination of the campaign, Patricia Wright from DREDF; Liz Savage, the lobbyists coordinator, then with the Epilepsy Foundation, Paul Marchand, lobbyist from the Associ-

ation for Retarded Citizens; Curtis Decker, lobbyist from the Association of Protection and Advocacy Agencies, Marylin Gouldin, the grassroots coordinator from DREDF; and a brief correspondence with attorney Karen Strauss, then with the National Association for Law and Deaf. During October 1997 and April 1988 telephone and personal interviews were conducted for the second time with Chai Feldblum and Arlene Mayerson, as well as with Tom Sheridan (during the ADA campaign the coordinating lobbyist for the AIDS related issues) and with attorney David Rappallo, with the Georgetown University Law Center Legislative Clinic.

14. The extent to which the groups in Washington actually represented the millions of people with disabilities in the United States is an issue that can, of course, be contested. I do not attempt to address this complex representation issue in this essay. CCD included about 70–80 members.

15. See Feldblum (1991). Interview with C. Feldblum, 11.26.96.

16. The lead strategist was Patricia Wright of DREDF.

17. Interview with Patricia Wright, 1.8.97; interview with attorney Arlene Mayerson, 11.19.96; interview with attorney Bonnie Millstein, 1.9.97; interview with lobbyist Curtis Decker, 1.11.97; interview with lobbyist Paul Marchand, 1.15.97.

18. Feldblum could not recall a particular meeting in which these topics were agreed upon expressively; nonetheless she confirms that these were the underlying assumptions on which the lawyers had operated. Interview with Feldblum, October 1997.

19. Attorney C. Feldblum, nevertheless, reflected that she had considered her responsibility to inform her immediate supervisors at the ACLU on all substantial developments and information that was conveyed to her. This does not necessarily mean that the ACLU was "the client," but that at times working for an organization may require establishing different relations with clients and others, compared to working directly with a client. Attorney James Weisman mentioned that when he started working on the ADA he considered the organization who "paid his salary" his client (Eastern Paralyzed Veterans of America), but that notion changed shortly and he regarded as his clients all people with disabilities, especially those with transit needs. Attorney David Capozzi also felt that his employer deserved his professional loyalty.

20. Model Rules of Professional Conduct (1995 ed), Rule 1.2 (a).

21. Ibid., Rule 1.4 (a).

22. Interview with Feldblum, October 1997; interview with Mayerson, April 1998.

23. The attorney was Robert L. Burgdorf. For a detailed description of the development of the ADA see, for example, Feldblum (1991), 523–31.

24. Feldblum (1991), 24–25.

25. The first version was introduced in the 100th Congress, but since it was not enacted before final adjournment, it needed to be reintroduced in the 101th Congress. The first bill was introduced by Senators Weicker (R) and Harkin (D) and twelve other sponsors on April 28, 1988, as S.2345 and in the House of Representatives by Rep. Coehlo (D) and forty-five other sponsors as H.R. 4498 on April 29, 1988.

26. Senator Harkin's staff lawyer at the time was Bobby Silverstein, and Senator Kennedy's was Carolyn Osolinik. See Feldblum (1991).

27. The ADA was introduced in the Senate as S. 933, 101st Cong., 1st Sess., 135 *Cong. Rec.* sec. 4984–98, and in the House as H.R. 2273, 101st Cong., 1st Sess., 135 *Cong. Rep.* H1791.

28. On the importance of maintaining such connections, see, e.g., Bellow (1996).

29. Halderman v. Pennhurst State School & Hosp. 74–1345 (E.D. Pa., May 30, 1974). On conflicts within the disability movement, see also Herr (1989).

30. *See*, for example, the explanations of Senator Hoyer as recorded in 136 *Cong. Rec.* H2509–01, H2604, May 22, 1990.

31. Interview with attorney David Capozzi and attorney James Weisman, who recalled the objection of a woman from St. Cloud, Minnesota, a small town that gets 65 inches of snow during the winter, who described the difficulties of using public transportation.

32. In the words of attorney D. Capozzi.

33. Interview with attorney James Weisman.

34. Interview with attorney David Capozzi. The ADA requires all public transit systems who operate regularly on a fixed route to install lifts on new buses they acquire. At the same time, these companies must provide paratransit services for those who cannot use public transportation (42 U.S.C. sec. 12162, 12182, 12183). According to Capozzi, now at the Architectural and Transportation Barriers Compliance Board, consequently, as public transportation has become more accessible, more persons with disabilities are using it. Paratransit has become a better service for those who are in real need. Nonetheless, as it has become better, the demand for it is growing, thus causing heavier financial burdens.

35. Interview with lobbyist Paul Marchand, 1.15.97.

36. Interview with lobbyist Curtis Decker, executive director of the National Association of Protection and Advocacy Agencies, 1.11.97.

37. 42 U.S.C.A sec. 12112 c.

38. For a very detailed description of the negotiations, see Feldblum (1991), 531–48.

39. Similar concerns occur in class actions. See Rhode (1982), 1238: "The more technical the issue is, the less the point in counting noses."

40. Consequently a compromise was reached, to allow the Center for Disease Control to determine what infectious disease would be restricted from employment protection in the food-handling business.

41. Interview with Patricia Wright, 1.8.97.

42. On participatory democracy, *see* Tribe (1970). Rhode, (1982), 1232–42.

43. Interview with Marylin Goldin from DREDF, 1.17.97.

44. This idea is similar to the "original concept" theory in political science, which assumes that once a path has been chosen in a democratic manner, representative democracy is easier to justify. Rawls (1970).

45. Interview with lobbyist Paul Marchand of ARC (The Association for Retarded Citizens), 1.15.97.

46. For reasons that will not be elaborated here, the vote was cast as a motion to recommit the bill, and fifty-one votes were needed in order to defeat the motion; otherwise, the bill in its entirety would be lost and would have to be reintroduced in the next Congress.

47. Lobbyist Tom Sheridan approached Congressman Orrin Hatch.

48. Telephone interview with Tom Sheridan, April 1998.

49. The term was borrowed from the Civil Rights Act, which served as the ADA's model.

50. Phone conversation with attorney Chai Feldblum, 12.3.96. CCD's involvement on this topic was also confirmed by attorney Arlene Mayerson, phone conversation, 11.10.1996.

51. Chai Feldblum's memo to CCD (unconfirmed date).

52. As it turned out, shortly after this agreement was reached, an amendment to the Civil Rights Act was introduced (by Senator Kennedy, among others), to expand the remedies available in the CRA to include compensatory and punitive damages. As a result, another whole series of debates arose, if "the deal" that was reached earlier included "freezing" the remedies under the ADA to those currently under the CRA, or that they would be changed as those may change. The disability representatives sustained a firm stand that the latter position would be accepted, and indeed the bill was passed without limiting the rem-

edies available under the ADA. On this point, and the debate about the remedies, see ADA annotated, Title I, pages 305–22. It is interesting to note that on this issue the votes were split, quite closely, between Republicans and Democrats reflecting the conventional partisan approaches to civil rights legislation (192–227), a relatively close vote, in which an amendment to restrict the remedies under the ADA was defeated. Id, at 322.

53. Interview with A. Mayerson, April 1998. This clarification does not appear in the definition of undue hardship in the law (Section 101(10)(A)), but rather in the report of the Judiciary Committee, which states: "Concerns were expressed that a court would look only at the resources of the local facility involved, or only at the resources of the parent company. The committee believes that both these alternatives are unsatisfactory. Instead, the committee intends that the resources of both the local facility and of the parent company, as well as the relationship between the two, be relevant to the undue hardship determination." *Cong. Rec.* 101st Cong., 2nd Sess. Rept. 101–485, May 15, 1990, p. 40. See also on this point, 136 *Cong. Rec.* H2441 (daily ed. May 17, 1990) (Statement of Rep. Sensenbrenner): "The financial resources of both the specific facility and the parent company are to be considered in determining an undue hardship"), and also 136 *Cong. Rec.* H 2631 (daily ed. May 22), statement of Rep. Gingrich: "Site-specific factors and parent company factors must be considered when determining if a reasonable accommodation for a disabled employee is an undue hardship or a barrier removal is readily achievable."

54. 42 U.S.C. 12201[c].

55. 42 U.S.C. 12187 (excluding from the statute "religious organizations and entities controlled by religious organizations, including places of worship").

56. 42 U.S.C. sec. 12102 (2).

57. See 135 *Cong. Rec.* s10765–86 (daily ed. Sept. 7, 1989). *Id.*

58. Arlene Mayerson, interview, April 1998.

59. 42 U.S.C. sec. 12183[a][2]. The Department of Justice determined that "disproportionate" in this context means more than 20 percent of the renovation costs (28 C.F.R. sec. 36.40333[f]).

60. Interview with Attorney Chai Feldblum, 11.26.96.

61. See, for example, Symposium: Backlash Against the ADA: Interdisciplinary Perspectives and Implications for Social Justice Strategies, Spring 1999. In April 1999, marking nine years to the passage of the ADA, a new Harris poll found that 67 percent of American adults have heard or read about the ADA, 87 percent of those support and approve of the ADA, and 75 percent think that the benefits to persons with disabilities are worth the additional costs to governments and businesses; 94 percent believe employers should not discriminate against persons with disabilities, 91 percent would like to see public transportation accessible, and support nondiscrimination policies for hotels, restaurants, and theatres, and 95% think that government should offer more home care services that would enable persons with disabilities to live at home and not institutions. The poll was conducted on behalf of the National Council on Disability and can be found through www.nod.org.

References

Aron, Nan (1989). *Liberty and Justice for All: Public Interest Law in the 1980s and Beyond.* London: Westview Press.

Beck, Ulrich (1994). "The Reinvention of Politics: Towards a Theory of Reflexive Modernization," in *Reflexive Modernization, Politics, Tradition and Aesthetics in the Modern Social Order*, Cambridge: Polity Press. Ulrich Beck, Anthony Giddens, and Scott Lash, eds.

Bellow, Gary (1996). *Steady Work: A Practitioner's Reflections on Political Lawyering*, 31 Harv. C.R.-C.L. L.Rev., 297, 304.

Burgdorf, Robert L. (1991) *The Americans with Disabilities Act: Implications of a Second Generation Civil Rights Statute*, 26 Harv. C.R.-C.L. L.Rev., 413.

Ellman, Stephen (1992). "Client-centered Multiplied: Individual Autonomy and Collective Mobilization in Public Interest Lawyers' Representation of Groups," 78 Va. L. Rev., 1103.

Feldblum, Chai (1991). "Medical Examinations and the Inquiries under the Americans with Disabilities Act: A View from Inside," 64 Temp. L. Rev., 521.

Fried, Charles (1997). "The Lawyer as Friend," 86 Yale L. J., 573.

Gabel, Peter, and Paul Harris, (1983). "Building Power and Breaking Images: Critical Theory and the Practice of Law," 11 N.Y.U Rev. L. & Soc. Change, 369.

Glennon, Michael J. (1998). "Who's the Client?: Legislative Lawyering through the Rear View Mirror," 61:2 (Spring) *Law & Contemporary Problems*, 21.

Handler, Joel F. (1996). *Down from Bureaucracy: The Ambiguity of Privatization and Empowerment*. Princeton, N.J.: Princeton University Press.

——— (1978). *Social Movements and the Legal System: A Theory of Law Reform and Social Change*. New York: Academic Press.

Herr, S. (1989). "Disabled Clients, Constituencies, and Counsel: Representing Persons with Developmental Disabilities," 67 *Milbank Quarterly*, 352, 368–71.

Klark, Kathleen (1998). "The Ethics of Representing Elected Representatives," 61:2 (Spring) *Law & Contemporary Problems*, 31.

Lopez, Gerald P. (1992). *Rebellious Lawyering: One Chicano's Vision of Progressive Law Practice*. London: Westview Press.

——— (1996). *An Aversion to Clients: Loving Humanity and Hating Human Beings*, 31 Harv. C.R.-C.L. L.R., 315.

Luban, David (1988). *Lawyers and Justice: An Ethical Study*. Princeton N.J.: Princeton University Press.

Macdougall, Harold A. (1991). "Lawyering for the Public Interest in the 1990s," 60:1 *Fordham Law Review*, 40–42.

Mayerson, Arlene (1993). "The History of the ADA: A Movement Perspective," in *Implementing the ADA: Rights and Responsibilities of All Americans*, Larry O. Gostin and Henry A. Beyer, ed. Paul H. Brooks.

McCann, Michael (1986). *Taking Reform Seriously: Perspectives on Public Interest Liberalism*. Ithica, N.Y.: Cornell University Press.

Nader, Ralph, and Wesley J. Smith (1998). *No Contest: Corporate Lawyers and the Perversion of Justice in America*. London House, New York.

Olson, Susan M. (1984). Clients and Lawyers: Securing the Rights of Disabled Persons 63–65. Westport, Conn.: Greenwood Press.

Pateman, Carole (1976). *Participation and Democratic Theory*. New York: Cambridge University Press.

Pepper, Stephen L. (1986). "The Lawyer's Amoral Ethical Role: A Defense, a Problem, Some Possibilities," A.B.Found. Res.J., 613.

Polikoff, Nancy D. (1996). "Am I My Client? The Role Confusion of a Lawyer Activist," 31 Harv. C.R.-C.L. L.Rev, 443.

Rawls, John (1971). *A Theory of Justice*. Cambridge, Mass: Harvard University Press.

Review Essay Symposium (1999). "*The Practice of Justice*, by William H. Simon," 4:51 *Stan. L. Rev.*, 867–991.
Rhode, Deborah L. (1982). "Class Conflicts in Class Actions," 34 Stan. L. Rev, 1183.
Rosenberg, Gerald S. (1991). *The Hollow Hope: Can Courts Bring about Social Change?* Chicago: The University of Chicago Press.
Rubenstein, William B. (1997). "Divided We Litigate: Addressing Disputes among Group Members and Lawyers in Civil Rights Campaigns," 106 Yale L. J., 1623.
Sarat, Austin, and Stuart Scheingold, eds. (1998). *Cause Lawyering: Political Commitments and Professional Responsibilities*. New York: Oxford University Press.
Scheingold, Stuart (1974). *The Politics of Rights: Lawyers, Public Policy and Political Change*. New Haven Conn.: Yale University Press.
Shapiro, Joseph P. (1993). *No Pity: People with Disabilities Forging a New Civil Rights Movement*. New York: Times Books.
Simon, William H. (1994). "The Dark Secret of Progressive Lawyering: A Comment on Poverty Law Scholarship in the Post-Modern, Post-Reagan Era," 48 U. Mia. L. Rev., 1099.
——— (1998). *The Practice of Justice: A Theory of Lawyers' Ethics*. Cambridge Mass: Harvard University Press.
Tribe, Lawrence (1988). *American Constitutional Law*, 2d ed. Mineola: Foundation Press.
Trubeck, Louise G. (1996). "Embedded Practices: Lawyers, Clients and Social Change." 31 *Harv. C.R.-C.L.L. Rev.*, 415, no. 2.
West, Cornell (1998). "The Role of Law in Progressive Politics," in *The Politics of Law*, David Kairys, ed., 708. New York: Basic Books.
West, Jane (1993) The Evolution of Disability Right in *Implementing the ADA, Rights and Responsibilities of All Americans*, edited by Larry O. Gostin and Henry A. Beyer, 3. Paul M. Brooks. (publisher).
Yoo, John C. (1998). "Lawyers in Congress," 61:2 (Spring) *Law & Contemporary Problems*, 1.

CHAPTER 9

The Global Language of Human Rights
Patterns of Cooperation between State and Civil Rights Lawyers in Israel

YOAV DOTAN

What are the relations between the concept of "cause lawyering" on the one hand and the concept of "the state" and "globalization" on the other hand? And how does the fast-growing phenomenon of cause lawyering influence the complicated interaction between the globalization of law in general, globalization of human rights law in particular, and preexisting power structures of national legal systems and local patterns of litigation? These are the issues that will be the subject of this chapter.

Current academic discussion of the legal profession distinguishes between two models of lawyers. The first is the conventional model of lawyering espoused by value-neutral "hired guns" providing their services to those able to pay for them. The second is the political or "cause" model of lawyers who commit themselves and their legal skills to further a vision of a just society and thus put a humane face on the profession at large (Sarat and Scheingold, 1998; Menkel-Meadow, 1998; Margulies, 1995). While different studies emphasize different aspects of cause lawyering, it is generally assumed that cause lawyers operate from within civil society, as opposed to operating from within the legal and professional apparatus of the state, which in their case becomes the object of their attacks in courts. Yet another assumption paints cause lawyers as legal warriors breaking the profession's neutral and apolitical paradigm in striving to achieve some broader social goals in the face of opposing social forces (normally supported by the current political regime or by powerful elites) within the framework of a competitive (and usually adversarial) legal system (Sarat and Scheingold, 1998; Menkel-Meadow 1998). In other words, common wisdom assumes that cause lawyers differ from other members of their profession in that they *take sides* in some social or ideological conflict (Scheingold, 1998; Luban, 1988: xx).

In this essay I wish to question these assumptions. I will do this by presenting a case study of the relationship between two groups of lawyers: those representing civil rights organizations in litigation concerning human rights of the Palestinian residents of the Occupied Territories, and their "adversaries," who represent the Government of Israel in the same type of litigation. The "battlefield" in which these two groups of lawyers meet is the Israeli Supreme Court—sitting as the Israeli High Court of Justice—which serves as the main tribunal authorized to dispose judicial review cases dealing with civil rights actions on behalf of the Palestinian residents of the Territories.

While one might expect the relationship between these two groups of lawyers to be purely adversarial and competative, I found that, in practice, patterns of cooperation are no less common and important than attitudes of fragmentation and competitive practices. I also found a common phenomena of professional mobility between the two groups, i.e., in a relatively large number of cases in which members of one group "crossed the lines" and joined the other group. For example, a lawyer-activist for Palestinian rights left his job in a civil rights organization and became a member of the legal department representing the government in the same field of litigation. This phenomenon raises a new series of questions as to the motivations and ideological commitments of cause lawyers. To present such questions, let me pose the example of a lawyer who works for several years for a "prochoice" organization, before taking a position representing a "pro-life" organization in litigation concerning abortion rights. Can we regard such lawyer as a cause lawyer? If so, *what is her cause?* What do such phenomena tell us about cause lawyering at large? Under what conditions is such a model of cause lawyering possible? These will be some of the questions that I will address here.

In the last part of the article I will deal with the relationship between the seemingly local phenomenon of lawyers crossing the lines and the broader phenomenon of the globalization of law in general, and the globalization of human rights law in particular. One way to understand institutions and institutional processes is to follow and analyze career patterns of individuals and to study the way *they* view the "social space" within which they operate (Dezalay and Garth, 1996: 16–17). I will argue that the description of the ways by which transnational institutions influence the careers and ideologies of "local" agents (i.e., lawyers) may serve to illuminate the ways by which globalizations contribute to the process of deconstruction of the state and reconstruction of its relationship with institutions within civil society.

Background: Palestinian Rights in the Israeli High Court of Justice

Since the beginning of Israel's occupation of the West Bank and the Gaza Strip, the residents of these territories have been allowed to petition Israel's courts to challenge the orders and actions of the military government (H. C. 302, 306/72

Hilu; H. C. 393/82 *El Masulia*; Shamgar, 1971). Since most judicial review cases are disposed in Israel by the Supreme Court, sitting as the High Court of Justice (HCJ), most of these petitions made their way to this court.[1] During the thirty years of the occupation, the HCJ has dealt with thousands of petitions of Palestinians.[2] These petitions deal with all kind of controversies between the Palestinian population and the Israeli military regime, including planning and zoning, licensing, and work permits. A significant part of them deal with civil rights issues, such as the freedom of Palestinians to leave or enter the Territories, and administrative arrests. During the last decade, and since the eruption of the Palestinian upheaval—the *Intifada*—both the number of hostile activities against Israeli forces in the Territories and the number of military actions infringing on the liberties of the Palestinian residents of the Territories have risen sharply. The number of petitions to the HCJ dealing with serious violations of human rights, such as administrative detention orders and house demolition orders, has also risen sharply.[3] In most cases Palestinian petitioners are represented in the HCJ either by civil rights organizations or by activist lawyers specializing in legal advocacy on behalf of Palestinian petitioners.[4] The two most dominant organizations representing Palestinian issues in the HCJ are the Association for Civil Rights in Israel (ACRI) and Hotline—Center for Defense of the Individual (Hotline).[5]

The government of Israel is represented in all judicial proceedings by the Attorney General Office. Before the HCJ, the government is represented by lawyers belonging to a department of that office specializing in litigation before the HCJ: *The High Court of Justice Department (HCJD)*. It is a small department, composed normally of no more than ten lawyers. They represent all public agencies belonging to the central government of Israel, including ministries, governmental departments, the army (and any other security agency), the police, and many other public corporations (other than local authorities, which are represented by their own lawyers).

Adjudication on behalf of Palestinian civil rights in Israeli courts thus takes place in a rather small circle. The "adjudicative game" is normally played by repeat players: the fourteen judges (i.e., the Supreme Court justices) who deal with almost all petitions; the ten government lawyers (of the HCJD) who represent all government agencies before this court, and about two dozen lawyers who represent the petitioners in the majority of the cases.[6]

Crossing the Lines in the Civil Rights Adjudicative Game

The Israeli-Palestinian conflict is a deep cleavage between two communities contesting each other's fundamental national rights. This conflict has national and political as well as ethnic and religious aspects. It has a history of violent clashes between the two communities that have become even more violent since the eruption of the *Intifada*. Some of the most sensitive and problematic aspects of this conflict, such as the property rights of Palestinians and Israeli right-wing activists in the West Bank, and the legality of severe sanctions imposed on Palestinians activists by the Israeli regime (expulsion orders, house demolitions, etc.), are fought in legal battles before the courts. Therefore, one might expect that the sides' counsels constantly involved in such battles would be typical hard-liners, ideologically committed to their causes and emotionally devoted to the rightness of the arguments of their clients. Such an expectation would exist particularly in the case of civil rights legal activists who hold key positions in civil rights organizations representing Palestinians in Israeli courts. In other words, if one were looking for a place to find "classic" cause lawyers, this would be the place.

Interviews that I conducted with some of these activist lawyers do confirm these expectations, at least to some extent. All the lawyers I interviewed *view themselves* as cause lawyers. They all said that their professional career matches their ideological and political convictions, and that their current position is the result of their personal interest in human rights advocacy. Many of them regard themselves as human rights activists no less then lawyers. They all believe that their professional work should and does serve political causes which conform to their own ideological convictions. They also stated that their decision whether to represent a client is influenced by ideological considerations no less (and normally more) than pecuniary calculations.[7]

Following the career patterns of lawyers in this field reveals, however, unexpected phenomena. Some of these lawyers have "crossed the lines" during their professional career, that is, they left jobs as lawyers for civil rights groups for jobs within the Ministry of Justice, to represent, in essence, the other side to the conflict; or, they left the government for jobs in civil right organizations.

Two such cases refer to two senior members of the Legal Department of ACRI. In both cases, the head of the legal department of ACRI moved to accept a position in the HCJD immediately after completing his tenure at ACRI. In one of these cases, the lawyer served in the HCJD for a short period (about a year) before being promoted to a senior job at the Legislative Advisory Department of the Ministry of Justice, where some of his responsibilities are related to legislation concerning the rights of Palestinians in the Territories. The second lawyer left her position as the head of the legal department of ACRI in 1995 to accept a position in the HCJD, and has served there as a staff member ever since. A third case involves a lawyer who, after completing his statutory clerkship at the district attorney's office,[8] continued to work as a lawyer in the district attorney's office and was involved in prosecution of Palestinians charged with violent activities (such as stone throwing) against the IDF soldiers during the *Intifada*. He "crossed the lines" and joined the legal department of ACRI, where he worked for six years before taking a job as the head of the legal department of Hotline.[9]

These career moves took place within a relatively short period of time (between 1990 and 1996) and within a community composed of little more than two dozen lawyers (on each side). Some of the lawyers involved served for long periods in key positions within an institution representing one side in the conflict before going to represent the other side.[10] In a series of interviews with some of these lawyers and their colleagues, I sought to study the explanations for this phenomenon and its implications on our understanding of the cause-lawyering phenomena in general.

Analysis

How then, could we explain this trend of lawyers in the civil rights field to cross the lines, and how does each explanation affect our understanding of the concept of cause lawyering?

The first possible explanation is simple. Those lawyers who crossed the lines are not, in essence, cause lawyers. They are driven by motives such as promotion or money—just like any other hired gun. This explanation, however, is wholly incompatible with the way in which the lawyers involved present *their own* personal perceptions. As one of them said:

> Q: Do you think that lawyering is a way to promote ideological goals?
> A: It can be. This is not the case for most lawyers [but] . . . I joined ACRI as a lawyer because it was always the thing I wanted to do. . . . I wouldn't have come to this job otherwise. . . . I believed in ACRI and in its goals.
> —H. N.[11]

Another lawyer said:

> From the moment I decided to immigrate to Israel and to study law I wanted to work in the civil rights field.
> —U. M.

A third lawyer who had crossed the lines said:

> I went to law school in order to deal with issues in the public interest such as civil rights . . .
> —A. N.

A second and more complicated explanation is that, in fact, those who moved to the attorney general's office from ACRI or vice versa *did not* cross the lines. They are representing the other side in the litigation—but *from their point of view they continue to serve the same causes.* As one of them articulated:

> The truth is, and I really believe this, that I see a close similarity between my views and feelings—as a civil rights advocate—of what the role of lawyers should be, and the views and feelings of my counterparts at the Office of the Attorney General. This is true particularly in the criminal law field. The public prosecutor strives to further the public interest and to safeguard the rights of the accused and the rules of due process. . . . When I am in contact with the members of the HCJD I feel

that I am talking to people who are like me; they more or less share these basic conceptions of what the law is and what we are striving for in the public interest.

—U. M.

In order to understand the "shared causes" argument, it is worthwhile to probe into the nature and characteristics of these two organizations. ACRI is considered among civil liberties activists to be the most "establishment" organization in the field. Many key figures in ACRI are (and have been) distinguished academic figures, retired Supreme Court or district court justices, and other respected figures within the Israeli community. Unlike some other civil rights organizations and cause lawyers who are working in the field of Palestinians' rights and are regarded by Jewish public opinion as outside the national consensus, ACRI always strives to preserve its image as an organization that appeals to the support of the mainstream. As one former member of the legal department of ACRI, currently a member of Hotline, emphasized:

> ACRI is a more "establishment" body [than Hotline]. Their attitude is more careful, they are concerned with their image among the general public, judges and the lawyers in the Attorney General's department. Here, at Hotline, we don't concern ourselves with this.
>
> —U. M.

In other words, the lawyers at ACRI, and in particular those lawyers who left to work for the government, do not see themselves as detached from the national narratives of Jewishness as the dominant criterion for complete Israeli affiliation, and national security as a major ethos that characterizes the broader legal community in Israel (Barzilai, 1997). These lawyers are all Jewish (like most lawyers in ACRI)[12] and have served in the Israeli Defense Forces, like most other Jewish Israeli citizens. They belong to a group of lawyer-activists classified by Lisa Hajjar as "Jewish Israeli Liberals": critical of the *form* of the Israeli rule in the Territories, to the extent that it involves the violation of the standards of the rule of law, rather than completely identifying with the national and political aspirations of the Palestinians in their struggle to put an end to the Israeli occupation (Hajjar, 1997: 9–10).[13]

If one looks at the other side of this "battlefield," one discovers that some important characteristics of the HCJD made these career moves even less problematic from the point of view of this group of lawyers. The lawyers of the HCJD do not always act as one might expect of lawyers representing a military regime in an adversarial environment. During interviews, they repeatedly emphasized that they view themselves as "officers of the Court," rather than merely as lawyers representing the government (Dotan, 1999). As one of them stressed:

> [As a lawyer in the department] you are not only a government lawyer but also an officer of the court, a gatekeeper of the rule of law, and you also have to watch your professional reputation.
>
> —I. N.

Another member described the department role as follows:

> The code of values guiding us here [at the HCJD] is to serve the client at any price.... We are guided by a different code of values. We serve the public, and this is our first priority. Serving the client agency comes only second to this priority.
>
> —K. S.

The HCJD members also pointed out that, from their point of view, whether the government wins a certain case is of secondary importance to them. What is more important is to ensure that the administrative action meets the legal standards of the HCJ.[14] In the words of one lawyer I interviewed:

> It is a million times more important for me to retain the court's trust in me than to win a certain case.
>
> —T. L.

Another lawyer added:

> The lawyer in the public service is committed, above all, to the rule of law, and to similar values, and not necessarily to what the client wants at a given moment. [We are committed] to long-term values and to public norms.
>
> —A. N.

The HCJD's lawyers are at liberty to adopt such an attitude to their professional role because they enjoy a high level of autonomy *vis-à-vis* their client agencies. On the institutional level, they are part of the ministry of justice and are not supervised by the client agencies. They do not view themselves as obligated to be completely committed, on either the policy level or on the institutional level, to the interests of the client agency. Moreover, according to the rulings of the Supreme Court, the attorney general's office enjoys the exclusive right to represent the government before the HCJ (H.C. 4267/93 *Amitai*). The HCJD members are well aware of the power that this exclusivity bestows on them on occasions when they do not believe in the case of their clients. Therefore, in disputes between the client agencies and the policymakers in the attorney general's office regarding the true "public interest," it is usually the view of the latter that prevails (Dotan, 1999). This high level of institutional autonomy enables these lawyers to represent the Israeli government and the Israeli authorities in the Territories, and yet to view themselves as committed to liberal values such as the rule of law and human rights.[15]

It can be concluded from the discussion above that those who crossed the lines were well aware of the implications of their career move on the level of their affiliation to legal institutions. They did not feel, however, that they had to pay a price in terms of their professional ideology. Therefore, they do not view themselves as hired guns. Rather, they view themselves as cause lawyers *whose causes are shared by the lawyers on both sides*: a deep commitment to the idea of the rule of law *and* a commitment to assure the safeguards of fundamental human rights as officers of the court. The lawyers who moved from ACRI to the government (or *vice versa*) did not, according to this line of reasoning, change their causes, but only their place of work. It is the shared ethos of the rule of law that unites lawyers both in the civil rights organizations (at least some of them, such as ACRI) and those representing the state on behalf of the ministry of justice. As one of the lawyers who made such a move said:

> Q: Do you think that when you moved from ACRI to the HCJD you crossed the lines?
>
> A: The *positions* of each side are different; otherwise they wouldn't be appearing in court. However, the *ideological causes* are not different in principle. We solve most cases before we get to the courtroom. The tools [each side uses] to analyze the case are more or less similar and so are each side's values. If there is an arguable case the role of the HCJD is to argue it in court. If there is no arguable case, [we] would handle the matter out of court. In other cases, in accordance with our commitment to the rule of law, it is possible to argue the case on behalf of each party.
>
> —A. N. (italics mine)

The above description illuminates another source of affinity between ACRI and the HCJD, that is, their tendency to cooperate in the daily practice of handling disputes. While it is generally the case that most petitions to the High Court of Justice are disposed through out-of-court settlements, and do not reach final judicial determination, it is particularly common for the HCJD to reach out-of-court settlements with ACRI or other Palestinian civil rights organizations (Dotan and Hofnung, 1997).[16] The working relationship between the HCJD and ACRI (as well as some other action groups) is so close that in many cases these organizations address the HCJD even *before* they take the action to the court in order to reach a pretrial agreement that would save the time and trouble of litigation (Dotan, 1999). These patterns of cooperation on the professional level are combined with social affiliations between these two groups of lawyers. The members of both groups live in the same relatively small community of lawyers in the same city (Jerusalem). Most of them graduated from the same law school and often have known each other since they were law students.[17] The two groups of lawyers meet on an almost daily basis for professional purposes (either in or out of court), and they also meet quite often at social events.

These relations may also serve as a complementary explanation for the phenomenon of line crossing, as just one aspect of the general phenomena of professional cooperation between these two groups of lawyers.

To the above explanations for the phenomenon of line crossing, one could add an explanation that has to do not with the political convictions or professional ideology of these lawyers but with personal characteristics. Some of these lawyers explained their ability and willingness to cross the lines in terms of their personal character—their tendency to look at every issue or problem from all possible angles, rather than to commit themselves completely to one side. As one of them said:

> It is no coincidence that I and A. N. could move from ACRI to work for the HCJD. There are some people at ACRI who I can't imagine doing this. I have always looked at things less in terms of black and white. When I was at ACRI, I always felt very strongly the dilemmas [concerning the case at hand]. There were nights that I couldn't fall asleep because of my concern that were I to defend the right of a suspected terrorist in court, the next day some bomb would explode. For me it is very difficult to be on one side. Some people believe in absolute values, such as freedom of speech. I have always seen the complexity.
>
> —H. N.

While this last explanation may be a useful illumination for the phenomenon of crossing the lines, it also raises some troubling questions and objections. One may question the rightness of a system in which activist lawyers, who advocate civil rights in an adversarial system, are led by a motivation to "serve the system" or some broad and vague concept of "the Rule of Law," rather than by dedication to an uncompromising struggle on behalf of the civil rights of their clients. Indeed, not all activist lawyers in the field are sympathetic to the career moves of the "line crossers." Some severely criticize ACRI's members' tendency "to cooperate" and play a "responsible" role, or to be cognizant of "the other parties position" while neglecting their roles as fighters on behalf of the Palestinians' civil liberties. For these "hardliners" the move of the two ACRI members to the HCJD was wholly unacceptable on both moral and ideological grounds, as one said:

> Q: What do you think of the phenomenon of attorneys leaving ACRI for jobs at the HCJD?
> A: The truth is that it is an embarrassment for ACRI, something they should be ashamed of. How could people just "jump" from one "pool" to another without any cooling-off period at all? I fully understand—both "pools" are very well "heated" and are very pleasant.... ACRI operates safely within the national consensus.... The move from one to the other doesn't look good at all.
>
> —A. L.

On the conceptual level, one may question the assumption that the above described group of lawyers can truly be called cause lawyers. The phenomenon of functional cooperation between lawyers belonging to opposing sides in a given adjudication, by reaching settlements, and by creating channels of communication in order to benefit their clients and themselves, is not rare. Nor is the phenomenon of social alliance, collegiality, and close personal amity between the members of such groups, even if formally they represent the opposing parties in court (such as between the public prosecutor and the public defense lawyer who work in the same town for many years; see, e.g., Sudnow, 1965; Coglianese, 1996). However, this kind of behavior seems to be compatible with the model within which the lawyers are part of a professional elite group whose members share a common social and academic background (they graduated from the same schools, belong to the same club, etc.), rather than with the model of cause lawyers. For example, one could argue that two barristers, who meet together for lunch and a glass of sherry after battling in court all morning—one as prosecutor and the other as defense attorney—share "the same cause" of "preserving the rule of law." From a more skeptical viewpoint, however, one may suggest that the only real "cause" they share is the common will to preserve the status of the profession and the prestige of the law school from which they both graduated.

Moreover, in the context of human rights litigation, cause lawyering "for the rule of law" may become an oppressive, rather than a liberating mechanism. This strong professional sense of unity shared by members of the legal profession may be seen as the reflection of a narrow legalistic discourse dominating the work of lawyers in the field of civil rights litigation. It is one thing when such discourse controls the perceptions of the legal bureaucrats representing the state. It is wholly a different situation when it becomes the controlling ideology of the legal community at large, and serves as a shared ethos of the legal representatives of both the state and the people whose basic rights are at risk as a result of the state's actions.

In this respect, one may argue that this common view shared by lawyers in different positions is one of the implications of the particular legal culture that has evolved in Israel. This legal ideology is based, on the one hand, upon a strong and often uncritical belief in the autonomy of the law. On the other hand, this ideology espouses a rather ambitious (if not wholly extravagant) concept as to the role of law in society, as reflected in the following words taken from a judgment of the Supreme Court:

> Any [human] action is susceptible to determination by a legal norm, and there is no action regarding which there is no legal norm determining it. There is no 'legal vacuum' in which actions are taken without the law having anything to say about them. The law encompasses any action.... The fact that an issue is "strictly political" does not change the fact that such an issue is also "a legal issue." (H.C. 910/86 *Ressler*)[18]

This rhetoric is but one aspect of a wider process of the rise of law in general, and of the High Court of Justice in particular, as a dominating social mechanism which is assumed to be able to correct all sorts of deficiencies in the work of other institutions in society and to resolve any sort of social, ideological, or cultural cleavages (Kretzmer, 1988; Shamir, 1995; Avnon, 1996). The rise of law as a dominating discourse may not come as a surprise in a society that suffers from both strong external pressures and deep ideological cleavages among its own members. The "rule of law" concept presents one of very few palatable choices in such a radically conflicted society. In this context the HCJ is conceived as a defender of civil rights (at least for the middle-class liberal population). As a result, this court also serves as a joint reference point for lawyers both inside and outside the state.

While the possible explanations for the phenomenon of "lawyering for the rule of law" vary, it is still worth considering the relations between this phenomenon and the general concept of cause lawyering. Can we actually talk about "cause lawyering" in this context? Or does the concept of cause lawyering assume some uncompromising ideological commitment to the causes of *your own side*? Can cause lawyering be compatible with a tendency to "understand" the other side's point of view, to "view the whole picture," and to be able to associate yourself with a professional group which includes "the other guys' " lawyers? In order to answer this question, I will now discuss "lawyering for the cause of the rule of law" by referring to some of the accepted parameters for cause lawyering in general (Sarat and Scheingold, 1998).

Lawyering for the cause of the rule of law does conform with some basic characteristics of cause lawyering in general. The people engaged in such activity are motivated by moral and ideological convictions rather than by exclusive concern for personal gain such as for pecuniary benefits or for professional promotion.[19] They work for a cause that has to do with their own conception of good society, rather than rent out their services solely to promote their client's interest. Therefore, the tension between their public cause and the interests of their client is as relevant as in any other case of cause lawyering. In fact, this tension may be even stronger in the case of this type of lawyering. Normally, cause lawyering involves tensions between the private interests of the individual client on one hand, and the general interests of the group to which she belongs on the other hand (Bell, 1976; Luban, 1988: 337; Ellmann, 1992; Petrara, 1994). In the case of cause lawyering for the sake of the rule of law, the situation is more complex. Sometimes, the lawyer may feel committed not only to the public ideas supported by the group to which her client belongs, but she may also feel committed to (or inhibited by) general considerations as to the public good, including those who may foster the interests of the *other party* to the litigation. For example, a lawyer employed by a "green" organization arguing a case against the destruction of a forest for the purpose of building a new highway, may be aware of the interest of the general public in creating modern and efficient transportation as well as being committed to the preservation of nature. Indeed, such an attitude may be incompatible with the common perception of lawyers' ethics according to the paradigm of lawyers' "role morality" within an adversary system (see, e.g., Luban, 1988: xx). In this respect, however, cause lawyering for the rule of law does not differ from cause lawyering in general, as a social phenomenon transforming the lawyer-client relationship of the conventional model of lawyering (Sarat and Scheingold, 1998).

Another attribute of cause lawyering is that it is directed at altering some aspect of the social, economic, and political status quo (Minow, 1991; Abrams, 1991). Indeed, for some scholars, this parameter of cause lawyering as a legal practice seeking to attack the current social and political status quo is the paramount factor that distinguishes these lawyers from their professional counterparts (Scheingold, 1988; Buchanan and Trubek, 1992; Menkel-Meadow, 1998). In this respect, it seems that cause lawyers for the rule of law would normally be regarded as belonging to the less radical end of the continuum of cause lawyering, or else be considered as wholly outside of the spectrum. This does not mean that such lawyers do not have their own vision of a good society. Unlike hired guns, they do not completely distinguish between their ideology and their professional duties as a lawyers. However, it may well be assumed that the strategies that they would adopt in order to carry out their vision would be much less radical than those of some other cause lawyers. The deep commitment of such lawyers to the (traditional liberal) value of the rule of law, and their tendency to always view "both sides' point of view," seem to be at odds with the conception of extreme and radical cause lawyers, who challenge established conceptions of professionalism with an effort to decommodify, politicize, and socialize legal practice in order to contribute to some sort of transformative politics that will redistribute political power and destabilize existing social structures (Sarat and Scheingold, 1998).

The last aspect of this model of cause lawyering that needs to be discussed is its relation to the state. Common wisdom assumes that there is an opposition between cause lawyers and the state. This case study proves, however, that this opposition should not always be taken for granted. Some kinds of cause lawyering may exist within the state and among state lawyers, rather than being carried out only by public action organizations or individuals using their professional skills to challenge state activities. Cause lawyering for the rule of law is surely one of these models of cause lawyering that may be practiced by state lawyers, much as it may be performed by lawyers in civil rights or other public action organizations. And, as demonstrated in the case of the "line crossers," it may be performed by the same people on both sides.

It is now worthwhile to get back to the question of the evaluation of the potential impact of this kind of lawyering: Is this kind of lawyering good or bad for defending human rights and promoting ideas of better society? What is the impact of such lawyering on the causes usually attributed to cause lawyering?

As mentioned above, there are several dangers that can be attributed to this type of professional practice. Lawyering for the rule of law may represent nothing more than cozy cooperation between those defending state infringements of human rights and those who are supposed to attack such infringements. It may also run the risk of cultivating a discourse in which formalistic legal values supersede human concerns and social values. It surely runs the risk of inhibiting any possibility of radical social change that may be considered inherent to the concept of cause lawyering. In other words, the danger of playing a minor ameliorative role, restricted to co-opting and conforming the established order and diverting energies from challenges to it (Abel, 1985; Rose, 1985; Sarat and Scheingold, 1998), is particularly relevant to this type of lawyering.

On the other hand, it may be argued that the definition of cause lawyering must be culturally located and so is the evaluation of its possible impact (Menkel-Meadow, 1998). Therefore, in order to evaluate the phenomenon of lawyering "for the rule of law," we need to look at the particular Israeli political and cultural setting. Previous studies prove that cause lawyers in Israel were much more successful when emphasizing formal legal arguments rather than when addressing general policy claims (Morag-Levine, 1998). This reality is partly the result of the failure of legal and other interest groups to effect popular social mobilization (Morag-Levine, 1998; Yishai, 1987; Yishai, 1992), and partly the result of the ambition of Israeli courts to preserve their image as professional, impartial, and apolitical agents of the rule of law idea. This has been the case particularly in cause lawyering advocating the civil rights of ethnic minorities. In litigation concerning the rights of minorities such as Bedouins living in the southern part of Israel and Palestinian residents of the Occupied Territories, arguments based on individualistic and particularistic claims proved to be much more successful than those based on collective appeals (Shamir and Chinski, 1998; Dotan, 1999). While cause lawyering may be properly defined as an activity that seeks to use law-related means in order to bring about legal and social reforms, it is sometimes forced to concentrate on a case-by-case struggle to prevent infringements on individual rights (Menkel-Meadow, 1998 n. 53). The tendency of some Israeli cause lawyers to cooperate with forces within the legal apparatus of the state, that are friendly to the ideas of civil rights, may serve as yet another example for the limitations on cause lawyering that operates within a social environment unsupportive of their causes.

Globalization and the Blurring of Institutional Lines

Thus far, I have dealt with the (unexpected) cooperation between human rights and government lawyers as a purely Israeli legal and cultural phenomenon. The blurring of institutional lines is, however, closely related to the globalization of law. The ideological alliance between these two groups of lawyers derives its stamina not only from the conditions described above but also from the shared commitment to what can be described as the global ethos of human rights. The process of the globalization of law in general, and of human rights law in particular (Bianchi, 1997; Teubner, 1997), has broad implications on the behavior of the Israeli legal system. The Supreme Court of Israel espouses the international language of human rights. The rulings of the court on the issues of human rights are heavily influenced by concepts and doctrines developed in other countries as well as by international treaties on human rights. The court frequently cites decisions of foreign courts, and more specifically decisions of American courts (Shachar et al., 1996). Constitutional terms such as "clear and present danger," "the marketplace of ideas," and "chilling effect" are frequently mentioned alongside citations from American decisions and academic writings as the basis for the rulings of the court (e.g., H. C. 1/81 *Shiran*; H. C. 399/85 *Kahana*; H.C. 680/88 *Schnitzr*). It is only natural that lawyers who appear before the court internalize these concepts.

The process of the globalization of human rights law is also reflected in the career structure of lawyers from both groups. Many of the lawyers serving in ACRI received part of their legal training at law schools and human rights organizations in the United States.[20] A number of lawyers in the HCJD also acquired legal education in the United States at some stage of their career.[21] Moreover, the three main figures that have crossed the lines, as well as others who made the same move, received their education (wholly or partly) in the United States.[22] Two of the three lawyers who crossed the lines were born and educated in the United States and were involved in human rights activities before they immigrated to Israel. The influence of this background on their professional ideology is reflected by the following words of one lawyer who grew up in the United States and immigrated to Israel:

> I think that the education of an educated person in the U.S. emphasizes human rights from a very early stage. My son studies now in the fifth grade, and I told him how when I was studying in the fifth grade I presented to my class the struggle of Afro-Americans for equality. The class was fascinated by my presentation and I was very proud of myself, and up to this day I remember this as one of the first speeches in my life.
>
> —U. M.

The third lawyer was born and educated in Israel but spent two years in the United States after graduating law school, where she received an LLM degree from an elite American law school and worked for the ACLU and other civil rights organizations. I asked her to refer to the influence of her experience in the United States on her perceptions as a cause lawyer:

> Q: Do you think that your experience at the ACLU contributed anything to your view of yourself as a lawyer?
> A: I think so. I mean, that you could see [while being there] that the work is not strictly legal, but that it goes much beyond this. I have learned about the variety of fields in which these lawyers operate, and I saw how it works in practice. The truth is that I knew it already [before I went to the United States], but then I saw how it works in the field. It was amazing to see the variety of different organizations, the number of areas in which they were involved and the amount of things they do. At the time I went to the US there were [in Israel] only ACRI and some very small organizations. That has changed a lot. There are many more organizations nowadays and I think one main reason for this is that many people who went to the US on scholarships brought these changes after they have seen how these things work [in the United States].
>
> —H. N.

The tendency of the lawyers in the two groups to cooperate may be explained by the fact that they view themselves as a part of a broader project that crosses not only institutional lines but also transnational boundaries. In this respect, the close cooperation between government lawyers and human rights legal activists serves as a manifestation of the implications of globalization on institutional structures. Globalization leads to reform of existing institutional arrangements through adoption and adaptation of transnational norms and doctrines (Teubner, 1997; Sarat and Scheingold, 2000). The ability of state and civil rights lawyers to create a sense of "civic professionalism" (Halliday, 1987), which is the basis for the above described patterns of cooperation, is based primarily on the fact that these two groups of lawyers share the common transnational ethos of human rights, which, with all its limitations and shortcomings, enables an ongoing cooperation between them. This ethos became part of their professional training, and is routinely reaffirmed by the rhetoric and practice of the Supreme Court before which both groups appear frequently. It serves as an explanation for their seemingly surprising career moves.

At the same time, the above described phenomenon of Israeli lawyers who cross the lines demonstrates the implications that globalization has on institutional lines. More particular, it illustrates *the ways* by which globalization blurs the distinction between the state and institutions of civil society. Globalization decenters the state (Shamir, 1998; Sarat and Scheingold, 2000) not only by exerting power and influence "from the outside," but rather, by enlisting forces *within the state* that cooperate with external forces (such as cause lawyers) in the course of reshaping the state and redefining the boundaries between the state and civil society. The influence of globalization is manifested through number of different channels of human activities such as immigration, education, institutional affiliation, and sponsorship. Globalization affects forces within the state through the "genealogy of ideas" as well as through the "genealogy of careers." Thereafter, there are some forces within the state that become more amenable (or more vulnerable, one may argue) to cooperation with forces "outside" the state that seek to reform state policies and practices (Dotan, 1999). This vulnerability may lead to cooperation between forces within and outside the state (such as in the case study above described), and this cooperation may ultimately help to bring about reforms in state practices. In other words, while the ability of cause lawyers to use litigation as a vehicle for social change may depend primarily on the creation of a support structure for legal mobilization (Epp, 1998), it is sometimes the state itself that contributes to the creation of the same support structure that is crucial for its own reconstruction.

Conclusion

Cause lawyering for the rule of law, unlike some other kinds of cause lawyering, does not involve an absolute commitment to the objectives of one group or to one side in a social or political conflict. It does, however, involve a commitment of the lawyer to moral and ideological values, and it does involve the use of the lawyers' professional skills to promote certain broader social goals. This model of cause lawyering may be espoused also by lawyers employed by the legal apparatus of the state or other agencies in the public sector. The model also explains the phenomenon of activist lawyers who, at some stage of their careers, serve one side of a social conflict and, at another stage, may represent the opposing side. Changing sides does not necessarily mean changing one's causes. Lawyers may, in some cases, serve the same causes while arguing a case for different, and even opposing, parties.

At the same time, the phenomenon of cause lawyers crossing the lines manifests the influence of globalization on institutional lines in Israel. It also demonstrates the ways by which transnational doctrines, processes, and institutions deconstruct and reshape institutions within the state and thereby help to create the support structure that is necessary for social reforms through litigation.

Acknowledgments

The research for this essay was supported, in part, by the Israel Science Foundation founded by the Israeli Academy of Sciences and Humanities, and, in part, by a grant from the Minerva Center for Human Rights at the Faculty of Law of the Hebrew University and the Harry S. Truman Research Institute for the Advancement of Peace. An earlier version of this study was published as "Cause Lawyers Crossing the Lines: Patterns of Fragmentation and Cooperation between State and Civil Rights Lawyers in Israel," 5 *International Journal of the Legal Profession* (1998), 193–208. I thank Ms. Einat Albin for her excellent work as a research assistant.

Notes

1. The High Court of Justice (HCJ) is one of the functions of the Supreme Court of Israel. In this capacity the HCJ serves as the principal judicial institution for judicial review cases in the country. When a civil or criminal dispute arises in Israel, it normally makes its way into a county court and then—on appeal—to a district court. Only a handful of such cases reach the Supreme Court as a third instance of *cassation*. The Supreme Court also functions as an appellate court for cases involving serious criminal offenses, or civil disputes where the value of the claim is particularly high. Such cases will make their way directly to a District Court and then, on appeal, to the Supreme Court. If, however, the dispute—no matter how minor and ordinary—concerns a public agency exercising its legal powers, it is brought directly before the Supreme Court, and is resolved by this court with no possibility of appeal. Therefore, the Supreme Court in Israel serves three different functions: as a court of *cassation*, as a court of appeal, and as a court of first (and last) instance for judicial review cases.

2. In this essay I use the term "Palestinians" to indicate Palestinian residents of the Territories, as distinct from Palestinian residents of Israel.

3. For example, during the first three years of the *Intifada* about 14,000 Palestinians were administratively detained. During the same period, more than 500 houses were either demolished or sealed. The frequency of the use of other infringing measures such as curfew and closure of schools has also risen sharply (Shalev, 1990; Straschnov, 1994: 72, 86–87;

B'Tselem report, 1990–91; B'Tselem report, 1989). This increase in the number of restrictive administrative measures was accompanied by a sharp rise in the number of petitions to the HCJ by Palestinians. For example, while during the twenty years between 1967 and 1986 557 petitions were submitted (Shamir, 1990), during the four first years of the *Intifada* (1988–91) 806 petitions were submitted (Dotan, 1999). Apart from judicial review cases, the Israeli judicial system dealt with a massive wave of criminal cases against Palestinians involved in disobedience activities during the *Intifada* (Strachnov, 1994).

4. For research concerning Palestinian petitions before the HCJ during the period of 1986–95, I checked the HCJ registers for two months (January and June) for each of these years. I found that in 58.6 percent of the cases the petitioners were represented by such repeat players (Dotan, 1999).

5. ACRI is the prominent civil rights organization in Israel. It deals with all kinds of civil rights issues, and its activities include litigation, education, and publication of reports. Hotline is a smaller organization, specializing in the field of Palestinian rights. It is involved mainly in litigation and in advising Palestinians of their legal rights. Apart from these two organizations, there are some other organizations that occasionally petition the HCJ, as well as a dozen activist lawyers who specialize in representing Palestinians in civil rights cases.

6. Criminal actions involving issues of civil disobedience (such as violent demonstrations, throwing stones at vehicles and soldiers) or terrorist activities are disposed mainly in military courts formed by the Israeli Government in the Territories, and only in a minority of cases by regular criminal courts in Israel itself (Edelman, 1994; Bisharat, 1995; Hajjar, 1997). The prosecution in such criminal cases is conducted by the criminal departments of the military advocate or the district attorney's department of the relevant region.

7. Interviews were conducted through 1996 and 1997. I interviewed twenty lawyers involved in litigation concerning Palestinian rights (both on behalf of civil rights organizations and on behalf of the Israeli government). Most interviews were taped and transcribed (including all those interviews from which the citations brought below were taken).

8. The training process of lawyers according to Israeli law includes a twelve month clerkship.

9. Two other such career moves were made by people who completed their statutory clerkship at the HCJD and then began working as lawyers at ACRI. In two additional cases, lawyers left the Ministry of Justice (but not the HCJD) to work for ACRI. In one case, a lawyer began her professional career as a clerk in ACRI, then worked as a lawyer in the Ministry of Justice, left the Ministry of Justice for a job with another ministry, and then went back to the legal department of ACRI. The other case is of a lawyer who did her clerkship in the Ministry of Justice and is now working for ACRI.

10. All these cases involved lawyers who worked for ACRI at some stage of their professional career, and in most of them the government agency involved was the HCJD. Therefore, I will concentrate on the relations between these two organizations.

11. I agreed not to publish identifying information about any of the lawyers interviewed. Therefore, they are identified by initials which are pseudonymous.

12. Some of the legal staff at ACRI are Arab-Israelis (i.e., Palestinians who are Israeli citizens). ACRI does not employ Palestinians from the Territories.

13. One of the former ACRI lawyers told me that even as an ACRI lawyer, he used to do his reserve military service for the legal department of the IDF, which dealt with (among other issues) prosecuting Palestinians for breaking the military laws in the Territories. This is probably the most striking example of the dilemma of "double loyalty" characterizing the role of ACRI lawyers in the context of their actions in favor of the Palestinian population in the Territories.

14. While all the lawyers of the HCJD that I interviewed emphasized their dual function (as representative of their client and as officers of the court), they all pointed out that the weight and intensity of each of these values vary among the different lawyers in accordance with their professional ideology, as well as with the policies of the head of the department at the time.

15. This does not mean that these lawyers feel comfortable with any specific action taken by the military authorities in the Territories. In fact, the "crossers" serving in the HJCD (as well as other lawyers in the department) emphasized that they have their "red lines," meaning that there are some types of action that they would object to defending in court. They also emphasized that such "red lines" are personal decisions and vary from one lawyer to another. They said that on the practical level they could avoid the dilemma to some extent, since there are usually other members of the HCJD willing to handle such problematic cases. The fact that both the HCJD and ACRI are relatively large organizations that deal with many issues (i.e., not only with civil rights of Palestinians) allows these lawyers leeway to avoid the need to deal with cases involving a moral dilemma for them. One lawyer who moved from ACRI to the HCJD said that she has not been required so far by her superiors to deal with cases of Palestinian rights.

16. For example, out of 75 petitions of ACRI to the HCJ during the years 1983, 1986, 1989, 1991, 1993, and 1995, only 23 reached the stage of final judicial disposition, while 47 were settled (and another five remained undecided); see Dotan and Hofnung, 1997.

17. Almost all the lawyers interviewed graduated from the Faculty of Law of the Hebrew University of Jerusalem.

18. *Ressler v. Minister of Defense*, 477, per Justice Aharon Barak (currently the president of the Supreme Court).

19. I do not claim, of course, that such lawyers may not be motivated to some extent by the wish to promote their own career, etc. The phenomenon of mixed motives (ideological and personal) is, however, relevant to any sort of cause lawyering (Sarat and Scheingold, 1998). It seems that cause lawyering of the kind discussed in the text does not differ from any other kind of cause lawyering in this respect.

20. ACRI is officially affiliated with the ACLU. Many of the lawyers in ACRI acquire advanced legal education and practical training in civil rights organizations through funding programs that are supported by the New Israel Fund.

21. Out of ten lawyers who served in the HCJD at the time of the research, four have received their education in the United States. The most important program in this respect is the program for advanced academic education in the United States offered by the Vaxner Foundation. While the program is offered (on a competitive basis) for all government officials at mid-career stage, several HCJD members managed to win seats in this program

22. Most other lawyers who made similar moves (see note *supra*) also received legal education in the United States at some stage of their career.

References

Books and Articles

Abel, R. L. (1985). "Law without Politics: Legal Aid under Advanced Capitalism," 32 *UCLA Law Review*, 474.

Abrams, K. (1991). "Lawyers and Social Change Lawbreaking: Confronting a Plural Bar," 52 *University of Pittsburgh Law Review*, 753.

Avnon, D. (1996). "'The Enlightened Public': Jewish and Democratic or Liberal and Democratic?" 3 *Mishpat Umimshal—Law and Government in Israel*, 417.
Barzilai, G. (1997). "Between the Rule of Law and the Laws of the Ruler: The Supreme Court in the Israeli Legal Culture," 152 *International Journal of Social Science* (June 1997), 193.
Bell, D. (1976). "Serving Two Masters: Integration, Ideals and Client Interest in School Desegregation Litigation," 85 *Yale Law Journal*, 470.
Bianchi, A. (1997). "Globalization of Human Rights: The Role of Non-State Actors," in *Global Law without State* G. Teubner, ed. Aldershot: Dartmouth Gower.
Bisharat, G. (1995). "Courting Justice? Legitimation in Lawyering under Israeli Occupation," 20 *Law and Society Review*, 349.
Buchanan, R., and L. G. Trubek (1992). "Resistances and Possibilities: A Critical and Practical Look at Public Interest Lawyering," 19 *Review of Law and Social Change*, 687.
Coglianese, C. (1996). "Litigating within Relationship: Disputes and Disturbance in the Regulatory Process," 30 *Law and Society Review*, 735.
Dezalay, Yves, and Bryant G. Garth (1996). *Dealing in Virtue: International Commercial Arbitration and the Construction of a Transnational Legal Order*. Chicago: University of Chicago Press.
Dotan, Y. (1999). "Judicial Rhetoric, Government Lawyers and Human Rights: The Case of the Israeli High Court of Justice," 33 (2) *Law and Society Review*, 319.
Dotan, Y., and M. Hofnung, (1997). "Legal Battles as Primary Means of Collective Action: The Judicial Politics of Israeli Interest Groups." Paper presented at the International Political Science Association XVII World Congress, Seoul.
Edelman, M. (1994). *Courts, Politics and Culture in Israel*. Charlottesville: University Press of Virginia.
Ellmann, S. (1992). "Client-Centeredness Multiplied: Individual Autonomy and Collective Mobilization in Public Interest Lawyers' Representation," 78 *Virginia Law Review*, 1103.
Epp, C. R. (1998). *The Rights Revolution: Lawyers, Activists and Supreme Courts in Comparative Perspectives*. Chicago: University of Chicago Press.
Hajjar, L. (1997). "Cause Lawyering in Transnational Perspective: National Conflict and Human Rights in Israel/Palestine," 31 *Law and Society Review*, 473.
Halliday, T. C. (1987). *Beyond Monopoly: Lawyers, State Crises and Professional Empowerment*, Chicago: University of Chicago Press.
Kretzmer, D. (1988). "Judicial Review of Knesset Decisions," 8 *Tel Aviv University Studies in Law*, 95.
Luban, D. (1988). *Lawyers and Justice*. Princeton, N.J.: Princeton University Press.
Margulies, P. (1995). "Progressive Lawyering and Lost Traditions," 73 *Texas Law Review*, 1139.
Menkel-Meadow, C. (1998). "The Causes of Cause Lawyering: Towards an Understanding of the Motivation and Commitment of Social Justice Lawyers," in *Cause Lawyering: Political Commitments and Professional Responsibilities*, A. Sarat and S. Scheingold, eds. New York: Oxford University Press.
Minow, M. (1991). "Breaking the Law: Lawyers and Clients in Struggles for Social Change," 52 *University of Pittsburgh Law Review*, 723.
Morag-Levine, N. (1998). "Global Networks, Local Cultures: Transplantation and Transformation in Israeli Environmental Cause Lawyering." Prepared for presentation at the 1998 Annual Meeting of the Law and Society Association, Aspen, Colorado.
Petrara, M. C. (1994). "Dangerous Identification: Confusing Lawyers with Their Clients," 19 *Journal of the Legal Profession*, 179.
Rose, N. (1985). "Unreasonable Rights: Mental Illness and the Limits of the Law," 12 *Journal of Law and Society*, 199.

Sarat, A., and S. Scheingold, (1998). Cause Lawyering and the Reproduction of Professional Authority: An Introduction, in *Cause Lawyering: Political Commitments and Professional Responsibilities*, A. Sarat and S. Scheingold, eds. New York: Oxford University Press.

Scheingold, S. (1998). "The Struggle to Politicize Legal Practice: A Case Study of Left-Activist Lawyering in Seattle," in *Cause Lawyering: Political Commitments and Professional Responsibilities*, A. Sarat and S. Scheingold, eds. New York: Oxford University Press.

——— (1988). "Radical Lawyers and Socialist Ideals," 15 *Journal of Law and Society*, 122.

Shachar, Y., R. Haris, and M. Gross (1996). "Practices of Citation in the Supreme Court— Quantitative Analysis," 27 *Mishpatim*, 119 (Hebrew).

Shalev, A. (1990). *The Intifada: Causes and Effects*. Tel Aviv: Papyrus (Hebrew).

Shamgar, M. (1971). "The Observance of International Law in the Administrative Territories," 1 *Israeli Yearbook of Human Rights*, 262.

Shamir, R. (1990). " 'Landmark Cases' and the Reproduction of Legitimacy: The Case of Israel's High Court of Justice," 24 *Law and Society Review*, 781.

——— (1995). "The Politics of Reasonableness: Discretion as Judicial Power," 5 *Theory and Review*, 354 (Hebrew).

Shamir, R., and S. Chinski (1997). "Destruction of Houses and Construction of Cause: Lawyers and Bedouins in the Israeli Courts," in *Cause Lawyering: Political Commitments and Professional Responsibilities*, A. Sarat and S. Scheingold, eds. New York: Oxford University Press.

Straschnov, A. (1994). *Justice under Fire*. Tel Aviv: Yedioth Ahronoth Books (Hebrew).

Sudnow, D. (1965). "Normal Crimes: Sociological Features of the Penal Code in a Public Defender Office," 12 *Social Problems*, 255.

Teubner G. (1997). "The King's Many Bodies: The Self-Deconstruction of Law's Hierarchy," 31 *Law and Society Review*, 763–87.

Yishai, Y. (1987). *Interest Groups in Israel: The Test of Democracy*. Tel Aviv: Am Oved and Eshkol Institute. (Hebrew).

——— (1992). "Interest Groups and Bureaucrats in a Party Democracy: The Case of Israel," 70 *Public Administration*, 269.

Cases

H.C. 4267/93 Amiti v. The Prime-Minister of Israel, 47(5) P.D. 441.
H.C. 393/82 El Masulia v. Army Commander, 37(4) P.D. 785.
H.C. 302,306/72 Hilu et al. v. Government of Israel, 27(2) P.D. 169.
H.C. 399/85 Kahana v. The IBA Board of Directors, 41(3) P.D. 255
H.C. 910/86 Ressler v. Minister of Defense, 42(2) P.D. 441
H.C. 680/88 Schnitzer v. The Military Censor, 42(4) P.D. 617
H.C. 1/81 Shiran v. IBA, 35(3) P.D. 365

Reports

B'Tselem report: Violations of Human Rights in the Occupied Territories 1990/1991.
B'Tselem report: Demolition and Sealing of Houses, September 1989.

CHAPTER 10

Local Advocacy, Global Engagement
The Impact of Land Claims Advocacy on the Recognition of Property Rights in the South African Constitution

HEINZ KLUG

Dispossession and forced removals were central to the apartheid project. These processes were not only the basic means of colonization but continued late into the twentieth century, as the darkest face of apartheid policy (see Desmond, 1971)—justifying the international community's designation of apartheid as a crime against humanity.[1] It is this legacy—in which millions were forced from their homes and declared pariahs in the land of their birth (Plaatje, 1916: 6); in which communities were dismantled brick by brick and their members scattered across the most barren wastelands of the country (see Surplus People Project, 1983); in which people clung to the land and refused to give up their claims (see Transvaal Rural Action Committee, 1988)—that set the stage for the recognition and shaping of property rights in postapartheid South Africa.

Although the degradation and pain of communities and individuals who had these policies thrust upon them can never be adequately documented (cf. Desmond, 1971, and Platzky and Walker, 1985), this paper explores the link between these struggles and the shaping of property rights in South Africa today. Central to this link is the work of a group of activists and lawyers. These included activists of the African National Congress, NGOs, church and community-based organizations, as well as practicing lawyers who represented a spectrum within the legal profession from liberal professionals, who believed in the neutral representation of their clients, and public interest lawyers, to classic cause lawyers. Most extraordinary were a number of individual lawyers whose commitments included constant attempts to both deploy the law and to understand their own role in the empowerment of communities resisting forced removals or reclaiming their land (see

Budlender, 1988, and Haysom, 1990). The "legal" product of these efforts has been the creation of a connection between restitution and the definition of legitimate property rights, including provisions for the legitimate redistribution of material resources, which have been incorporated into the very understanding of constitutionally protected property rights in the 1996 Constitution. The result is that the legacy of dispossession and forced removals has become as central to the project of building justice in a postapartheid South Africa as these processes were in perpetuating the injustices of apartheid.

Embedded in this outcome is the role of lawyers and activists, transformed from what might have been understood as classic cause lawyering—sharing responsibility with their clients for the ends being promoted and using their professional work as a vehicle to build the good society (Sarat and Scheingold, 1998 :3)—to full participation in the state where their commitments and relationships to their goals and their former clients remain both unwavering and fundamentally transformed. Many of the most prominent cause lawyers who participated in the antiapartheid movement as lawyers or activists have now gone into the new democratic state. Among the former staff of the Legal Resources Centre—South Africa's premier public interest law practice—there is now the president of the Constitutional Court, two justices of the Land Court, the director-general of Land Affairs, two land claims commissioners, one commissioner on the Truth and Reconciliation Commission, and judges in the Labour Court and regular High Court. Of those who were active as members of the ANC's Constitutional Committee, three became members of the Constitutional Court, including its president and later its deputy-president; one became chairperson of the upper house or Senate and is now National Director of Public Prosecutions; three became members of the cabinet, including the minister of justice; and one became legal adviser to President Mandela.

While as participants in the struggle against apartheid and as advocates for land claimants in particular, activists and lawyers could see themselves in Richard Abel's eloquent term as "speaking law to power" (Abel, 1998: 69), with the democratic transition they have walked through the mirror. If in the past their role and self-image were defined in opposition to the state, the task ahead is to build the institutions of the democratic state. Now this community works to shape the law and is engaging and wielding power in its attempts to further the cause. For most, there is no contradiction between the democratic goals shared by those who opposed apartheid and the new roles they have been called upon to play within the state. Arguing that the "struggle was always for law," Constitutional Court president Arthur Chaskalson notes that South Africa is in a postrevolutionary situation and that "institutions need to be developed" (interview with author, 1998). While specific positions may require an explicit distancing from former political party memberships,[2] office bearing and advocacy roles,[3] Constitutional Court deputy president Pius Langa sees no tension between his past role as a cause lawyer under apartheid—in which as an Advocate he defended accused in political trials and served as president of the National Association of Democratic Lawyers—and his new role as a Constitutional Court judge, for in his words, "I always fought for the rule of law" (Interview, 1998). Although he would never have taken a judicial appointment under the old regime, he is now in the position he argues to work toward that ideal by giving, through his work on the Court, a collective, communal meaning to rights that he is concerned the majority of South Africans will feel alienated from if they are given a narrow individualistic focus (ibid.).

Unlike most assumptions about cause lawyering, which envisions the practice as oppositional, and the law as checking power, South Africa's democratic transition provides an illustration of cause lawyering being transformed. Now as either senior government members, judges, civil servants, or consultants to government, commitments to communities and clients and their demands have become mediated by a responsibility to democratic accountability and policy work that requires a shift in focus to include needs and constraints beyond those which formed the heart of these lawyers' causes. In this paper I will try to explore this transformation by focusing on the constitution-making process as a moment of passage through the looking glass, and by looking at some of the consequences this specific commitment to the land issue might have on the framing of property and power in the postapartheid era.

Bound to the Land: Forced Removals and Commitment to the Cause

Understanding the role of cause lawyers, and their commitment to an issue through multiple transformations of both the issue and their own roles, requires, I believe, an acknowledgment of the impact that exposure to the particular circumstances and role of the law, as well as the building of relationships with clients, has on these lawyers as individuals. My own exposure to the horrors of forced removals came in early 1977, when as a student activist at the University of Natal in Durban I was asked to help provide alternative shelter for a community in Clermont whose homes were being destroyed.[4] As I arrived in the "township," in the midst of a tropical downpour, to meet a community organizer whose home bordered the settlement being destroyed, I was met by a sight of despair I shall never forget. Standing up against the side of the house for shelter against the torrential rain was a host of middle-aged women looking out over a ravine to their partially demolished homes, as government workers, with the aid of a front-end loader, methodically destroyed what these families had worked so hard to build. As I approached I was struck by the eery stillness—the only sounds being the drumbeat of the rain and the occasional cracking sounds which came from a pile of salvaged plywood furniture that swelled and cracked as it soaked in the rain—and the sight of the women's faces as their eyes stared blankly out, ignoring the tugs of children at their skirts, with tears coursing silently down their cheeks.

As the initial shock wore off, the chaos of destruction gave way to the urgent task of regrouping. Workers who had returned from their jobs, to find their homes demolished and the area cordoned off by police, now came looking for their families, retrieving what possessions they could, and seeking shelter from the persistent rain. Later that night as we erected canvas tents in the muddy yard of a local church, amidst families trying desperately to cook a meal, clean children, and find a dry place for sleeping babies, I was amazed by the community's grim determination to stand its ground, to rebuild and to continue to assert their presence despite the callous brutality of apartheid law and its dictate that they should go away—to some rural "homeland" for migrant workers imagined by the architects of "separate development." It was in the midst of these experiences that communities, activists, and lawyers found each other and sought ways to stop the machine (White, 1988). On the one hand, activists such as the Reverend David Russell, an Anglican priest working in the community, protested the demolitions by lying down in front of the bulldozers at the Modderdam settlement outside Cape Town (South African Institute of Race Relations, 1978: 452), facing arrest and subsequent banning (ibid., 126), while on the other hand, lawyers began searching for creative ways to deploy the law.[5]

While personal commitments may be forged in the horror of experience, there remained, in apartheid South Africa, a vast gulf between injustice and the ability of lawyers to deploy the law in the face of apartheid barbarism (see Budlender, 1990). It was this task that was taken up by the Legal Resources Centre and other sympathetic lawyers, and in the end, even though, as Richard Abel has so clearly shown (see Abel, 1995: chap. 10, 11, 12), any plain reading of law and practice gave little hope for legal remedies against the apartheid state, the combination of resistance, public exposure, and creative lawyering threw so much sand into the cogs that the bulldozers ground to a halt. But stopping the machine was only the beginning. Even after the old regime conceded that forced removals must end, after their claims of "voluntary" removals were exposed, and after they abolished the laws denying Africans a right to land and even provided a mechanism for the recognition of some claims, they still insisted that all existing property rights were perfectly legitimate. Even when the "interim" Constitution recognized land claims and required the establishment of mechanisms to address these claims, the representatives of the old order resisted the need for land reform or any other form of redistribution as a prerequisite to the legitimation of all property rights. I will argue that it was the assertion of land claims in this context that provided the key that kept open the door in the debate over property rights. It was the continuing resistance of those communities and their connection with the activists and lawyers with whom they had worked in the struggle against forced removals that gave birth to the return to land movement during the democratic transition, keeping these claims on the political agenda and propelling some of the key players into the new government and into the Department of Land Affairs in particular. It is from within the regional Land Commissions and from within the government that these same activists, and some of their lawyers, have been working to implement land restitution and land reform in the new South Africa.

Claiming Land and Protecting Property

The debate over land began in the African National Congress (ANC) in late 1989 and coincided with de Klerk's February 1990 public announcement of the political opening that would set the stage for South Africa's democratic transition. At that moment the ANC in Lusaka, Zambia, organized a workshop on the "Land Question" initiated by ANC activists Bongiwe Njobe and Helena Dolny. While the workshop focused on analyzing the state of rural South Africa, all the participants—ANC members who ranged from scholars and traditional leaders to peasant activists—seemed to assume that nationalization of existing land holdings, given a history of dispossession and the vast inequalities in land holdings between black and white (see Claassens, 1991; and Robertson, 1990), would be high on the agenda of an ANC government. This shared assumption was based in no small part on our commitment to the 1955 Freedom Charter—recognized by the ANC as expressing the will of the South African people—which declared in part that the "national wealth of our country . . . shall be restored to the people," and "all the land redivided amongst those who work it, to banish famine and land hunger" (The Freedom Charter, 1955).

Despite these assumptions and the liberation movement's general rhetoric on the "Land Question," activists at the workshop had a realistic view of the low priority rural issues had on the mainly urban-based ANC's political agenda in the late 1980s. They were, however, encouraged by the "Economy and Land" sections of the ANC's Constitutional Guidelines, which had been issued in 1988 as part of the ANC's preparations for negotiations with the apartheid regime. Here, the ANC signaled its future intentions to both the international community and the apartheid regime, by announcing its intention to constitutionally protect property. While this promise went further than what might have been expected, given the rhetoric of socialization, nationalization, and redistribution so dominant in the ANC at the time (see ANC, 1969), the limited focus on property for "personal use and consumption," allowed these conflicting visions of redistribution and property rights to coexist. This coexistence was aided by the document's commitment to "devise and implement a land reform programme . . . in conformity with the principle of affirmative action, taking into account the status of victims of forced removals" (ANC, 1988). With the exact modes of implementation still open to debate, the Lusaka workshop opted to institutionalize the issue within the ANC by calling for the formation of an ANC Land Commission to address the lack of specific policies within the organization.

It was as a member of the ANC Land Commission's secretariat (first alone and joined later by two others)[6] that I returned to South Africa in June 1990. In setting up the Land Commission we soon began to work with the already well-established community of lawyers, NGOs, and activists who had long struggled against forced removals in the courts and on the land (see Abel, 1995). This informal coalition provided the organizational basis, knowledge, and experience that sustained the struggle for the recognition of dispossessed land rights during the political transition and constitution-making process. While the ANC Land Commission had access to the ANC's internal policy-making processes and could evoke strong public reaction as a voice of the ANC,[7] it was the return to land campaigns of land claimants, and their lawyers' continued engagement with the de Klerk government, that frustrated the apartheid regime's attempts to preempt future claims. This the apartheid government attempted to do by repealing the Land Acts in 1991 (see Abolition of Racially Based Land Measures Act 108, 1991) and establishing an Advisory Commission on Land Allocation (ibid., sections 89–96) with the purpose of settling all claims before the political transition to democratic rule could be completed.

The debate over land reform[8] and property rights centered first on the ANC's draft bill of rights published in 1990, which contained a single article addressing the "economy, land and property" (ANC Constitutional Committee, 1990: Art. 11). Within the ANC, the Land Commission began hearing from its constituency and opening debates on land reform, nationalization, and restitution. This process began with newly formed branches and communities locked in land conflicts around the country, but increasingly focused on a series of internal discussions, joined at times by activists and lawyers of the land movement, with members of the Constitutional Committee[9] as well as in engagements with other activists and sectors in a series of conferences initiated by the Constitutional Committee—at which special sessions or subgroups focused on the issue of land and property. Outside the ANC, the Land Commission built links and worked closely with lawyers and activists of the return-to-land movement and became engaged in wider public debates over land claims and land redistribution. It was here then that those cause lawyers who had long opposed government action began to participate in a process aimed at shaping the future law in this area. Central to these debates was the status that property rights would have in a future constitution.

Although the ANC's draft bill of rights only protected, in our view, limited rights to personal property, it became clear at the May 1991 conference convened by the ANC Constitutional Committee that the ANC was under a great deal of pressure to grant greater recognition to property rights. In fact, attempts at that conference to question whether there should be any constitutionally protected property rights at all elicited a highly charged response from one member of the Constitutional Committee who warned that the rejection of property rights would directly endanger the democratic transition. In response the participants at the conference called for a reworking of the draft in which land would be recognized as a specific form of property and treated separately from property in general. As such, concern was expressed about the recognition of property rights before the implementation of the necessary process of redistribution. Furthermore, participants made a commitment to include positive rights to land for the landless (see Centre for Development Studies, 1991: 129–32).

While this internal debate sought simultaneously to limit the reach of existing property rights and to secure a more equitable distribution of property in the future, the response of the regime and the existing economic interests was expressed most clearly by the South African Law Commission—a nominally independent statutory body. In its August 1991 "Interim Report on Group and Human Rights," the Law Commission launched a sustained attack against the ANC Draft, charging that the "ANC's bill ... provides, in a manner which hardly disguises the aim, for nationalization of private property without objectively testable norms for compensation," and that what the ANC intended was "in fact nothing but nationalization under the cloak of expropriation ... designed to secure state control over property" (South African Law Commission, 1991: 359–65).

Instead, the Law Commission called for the protection of private property and for the payment of just compensation in the event of expropriation in the public interest. Likewise, the Democratic Party, traditionally the party of big capital and white "liberals," proposed a comprehensive right to property that could only be derogated by lawful expropriation in the public interest, and only then, when subject to the "proper payment of equitable compensation, which in the event of dispute, shall be determined by an ordinary court of law" (Democratic Party, 1993: Art. 9). Neither of these proposals provided for the restitution of property taken under apartheid and as such failed to comprehend the threat to property rights, and even the very notion of constitutional rights, that the legal entrenchment of the apartheid's spoils entails.

While attention was focused on the question of property rights, the ANC Land Commission continued to hold meetings around the country to discuss land issues,[10] both as a means to increase awareness within the ANC, as well as to begin the formulation of a land policy for adoption by the movement. The first target of this campaign was to commit the organization to a set of principles upon which a policy could be built. With this as its goal, the ANC Land Commission held a national conference in June 1991 at which we produced a set of guidelines for the development of land policy. These guidelines were then presented and adopted at the ANC's National Conference in July 1991. The most important features of the Land Manifesto were: its simultaneous commitment to both land restitution and land redistribution; its recognition of a diversity of land tenure forms; and the advancement of a policy of affirmative action as the main device to achieve specific policy goals (ANC Land Commission, 1991). With these guidelines the ANC effectively endorsed a strategy against the simple constitutional recognition of private property as recognized by the apartheid state. First, by demanding both restitution and land reform, it questioned and threatened the legitimacy of existing property rights. Second, the recognition of different forms of tenure decentered private land ownership and provided a basis for the recognition of communal and other forms of land tenure. Finally, the manifesto recognized that affirmative action–type polices would provide a structure in which the multitude of specific policy goals and claims of different constituencies within the ANC could be accommodated and targeted to address land issues and the interests of the rural poor.

At the October 1991 National Conference on Affirmative Action, convened by the ANC Constitutional Committee, a report back to the plenary session from the subgroup on land concluded that a "wealth tax" would be necessary to fund land redistribution. Given the demand that any expropriation be compensated, the group concluded that the only way to achieve the redistribution of land necessary to overcome the legacy of the 1913 Land Acts was to create a specific compensation account. In order to achieve the equitable redistribution required, this dedicated account would need to be funded by those who benefitted from the limited land market created by the Land Acts, which had reserved 87 percent of land for white ownership and control (see Robertson, 1990). This could be achieved, it was argued, by the imposition of a "wealth tax" similar to the equalization tax adopted in the Federal Republic of Germany in the aftermath of World War II. While the idea of special taxes to overcome the vast disparities created by apartheid has continued to raise interest and was used in 1994 as a once-off surcharge to cover the costs of the transition, in 1991 the reaction was immediate—the major white-controlled newspapers went ballistic, and within hours ANC members involved were once again receiving death threats from those who had attempted to silence opposition during the height of apartheid. Although senior ANC leaders supported the holding of a debate on the "wealth tax" it also became clear that any attempt to conduct an effective redistribution of land rights would meet extremely stiff opposition from the ancien régime as well as conflict with alternative demands for resources among the ANC's own constituencies.

While activists and lawyers in the antiapartheid movement had long engaged the state on issues of land, in the classic cause-lawyering sense of "speaking truth to power" as they campaigned against forced removals, the democratic transition unsettled this paradigm. As power shifted, away from the old regime and into a contested realm of negotiations, so the role of cause lawyers was transformed. At first, the need to pursue and claim the rights of land claimants—in the return-to-land movement—remained a central activity, but soon the focus began to shift toward participation in defining the future. This brought these cause lawyers into a different realm, one in which the claims of their clients had to be placed in the context of broader social policies and concerns—including the often contradictory needs of the democratic transition itself. Instead of working to secure the immediate goals of the cause as represented by their clients' claims to land, the formulation of constitutional and policy options required concern for a myriad of competing concerns, including issues of procedural fairness and feasibility—issues that are of secondary importance to those whose focus is the cause of rights claimants.

Despite the fierce public exposure which followed the proposal of a wealth tax, when formal negotiations began at Codesa in December 1991, it seemed as if the land issue would, once again, be pushed into the background as the parties clashed over the very nature of the political transition. As far as property issues were concerned, they were subsumed in the larger debate over whether the purpose of Codesa was to produce a detailed interim constitution or broad constitutional principles that would guide but not frustrate the work of a future democratically elected constitution-making body. Despite this marginalization of substantive issues in the negotiations, for land claimants and those active in support of their demands, the struggle over land and property rights continued simultaneously on two planes. First, in actual land occupations and attempts to return to land, from which communities had been forcibly removed—whether by occupation or legal and administrative negotiations with ACLA[11] and the de Klerk government. Second, at the level of ideas, with debates over different policy options continuing at a series of conferences and meetings, either organized by the ANC Constitutional Committee together with various university-based institutes or directly by the academy. One of the most important of these was organized by long-time land activist Aninka Claassens through the Centre for Applied Legal Studies (CALS), to discuss "the effect that a constitutionally entrenched right to property might have on future land reform legislation and programmes" (see Claassens, 1992).

The opening of a discussion on particular options for the recognition of land rights and the consequences a property clause might have on land claims was, at this stage, a vital intervention, making it clear that the issue of land rights could not be divorced from the wider question of property. Furthermore, when this conference is placed in the context of the series of conferences, meetings, and workshops held in this period,[12] its significance, as one in a series of intellectual loci of the South African transition, may be recognized. At these events, new substantive ideas were introduced into the public debate while simultaneously being framed through their presentation in the context of different international histories and examples. Among the important substantive interventions made at the CALS conference was the public floating of the suggestion for a land claims court—in the form of a report to the conference from a group of lawyers and activists from the "land claims movement" who were working on this option at the behest of the ANC Land Commission (see Swanson, 1992).[13] Other important substantive interventions at this conference included Geoff Budlender's construction of a legal right to land for the landless (Budlender, 1992a),[14] as well as the work of Catherine Cross, who demonstrated the continued vitality and existence of an alternative understanding of land rights in opposition to the prevailing legal notions of individual private property rights (Cross, 1992). Presentation of the Canadian decision to preclude the explicit recognition of property rights from their 1982 Charter of Rights (Bauman, 1992) and the history of constitutional conflict over land reform in India in the postindependence years (Murphy, 1992) introduced both substantive examples of alternative approaches and provided grist for debate over the dangers of, and alternatives to, the constitutional enshrinement of property rights.

It was these interventions that forced the ANC to reevaluate its own proposed Draft Bill of Rights. After several meetings with land activists and members of the Land Commission, Albie Sachs[15] proposed new sections on Land and the Environment as well as a separate Property clause for the revised text of the ANC draft bill of rights (see ANC Constitutional Committee, 1992, and see also ANC Constitutional Committee, 1993). These new sections essentially expanded the ANC's proposals making it clear that land rights would remain a central claim of the antiapartheid movement and that the protection of property would remain subject to these claims. While property rights were given separate recognition for the first time in the new text, the text also suggested that these references to property, along with all other "principles governing economic life" might be better placed outside the bill of rights in a nonjusticiable section of the Constitution defined as "Directive Principles of State Policy"—which is the case with similar sections of the Irish and Indian constitutions.

By the time this revised text was first published in May 1992, negotiations with the de Klerk government had formally broken down—collapsing Codesa into a morass of mutual recriminations (see Friedman, 1993). At the same time the government's land claims forum was being rejected by communities[16] who were threatening to physically reoccupy their lands[17] and the ANC Land Commission was being thrust into an engagement with new actors—both national and international—who had recognized the centrality of land to the struggle over property rights. The first engagement, which culminated in a meeting in December 1992, was with the Urban Foundation, a policy institute funded by South African big business, who asked for a meeting with the ANC Land Commission to discuss land claims and the question of creating a land claims court. At this meeting the ANC delegation, which included members of the Constitutional Committee as well as the Land Commission and its allies in the land movement, were presented with the argument that while some form of limited land claims process might be necessary to legitimize future property relations, both the demand for land among the African majority and the reality of resource needs and allocations for future development, required that this process be tightly circumscribed. However, at this stage in the shift from pure advocacy to the responsibility of weighting alternative policy options, procedures, and consequences, the cause of the land claimants remained paramount. While the ANC-aligned participants recognized the problem of competition over resources under a future democratic government, we argued that any attempt to engage in an all but symbolic process of restitution would fail to build the legitimacy that the Urban Foundation and its corporate constituency seemed to recognize was needed to secure property relations in the new South Africa.

The second of these new engagements began in mid-1992 when the World Bank launched their own initiatives in South Africa. Our immediate response was to ask who had invited them to South Africa, and to reject the notion of engagement with this institution. Soon, however, we realized that the World Bank was developing its own strategy towards the "new" South Africa (see World Bank Southern Africa Department, 1994)[18] and would continue to do so whether or not we engaged. Refusal by definition meant lack of knowledge and influence. The bank, at the same time, had been rebuffed by other sectors of the antiapartheid movement—particularly the urban sector activists—and responded to our own hesitations by organizing an initial seminar outside South Africa, in Mbabane, Swaziland, in November 1992. To this event they invited representatives from different South African political groupings, government and nongovernment bodies to discuss a set of papers prepared by the World Bank and its consultants (see World Bank, 1992).

These two engagements presented radically alternative possibilities and opportunities. While the Urban Foundation (UF) was convinced that the demand for land reform among Africans was being grossly exaggerated, Hans Binswanger, the senior World Bank adviser who dominated the Swaziland seminar, presented a vision of world development dependent upon the carrying out of a successful land reform (see Binswanger and Deininger, 1993). While the UF suggested a limited process of restitution in order to legitimize property rights, Binswanger argued that land claims and even land invasions would drive a process of land reform and suggested that by facilitating land reform the government would be providing an essential catalyst for sustained economic development. Although the ANC Land Commission remained extremely skeptical of the equities of the World Bank's proposals—for a market-driven reform focused on small-scale producers—we realized immediately that the World Bank's position could be deployed as a way to keep the issue of land reform on the political agenda. With this aim we encouraged Hans Binswanger to persuade the de Klerk government that land reform was an essential part of South Africa's political transition. At the same time we introduced Binswanger to members of the ANC's leadership, including the Constitutional Committee, facilitating ANC agreement to engage with the World Bank on these issues.

This engagement was pursued through the newly formed Land and Agricultural Policy Centre (LAPC) and was structured by the tension between the ANC's historic concerns about the role of the Bretton Woods institutions and by our concerns to retain some influence over the bank's activities in the political transition. As we began to negotiate our working relationship with the bank's representative, Robert Christiansen, I attended a meeting of NGOs in Johannesburg at which Martin Khor of the Malaysia-based Third-World Network and representatives of a World Bank–monitoring group from Washington, D.C., explained the structure and workings of the institution. Although we had already experienced the dramatic impact that interest by the bank could have on an issue, the understanding we gained from these activists of the manner in which the bank's missions operated, convinced us of the need to engage the bank closely and to retain some influence over the bank's own information gathering and analytical process.

While the World Bank both wanted and needed our endorsement of their plan to prepare a Rural Restructuring Program (RRP) for South Africa, we demanded that the initial research work be conducted by and remain under the control of South Africans. This was made possible through the creation of terms of reference for the preparation of a series of background reports that would form the basis of the preparation of the RRP. The resulting "aide memoire" was concluded on June 15, 1993, in which Christiansen committed the bank to a process that would "be fully transparent, consultative and collaborative at all stages" (Christiansen, 1993). To this end, various South Africans were asked to head different aspects of the research, including the legal team which had to prepare a report on the constitutional requirements of a land restitution and reform process. Later, as a member of the World Bank's mission to South Africa in late 1993, I participated in the formulation of the bank's proposal for a Rural Restructuring Program for the country. While there were many parts of the report with which to disagree, its importance from the perspective of the ANC Land Commission lay in its clear assertion that both land restitution and land reform were central to rural restructuring (see World Bank, 1993). Furthermore, even though our argument that a constitutionalized property right would impede land redistribution was excised at the last moment, in favor of the bank's ideal of a market-driven process, the report contained a clear statement to the effect that land restitution and even redistribution were so important that in the event of market failure, government intervention would be both justified and necessary.[19] Here, then, the rigors of policy formulation, in which arguments of feasibility and consequence begin to predominate, begin to shift the ground upon which the cause lawyer stands. Instead of speaking truth to power, the task becomes one in which the participants seek to establish a new truth (or policy) through which democratic power might be exercised.

But here there is the danger of running ahead. Prior to the beginning of substantive constitutional negotiations in early 1993, the ANC and government still held dramatically alternative notions of how property should be constitutionally protected. On the one hand, the ANC was willing to protect the undisturbed enjoyment of personal possessions, so long as property entitlements were to be determined by legislation and provision was to be made for the restoration of land to people dispossessed under apartheid (ANC Constitutional Committee, 1993: Art. 13). The government's proposals, on the other hand, aimed at protecting all property rights and would only allow expropriation for public purposes and subject to cash compensation determined by a court of law according to the market value of the property (see Republic of South Africa, 1993). In response, the ANC suggested that no property clause was necessary.[20]

As negotiations with the de Klerk regime gained momentum in 1993, conflict over the property clause began to focus on specific issues. Although the ANC had initially insisted that an "interim" constitution contain only those guarantees necessary to ensure a level political playing field, the momentum for entrenching rights could not be slowed, and before long we recognized that we were in the process of negotiating a complete Bill of Rights. It was in this context that the apartheid government insisted that property rights be included in the "interim" constitution and that the measure of compensation include specific reference to the market value of the property. In response, the ANC insisted that the property clause not frustrate efforts to address land claims and that the state must have the power to regulate property without being obliged to pay compensation unless there was a clear expropriation of the property. Although the regime agreed that explicit provisions guaranteeing and providing for land restitution should be included, its negotiators insisted that such provisions should not be located within the property clause. Instead, it was proposed that if they were to be included, they should be incorporated into the corrective-action provisions of the equality clause.

Mass action played an important part in the ANC alliance's campaign to shape the transition, and various forms of public display of claims, outrage, and strength were employed by groups on all sides, to ensure that their concerns or demands be placed on the agenda at the multiparty talks. Marked by protests, demonstrations, campaigns and even an invasion of the World Trade Center in Kempton Park, the site of the multiparty negotiations, mass participation in the constitution-making process exhibited both a diversity of claims and a degree of popular frustration with an undemocratic negotiating process. Among these were representatives of communities who were forcibly removed under apartheid, who marched on the World Trade Center protesting the proposed constitutional protection of property, which they saw as an entrenchment of the apartheid distribution of property, and demanding constitutional recognition of their right to return to their land.[21]

Answering these demands and conflicts, the interim 1993 Constitution provided a separate institutional basis for land restitution, which was guaranteed in the corrective action provisions of the equality clause (Constitution, 1993 [section 8(3)(b)]), and compromised on the question of compensation by including a range of factors the courts would have to consider in determining just and equitable compensation (ibid. [section 28(3)]). Significantly, as Matthew Chaskalson argues, the final outcome in terms of the specific wording adopted was as much a result of serendipity, legal ignorance, and the particular quirks and concerns of the individual negotiators, as the logical product of an informed or even interest-based political debate and compromise (Chaskalson, 1995). This is demonstrated most aptly in the choice of the terminology of public purpose over public interest in the expropriation clause despite agreement among the parties to give the state as much leeway as possible in this regard.

However, even then, the substance of the outcome reflects both the general contours of the political conflict over the property clause and the bounded alternatives available to the parties—from the recognition of existing property rights on the one hand to the recognition of land claims on the other. Significantly, the factors to be considered in the determination of just compensation reflect this outcome. On the one hand, they were directed at the problem of land claims and included "the use to which the property is being put, the history of its acquisition, the value of the investments in it by those affected and the interest of those affected" (Constitution, 1993 [section 28(3)]), while on the other hand, at the insistence of the ancien régime and making possible the inclusion of other factors, it enshrined "market value." This compromise marked both the success and limit of those cause lawyers and activists committed to securing land for the dispossessed, and it was under this constitutional regime that Mandela's government and South Africa's first democratic parliament began to address land claims. Acting in terms of the specific clauses of the 1993 Constitution which provided for the establishment of a land claims process, parliament passed the Restitution of Land Claims Act in 1995, setting up regional Land Claims Commissions and the new Land Claims Court (see Klug, 1996).

Despite predictions that there would be very little change in the Constitution during the second phase of the constitution-making process, particularly on such sensitive issues as the property clause and the Bill of Rights, the property issue, in fact, once again became one of the unresolvable lightning rods in the Constitutional Assembly. Although the committee charged with reviewing the Bill of Rights was at first reluctant to change the formulation of the 1993 compromise, challenges centered on the question of land restitution and reform (see Constitutional Assembly, 1995c; Constitutional Assembly, 1995d, and Constitutional Assembly 1995e) once again forced open the process.[22] In this case the impetus came from a Workshop on Land Rights and the Constitution organized by the Constitutional Assembly's subcommittee, Theme Committee 6.3, whose task it was to resolve issues related to specialized structures of government such as the Land Claims Commission and Court provided for in the 1993 Constitution. Focusing on the land issue, this meeting once again brought together those committed to the cause of land redistribution and raised the problem of property rights in the Constitution. While some participants again raised the question about whether there should be any property protection within the final Constitution, the major change from the period in which the 1993 Constitution was negotiated was that the participants in this workshop, even those representing long-established interests like the National Party and the South African Agricultural Union, now agreed on the need "to rectify past wrongs" and for land reform. Disagreement here was over the means. The South

African Agricultural Union, for example, continued to assert that "it should be done in a way without jeopardising the protection of private ownership," while the National Party now embraced the World Bank's proposals, arguing that land reform should "be accomplished within the parameters of the market and should be demand-driven."

The outcome of this workshop and the submissions made to Theme Committee 6.3 was a report to the Constitutional Assembly which both challenged the existing 1993 formulation of property rights and called for a specific land clause to provide a "constitutional framework and protection for all land reform measures" (see Constitutional Assembly, 1995c). While Theme Committee 4, which was responsible for the Bill of Rights, had until that point uncontroversially adopted a property clause that merely incorporated the 1993 Constitution's restitution provisions into the property clause itself, the report on land rights threw the proverbial cat among the pigeons. Some objected to Theme Committee 6.3's very discussion of property rights, while others sensed an opportunity to reopen the debate on property rights and to once again question their very inclusion in the Bill of Rights. As a result, the Draft Bill of Rights published by the Constitutional Assembly on October 9, 1995, included an option that there be "no property clause at all."

It was in this context that an alternative option, a property clause including within it specific land rights as well as a subclause insulating land reform from constitutional attack began to gain momentum. While a strategy to insulate land restitution and land reform from constitutional attack had been implicit from early on in the debate, it was now suggested in a submission to Theme Committee 6.3 that the property clause include a specific subclause insulating state action aimed at redressing past discrimination in the ownership and distribution of land rights (see Constitutional Assembly, 1995e: 13–41). The negotiators were able to rely on this formulation as a compromise between those demanding the removal of the property clause and those, like the Democratic Party, who remained opposed to even the social democratic formulation modeled on the German Constitution. Still the debate raged on, and the draft formulations of the property clause continued to evolve.[23] Political agreement on the property clause was only finally reached at midnight on April 18, 1996, when subsection 28(8), the "affirmative action" or insulation subclause of the property clause, was modified so as to make it subject to section 36(1), the general limitations clause of the Constitution (see Bell, 1997).

The final property clause thus reflects both the democratic origins of the Constitutional Assembly as well as the continuing influence of the cause-lawyering community in this area. It not only guarantees the restitution of land taken after 1913 (Constitution, 1996 [section 25(7)]) and a right to legally secure tenure for those whose tenure is insecure as a result of racially discriminatory laws or practices (ibid. [section 25(6)]), but also includes an obligation on the state to enable citizens to gain access to land on an equitable basis (ibid. [section 25(5)]). Furthermore, the state is granted a limited exemption from the protective provisions of the property clause so as to empower it to take "legislative and other measures to achieve land, water and related reform, in order to redress the results of past racial discrimination" (ibid. [section 25(8)]).

Despite agreement in the Constitutional Assembly the property clause was presented to the Constitutional Court as violating the Constitutional Principles and therefore as one of the grounds for denying certification of the Constitution.[24] Two major objections were raised: first, that unlike the interim Constitution, the new clause did not expressly protect the right to acquire, hold, and dispose of property; second, that the provisions governing expropriation and the payment of compensation were inadequate (First Certification Case: para. 70). The Constitutional Court rejected both of these arguments. First, the court noted that the test to be applied was whether the formulation of the right met the standard of a "universally accepted fundamental right" as required by Constitutional Principle II. Second, the court surveyed international and foreign sources and observed that "[i]f one looks to international conventions and foreign constitutions, one is immediately struck by the wide variety of formulations adopted to protect the right to property, as well as by the fact that significant conventions and constitutions contain no protection of property at all" (ibid., para. 71). In conclusion the court argued that it could not "uphold the argument that, because the formulation adopted is expressed in a negative and not a positive form and because it does not contain an express recognition of the right to acquire and dispose of property, it fails to meet the prescription of CPII" (ibid., para. 72). The second objection met the same fate, with the court concluding that an "examination of international conventions and foreign constitutions suggests that a wide range of criteria for expropriation and the payment of compensation exists," and thus the "approach taken in NT 25 [new text section 25] cannot be said to flout any universally accepted approach to the question" (ibid., para. 73).

Conclusion

From the moment negotiations began for a new Constitution, through the 1994 elections and the formation of Nelson Mandela's cabinet in the Government of National Unity, the terrain of cause lawyering in South Africa was transformed. Instead of searching for ways to deploy the law, as a means of political struggle against injustice, "cause lawyers" and the activists working with them—guiding, pushing, chastising—began to seek ways to structure power in furtherance of the cause. By early September 1995, Geoff Budlender, former national director of the Legal Resources Centre, then working full time as a ministerial adviser for the minister of land affairs, presented the summary address to the first National Conference on Land Policy, emphasizing a collective agreement "that land reform was a necessity because it was essential for the future of the country."[25] Instead of advocating for the victims of forced removals against government, Budlender now called for a partnership between government, community groups, NGOs, commercial farmers, and commercial institutions. Now, instead of speaking to power, Budlender was required to explain the limitations of power, to promise alternatives for those whose claims had been denied by the 1913 cut-off, and to acknowledge that the constitutional protection of property rights and the realities of government financing imposed potential limitations on the redistribution of land. Instead of a responsibility to specific clients, there is now a democratic responsibility in the formulation of government policy and an accountability to elected representatives. Democratization in South Africa transformed the role of cause lawyers, providing new opportunities and resources but also raising new complexities and wider responsibilities.

Rejecting the notion that participation in the democratic state is at all in contradiction to the goals of antiapartheid cause lawyering, Geoff Budlender argued that he was in fact still lawyering (interview, 1998). While he accepts that the modalities of his lawyering praxis changed, Budlender notes that since cause lawyering is about engaging with and managing social power—through litigation, intervention with the bureaucracy, advocacy, and organizing—the movement into the state, into policy-making roles, and to control the levers of state power is in many ways the logical outcome of cause lawyering (ibid.). The purpose, however, for Budlender at least, was not to remain within the state, but rather to use the opportunity to put in place "a platform of rights and processes" that will allow people to continue to fight and struggle for what they want (ibid.). Although Budlender intended, personally, to return to some form of advocacy role when his contract as director-general of land affairs expired,[26] he argued in August 1998 that the big difference in praxis between advocacy—which is the main activity of cause lawyers—and the exercise of social power within the state is the need to consider a whole range of factors inherent to this new role, including: the likely response from various social sectors; whether any particular option is implementable; the fiscal implications of each option; and their likely impact on other policies. This process is distinctly different from merely advocating for the rights and interests of one group of clients and cannot be merely adversarial (interview, 1998). Instead of speaking truth to power, the role of cause lawyers has been transformed into defending the "democratic" truth of the new society. Whether this means defending power or opposing power in the name of new democratic claims will depend on the context—it is no longer as simple as it was.

Walking through the looking glass, the cause lawyers and activists who had opposed apartheid's land policies turned their attention to shaping the future. This transformation began to work its changes in exposure to the internal conflicts of interest within the liberation movement during the constitution-making process. And while it was the impact of local histories, ideas, and struggles that shaped the property clauses' ultimate form, it became both possible and necessary to deploy international influences, examples, and legal sources in arguing for our desired outcome in the debate over the property clause. Through the two-stage constitution-making process, these activists fought for the recognition of legitimate claims to restitution. Even if these claims were narrowly defined in the 1993 "interim" Constitution, they became the basis for the explicit limitation of property rights in the final constitution. Not only was the right of restitution brought into the property clause, where it logically belonged, but the shift in power enabled the Constitutional Assembly—despite desperate struggles to the contrary—to include positive rights to land and an explicit affirmative exception for future land and water reform within the property clause of the final constitution.

Finally, despite the obvious gains made by those of us who participated in the struggle for the restitution of land taken by the apartheid regime through acts of forced removal, we must also face up to the unintended consequence of our victory—the protection of the wealth of apartheid's beneficiaries. While it may be argued—and indeed was argued, at the ANC conference on a future bill of rights in 1991—that a peaceful transition to democracy required important compromises, including the recognition of existing property rights, it is also true that the focus on land left the country's real wealth—now in companies, mines, stocks, and bonds, as well as urban housing—completely unchallenged.

Notes

1. See: United Nations General Assembly Resolution: The Policies of Apartheid of the Government of the Republic of South Africa, G. A. Res. 2202, U.N. GAOR, 21st Sess., U.N. Doc. A/RES/2202 A (1966); United Nations General Assembly Resolution: The Policies of Apartheid of the Government of South Africa, G. A. Res. 2396, U.N. GAOR, 23rd Sess., U.N. Doc. A/RES/2396 (1968); United Nations General Assembly Resolution: International Convention on the Suppression and Punishment of the Crime of Apartheid, G. A. Res. 3068, U.N. GAOR 28th Sess., U.N. Doc. A/RES/3068 (1973), reprinted in United Nations, *The United Nations and Apartheid, 1948–1994* (1994).

2. See statement of facts read in open Court on May 4, 1999, and referred to in the Judgment on Recusal Application of the Constitutional Court in President of the Republic of South Africa et al. v. South African Football Union et al. CCT 16/98 delivered on June 4, 1999, in which it was stated that "[i]t is a matter of public record that justices Langa, Mokgoro, O'Regan, Sachs and Yacoob were, prior to their appointments to the Court, members of the African National Congress (ANC). All these judges severed their ties with the ANC before or immediately upon their appointment to the Court. . . . No member of this Court is a member of any political party" (para. 23).

3. Constitutional Court judge Albie Sachs is adamant that in his position as a judge he is playing a judicial role and is no longer an advocate pursuing the agenda of the ANC Constitutional Committee. Interview with author, 1998.

4. Approximately 5,000 homes in Clermont, housing approximately 20,000 people, were demolished between 1974 and 1978 (see South African Institute of Race Relations, 1979: 357).

5. One example of this creative use of the law was the application of the South African common law remedy to protect possession, the *mandament van spolie* (spoliation order), in

which squatters asserted the violation of their peaceful possession, and which in one case led to the courts ordering the Stellenbosch Divisional Council to reerect homes that the council had demolished (see Fredericks v. Stellenbosch Divisional Council, 1977).

6. Bongiwe Njobe, now director general (the most senior civil servant) in the Department of Agriculture, and Derek Hanekom, minister of land affairs and agriculture in Mandela's cabinet, 1994–99.

7. As we experienced in the public furors over a suggested wealth tax to pay for compensation to landowners whose land would be expropriated for redistribution, or when suggestions were made about claims on land within the national parks.

8. For an example of an early contribution to the land reform debate from the perspective of the ANC Land Commission, see Dolny and Klug, 1992.

9. The Constitutional Committee was chaired by Zola Skweyiya, head of the ANC's legal department, under whose authority the land commission initially fell. Skweyiya's interest in and commitment to these issues are reflected in Skweyiya, 1990.

10. It should also be noted that at the same time activists working in or identified by the ANC Land Commission were being exposed to international experiences of land reform, including a Ford Foundation–funded, six-week minicourse organized by the Land Tenure Center at the University of Wisconsin—Madison.

11. For a critique of the government's Advisory Committee on Land Allocations (ACLA), see Klug, 1996: 166–71.

12. These included the following conferences: "Towards a Non-Racial, Non-Sexist Judiciary in South Africa," Constitutional Committee of the ANC and the Community Law Centre, University of the Western Cape, Cape Town, March 26–28, 1993; "Structures of Government for a United Democratic South Africa," the Community Law Centre, University of the Western Cape, ANC Constitutional Committee, Center for Development Studies, University of the Western Cape, Cape Town, March 26–28, 1992; "National Conference on Affirmative Action," ANC Constitutional Committee and Community Law Centre, University of the Western Cape, Port Elizabeth, October 10–12, 1991; "Conference on a Bill of Rights for a Democratic South Africa," Constitutional Committee of the ANC and the Centre for Socio-Legal Studies, University of Natal, Durban, Salt Rock, Natal, May 10–12, 1991; "Constitutional Court for a Future South Africa," ANC/CALS/Lawyers for Human Rights, Magaliesberg, February 1–3, 1991; and "Seminar on Electoral Systems," Centre for Development Studies (CDS)/ANC Constitutional Department, Stellenbosch, November 2–4, 1990.

13. While I participated erratically in the meetings of this group, I did submit a memorandum on the experience of the Indian Claims Commission in the United States as both an example of a land-claims process and as a warning against limiting the claimants' remedies to monetary compensation instead of the return of land which was the basic demand of claimants. In the debates that followed, we were able to use the experience of the ICC to argue that cash settlements could never satisfy demands for the return of land, pointing to the fact that despite thirty years and millions of dollars Native American claims remain unsatisfied.

14. Budlender served as director-general of the Department of Land Affairs, the highest-ranking civil servant in the department from 1995 to 2000.

15. Albie Sachs, then a member of the ANC's Constitutional Committee and now a judge of the Constitutional Court, made important contributions to the debate over land and property rights (see Sachs, 1990: chapter 9, and Sachs, 1992 chapter 6).

16. See Statement from 19 Communities on the Government's Advisory Commission on Land Allocation, September 15, 1991; see also Budlender, 1992b.

17. See, letter dater July 31, 1991, from J. De Villiers, Minister of Public Works and Land Affairs, responding to a letter from lawyers representing a claimant community and stating in part, "I do appeal to you to advise your clients not to take the law into their own hands because that would unnecessarily complicate consideration of possible claims. It would only serve to increase the temperature of the debate rather than to arrive at a solution."

18. An example of one in the World Bank's series of "Informal Discussion Papers on Aspects of the Economy of South Africa," published between 1992 and 1994.

19. When the World Bank's Rural Restructuring Programme was presented in South Africa at the LAPC-organized Land Redistribution Options Conference in October 1993, it had to compete with a range of suggestions and received serious academic and political criticism. As a result the program never gained a life of its own but became yet another source of the smorgasbord of alternatives both enabling and constraining the options available to policymakers in the new South Africa. Its most enduring impacts may be its endorsement of land restitution and reform, on the one hand, and the emphasis upon the market in achieving these reforms, on the other.

20. As late as October 1995, the Draft Bill of Rights being considered by the Constitutional Assembly's Theme Committee 4 included as Option 2, "No property clause at all" (see Constitutional Assembly, 1995a, and Constitutional Assembly, 1995b: 126–40, which includes a discussion of the nature of the right to property in international law).

21. A march on the World Trade Center in June 1993, in which a land-rights memorandum was delivered to the negotiators, was followed by a march in central Pretoria in September 1993, in which about 600 people from 25 rural communities threatened to reoccupy land from which they had been removed by the apartheid government as a way of highlighting their demands for the unconditional restitution of land, the establishment of a land-claims court, and guaranteed security of tenure for farm workers and labor tenants. The Transvaal Rural Action Committee which organized the march also called for the rejection of the proposed property clause in the constitution (Hadland, 1993).

22. It is important to note that even senior ANC leaders who had been very supportive of claims for restitution were at first reluctant to renegotiate the property clause, feeling that the 1993 compromise provided an adequate means to address the issue. Again it seems that the demands for land reform clashed with the needs of the ANC's urban constituency. Faced, however, with the claims of rural communities, the ANC members of the Constitutional Assembly were quick to respond.

23. New versions were published in the October 30, 1995, Refined Working Draft (2nd ed.) of the Constitution; and another ANC proposal was published in the February 9–16, 1996, edition of *Constitutional Talk*—the official newsletter of the Constitutional Assembly—and yet another was published in the April 22–May 18, 1996, edition of *Constitutional Talk*.

24. Under the original political compromise, the Constitutional Assembly was to be constrained by the Constitutional Principles negotiated between the parties and appended to the 1993 interim Constitution. The Constitutional Court was empowered to certify whether a draft Constitution prepared by the Constitutional Assembly met the requirements of the Constitutional Principles. The Constitutional Court in 1996 first declined to certify the draft and then certified the new text adopted in response to the Court's first certification judgment.

25. See Proceedings of the National Land Policy Conference, Department of Land Affairs, August 31, 1995–September 1, 1995, World Trade Centre, Kempton Park, Gauteng. (On file with author).

26. Budlender resigned from his position as director-general of land affairs in December 1999.

References

Interviews

Budlender, Geoff. Author's interview with Director-General, Department of Land Affairs, Geoff Budlender, August 4, 1998, Pretoria.
Chaskalson, Arthur. Author's interview with Constitutional Court President Arthur Chaskalson, July 30, 1998, Johannesburg.
Langa, Pius. Author's interview with Constitutional Court Deputy President Pius Langa, July 27, 1998, Johannesburg.
Sachs, Albie. Author's interview with Constitutional Court Judge Albie Sachs, by telephone, August 1, 1998, Cape Town.

Books and Articles

Abel, Richard (1995). *Politics by Other Means: Law in the Struggle Against Apartheid, 1980–1994.*
Abel, R. (1998). Speaking Law to Power: Occasions for Cause Lawyering, in *Cause Lawyering: Political Commitments and Professional Responsibilities*, A. Sarat and S. Scheingold, eds.
African National Congress (1971). "An Analysis of the Freedom Charter, the Revolutionary Programme of the African National Congress," as presented at the Morogoro Conference, Tanzania, May 1969, reprinted in *Apartheid: A Collection of Writings on South African Racism by South Africans*, Alex La Guma, ed.
African National Congress (1989). "Constitutional Guidelines for a Democratic South Africa (1988)," reprinted in 12 *Hastings International and Comparative Law Review*, 322.
ANC Constitutional Committee (1990). "A Bill of Rights for a New South Africa: A Working Document of the ANC Constitutional Committee," Centre for Development Studies.
ANC Constitutional Committee (1992). "ANC Draft Bill of Rights: Preliminary Revised Version 1.1."
ANC Constitutional Committee (1993). "A Bill of Rights for a New South Africa: Preliminary Revised Text, February 1993" Centre for Development Studies, UWC.
ANC Land Commission (1991). "Land Manifesto for ANC National Conference, July 1991."
Bauman, R. W. (1992). "Property Rights in the Canadian Constitutional Context," 8 *South African Journal on Human Rights*, 344.
Bell, P., ed., (1997). *The Making of the Constitution: The Story of South Africa's Constitutional Assembly, May 1994 to December 1996*. Churchill Murray Publications, South Africa.
Binswanger, Hans, and Deininger Klaus (1993). "South Africa Land Policy: The legacy of history and current options," 21(9) *World Development* pp. 1451–1476.
Budlender, Geoff (1988). "On Practising Law," in *Essays on Law and Social Practice in South Africa*, Hugh Corder, ed.
——— (1990). "Urban Land Issues in the 1980s: The View from Weiler's Farm," in *No Place To Rest: Forced Removals and the Law in South Africa* Christina Murray & Catherine O'Regan, eds.
——— (1992a). "The Right to Equitable Access to Land," 8 *South African Journal on Human Rights*, 295.
——— (1992b). "*Lessons* Learnt from the Land Mistake," Review/Law: Special Supplement to the *Weekly Mail*, December 11, 1992, p. 2.
Centre for Development Studies (1991). "A Bill of Rights for a Democratic South Africa:

Papers and Report of a Conference convened by the ANC Constitutional Committee, May 1991."
Chaskalson, Matthew (1995). "Stumbling Towards Section 28: Negotiations over Property Rights at the Multiparty Talks," 11 *South African Journal on Human Rights*, 222.
Christiansen, Robert (1993). "Aide Memoire: Preparation of a Rural Restructuring Program" (Document in author's possession).
Claassens, Aninka (1991). "For Whites Only: Land Ownership in South Africa," in *Harvest of Discontent: The Land Question in South Africa*, M. de Klerk, ed.
——— (1992). Editorial, 8 *South African Journal on Human Rights*, v.
Constitution of the Republic of South Africa, Act 200 of 1993.
Constitution of the Republic of South Africa, Act 108 of 1996.
Constitutional Assembly (1995a), Theme Committee 4, Draft Bill of Rights, October 9, 1995.
Constitutional Assembly (1995b), Constitutional Committee Sub-Committee: Draft Bill of Rights, Volume 1, Explanatory Memoranda, October 9, 1995.
Constitutional Assembly (1995c), Constitutional Committee Sub-Committee: Documentation: Land Rights, October 9, 1995.
Constitutional Assembly (1995d), Theme Committee 6.3: Specialized Structures of Government: Land Rights, Documentation, September 11, 1995.
Constitutional Assembly (1995e), Theme Committee 6.3: Specialized Structures of Government: Documentation Volume 2A: Land Rights, September 15, 1995.
Cross, C. (1992). "An Alternative Legality: The Property Rights Question in Relation to South African Land Reform," 8 *South African Journal on Human Rights*, 305.
Democratic Party (1993). "Freedom under the Rule of Law: Advancing Liberty in the New South Africa," Draft Bill of Rights, May 1993.
Desmond, Cosmos (1972). *The Discarded People: An Account of African Resettlement in South Africa* (orig. 1971). Penguin African Library.
Dolny, Helena, and Heinz Klug (1992). "Land Reform: Legal Support and Economic Regulation," in *South African Review 6: From 'Red Friday' to Codesa*, G. Moss and I. Obrey, eds.
Friedman, Steven, ed. (1993). *The Long Journey: South Africa's Quest for a Negotiated Settlement*. Johannesburg: Centre for Policy Studies.
Hadland, Adrian (1993). "Demonstrators hand govt land ultimatum," *Business Day*, Sept. 2.
Haysom, Nicholas (1990). "Rural Land Struggles: Practising Law Democratically," in *No Place to Rest: Forced Removals and the Law in South Africa*, Christina Murray and Catherine O'Regan, eds.
Klug, Heinz (1996). "Bedeviling agrarian reform: the impact of past, present and future legal frameworks," in *Agricultural Land Reform in South Africa: Polices, markets and mechanisms*, J. Van Zyl, J. Kirsten, and H. P. Binswanger, eds.
——— (1996). "Historical claims and the right to restitution," in *Agricultural Land Reform in South Africa: Policies, markets and mechanisms*, J. Van Zyl, J. Kirsten, and H. P. Binswanger, eds.
Murphy, John (1992). "Insulating Land Reform from Constitutional Impugnment: An Indian Case Study," reprinted in 8 *South African Journal on Human Rights*, 362.
Plaatjie, Sol T. (1987). *Native Life in South Africa* (orig. 1916), B. Willan, ed.
Platzky, L., and C. Walker (1985). *The Surplus People: Forced Removals in South Africa*.
Republic of South Africa (1993). "Government's Proposals on a Charter of Fundamental Rights," February, 2.
Robertson, Michael (1990). "Dividing the Land: An Introduction to Apartheid Land Law,"

in *No Place to Rest: Forced Removals and the Law in South Africa*, C. Murray and C. O'Regan eds.
Sachs, Albie (1990). *Protecting Human Rights in a New South Africa*.
Sachs, Albie. Advancing Human Rights in South Africa (1992).
Sarat, A., and S. Scheingold (1998). "Cause Lawyering and the Reproduction of Professional Authority: An Introduction," in *Cause Lawyering: Political Commitments and Professional Responsibilities*, A. Sarat and S. Scheingold, eds.
Skweyiya, Zola (1990). "Towards a Solution to the Land Question in Post-Apartheid South Africa: Problems and Models," 6 *South African Journal on Human Rights* 195.
South African Institute of Race Relations (1978). "Survey of Race Relations in South Africa, 1977."
South African Institute of Race Relations (1979). "Survey of Race Relations in South Africa, 1978."
South African Law Commission (1991). "Interim Report on Group and Human Rights," August.
Surplus People Project (1983). *Forced Removals in South Africa: The Surplus People Project Reports*, vols. 1–5.
Swanson, E. (1992). "A Land Claims Court for South Africa: Report on Work in Progress," 8 *South African Journal on Human Rights*, 332.
"The Freedom Charter" (1989; orig. 1955), reprinted in 12 *Hastings International and Comparative Law Review*, 318.
Transvaal Rural Action Committee (1988). "A Toehold on the Land: Labour Tenancy in the South Eastern Transvaal," May.
White, Lucie (1988). "To Learn and Teach: Lessons from Driefontein on Lawyering and Power," 1988 *Wisconsin Law Review* 699.
World Bank (1992). "Experience with Agricultural Policy: Lessons for South Africa."
World Bank (1994). "Summary: Options for Land Reform and Rural Restructuring," in *Land Redistribution Options Conference 12–15 October 1993: Proceedings*. Land and Agricultural Policy Centre.
World Bank, Southern Africa Department (1994). "South African Agriculture: Structure, Performance and Options for the Future."

Cases

Ex Parte Chairperson of the Constitutional Assembly: In Re Certification of the Constitution of the Republic of South Africa, 1996, 1996 (4) SA 744 [hereinafter First Certification Case].
Fredericks v. Stellenbosch Divisional Council 1977 3 SA 113 (C).
President of the Republic of South Africa and others v. South African Rugby Football Union and others CCT 16/98 (4 June 1999) 1999 (7) BCLR 725 (CC).

CHAPTER 11

State-Oriented and Community-Oriented Lawyering for a Cause
A Tale of Two Strategies

RONEN SHAMIR AND NETA ZIV

The form and substance of politics—as we habitually tend to think of the term—undergo fundamental changes. By and large we still tend to locate politics in institutional arenas and to focus on the political action of state and quasi-state agents: parliaments, political parties, courts, government agencies, and labor unions. Yet this top-down view of politics misses the intensity and vitality of a new politics from below, loosely organized and sustained by individuals, groups, and non governmental organizations. The same can be said about political consciousness and the ways it is molded and reproduced in the media. The media scrupulously scrutinize the Prime Minister's declarations, the foreign minister's journeys, the plans of the education ministry, and the fate of Supreme Court litigation. And each headline, editorial, and commentary affirms the extent of politics "up there." But is it possible that only too often we pursue the political in the wrong places and on the wrong pages of our newspapers? (Beck, 1994).

Researchers from disparate theoretical viewpoints and ideological positions tend to acknowledge that late modernity is characterized, among other things, by "new" politics. In the context of social change, the new politics relies on specific targeted initiatives of expert organizations, ad-hoc coalitions of committed activists, and, at times, individuals engaged in micro-change. The "old" politics, many seem to agree, is in "crisis" or "decline." Mass parties and social movements formed a prominent, if not an exclusive, means for social activism in the past. Nowadays they form only part of a complex landscape consisting of individuals, groups, and organizations that employ diverse organized and semiorganized strategies.

The pessimist interpretation of this new political landscape centers on the regress of the public sphere and the triumphant rise of inwardly looking individuality. Communitarians, in particular, lament the rise of a market-driven "psychological person" who undermines the vitality of the "sociological person": an individual interested primarily in his own well-being and her most immediate surroundings; a person with weaker commitments to the community and the public interest in general (Rieff, 1966; Lasch, 1979). Accordingly, studies in this vein pronounce the long decline of that civil society admired by Tocqueville: a vibrant public spirit characterized by heightened citizens' engagement in organizations, clubs, and voluntary associations.

The postmodern view, on the other hand, perceives the new politics as social activism that encroaches, discretely and secretively, on hegemonic structures. At times pessimist, often prudently and soberly hopeful, the postmodern vocabulary consists of terms such as subversion and empowerment, and it uses these terms to describe the only real possibilities under the conditions of late global capitalism. To a large extent, the postmodern position despairs in face of the enormous powers of political and economic machines whose extensions reach the most discrete corners of the human existence. Social activism is conceived in terms of local practices of guerrilla warfare. Individuals and ad hoc groups search for openings through which tentative challenges to the existing order may bring about piecemeal changes or, at least, a sense of empowerment for those who have managed to evade or privately undermine hegemonic structures.

The complexity of the new politics and its interpretations is also reflected in literature relating to lawyering for social change. The "conventional" public interest practice—legal representation on behalf of disadvantaged groups that centers on impact litigation and aims at general policy change—has been contested by critical approaches to lawyering. On the one hand, the critics are skeptic of law's capability of bringing about social transformation without collective support from below, and fears the subjugation of the community to the lawyer-experts (Bachman, 1984; Quigley, 1995). Accordingly, cause lawyers are urged to integrate their legalistic strategies with community empowerment and grassroots activity. Lawyers are expected to adopt a less hierarchical relationship with their clients, to be reflexive of the power disparities between them and their clients, and to treat representation as an emergent interactive process. This view, in short, sees personal empowerment as key for social and political change (White, 1988; Alfiery, 1991). On the other hand, postmodern critics acknowledge the contradictions of legal work for a cause inherent in the very necessity to depend on the legal system while challenging its fundamental premises. Yet they try to find openings through which lawyers can introduce subtle and ad hoc acts of resistance (Gabel and Harris, 1982; Lopez, 1992). Some writers see real opportunities in such subversive micro-change-oriented activities. Others are less hopeful and doubt the prospects of bringing about actual change by legal means (Handler, 1992; Fitzpatrick, 1992; Handler, 1996; Scheingold, 1998; cf. Trubek and Kransberger, 1998).

Generally speaking, it seems that these approaches tackle both subpolitics and lawyering for social change in the context of an American experience: an experience that historically assumes a weak state and a vibrant civil society, one in which the legal profession assumes a central and leading role in civic life. Considering Israel's different history, we ought to be cautious in applying these analytical frameworks to Israeli society.

Perhaps Ulrich Beck's approach, working from within a tradition of a strong German state, may be more relevant for our analysis. According to Beck, the public issues of the future will not emanate from foresighted leaders or from parliamentary struggles, but will be placed on the political agenda by citizens' initiative groups, issue-related organizations, and voluntary associations. Fragmented and unstable, and sustained through multiple and semiorganized strategies, that new politics are conceptualized by Beck as "sub-politics." Subpolitics is a concept that describes political action from below, carried out through agents situated outside conventional political structures, who nonetheless actively take part in policy shaping, in the distribution of social power and in setting the political agenda (Beck, 1994: 23). Following Beck, our frame of reference is concerned with different options available to cause lawyers in the context of a general process of state decentering. Our concern will not only engage forms of representation per se, but also the relationship between such forms and the changing locus of politics.

In this article we explore the relevance of the new politics to the analysis of social activism against ethnic discrimination. We organize this exploration around a specific case: the struggle against the attempt to prevent Arab citizens of Israel from living in the community township of Katsir. This struggle currently involves two forms of political activism. One course of action is a strictly legal one. It challenges the discriminatory policy in a petition to the Supreme Court of Israel. The petition was submitted by Adel and Iman Kaadan, an Arab couple who were rejected from Katsir on grounds of their ethnic identity. The petition—which had been prepared and handled by the Association for Civil Rights in Israel (ACRI)—challenges one of the basic tenets of Zionism, i.e., the drive to establish Jewish towns and settlements as a basic form of socio-spatial national presence. These settlements, at least in Israel's early years, were also to serve the instrumental purpose of marking its borders and of dotting the landscape with signposts of sovereignty, especially in areas of the country that were densely populated by Arabs.

The second form of action had been, at first, less publicly visible. A certain Mahamid family from the neighboring town of Um-El-Fahem managed to buy land and build a home in Katsir through the mediation of a Jewish person who acquired the land on their behalf without disclosing the fact that the land was intended for an Arab family. This affair was exposed to the public when the keys of the house were handed over to the Arab family in a public ceremony, an act that led to an attempt by some residents of Katsir to prevent the transaction through legal action. At the background of this action, however, stood a lawyer and a voluntary organization named El-Beit, who planned and orchestrated the transaction.

An analysis of the two forms of action in terms of new politics calls for an explanation. In general, there is widespread agreement among students of Israeli society that it has been historically organized around a strong and highly centralized state. Such a society heavily depends upon the state for resource distribution and market activity. It is characterized by the salience of institutionalized and beaurocratic mechanisms that mediate between the citizen and the state. The boundaries between state and society are blurred: the state is conceived as the very incarnation and representation of society and as an exclusive source of social identity. Challenges to the state's hegemony as the sole legitimate source of identity are perceived as a threat to the social fabric. A society organized around a strong state sanctions cultural homogeneity that mirrors society's hegemonic social groups. Concurrently, a strong state entails a relative weakness of individuals, groups, and other civil society associations. The political culture of a central state identifies civic participation with a "contribution" to the state, sanctions political participation to broadbased political parties, and consists of deep skepticism concerning the ability of nonorganized forces to change the existing order. Stated differently, a civil society of this sort provides only a limited space for social activism and political change from below.

At the same time, there seems to be a widespread agreement among Israeli researchers that the last two decades were marked by an at least relative erosion in the centrality of the state. The most significant marker for this process is economic. From the 1980s onward, dominant forces in the Israeli society embraced a neoliberal market ideology. Israel has engaged in a policy of privatizing governmental companies, has witnessed the disintegration of organized labor, and has seen the rising power of market forces in shaping economic policy. At the same time, there are many indications to the declining capacity of the state to act as an exclusive cultural agent that is able to suppress and marginalize attempts to develop ethnic and cultural distinctions independently of the statist framework. One indication of this process is the substantial increase in the activity of nongovernmental voluntary organizations, which pursue various public causes, defend underprivileged minorities, and represent the interests of specific groups in Israeli society.

The role of these organizations in shaping contemporary public policy is quite significant, yet little attention has been given to them in social and political research. We still look for politics "up there," on the wrong pages of the newspaper. Yet while we follow and debate the significance of, for example, the constitutional revolution,[1] it has hardly been noticed that some of the most important legislative initiatives in recent years, let alone some of the most pressing public issues, were placed on the agenda, planned, and carried out by voluntary groups and organizations.[2]

In describing the practices of these organizations as novel forms of politics, we have to distinguish between two generic types of subpolitics: one is premised on popular mobilization or on social movements with a more or less wide social basis. The other is based on various forms of "private" initiatives and on the activities of issue-specific professional organizations. The latter are often funded by international foundations and rely on a limited number of employed activists and expert advisers. The typical activism of these organizations, at least in Israel, has been marked by overrepresentation of lawyers and the development of strong legal departments. We argue that the so-called awakening civil society in Israel, at least up until now, is largely characterized by social activism of the latter type and not by broad popular action from below.[3]

Legal action led by cause lawyers constitutes a central venue of activism for these groups. Nevertheless, we also argue that it is possible to locate different versions of social activism and different roles for the lawyer-experts within this latter type of politics. In this regard, we will distinguish between state-centered political activism and a community-centered form of political activism. As we shall see, these two types of political action were also matched, in the present case, by two distinct types of cause-lawyering strategies.

The struggle against Katsir allows us to examine these two versions of expert-based political activism. The aforementioned petition to the Supreme Court was submitted by cause lawyers from ACRI, an organization that has been intensively active in various cases of discrimination and social inequality in Israel. The idea of purchasing land for the Mahamid family, on the other hand, had been jointly developed by an activist and a lawyer from an Arab-Jewish association by the name of El-Beit. El-Beit targets the housing needs of the Arab population in Israel and monitors violations of Article 13 of the Universal Declaration of Human Rights, which guarantees freedom of movement and residence.

In both cases the challenge of the discriminatory policy was led by nongovernmental voluntary organizations. Neither of these organizations operates by way of recruiting members and mobilizing a broad constituency. Both rely on skilled experts and selected activists—cause lawyers in particular. The organizations often enlist individuals (in this case Kaadan and Mahamid) for ad hoc action or as representatives of precedent-setting legal test cases. Still, the two forms of activism differ in their use of law and of lawyer-experts. As we shall shortly see, in each of the cases we describe, the cause lawyer assumes a different orientation to legal action and undertakes a different representation role in furthering the social cause. In what follows we shall describe and compare in detail these two forms of legal action and situate each in the context of contemporary theory concerning the meaning of the new politics and the relevance of the declining centrality of the state.

The Story

The challenge to Israel's land-segregation policies touches upon the core of Jewish-Arab relations in the country. For decades Israel has designated state-owned land (95 percent of total land in the country) solely for Jewish settlement. This policy is considered to fulfill a basic national goal: settling Jews in all regions of the country and creating Judified belts of presence, especially crucial in areas densely populated by Arabs. Moreover, Jewish settlement aims to fulfill not only a demographic purpose but also a spiritual one; it is perceived as a means for the social transformation of Jews into "productive" participants in the nation-building process.[4] However, the state is constitutionally barred from distributing land on the basis of discriminatory criteria such as gender, race, or ethnicity. Accordingly, a variety of mechanisms have been devised in order to bypass this restriction. The principal methods for circumventing these restrictions are based on the following: [a] the state leases its land to the Jewish Agency, which is a special status organization that promotes the interests of the Jewish nation within Israel and abroad, and is funded by Jews living outside Israel. The transfer of land from the state to the Jewish Agency enables the latter to designate the land for the use of Jews only. [b] State land is leased to an *association* or *communal corporation* [recognized as such by state law] which, in turn, is granted autonomy to screen potential candidates for membership and residence in the association. The two methods are frequently fused: in the case of Katsir, land had been leased to the Jewish Agency which in turn handed part of it to the communal association. Consequently, the Katsir screening committee was the body that ultimately rejected the request of the two Arab families to live in the community. Another area within the jurisdiction of Katsir remained "open" in that settlers dealt directly with the state and were not required to go through the above-mentioned screening procedure. This latter area is known as "the central hill," while the former is known as "the western hill."[5]

In 1993 attorney Taufiq Jabarin, an Arab lawyer with a known reputation in matters relating to Arab rights, tried to buy land on the western hill of Katsir. He was rejected by the screening committee. Following his resolved to challenge the refusal through legal action, the state offered Jabarin a chance to buy a housing unit on the central hill, an area that is considered somewhat less affluent than the western hill. Jabarin accepted the compromise and he and his family moved into Katsir.

In 1995, Adel and Iman Kaadan from the nearby Arab town of Baka el Garbiya also tried to buy a lot in the western part of Katsir. The Katsir screening committee rejected the request on the basis of their Arab identity, and the Kaadan family approached attorney Jabarin for assistance. Jabarin decided not to handle the case himself and referred them to the Association for Civil Rights in Israel. He reasoned that representation by ACRI, a reputable organization to which the court tends to lend an attentive ear, may be more effective in such a politically delicate case.

Moreover, he wanted Jewish lawyers to be involved in representation so as not to create the impression that Jews and Arabs were poised on opposite sides of the dispute. The Association for Civil Rights considered the matter as a suitable test case for challenging the discriminatory land policy and assumed representation. Jabarin remained involved in the petition from behind the scenes and was consulted and informed about the proceedings.

At the same time, and without informing the lawyers at ACRI, Jabarin began to construct a parallel clandestine scheme to challenge discrimination in Katsir. Jabarin contacted Fat'hi Mahamid from the neighboring Arab town of Um el Fahm. Mahamid also tried to buy land in Katsir and, like Ka'adan, was rejected by the screening committee. Acting on Jabarin's advice, Mahamid decided not to initiate legal action. Instead, Jabarin introduced Mahamid to Uri Davis, a Jewish human rights activist and Jabarin's cofounder of El Beit, the newly founded association that had been advocating against the housing discrimination of Arabs in Israel. In the course of joint meetings among the three, Jabarin proposed to construct a covert agency contract (a recognized device under Israel's Agency Law) between Davis and Mahamid, that would have allowed Davis to purchase the lot in Katsir on behalf of Mahamid. In short, Jabarin simultaneously initiated two forms of resistance to the de facto segregation practices undertaken by Katsir, the Jewish Agency and the State of Israel: an open and well-publicized Supreme Court petition that had been based on Israeli constitutional law, and a covert agency contract that exploited an opening in Israel's civil commercial law. In order to realize these schemes, Jabarin engaged two Jewish "wardens": attorney Neta Ziv from the ACRI on behalf of the Kaadans and Uri Davis on behalf of the Mahamids.

Between Katsir and Jerusalem: The Chronicle

The succeeding chronicle is rather typical of a legal process. Legal proceedings often impress the petitioner as slow and cumbersome and often deprive her or him of having a sense of control over the pace, nature, and career of the grievance.

Adel and Imman Kaadan approached ACRI in June 1995. Following some correspondence with the state and other adversaries, the petition was filed before the Supreme Court in October 1995. The petitioners obtained a temporary injunction preserving one lot in the western part of Katsir in case their claim prevailed. The Kaadans were represented by lawyers from ACRI, the state by the attorney general's office, and the Jewish Agency and the Association of Katsir by private law firms. The Supreme Court held two sessions, one in June 1996 and another in March 1997, and preliminary arguments by both parties had been heard. From the outset, the judges implored the parties to reach an out-of-court settlement and indicated that they preferred not to rule on the merits of the case. The court ordered the parties to summarize their arguments in writing, a process that caused further delay and extended over several months.

The next hearing was held in February 1998. Chief Justice Aharon Barak, presiding, indicated that the petition was one of the hardest he had ever encountered and contemplated whether the public was sufficiently "ripe" for a resolution of this sort. The judges repeated their call to settle the case and directed the parties to a mediating process in the hope that it would facilitate a compromise. The mediator was appointed in February 1998 and was guided by the court to conduct and conclude the mediation within two months. Despite the tight schedule set by the court, the mediation extended over the next ten months. The mediator conducted about five hearings and paid a visit with the parties and their lawyers to Katsir. The process was marked by continuous and repetitive delays due to difficulties in setting "convenient" times for meetings.

Throughout this time, the petitioners rather passively waited for progress on the judicial front. Realizing that the resolution would be delayed beyond their expectations, and after the birth of their third child, the Kaadans began to expand their existing house in Baka el Garbiya.

The mediation efforts failed. The solution offered by the representatives of the state undermined the very logic of the petition, as the Kaadans were asked to buy land that lay outside the municipal boundaries of Katsir. Acting on the advice of ACRI, and themselves progressively enraged by the offer, the Kaadans rejected the proposal. The final mediation hearing was conducted in December 1998, and on the same day an ACRI lawyer notified the court of the failure to reach a settlement and asked for a judicial resolution. In early March 2000, after the completion of this manuscript, the court rendered a decision in the case (see "Epilogue").

Between Katsir and Hadera: The Chronicle

Uri Davis returned to Israel from a prolonged stay abroad in December 1994. Shortly afterward he met Jabarin, and the two established the El Beit association. It was in the context of initiating political activism on behalf of Arabs in matters pertaining to housing and residence issues that they developed the idea to use the law of agency as a mechanism for buying land in Katsir. Jabarin knew Fat'hi Mahamid, a building contractor who had the financial means for buying and building a house in Katsir, and, following his rejection by the screening committee, enlisted him to the scheme. Jabarin drafted the necessary documents, and Davis approached the Katsir screening committee without disclosing the fact that he was acting on behalf of Mahamid. Davis was admitted to Katsir, paid for the land with moneys he had received from Mahamid, and signed all necessary documents with the Jewish Agency and the Israel Land Authority. In 1996 Mahamid began to build his house. The house was ready for residence in mid-1999.

In May 1999 Davis and Mahamid invited a selected group of activists, journalists, and guests to a housewarming ceremony. The scheme was publicly disclosed. Uri Davis publicly handed the keys of the house to Mahamid and congratulated the residents of Katsir for being selected to serve as a vanguard in this new cohabitation project. He spoke against discrimination and about his hopes for a new future of Arab-Jewish coexistence. The residents of Katsir therefore realized that an Arab had moved into their neighborhood under most embarrassing circumstances. In June 1999, the Katsir communal association appealed to the magistrate court in the neighboring Jewish town of Hadera, asking for a temporary injunction that would prevent the Mahamid family from moving into their house. On July 14 the judge on duty, Sabri Muhassen [incidentally, an Arab] rejected the petition for injunctive relief. He reasoned that sufficient evidence was provided for showing that the Mahamid family had already moved into their house. At the hearing, the judge was notified of the pending Supreme Court petition on behalf of Kaadan, but he did not mention it in his decision. Katsir's petition to remove the Mahamid family from its house is still pending at the court.

In sum, concomitant to the ongoing proceedings in the Kaadan case that have been taking place in the last five years, a new reality has been forged in Katsir as the Mahamid family built its house and moved in.

Private and Public in a Struggle for Social Change

It is worthwhile to underscore some of the basic elements in each form of resistance described above. Litigation before the Israeli Supreme Court is a highly visible and publicized process; in fact, visibility is an inherent part of a court-centered strategy and is often contemplated as an important component in its prospects of success. The Kaadan petition, known as "the Katsir case," indeed received broad coverage in the local and international media. Mahamid's action, on the other hand, was clandestine and discrete. Until he decided to expose himself as the true owner, Mahamid's construction of his house, while visible and public, was probably considered by neighbors as a most common market relationship between a Jewish landowner and an Arab contractor.

The first issue we would like to raise here concerns the implications of a public court-centered action against discrimination on the subjective standing of the petitioner-clients. We suggest that one of the consequences of opting to petition the court and the subsequent publicity that followed was that the Kaadans have been transformed, objectively and subjectively, from being a "private" family striving to improve its quality of life to a public asset that symbolized the struggle against ethnic discrimination. When the Kaadans began their legal struggle, they did not consider themselves as principled social reformers. They emphasized the private nature of their quest to live in Katsir, namely the higher quality of life there (a better educational system, good public services, etc.) and underscored their personal insult and humiliation due to their rejection. As time went by, however, subsequent to the court hearings and extensive media coverage, the couple came to see themselves and to be seen by the public as symbols for the principled struggle.

The sense of personal satisfaction and empowerment that may be derived from becoming a symbol in a legal struggle should not be underestimated. Yet it should be noted that such a sense of empowerment is inherently constrained. Filing the petition to the Supreme Court also meant that the management of the case was passed over to ACRI's legal experts. The Kaadans became represented, and entered an expert-client relationship. This power-based relationship is not an equal one to begin with, and is augmented when the lawyer belongs to the majority group and the client to the minority. Lawyers are equipped with knowledge unavailable to clients, which affords them extensive control over the legal process. In addition, the institutional and procedural framework of litigation often leaves the client in suspension even under optimal conditions of high visibility and close contact with the lawyer. After all, lawyers govern the court hearings, draft the documents, file the motions, and conduct negotiations; the client is at best informed about the proceedings. Ultimately his fate is not in his hands. This relative passivity is especially critical in activities that are aimed at social change. In other words, the individual client practically exhausts his active participation in the process by becoming an icon of a public issue.

Mahamid's actions stand in sharp contrast to the above-mentioned disposition. Concomitant to the prolonged albeit publicized legal proceedings that took place in the Supreme Court, the secrecy of Mahamid's scheme enabled him to become an active participant in the struggle for social change and to assume personal responsibility (and risk) for building his house in Katsir. This local subversive activity was transformed into a political conduct that empowered him to take initiative, assume control over his fate, and secure his acclaimed interests.

To be sure, Mahamid was also guided and accompanied by a lawyer. Attorney Taufiq Jabarin employed his professional skill as a transactional lawyer to establish the legal framework necessary for purchasing the land and building the house. Mahamid and Jabarin, therefore, also entered a lawyer-client relationship. It seems, however, that the nature of the lawyer-client relationship in this line of action has been substantially different from the relationship between the Kaadans and the attorneys of ACRI. In the case of Mahamid, legal intervention, important as it was, served only as the formal framework for the real action that changed the social reality in Katsir. Jabarin acted behind the scenes and Mahamid performed at the front stage. This type of representation situated the client in an active position, coherent with beliefs that actual social and political change must involve active participation and personal empowerment of disadvantaged individuals and groups. In contrast, legal representation at the Supreme Court occupied center stage, both formally and substantively, leaving the Kaadans in the background.[6]

The second issue we wish to raise concerns new ways of thinking about cause lawyering. Supreme Court litigation is compatible with the prevailing format employed by most cause lawyers in most rights organizations. These lawyers typically display a legalistic orientation to social change: litigation is a primary means for challenging state policies, and principled constitutional arguments by skilled experts are the highroad to success. Kaadan's petition is typical in that vein of struggle. The petition uses the individual case as a harbinger for the general principle. The specific needs and expectations of the Kaadans are reconceptualized to meet the demands of legal discourse, namely the legality of the land-transfer arrangements between the State and the Jewish Agency and its relationship to issues of equality.

Moreover, lawyers who adopt a legalistic orientation tend to uncritically accept the acclaimed "proper" professional rules governing this type of activism. These same rules, however, did not play a central role in the route undertaken by attorney Jabarin. Jabarin did not use his legal expertise to ground his clients' action within doctrines of fundamental rights and constitutional principles. He operated as a commercial-transactional lawyer who simply offered his clients an effective mechanism, namely a covert agency contract. This legal device is a recognized and legitimate concept in commercial relations. Market economy tolerates, sometimes even encourages, a certain degree of concealment and deception in commercial activities. The "trick" was that Jabarin used an innocent legal tool to obtain a political goal and to further a "cause." The law, in this case, was not activated in its majestic constitutive form; a form that presupposes that the very recognition of constitutional rights in and of itself constitutes the desired change in the existing order. The law was rather activated as a technical device, stripped of its regal qualities, lacking any substantive meaning of its own, subordinated to prevailing commercial norms. It was used, in other words, as a resource for community-oriented political activism.[7]

By misleading the screening committee of Katsir, Davis and Mahamid employed a form of resistance that coincided with postmodern conceptions of personal empowerment and subversion. Yet this mode of action is in tension with the legalistic orientation described above. The legalistic approach includes an at least silent expectation that challenges to discriminatory policies should be conducted upfront—*bona fide*—and should rely upon the "ethical/normative" principles of constitutional and administrative law. The use of the law in its constitutive form, in other words, entails adherence to standards of candor, transparency and fairness that oftentimes stand in discord with the norms of commercial life. From this perspective, even if the course of action undertaken by Mahamid had been formally lawful, it still failed to obey the codes of a "proper" challenge. Yet it is noteworthy to comment that the question of adhering to the "proper" rules of the game is incongruous in the context of localized and community-oriented activism. On the contrary, adherence to issues of proper decorum may distort what is at stake as it shifts the debate from the political and historical injustice incurred on Arabs in Israel to a decontextualized and abstract polemic about fairness and decency.

The normative tension between the two legal practices employed in this case originates from the different sociological significance of each respective form of activism. A petition to the Supreme Court is essentially state oriented. It aims to change the existing order through a principled change in the rules of the game and by using one state apparatus (the court) against another (an administrative agency). Lawyers who locate politics at the level of the state inevitably speak the language of the state, i.e., the language of constitutional law. They typically employ a rights discourse as the paramount venue for improving the status of disadvantaged minorities and they typically expect meaningful change to occur from above, through courts and judges that confer fundamental rights.

The form of activism utilized by Mahamid, in comparison, was community oriented and place oriented. It aimed to create a concrete change at the contested scene without directly confronting the state. Moreover, it caused those residents of Katsir who wanted to prevent the Mahamids from moving into their neighborhood to activate a state-centered approach: appealing to a court for remedy. In this way, the community-based action reversed or at least confused the "natural order of things": it drove the majority group—Jews—to ask the state for "protection" from the minority, and it forced the majority to actively fight in order to sustain their discriminatory policies. Consequently, and not unlike the current position of the still patiently waiting Kaadans, Jewish residents of Katsir are now passively awaiting the decision of the Supreme Court.

Obviously, these two forms of activism against discrimination are not opposites and do not negate each other. Rather, they are mutually constitutive. The act of Mahamid is not external to the anticipated ruling of the Supreme Court in the matter of Kaadan. It has become part of the context, now also a publicly contested one, to which the court's justices must respond. The mundane reality of copresence that Mahamid imposed on Katsir serves to undermine Katsir's reply to Kaadan's petition. In that reply, attorneys for Katsir projected a number of scripts according to which the copresence of Arabs and Jews would be disruptive to community life. The petition to the Supreme Court, a state-centered action, challenged the segregation policy from above. Mahamid's action, conceived by Jabarin and executed by Davis, challenged this same policy from below, by centering on the community itself. These two forms of activism intersect once again as a result of Katsir's appeal to the local court: this time not as respondents but as plaintiffs. Here, Kaadan's petition sets part of the context that the local judge must take into consideration.

Finally, the mutually constitutive relation of these two forms of activism emphasizes the interplay of two venues for cause lawyering. Whereas a state-centered approach—litigation and legislation—dominates cause-lawyering activities, the case we discuss demonstrates the relevance of exploiting commercial law and utilizing transactional lawyering to further social change. The possibilities for transactional cause lawyering encompass the whole range from enlisting individuals to single acts of defiance to mobilizing whole communities for economic development or civic organization (Suggs, 1995). In the case we discussed, certainly unique in its features, a transactional activity supported an individual challenge to a discriminatory policy. This form of cause lawyering may be particularly useful when targeting an issue not by directly confronting the state but rather by disturbing the embedded prejudices and routine bureaucratic practices born out of a longstanding state policy. This disturbance necessarily focuses on local and practical situations, immediately bearing on the lives of those involved.

By focusing on the market rather than on the state, transactional cause lawyering may overcome or avoid some of the concerns raised by the critical literature concerning cause lawyering. Cause lawyering is sometimes described as a contradiction in terms because lawyers attempt to resist and undermine the very same institutions upon which they rely in their professional activities and which provide them with the platform for their cause of action, i.e., state institutions. Therefore, shifting advocacy from the state to the market eases this difficulty. Directing activities toward the market relieves lawyers from the need to conform to some of the strict rules of the game discussed above because the market carries lesser expectations of adherence to the norms associated with rights advocacy. More important, market-oriented transactional law opens up diversified opportunities for poor people or disadvantaged groups to assume greater control over their lives. They are situated not only as receivers of rights and entitlements that are bestowed upon them by the state. Rather, they engage in enterprise building—as vendors and buyers, employers, business entrepreneurs and contractors that use the private-market for their advantage. Finally, transactional cause lawyering can be practiced on an individual as well as a collective basis. As shown in this article, lawyers regularly represent individual clients in commercial transactions and they can do so to promote social justice. But cause lawyers can engage in transactional legal work on behalf of neighborhoods or communities. CED (community economic development) projects have sprung up in recent years in hundreds of low-income neighborhoods in the United States. These projects offer new venues for lawyers and their clients to further economic justice (Jones, 1997).

The case we discuss here, therefore, illustrates the important distinction between subpolitics directed at the state and subpolitics that avoids direct confrontation with it. This latter type of cause lawyering may be directed against specific locales, against specific market or commercial practices, or against a state policy, yet without initiating litigation in the courts of the state and with no direct appeal to principled constitutional arguments. Extending our argument beyond the present case, we believe that this latter type of activity may become more salient in the future as a result of state-decentering processes. When speaking of state decentering, we refer to the erosion in the standing of the state as a hegemonic source for political initiative and political change. State decentering has to do with the rapid development of suprastate politics that constantly erode and undermine state sovereignty from above and the development of subpolitics that erode state centrality from below. In law, suprastate politics appear in the form of international and regional treaties and conventions, the growth of lex-mercatoria, the spread of a universal human rights regime, and an enhanced presence of transnational nongovernmental organizations. Subpolitics, often in conjunction with suprastate processes, are visible in law in the form of nonstate legal arrangements, community justice mechanisms, and a growing demand for legal recognition of identity-politics practices (Ram, 1999; Santos, 1992). Accordingly, our modest contribution in respect to the notion of subpolitics is that we have to distinguish, for analytical purposes, between politics from below, which is still state centered (e.g., constitutional litigation), and community- or market-oriented legal action, which bypasses, avoids, or simply moves politics away from state arenas. The case we describe, although unique, does open up the question of cause lawyering which simultaneously is locale-oriented and relies on utilizing the law in its market appearance rather than in its normative-constitutive one. From this perspective, the type of transactional-lawyering activity we describe is not only a reflection but also a contribution to the erosion of the centrality of the state as a locus of politics. It calls attention, finally, to a broadening landscape of cause-lawyering activities and new possibilities for mobilizing the law for social change.

Subpolitics as Middle-Class Politics

In the final part of this essay, we would like to situate the challenge to Israel's land-discrimination policy in its immediate context of Arab-Jewish relations in Israel. Specifically, we would like to inquire into another aspect of Beck's notion of subpolitics, namely the idea that subpolitics should be conceptually tied to processes of individualization in late modernity. Unlike those who associate individualization with atomization, alienation, and retreat from the public sphere, Beck more neutrally describes it as a situation in which individuals have to invent, produce, and orchestrate their biographies on their own (1994: 22). Politics assumes a novel dimension that does not obey "old" categories of collective identity. The new politics, writes Beck, blurs the classic oppositions between 'right' and 'left,' 'radical' and 'conservative,' 'democrat' and 'anti-democrat,' 'majority' and 'minority.' Instead, the new politics is issue specific, contingent upon ad-hoc coalitions, individual or local initiatives, corresponding to practical possibilities for action.

The stories of Kaadan and Mahamid provide us with the opportunity to examine Beck's argument in action. On the face of it, the struggle against Katsir is one that takes place in the framework of "classic" categories. After all, it involves the struggle of citizens against discrimination on the basis of their ethnicity. The purpose of the struggle, in terms of the "old" categories, is social integration. Yet we doubt whether ethnic integration, as a political goal, is a term that captures the nature of the struggle in Katsir. The Jewish residents of Katsir are not altruistic pioneers, and the Arabs who wish to live there are not "backward" villagers. Both belong to the new Israeli middle class that identifies a place of residence with global criteria of "quality of life." The political activism we describe here was directed against an affluent middle-class community and, not coincidentally, was carried out by Arab families who had the necessary material means and social skills to establish a claim for residence in that community and to pursue it with the assistance of cause lawyers.

Integration between Arabs and Jews, as a principled political objective, does not necessarily express the urgent expectations and desires of the Israeli-Arab population as a whole. As the struggle against Katsir gained momentum and visibility, other voices had been heard, arguing that the true needs of the Arab population lie elsewhere, first and foremost in a more egalitarian distribution of resources between Jewish and Arab municipalities and local governments. In other words, discrimination against the Arabs in allocating state resources and in developing local health, education, and infrastructure in Arab towns and villages is a more pressing issue, albeit somewhat overshadowed by the visibility of the struggle against segregation. This latter point cannot be overstated. The wish to live in an affluent neighborhood, in a comfortable house with a backyard and a magnificent view, and the wish to enjoy high-quality community services, and not integration per-se, are what seem to be at stake in the present case. This latter statement, of course, is not meant to diminish the significance of the struggle or to trivialize it. Rather, it is meant to emphasize that the struggle we analyze here is a struggle of *individuals* who share middle-class social dispositions with their Jewish 'adversaries' and who are able to press claims on the basis of their material and cultural capital.

The cause-lawyering strategies that we analyze here, accordingly, were made available to and worked at the service of particular clients. It is beyond the scope of the present article to develop the possible links between middle-class politics and subpolitics. Yet as a general direction for further inquiry, we suggest looking more closely at such a relationship. At minimum, the degree to which the new politics we discuss is generated at the service of, is most accessible to, and is most responsive to middle-class recipients, opens questions about the options of the truly disadvantaged: those groups who may find it ever more difficult to articulate their needs and to find vehicles of mobilizing for change. We leave it here, however, as an open question for future studies.

Epilogue

As we go to press, the Supreme Court has rendered its decision in the matter of the Kaadans (HCJ 6698/95, 8.3.00). The court accepted the petition on grounds of a principled equality doctrine that forbids the state, directly or indirectly, to discriminate in allocating land on the basis of nationality or ethnicity. However, it is noteworthy that the actual remedy granted by the court to the Kaadans has been significantly restricted. On the one hand, the court transcended the individual case by describing its decision as a "future-oriented" one; that is, a decision that should apply in future cases of land transfer to the Jewish Agency. On the other hand, the court did not grant the petitioners the actual right of residing in Katsir. Rather, it advised reconsideration of the application in light of the equality doctrine on the one hand and in light of the fact that Jewish residents had a basic right of reliance on their past expectations to live in an Arab-free neighborhood. In the polite words of the court:

> What, then, is the remedy for the petitioners? The answer is not simple at all. The petition, as the petitioners say, looks to the future. But we must not forget that the state allocated the land on which Katsir was established to the Jewish Agency in 1986. Moreover, the residents bought houses in the place and moved to reside there, while relying on the situation that existed at the time. These facts raise difficult problems... not only from a social standpoint, but also from a legal standpoint.... We cannot ignore these problems. In this state of affairs, [a] we declare that the state had no legal right to allocate state land to the Jewish Agency in order to establish a communal neighborhood on the basis of discrimination between Jews and non-Jews. [b] the state must consider the application of petitioners to buy land in Katsir in order to build a house, on the basis of an equality principle, and while taking into account other relevant considerations—including considerations pertaining to the Jewish Agency and the settlers—and including the legal problems associated with the matter. On the basis of such considerations, the state must rapidly decide if it can allow petitioners, within the law, to build a house in Katsir.

A legal victory it is. However, we believe that its symbolic and practical implications should be evaluated in light of the theoretical parameters provided in this essay.

Notes

1. The term "constitutional revolution" refers to Israel's new laws affirming and embodying basic constitutional rights. The term was coined by the chief justice of the Supreme Court, and its adequacy is hotly debated in academic and public discourse.

2. For example, the new disability law, or the new sexual harassment legislation. Both were drafted and planned by nongovernmental organizations.

3. Two notable exceptions of the past twenty years concern the pro-peace and pro-Jewish settlement movements, Peace Now and Gush Emunim, respectively.

4. See Oren Yiftachel, 1998; Sandy Kedar, 1998.

5. The second neighborhood was developed during the mass immigration of Jews from the former Soviet Union with intention to facilitate their absorption. To expedite and facilitate the housing of the newcomers, the state had built small prefab housing units on the central hill.

6. The case had become known as the "Katsir case" rather the "Ka'adan case." This is yet another example of "Hebrewtizing" cases filed by Arabs. Symbolically, a petition to court might lead to erasing the identity of Arab petitioners, creating the impression that Jews "grant" Arabs their rights within a Jewish rights discourse.

7. Our discussion here draws upon and hopefully expands Fitzpatrick's distinction between two dimensions of law: a relational (practical, operative) dimension and a surpassing (above and outside specific social relations) dimension. See Fitzpatrick, 1992: 45–46.

References

Alfiery, Anthony (1991). "Reconstructive Poverty Law Practice: Learning the Lessons of Client Narrative," 100 *Yale Law Journal*, 2107.
Bachman, Stephen (1984). "Lawyers, Law and Social Change," 13 *New York University Review of Law and Social Change*, 1.
Beck, Ulrich (1994). "The Reinvention of Politics: Towards a Theory of Reflexive Modernization," in *Reflexive Modernization*, U. Beck, A. Giddens, and S. Lash, [eds.] Stanford, Calif.: Stanford University Press, 1–55.
Fitzpatrick, Peter (1992). "Law as Resistance," in *The Critical Lawyer's Handbook*. Ian Grigg-Spall and Paddy Ireland, eds. London: Pluto Press, 44–48.
Gabel, Peter, and Paul Harris (1982). "Building Power and Breaking Images: Critical Legal Theory and the Practice of Law," 9 *Review of Law & Social Change*, 369–411.
Handler, Joel (1992). "Postmodernism, Protest, and the New Social Movements," 26 (4) *Law and Society Review*, 697–731.
Jones, Susan R. (1997). "Small Business and Community Economic Development: Transactional Lawyering for Social and Economic Justice," 4 *Clinical Law Review*, 195.
Kedar, Alexander (1998). "Majority Time, Minority Time: Land, Nation and the Law of Adverse Possession in Israel," 21 (3), *Iuney Mishpat*, 665–746 [Heb.].
Lasch, Christopher (1979). *The Culture of Narcissism*. New York: W. W. Norton.
Lopez, Gerald P. (1992). *Rebellious Lawyering: One Chicano's Vision of Progressive Law Practice*. Boulder, Col.: Westview Press.
Minnow, Martha, and Elizabeth Spelman (1990). "In Context," 63 *Southern California Law Review*, 1597–652.
Quigley, William P. (1995). "Reflections of Community Organizers: Lawyering for Empowerment of Community Organizations," 21 *Ohio Law Review*, 455.
Ram, Uri (1999). "Between Market and Arms: Liberal Post-Zionism in the Glocal Age," in *Ethnocracy and Glocalization: New Approaches to the Study of Society and Space in Israel*. U. Ram and O. Yiftachel, eds. Ben-Gurion University, 43–100 [Heb.].
Rieff, Philip (1966). *The Triumph of the Therapeutic: The Uses of Faith after Freud*. London: Chatto and Windus.
Santos, Boaventura de Sousa (1992). "State, Law and Community in the World System: An Introduction," 1 (2) *Social and Legal Studies*, 131–42.
Scheingold, Stuart (1998). "The Struggle to Politicize Legal Practice: A Case Study of Left-Activist Lawyering in Seattle," in *Cause Lawyering: Political Commitments and Professional Responsibilities*. A. Sarat and S. Scheingold, eds. New York: Oxford University Press, 118–148.
Suggs, Robert E. (1995). "Bringing Small Business Development to Urban Neighborhoods," 30 *Harvard Civil Rights and Civil Liberties Law Review*, 487.
Trubeck, Louise, and Elizabeth Kransberger (1998). "Critical Lawyers, Social Justice and the Structures of Private Practice," in *Cause Lawyering: Political Commitments and Profes-*

sional Responsibilities. A. Sarat and S. Scheingold, eds. New York: Oxford University Press, 201–26.

White, Lucie (1988). "To Learn and to Teach: Lessons from Driefontein on Lawyering and Power," 1988 *Wisconsin Law Review*, 699.

Yiftachel, Oren (1998). "The Internal Frontier: Territorial Control and Ethnic Relations in Israel," in: *Ethnic Frontiers and Peripheries: Landscapes of Development and Inequality in Israel.* A. Meir and O. Yiftachel, eds. Boulder, Col.: Westview Press, 39–68.

PART III

The Globalization of Cause Lawyering

CHAPTER 12

Latin American Cause-Lawyering Networks

STEPHEN MEILI

Cause-lawyering networks have become prevalent in Latin America over the past two decades, coinciding with—and in many instances the result of—the transition to democracy in several countries of the region. This increase in transnational cause-lawyering networks parallels—and is part of—the recent proliferation of international linkages among a host of actors from nongovernmental, governmental, and intergovernmental organizations mobilized around particular issues. These international linkages, referred to in some of the relevant literature as "transnational issue networks," have been organized primarily to exchange information among activists and exert pressure on governmental actors who are otherwise resistant to entreaties from domestic forces.[1] Such networks are normally formed as a result of the shared ideas or values of their members.[2] In most instances they seek to frame public debate, put issues on the agenda, influence the behavior of decision makers, and affect public policy.[3]

Substantively, Latin American cause-lawyering networks cover a wide range of issues, including human rights, environmental protection, women's rights, children's rights, the rights of indigenous persons, labor law, consumer law, and various economic and social rights such as housing, health care, and education. The networks relevant to some of these issues—most notably those concerned with human rights and environmental protection—are more established and have achieved significant objectively measured victories.

Structurally, there are networks of cause lawyers across national boundaries within the region, and between lawyers in individual Latin American countries and other parts of the world, most notably the United States and Western Europe. For example, networks on human rights and environmental protection include domestic organizations from several Latin American countries, as well as transnational organizations based in the United States and Western Europe. On the other hand, networks of grassroots community-based cause lawyers, who focus primarily on social and economic rights, are almost exclusively comprised of cause lawyers from Latin America.

There are obvious advantages and disadvantages to both types of networking structures. Linkages with groups from outside the region (or sponsorship of conferences and other initiatives that include outside groups or individuals) provide the kind of informal contacts and official meetings that increase exposure and the opportunities for the funding necessary to sustain such networks. This is critical, since much of the funding for the conferences and other projects which support Latin American cause-lawyering networks comes from outside the region. On the other hand, the participation of cause lawyers from the United States and Western Europe always carries with it the potential for cultural bias, insensitivity, and domination. Of course, such adverse cultural dynamics exist between countries within Latin America, as well.

The methodology of Latin American cause lawyers falls into two general categories: advocacy that consists primarily of traditional forms of lawyering such as litigation and lobbying, and advocacy that rejects such traditions and focuses instead on client-centered, less conventional strategies such as community organizing and citizen empowerment. The cause lawyers who pursue the latter methodology are frequently identified by one of several terms, including "alternative lawyers," "new lawyers," or "change-oriented lawyers." Alternative lawyers promote conflict resolution and collective enforcement of rights outside traditional legal structures. Frustrated by inefficient, expensive, and frequently corrupt legal systems, as well as historically nonindependent judiciaries, these lawyers work collaboratively with grassroots community groups, frequently in urban shanty towns and rural land occupations. They usually act more like legal consultants to an already organized community or movement, rather than as the traditional legal representatives for an individual client. They often advise these groups on alternative means of resolving local disputes, thereby enabling the community to resolve future disputes on its own, without recourse to court.[4] Rather than dictate strategy to a particular community group or movement, they offer advice concerning the legal consequences of contemplated actions, such as land occupations by the Brazilian Landless Peasant Movement. [5]

This chapter examines the role and dynamics of cause-lawyering networks in postauthoritarian Latin America. It is based primarily on interviews conducted with cause lawyers and law professors in several Latin American countries between 1994 and 1999. It begins with a theoretical framework, reviewing relevant literature on transnational issue networks, particularly those devoted to some of the causes traditionally associated with cause lawyering (e.g., human rights and environmental protection). This part of the chapter also outlines the circumstances that normally contribute to the formation and maintenance of such networks, and the means by which the networks seek to identify and achieve their goals.

The chapter then describes cause-lawyering networks in Latin America. Drawing on interviews with, and the writings of, Latin American cause-lawyers, it analyzes the different kinds of cause-lawyering networks, how they are formed, the forces that impede them, and their relationship with the organized bar.

The chapter next discusses some of the tensions between cause lawyers and the networks of which they are a part. These tensions result from conflicts over the relative importance of different causes in postauthoritarian Latin America, methodologies for promoting those causes, and diverse views of the role of law and the rule of law in newly emerging democracies that must operate within a context of increased globalization. In particular, this part of the chapter will focus on some of the conflicts between cause lawyers who emphasize political rights (e.g., human rights) and those who emphasize social and economic rights (e.g., housing and health care).

Finally, the chapter analyzes the difficult issue of how to measure the effectiveness of cause-lawyering networks. This question is related to the conflicts between different types of cause lawyers noted above, since each group has its own ideas about what constitutes effectiveness in the cause-lawyering context.

Underlying the discussion in this chapter are two of the major themes of this volume: democratization and globalization. Many Latin American cause lawyers have a somewhat conflicted attitude toward democratization; that is, while they push for greater democratization of state processes (i.e., expansion of political and civil rights), they also challenge the reliance on rights-based strategies for social change as democratization proceeds. Similarly, globalization has created—or in some sense recreated—patterns of dependency and domination between the region and the rest of the world (primarily the United States and Western Europe). In this context, the chapter considers the extent to which the origins and financial support for Latin American cause-lawyering networks (much of which comes from abroad) affect the agenda setting, legitimacy, and efficacy of these networks. Thus, while globalization provides opportunities for cause lawyers to benefit from alliances beyond national borders, the extension of the rule of law to newly emerging democracies may be another form of imperialism and neocolonialism.

Theoretical Framework

Transnational Advocacy Networks

In theoretical terms, cause-lawyering networks are perhaps best viewed as a hybrid between transnational advocacy networks and epistemic communities. According to Keck and Sikkink, advocacy networks "are organized to promote causes, principled ideas, and norms, and they often involve individuals advocating policy changes that cannot be easily linked to a rationalist understanding of their 'interests.' "[6] Moreover, "by building new links among actors in civil societies, states, and international organizations, advocacy networks multiply the channels of access to the international system. In such issue areas as the environment and human rights, they also make international resources available to new actors in domestic political and social struggles. By thus blurring the boundaries between a state's relations with its own nationals and the recourse both citizens and states have to the international system, advocacy networks are helping to transform the practice of national sovereignty."[7]

Many of the issue-oriented linkages between Latin American cause lawyers discussed in this chapter are advocacy networks. Most have been organized to promote causes, principled ideas, and norms. Many—particularly in the areas of human rights and environmental protection—have made international resources available to new actors in domestic political and social struggles. They use both traditional legal strategies (e.g., litigation) and innovative methods (e.g., grassroots community organizing) to advance the interests of the individuals or groups for whom they advocate.

According to Keck and Sikkink, transnational advocacy networks are most likely to emerge when three conditions are present:

> (1) channels between domestic groups and their governments are severed or hampered or where such channels are ineffective for resolving a conflict, (2) activists believe that networking will further their missions and campaigns, and actively promote networks, and (3) conferences and other forms of international contact create arenas for forming and strengthening networks.[8]

In elaborating on these points, the authors describe a "boomerang pattern" of pressure exerted on governmental actors by advocacy networks: when the channels between a particular state and its domestic actors are blocked, NGOs bypass their state apparatus and seek out international or transnational allies to bring pressure on their states from outside. This is particularly evident in the case of human rights campaigns.[9] Keck and Sikkink also note that activists create transnational issue networks "when they believe (and can convince others) that networking will further their organizational missions—by sharing information, attaining greater visibility, gaining access to different publics, multiplying channels of institutional access, and so forth."[10]

Keck and Sikkink also identify several criteria by which to measure the success of an advocacy network: (1) framing debates and getting issues on the agenda; (2) encouraging discursive commitments from states and other policy actors; (3) causing procedural change at the international and domestic level; (4) affecting policy; and (5) influencing behavior changes in target actors.[11] According to these criteria, such networks are more successful when they concentrate on issues with broad public consensus and vulnerable decision makers whom the network is trying to influence.[12] While certainly useful in a discussion of Latin American cause-lawyering networks, these yardsticks are objective, institution-based measures of success that do not take into account more subjective criteria such as whether cause lawyers believe they have achieved what they had hoped to accomplish in a particular endeavor, and the extent to which a network has satisfied the desires of the communities it purports to represent or for whom it advocates. For while some networks may "succeed" with an agenda developed by its leadership (e.g., achieve certain legislative victories), its members may nevertheless feel frustrated and the grassroots community for which it speaks may feel alienated, marginalized, or ignored. Conversely, some networks that fail to meet certain objective goals may nevertheless achieve favorable results for their communities in ways that no one may have predicted. We will see some of the latter phenomena during the course of this chapter. They illustrate that cause-lawyering networks in Latin America are diverse and constantly shifting, reflecting the ever-changing needs and realities of postauthoritarian civil society.

Epistemic Communities

An epistemic, or "knowledge-based," community is a group or network of professionals on whom policymakers rely for information and expertise. According to Haas, "as demands for such information arise, networks or communities of specialists capable of producing and providing the information emerge and proliferate. The members of the prevailing community become strong actors at the national and transnational level as decision makers solicit their information and delegate responsibility to them."[13] Haas notes that the members of an epistemic community share the following:

> (1) a set of normative and principled beliefs, which provide a value-based rationale for the social action of community members; (2) causal beliefs, which are derived from their analysis of practices leading or contributing to a central set of problems in their domain and which then serve as the basis for elucidating the multiple linkages between possible policy actions and desired outcomes; (3) notions of validity—that is, intersubjective, internally defined criteria for weighing and validating knowledge in the domain of their expertise; and (4) a common policy enterprise—that is, a set of common practices associated with a set of problems to which their professional competence is directed, presumably out of the conviction that human welfare will be enhanced as a consequence.[14]

While epistemic communities are usually associated with scientific and technological issues, they can appear in other contexts, as well. Epistemic communities have been identified in such issue areas as international food aid, banking, postwar settlements, and international cooperation.[15] The Mexican Center for Human Rights exhibits characteristics of both an advocacy network and an epistemic community: it combines traditional and innovative advocacy efforts (i.e., litigation and community organizing) with consulting work for the state within its area of expertise.

It is useful to analyze Latin American cause-lawyering networks against the theoretical framework outlined above. That framework is particularly helpful in describing the various cause-lawyering networks that have emerged within the region in recent years, noting the reasons for their emergence, and beginning to think about how one might articulate the degree to which these networks have met the goals of the cause lawyers who comprise them and the communities who are affected by their actions.

Description of Latin American Cause-Lawyering Networks

Reasons for Forming Networks

Cause lawyers in Latin America articulate two principle reasons for forming or participating in cause-lawyering networks: the need to exchange information with other cause lawyers, advocates, and affected groups; and to attempt to alter the behavior of domestic decision makers who would otherwise ignore their demands. Comments from individual cause lawyers are illustrative. According to Soraya Long, of the human rights organization CODEUCA (Commission for Human Rights in Central America) in Costa Rica, the major benefit of linkages with cause lawyers active in other advocacy groups is what she terms "retroalimentacion," or nourishment: By working with and sharing information and strategies with each other, cause lawyers give and receive support for their causes. In addition, the notoriety created by regional and international linkages has allowed cause-lawyering organizations to mount successful human rights campaigns; i.e., they have used international pressure and publicity to influence government officials in their own countries.[16]

Other Latin American cause lawyers echo Long's sentiments. Jaime Benvenuto, an attorney and the director of the Legal Assistance Group for Popular Organizations (GAJOP) in Recife, Brazil, says that the driving force behind emerging cause-lawyering networks is that "isolation does not work. We sometimes feel like we are reinventing the wheel, and the idea is to try and establish mechanisms of enforcement of human rights. We can learn from the triumphs and mistakes of others."[17] Cristian Riego, a professor at Diego Portales University in Chile who has been active in revising Chile's criminal code, states that "we are just starting to learn the importance of cooperation at the international level after a very long tradition of isolationism. For me, the most important [thing about such contacts] is the possibility of receiving influences and ideas from sources different from the traditional continental European legal culture that has been so strong in Latin America."[18] Amanda Romero of ILSA (the Latin American Institute for Alternative Law), based in Bogota, Colombia, says that the goal of her organization's networking efforts with community-based legal groups throughout the region is to help as many people as possible learn how to advocate for themselves before various tribunals and other decision-making institutions.[19] In addition, many cause lawyers in newly emerging democracies believe that these linkages will help them devise litigation and lobbying strategies, as well as ideas for educating judges about the social and political rights contained in new laws and constitutional provisions, and the judiciary's critical role in the development and enforcement of those laws.[20]

Three Categories of Cause-Lawyering Networks

1. AD HOC OR CRISIS-ORIENTED CONTACTS

The most common type of cause-lawyering network in Latin America, according to Alejandro Carrió, an Argentine lawyer who recently established a civil rights law firm in Buenos Aires,[21] is a group of informal contacts. These, by their very nature, are difficult to document in any systematic manner. They tend to be ad hoc, based on professional and academic ties established during previous conferences, educational experiences, and professional collaborations. While they may not always concern issues of legal substance, they sometimes lead to the more formal linkages described in detail below.

These ad hoc linkages are frequently established to address a specific problem or crisis; i.e., one cause lawyer needs assistance on a given case and turns to another cause lawyer with expertise or experience in that area. For example, Fundo Publico, based in Bogota, has earned a reputation for its effective use of the legal system in asserting collective rights, particularly concerning the environment.[22] As a result, it receives requests for assistance and participation from virtually every country in Latin America. And the Center for Rights and Society, in Quito, Ecuador, which works with grassroots organizations to mediate community disputes, receives requests for help from lawyers who have been unsuccessful in resolving problems through the traditional legal system.[23] These organizations and the cause lawyers with whom they share information thus exhibit some of the characteristics of epistemic communities, although that information is generally given to other members of the community, rather than to the state.

It is unclear how much this type of informal or ad hoc networking lends itself to a sustained transnational exchange of information. On the one hand, according to Miguel Pressburger, the director of the Institute for Popular Legal Support (AJUP), a clearinghouse for cause lawyers in Rio de Janeiro, these one-way linkages are too crisis specific to result in long-term relationships between cause-lawyering entities.[24] And some of the cause lawyers who provide issue-specific expertise feel that these exchanges have limited benefit for their own work.[25] On the other hand, cause lawyers who achieve notoriety because of their work in certain areas are able to establish numerous and frequently ongoing contacts with nongovernmental organizations and other groups in need of their services. For example, Maria Elba Martinez, a cause lawyer based in Cordoba, Argentina, has developed an international reputation for her work in the area of human rights, most notably on behalf of the "disappeared" during Argentina's "dirty war," and for prison inmates and the victims of police violence since then. As a result, she receives numerous requests from NGOs to work on human rights cases.[26] For the most part, then, these informal contacts are more focused on individual cases or disputes than on promoting any larger cause or agenda.

2. INFORMALLY ORGANIZED NETWORKS

Several organizations in Latin America have established networks that are more organized and sustained than the ad hoc arrangements described above, though not formally linked to international movements or networks. One example of this is the network of lawyers working with grassroots community groups that has been developed by ILSA. Founded in 1978 in order to emphasize an alternative to the Law and Development movement's focus on judicial and legal reform, ILSA advocates community legal education and views "access to justice" not as an increased opportunity to place a dispute before a tribunal but as a wider concept of promoting the enforcement of social and economic rights through a variety of measures, including hunger strikes and demonstrations.[27] Many of the lawyers who are part of the ILSA network spend at least part of their time practicing "alternative" law. Over the past two decades, ILSA has sponsored more than fifty conferences and seminars in numerous Latin American countries dealing with a wide range of cause-lawyering issues.[28]

Another example of an informal cause-lawyering network is the consortium of six law school clinical programs from Argentina, Chile, and Peru that, under the auspices of the Ford Foundation, has recently sponsored conferences at which participants discuss their work on public interest litigation involving gender and race discrimination, protection of minorities, prisoners' rights, the rights of indigenous persons, and consumer and environmental protection. The conferences have also included a handful of clinical teachers from law schools in the United States. The participating clinics have established cooperating agreements with several NGOs in each country that focus on human rights, women's rights, and environmental protection. The conferences provide an opportunity for cause lawyers from the participating countries to learn about the issues affecting their colleagues' work, and to devise strategies for maintaining such communication in the future. According to the postconference report prepared by the organizers, "Experts from disciplines traditionally separated, such as human rights, consumer protection, environmental matters and others, have been convened to work together on a systematic basis, something unprecedented in Latin America."[29]

One of the most important ways that these informal, intercontinental networks are created and maintained is through data banks established by private NGOs that facilitate information exchange. As noted above, ILSA has developed a database of cause lawyers throughout the region.[30] AJUP in Rio de Janeiro and GAJOP in Recife, Brazil, serve as clearinghouses for cause lawyers in Brazil. They receive requests for legal assistance from grassroots groups and make referrals to attorneys with expertise in the relevant area who may be willing to provide help at no cost.[31]

3. FORMALIZED-ISSUE NETWORKS

The third type of Latin American cause-lawyering network is more formally organized than those described above. It typically involves groups of lawyers from several different organizations or institutions in countries both within and outside Latin America who specialize in a particular issue or cause. These networks are frequently sponsored by an existing organization, although in some cases the cause-lawyering networks themselves have created an entirely new organization. They are often sustained by periodic conferences and more frequent informal information exchanges. They typically receive funding from international foundations. Indeed, the extensiveness of such networks makes funding more readily available.[32] These networks generally do not encounter as many barriers as the more informal networks described above.

The most prominent formal networks of cause lawyers in Latin America are in the areas of human rights and environmental protection, particularly the former. On a global scale, groups working on these issues, as well as women's rights, constitute over half the total of international nongovernmental organizations working for social change.[33] As Dezalay and Garth explain in their chapter in this volume, lawyers have become prominent in human rights organizations, helping to create an international field of human rights that operates outside the influence and limitations of individual countries and legal systems.[34] Cause lawyers working in these areas have the advantage of affiliating with existing—and extensive—international networks devoted to these issues. As Cristian Riego of Diego Portales University notes, "It is easier to establish networks on issues in which those networks already exist ... like in human rights and environmentalism."[35] And as Halliday and Karpik observe, the commitment to such political rights is spreading because it is reinforced by a kind of political globalization.[36]

The list of organizations working on human rights in Latin America includes domestic NGOs like the Center for the Study of Law and Society (CELS) and the Latin American Peace and Justice Service (SERPAJ) in Argentina, the Commission for Human Rights in Central America (CODEUCA) in Costa Rica, and the Academy of Human Rights in Mexico, as well as transnational organizations such as the UN Commission on Human Rights, the UN Committee on Human Rights, the Inter-American Commission on Human Rights, Amnesty International, Americas Watch, and the Washington Office on Latin America.

There is a similarly large group of NGOs devoted to environmental protection issues in Latin America, including domestic organizations like the Mexican Foundation for Environmental Protection, the Peruvian Society for Environmental Rights, the Foundation for the Environment and Natural Resources in Argentina, the Public Fund in Colombia, and Latin American Future in Ecuador, as well as the National Wildlife Federation, Greenpeace, the Environmental Defense Fund, Oxfam, and Friends of the Earth.

A good example of the way in which the more formal Latin American cause-lawyering networks function both within and outside the region is the Mexican Center for Environmental Rights, based in Mexico City. On the national level, it works with other environmental groups in Mexico, such as Greenpeace, the Mexican Foundation for Environmental Education, and the Committee for the Protection of Natural Resources. On the regional level, in addition to being a member of the newly formed Network of NGOs for Environmental Rights in Central America, the Center has ties to environmental groups throughout Latin America, including the Peruvian Society for Environmental Rights, the Foundation for the Environment and Natural Resources (Argentina), the Public Fund (Colombia), and Latin American Future in Ecuador. These groups meet both formally and informally to discuss enforcement of environmental laws, including preparation for the impact that free trade in Latin America will have on the environment.[37] On the international level, the Center has established linkages with several environmental groups in the United States. It has received support (financial assistance, research tools, and books and other publications) from the National Wildlife Federation. Some of the organization's funding also comes from consulting work it performs for Mexican business and the government.[38]

Who Creates the Networks?

A question related to why cause lawyers form or join networks is who creates them and what impact that has on the setting of the network's agenda. It is clear from the research leading to this chapter that most of the formal networks related to political and civil rights were created by individuals and organizations outside the region, and that the Latin American cause lawyers who belong to those networks have only a limited role in determining their agendas. Since the goal of many of these networks is to press for compliance with international agreements promulgated in the past, a significant part of their agendas has been previously determined. As Dezalay and Garth note, the agendas of cause-lawyering networks on human rights must be legitimated in the north because of the need for funding and other means of outside support to sustain the network.[39]

On the other hand, the Latin American cause-lawyering networks devoted to social and economic rights were, for the most part, created by cause lawyers within the region, who maintain control over their agendas. This allows these networks to remain flexible in setting goals that reflect differences between the various countries in the region. The alternative lawyers within this category would assert that their networks' agendas are set by the grassroots community groups with which they work; i.e., the cause lawyers must adapt their strategies to the needs and strengths of the "client" group, rather than the other way around. Thus, depending on the desires, dynamics and sophistication of a particular community group, such cause lawyers will participate in or offer advice about demonstrations, land occupations, hunger strikes, community organizing drives, and negotiations with governmental officials, as well as direct client representation before a tribunal.

Of course, the answer to the question of who actually creates an agenda can be complicated and multilayered. For example, although the clinical law professors in Argentina, Chile, and Peru who have formed an informal network choose which cases they will litigate, the group has been sustained through funding from the Ford Foundation, and its strategy for promoting social rights through litigation was inspired by the experience of cause lawyers in the United States.[40] And since their litigation choices are constrained by existing statutes or constitutional provisions, their agenda is also partially set by the legislative and executive branches. Moreover, to the extent that groups like ILSA have recently begun to seek vindication of social, economic, and cultural rights through enforcement of international instruments such as the International Covenant on Economic, Social and Cultural Rights, they have effectively surrendered some control over their agenda setting.

Obstacles to Cause-Lawyering Networks

One of the greatest obstacles to the formation and maintenance of cause-lawyering networks in Latin America is that there are not many lawyers involved in them. According to Cristian Riego of Diego Portales University in Chile, the main impediment to networking among public interest lawyers in Latin America is that it is "a very very little group of people."[41] Unlike in the United States and Western Europe, where numerous cause-lawyering organizations concerned with a host of public policy and legal issues have the financial and technological resources to communicate regularly about the substance and methodology of their work, networking among Latin America cause lawyers is limited by the same shortages that make the work of individual cause lawyers in the region so difficult. Although the increasing prevalence of email has made transnational communication much easier, a dearth of money and technology forces most cause lawyers to focus their efforts on the daunting tasks at hand, rather than on establishing links with their colleagues across national and continental borders.[42] This is particularly true among cause lawyers who work outside the areas of human rights and environmental protection, where networks are less well established. These time and money pressures are exacerbated by the fact that most cause lawyers in the region can only afford to do such work on a part-time basis.[43] For many Latin American cause lawyers, the international conferences and seminars that make large-scale networking possible in other parts of the world are an overly expensive and time-consuming luxury.

Second, several cause lawyers feel that most Latin American countries lack a public interest lawyering tradition, which makes it difficult to establish linkages with cause lawyers elsewhere. According to Christian Courtis of the University of Buenos Aires, there is not a clear understanding of what public interest law is. He adds that poverty law is generally not even seen as a separate branch of the law, but simply as the application of traditional civil law issues for people without resources.[44] In a similar vein, Cristian Riego notes that there is not a public interest legal community within each country, which he attributes in part to "the lack of an adequate legal frame, the weakness of the role that the judiciary plays in the political system, the lack of a tradition in this kind of activity, and the weakness of civil society."[45]

Moreover, many cause lawyers believe that Latin American law schools do not provide adequate training in the sociology of law and in thinking of new ways to use the law in order to challenge the status quo. Most law school professors are practicing attorneys who appear before local judges, or who otherwise have significant ties to the judiciary, and are thus unwilling to criticize the dominant legal structure, or to encourage law students to think of ways that it might be altered or challenged.[46]

There are additional obstacles to cause-lawyering networks that are particularly of concern to those cause lawyers who promote social and economic rights. The issues with which these cause lawyers are concerned—housing, health care, food, consumer protection, and domestic violence—do not enjoy the kind of transnational consensus that supports work in defense of human rights and the environment. Most people throughout the world support a clean environment and the right to live free from state repression; indeed, many people are willing to donate money to support these causes. On the other hand, the struggles for adequate housing and health care, for example, are not as universally embraced or funded. This lack of consensus results in less financial support for social and economic rights cause-lawyering networks.

Social and economic rights issues also tend to be more locally oriented and culturally specific, and have few discernable repercussions in other parts of the continent or the world: while rain-forest depletion in Brazil has an obvious impact on the United States and Western Europe, the political and social dynamics of, say, Brazil's urban shanty towns (*favellas*) are very different from those in the inner cities of the United States, or even those in Argentina's *villas miserias*.

Accordingly, the strategies and methodology of cause lawyers who work with community groups in these countries are also dissimilar. As Dennis Lynch of ILSA notes, "It is difficult [for some lawyers] to justify the expense of cross-border information when the problems that need addressing are nationally or regionally specific."[47] Moreover, as Halliday and Karpik note, despite all of the discussion of globalization among academics, most lawyers—including, presumably cause lawyers—maintain a nation-state focus and are unaffected by global commercial traffic.[48]

Indeed, the heterogeneity of the Latin American region is a significant barrier to the networking efforts of cause lawyers, regardless of the issues on which they focus. Each country is unique in its stage of development, legal culture, judicial institutions, and political traditions. Thus, notes Cristian Riego, public interest lawyers often have very different perspectives and interests: "In some countries the issue is to protect people from being murdered by the military, and they have very little in common with lawyers addressing issues of discrimination or consumer protection."[49] And cause lawyers in Brazil note that the language difference between their country and the rest of the continent makes such linkages all the more difficult.

Latin American Cause-Lawyering Networks and Bar Associations

It is difficult to make generalized conclusions about the attitude of the organized bar in Latin America toward cause-lawyering networks. That attitude is different within each country, as well as between the national bar association and local bars. For example, although the Chilean Bar Association is, according to Sebastian Cox of FORJA, one of the most traditional institutions in the country, it has been supportive of his group's community education program, which trains community leaders to teach other members of the community how to assert their legal rights without the assistance of lawyers. On the other hand, some of the local bar associations in areas where the program has become active have been critical of its use of "fake" lawyers.[50] They also "went berserk" when the program's written materials were used in a lawsuit involving members of a community group.

Some national bar associations, most notably in Brazil, are quite supportive of cause lawyers and their networking activities.[51] Others, such as the one in Ecuador, have at times been openly hostile to cause-lawyering activities: for example, Ecuador's Center for Rights and Society (CIDES), which promotes mediation and other forms of alternate dispute resolution, has been sued by the national bar association for taking jobs away from other attorneys.[52] Most of the time, however, national and local bar associations have displayed detachment and disinterest toward most cause-lawyering activity, most likely because their small numbers and the kind of work they perform do not pose a threat to the livelihood of the organized bar.

Conflicts between Cause Lawyers

1. POLITICAL RIGHTS CAUSE LAWYERS V. SOCIAL RIGHTS CAUSE LAWYERS

As the discussion in this chapter suggests, there are several points of conflict between cause lawyers in Latin America. One such conflict is the division between those cause lawyers devoted to increasing civil and political rights on the one hand, and those who promote social and economic rights, on the other. This split is reflected not only in the kind of issues on which the network focuses (e.g., human rights v. housing or health care), but in the methodology, and, to some extent, the ideology of the lawyers who participate in those networks. Indeed, the recent growth of cause-lawyering networks in postauthoritarian Latin America has exacerbated the split between these two types of cause lawyers. According to Soraya Long of CODEUCA in Costa Rica, cause-lawyering linkages have created a tendency to shift emphasis from social rights, where—in her view—cause lawyers' efforts are least effective, to legal rights.[53] Legal rights, at least in the area of human rights, are generally easier to enforce because of national and international agreements, and their successful enforcement is far more tangible than social rights'. The resulting higher profile is continually reinforced by the greater accessibility to funding for this type of work. As ILSA's Amanda Romero notes, it is much easier for a cause-lawyering organization to gain support (financial and otherwise) by saying "we freed a political prisoner," than by reporting that it has helped a grassroots community group advocate on its own for adequate health care or housing. A similar concern was expressed by Flavia Piovesan, an attorney for the State of São Paulo in Brazil, who notes that on the international level there is a distinct separation of civil and political rights from economic, social, cultural, and environmental rights: "The international community and system is set up to address the former rather than the latter of these interests."[54]

Social rights cause lawyers think that the traditional definition of human rights is excessively narrow, and should be expanded. According to Adolfo Pérez Esquivel, Nobel Peace Prize winner and director of SERPAJ (Latin American Peace and Justice Service) in Argentina:

> States tend to offer normative answers—laws that are positive to the extent to which they recognize rights. However, national laws, together with the international covenants and treaties, cannot stand up to a comparison with the reality of the infinite number of daily violations which arise from the privation of the right of all people and all peoples to meet their basic needs.... The systematic application of economic, social and cultural policies that benefit 20 percent of the population while excluding the other 80 percent presupposes the inadequacy of the rule of law.... The logical consequence of this combination is the systematic violation of human rights.... There is a marked tendency, however, to limit the conceptualization of human rights, and hence the situations under which they are violated, to that of civil and political rights. This tendency must be reversed.[55]

The need to broaden the definition of human rights has an economic dimension, as well. Cause-lawyering organizations that focused on traditional human rights issues during recent military dictatorships (by, among other things, advocating against murder, torture, and "disappearances" by the military and paramilitary forces) have generally had less success raising money in the postauthoritarian period; once ostensibly democratic transitions have taken root, many donors consider that the worst is over and any future problems can be solved through the democratic process.[56] Being able to include issues of health care, housing, and education within the overall rubric of human rights may make it easier to raise outside financial support for such work.

At the same time, there has been something of a backlash against this effort to broaden the concept of human rights. According to ILSA's Amanda Romero, those cause-lawyering groups which have built networks concerning social, economic and cultural rights have been criticized by political rights advocates (particularly those who continue to seek redress for the relatives of those killed, tortured or "disappeared" by various military regimes) as detracting from their cause.[57]

2. CASE V. CAUSE

Though most Latin American cause lawyers generally view cause-lawyering networks as a positive development, others seem less convinced. One of the main sources of criticism is that these networks divert scarce time, energy, and money from the overwhelming problems of poverty faced by the individuals and communities they are trying to serve. According to Beatriz Galli, an attorney for the Center for Justice in International Law in Brazil, it is difficult to work on or participate in international networks when there is so much work to be done and few resources to support such efforts.[58] Similarly, Sebastian Cox, director of FORJA (Institute for Juridical Formation) in Santiago, Chile, which sponsors community-based legal training on a variety of issues, observes that advocates sometimes get "tangled up in networks" and lose their focus.[59] He stresses that there must be coherence between what is going on at the local, national, and international levels.

This conflict between *case* (i.e., attending to the immediate demands of individuals or communities, which is the fundamental work of most cause lawyers) and *cause* (focusing on building and maintaining networks) plays out on several levels. For example, community-based cause lawyers, who typically work on social rights issues, seem more skeptical of networking and the lawyers who engage in it, while political rights cause lawyers are more apt to appreciate the benefits of such networks. Indeed, at least according to some observers, networking has contributed to many of the victories enjoyed by political rights cause lawyers.

On the other hand, there seems to be a feeling among some cause lawyers that transnational networking is largely an intellectual/elitist endeavor reserved for those supported by adequate resources, far removed from the day-to-day struggles of ordinary people and the lawyers committed to helping them. According to one cause lawyer, "There is an undercurrent of tension between academicians in the area of public interest law and those who are activists in the area."[60]

This conflict reflects one of the debates fundamental to the entire notion of cause lawyering: what, indeed, constitutes a "cause." For some cause lawyers, the individual case *is* the cause; i.e., the attorney's job is to vindicate the rights of the marginalized client or community which she represents, regardless of how this particular case might relate to larger issues of social justice, equality, and the like. As Shamir and Chinski suggest, such lawyers do not consciously orient their professional lives toward promoting a particular cause.[61] Indeed, many of them do not necessarily see much of a distinction between their cause-lawyering work and the other kinds of legal work that most lawyers—including themselves—perform in order to make money. To the extent that such lawyers are involved in networks, they are most likely to limit themselves to the ad hoc, informal contacts described above, through which they can obtain information necessary to advocate effectively on behalf of their client in a particular case.

On the other hand, there are cause lawyers who—to the extent they work on individual cases at all—view such cases much more as the means to promote a larger ideal than to serve the interests of a particular individual or group. The latter category of cause lawyers are much more likely to see the value in more formalized networks among like-minded lawyers as a means to advance that larger cause and to exchange ideas and strategies.

Of course, such divisions between types of cause lawyers are rarely so tidy. Indeed, many lawyers in Latin America are more "case-centered" at certain times and more "cause-centered" at others, depending on the kind of issue they are addressing and what they perceive to be the best way of addressing it.

3. DIFFERING CONCEPTIONS OF THE IDEAL LIBERAL STATE, THE RULE OF LAW, AND LEGAL INSTITUTIONS

A third area of conflict between social and political rights cause lawyers is their differing views of the ideal liberal state, the rule of law, and legal institutions. Indeed, differences over these issue is fundamental to understanding cause lawyering generally, since much cause lawyering is directed toward altering state behavior or policy. Most political rights cause lawyers emphasize what McCann terms "procedural liberalism," i.e., the importance of due process and other procedural rights as a check against unbridled state power.[62] For many of these cause lawyers, the rule of law *is* the cause; i.e., procedural rights are fundamental to the modern liberal state, more important than the result in a given legal struggle or case. In this way, they resemble lawyers—described by Dotan in this volume—who have represented both sides in the dispute over the occupied Territories in Israel (i.e.,

Palestinians and the State of Israel) who consider themselves cause lawyers upholding the cause of the rule of law.[63]

Juxtaposed to this view of the modern liberal state is what McCann terms "social rights liberalism," which focuses on more humanistic goals involving social welfare.[64] Cause lawyers who espouse this view tend to be more concerned about problems stemming from economic and social inequality, rather than the power of the state per se (though, of course, the state in many authoritarian and postauthoritarian regimes promotes and/or helps to maintain inequality and the conditions that lead to poverty, poor health care, and the like). For the more traditional social rights cause lawyers (i.e., those who utilize traditional forms of cause lawyering such as litigation), the rule of law is the means to an end (e.g., the elimination of inequality and poverty), rather than an end in itself. On the other hand, among some community-based "alternative" cause lawyers, who use nontraditional advocacy strategies, the rule of law is viewed as both product and reinforcer of state and corporate power—and thus something to be avoided or confronted, rather than promoted or embraced.

These differing views of the rule of law and the ideal modern liberal state are summed up well by the following statement by Adolfo Pérez Esquivel:

> One hundred years ago we could have said, from a Latin American perspective, that a system is democratic to the extent that it can be identified with the rule of law. In other words, the extent to which it includes the following characteristics:
>
>> The rule of law, as an expression of the general will manifested through its representatives
>> The separation of powers
>> A legally-constituted administration
>> Basic rights and freedoms
>
> As we enter the twenty-first century, these standards of the rule of law are insufficient for determining the existence of a "process of democracy building." It is important to recognize that every democratic system can be improved upon, and that such improvement permits the possibility of advancement. To reject this possibility is to take a step backwards.[65]

For many cause lawyers like Esquivel, forming or joining networks is a means of pushing for a democratic ideal that goes beyond the rule of law; such networks offer a chance to broaden the debate over the postauthoritarian democratization process to include social, economic, and cultural rights. And for "alternative" cause lawyers, networks provide an opportunity to create a democratization process that ignores or rejects the rule of law as inherently oppressive and antidemocratic.

The division among cause lawyers over the modern liberal state and the rule of law also manifests itself in differing attitudes toward the role of the judiciary in postauthoritarian Latin America. This is a critical issue, given that new constitutional provisions and statutes throughout the region grant a wide array of social rights and other legal protections to various segments of the public.[66] Enforcement of such rights is still in question, however, given the legacy of executive and/or military control of the judiciary in most Latin American countries. As Thome notes, "Supreme Court justices ... while paying lip service to reform may actually perceive it as threatening to their corporate prerogatives and thus operate behind the scenes to undermine or defeat the reform proposals."[67]

The more traditional cause lawyers (whether of the political or social rights persuasion), who place more faith in the rule of law and legal institutions, are attempting to use this democratic opening to promote a more informed and independent judiciary. To these cause lawyers, cause lawyering includes convincing judges that they have the authority to take a more activist role in protecting the rights of disenfranchised groups and previously marginalized causes. The report following the 1997 meeting of public interest lawyers and clinical professors in Buenos Aires reflects this aspect of cause lawyering:

> Making the judges familiar with the language of public interest law and persuading them about their key role in this matter seems to be the toughest challenge to confront. Latin American judges usually are not aware of the scope of their role, as they consider the Parliament to be the forum where the most important issues are to be discussed and resolved. This perspective is based on a formalistic approach to Law, according to which judges make an automatic application of the legislation rather than envision different potential ways of interpreting it. This formalistic approach also leads to the conviction among judges that separation of powers prevents them from challenging the legislation on grounds of unconstitutionality except under extraordinary circumstances. As a result, judges not only rarely make progressive interpretations of the legislation, but as a matter of fact they [are] ineffective or, at best, only partially effective [in guaranteeing] constitutional rights.... [A]lthough constitutional and legislative reform can be relevant on public interest matters, a change in the way judges assume their role is indispensable. For this purpose, two basic means are envisioned. The first is to increase and make more systematic the litigation on public interest matters, calling public attention about such litigation. This should help judges realize the magnitude of their role. The second consists of convening judges at seminars, workshops, training programs and other fora to make them aware of their role in public interest matters.[68]

Felipe Gonzalez, of Diego Portales University in Chile, and one of the architects of this network of clinical law programs, reinforces this view: "We are enthusiastic at these early stages about the initiatives, the dynamics of those involved, and the possibility of bringing actions before judicial tribunals in a systematic way. Traditionally, the tribunals in Latin America have been extremely passive, being very slow to recognize the constitutional rights of citizens."[69]

Thus, while the decision makers at whom the efforts of transnational advocacy networks are normally directed are members of the executive or legislative branches, the more traditional social rights cause-lawyers in Latin America quite explicitly seek to alter the perspective and function of the judiciary, seeing such change as critical to achieving their larger cause lawyering goals. In this way, cause lawyers have become a part of (or perhaps part of the engine driving) the judicial and legal reform that is gaining momentum throughout Latin America today. In this way, certain cause lawyers are using networks to foster the rule of law.

The emerging network of "alternative" lawyers is less concerned about influencing the judiciary in any systemic way, since most members of this group promote strategies that seek change outside the courtroom and other traditional legal fora. For these lawyers, the primary purpose of networking would appear to be altering the behavior not of an outside decision maker, but of the members of the network itself; i.e., by encouraging lawyers to be less hierarchical and to emphasize the role of citizens, rather than lawyers, in resolving conflict. In some ways, this is the polar opposite of the justification for other cause-lawyering networks which—whether explicitly or implicitly—seek to expand the role and influence of cause lawyers and the rule of law within civil society.

The Relative Success of Latin American Cause-Lawyering Networks

One must be very careful in attempting to evaluate the success of a cause-lawyering network (not to mention a cause lawyer herself). There is little empirical data on the subject, particularly in situations where "success" cannot be measured in terms of cases won or proposed legislation enacted. The criteria by which Keck and Sikkink judge the success of transnational issue networks are objectively measured factors such as framing debates, encouraging commitments from states and other policy actors, and affecting policy.[70] By these kinds of measures, the political rights networks have been far more successful than the social rights networks. Latin American cause lawyers active in human rights, for example, are frequently members of, or otherwise affiliated with, one or more of the kinds of organizations identified above. In most cases, these networks have brought pressure to bear on individual states that are unresponsive to domestic calls for change. These cause lawyers generally believe that networking will improve the effectiveness of their domestic advocacy, along the lines of the "boomerang pattern" described by Keck and Sikkink.[71]

There are several reasons for the objectively measured success of the political rights cause-lawyering networks. One is that there is regional and global consensus on the causes that those lawyers espouse. At this point in history, for example, few people would openly support a state's repression of its own people (though one must allow for significant anomalies here, such as public opinion in favor of the death penalty in the United States). This consensus makes it easier for human rights organizations and the cause lawyers who work for them to raise the money necessary for the maintenance and support of the networks. The growth in size and influence of these networks, in turn, leads to the objectively measured successes (e.g., passage of additional human rights protections at the international level, freeing of high-profile political prisoners, etc.) that encourage further networking (and funding of such networking).

Second, much of the objectively measured success of the political rights cause-lawyering networks stems from relevant and enforceable international agreements or codes of conduct. This leads to what some cause lawyers refer to as a "standardized agenda."[72] The most compelling example is the 1948 Universal Declaration of Human Rights, which sets forth common principles and standards around which consensus can be built and advocacy campaigns organized. Cause lawyers active in human rights have used the enforcement (or lack thereof) of such international agreements by individual states as a rallying cry in support of networking and grassroots organizing. The enforcement of such agreements has also been a useful benchmark for these networks to evaluate their success in changing state policies. Examples include the efforts of various NGOs in Argentina both during and after that country's "dirty war" between 1976 and 1982, which eventually led to the trials of numerous military personnel; more recent international and domestic pressure on the Mexican government, which has contributed to a decline in human rights violations and a strengthening of democratic institutions in that country; and the worldwide campaign to reduce deforestation in the Brazilian Amazon.[73]

By comparison, networks that promote social and economic rights in Latin America have been less successful, at least according to these objective standards. For one thing, the issues around which these networks are organized do not enjoy universal support. There is no global (or regional) consensus on the right to adequate health care or housing; nor on the way that an intercommunity dispute on land use or domestic violence should be resolved. As a result, it is difficult for cause lawyers who focus on these issues to attract the kind of media attention and international financial support that political rights cause lawyers have used to support a widespread network and movement. Moreover, the few international agreements on social and economic rights that exist have not received the same level of general acceptance and support enjoyed by human rights declarations. Accordingly, the social and economic rights cause lawyers have been generally unable to use these agreements and declarations to build their own movement.

On the other hand, if one evaluates the work of these networks more subjectively, i.e., from the perspective of the goals of the cause lawyers themselves, the social and economic rights cause lawyers have enjoyed a significant amount of success. As noted above, many social and economic rights cause lawyers, particularly those who fall within the category of "alternative" lawyers, cite as one of their main goals the empowerment of their clients and the communities in which they reside, rather than some objectively measured "victory," such as the passage of a law or the winning of a lawsuit. Since, as Menkel-Meadow suggests, these lawyers stress less legalistic and more client-centered goals, one must view the results of their advocacy on much more of an individualistic basis, rather than a database of wins and losses.[74]

An example from ILSA's advocacy on behalf of childcare workers in Colombia is illustrative. Perhaps taking a cue from the objectively measured successes of the more formal networks that have pressed for compliance with international agreements on human rights, ILSA has recently begun a grassroots campaign to induce compliance with the International Covenant on Economic, Social and Cultural Rights ('ICESCR'), which addresses issues such as housing, health care, and education.[75] One of these efforts involved a group known as the Community Mothers, comprised of childcare workers employed by the Colombian government at substandard wages to take care of as many as fifteen children at one time in poor neighborhoods. Together with representatives of ILSA, members of this organization traveled to Geneva to meet with a United Nations committee and demand compliance by the Colombian government with the ICESCR and International Labor Organization standards. The U.N. committee agreed with their demands, but the Colombian government has not implemented any changes. Nevertheless, the Community Mothers (of which there are about 70,000) have formed a union, become more informed about their rights, and convinced the government to extend social security benefits to them.

There are several fascinating aspects to this story. The first is that ILSA, a long-term advocate of alternative lawyering, chose a rather traditional judicial forum—a U.N. committee—to make its demand. Second, according to the objective measurements espoused by Keck and Sikkink, ILSA failed in its effort to change state behavior through an entreaty to an international actor (a goal that one assumes was fashioned by the lawyers rather than the community). On the other hand, ILSA's goal of community and client empowerment was met, even if in an unintended way; the Community Mothers have become a considerable grassroots political force and presumably will be able to advocate on their own behalf in the future.

According to ILSA's Amanda Romero, helping people organize is more important than the actual implementation of the U.N.'s recommendations. [76] She refers to the kind of change sought by ILSA and other organizations concerned more with social and economic rights than with political or civil rights as more of a cultural process where one cannot see the results of a network's efforts in a short period of time: "Here, there is a social approach to the law; sociology of the law is very complex; it is not just costs and benefits."[77] According to Romero, the success of advocacy efforts that focus on more traditional legal strategies, such as litigation, are easier to measure.[78]

One of the most intriguing aspects of the goals of alternative lawyers is that if they are met, these lawyers will have made themselves unnecessary. Since these lawyers seek to diminish and demystify the role of lawyers (and the rule of law) and enable grassroots communities to advocate for themselves in the process, a "successful" cause-lawyering network in this regard will be one that renders itself irrelevant. This is quite different from the goal of the more traditional cause lawyers who, if anything, seek to augment the role of lawyers (and the rule of law) in postauthoritarian Latin America.[79]

Conclusions

This chapter's findings appear to be at least somewhat consistent with the models outlined in the theoretical literature on transnational advocacy networks. For example, the conditions that Keck and Sikkink view as necessary for the emergence of such networks are present in the Latin American cause-lawyering context: in each of the cause-lawyering networks analyzed in this chapter, the channels between cause lawyers and their governments have broken down or are ineffective in resolving conflicts (indeed, in the case of many "alternative" lawyers, the channels have broken down *because* the governments were ineffective in resolving conflicts). And in each case, but particularly with respect to the human rights and environmental lawyers, transnational conferences have created arenas for forming and strengthening networks. However, the networks discussed here diverge on a third criteria articulated by Keck and Sikkink: while it appears that most political and civil rights lawyers (those involved in issues such as human rights) promote networking because they believe that it advances their causes, at least some of the cause lawyers involved in "social rights" issues are more skeptical. Indeed, some view it as a one-way, time-consuming distraction (particularly when their expertise is sought or when it otherwise causes them to lose their focus) largely irrelevant to their work. In addition, some cause lawyers view such networks as a reflection of the professional bias in favor of more "glamorous" cause-lawyering issues like human rights and environmental protection.[80]

Second, as the literature suggests, it appears that Latin American cause-lawyering networks are more extensive and objectively successful when there are relevant and enforceable international agreements or codes of conduct around which they can organize, advocate, and generate publicity. Thus, while cause lawyers active in human rights or environmental issues have used international agreements to set agendas, influence public debate, and affect public policy, cause lawyers active in most other issue areas have generally not had this advantage. On the other hand, those more traditionally oriented cause lawyers working on social rights issues seem to be using postauthoritarian constitutional provisions and legislation in much the same way as human rights activists have used international agreements: as both an educational tool for members of the network and the public generally, and as a means of enforcing rights that the state might otherwise ignore. In this way, these Latin American cause lawyers may become increasingly influential in setting future public-policy agendas throughout the region.

Third, this chapter illustrates that there are several factors that determine the scope of—and support for—transnational networks of cause lawyers in Latin America. Those networks are more extensive and financially supported where: (1) the cause lawyers involved in them work on a single issue (e.g., human rights) that enjoys widespread international support, particularly from Western Europe and the United States and is the subject of enforceable international agreements; (2) the cause lawyers employ a form of lawyering (e.g., litigation) that is practiced and accepted in the United States and Europe; (3) the cause lawyers believe they benefit from the time and resources necessary to sustain these networks; and (4) through the networks, the cause lawyers have been able to alter the behavior of relevant decision makers. When measured against these standards, cause-lawyering linkages have been most successful in attracting support in the areas of political and civil rights, and somewhat less so with social, economic, and cultural rights. What is more difficult to measure by any objective criteria is the degree to which cause lawyers who follow more of an alternative model have been able to meet their goals of client-centered lawyering and community empowerment.

Fourth, this chapter suggests that cause lawyering networks are likely to play a critical role in at least two significant sociolegal issues in postauthoritarian Latin America. The first is the ongoing debate over legal and judicial reform throughout the region. Through public interest litigation and popular education, cause-lawyering networks are likely to assist cause lawyers from individual countries exert pressure on the judiciary to take a more active role in enforcing rights created, clarified or expanded in postauthoritarian constitutions and laws. The second critical issue is the very role that cause lawyers will play in the ongoing social struggles within the region. While the work of more traditional cause-lawyering networks will inevitably expand the role (and probably the number) of such lawyers actively addressing these struggles, the work of "alternative law" networks seeks to deemphasize that role.

Finally, Latin America's cause-lawyering networks have been influenced significantly by democratization and globalization, two of the overall themes of this volume. For example, the work of these networks, and the tensions between and among them, is emblematic of the ambivalence that Latin American cause lawyers have toward democratization generally. While for some cause lawyers, democratization is more or less synonymous with the recognition and enforcement of political and civil rights, for others it should mean the protection of social, economic, and cultural rights that have long been ignored within most Latin American countries, particularly during military regimes. Thus, democratization has intensified the struggle between political and social rights cause lawyers for scarce resources to perform their lawyering and for the attention of the judiciary and other decision makers who must determine how they will function in postauthoritarian civil society. Given this competitive milieu, networks have helped cause lawyers increase their influence both within their home countries and in the more globalized arena of foundations and universities that provide them with financial support and a certain degree of legitimacy. In addition, the increased reliance on such outside sources of funding and ideas has raised concerns about the degree of control such sources exert on cause-lawyering networks, the goals they set, the strategies they follow, and the ways they serve their clients and society generally.

Acknowledgments

I received invaluable research assistance in preparing this chapter from University of Wisconsin Law School students Leticia Camacho and Chela O'Connor. I would also like to thank all of the contributors to this volume, as well as Michael McCann and Terrence Halliday, for their insightful comments on earlier drafts of this chapter.

Notes

1. Margaret E. Keck, and Kathryn Sikkink (1998), *Activists Beyond Borders: Advocacy Networks in International Politics*, Ithaca: Cornell University Press; Margaret E. Keck, and Kathryn Sikkink (1995), "Transnational Issue Networks in International Politics," paper presented at the 91st Annual Meeting of the American Political Science Association, Chicago; Kathryn Sikkink, (1993), "Human Rights, Principled Issue-Networks, and Sovereignty in Latin America," 47 *International Organization*, 411–41; David M. Trubek, Yves Dezalay, Ruth Buchanan, and John R. Davis (1993), "Global Restructuring and the Law: The Internationalization of Legal Fields and the Creation of Transnational Arenas," 1 *Global Studies Research Program Working Paper Series on the Political Economy of Legal Change*; Leon Gordenker, and Thomas G. Weiss, "Pluralising Global Governance: Analytical Approaches and Dimensions" (1995), 16 *Third World Quarterly*, 357–87.
2. Keck and Sikkink (1998: 1).
3. Keck and Sikkink (1998: 201).
4. Fernando Rojas (1988), "A Comparison of Change-Oriented Legal Services in Latin America with Legal Services in Latin America and Europe," 16 *International Journal of the Sociology of Law*, 203–56; Stephen Meili (1993), "The Interaction Between Lawyers and Grass Roots Social Movements in Brazil," 3 *Beyond Law*, 61–81.
5. Stephen Meili (1998), "Cause Lawyers and Social Movements: A Comparative Perspective on Democratic Change in Argentina and Brazil," in *Cause Lawyering: Political Commitments and Professional Responsibilities* Austin Sarat and Stuart Scheingold, eds., New York: Oxford University Press.
6. Keck and Sikkink (1998: 8–9).
7. Keck and Sikkink (1998: 1–2).
8. Keck and Sikkink (1998: 12).
9. Keck and Sikkink (1998: 12).
10. Keck and Sikkink (1995: 8).
11. Keck and Sikkink (1998: 201).
12. Keck and Sikkink (1998: 201–2).
13. Peter M. Haas (1992), "Introduction: Epistemic Communities and International Policy Coordination," 46 *International Organization*, 3–4.

14. Haas (1992: 3).
15. Raymond F. Hopkins (1992), "Reform in the International Food Aid Regime,"46 *International Organization*, 225; Ethan Barnaby Kapstein, (1992), "Between Power and Purpose: Central Bankers and the Politics of Regulatory Convergence," 46 *International Organization*, 265; G. John Ikenberry, "World Economy Restored: Expert Consensus and the Anglo-American Postwar Settlement," 46 *International Organization*, 289; James K. Sebenius, (1992), "Challenging Conventional Explanations of International Cooperation: Negotiation Analysis and the Case of Epistemic Communities," 46 *International Organization*, 323.
16. Soraya Long, telephone interview conducted by Leticia Camacho, April 1996.
17. Interview with Jaime Benvenuto, conducted by Chela O'Connor, Recife, Brazil, April 2, 1997.
18. Cristian Riego, interview conducted by author, via email, May 11, 1998.
19. Amanda Romero, ILSA, interview conducted by author, Madison, Wisconsin, May 13, 1999.
20. Report on International Seminar and Workshop on Public Interest Law, Buenos Aires, December 1997.
21. Alejandro D.Carrió, telephone interview conducted by Leticia Camacho, April 1996. The Association of Civil Rights, which Carrió describes as the Argentine equivalent of the American Civil Liberties Union, is based in Buenos Aires and staffed by five full-time attorneys. It is funded by the Ford Foundation and the Argentine Fundacion Antorchas.
22. Claudia Mora, telephone interview conducted by Leticia Camacho, April 1996.
23. Maria Eugenia Tamariz and Jaime Vintimilla, telephone interview conducted by Leticia Camacho, April 1996.
24. Miguel Pressburger, telephone interview conducted by Chela O'Connor, March 1996.
25. Maria Elba Martinez, telephone interview conducted by Leticia Camacho, April 1996; Sister Michael Mary Nolan, telephone interview conducted by Chela O'Connor, March 1996.
26. Martinez, interview.
27. ILSA 20h Anniversary Report (1998), at Section 1; Romero, interview.
28. ILSA 20th Anniversary Report.
29. Report on International Seminar and Workshop on Public Interest Law, Buenos Aires, December 1997.
30. Dennis Lynch, telephone interview conducted by Chela O'Connor, March 1996.
31. Miguel Pressburger (1991), "Case Studies on the Transformative Potential of Legal Services: A View from Brazil," 1:3 *Beyond Law*, 35–42; Eliane Botelho Junqueira, "Legal Services: A Two-Way Movement," paper presented at the annual Law & Society Meeting, Toronto, June 1995.
32. Christian Courtis, interview conducted by author, via email, May 19, 1998.
33. Keck and Sikkink (1998:12).
34. Yves Dezalay and Bryant B. Garth (2000), "The Reformist Establishment Out of Power: Temporarily Converging North-South Strategies in the Construction of the Field of International Human Rights," chapter 14 in this volume.
35. Riego, interview.
36. Terrence C. Halliday and Lucien Karpik (1997), "Lawyers, Political Liberalism, and Globalization" in *Lawyers and the Rise of Western Political Liberalism*, Halliday and Karpik, eds., Oxford: Oxford University Press, pp. 349–370.
37. Gustavo Alaniz, telephone interview conducted by Leticia Camacho, April 1996.
38. Alaniz, interview.

39. Dezalay and Garth (2000).

40. Felipe Gonzalez, interview by author, tape recording, Santiago, Chile, December 29, 1998.

41. Riego, interview. This comment may be difficult to reconcile with the ILSA database, which lists a total of approximately 320 organizations working on public interest issues in the region (the issues include human rights, environmental protection, and the rights of women, children, campesinos, workers, indigenous peoples, and residents of shanty towns). However, it is unclear how many cause lawyers actually work at these organizations, and how much time they devote to them, since many Latin American cause lawyers cannot afford to do such work on a full-time basis.

42. Romero, interview.

43. The fact that most Latin American cause lawyers can only afford to do such work on a part-time basis raises the question, posed articulately by Menkel-Meadow, of whether a cause lawyer is a cause lawyer in all aspects of her job, or only when she is performing cause-lawyering work. See Menkel-Meadow (1998), "The Causes of Cause Lawyering: Toward an Understanding of the Motivation and Commitment of Social Justice Lawyers," in *Cause Lawyering: Political Commitments and Professional Responsibilities*, Austin Sarat and Stuart Scheingold, eds., Oxford: Oxford University Press.

44. Courtis, interview.

45. Riego, interview.

46. Romero, interview.

47. Lynch, interview.

48. Halliday and Karpik (1997: 360).

49. Riego, interview.

50. Cox, interview.

51. Eliane Junquiera, "The Brazilian Bar Association in the Struggle for Human Rights," paper presented at the Annual Law & Society Meeting, Aspen, Colorado, June 1998.

52. Tamariz and Vintimilla, interview.

53. Long, interview.

54. Flavia Piovesan, comments at a conference on economic, social, cultural and environmental rights, Rio de Janeiro, April 2–4, 1997.

55. Adolfo Pérez Esquivel (1996), "Conditionality, Human Rights and Democracy: The Latin American Experience," *Beyond Law*, 5:15/16 75–91.

56. Alicia Curiel, interview by author, tape recording, Buenos Aires, July 15, 1994 (translated by Sandra Beuchert).

57. Romero, interview.

58. Interview with Beatriz Galli, conducted by Chela O'Connor, April 1997.

59. Sebastian Cox, director of FORJA, interview conducted by author, *tape recording*, Santiago, Chile, December 30, 1998 (translated by Leigh Payne).

60. Lynch, interview.

61. Ronen Shamir and Sara Chinski (1998), "Destruction of Houses and Construction of a Cause: Lawyers and Bedouins in the Israeli Courts," in *Cause Lawyering: Political Commitments and Professional Responsibilities*, Austin Sarat and Stuart Scheingold, eds., Oxford: Oxford University Press.

62. Comments by Michael McCann at the cause lawyering conference at Bellagio, Italy, June 1999.

63. See Yves Dotan (2000), "The Global Language of Human Rights: Patterns of Cooperation between State and Civil Rights Lawyers in Israel," chapter in this volume.

64. Dotan (2000).

65. Esquivel (1996: 76).

66. Joseph R. Thome, "Searching for Democracy: The Rule of Law and the Process of Legal Reform in Latin America," paper prepared for the Workshop on Reforma Judicial, Motivaciones, Proyectos, Caminos Recorridos, Caminos por Recorrer, Insituto Internacional de Sociologia Juridica, Onati, Gipuzkoa, Spain, April 6–7, 1998.

67. Thome (1998: 1).

68. Report on International Seminar and Workshop on Public Interest Law, Buenos Aires, December 1997.

69. Felipe Gonzalez, e-mail message, April 29, 1996.

70. Keck and Sikkink (1998: 201).

71. Keck and Sikkink (1998: 12–13).

72. Courtis, interview.

73. Keck and Sikkink (1998: 103–16, 135–50).

74. Menkel-Meadow (1998: 36–37).

75. The ICESCR was passed in 1967 and became effective in 1976.

76. Romero, interview.

77. Id.

78. Id.

79. Comments of Terrence Halliday at the cause lawyering conference at Bellagio, Italy, June 1999.

80. A similar tension may exist in the United States between lawyers who work for civil rights and environmental organizations (ACLU, NAACP, NRDC) on the one hand, and community-based legal services organizations on the other.

CHAPTER 13

The Politics of Imported Rights
Transplantation and Transformation in an Israeli Environmental Cause-Lawyering Organization

NOGA MORAG-LEVINE

The fusion of legal practice with social movement activism is epitomized in the work of American groups such as the ACLU and the NAACP and the combined legal/political campaigns with which they are associated. The model they chartered was adopted by the 1960s and 1970s by advocates on behalf of myriad minority, social equity, consumer and environmental interests (Handler, 1978). This trend was part of a larger growth in the number and visibility of professional Social Movement Organizations (SMOs) during that era, primarily as a result of increased private foundation support for such ventures (MacCarthy and Zald, 1987). This money facilitated the creation of social change–directed nongovernmental organizations, offering in the process novel social-movement-affiliated career opportunities for practitioners in a number of professions, including law.

The various "legal defense" organizations established during that era transformed cause lawyering from an individual, and often risky, professional choice into an established career path. These groups, henceforth termed Cause Lawyering Organizations (CLOs), created an institutional venue in which transformative commitments and legal professional practice could comfortably coexist.[1] In the United States, however, CLOs have succeeded in conferring visibility and stature upon this mode of lawyering in a manner that all but moved it into the mainstream of the profession. As much of the work in this and the previous volume in this project (Sarat and Scheingold, 1998) shows, cause lawyers can be found in widely divergent professional settings.

In the United States the assumption that lawyers can constructively advance the agendas of social movement organizations and belong within them gave rise to the CLO model. That assumption was, in turn, grounded in a broader set of understandings regarding the relationship between litigation and collective action. Social movements by definition engage in "collective challenges, based on common purposes and social solidarities" (Tarrow, 1998: 4). Lawyers conventionally engage in case-by-case litigation and the processing of particular legal or policy problems. Social movements will have use for such services only to the extent that they expect litigation to yield aggregate social-change benefits greater than the isolated legal interventions individual lawsuits may produce. In other words, without a belief in law's capacity to effect larger processes of social change, CLOs make little organizational or political sense.

Until the 1980s CLOs were an almost uniquely American phenomenon. A 1978 survey of "Public Interest Law Firms" concluded that this "American model is not important elsewhere in the world" (Sward and Weisbrod, 1978). Today, however, groups patterned after this originally American model can be found in diverse countries across the globe (e.g., Gleason and Johnson, 1995; Lev, 1998; Meili, 1998). As was earlier the case in the United States, private foundations, often American-based, are behind many of these transplanted CLOs. But whereas in the United States CLOs were an extension of a liberal/pluralist tradition to which law and rights were inherently salient, the model's transplanted variants operate in locales chosen despite, and at time because of, their lack of parallel pluralist background.

The impact of tensions between national and transnational frameworks or fields on the work of relevant lawyers and activists is a major theme cutting across recent studies of the effects of globalization on both legal professional practice and various economic and social-change agendas (Dezalay and Garth, 1996). On the legal side Halliday and Karpick (1987: 360) have suggested that imported foreign models are likely to take root only to the extent that they are "made consistent with national traditions and institutions." Where social movements are concerned, Keck and Sikkink (1998) have pointed to the parallel need of those working within transnational advocacy networks to invoke mobilizing symbols and structures capable of resonance within the particular target audiences they wish to activate.

Because transplanted CLOs straddle both the legal professional and social-movement domains, they face the need to adjust both to the specific legal professional traditions of the countries they enter and the larger political culture of those locales. Moreover, their adaptive capability is hampered by an a priori commitment (as a result of the imported blueprint they follow and the expectations of their often American funders) to law as a cornerstone of organizational identity and a primary mobilizing structure. How these organizations negotiate the tension between commitments inherent to their transnational origins and the support structures and the conditions of the locales they wish to influence is at the center of this chapter. This question is examined through the evolution of one such transplanted group, the Israel Union for Environmental Defense (IUED), an Israeli environmental law group patterned in large after the American Natural Resources Defense Council (NRDC).[2]

The organizational model that transplanted CLOs tend to carry to their adopted locales assumes and seeks to build upon symbiotic interactions between litigation and social-movement mobilization. Beyond any direct legally defined goals American CLOs have used lawsuits to capture the attention of foundations, potential members, the media and through it the public at large. In return, financial and political resources generated in this fashion help support further legal campaigns. The audience American CLOs target through such legal mobilization tactics divides into two general categories: The first consists of the narrow but influential segment of political actors upon which CLOs depend for financial support and organizational legitimacy, i.e, foundations and members. The second category includes those in the media, government, and the public at large whose attitudes, actions, and commitments toward particular social movement goals CLOs hope to change through legal discourse and litigation. The significant organizational success that CLOs have continued to enjoy in the United States suggests that at least where funding and membership is concerned, litigation has been an effective organizational tool, though the extent to which this organizational success has been matched by broader social movement benefits is a subject of debate.

The primary skeptic in this regard is Rosenberg (1991), who argues that empirical evidence in support of litigation's capacity to mobilize significant political action is largely missing and contends that courts (and by implication CLOs) can at best offer secondary support for social-change agendas that other political actors have already embraced. In contrast, Scheingold (1974) and McCann (1994) have been among those most closely associated with the claim that lawyers and litigation can themselves be important catalysts for social change. Scheingold links this potential to the strength of a culture and ideology of rights in American politics and the forms of transformative behavior that they facilitate. Rights and law matter in America because Americans expect them to matter and thus take notice when activists couch their claims in terms of rights deprivation. Through this process a "myth of rights" generates a "politics of rights" allowing litigation to make "an important, if ancillary, contribution to political change" (Scheingold, 1974:96). Similarly for McCann (1994: 100), it is "the rich legacy of rights-based legal reform within modern American political culture" that accounts for their transformative power.

Law and legal instruments serve, under this argument, as what social movement theory has termed a "collective action frame" (Snow et al., 1986). Movements rely on such frames "in the production and maintenance of meaning" and invoke them "as accenting devices that either underscore and embellish the seriousness and injustice of a social condition or redefine as unjust and immoral what was previously seen as unfortunate but perhaps tolerable" (Snow and Benford, 1992:

136, 137). The mobilization potency of such frames is said to increase with the closeness of its fit with extant beliefs. The ability of social movements to mobilize for social change increases the more able they are to explain the need for such change in a manner consistent with their target audience's worldview and existing norms. The "politics of rights" is, as such, an argument about the tight fit between rights-oriented social-movement frames and American legal-cultural predispositions rooted, in turn, in a liberal pluralist tradition.

Transplanted CLOs, unlike their American counterparts, seek to implement their law and social change project away from its pluralist roots within corporatist political traditions governed by the "politics of deference" or "consensus" rather than rights. Corporatist systems, long associated with smaller European countries such as Sweden and Austria, are marked by the existence of a relatively small number of associations spanning economic sectors and operating in close alignment with the state (Schmitter, 1974:15). Unlike pluralism, the governing paradigm within corporatist systems is that of political partnership rather than competition, and the pursuit of individual or group interests outside state channels is seen as both superfluous and inappropriate (Williamson, 1989; Crepaz, 1995).

If, as social-movement theory suggests, the success of collective-action frames depends on their capacity to resonate with the movement's target audience, what is the logic of employing, as transplanted CLOs do, legal tactics and rights-focused frames likely to encounter apathy if not outright hostility in those they hope to mobilize? This study explores this question through analysis of IUED's history in Israel and suggests that an attachment to law conferred important benefits where IUED's ability to mobilize American-based or influenced sources of support but may have detracted from its capacity to reach and mobilize a domestic Israeli constituency. In response to this concern, IUED has gradually redefined its organizational mission in a less litigation-focused fashion.

During its first years in Israel the organization made little effort to align its imported American legal frames with those of its Israeli audience. Instead, it followed a bifocal strategy, dividing what under the original CLO model was envisioned as a unified organizational whole into two parallel local and transnational tracks.[3] Under this system, legal instruments were domestically employed and utilized in the mobilization of external sources of support. This strategy later shifted, however, when in the face of a major legal defeat IUED came to recognize that its legal mission could not succeed in the absence of a local Israeli constituency, and that the development of such a constituency required it in turn to reframe its local mission in distinctly less legal terms. It remains to be seen whether this shift will result in permanent substitution of legal with more directly political collective action frames in IUED and perhaps other such transplanted CLOs, or whether this shift represents only a temporary adaptation on the way to a pluralist legal culture in which imported legal frames will gain greater local resonance.

Rights and Politics in IUED

IUED was established in 1991 by Alon Tal, an American immigrant and an Israeli-trained attorney. As in all new enterprises, naming the organization was one of its first decisions. Tal opted for two, distinct Hebrew and English names. The Israel Union for Environmental Defense, IUED's English title, aligned the new initiative with parallel American environmental law groups such as the NRDC and the Environmental Defense Fund (EDF). In contrast, the organization's Hebrew name, Adam, Teva V'Din (Man, Nature and Law), evokes a native Israeli identity tinged with appeal to traditional Jewish sources.[4] This double name is indicative of the two constituencies, one domestic and one transnational, the new organization sought to address from its inception. This duality has remained with the organization ever since.

IUED met in Israel a binary challenge grounded in that country's particularly trenchant corporatist traditions and the marginality of environmental concerns in Israel's political agenda. Observers of Israeli politics up until the early 1990s describe a political arena in which "groups do not provide a key link between the people and their government and groups do not compete with one another" (Arian 1993: 185). Instead, in traditional corporatist fashion political organizations displayed deference toward collective state goals and refrained from challenging dominant understandings of national interests (Yishai, 1991: 362).

Relative to similarly developed nations, Western environmental ideologies have been slow to penetrate Israel's political agenda and public discourse (De-Shalit and Talias, 1994; Vogel, 1998; Morag-Levine, 1999). Israeli environmental activism, until the coming of IUED, was essentially the province of one traditionally corporatist, and up to that point largely consensualist, organization, the Society for the Protection of Nature (SPNI) (Yishai, 1991). Few environmental lawsuits of any kind were brought before Israeli courts prior to the 1990s (Gabai, 1994). All but absent were environmental lawsuits aiming at larger policy or social-movement mobilization.[5]

Soon after launching IUED, Tal explained in an interview with an Israeli newspaper: "This is the American model: citizens taking matters into their own hands."[6] Implementing this American model required primarily American financing. Of the foundations offering such support, some, such as Ford, have long been associated with similar efforts elsewhere. Others, such as the Nathan Cummings, Bronfman, and New Israel Fund have strong Jewish or exclusively Israeli orientations and are currently behind multiple other new civil associations in Israel. In addition, IUED receives some support from those in the American Jewish community who are sympathetic toward both its Zionist and environmental mission. The willingness of these various sources to wager their money on the initiative of a young and generally inexperienced individual is a tribute to Tal's charisma and professionalism, but was also the result of his American audience's familiarity with the organizational model and legal mission that he sought to implement in Israel.

Following the example of the civil rights movement, American environmentalists quickly, and with an initial degree of success, turned to the courts. The names of cases like *Scenic Hudson* (1965) and *Calvert Cliffs* (1971) are to this day intertwined with the American environmental movements' early momentum. Writing in 1978, Handler went as far as to say that "it could be argued that extrajudicial uses of the courts have been the most important accomplishment of the environmentalists todate.... The courts were used for consciousness-raising, for dramatizing issues, and for arousing political and social concern for environmental issues" (1978: 63). For American environmentalists raised on this example, the ideal of cloning this effort in Israel made good political sense.[7]

Beyond funding, IUED relied on a network of American and other English-speaking sympathizers in Israel and abroad to boost its membership roster (and its organizational legitimacy) and link it with a larger transnational environmental community.[8] But the legal instruments so crucial to the cultivation of its external links ultimately cut against the establishment of a local base of support.

IUED's leadership was cognizant from the beginning of the importance of cultivating an Israeli constituency and took various measures toward that goal. Tal was careful to include native Israelis in the organization's first board of directors and, in order to help establish a more authentically Israeli organizational identity, encouraged IUED's English-speaking staff to speak Hebrew while on the job. More substantive, in 1993 IUED turned to the Israeli public and invited it to become part of the organization by instituting a very moderately priced membership program. Most who responded to this call came from the ranks of American and other English-speaking immigrants to Israel and Israelis acquainted with the CLO model through their own extensive stays abroad. The obstacles that IUED faced in developing a broader Israeli constituency began with weak Israeli environmental consciousness and continued with the absence of a tradition of membership in civic associations. But IUED's appeal was additionally hampered by the difficulty even Israelis with general sympathy to IUED's environmental mission had in relating to the organization's legal focus or in understanding what their own role in it could be.

Rather than attending to the seeming dissonance between its imported legal collective-action frame and the political sensibilities of its new environment, IUED, during its early years, relied instead on a transnational network of support to step in where local financial and political resources were inadequate to sustain the joint legal/political components of the CLO model. IUED modified this strategy, however, when it came to see the absence of stronger popular Israeli backing as an impediment to success in the courts.

Lawyers and Litigants: Starting from Scratch

The most immediate challenge IUED faced after its establishment followed from the novelty of its enterprise and the attendant absence in Israel of a developed environmental law infrastructure, most notably lawyers and litigants able and willing to bring environmental lawsuits. Whereas IUED could turn outward for funding and even membership, the implementation of its primary legal mission required direct participation by Israelis with the relevant local environmental and legal knowledge—in other words, it demanded changes in the structure of the Israeli legal profession and legal education.

Lawyers

Bringing environmental lawsuits in Israel required IUED to employ locally trained attorneys with the necessary professional, language, and cultural skills. Yet no more than a handful of Israeli attorneys with significant environmental legal experience were active in Israel prior to IUED's arrival. The creation of a cadre of Israeli environmental lawyers was among the tasks Tal undertook, soon after establishing IUED, through an environmental law clinic linking Israeli law students with IUED's work. In the short term Tal resorted, however, to hiring attorneys with no previous environmental experience or interests, who, to varying degrees, converted to the cause while on the job.

This pattern has largely persisted. The biographies of most attorneys IUED hired during its first eight years show little earlier interest or engagement with environmental causes. Exceptions include two temporary attorneys who each worked in IUED for a year under a fellowship provided by the New Israel Fund (an American Jewish foundation which has actively supported civil rights and other forms of cause litigation in Israel). The third attorney whose environmental credentials predate his employment at IUED is a graduate of Alon Tal's first environmental-law clinic. The remaining attorneys came to their job after having worked or interned for private law firms or various governmental bodies.

IUED offers its attorneys an informal and flexible work environment and salaries that, in recent years, have become more competitive. Whereas the organization began its operations in a cramped facility and with little support staff, its current offices are spacious and well equipped, though less opulent than most large private law firms. These factors, coupled with an Israeli legal market glutted with graduates of private law schools established in the past decade, have made IUED an attractive legal-employment option even for attorneys with little or no prior environmental commitments. For its part, in selecting among a steadily growing applicant pool IUED has tended to favor legal expertise above environmental credentials.

Whereas this choice was initially dictated by the scarcity of environmentally trained and committed attorneys, by the late 1990s it seemed better to reflect a conscious organizational policy grounded in IUED's desire to meet its increasingly sophisticated and adversarial opponents on their own terms. As subsequently discussed, IUED in recent years has squared off against both a major transnational conglomerate and one of Israel's largest construction companies. The attorneys it faces in court come from some of Israel's most prestigious law firms. Winning against them, IUED has come to believe, requires, first and foremost, an ability to beat its opponents at their own game. The resulting emphasis on legal expertise has signaled increased compartmentalization of the CLO's legal and social-movement components.

Litigants

In an effort to reach the Israeli public, establish its presence, and attract potential plaintiffs, IUED established, soon after it opened, a complaint line offering free environmental legal advice. In 1991 the organization responded to 100 such complaints, and by 1994 the number grew to 250. Though the number of complaints continued to grow over the next few years, few complainants joined the organization or turned to other modes of environmental activism. Furthermore, the complaints (which most commonly related to noise disputes between neighbors) rarely touched on the type of larger environmental policy concerns that IUED deemed worthy of litigation.

IUED's early emphasis upon citizens' complaints followed in part from concerns over its own ability to gain independent standing in the courts and its desire to generate a steady flow of potential litigants. Standing, however, never emerged as a serious obstacle due to the Israeli Supreme Court's increasingly liberal stance on this issue. Independent organizational standing freed IUED of the need to include local citizens in its lawsuits, but as the history of the following three cases suggests, at the same time it may have contributed to its isolation and negatively affected judicial and public perceptions of its mission.

Global-Local Tensions in Three IUED Legal Campaigns

IUED's annual report for 1997–98 described an organization that at any given time juggled the litigation and preparation of approximately one hundred legal cases. In 1995–96 IUED's docket showed thirty-two primary cases dealing with problems of water, air, and noise pollution, land use and waste disposal. These cases have come before all levels of the Israeli judiciary, from the Supreme Court to local municipal magistrates. In view of the sparse interest-group environmental litigation prior to IUED's coming, the scope of the organization's legal activity is a significant achievement. Nonetheless, its legal success record has been mixed. Though it has suffered few outright losses, neither has it produced many clear victories of the type that sustained the early efforts of environmental law groups in the United States, and a significant number of its cases have languished in protracted legal limbo.

The following discussion reviews the history of three of IUED's most important cases during the period covered here. The first, brought before the Supreme Court, ended in defeat. The second concluded in a settlement that IUED justifiably considers a major victory, while the third, litigated before the Haifa District Court, ended more or less in a draw. All three cases illustrate both the process through which IUED sought to transplant American-modeled environmental litigation to Israel and the local factors that prompted later transformations of this approach.

The Trans-Israel Highway Case

IUED began with significant optimism regarding its prospects before the courts, especially the Israeli Supreme Court, which beginning with the 1980s assumed a more activist, rights-supportive orientation. The primary indication that the court may extend this activism to environmental litigation came from a 1989 decision colloquially known as the "Voice of America" case in which the court, citing an inadequate EIS review process, delayed construction of a massive radio transmission station in Israel's Arava desert (Regional Council for the Central Arava et al. v. The National Planning and Building Council [1989]). [9] The opinion, broadly celebrated in Israeli environmental circles, was, however, both brief and circumscribed and as such offered little substantive legal ground for future environmental litigation. More significant, it remains one of a tiny number of victories the Supreme Court has granted environmental interests. An attempt by IUED to build upon and go beyond the Voice of America success through a challenge to EIS procedures employed in planning the Trans-Israel Highway was IUED's most ambitious and ultimately most disappointing litigation venture.

The Trans-Israel Highway is a planned, 300-kilometer toll road that is slated to cut through much of the country. Fashioned after the U.S. interstate system and similar projects worldwide, the highway will profoundly alter Israel's landscape and the course of its future transportation and land-use policy. Nevertheless, the project, since 1990, moved swiftly through the various pertinent planning stages and was the object of little if any public discussion or debate. Against this background, IUED, in a last-ditch effort to place the road on the country's legal and political agenda, brought suit before the Supreme Court.

Its petition argued that the absence of a comprehensive EIS evaluating the road's cumulative environmental effects invalidated the decision by the National Planning Board to approve it (six partial studies pertaining to particularly sensitive segments of the road were prepared). It was a bold argument, similar in its nature to the one that U.S. environmental law groups had employed in the course of litigation aimed at expanding procedural EIS requirements included in the 1969 National Environmental Protection Act (NEPA). The brief IUED submitted in the case was replete with references to norms and practices governing the EIS process in Europe and the United States and backed with expert opinions solicited from Israeli and American academics. It was the culmination of extensive efforts in which IUED mobilized colleagues and supporters, many of them in the United States, on behalf of this project.

Though the brief referred to the scope of pertinent EIS regulations, the status of the various national plans in which the road was incorporated and the nature of the relevant National Board's authority, the weight of the argument, following the American NEPA model, was policy oriented. Whereas in the United States this strategy was successful, at least initially, IUED's parallel attempt met with failure. The court deferred to the authority of the National Planning Board and warned against "uncritical emulation of EIS laws and procedures customary in foreign legal systems" (Adam Teva V'Din v. The National Planning and Building Council, 1996: 1182). Rejecting IUED's appeal to policy, Justice Heshin, writing for the unanimous three-judge panel, declared: "We judge from the seat of justice, our language is the language of law, and in that language we will speak. The way of the law is the one open before us, and in it we will march" (ibid.).

The legalistic undertone of this response contrasts with the Israeli court's generally activist reputation under the leadership of its current chief justice, Aharon Barak. Chief Justice Barak did not sit on the panel that decided the Trans-Israel Case, and Justice Heshin's language in the opinion may in part reflect internal divisions on the court regarding its proper role within public-policy disputes. Nevertheless, the chief justice's decision not to assign himself to the panel of judges hearing this case suggests that the issue was marginal to his own judicial agenda. Consequently, rather than the activist policy–oriented court it structured its strategy in the case around, IUED found itself in a much more legal-formalistic judicial arena.

The litigation strategy IUED employed followed to a significant extent in the footsteps of the environmental law groups who through the courts succeeded in pouring life into the seemingly declaratory EIS provisions of NEPA. Relative to these groups, IUED was disadvantaged not only by the absence of broader political support of the type its American counterparts enjoyed, but by the evolution of EIS doctrine and theory in the United States since the early 1970s. Rodgers (1990) describes NEPA's EIS provisions as "sleepers" and attributes environmentalist success in this area to an opposition caught off guard by a surprise attack. Once this organization awakened, early court victories were overturned in subsequent litigation, as was the case with *Calvert Cliffs*. IUED acted without the benefit of such "sleeper provisions" because its own transnational mobilization efforts were met by countervailing Israeli and American expert opinions detailing current skepticism in the United States over the desirability of extensive EIS requirements. By framing the matter in terms of foreign experience and expertise, IUED ended cornering itself into an arena in which it was ultimately outgunned.

Perhaps more significant, the emphasis that IUED placed on mobilizing outside experts and external sources of support came at the expense of efforts to generate domestic momentum behind the lawsuit. IUED stood before the Israeli Supreme Court practically alone (it was joined by a small number of former members of Knesset and professors). It failed to bring aboard any additional environmental group or representatives of the settlements located directed along the planned road. Whether a more broad-based lawsuit and evidence of larger political interest would have changed the legal outcome is difficult to tell. As things stood, though, it is hardly surprising that the Israeli Supreme Court, already embroiled in more than its share of controversy, did not expend its dwindling political capital on a case about which so few Israelis seemed to care.

The Haifa Chemicals Case

If the Trans-Israel Highway case was IUED's sorest loss, Haifa Chemicals stands as a major success. The case began with a criminal complaint (which, under Israeli law, private citizens and groups can file in some such instances) that IUED brought in 1995 against Haifa Chemicals, the world's largest producer of the fertilizer potassium nitrate. The company, which like the bulk of Israeli industry was previously state-owned, became a fully owned subsidiary of the American company Trans Resources Inc. The complaint charged the company with dumping in the order of 1.5 million cubic meters of untreated highly acidic wastes in the nearby Kishon River and directly into the Mediterranean Sea. The case concluded in 1996 with a court-approved settlement the likes of which have never existed in Israel. Haifa Chemicals committed to building, within five years, extensive waste-treatment facilities at a cost of $16 million. In addition, it agreed to pay $250,000 to an environmental trust fund and $475,000 in legal fees to IUED.

The settlement, while novel in the Israeli context, followed a well-recognized model of environmental dispute resolution in the United States and was facilitated by Haifa Chemicals' transnational identity and interests. The criminal lawsuit personally threatened the company's American directors and the standing of its stock offerings on Wall Street. The pollution problem had already become the object of negative international publicity through the intervention of Green Peace. Furthermore, among the legal firms representing Haifa Chemicals in Israel was one of Israel's most prestigious American-styled mega firms. For all of these reasons in this dispute IUED played, and ultimately won, on its own originally American home turf.

Among the questions disputed by the parties was the type of waste disposal standards and technological solutions employed by companies engaged in similar production processes in the United States. In search of answers to this question, IUED once again activated its extensive transnational connections, most notably its membership within Environmental Law Alliance Worldwide (E-LAW) an international organization linking environmental law groups in more than forty countries.[10] E-LAW informed IUED that the EPA has regulated effluents of the type released untreated by Haifa Chemicals since 1972. When IUED cited this information in support of its own demands for enforcement, attorneys for Haifa Chemicals filed a motion demanding release of all of IUED's internet communications with E-LAW in connection with the case. IUED refused, invoking a confidentiality pledge that all E-LAW members take and successfully argued that the information was immaterial to Haifa Chemicals' own legal responsibilities in Israel and thus to the question before the court. Whereas that indeed was the disputes' legal parameters, the terms of the extralegal settlement suggest that these American standards may well have been highly pertinent to the solution ultimately negotiated between the parties.

The Haifa Chemicals settlement was a significant environmental and organizational success, and one that IUED was unlikely to reach through judicial intervention. Nevertheless, settlements are difficult to market, even for U.S. environmental groups. This difficulty is exacerbated in Israel where the status and mission of CLOs leave significant portions of the public confused. A pointed attack on the settlement came in an extended article published in July 1997 in the popular Israeli daily *Yediot Aharonot*. The article singled out for criticism two interrelated elements in the agreement: the meager payment it provided fishermen whose complaints helped IUED to establish its right to sue during the dispute's early stages, and the significant legal fees IUED itself received under the settlement. More specifically, the article accused IUED's attorneys of making significant personal profit of the deal while leaving little to the fishermen whom they ostensibly represented (Ringel-Hofman, 1997). The latter claim was patently false and at best evinced a fundamental misunderstanding of the difference in the incentives driving private legal practice and salaried lawyers within a nonprofit CLO such as IUED.

More complicated was the claim regarding the small size of the compensation, 150,000 NIS (approximately $40,000), allocated to six fishermen under the settlement. The fishermen whose union was active in calling attention to water-pollution problems were invited by IUED to join the case because as the law then stood only directly affected parties could bring a private criminal complaint of this sort. The law was subsequently changed so as to allow citizen groups such as IUED independent standing and the fishermen were not a party to the agreement that IUED ultimately reached with Haifa Chemicals. The change in the relevant standing requirements relieved IUED of its dependence upon the fishermen and accorded with the organization's imported CLO mission. But IUED's adherence to this model here, as in the Trans-Israel Highway case, ultimately interfered with opportunities to reach to and sustain connections with broader segments of its local Israeli audience. The threat that an insufficient local base could ultimately pose for the organization became all too evident when, in response to a lawsuit IUED brought against a major development project, known as the Carmel Beach Towers, its opponent set out in direct attack against it.

The Carmel Beach Towers Case

The Carmel Beach Towers are a group of high-rise hotels and residential buildings built or planned for construction directly adjacent to the Haifa seashore. The specific project and company behind it are among the largest in the country. In 1996

IUED brought suit against these developers. For IUED, it was a high-stakes gamble and a coming-of-age experience.

The case was part of a coordinated IUED campaign aimed at halting a wide string of luxury beachside development projects in a number of Israeli coastal cities. This campaign, which began shortly after the failed Trans-Israel case, followed an opposite strategy. Rather than criticizing the development on environmental-policy grounds, the suit focused on incompatibilities between the planned projects and the rules of pertinent permits and plans, most notably the National Plan for Coastlines. This narrowly constructed legal argument earlier resulted in favorable decrees issued by both the Tel Aviv and Haifa district courts.

The Carmel Beach Towers suit followed the same strategy. In a statement echoing the Supreme Court's legalistic tone in the Trans-Israel opinion, IUED stated in its brief: "[T]he court does not sit as an ultimate planning body and should rule on questions of law alone."[11] In response, the Haifa District Court issued a temporary stop-work order. Though the order expired when IUED did not provide judicially required financial guarantees, work on the project was essentially halted in the wake of this litigation, sales slowed down, and, according to an affidavit submitted by the developers, the entire project was in danger of collapse (Ma'ariv, 1997).

The project developers responded with a direct and multifaceted attack on IUED. The first prong of this strategy was a legal challenge to the CLO's incorporation procedures and its internal decision-making processes. Next, in what appears to have been the first direct environmental SLAPP (Strategic Lawsuits Against Public Participation) threat in Israel (Pring and Canan, 1996), the company informed IUED of its intention to sue the organization for damages. In addition, the purchaser of one unit in the contested complex, who joined IUED as a member during the year in which its suit against the project was undertaken, sought to inform all other thousand or so IUED members of their potential personal liability for the damages the developers claimed to have suffered. In March 1997, days before IUED's annual meeting was scheduled to take place, a string of new membership applications arrived in IUED's offices. Some, rather unusually, were delivered by a special business messenger, and others arrived as faxes that bore the address of one of the primary investors in the project. IUED accused the developers of attempting to infiltrate the organization and change its decisions from the inside. The 1997 annual meeting was overshadowed by these events and resulted in a vote to revoke the membership of the Carmel Beach Towers purchaser.

In January 1998, the district court handed down a decision that granted some but not all of IUED's demands. Both sides declared victory following the decision, and both appealed to the Israeli Supreme Court. Soon after the district court issued its decision, one of the investors in the project repeated the SLAPP threat and said: "We have suffered a terrible injustice. It is not right that an organization like this will halt a project without first considering the legal process and its likely outcome.

Someone will have to pay for our damages. It is not right that this organization will scare developers as is presently the case, from building along the country's coasts" (Morgenstern, 1998).

The scope of the assault triggered by the Carmel Beach Towers case is indicative of the significance of the threat that IUED's litigation in this area poses to the Towers' and other developers in Israel. Through this lawsuit and others like it, IUED is currently challenging Israeli planning practices that have all too often honored statutory planning restrictions in the breach. Governmental planning committees have long turned a blind eye when development projects supported by business and local municipal interests violated pertinent planning provisions. IUED intruded into this arrangement and in the process threw a pall of uncertainty over a host of development projects. Yet the seeming attempt to infiltrate the organization in order to change its policies from within is also indicative of an organizational vulnerability grounded in its perception as an imported American façade devoid of Israeli membership and local sources of support.

In an attempt to build on this perception and cast IUED as a meddlesome foreign interference, one of the investors in the Carmel Beach Towers project stated in a newspaper interview: "A few Americans immigrated to Israel. Half went to Hebron [i.e., became ultranationalist West Bank settlers] and half to IUED" (Ma'ariv, 1997). IUED succeeded in fending off the Carmel Towers attack, but the ordeal exacted significant costs in terms of both resources and organizational morale. Writing in the conclusion of a legal brief he submitted toward the end of the Carmel Towers litigation, IUED's attorney noted with regret the organization's failure to include as plaintiffs in the case the people who live in proximity to the Towers and would thus be most directly affected by their construction. That decision, he explained, derived from the belief that the issue was not primarily local but rather a question with national rule-of-law and environmental-policy implications. In retrospect, however, the brief continued, IUED has come to recognize that the inclusion of local Haifa residents would have improved its position by putting the project's environmental impacts, rather than IUED itself, at the center of the case.[12] The absence of local litigants in the Trans-Israel Highway case, and their marginalization in Haifa Chemicals, negatively affected IUED's legal and or political missions in both instances. But it took the Carmel Towers' trial by fire for IUED to come to terms with the limits of going at it alone.

Reaching Out

Soon after its defeat in 1995, IUED came to recognize that success in the courts, especially the type of larger, politically mobilizing victories it hoped to secure, required a more deeply rooted presence in Israel. A comparison between two fundraising letters, both written by then–Executive Director Alon Tal, documents this change. The first letter, dated March 24, 1994, optimistically announced: "Next week a year of intensive work will culminate in the filing of a supreme court petition against the establishment of the Trans-Israel Highway, *without the preparation of an environmental impact statement* in contravention of Israeli law." In contrast, the letter written after the Trans-Israel loss on June 15, 1996, stated: "We realized this year that for our legal and scientific initiatives to really take hold, the public must be aware, involved and empowered. Although our staff is skilled and dedicated to the protection of Israel's environment, we can not do it alone."

Recognizing that the route to the Israeli public did not go through the courts, IUED subsequently realigned the frames defining its mission in Israel in a distinctly less legal direction. Most notably this move was reflected in IUED's turn toward popularly directed environmental campaigns with little or no legal content. The first such campaign involved the organization of a mass rally in opposition to plans to open parts of Tel Aviv's Yarkon River park to restaurants and other tourist-oriented development. Where IUED's membership recruitment goals are concerned, this campaign was well chosen. Tel Aviv, the most wealthy and cosmopolitan of Israel's metropolitan areas, is IUED's backyard and primary membership reservoir. Furthermore, the Yarkon park is itself adjacent to some of Tel Aviv's more upscale neighborhoods and the populations most likely to heed IUED's environmental message.

In a second such campaign undertaken in 1996, once again in Tel Aviv, IUED pressured city officials to release air-pollution-monitoring information they refused until then to divulge. Toward that goal, IUED scientists and volunteers, some dressed in potently symbolic gas masks, orchestrated a week of public protest. In addition, they conducted independent air-pollution monitoring along some major Tel Aviv thoroughfares. The campaign led Tel Aviv's municipal authority to allow the Environmental Ministry to operate new pollution-monitoring stations in the city, and it provided IUED with extensive media coverage and a valuable public relations victory. In addition, almost five hundred new Israeli members joined IUED during that year.[13]

Reflecting upon IUED's role in the Yarkon park campaign, Alon Tal wrote in the January 1996 edition of the *Eco-Advocate*, the organization's English-language newsletter:

> Our organization has always been, foremost, a professional advocacy group. Based on American models such as the Sierra Club, Legal Defense Fund, NRDC and EDF, we have never sought out issues that didn't offer a legal angle. But the Yarkon River is a natural treasure, which to many is more significant than remote Nature Reserves. So we took a leap of faith and headed into the fray. A rally at the Tel Aviv City Hall, attracted hundreds of citizens.... The battle has just begun. We will remain predominantly a public interest law organization, but it is good to know that when legal action is not promising, we too are capable of taking to the streets.

This message, directed at IUED's American-oriented constituency, seems to hint at Tal's own ambivalence regarding this transformation. More significant, however, it points to the continuing relevance of IUED's original legal frames where its contacts with its transnational American supporters are concerned.

The transition that began in 1995 accelerated significantly with IUED's receipt during 1998 of a large grant earmarked for building a more environmentally active Israeli citizenry. IUED's membership roster, which numbered fewer than 100 in 1994, stood at close to 2,000 in 1998. This growth was the result of a concerted, domestically oriented campaign, in which law and environmental litigation were rarely mentioned. As part of that campaign, IUED substituted a new graphic logo for the logo that had served the organization until then. Whereas the old logo was "homemade" on Alon Tal's computer, the professionally designed one reflected the organization's increased professionalism and secure financial base. More significant was the change in the message implicit in each of the logos. At the center of the first stood the scales of justice and in the background graphic representations of a person and a tree (responding to each of the elements in the organization's tripartite Hebrew name, Adam, Teva V'Din [Man, Nature and Law]). Of the three elements a tree and a human hand appear in IUED's new logo, but gone are the scales and with them the appeal to law as a central legal collective-action frame.

Conclusion

The extent to which this story is indicative of the experience of transplanted CLOs elsewhere requires additional comparative case studies.[14] Nevertheless, there are good reasons to expect that its central themes are not unique to IUED or to its Israeli context, and that the lessons it imparts are of relevance to parallel cause-lawyering transplantation efforts currently taking place across the globe.

The dissonance between IUED's imported pluralist legal mission and the corporatist sensibilities of its Israeli audience is inherent in the work of similar transnational enterprises. Like IUED, other transplanted CLOs seek locales in which civil associations have traditionally been few and social-movement litigation rare. By definition they have to rely upon financial and organizational resources outside the domains they enter for the support needed to launch their enterprise. The result in IUED's case was the creation of a bifocal organization that turned outward for money, expertise, and even membership while directing its attention in Israel toward building, essentially from scratch, an environmental-law infrastructure.

IUED's success in building this infrastructure and in disturbing long entrenched illegal practices by industrial polluters and land developers in the country has been significant. At the same time IUED has found it difficult to win the type of broad policy-laden and symbolically potent legal victories that it needed to persuade its Israeli audience of the importance of law-based environmental strategies and to meet the expectations of its largely external supporters. This difficulty in part stemmed from litigation strategies that relied heavily on foreign doctrines and expertise to the neglect of local litigants and domestic contacts. In particular, the liberalization of Israeli standing doctrines, a result for which IUED actively lobbied, may have paradoxically hurt the organization by increasing its isolation from its local Israeli context. In addition, as became all too evident in the Carmel Beach case, the perception that IUED was a rootless American import made it vulnerable to extraordinary, disruptive, and potentially destructive attacks.

In response to the realization that the success of its legal mission depended upon the creation of broader Israeli engagement and support for the organization, IUED, from 1995 onward, began to shift its bifocal gaze inward and actively turned to building a domestic Israeli constituency. Doing so, however, required a shift away from law toward alternative mobilization tactics more likely to resonate with its Israeli audience.

There may be grounds to expect, however, that the longer term will result in closer alignment between IUED's pluralist and litigation-directed environmental mission and the sensibilities of its once corporatist, but increasingly pluralizing, locale. What a decade ago began as an obscure group struggling for media, judicial, and government attention is today a well recognized and increasingly respected actor in Israeli environmental politics. IUED is yet to win a major catalytic environmental victory in the Israeli Supreme Court, but its recent successes in winning more narrowly tailored procedural lawsuits have caught the attention both of its opponents and of the Israeli public. Though IUED remains the only Israeli environmental law group of its kind, the 1990s have seen in Israel visible growth in the number of civil associations and in the frequency with which they take to the courts. Where environmental groups are concerned, the growth both in the number of organizations and in their propensity to litigate has been especially pronounced (Bar-David and Tal, 1996).[15] Whether the country's pluralist turn will ultimately bridge imported "rights" with Israeli "politics" or yield a distinct transplanted variant of the CLO model is at present too early to tell.

Acknowledgments

The author acknowledges with gratitude the assistance and cooperation extended to her by the staff of the Israel Union for Environmental Defense. Special thanks are due to Alon Tal and Daniel Fisch for many illuminating conversations and to Philip Warburg for detailed and helpful comments on work related to this project. Errors of fact or interpretation remain, of course, my own. A fellowship from the the Lady Davies Trust provided funding for this study.

Notes

1. The term Public Interest Law Firm has been commonly used in reference to these organizations, but is misleading to the extent that it suggests a public consensus behind the agendas these groups address.

2. The study covers the history of IUED between its founding in 1990 and 1998.

3. The term bifocal is borrowed from Michael P. Smith who uses it to uses it to be describe transnational migrants engaged in on going "migratory circuits" as "bifocal subjects" (1994: 15).

4. The organization is legally registered in Israel only under its Hebrew name: Adam Teva v'Din.

5. A search I conducted of reported supreme and district court cases for the period 1980–87 revealed only one environmental case brought by an interest group.

6. *Yediot Ahronot*, July 3, 1991 (English translation in *The EcoAdvocate*, August–September 1991).

7. IUED's budget for 1996 was approximately $580,000 and in 1997 approximately $400,000 (the difference between the two years is due to payments IUED received as part of a legal settlement in 1996. The case, Haifa Chemicals, is discussed in a later section of IV of this study).

8. In January 1997 IUED's list of addressees receiving its English-language publications included 628 entries. Of these, 258 were English-speaking members of IUED living in Israel, 156 were overseas donors, 47 were foundations and the other 157 were categorized as Israeli and overseas colleagues, personal contacts, and VIPs (IUED English Mailing List, January 21, 1997).

9. The transmitter was intended for the Voice of America and was a joint venture of the U.S. and Israeli governments. Following the court's order, construction was delayed pending the preparation of a new EIS, but the project was ultimately canceled when changing geopolitical circumstances following the collapse of the Soviet Union made its previous rationale obsolete.

10. An article written by two E-LAW staff attorneys describes the organization, which in 1989 was established at a public interest lawyers' conference at the University of Oregon, as "one model wherein U.S. attorneys have helped advance sound legal protections for the environment beyond U.S. borders" (Gleason and Johnson, 1995:68). E-LAW's center of operation is its U.S. office in Eugene, though the organization is structured as a loose international federation linking twenty independent national law offices.

11. Plaintiff's Brief, Adam Teva V'Din v. The Haifa Regional Planning and Building Commission, p. 4.

12. Final Brief submitted in the case of *Adam, Teva V'Din* (Iued) v. *The Regional Planning and building Commission and others*. p. 61 (In Heberw)

13. Interim Report for General Support Grant, submitted to the New Israel Fund by the Israel Union for Environmental Defense, August 1, 1996.

14. Meili's analysis in this volume of the obstacles encountered by environmental and civil rights lawyers in Latin America evokes some parallels to the story of IUED.

15. Financial and organizational support for this development has come from a number of foreign Jewish foundations. In 1997 two such foundations the Canadian CRB and the American-based Nathan Cummings Foundation joined to form SHELI, a fund specifically directed at the promotion of grassroots environmental mobilization. SHELI has provided grants to 31 such groups in 1997. These monies have been disbursed through the intermediary

services of IUED, which in some of the cases has provided legal advice and representation to some of these groups.

References

Books and Articles

Arian, Asher (1993). "Israel: Interest Group Pluralism Constrained." *First World Interest Groups*, ed. Clive S. Thomas. Westport, Conn.: Greenwood Press.
Bar-David, Shirli, and Alon Tal (1996). *Harnessing Activism to Protect Israel's Environment: A Survey of Public Interest Activity and Potential.* Tel Aviv: Adam Teva V'din–The Israel Union for Environmental Defense.
Cameron, Roderick A. (1990). "Of Milk and Honey," *Acorn Days*, ed. Marion L. Rogers. New York: Environmental Defense Fund.
Crepaz, Markus M. L. (1995). "Explaining National Variations of Air Pollution Levels: Political Institutions and Their Impact on Environmental Policy-Making," 4:2 *Environmental Politics*, 391–414.
De-Shalit, Avner, and Moti Talias (1994). "Green or Blue and White? Environmental Controversies in Israel," 3:2 *Environmental Politics*, 273–94.
Dezalay, Yves, and Bryant G. Garth (1996). *Dealing in Virtue.* Chicago: University of Chicago Press.
Edelman, Martin (1995). "Israel," in *The Global Expansion of Judicial Power*, eds. C. N. Tate and Torbjörn Vallinder. New York: New York University Press.
Gabai, Shoshana (1994). *The Environment in Israel.* Jerusalem: Ministry of the Environment.
Gleason, Jennifer M, and Bern A. Johnson (1995). "Environmental Law Across Borders," *Journal of Environmental Law and Litigation*, 67.
Halliday, Terrence, and Lucien Karpick (1999). *Lawyers and the Rise of Western Political Liberalism.* New York: Oxford University Press.
Handler, Joel F. (1978). *Social Movements and the Legal System.* New York: Academic Press.
Keck, Margaret, and Kathryn Sikkink (1998). *Activists Without Borders: Transnational Advocacy Networks in International Politics.* Ithaca, N.Y: Cornell University Press.
Lev, Daniel (1998). "Lawyers' Causes in Indonesia and Malaysia," in *Cause Lawyering: Political Commitments and Professional Responsibilities*, Austin Sarat and Stuart Scheingold, eds., New York: Oxford University Press.
Ma'arive (1997). "Storm at Haifa Beach (in Hebrew)," (3 March), 4.
McCann, Michael W. (1994). *Rights at Work.* Chicago: University of Chicago Press.
McCarthy, John D., and Mayer N. Zald (1987). "The Trend of Social Movements in America: Professionalization and Resource Mobilization," in *Social Movements in an Organizational Society*, Mayer N. Zald and John D. McCarthy, eds. New Brunswick: Transaction Books.
Meili, Stephen (1998). "Cause Lawyering and Social Movements: A Comparative Perspective on Democratic Change in Argentina and Brazil," in *Cause Lawyering: Political Commitments and Professional Responsibilities*, Austin Sarat and Stuart Scheingold, eds., New York: Oxford University Press.
Morag-Levine, Noga (1999). "Outsiders, National Partnerships and the Judicialization of Politics: Declining Corporatism and the Growth of Environmental Interest Group Litigation in Israel." Paper presented at the 1999 Annual Meeting of the Law and Society Association, Chicago.

Morgenstern, Ronit (1998). "Court Rejects Request by 'Adam, Teva V'Din' to Halt Construction in Carmel Towers (in Hebrew)." *Ha'Aretz.*
Pring, George W., and Penelope Canan (1996). *SLAPPs: Getting Sued for Speaking Out.* Philadelphia: Temple University Press.
Rinat, Tsafrir (1997). "Trojan Horse Style (in Hebrew)." *Ha'Aretz* (4 May), B4.
Ringel-Hofman, Ariella (1997). "The Kishon Stinks from the Head (in Hebrew)." *Yediot Ahronot,* Musaf (7 July), 23.
Rodgers, William H., Jr. (1990). "NEPA at Twenty: Mimicry and Recruitment in Environmental Law," 20 *Environmental Law,* 485.
Rosenberg, Gerald (1991). *The Hollow Hope: Can Courts Bring about Social Change?* Chicago: University of Chicago Press.
Sarat, Austin, and Stuart Scheingold (1998). *Cause Lawyering: Political Commitments and Professional Responsibilities.* New York: Oxford University Press.
Scheingold, Stuart A. (1974). *The Politics of Rights.* New Haven, Conn.: Yale University Press.
Schmitter, Phillippe (1974). "Still the Century of Corporatism," 26 *Review of Politics,* 85–131.
Smith, Michael P. (1994). "Can You Imagine? Transnational Migration and the Globalization of Grassroots Politics," 39 *Social Text* 15.
Snow, David A., E. Burke Rochford, Steven K. Worden, and Robert D. Benford (1986). "Frame Alignment Processes, Micromobilization, and Movement Participation," 51 *American Sociological Review,* 464.
Snow, David A., and Robert D. Benford (1992). "Master Frames and Cycles of Protest," in *Frontiers in Social Movement Theory,* Aldon D. Morris and Carol McClurg Mueller, eds. New Haven, Conn: Yale University Press.
Sward, Ellen, and Burton A. Weisbrod (1978). "Public Interest Law Activities outside the U.S.A," eds *Public Interest Law,* eds. B. A. Weisbrod, J. F. Handler and N. K. Komesar. Berkeley: University of California Press.
Tarrow, Sidney (1998). *Power in Movement,* 2d ed. Cambridge: Cambridge University Press.
Turner, Tom (1988). "The Legal Eagles," 10 *The Amicus Journal* (Winter), 25.
Vogel, David (1998). "Israeli Environmental Policy: An International Perspective," 5 *Israel Affairs* (Winter), 245.
Williamson, Peter J. (1989). *Corporatism in Perspective.* London: Sage Publications.
Yishai, Yael (1991). *Land of Paradoxes: Interest Politics in Israel.* Albany, N.Y.: SUNY Press.

Cases

H.P. 524/96, Adam Teva V'Din v. Haifa Regional Planning and Building Council (unpublished opinion) [in Hebrew].
H.C. 2920/94, Adam Teva V'Din v. National Building and Planning Council, available in TAKDIN-ELYON, 96(2) 1175 [in Hebrew].
Calvert Cliffs Coordinating Comm. v. Atomic Energy Comm'n, 449 F.2d 1109 (D.C. Cir. 1971).
H.C. 594/89, Regional Council for the Central Arava et al. v. The National Planning and Building Council, 44 (1) P.D. 558 [in Hebrew].
Scenic Hudson Preservation Conference v. Federal Power Comm'n, 354 F.2d 608 (2d Cir. 1965), cert. denied, 384 U.S. 941 (1966).

CHAPTER 14

Constructing Law Out of Power
Investing in Human Rights as an Alternative Political Strategy

YVES DEZALAY AND BRYANT G. GARTH

Proliferating in the 1970s and especially the 1980s, human rights organizations became thriving examples of successful cause lawyering outside the United States (Keck and Sikkink, 1998). They attacked authoritarian states in Latin America, Asia, and Africa, helping to bring new elections and transitions to democracy (Abel, 1995; Brysk, 1994). Human rights lawyers actively constructed law and developed legal approaches through such entities as the Inter-American Commission on Human Rights, truth commissions, and international criminal courts. Increasingly human rights organizations also became linked through the internet and transnational exchanges and meetings (Riles, 1999). This proliferation of transnational activities has produced an international field of human rights with substantial autonomy from national states and legal systems. As with respect to the efforts to make Pinochet accountable in England and Spain for his human rights violations in Chile, national and transnational advocates can use the power of the international community to put pressure on local human rights violators. This international movement of cause lawyers invoking universally recognized standards against states and against transnational organizations has led academics to posit a new stage of progressive international law (Koh, 1997). Seen in relation to a counterpart in the world of business, namely the field of international commercial arbitration (Dezalay and Garth, 1996), the emerging field of international human rights can provide an emancipatory counterpoint to business norms and the lex mercatoria.

This optimistic story of the field of international human rights provides only a partial picture of a complex phenomenon. It depends on a particular reading of cause lawyers, human rights, and the law, and it works better for the 1980s than the 1990s. What can be presented as the steady progress in institutionalizing the lofty goals of human rights and the law, or even a militant struggle to overcome the forces of evil represented by dictatorships and apartheid, is also the product of particular palace wars in the north and the south. As with respect to the law, more generally, the field of human rights was constructed out of the tools and resources that were available to particular actors at discrete moments. In this process of social construction, power is exchanged for law in order to gain legitimacy.

We can trace the processes that have produced this field through the careers of individuals in law and politics. Our larger research project uses careers and, more generally, relational biography, to situate individuals in relation to others in fields that are constantly changing. This chapter uses this approach to explore the prospects of cause lawyering in the United States and elsewhere, especially in Latin America. Following Bourdieu and our prior work, we use biographical accounts of individual choices and career strategies to understand the hierarchical structures and institutions in which actors operate. Instead of studying those who seem to fit a category of "cause lawyers" or even "activists," we use biographies to see relationships and influences that come together to construct a field. Similarly, we do not focus on the goals of the actors, or whether they are ideologically driven, playing power politics, or simply building careers. It does not matter how we label them. Our purpose is to see what channels are available at particular moments for idealists and idealism, since those who invest in idealism must find ways to get attention, resources, and power in competitive fields. Individual stories, in addition, are less important than the collective accounts that emerge from such stories and serve to reveal what Bourdieu terms the habitus and doxa of the field (Bourdieu and Wacquant, 1992). Ideally we will be able to see how groups move into the field of state power, what they bring, how they operate, how they are oriented, and what changes are produced in the institutions and organizations operating in the field.[1]

Our interviews took place primarily in the United States and Latin America. This geographical focus means that we do not have a full picture of the history of international human rights nor the role of human rights organizations around the globe. In defense of our choice of priorities, Latin America was essential to the legitimation and development of the movement in the 1970s and 1980s, and the most important international human rights organizations are those centered in the United States (e.g., Korey, 1998). The powerful role of models and connections to the United States in the development of the field more generally—and cause lawyering internationally—is seen also in a number of the chapters in this volume (e.g., Morag-Levine; Meili; Dotan). This importance, we should also note, is not meant to ignore the particular local factors that determine when human rights strategies will be found in particular places and how they will be shaped. Fundamental to our research—including what we report in this chapter—is the recognition that the human rights movement could only occur because of a particular coincidence of structural factors in the north and the south.

The important role of the United States means that the politics of the Cold War were central to the construction of this international field of human rights, and the close relationship to the U.S. state has continued as the field has undergone dramatic change and growth. The human rights organizations centered in the United States, as we suggested above, are the most important globally, and they have gained further legitimacy through a kind of brain drain that relates to the different positions of law in the United States and Latin America (and probably elsewhere as well). In order to show both the development of the human rights movement in the 1970s and 1980s and the recent transformations, our account presented here will concentrate on two moments in this story of human rights.

The first moment was the challenge to power made possible because of parallel positions in the fields of state power in the north and the south. Drawing in particular on the Chilean experience, we can see how the Vicariate for Solidarity— the most famous Chilean human rights organization—built ties with a particular group at the Ford Foundation and in the field of state power in the United States at a very specific moment in the mid-1970s. Each side pursued a strategy that suited a domestic reformist establishment that had temporarily lost power as part of the Cold War. The kind of cause lawyering connected with international human rights is a product of that moment.[2]

The second period, however, presents an important divergence. The structural parallels between the United States and Chile were not sustained. When the challengers from the human rights community succeeded in gaining political power in Latin America, they reconnected with the state. In the south, at least in the countries that we studied, this meant that the human rights movement largely disappeared. Key actors went back into politics or took positions abroad. The Vicariate, for example, is now merely an archive. The same processes that could construct the human rights movement at a particular political conjuncture could also unravel as the first generation moved back into the field of state power. The human rights institutions in the south often remained, but they were emptied of the content they had in their flourishing period. In contrast, the institutions of the north continue to thrive and evolve. Instead of remaining at the forefront of the battle against the state, the human rights organizations of the south have increasingly become appendages of the human rights organizations centered in the north. The stories in the north and south, therefore, diverged in this second moment.

Our conclusion will thus be one of caution. While there is no agreed-upon definition of cause lawyering, the idea is associated with the use of legal strategies for political ends. Cause lawyering seeks to take advantage of the relative autonomy of the law and institutions that promote legal autonomy, namely the courts and the legal academy; and of the power that comes when courts and legal institutions occupy a relatively strong place in the structures of state power. The United States historically has provided the best—even the unique—example of this kind of role for law and legal strategies. Law graduates with political ambitions and agendas elsewhere have tended to act very differently—taking advantage of other political and institutional configurations. The development of cause lawyering outside the United States—in the sense we have described—has tended therefore to draw heavily on the U.S. experience and U.S. models, which activists in the United States have been eager to export. In order to be imported with any success, however, the U.S. models must combine with domestic contexts in a way that changes the space of possibilities for political-legal-moral activity. There must be a local structural basis in the field of state power for this alternative politics combining law and moralism.

The experience we describe suggests two cautions for those who would like to see cause lawyering develop further in Latin America. First, the development of the human rights field—in terms of practices and substantive agendas—cannot be separated from the influence of the field of state power in the United States. The successes of human rights required a strong investment and translation of U.S. power into law. As we already suggested, there is an international field of human rights that provides a transnational legal space of some importance and autonomy, but that relative autonomy has been constructed very close to the U.S. state. What practices and norms are accepted as legitimate internationally relate to what is considered legitimate with the major human rights NGOs in the United States. The understandings can be challenged, of course, and domestic experiences can and will vary, but, just as the international field of economic expertise is dominated by what is considered legitimate economics in the United States, the field of human rights expertise is dominated by the influence and prestige of the U.S.-based multinationals.

Second, absent a change in the position and role of law in the structures of state power in countries where a tradition does not exist of moral investment in law, the prospects for this kind of cause lawyering are relatively weak. We can trace processes of change that are still at work, but we cannot say what the prospects are for a greater convergence on the basic elements of the U.S. model of cause lawyering. To some extent, the situation is reminiscent of the progressive era in the United States. We see business lawyers beginning to invest both in the autonomy of law and in reformist political strategies (Gordon, 1984), but those outside of the business law firms who invest in legal causes do not (yet?) have career options that can be built on their legal and moral investment. "Public interest lawyers" are recognized and validated by leading law schools and elite corporate lawyers in the United States. Their contribution to the legitimacy of law is rewarded with some prestige that can even be converted into careers in business law. In Latin America, in contrast, the situation remains closer to the one lawyers from the Bar Association of the City of New York found when they visited Buenos Aires in the early 1970s in the name of human rights. The corporate bar in Buenos Aires could not understand why lawyers from elite law firms in New York would have anything to say to the communist or radical lawyers who went under the name of human rights. The professional route of investment in legal moralism simply did not exist.

Chile and the Invention of the Vicariate as a Cause-Lawyering Organization on Behalf of International Human Rights

Chile occupies a central place in the institutionalization of the international human rights movement in the 1970s and 1980s (see Keck and Sikkink, 1998: 88–92; Korey, 1998: 172–73). At the time of the Pinochet coup in 1973, legality was not a key issue in Chile in any domain. Lawyers mainly supported the coup, and there was no autonomous human rights movement or discourse under which lawyers could gain any distance from politics. A petition circulated against the military coup in 1973, but it gained only twelve signatures. Within a few years, however, the Vicariate in Santiago became an international symbol and model human rights organization—equipped with a large and active legal staff.[3]

The human rights story in Chile begins with the response to Pinochet's violent persecution of those who had participated in the Allende government. Many of these politicians who were suddenly in the opposition sought to gain some protection through an alliance with the Catholic church, which itself still contained many holdovers from Catholic progressive social thought (see generally Snyder, 1995). As one observer reported, "Only churches remained to provide some umbrella."[4] A few bishops joined with a group of lawyers and activists to form a Peace Committee, which later evolved into the now famous Vicariate of Solidarity. This Peace Committee quickly established a legal department, initially headed by Jose Zalaquett.

The legal department of the Peace Committee, which soon grew to some seventy-five people, drew on the discredited but nevertheless existing legal tradition, filed habeas corpus petitions in every case possible, and also helped to provide lawyers for defense in the military courts. Some individuals asked "at the beginning" whether they were "legitimating the system" by using the courts, but, as one activist noted, "we didn't have any other forum." While the courts granted at most two or three writs altogether, it turned out that the writs served "collateral purposes" in helping to provide some documentation.[5]

The connection between Chile and the emergence of the international human rights movement emerged in part because of the central role that Chile had already been playing in northern political struggles. Chile was a focus of international contestation and concern about Allende and democratic transitions to socialism, and it remained very much in the news after Pinochet came to power. The Peace Committee—kept alive initially through the umbrella of the church—maintained links with "*Le Monde, Time,* the U.N., Amnesty International," the *New York Times,* and others who "were coming by every day" to report on the Chilean situation.

"Chile was news"—the "hot case of the day," reflected in the strong international presence. This attention helped to internationalize the strategies that the activists utilized. The people at the Peace Committee soon learned of Amnesty International, the International Commission of Jurists (ICJ), the Organization of American States, and the international human rights instruments that had been created under U.N. auspices and were, in some cases, just coming into effect. The Vicariate soon became recognizable as a human rights organization.

The story of Jose Zalaquett, one of the most famous of the Chilean human rights leaders, helps reveal this transformation. He graduated in 1967 from law school and became a law professor and criminal defense lawyer. These activities were consistent with the careers associated with the legal elite, and he also worked briefly on agrarian reform in the Allende government. He was a Christian Democrat, linked to the progressive wing of Catholic thought. When Zalaquett joined the Peace Committee immediately after the coup, the committee had a more "political" than "legal" valence. While the Peace Committee quickly gained the support of a number of lawyers, only two were relatively conservative in their politics and only a handful were Christian Democrats who had actually opposed Allende. The large majority, typified by Zalaquett, had "sympathized with the Allende government" and joined the Peace Committee as a way to save some "comrades who had been jailed." Their effort, as one member put it, was part of a "humanitarian front of a political committee that had suffered a setback." As stated by another, the lawyers were "left of center, politically-oriented lawyers" who began "using professional tools"—in effect beginning to turn politics and what was left of their political power into law. The activity transformed slowly as it began to "sink in that certain values" had "universal" appeal, which is to say they gained widespread international support. While at the beginning of the resistance to the coup, therefore, lawyers spoke about "the constitution" or the "rights of defendants," within a few months they spoke of "human rights" and began, for the first time, to systematically seek to activate U.N. machinery. When Zalaquett was expelled in 1976 after his second arrest, he went to work for Amnesty International—at the time still not part of the international mainstream. There he became a Board member of the U.S. section in 1977 (the year Amnesty won the Nobel Peace Prize), began service on the International Executive Committee in 1978, and ultimately became chair in 1979. Because of these activities, he became the first non–U.S. citizen to win one of the famous MacArthur "genius" awards.

Chile became a model for human rights organizations around the world. That does not mean, however, that human rights organizations occupied the same political space in every country. Among the countries that we have studied, the situation in Brazil was quite close to what occurred in Chile. Argentina and Mexico, because of their very different state structures, did not initially develop as close parallels to the Chilean cause lawyers. Nevertheless, they also developed strong human rights entities and activists who became quite prominent in the 1970s and

1980s. For present purposes, we will concentrate on the structural parallel between Chile and the United States, since it made for an institutional success that became celebrated as a model for struggles elsewhere.

Cause Lawyering, Human Rights, and the Decline of the Cold-War Consensus

There was nothing that could be labeled an "international human rights movement" in the early 1970s.[6] Amnesty International, founded in 1961 in England, was building its legitimacy very carefully as a nonpolitical organization seeking some distance from the Cold War.[7] Despite at one time having both Joan Baez and William Buckley on its board, Amnesty still had to work hard to sever the connection between human rights and cold-war politics—particularly leftist politics. At the Ford Foundation, even as late as 1976, according to one human rights supporter within the Foundation, "back then, some of our colleagues back at the Ford Foundation still believed... what they knew about Amnesty International suggested that it was a communist front organization." By then, however, Amnesty was gaining considerable credibility in part through its investment in South America.

A number of indicators illustrate Amnesty's growing success and legitimacy. In the 1960s, 900 prisoners were the focus of Amnesty campaigns with a staff of one full-time and one part-time salaried persons. The budget was only £10,000. In 1976, the staff was about 40. The newly found prosperity evident in the winning of the Nobel Prize in 1977[8] was also clear in the membership and budget figures. By 1981, Amnesty supported the campaigns of 4,000 prisoners with 250,000 members, a budget of £2 million and a staff of 150 persons.[9] The field began to develop.[10]

A key factor in the successes of Amnesty and in the development of the Vicariate was the conflict found in the United States. In particular, by the late 1960s, as evident in the Vietnam War and the student movements, the cold-war consensus had been shaken. Prior to that time, the members of a relatively small elite group, often called the Foreign Policy Establishment,[11] controlled all the positions of power in the state and around the state—the elite universities, the major foundations, the World Bank.[12] This break in the establishment—as we shall see—became quite important in relation to Chile.

Within the United States, in addition, lawyers in the 1960s linked to the establishment institutions—at that time reformist in orientation—were channeling moral and legal investment into the civil rights movement and the War on Poverty's neighborhood law firms (Johnson, 1974). That investment flowed also into the new public interest law firms. The leading institution in this flowering of cause lawyering was the Ford Foundation, which underwent a major change with the presidency of MacGeorge Bundy, a pillar of the eastern establishment.[13] Bundy joined the foundation in 1966 after deciding not to continue his role as a cheerleader for the

Vietnam War (Bird, 1998). At the Ford Foundation, stating that white racism was the cause of inequality and poverty, he quickly funded the NAACP, the Urban League, the Southern Christian Leadership Conference, and even the more radical Congress on Racial Equality (Bird, 1998: 381).

In 1968, the Ford Foundation gave over a half a million dollars to the Southwest Council of La Raza and some $2.2 million for a multiyear litigation strategy of the Mexican-American Legal Defense and Education Fund. As Bird notes, "it was Bundy who pushed Ford into the contentious territory of public interest law" (1998: 390). Indeed, Bundy saw this as a consciously leftist strategy. Bird cites an internal memo from 1975 where Bundy stated that Ford's position was to seek the "redress of inequity" or a more just "distribution of the material and nonmaterial things that society prizes most" (ibid.).[14] Bundy's reformism at home was for him quite consistent with a militant cold-war stance abroad. The human rights movement was a vehicle for him to moderate his cold-war strategy abroad.

The foreign policy of the 1960s translated into the Nixon election in 1968 and the subsequent divide between Democratic doves, their opponents in the Democratic party, and the Cold Warriors in the Nixon administration. This split had important repercussions for the development of the field of human rights. The doves were quite unhappy with the Nixon involvement in the destabilizing of the Allende government and in promoting and assisting the coup that brought Pinochet to power. The Democratic doves—now soundly out of power with the 1972 election—sought to mobilize new arguments that could be used to attack the Nixon administration's involvement in Chile. The congressional mandate to take human rights into account in foreign policy was sponsored by Donald Fraser, a Minnesota congressman who had been a leading liberal protégé of Hubert Humphrey. Reacting to the revelations of the role of the CIA in the fall of Allende, he and some activist congressmen, including Father Robert Drinan, sought to "put the country on the side of angels, by using human rights as the touchstone of U.S. foreign policy." In the words of one congressman at the time, the initiative in Congress "came because we in Congress were very, very annoyed at the administration, particularly after we found out that the Nixon administration had destabilized the regime of... President Allende of Chile."

Academic idealists who had been promoting the principles of the Universal Declaration of Human Rights, and who had made some connections with Amnesty International and the International Commission of Jurists, were essential in the strategy of the congressional doves. Following an approach that was the exact counterpart of that followed by the Vicariate in Chile, they mobilized the neutral principles of the international law scholars, Amnesty, and the ICJ in a series of congressional hearings that exhibit a who's who of international law and human rights at the time (International Protection of Human Rights, 1974). These international law scholars, drawing on the postwar experience in Europe, had begun to write articles and books suggesting that the "soft law" of the Universal Declaration on

Human Rights and the U.N. Charter might come to constitute a customary law of human rights and that U.N. machinery should be reformed to allow at least some measures of enforcement. At the time, however, international human rights law was still relatively marginal—the domain of a few immigrant scholars with histories that made them especially interested in the field.[15]

Frank Newman, not traditionally an international law scholar, was a key figure in linking the academics and the Democratic doves. Newman had been the dean of the law school at the University of California at Berkeley prior to taking a sabbatical in Geneva—ostensibly to explore the administrative law of the United Nations. He became connected to the International Commission of Jurists and helped the ICJ participate in activities brought before the Council of Europe against the Greek colonels. Similarly, other scholars, such as Thomas Buergenthal, drew on the experience of the Council of Europe and the European Court of Human Rights to promote similar developments in the Inter-American Commission. The linking of these academic idealists, the few existing human rights organizations,[16] and the doves in Congress helped to build credibility and promote an expansion that related very closely to the U.S. division about such regimes as that in Chile. Just as the Chilean opposition had been able to gain some power and credibility by exchanging leftist politics for a discourse of human rights coming largely from the north, those in the north who were questioning the traditional cold-war strategies—and left reformism in the United States—could build their own positions by investing in a neutral discourse that could attack Nixon for his role in Chile and elsewhere. Success in this human rights strategy helped to persuade Jimmy Carter to make human rights rhetoric an essential part of his political campaign and subsequently his foreign policy.[17]

The development and universalization of human rights activity was then greatly accelerated by the activities of the large philanthropic organizations, especially the Ford Foundation. But in Chile, as in Brazil, the Foundation investment in human rights only came as an outgrowth of earlier investments in social science. As suggested above, the Bundy position for public interest law in the United States was not inconsistent with an aggressive cold-war stance. At the time of the Pinochet coup, in 1973, there was no way that the Ford Foundation could fund the Vicariate.

The Ford Foundation assistance in the 1960s was geared toward upgrading social science, including economics, but there was conflict—partly generational—about what this policy meant in Chile and elsewhere.[18] Contrary to the specific advice of the CIA, which strongly opposed Allende when elected in 1970, the young idealists in the Ford Foundation office in Chile decided to work with the Allende government rather than to seek to destabilize it.[19] This approach led directly to the Ford Foundation's position after the coup. As one Ford official noted, the economic survival of social science was threatened by the military government.[20] The Ford people in Chile thus naturally asked themselves, "What can we do in a repressive regime?" The Vicariate was already gaining prominence but, as stated by one of the officials of the Ford Foundation, it did not "fit our program." The Santiago office of the Ford Foundation thus recognized the need for "distance" from Pinochet, but in human rights—a term that was not so prominent then—the foundation "did not know what it ought to do."

After the first few years of the Pinochet regime, however, the question about the Vicariate and others, according to one Ford Foundation official, became, "how can we do this and not get involved in politics." Ford Foundation officials began to debate whether it was "human rights or partisan political" activity. The closer it was to "law," the more the activists in the foundation could legitimately get behind it—even if for activist political reasons. The foundation officials "tried to distinguish" politics from law in part by "getting to know the people." The impressive documentation at the Vicariate—"people could pull out empirical data"—impressed the Ford Foundation trustees when they visited Chile. They could recognize the Vicariate, in fact, according to the model of public-interest law firms that the foundation was then funding aggressively in the United States. The Vicariate was "not just people yelling and screaming," but rather was "curiously legalistic." Those who had embraced legal activism at home saw a place to develop this new strategy abroad—and to fight with legal instruments those who resisted reform domestically and in foreign policy.[21]

The Ford Foundation leaders converted to the cause of human rights, at least as represented by the relatively legalistic Vicariate. As part of that conversion, the foundation programs also began to encourage the building of "international networks that can help each other" in the domain of human rights. As a foundation official who had been in Chile stated, by the late 1970s, the "model was in place," and it "worked in Chile." The Ford Foundation had a formal program in human rights by 1977, and in 1981 Human Rights and Governance became one of the five program areas (Keck and Sikkink, 1998: 101). One of the Ford Foundation individuals who helped work out the human rights program, Peter Bell, then made human rights the centerpiece of the Inter-American Foundation, which he headed from the late 1970s until early in the 1980s (see ibid., 1998). Another, William Carmichael, became vice president of the Ford Foundation and later brought the model to South Africa, among other places (see Abel, 1996). Both later became very involved also with Human Rights Watch.

The field was growing, and the investment of the Ford Foundation and others led to much greater growth. According to Keck and Sikkink (1998: 99), the total U.S. investment in human rights organizations went from $1 million in 1977 to just over $3 million in 1982. Among the new organizations in the United States created with the help of the Ford Foundation were the Lawyers Committee for Human Rights and the International Human Rights Law Group, both formed in 1978.[22] The international human rights community, modeled on the Vicariate and

U.S. legal advocacy, also began to prosper. Events centered in the United States in the 1980s helped then to expand the global reach further while transforming the leading human rights organizations.

Competition and Professionalization on the Market of Civic Virtue

The success of the relatively activist strategy of the Ford Foundation and others in the 1960s and 1970s unleashed a domestic dynamic with profound consequences for this emerging field of human rights. The foundation and its allies became the scapegoats of a conservative counterrevolution, which mimicked Ford's strategy of mobilization of the learned world in the service of a political project.[23] They also decided that they needed to bring business principles to this effort to make government more responsive to business.

The Heritage Foundation, formed in 1973, is a key institution in this transformation. According to the director of research of the Heritage Foundation, who began there in 1977, "we had one major goal in mind: to create a think tank unlike any Washington had previously known.... One of the most important decisions we made right at the start was to run Heritage like a business. That meant identifying our market niche, creating a unique product and aggressively marketing it. ... We then redesigned Heritage's 'product line' to meet their [Capital Hill, the Executive Branch, the news media, and other conservative groups] needs. That's when we created the Heritage Backgrounder series ... a short 5,000-to 10,000-word journalistic study, rather than a book. Today, nearly every think tank produces similar studies.... The third thing we did is go out and recruit the best and brightest researchers and marketing professionals we could afford" (Heritage Foundation, 1996).[24]

The effects of this conservative strategy were contradictory. On the one hand, the development of the activism of the right worked an almost mechanical repositioning of the reformist institutions like the Ford Foundation. They moved closer to the social movements representing the disadvantaged. As against these centrifugal effects, however, the similarity of approaches that characterized the new right and the more liberal foundations helped to facilitate institutional exchanges. As we shall see, "cause lawyering" domestically and abroad was transformed by the changes in the dynamic of this field organized around state power.

Professionalization and Mediatization

The ultraconservative right, building on the successes in legitimating neoliberal economics and the campaigns of the conservative think tanks, came to power with Reagan in 1980—uniting cold-war hawks and critics of the welfare state.[25] Human Rights Watch, the leading human rights organization in the 1980s and 1990s, came out of a counterattack, as much domestic as international, against the Reagan administration. In this fight, the potential new elite linked to the organizations and strategies of the reformist and antiwar 1960s and 1970s[26] was quite prepared to mobilize their social capital of personal relations as well as the professional institutions that they controlled.[27] The space of human rights then became the stakes of a political fight between the new conservative holders of state power and a large coalition of reformers from places like the civil rights movement and the liberal foundations. Palace warriors applying their 1970s strategy continued to match quite well with their counterparts in the south, who continued to find themselves and their reformist approaches outside of political power. Both sides sought to invest in more technical and international strategies to build their own power bases. The human rights movement moved to another level.

The targets of the human rights movement in the Reagan era were the military dictatorships inherited from the Cold War and converted by the "Chicago boys" into a new religion of the market. The symbolic target was Jeane Kirkpatrick, the former Humphrey Democrat isolated by the left turn of the Democratic Party in 1972.[28] Her rationale for the support of Pinochet and the Argentine generals was that authoritarians—as distinguished from communist totalitarians—were by definition better than communists.

The forerunner of Human Rights Watch, the U.S. Helsinki Watch Committee, was initially created at the instigation of Arthur Goldberg in 1979 [29] in order to support the actions of the Helsinki monitors in the United States. An early newspaper account suggested that the committee would monitor compliance by the United States with human rights provisions in the Helsinki Accord. The group, however, found much more opportunity in taking on human rights violations abroad than trying to put more life into the civil rights and antiwar movements in the United States. The media strategies of the conservative think tanks, fortified with Chicago economics and business resources, delegitimated the reformist movements for social equity.

The Helsinki Watch Committee was transformed in 1982 into Human Rights Watch, along with a new branch termed Americas Watch. The director was Aryeh Neier, a prominent former leader of the ACLU with strong connections also to public interest law, and the early board included establishment lawyers identified with opposition to the Vietnam War. As one of the founding individuals noted, the focus was on the state at home even though the investigations were conducted abroad: "[W]e were oriented toward Washington, D.C. at the time."

This new elite of human rights involved a number of the important lawyers from the beginning, but the initiative came principally from the publishing industry. Robert Bernstein, in particular, came to Helsinki Watch through a concern that began in the early 1970s to protect the freedom of expression of Soviet and Eastern European dissidents.[30] Their work was in fact published by Random House—where Bernstein was president.

This anchor of human rights in the literary and journalistic world is not simply of anecdotal interest. It came to reinforce the strategy of "mediatization" in a new context. Earlier human rights organizations had of course relied considerably on the media, as had public interest lawyers generally, but the new context increased the importance of media strategies. This influence of the media thus weighed heavily on the choice of an organizational model. Indeed, the new geopolitical configuration that came to be inscribed durably in the structures of this field of practice can be traced to this strategy.

The new context can be traced to increases in the competition in the field of state power. As human rights organizations multiplied in number, the competition increased in the media and in the domain of philanthropy. The competition was exacerbated because the success of human rights organizations in gaining exposure in the media determined in large part their visibility, their capacity to recruit, and finally even their budget. The individual contributions made to these enterprises and, to a certain extent, their support from the foundations, were closely connected to their notoriety. In this new context, the professionals that they recruited were anxious to operate with objectives and methods that appeared to be most effective pursuant to this media-oriented strategy. They moved to the approach that was explicit also in the new conservative think tanks epitomized by the Heritage Foundation.

In the same way that Amnesty International constructed its identity in opposition to the politicized human rights organizations of the early Cold War, the new organizations for the protection of human rights—developed after the Helsinki Accords—were defined in relation to what they perceived as limits, even lacunae, in Amnesty's type of mass mobilization. According to a longtime participant in Human Rights Watch, "I think where Human Rights Watch has been particularly successful is in moving to . . . the next step [from Amnesty]. First in terms of using the press as a major tool on behalf of human rights, and we pride ourselves in being able to present human rights information in a way that is interesting to the press, and that is a regularly evolving process—and one that requires knowing what journalists revere as pushing the envelope and interesting to the readers and beyond what they could have done on their own so that they will be inclined to incorporate this information." Further, drawing on foundation support, HRW emphasized a flexible and professional staff. "Human Rights Watch, I think, consciously saw Amnesty as a model, tried to take the best of what Amnesty had in terms of its accuracy, it's reporting, it's impartiality, but felt that Amnesty had a too limited mandate and moved too slowly and that they could do it, you know, sort of more quickly."

For the promoters of these structures, who were often also former activists within Amnesty, Amnesty was seen as a model to "go beyond." The new structures like Human Rights Watch sought to be lighter in order to have the power to invest more easily in new and more political and policy-oriented terrains, such as humanitarian law[31]—and to develop new strategies and modes of action like trade sanctions or boycott campaigns.[32] They also emphasized their technical skills and links to cutting-edge law.[33] Indeed, the media emphasis and exacerbated competition of the field made it increasingly important to use celebrities to gain attention to particular causes and concerns. While the new breed of activist organizations could act with commando-like swiftness, the problem was that they were also dependent on the philanthropic foundations.[34]

Within the emerging field of international human rights, as in other domains, the competition permitted this space of practice to develop itself and to professionalize under the impulse of policy entrepreneurs. The adversarial marketing that helped the conservative think tanks attack the foundations and their strategy of gradual reformism matched perfectly with the new generation of human rights organizations epitomized by HRW. The human rights field, in particular, prospered enormously in the 1980s from the widely reported debates between Reagan administration officials, especially Elliot Abrams, and human rights advocates such as Aryeh Neier and Michael Posner.[35] The media success on both sides of these debates ensured that, in the words of a *New York Times* editor, "the American public has made it fairly clear that it sees human rights as an absolute good—a universal aspiration to be pursued for its own sake..." (Jacoby, 1986). The debates also forced the human rights movement to "balance" their reporting in terms of the countries that were looked at,[36] and to upgrade the quality of the work that was produced.[37] The adversarial media campaign organized around human rights also gave legitimacy and importance to law and to lawyers in debates around foreign policy. Neier and Abrams argued both about facts and about the legal requirements.[38] The expertise of the new generation of lawyers gained a more prominent place (along with many journalists as well).[39]

The human rights field gained a certain autonomy in relation to these and similar debates, which brought both the conservatives and the relatively liberal activists to occupy the same field. It was also legalized to a much greater extent, and the leading human rights organizations began to recruit increasingly from the most elite law schools—which cemented their relationships through human rights programs and internships.[40] One indicator of the success of this field is the circulation of individuals. There is mobility within the human rights community,[41] between the human rights community and the foundations that support it, and between the elite human rights organizations and the legal academy.

Another indicator of the development of the field is the tendency to use the existing human rights community to evaluate other potential human rights organizations. According to a senior Human Rights Watch official, "The funders will ask us, we would like to help in this or that country, you know 'who would you recommend?' It's sort of a practical or pragmatic level, we help with... I mean at times we fund... we're not funding organizations but we'll steer groups to funders. We also try to help through training because and it could be training in anything from 'how do you conduct an investigation?' to 'how do you administer a human rights organization?' to 'how do you operate in Brussels?' or 'how do you operate in Geneva?' "

From the perspective of the late 1980s in Chile and somewhat earlier elsewhere in Latin America, snapshots gave reason for cause lawyers to be optimistic. The human rights movement gained considerable power through its link to the north, to what was now seen as "law" in the international center of power, and to the simultaneous and closely related de-legitimation of the politics, if not the economics, of the authoritarian states. Young law graduates in the United States, Chile, and elsewhere were attracted to this idealistic politics of law, suggesting a convergence toward U.S.-style cause lawyering for progressive causes everywhere. It is true, of course, that there was a structural inequality built into the emerging transnational field. The strongest NGOs were in the United States, and U.S. foundation funding was as crucial to global cause lawyering as it was to public interest law in the United States. The different histories and structures of power, however, then produced quite a strong divergence in this field.

A Second Stage: Southern Institutional Depletion and the Human Rights Brain Drain

The human rights strategy worked very well in the transitions to democracy in Argentina, Brazil, Chile, and even Mexico, where elections became much more contested and legitimate. The opposition to Pinochet in Chile, for example, succeeded in promoting an open election in the late 1980s because the Reagan administration had converted to the idea that democratization was necessary to legitimate the economic changes that had taken place. At that point, there was still a nice structural identity between the human rights organizations attacking Pinochet in Chile and counterparts in the north who were constantly putting pressure on the Reagan administration to promote the respect of human rights. Both sides thrived.

Once the actors in the human rights movement succeeded in gaining power in Chile and elsewhere, however, they abandoned institutions like the Vicariate in order to invest in the new state. That is to say, they returned to their more traditional strategies as "power lawyers" on a political track. The human rights movement hardly exists anymore in Chile in the sense of a movement seeking to invest in law in support of progressive politics against the state. The same conclusion in general could be reached for Argentina, Brazil, and Mexico. For example, Raul Alfonsin in Argentina—the first president after the military dictatorship—came from human rights to elite party politics and the institutions of the state. In all the countries we studied, in fact, the investment of the first generation in human rights provided an excellent base for political activity after the transition. In both Argentina and Chile, for example, studies of NGOs that were completed recently both emphasized the depletion and transformation of the NGO community after the change in politics (Bebbington and Bebbington, 1997; Thompson, 1994).[42] This is not just a matter of a revolving door. What was left behind was not replenished by a new generation eager to mimic the careers of their predecessors. The reason is that the particular conjuncture that united moral activism with law through the church and international actors did not continue. The newly created institutional structures that built the human rights NGOs unraveled, revealing the structures that had been in place prior to the 1970s.

Moral investment by lawyers in politics and law is still not recognized and validated as a viable career strategy in Chile and probably outside the United States more generally. The generation that invested in international human rights in the 1970s and 1980s had few other options, and their relatively risky investments were ultimately rewarded. For those who came later, however, the situation was different. In Chile and also the other countries we studied, the best-credentialed and most ambitious students in law do not invest in a professional moral strategy.[43] Some legal investment may be convertible into local politics, but it does not translate into local professional distinction and credibility. The situation was different when the only political space for a relatively well-connected political group was through international alliances legitimated through law. In the United States, in contrast, an important fraction of the best students will invest in public interest careers that gain them high status and open up professional options. Outside the United States, however, neither the law faculties, the courts, nor the law firms provide any real recognition of moral investment in the law. The moral dimension worked for a time because of the particular circumstances of the 1970s and 1980s, but the U.S. model of legal idealism did not gain a secure base.

In contrast, another relatively recent import that draws on a U.S. model is thriving. Building on a long legal tradition of serving foreign interests and receiving excellent remuneration for doing so, business law firms have become well institutionalized. They have become well integrated into the international market for legal services and U.S.-style legal practices. Indeed, it is increasingly a requirement for employment in business firms in Latin America that lawyers receive a graduate degree in the United States—preferably combined with a U.S. apprenticeship in international legal practice. Transitions to democracy helped to build the position of these corporate lawyers who combine their foreign-based expertise with local connections to business and political power.[44]

Nevertheless, local organizations of human rights, once formed, can continue to exist in the south even if they no longer resemble what they represented earlier. Many, for example, have converted to causes and issues such as the control of crime or the prevention of violence against women. They are much more outposts of international development assistance than activist legal institutions challenging the state. This pattern may of course change.

There may also be some exceptions in the south involving institutions that continue to follow the approach of moral investment in law against the state. In Brazil, for example, Viva Rio is one example of a mix between social movements, religion, politics, and law. Its activities, which grew out of the human rights movement, focus on crime, hunger, and police violence in Rio de Janeiro, and it draws on elite lawyers as well as social activists. In Chile, activities centered at the University of Diego Portales, a private university originally designed to produce business lawyers, continue to emphasize human rights and public interest law. Argentina, in particular, seems to offer the most promise for cause lawyering, since there is a long tradition of professionals investing in institutions and organizations outside the state. The tradition—inspired largely in order to protect professionals from the purges that plagued Argentina and made it highly dangerous to invest in the state—made it difficult for Argentina to develop an effective state, but it also gave Argentine professionals an orientation that suited the construction of organizations around the state. A number of individuals with close ties to Yale have sought to reproduce public interest law in Argentina. Such entities as Poder Ciudadano and a recent and related entity termed the Association for Civil Rights (Associacion por los Derechos Civiles–ADC), which is dedicated to the protection of civil liberties in Argentina and funded primarily by the Ford Foundation, provide examples. Argentine history has produced an internationalized setting that may be particularly conducive to the creation of internationally oriented NGOs outside of the state. The "dollarized" economy in Argentina may translate also into a dollarized state.

In contrast to the general pattern in the south, the leading international human rights organizations in the United States could convert to power lawyering, U.S.-style, without missing a beat. Instead of abandoning their investment in legal expertise to join political parties and movements, human rights organizations continue to thrive by investing in the cutting edges of U.S. foreign policy. As with power corporate lawyers in Washington, D.C., some go into the government on the basis of their experience and expertise, but the legal bases continue to thrive through their symbiotic relationship with the state.

Two further developments relate to the structural asymmetry of the present period. First, those who have continued to invest in the field of human rights from the south have tended to go abroad, where their expertise and investment in international human rights remains validated and recognized. One example is Jose Vivenco of Chile, who is one of the key figures today in Americas Watch and in activities before the Inter-American Commission and Court of Human Rights. The institutions located in the United States or close to the U.S. field of power provide places where moral investment in the law continues to be valued. Similarly, Jose Zalaquett, after returning to Chile and working on the Truth Commission, spends much of his time working with international NGOs on similar issues in other countries. Roberto Garreton, the leader of the legal department of the Vicariate for most of the Pinochet period, first went into the government as Ambassador of Human Rights and now is well known for his international activities as Special Rapporteur for the United Nations on the situation of human rights in Zaire.[45]

This brain drain from the south to the north helps to legitimate the international human rights organizations based in the north. The northern organizations can modify their approaches to take into account the perspectives of those who come from the south while further building their leadership in the international movement.

Conclusions

The convergence of strategies and structural positions between an establishment out of power in Chile and the United States (and other countries as well) built a transnational field of human rights. In order to fight in their own palace wars, each side helped to convert some of its power into law. That investment paid off personally and professionally when it forced the Reagan administration and even the Pinochet administration to fight in terms of the discourse of human rights. Pinochet submitted to elections and gave up power. The Chilean example was an especially important one, but other countries drew on it and replicated the same kinds of results. Cause lawyers fought together and competed to build networks and this relatively autonomous field.

The model of cause lawyering promoted by the Ford Foundation in the north and the Vicariate in the south, however, did not thrive equally in both places after the supporters of the authoritarian states left power. The leading organizations of the north continue to attract top recruits, compete aggressively for attention and influence, and play a strong role in foreign relations on their own terms and through the revolving door of Washington politics. In contrast, the legal activists of the south either went directly into politics, where legal strategies are relatively unimportant (and there are no remaining cause-lawyering groups out of power to push legal strategies), or they continued to stay in the field of human rights by joining the major organizations centered in the United States. Cause lawyering is not thriving in these settings.

Our microhistories mainly demonstrate the importance of structural factors in determining how innovations such as cause lawyering for human rights get invented and legitimated in different ways in different places. For the purpose of this chapter, however, we can offer three points that we think must be considered by those who adopt the stance of promoting a progressive politics outside the United States through investment in cause lawyering.

First, the field of human rights was constructed out of palace wars in the north and south, including especially those related to the Cold War, and U.S. politics were therefore crucial. The major human rights groups gained their substantive agendas and their tactics not simply through the adoption of "pure law" and "pure enforcement," but rather through media strategies designed to gain influence *in Washington*, first against Reagan and more recently to guide Clinton. Just as the field of international commercial arbitration builds its autonomy close to business power and U.S. litigation, the field of international human rights has a tilt toward U.S. state power. It is an autonomy constructed to be consistent with U.S. foreign policy, even if often disagreeing with particular details (including how to fight the Cold War). We do not have space to elaborate on this point, but we caution promoters of transnational cause lawyering to investigate critically the norms that gain legitimacy, funding, and media attention in the places that count.

Second, given the relative lack of success of the public interest law model of cause lawyering outside of the United States, despite its seeming great promise in the 1980s, it may be necessary to question whether "innovative legal services" should be privileged as a political strategy outside the United States. For the time being, at least, legal politics tends to come more with politics than law. Law graduates may use their networks to move into politics, but they do not invest much in the autonomy of the law in state governance. It is a different approach than trying to use the relative autonomy of the law and legal institutions to promote change, whether through courts, legal scholarship, media strategies, or even social movements in which legal strategies are central. To overstate the difference, those who seek to speak for marginal groups in the United States can gain professional stature and influence. There is a place in law for this investment in idealism. Those who do the same in Chile may gain political stature and influence, but they will not gain many professional dividends from a combination of idealism and technical legal skills and arguments on behalf of those with little power. Internationalization, as we have suggested before, is breaking down categories and dichotomies, including this one between idealistic lawyers who gain legitimacy and influence through politics and those who do so more through law, but promoters of cause lawyering might be more specific in distinguishing U.S. models from approaches that are more salient elsewhere.

Finally, the relative weakness of cause lawyering in the south, coupled with the power and potential biases of the leading organizations in the north, counsels caution in examining campaigns that seem to involve north-south partnerships to promote the "modern politics" of cause lawyering and public-interest law.

Notes

1. The emphasis on biography should not be construed as acceptance of the "truth" of individual stories. It is not simply a matter of finding out a personal history for its own sake but, rather, to see conflicts and the ways in which particular positions relate to other positions in the field. An individual can act as a political scientist in one context, for example, and a lawyer in another; a spokesperson for "Asian values" in one context, a booster of the "rule of law" in another. The international arena multiplies the possibilities for double strategies of smugglers, compradors, and brokers, since there are many potential uncertainties and mistranslations surrounding individual positions. This confusion, indeed, helps make international strategies attractive as a way to build national careers.

2. With the help of the foundations—especially the Ford Foundation—in both funding and building networks, the model became influential in numerous countries around the world. As our own research also shows, there were quite similar kinds of developments in Argentina, Brazil, and Mexico (Dezalay and Garth, forthcoming). The success in Chile helped give legitimacy to the particular model, which then could be exported elsewhere. Of course, where and how it took root depended on local circumstances. The pattern that we describe in detail for Chile and to some extent in the other Latin American countries is thus important for developing the model and indicative of subsequent developments that we document here and that we can also show for the other Latin American countries we studied. We suggest that researchers will find similar origins and later developments in other places where human rights cause lawyering has developed, but we have done no detailed research on this point.

3. According to Aryeh Neier in 1987, "The Vicariate is the flagship of human rights groups in Latin America, the class act" (Graham, 1989: G12).

4. Quotations are from individuals we personally interviewed in the 1997–99 period.

5. The Peace Committee was able to make some use of the courts' passive nature. The courts, seeking to remain apart from political developments, would simply send a note to the government when a petition was filed. The note would signal the filing of a petition alleging the taking of a person. If the government replied, the petitioning parties knew that there was "no risk of death." But if they "never heard" from the government, they would "pull the alarm." The legal strategies therefore helped at least to shape the extralegal strategies.

6. It is partly a matter of perspective, of course. There was an emerging discourse found in a few places and among some academics influenced especially by Europe. But there was no active and institutionalized movement relatively autonomous from cold-war politics.

7. Amnesty was created in part as a reaction to the cold-war politics closely connected to the main organizations existing under the human rights banner in the 1950s—the International Association of Democratic Jurists, linked to Communism and centered in Brussels, and the International Commission of Jurists, funded covertly by the CIA and located in Geneva (Tolley, 1994).

8. In 1980 the award went to Adolfo Perez Esquivel, an Argentine human rights activist.

9. According to someone who participated in the changes after 1976, "I mean when I started in '76, there were probably 40 people at the whole secretariat. A lot of the researchers were people that, you know, had sort of walked in the office and said, 'Is there something I can do?' " By 1983 the number was 200, "and it was becoming increasingly professionalized and it was growing and it was under scrutiny as never before."

10. The growth then accelerated, largely through the influx of Americans. The number of members tripled to some 400,000 members from 1985 to 1989. In 1991, after thirty years, Amnesty International had 1 million members (half from the United States), a budget of 11 million pounds (against $23 million for Amnesty International–U.S.), and a staff of 260. The staff, furthermore, was recognized as one of the essential sources of expertise in matters of international human rights—and therefore one of the privileged places to acquire competence in human rights. There were some 500 candidates for every position that was open (Wade, 1995; see also Page, 1992).

11. Emblematic of the foreign-policy establishment is, of course, John McCloy. McCloy's career reveals perfectly the links between state and nonstate in this group. He pursued a strategy of a double game that is emblematic of these careers. "At one time or another, he was an assistant secretary of war, president of the World Bank, high commissioner to occupied Germany, chairman of Chase Manhattan Bank, chairman of the Ford Foundation,

chairman of the Council of Foreign Relations, and chairman of the President's Advisory Committee on Arms Control and Disarmament. He was legal counsel to all 'Seven Sister' oil companies, a board director for a dozen of America's top corporations, and a private, unofficial adviser to most of the presidents in the twentieth century.... He had no constituency—except for his ties to Rockefeller family interests on Wall Street—and even in this case, for most of his career, he managed to make it seem that he was always able to rise above these private interests in order to discern the public interest" (Bird, 1992: 18–20).

12. The climate of consensus among notables that facilitated this division of tasks is well illustrated by the movements of personnel. David Rockefeller, for example, the president of the Council of Foreign Relations, proposed to his friend Allen Dulles that Dulles became the president of the Ford Foundation if he would forego his ambitions to be the director of the CIA (Grose, 1994: 336). Richard Bissell went from the Ford Foundation to covert operations in the CIA, and Dean Rusk went from the head of the Rockefeller Foundation to become Kennedy's secretary of state. David Rockefeller was also active in the 1950s and 1960s in the Bilderberg Conference, along with many European and U.S. leaders. These connections are well documented also in Kai Bird's recent biography of the Bundys (1998).

13. A descendant of the Lowell family whose father was a prominent lawyer and key aid to Henry Stimson, Bundy was the dean of Harvard's College of Arts and Sciences prior to moving into the Kennedy administration as the most visible of Kennedy's "best and brightest."

14. The Ford Foundation's dramatic domestic role was evident in a survey by the council for Public Interest Law, created initially by the Ford Foundation, of 86 "public interest law" programs in 1975. The council found that 70 percent were established from 1969 to 1974 (including the National Resources Defense Council, the Environmental Defense Fund, the Center for Law and Social Policy). Of some $61 million given by foundations in the period 1969–75 to these groups, the Ford Foundation was responsible for a little more than half (Council for Public Interest Law, 1976: 85, D-15, D-16. The 86 centers employed 589 salaried attorneys in 1975 (1976: 82).

15. The first casebook on international human rights was published in 1973 by Louis Sohn and Thomas Buergenthal, both of whom had been refugees from the Nazis. Oscar Schachter, another important figure in these developments, reported that as late as 1968, when he was the president of the American Society of International Law, Dean Acheson severely criticized scholars who, he said, were trying to use international law to promote their ideals rather than to restate precisely what the law was.

16. Including also the International League for the Rights of Man.

17. The Carter approach is seen especially in some of the activities in the United Nations (see Guest, 1990). At the time, however, the field was not developed to the extent where Carter was really held accountable to a community of human rights organizations and activists. Only after the 1980s did the law of human rights gain a relatively prominent role in foreign policy—still with limits, of course.

18. Several of the same actors had earlier been involved in Brazil, where there was also conflict about funding social scientists associated with the left. Despite the wishes of the CIA and the diplomats assigned to Brazil, the Ford Foundation funded first Bolivar Lamounier and then Fernando Henrique Cardoso—allowing Cardoso to remain in Brazil as part of an independent think tank funded from abroad.

19. Describing the two generations at the Ford Foundation, the 1950s and early 1960s, one former official said they were concerned with "economics and development as economists conceived of it" during that period. In contrast, "[s]everal of the younger generation had Peace Corps experience and they were not economists by and large. Their formal train-

ing was in some cases in law and in other cases in the noneconomic social sciences. And these people were much quicker to move into social justice."

20. The support of human rights grew out of what one former Ford Foundation official described as "a natural transition from previous times, you know before the crisis.... [We were] protecting our investments, past investments." The independent centers for research that Ford funded after the coup led to the support of human rights organizations that were both linked and analogous in their approaches. As another former official stated, the initial beneficiaries in the mid-1960s were "mostly the academic elites. We were helping those people who were under threat of life or at least livelihood get out of the country and things like that. So, in a certain sense, that was a human rights–oriented or at least influenced kind of activity. We began to broaden that in the Brazilian context, and then we went squarely into supporting groups that would have to be called human rights groups in the Chile post-1973 period."

21. James Gardner's *Legal Imperialism*, published in 1980, reveals this transition perfectly. Gardner, a Ford Foundation official during this period, was heavily critical of policies that tried to train lawyers to serve in the cause of development. While the book is typically read as an attack on the effort to export U.S. legal approaches to Latin America, it is more accurate to see the book as an effort to kill law and development in the name of legal activism—again largely U.S. style—against the authoritarian states of Argentina, Brazil, and Chile.

22. This new competition was also a lever for a transformation of Amnesty International. Thus, following the development of more specialized organizations on the terrain of law, such as the Lawyers Committee for Human Rights, Amnesty International upgraded its legal department by hiring as the new leader a lawyer who had studied human rights with Father Drinan at Georgetown and had served his apprenticeship at the Lawyers Committee.

23. This mimicry is captured in an account of the history of the conservative movement. As many authors have noted, the conservative movement was very weak in the 1960s, as evidenced by the landslide defeat of Barry Goldwater in 1964. The universities, the foundations, and the establishment were all relatively reformist in orientation. The split of the establishment around issues of foreign policy provided new opportunities for the conservatives. Paul Weyrich, one of the founders and the first president of the Heritage Foundation, created in 1973, attended "a civil rights strategy meeting" as a member of the staff of a Republican senator in 1969. " 'There before my eyes was unveiled how the other side operated,' he says. 'It was the single most important meeting I have attended in my political lifetime.' The meeting drew together disparate groups from the Left—among them, the Brookings Institution, the liberal National Committee for an Effective Congress, the ACLU—to discuss how to pool their discrete resources into an effort to torpedo a Nixon Administration housing initiative. Weyrich left the meeting a right-wing version of the Ancient Mariner. 'Nobody wanted to see me coming from that time after because [to] everybody I met I said, "You've got to understand this is how they operate. And we don't have anything like that' " (Lowry, 1995). He and a small group of friends finally found funding from Joseph Coors. The American Enterprise Institute—another prominent think tank of the right—was founded much earlier, in 1943. A description of the AEI in 1995 describes it as having "twice as much history and half the funding as Heritage but prides itself on original research and the eminence of its senior scholars" (Burton, 1995).

24. James Pierson, executive director of the Olin Foundation, which invested substantially in "law and economics" and in the right-wing think tanks, stated, "We invested at the top of society, in Washington think tanks and the best universities, and the idea is this would have a much larger impact because they were influential places" (People for the American

Way, 1996: 8). Michael Joyce of the Lynde and Harry Bradley Foundation, another key funder of the right, stated, "Elite opinion is formed in America at the top of a pyramid. ... [E]lite institutions [are] important in the shaping of public policy" (ibid., 12).

25. This process was evident even as the Reagan administration took office. Aryeh Neier was quoted in the *New Republic* as saying that Americas Watch "was founded in reaction to the arrival of the Reagan administration. 'Those of us who created Helsinki Watch,' he said, felt that it [the Reagan administration] 'threatened to undercut Helsinki Watch because it politicized the issue of human rights in the Soviet Union.' When Jeane Kirkpatrick—who had been a Democrat until the split of the Democrats in the late 1960s—suggested treating friendly authoritarian regimes more charitably than hostile totalitarian ones, 'We felt that the only way we could be credible in dealing with human rights in the Soviet Union, and not subject to the charge of waging a cold war attack, was if we were even handed and were concerned with human rights abuses in friendly authoritarian countries" (Kondracke, 1988).

26. In fact, in several important respects, it bolstered the declining domestic political fortunes of the lawyers associated with the civil rights movement, which was losing momentum in the United States in the new era of conservatism. According to one law professor who became active in human rights in the late 1970s, "I did all sorts of First Amendment work and a lot of other sorts of cases. But as the '70s wore on, the tide began to turn against us and we started to repeat ourselves and I don't know. I just got tired of it. And, so I was offered this job here teaching ... after the middle '70s, ... about the time I started teaching, international human rights became a hot issue about which I knew absolutely nothing. I mean I didn't even know what the documents were that set forth the rights, initially. But, as far as how people get into international human rights work. One of the ways is that people who have been mixed up in civil rights, you know, public interest people have tended to syphon into human rights." According to another individual who joined Amnesty in the mid-1970s, "Now, you know, it was a time when ... both the civil rights movement and the anti-war movement had hit rough times and largely disappeared and I was fortunate that at that time I got some people who had also been very active in the anti-war movement who had gotten involved with Amnesty International." Similarly, the comments of Jerome Shestack about the Lawyers Committee for International Human Rights are instructive: "In 1976, towards the end of '76, '77, I thought that lawyers were not really involved in international human rights the way they should be and the way they had become involved in the civil rights movement. So, together with John Carey, who [had been] ... President of the International League of Human Rights or had just left that office (I was then president), we started to involve lawyers in human rights. There was at that time a group called Law Associates or Associates in New York, lawyers dedicated to do pro bono work. And I enlisted them in the cause and formed the Lawyers Committee for International Human Rights as a subsidiary of the International League for Human Rights. I became the first chair of that and asked Carey Bogan to be my co-chair. Carey Bogan had been chair of the Section of Individual Rights of the ABA." Michael Posner, the first director, "had tried unsuccessfully for jobs with Ralph Nader and the American Civil Liberties Union" (Singer, 1987: 7). Aryeh Neier, who became the leader of Human Rights Watch, had been the director of the ACLU in the 1970s. The ACLU underwent a substantial decline in the late 1970s, from 270,000 members in 1974 to 185,000 in 1978 (Garey, 1998: 177).

27. The chairman of the U.S. Helsinki Watch Committee was Robert Bernstein, the president of Random House and formerly the president of the Association of American Publishers. He had earlier organized a group to support freedom of expression in Eastern Europe and the USSR. The two other officers, Orville Schell and Adrian DeWind, were partners in leading Wall Street law firms and had been or were at the time president of the

New York City Bar. The latter's career includes also serving as the chair of the Natural Resources Defense Council, one of the most active NGOs in the domain of the environment. Schell was also a member of the select Council for Public Interest Law funded by the Ford Foundation in the mid-1970s. Along with this group associated with Helsinki Watch were presidents of major universities, including Chicago, MIT, and Columbia; leaders of great banks, including Lazard Freres and Salomon Brothers; and also representatives of the literary world, including the authors E. L. Doctorow, Toni Morrison, and Robert Penn Warren, as well as well-known editors and literary critics.

28. "After the 1972 Democratic convention they found themselves shut out of the decision-making process, and formed the Coalition for a Democratic Majority that included Humphrey, Henry Jackson, Norman Podhoretz and his wife Midge Decter, Michael Novak, Austin Ranney, Daniel Moynihan, Ben Wattenberg, Kirkpatrick and others who sought to reclaim the party from the McGovernites. The group was characterized as neoconservative" (Conaway, 1981). Kirkpatrick became affiliated with the American Enterprise Institute and maintained close ties to *Commentary*, the leading neoconservative publication. Moynihan began his political career working for Averill Harriman, when Harriman was governor of New York in the early 1950s.

29. This ambassador-at-large for President Carter was the key figure in taking the Helsinki Accords negotiated under the Republican administration, which contained a relatively unknown "basket" on human rights, into a major public forum to attack the treatment of dissidents who had used the language of the accords to organize and legitimate oppositional activities. He asked Bernstein and his group to become involved in Helsinki monitoring. Goldberg came from a poor family and built his career on his representation of labor. He was general counsel for the steelworkers union for many years and helped engineer the merger between the AFL and the CIO. His negotiating ability on behalf of the unions helped keep peace in the unions, and he was even credited with delivering the blue-collar vote to Kennedy, who rewarded him with the position of secretary of labor and later associate justice of the Supreme Court and ambassador to the United Nations. He resigned over his opposition to the Vietnam War. He joined the Wall Street establishment briefly as a partner at Paul Weiss. Among other activities, he had also been a president of the American Jewish Committee in 1968–1969.

30. Especially with the creation in 1973 of the International Freedom to Publish Group within the Association of American Publishers.

31. Human Rights Watch thus reportedly relied on Theodor Meron of NYU Law School and Robert Goldman at American University: "[T]hey introduced us to the laws of war. They guided us through the complex set of commandments and got us comfortable in dealing with something that was really not considered a human rights issue."

32. According to a HRW leader, "You have to be aggressive and innovative.... You have to find new avenues for pressure, like trade sanctions." Similarly, "we have always been willing to innovate and to be result oriented. And while on the one hand we abide very strictly by certain principles of objectivity, of impartiality in our fact-finding, and we also try to apply what are not impartial standards, but are internationally accepted standards of human rights.... [W]ithin that framework we try to be as creative and as aggressive as possible in finding avenues to put pressure on these governments."

33. In Human Rights Watch, for example, "in the beginning we were very careful about having sort of a list of advisory committee members who were very prominent people; who could open doors for us. And so that kind of personal diplomacy built on sort of pre-existing relationships was much more important in the early years. As time went on we didn't need others to create access for us. It came both through respect for

our work and also through respect for the fact that we were going to be able to get to the press. I mean it was clear that we had credibility with the press. And so policymakers understood that they ignored us at their peril. And so it was ... as time goes on the work, more and more, had spoken for itself ... that kind of derivative access" is "less important now."

34. The Ford Foundation gave Helsinki Watch its first $500,000 in 1978 (Kondracke, 1988). Other major funding sources in the 1980s were the MacArthur Foundation, the Revson Foundation, the J. M. Kaplan Foundation, and George Soros, who ultimately hired Aryeh Neier to head his own foundation.

35. An article in the *New Republic* noted that, "As combatants go, you could not ask for a better match—in terms of intelligence, assurance, activism, sometimes savage partisanship, and argumentative skills, than Abrams and Neier" (Kondracke, 1988). From an insider's perspective, "Americas Watch ... was designed to show that we were going to apply the same standards not only to the communist governments that had been the subject of Helsinki Watch but also to the right-wing governments that were subject of Americas Watch in Latin America. And that movement into head-on confrontation with the administration in Washington over its human rights policy, be it supporting the Salvadoran regimes, supporting the Contras in Nicaragua, you know, tolerating Pinochet in Chile or the Junta in Argentina, that very adversarial relationship was very interesting to the press and we found that the argument ... because the Reagan administration couldn't say human rights are irrelevant or 'we don't mind if we're supporting human rights abusers.' They tended to try to apologize for and defend the human rights records of these very repressive right-wing governments and they did it by lying about the facts. And so we ... that sort of pushed us into our methodology which was to be absolutely certain that we got our facts right and it forced us to be much more sophisticated, to go out into the field in the middle of the war zone and get the firsthand witnesses who can reliably tell you what happened and then to put that information out in a way that could affect the policy debates in Washington about whether to continue funding the Contras or whether to cut off aid to the Salvadoran government."

36. They had been "skittish" about trying to monitor "closed" countries, but they "began to figure how to crack the walls" using "refugee testimony" and other new tactics. Ultimately, according to one activist, this was a "positive effect."

37. According to Jacoby (1986: 1082), "[T]he human rights community claims that its factual disputes with Abrams—generally about the extent of abuses and who exactly was responsible—have on the whole had a beneficial effect, encouraging both the Administration and its critics to upgrade their reporting efforts. Monitoring groups that used to issue skimpy flyers, designed merely to draw attention to an offending country, now publish lengthy, detailed reports.... They also time their studies carefully to coincide with congressional decisions and regularly revise them to keep abreast of events." In the words of this *New York Times* editor, this "public disputation" on many occasions "seemed to serve a useful purpose, conferring new legitimacy on human rights issues and providing the noisy background clamor—the evidence of domestic American concern—that was often needed to give some meaning to the Administration's quiet diplomacy" (ibid.). When a quieter individual succeeded Abrams, "activists worry that human rights may suffer in the long run from a lack of publicity" (ibid.).

38. Ehrman provides a fascinating account of how Elliot Abrams used human rights as a platform to assert the importance of law and his own importance with respect to Jeane Kirkpatrick and the Reagan administration (1995: 155–62). Abrams's campaign on the terrain on law was successful enough to lead the administration to invest in democracy more generally, including the creation of the National Endowment for Democracy in 1983 (1995: 163).

The revival of what can be termed a new law and development in Washington owes much to this revival of interest in law as a tool of foreign policy in the 1980s (see also Carothers, 1991; 1998).

39. As a lawyer in Human Rights Watch stated, "[T]he goal is to try to enforce the law without a legal system in any traditional sense. If you have a functioning legal system you can call on organizations that look more like the ACLU, where there is a prominent role for lawyers. But most of the countries where we work are... have much more rudimentary if any legal systems and so the challenge of the human rights movement is to create surrogate forms of protection pending the establishment of legally based rights, and the process of doing that doesn't require a law degree. I mean, a law degree is very helpful, but if you look at... our employees, maybe a third of them are lawyers but the rest are journalists, they are regional experts."

40. As our main informant at Human Rights Watch thus noted, "We get the top people from the top law schools and the top every other school."

41. "We get a lot of people who come to Human Rights Watch who've worked for another human rights group."

42. "With the end of the military dictatorship in 1990, it soon became difficult for NGOs to justify their existence in the ways that they had previously done so. They were now operating in a democracy in which political resistance per se was not sufficient to justify supporting NGOs.... If this wasn't hard enough, the NGOs now had to compete with the state. This was a democracy whose public institutions became new homes to people who previously worked in the NGO sector.... [T]he state gained the confidence of donors who had previously channeled funds to NGOs. It also slowly became quite critical of NGOs. External funding to NGOs began to fall and has continued to do so" (Bebbington and Bebbington, 1997: pt. 3).

43. It would thus be more likely that the law graduate would move into politics or political parties and play down any investment in technical law.

44. On the basis of relatively limited data, we can suggest that these business lawyers may gradually be moving toward greater investment in human rights and moral legitimacy. This phenomenon is especially evident in Mexico, where business lawyers from traditional elite families have used international human rights strategies focusing on elections to move back into political power. They have gained a credibility and international legitimacy that has allowed them to cross a boundary that existed since the Mexican Revolution early in the century. They followed the path of their counterparts in the United States to bridge the divide between the political elite and the business elite. Lawyers who return from the United States can be seen to be building their careers in part through activities that could be linked to human rights, the environment, or other social causes. As with respect to the progressive-era lawyers in the United States, however, this corporate noblesse oblige does not translate to professional rewards for those who might be considered cause lawyers. Business lawyering is thriving, with some quite limited investment in causes such as human rights. But human rights or cause lawyering faces much more difficult obstacles.

45. From Brazil, Paulo Sergio Pinheiro, one of the key figures in human rights remaining outside the government, was the Special Rapporteur on the situation of human rights in Burundi.

References

Abel, Richard (1995). *Politics by Other Means: Law in the Struggle Against Apartheid, 1980–1994*. New York: Routledge.

Bebbington, Denise, and Anthony Bebbington (1997). *Evaluating the Impact of Chilean NGOs: Evaluation and the Dilemmas of Democracy.* Boulder, Colo.: Institute of Behavioral Science.

Bird, Kai (1992). *The Chairman: John J. McCloy, the Making of the American Establishment.* New York: Simon and Schuster.

––––– (1998). *The Color of Truth: McGeorge Bundy and William Bundy: Brothers in Arms.* New York: Simon and Schuster.

Bourdieu, Pierre, and Loïc J. D. Wacquant (1992). *An Invitation to Reflexive Sociology.* Chicago: University of Chicago Press.

Brysk, Alison (1994). *The Politics of Human Rights in Argentina: Protest, Change, and Democratization.* Stanford, Calif.: Stanford University Press.

Burton, Douglas (1995). "To Win the Battle of Ideas, Send in the Conservative Think Tanks," *Insight on the News* (March 6).

Carothers, Thomas (1991). *In the Name of Democracy: U.S. Policy toward Latin America in the Reagan Years.* Berkeley: University of California Press.

––––– (1998). "The Rule of Law Revival," 77:2 *Foreign Affairs,* 95–106.

Conaway, James (1981). "Jeane Kirkpatrick: The Ambassador from 'Commentary Magazine.'" *Washington Post Magazine* (November 1), 11.

Council for Public Interest Law (1976). *Balancing the Scales of Justice: Financing Public Interest Law in America.* Washington, D.C.: Council for Public Interest Law.

Dezalay, Yves, and Bryant Garth (1996). *Dealing in Virtue: International Commercial Arbitration and the Construction of a Transnational Legal Order.* Chicago: University of Chicago Press.

––––– (forthcoming). *The Internationalization of Palace Wars: Lawyers, Economists, and International Restructuring of the State.* Chicago: University of Chicago Press.

Ehrman, John (1995). *The Rise of Neoconservatism: Intellectuals and Foreign Affairs, 1945–1994.* New Haven, Conn.: Yale University Press.

Gardner, James (1980). *Legal Imperialism: American Lawyers and Foreign Aid in Latin America.* Madison: University of Wisconsin Press.

Garey, Diane (1998). *Defending Everybody: A History of the American Civil Liberties Union.* New York: TV Books.

Gordon, Robert (1984). "The Ideal and the Actual in the Law: Fantasies and Practices of New York City Lawyers, 1870–1910," in *The New High Priests,* G. Gawalt, ed. Westport, Ct.: Greenwood Press.

Graham, Bradley (1989). "Chilean Oppressed Turn to Vicariate." *Washington Post* (May 2).

Grose, Peter (1996). *Gentleman Spy: The Life of Allan Dulles.* Boston: University of Massachusetts Press.

Guest, Iain (1990). *Behind the Disappearances: Argentina's Dirty War against Human Rights and the United Nations.* Philadelphia: University of Pennsylvania Press.

Heritage Foundation (1996). *Annual Report.* Washington, D.C.: Heritage Foundation.

International Protection of Human Rights (1974). *International Protection of Human Rights. The Work of International Organizations and the Role of U.S. Foreign Policy.* Hearings of the Subcommittee on International Organizations and Movements. Foreign Affairs Committee, 93d Cong., 1st Sess.

Jacoby, Tamar (1986). "The Reagan Turnaround on Human Rights," 64 *Foreign Affairs,* 1071–72.

Johnson, Earl, Jr. (1974). *Justice and Reform: The Formative Years of the OEO Legal Service Program.* New York: Russell Sage.

Keck, Margaret, and Kathryn Sikkink (1998). *Activists Beyond Borders.* Ithaca, N.Y.: Cornell University Press.

Koh, Harold (1997). "Why Nations Obey International Law." 106 *Yale Law Journal*, 2599.
Kondracke, Morton (1988). "Broken Watch: Human Rights or Politics," *New Republic* (August 22), 8.
Korey, William (1998). *NGOs and the Universal Declaration of Human Rights: "A Curious Grapevine."* New York: St. Martin's Press.
Lowry, Rich (1995). "How the Right Rose," *National Review*. (December 11, 1995), 66.
Page, Nigel (1992). "Workers for Freedom," *Legal Business Magazine* (June), 28–31.
People for the American Way (1996). *Buying a Movement*. Washington, D.C.: People for the American Way.
Riles, Annelise (1999). *The Network Inside Out*. Ann Arbor: University of Michigan Press.
Singer, Amy (1987). "Human Rights Defender Michael Posner," *American Lawyer* (September), 97.
Snyder, Margaret (1995). *Transforming Development: Women, Poverty and Politics*. London: Intermediate Technology Publications.
Sohn, Louis, and Thomas Buergenthal (1973). *International Protection of Human Rights*. Indianapolis: Bobbs-Merrill.
Thompson, Andres (1994). *Think Tanks en la Argentina Conocimiento, Instituciones y Políticas*. Buenos Aires: CEDES.
Tolley, Howard, Jr. (1994). *The International Commission of Jurists: Global Advocates for Human Rights*. Philadelphia: University of Pennsylvania Press.
Wade, G. (1995). "Cancer Doctor: Lawyers Queue for Amnesty," *The Guardian* (June 10).

CHAPTER 15

Cause Lawyering and Democracy in Transnational Perspective
A Postscript

STUART A. SCHEINGOLD

In concluding this volume, it makes sense to take stock of cause-lawyering research following two collaborative projects. As is noted in the introduction to this volume, the initial collection of cause-lawyering essays focused on cause lawyering as a *process*. Cause lawyering was, so to speak, the dependent variable, and the objective of the collection was to shed light on the professional and political conditions that promote and/or inhibit the development of cause lawyering. In this collection, the focus shifted in a more *substantive* direction to the intersection of cause lawyering with two pervasive features of the current ethos: globalization and democratization.

Further complicating these efforts to reflect are the breadth and diversity of the cause-lawyering enterprise. Geographically speaking, it has become increasingly clear that cause lawyering is widespread—although just how widespread is difficult to say, given the partial coverage of the available research. Still, cause lawyering has been documented in parts of Europe, Asia, Latin America, the Middle East, and Africa, as well as in North America. It has also been found in both established and emerging democratic polities and in authoritarian settings. Moreover, cause lawyering is spread across the full range of professional venues: large and small private firms; salaried practice for national and transnational NGOs; and government and publicly funded lawyering.

To say that cause lawyering is, therefore, all over the world is not, however, to say that it is *the same* all over. Indeed, what is most striking about the findings is how much cause lawyering varies from time to time and place to place. The research record reveals that cause lawyers are associated with different causes, functioning with varying resources and degrees of legitimacy, and seeking a variety of goals. On the one hand, this variation and indeterminacy means that cause lawyering is in continuous transition. Wherever it is found, it must constantly adjust to changing political and professional circumstances as well as to new configurations of state power in general and to globalization and democratization in particular. On the other hand, there are some constants that transcend time and place—thus revealing cause lawyering as a conceptually coherent enterprise. Accordingly, cause lawyering emerges as both contingent and coherent—contingent in that it functions in diverse settings that are in continuous flux and coherent in that cause lawyers in all these settings face commensurable challenges and opportunities.

The formidable task of this essay is then to construct a synthesis that manages to identify the elements of coherence while at the same time honoring diversity and contingency. Contrary to what used to be the case, the goals that lawyers can realistically hope to reach are now subject, albeit to different degrees, to the forces unleashed and nurtured by globalization. In addition, the available research indicates that cause lawyering is regularly driven by what may reasonably be characterized as democratic aspirations—albeit democracy inflected in distinctly different ways. Finally, the evidence also indicates that cause lawyers have to work their way through roughly the same strategic choices, although they respond to these choices in quite different ways.

Accordingly, this final essay is constructed around the constants of democratic objectives, strategic choice, and globalization—while being sensitive to variation in how cause lawyers respond to each of them.

- While the *democratic aspirations* of cause lawyering are manifest and pervasive, distinctly different democratic narratives emerge from the available research. Both researchers and cause lawyers themselves tend to distinguish between two visions of democracy.[1] The liberal democratic vision is directed at securing political accountability, basic human rights, and the rule of law—and, thus, at a political and legal iteration of democracy. A more expansive vision of social and economic democracy enlists cause lawyering into a struggle on behalf of egalitarian values and redistributive policies. The evidence generated by the available research is indicative of a mutually constitutive relationship between liberal democracy and cause lawyering and a much more contingent and problematic relationship with social and economic democracy. This evidence also reveals the challenges to, and responses of, cause lawyers functioning under the special circumstances of neocorporatist regimes.
- As for strategic choice, two core questions that confront virtually all cause lawyers emerge over and over again in the research record. The more familiar of these questions is whether and to what extent cause lawyers should privilege legal as opposed to political strategies. Secondly, cause lawyers must decide how to position themselves between maintaining their distance from the state and operating in close proximity to it. What emerges from the evidence is that, contrary to the conventional wisdom, the former choice is more fraught with professional than policy consequences while the latter choice has decisive consequences for what cause lawyers can hope to accomplish.

- Globalization feeds into this mix in an ambivalent fashion, as was made clear in the introductory essay to this volume. "For cause lawyers . . . globalization and state transformation may be a mixed blessing. In some contexts it may help to provide a political structure wherein minimal rights claims and legal defenses against abuses of state power become meaningful. In other contexts, it may erode support for the kinds of social changes which these lawyers, and the movements with which they are affiliated, seek to advance." Generally speaking, this proposition stands up well to empirical scrutiny, which also reveals a number of interesting variations on this important theme.

In sum, while these matters are dealt with in divergent ways across the multiple and mutable settings in which cause lawyering is conducted, discernable parameters of practice do emerge, as do explanations of the causes and consequences of variation within the overall cause-lawyering enterprise. And the overall message that emerges is that cause lawyering and democracy are inextricably and productively linked to one another.

Of course, these are early days in cause-lawyering research, and any stocktaking can only yield provisional answers. Thus the spirit of this postscript is prospective even though its substance is largely retrospective. Indeed, this postscript will have served its purposes insofar as it prompts additional research and conceptual inquiry on the cause-lawyering enterprise.

Strategic Choices

The strategic questions that confront cause lawyers across the full range of settings in which they practice have to do with how they position themselves in relationship to the law and to the state, respectively.

- Should cause lawyers work within the accepted confines of legal advocacy, or should they engage in political action and/or support the political action of others?
- Should cause lawyers cultivate linkages to, and leverage within, state structures or maintain independence from, and an adversarial posture toward, the state?

Both cause lawyers themselves and those of us who study them believe that these questions—or, more accurately, the answers to them—are of crucial importance. This is not only because the questions intrude so persistently and pervasively into the world of cause lawyering but also because they are at the very core of the whole cause-lawyering enterprise. They prefigure the aspirations of cause lawyers; decisively shape tactics and impact; and also shed light on the relationship of cause lawyering to the mainstream of the legal profession. This relationship has a direct bearing on the social capital of cause lawyers and on their capacity to recruit and reproduce a cause-lawyering cadre.

With all that said, the available cause-lawyering research on these questions and answers does reveal some unexpected findings. Contrary to what seems to be a widely held view, the answers to the second question provide the more telling indications of what cause lawyers will, or will not, accomplish. Decisions about proximity to the state have especially strong implications for, and to some extent seem driven by, calculations about the impact of cause lawyering. In contrast, the answers to the first question reveal more about the cause-lawyering enterprise itself and the prevailing professional/political ethos. While by no means devoid of substantive consequences, where cause lawyers locate themselves on the presumptive continuum between the political and the legal is much more a reflection of, and an influence on, their own professional standing and on the standing of the cause-lawyering enterprise itself. In sum, the strategic choices posed by these questions are crucially linked to both the long-term professional vitality of cause lawyering and to its relevance to public policy, political discourse, and social values.

All of this will be explored and explained more fully below. Suffice it to say at this point that while the two core questions are conceptually distinct from one another, in practice they are intensely interdependent. The decision to practice cause lawyering in proximity to the state is consistent with both legal and political strategies, but proximity to the state does decisively influence the political and policy impact of cause lawyering. By the same token, the professional conditions and considerations that induce cause lawyers to engage legally rather than politically will influence whether or not they practice in proximity to the state. Before analyzing how these complex interactions play out, it is important to explore in some detail the conceptual foundations of each of the strategic choices.

The Legal and the Political

The distinction between law and politics has been subjected to relentlessly skeptical intellectual scrutiny, going back at least as far as legal realism. Nonetheless, it remains a prominent discursive presence in socio-legal scholarship and in the everyday thinking of cause lawyers themselves—as can be readily observed in the essays presented in this collection and in other cause-lawyering research. Irrespective, then, of the suspect conceptual integrity of the law-politics distinction, it offers access to the working consciousness of cause lawyers and, in particular, to how *they* understand their constraints and opportunities.

The choice between law and politics is seen, in the first place, as likely to have a substantial impact on the professional costs incurred in cause lawyering. Generally speaking, to engage *legally* means functioning at least partially, if ambivalently, within the boundaries of mainstream professionalism (Sarat and Scheingold, 1998: 3–4). This terrain may well be controversial and, as will be explained below, can even become a professional minefield for those who are deemed to be representing a socially constructed "other" in what is deemed to be too aggressive a way. On the whole, however, legally engaged cause lawyering may actually embellish an attorney's professional reputation (Sarat and Scheingold, 1998). In contrast, to politicize one's legal practice is to test and probably to violate the nethermost boundaries of mainstream professionalism, and this ordinarily means incurring substantial career costs. To understand how, why, and to what extent these generalizations hold true, it is necessary to look more carefully at the admittedly murky law-politics distinction as it plays out among cause lawyers.

Legal strategies are constructed around the articulation of difference and separation between cause lawyers and the causes and clients that they represent. Thus, to choose the legal route is to accept "the ideology of advocacy"—"neutral but partisan" representation (Simon, 1978; see also Luban, 1988). To conduct cause lawyering in accordance with the accepted rules of legal advocacy entails a willingness, indeed a commitment, to work on behalf of clients whose means and ends the lawyer may find objectionable—even abhorrent. Consider, by way of example, Dotan's analysis in this volume[2] of Israeli civil rights lawyers who defend Palestinian "terrorists" against "torture" by Israeli security officials. In this instance, the sensibilities of the Israeli civil rights lawyers certainly do not identify with the "terrorists"—meaning that the civil rights lawyers accept and, indeed, seem to embrace the distance and impersonality entailed in the ideology of advocacy. At the same time, they find "torture" a betrayal of the rule-of-law ideals of the Israeli state. Legality and constitutionality, then, become their cause.

It could be argued that this is not cause lawyering at all, but not by those who engage legally—nor, indeed, for purposes of this chapter. Legally engaged cause lawyers deny that an apolitical, rule-of-law mode of cause lawyering is, as some might have it, a contradiction in terms. Irrespective of whether they are familiar with the term *cause lawyering*, lawyers who work on behalf of legality, constitutional rights, and the rule of law see these objectives as a vocation, something of a higher calling. And as far as this essay is concerned, rule-of-law cause lawyering will be associated with what emerges as the dominant, albeit limited, democratic paradigm. As was suggested above, this version of cause lawyering tends to be in sync with the rule-of-law cutting edge that drives globalization. Of course, in autocratic states—with apartheid South Africa as a case in point, to consider only one of a host of examples—to introduce rule-of-law practices is to take a major step, perhaps a transformative step, forward.

In contrast to the liberal-legal version of cause lawyering, politicization is all about solidarity with clients and/or their causes. This means overt identification with and commitment to the political agenda of one side in conflicts over constitutional rights, public policy, regime structure, etc.—rather than identification with rights, legality, and constitutionality as ends in themselves. Solidarity is a marker of political cause lawyering, in part, because cause lawyers who thus become enmeshed in their clients' agendas do so in order to make a political statement and are ordinarily perceived as doing so by outsiders. More fundamental, the logic and the trajectory of solidaristic representation leads inevitably to privileging cause over legal and ethical constraints—and even over the immediate interests of the clients themselves (Sarat, 1998). Moreover, whereas rule-of-law cause lawyering privileges litigation, political cause lawyering tends to function in multiple venues: in legislative, administrative, and judicial institutions, as well as in the media and at the grassroots (McCann and Silverstein, 1998)—even in law offices themselves (Trubek and Kransberger, 1998).[3] For both of these reasons, politicized cause lawyering tends to be professionally suspect and is likely to have a negative impact on status and acceptance within the legal profession as well as opening up these lawyers to charges of ethical violations.

With all of that said, it is important to realize that cause lawyers regularly cross and recross the line dividing political from legal cause lawyering. As has already been suggested, politically engaged cause lawyers do not see political and legal strategies as mutually exclusive—although they are inclined to distinguish one from the other along the lines developed above. Coutin notes that U.S. immigration lawyers working for an advocacy group deploy both political and legal strategies simultaneously—albeit in different institutional arenas. When acting in the legal arena, the immigration cause lawyer ipso facto becomes the classic double agent, cooling out clients and imposing on them the prevailing legal culture. Coutin describes such an interaction as follows:

> As he answered these questions, the attorney urged immigrants to use their rights, to keep their spirits high, and to withstand the alienating affects of immigration bureaucracy. He advised one man that going to immigration court was "like science fiction, because they don't care about your name, they go by your number." The attorney's parting comment implied that legalization was almost a matter of life and death. Suggesting that a particular audience member ought to try his chances in court, the attorney said, "It's like a battle with cancer. If someone gives you a 50% chance, do you take it?" "You take it," the audience member agreed.

But Coutin also points out that "cause lawyers' advocacy work was not limited to helping immigrants discover ways to manipulate U.S. immigration law and thus to win in court." She goes on to provide an account of "political advocacy."

> This work required cause lawyers to participate in broad-based movements that sought justice for Central American immigrants. These movements were transnational in character, drew on both official and clandestine networks, and promoted multiple models of statehood, membership, and legitimacy. Attorneys sometimes participated in these movements directly. In addition, as members of organizations that were involved in political advocacy, attorneys were implicitly supporting this work.

Note that for Coutin, political advocacy is synonymous with a subversive reading of the political status quo and with acts of resistance to it.

Similarly, Shamir and Ziv identify a two-track strategy among lawyers working against Israel's land-segregation policies. The legal track entailed antidiscrimination litigation on behalf of excluded Israeli Arabs by the Association for Civil Rights in

Israel. At the same time, "a parallel clandestine scheme" was undertaken to subvert land-segregation policies. A willing Israeli surrogate was employed under a covert agency agreement ("a recognized device under Israel's Agency Law") to purchase land on behalf of, and turn it over to, an Arab buyer. While the clandestine track was, strictly speaking, legal, it was arguably political—"subpolitics," according to Shamir and Ziv—because the objective was not to vindicate the law but to subvert it in order to advance values and an agenda to which the lawyers were themselves committed.

From this perspective, political advocacy would seem to be all about expressing rather than sublimating one's values and objectives. The Latin America grassroots cause lawyering that Meili reports on is another case in point. Sarat finds much the same thing among *some* death penalty lawyers (1998). Moreover, this understanding of political cause lawyering is widely shared among both activists and researchers (see generally Scheingold, 1988, and 1998).

There is, however, another much more constraining version of political cause lawyering portrayed in a number of essays. In this version—exemplified by Ziv's research on disability cause lawyers—the locus of advocacy shifts from courts to legislatures and bureaucracies. Of course, the key to success in legislative and bureaucratic politics is finding a middle course, ordinarily in terms of a least-common-denominator resolution. As Ziv puts it, with respect to the legislative arena:

> It is common and acknowledged that the legal argument will not necessarily form one's position on a debated issue, but political realities and mainly their constraints. In contrast to adjudication, where the basic theoretical assumption is that if each party will assert its arguments zealously the process will yield the most just result (or the truth), this is not the legitimizing basis underlying the legislative political process. *In this setting the "best" law is the consequence of the consideration and accommodation of competing interests, procured through negotiation and compromise.* (Italics added)

This bargaining need not necessarily put the underlying cause at risk, and Ziv concludes that the ADA legislative campaign "illustrates how cause lawyers, as representatives of disadvantaged social groups and movements, can develop mechanisms that ameliorate imbalances between disadvantaged and privileged segments of society through mainstream political institutions." But co-optation is always a hazard of accommodation, and, at any rate, in this setting the cause lawyer is most certainly not a free agent. Note, however, that insofar as accommodation is a co-opting trap, the problem lies not in political cause lawyering as such, but in political cause lawyering in proximity to the state—an issue that will be taken up in the next section of this essay.

Note also that legislative and bureaucratic cause lawyering means, in effect, mainstream political advocacy. As such, it is much less likely to lead to professional marginalization. In principle, both *accommodative* political cause lawyering within legislatures and bureaucracies and *confrontational* political cause lawyering at the grassroots should be professionally suspect. In practice, however, organized legal professions have regularly tolerated, even honored, mainstream political advocacy because, among other reasons, it is unlikely to put professional privilege in harm's way and may even bolster privilege. Thus, while the reputation of lawyers who are perceived to be "political fixers" may well suffer, cause lawyers who are given to compromise and accommodation are unlikely to incur much, if any, professional opprobrium.[4]

Proximity to, Distance from, the State

Irrespective of their agenda, cause lawyers must, even in this era of globalization, negotiate relationships with state structures. Ordinarily, these relationships are direct, with cause lawyers calling on national and/or subnational institutions to protect and extend legal rights. Among the issue areas where cause lawyers typically work are immigration (Coutin), capital punishment (Sarat), the rule of law (Hajjar), redistribution of land (Klug; Shamir and Chinski), the environment (Morag-Levine), labor standards (Bloom), and so on. In addition, cause lawyers may relate to the state indirectly—invoking the authority of supranational institutions to bring pressure to bear on states from above, so to speak, or through mobilizing grass roots movements to pressure the states from below.

In all of these instances—whether approaching the state directly or indirectly, independently or in concert with social movements and/or transnational networks—the objective is to get the state to right, or at least to ameliorate, a wrong. This may be the state's own wrong or the wrong of individuals and corporations over which the state has at least partial jurisdiction (Bloom). In short, while one of the major themes of this volume is the destabilization of the state, state structures, albeit disaggregated state structures, remain central to the opportunities and problematics of cause lawyering.

Because of this centrality, and irrespective of the route taken, cause, lawyers must position themselves in relationship to the state. The research findings indicate that this positioning can be boiled down to the question of proximity to, and distance from, the state. Positioning can be measured along *an institutional continuum*, ranging from participation in, and cooperation with, state structures to maintaining an arm's-length relationship with the state through construction of adversarial and confrontational strategies.[5] Both Klug's research on cause lawyering in post-apartheid South Africa and Dotan's research on Israeli civil right attorneys, reveals cause lawyers working within state structures—analogous to the cause lawyers in Castro's Cuba, as analyzed in the first volume by Michalowski (1998). Ziv's disability rights lawyers who engage politically with bureaucrats and legislators can also be seen, albeit perhaps to a lesser extent, as working within the state:

The circumstances under which the language for the compromise was drafted blur the lines between official and unofficial law making. The task of obtaining enough votes to refute the amendment was left in the hands of the disability lobbyists; the ADA lawyer provided the final wording of the law. Lawyering under these circumstances allowed for direct participation and input by handing over official state tasks to representatives of the citizenry.

Of course, to thus become, in effect, part of the state raises a familiar question: is cause lawyering inside the state a contradiction in terms? Both the researchers and their respondents believe that cause lawyering can and does survive under these atypical circumstances on behalf of civil rights (Dotan), land redistribution (Klug), disability rights (Ziv), economic development (White), and so forth. But, as has already been suggested, working in such close proximity to the state does shape the character of cause lawyering. Shamir has argued in a different context that moderation is an inevitable consequence of proximity to the state. The implication of his research on New Deal lawyers in the United States is that the moderation of realist ideals was inadvertent. It was simply the unintended consequence of the state centered character of the New Deal project—of realist lawyers, as he puts it, "trapped" by a "growing involvement with the ongoing affairs of the administration" (Shamir, 1995: 174).[6]

By and large Shamir's propositions hold true for cause lawyers who choose proximity to the state. Note the prominence, and taken-for-granted tone, of "compromise" in Ziv's discussion of the quasi-legislative role of her disability cause lawyers. Some sense of the significance of compromise and moderation attendant to proximity to the state is revealed in the other chapters. In South Africa, there is a sharp and painful retreat from a pre-takeover ANC promise to redistribute land (Klug). Similarly, Israeli civil rights lawyers have been willing to draw back from significant elements of the rule of law in a show of solidarity with the state (Dotan).

Of course, it is important to keep in mind that cause lawyering, like politics in general, can never escape an element of compromise. Certainly this is true of what might be termed the classic cause lawyering associated with the adversarial legalism that comes up again and again in both cause-lawyering volumes. While working at arm's length from the state, the litigation in support of a moratorium on capital punishment (Sarat) in effect compromises the more sweeping objective of abolition (Sarat, 1998). Even those cause lawyers who are committed to fundamental political transformation and pursue a confrontational mode are, at least implicitly and contradictorily, dependent on the state that they wish to transform. Alan Thomson has captured this contradiction as an effort to deploy "the law to fight the system which (theory tells us) law maintains" (1992: 6). Aware of this contradiction, some cause lawyers make an effort to disengage from both state structures and formal law. Meili reports on Latin American cause lawyers who are working at the grassroots and who organize in opposition to the state and aim to destabilize and/or transcend state structures. To follow this trajectory is, of course, to move beyond lawyering and to make one's work indistinguishable from political activism as such.

The obvious question posed by all this is, how and why do cause lawyers distribute themselves along the continuum between proximity to, and distance from, the state? There are what might be termed both general and particular answers to this question. Most generally speaking, the available research strongly suggests that this positioning is substantive—driven, that is, by the cause itself. What is at play, in other words, are the results that cause lawyers wish to achieve, what they are willing to settle for, and how best to achieve their goals.

Posed in these latter terms, the question begs for reformulation along much less general lines. Why, for example, do some cause lawyers put themselves in such close proximity to the state that they thereby compromise their ostensible objectives? Conversely, why do other cause lawyers attempt to create so much distance between themselves and the state that they seem to be virtually giving up on lawyering? The answer to these questions will be taken up in detail in the next section. Suffice it to say for the time being that cause lawyers, irrespective of how they choose to construct their relationship to the state, do so for both pragmatic and ideological reasons—often in combination with one another. How can we, they seem to be asking themselves, maximize the consonance between what we believe in politically, socially, and economically and what we do professionally?

Explaining the Forms and Limits of Cause Lawyering

To explore why cause lawyers position themselves as they do along the law-politics and proximity-distance continua is to pursue an investigation of the sort referred to by Menkel-Meadow in the initial cause-lawyering volume as "the causes of cause lawyering" (1998). But the inquiry here is less about the causes of cause lawyering per se, than about *variation* in the way in which cause lawyering is practiced— and, specifically, about what kind of democratic agenda they are likely to pursue. The choice boils down, as was discussed in the introductory section of this essay, to a liberal versus egalitarian democratic agenda. Either way, the evidence reveals a mix of idealistic and careerist forces at work. In balance, these forces tend to lead cause lawyering toward liberal rather than egalitarian democracy. Only infrequently, and even then usually ephemerally, has cause lawyering been able to thrive on an egalitarian, participatory, and redistributive democratic agenda.

To understand why this is the case, it is necessary look at the different forces that are said to be driving cause lawyering. Menkel-Meadow (1998) traces cause lawyering primarily to ideology and altruism. In sharp contrast, Dezalay and Garth believe that cause lawyers, just like other lawyers, respond primarily to career-based, mostly material incentives. Hence, as they see it, cause lawyering is dependent on opportunities to build social capital.[7] Shamir and Chinski (1998) see all this in terms that are more fluid and multidimensional. For them, cause lawyering is constructed, reconstructed, and deconstructed, in response to a unstable mélange of factors and forces that shape the conditions of practice, the circumstances of the practitioners, and the opportunities to effectively serve the cause.

All of these explanations of the *causes* of cause lawyering will be appropriated for this inquiry into variation within the cause-lawyering enterprise. None of them is sufficient, but taken together they do provide a revealing account of the possibilities and limits of deploying cause lawyering in support of a democratic agenda. This is not to say, as will become readily apparent, that these explanations work in concert with one another. On the contrary, they often are at cross-purposes and thus require cause lawyers to negotiate among competing claims. Nonetheless, as cause lawyers calculate their relationship to the state and to the profession (and thus to their careers), all of these factors and forces come into play in ways that account for variation in both the democratic potential of the cause-lawyering enterprise and its own long-term vitality.

But, to repeat, for all of this complexity, the overwhelming message of the research conducted so far is that circumstances conspire to privilege a liberal democratic agenda built around accommodation with states, basic human rights, and incremental legalism. Cause lawyers with more ambitious agendas—directed at achieving grass roots and egalitarian democracy are much more likely to be marginalized professionally and to have their political objectives thwarted by countervailing pressures associated with the limitations of state structures, the difficulty of preserving social capital, and the neoliberal values driving globalization.

This is not to say that democratic aspirations, however defined—whether as "principled altruism" (Menkel-Meadow, 1998), civic professionalism (Halliday, 1999), or political ideology (Scheingold, 1988, and 1998)—are superfluous or negligible. Indeed, there is every reason to believe that the search for something to believe in—something, that is, beyond the ideology of advocacy—is the life blood of cause lawyering (Halliday, 1999). Absent this motivation, however formulated, why, after all, would attorneys choose to do good rather than to do well? Consider the personal injury lawyers who represented Costa Ricans employed by U.S. corporations in cross-border litigation directed at improving wages and working conditions. Bloom discovered that these lawyers were complicit in the passage of legislation that overturned a judicial decision favorable to their clients. She sees this as a conscious decision by personal injury practitioners "whose status as 'cause lawyers' is a matter of some debate" to head off unwelcome tort reform at the expense of their clients.

While Bloom presents us with a clear example of social capital trumping cause, her work also demonstrates that cause lawyering is not only about social capital.[8] If social capital were the whole story, then it would be difficult on the basis of research so far conducted to explain the pervasive presence of cause lawyering throughout the world.[9] It is clear from the research that has been conducted that cause lawyering is only rarely an avenue to professional prestige and material affluence. Dezalay and Garth's analysis of the construction of a human rights network in Latin America is one such example. An analogous and related example may be drawn from the heyday of cause lawyering in the United States from roughly the mid-1960s to the mid-1970s (Scheingold, 1998). Even under those relatively propitious circumstances, cause lawyering garnered neither the prestige nor, of course, the material rewards that are part and parcel of corporate practice. In short, cause lawyering almost always entails relative material and status deprivation.

On the other hand, altruism, political aspiration, and civic professionalism only go so far in explaining how cause lawyering will be practiced. Generally speaking, the evidence suggests that attorneys are drawn to cause lawyering for other-regarding reasons, but it is much less clear that these motivations are good predictors of the staying power of cause lawyers or of the kind of cause-lawyering practice that they will develop. Leave aside the putative impurities that can drive cause lawyers—that is, the notoriety that can accrue to prominent cause lawyers and the financial rewards of some kinds of tort litigation. Irrespective of impurities, cause lawyering must be practiced in a world shaped by the market for legal services, the neoliberal values associated with globalization, and state structures that, whether directly or indirectly, cause lawyers must ultimately confront, cajole, and accommodate.

The vagaries and complexities of all of this are captured in the research of Shamir and Chinski (1988), who compared two groups of lawyers representing Bedouins. This work was initiated by self-conscious cause lawyers, ostensibly motivated by altruism, trained in prestigious law schools, and working under the auspices of relatively well-funded social advocacy organizations. Subsequently, marginal practitioners who were searching for clients, not causes, got involved with the Bedouins. Shamir and Chinski's counterintuitive finding was that the *accidental* cause lawyers were more steadfast than the *intentional* cause lawyers in their advocacy on behalf of Bedouin land claims. Clearly, this could be read as lending credence to Dezalay and Garth's social-capital explanation. On the other hand, Halliday (1999) has chosen to view this as evidence of the power of civic professionalism.

Shamir and Chinski would probably agree that neither explanation is sufficient, although each of them may well be necessary to an adequate understanding of the etiology of cause lawyering. Put somewhat differently, the underlying message seems to be that cause lawyering is a social practice that is constructed and deconstructed out of "complex and conditional interactions," among a variety of variables (Scheingold and Bloom, 1998: 219). The strategic calculations made by cause lawyers are inevitably composed from a fluid, and unpredictable, amalgam of their own values (or ideological commitments), their interests (in terms of career objectives), and their political opportunities (in terms of the state structures that they confront). It is, then, around the fluid and indeterminate interactions among these three explanatory variables that the following analysis will be developed. But irrespective of the vagaries of the constitutive processes driving cause lawyering, the evidence lends substantial, if preliminary, credence to the proposition that cause lawyering is ordinarily and perhaps inevitably driven toward limited, discrete, and primarily liberal-legal objectives and away from a broadly egalitarian democratic agenda.

The Correlates of Egalitarian Democratic Cause Lawyering

Cause lawyers with egalitarian and redistributive democratic aspirations tend to be especially idealistic and prepared to forego many of the material rewards and the personal prestige that are available to talented and upwardly mobile legal professionals. Thus, even if all other things were equal, it would be predictable that egalitarian democratic cause lawyering would be the exception—and not only within the profession but among cause lawyers. But all other things are not equal, and the several additional burdens imposed on egalitarian cause lawyers mean that only an exceptional few within this already exceptional cadre are likely to stay the course. The multiple costs associated with egalitarian democratic cause lawyering make it the most unstable cause-lawyering cohort.

It should come as no surprise, therefore, that the available literature reveals very few instances in which an egalitarian and redistributive model of cause lawyering has been able to establish a significant and dependable professional presence. The United States has been the most hospitable to egalitarian democratic cause lawyering—particularly in the heady days of the late 1960s and early 1970s (Scheingold, 1998), but it has reappeared from time to time among lawyers allied with social movements (McCann, 1994; Silverstein, 1996; Olson, 1984). Elsewhere, the vision of cause lawyers enthusiastically and with some success brandishing an egalitarian democratic sword is found only rarely and episodically—as in the United Kingdom prior to, and during the early years of, the Thatcher regime (Scheingold, 1988, 1994).

More typically, such lawyers find themselves beleaguered like the anti–death penalty cause lawyers that Sarat (1998) characterized as *lost*-cause lawyers. These *lost*-cause lawyers were committed to doing pretty much whatever it took to realize a democratic vision that they knew was beyond reach. Thus, in the name of producing a historical record on the one hand and extending lives of their clients for as long as possible on the other, they were willing to marginalize themselves both politically and professionally. A comparable cloud of alienation and marginalization seems to hang over the grassroots transnational cause-lawyering networks in Latin America. These networks, Meili tells us, find themselves working at the periphery of their national political communities on behalf of social and economic equality in settings where, at most, a thin and minimalist version of democracy is accepted. Their best hope is that transnationalism will allow them to draw strength and resources from one another. While the transnational whole may well be greater than the sum of its national parts, the infusion of resources in support of egalitarian and redistributive social and economic democracy from established global or regional human rights networks seems unlikely (Dezalay and Garth).

There are at least two ways to read the cause-lawyering trajectory illustrated by Sarat's *lost*-cause opponents of the death penalty. The most positive inflection is to dub this "critical" cause lawyering (Trubek and Kransberger, 1998; Grigg-Spall and Ireland, 1992) and to see it as an effective and appropriate adaptation to the postindustrial condition. Critical cause lawyering

> locates domination at micro-sites of power and in cross cutting social cleavages. It, therefore, becomes appropriate to organize resistance around any of these cleavages—race, gender, sexual orientation, age, etc. Similarly any of the multiple sites of domination are appropriate as targets: the family, the work place, schools, social service agencies, etc. (Scheingold, 1998: 143)

According to Peter Fitzpatrick, writing with reference to popular justice in the "Third World," the secret of effective resistance to a seemingly impregnable hegemony is precisely to "create legal processes that resist state law and *operate beyond its bounds*" (1992: 47; italics added). In this same vein, Shamir and Ziv show that covert action by way of the civil law, subpolitics as they characterize it, puts the defenders of Israeli's land segregation laws on the defensive.[10] In other words, with big targets effectively out of reach and/or inappropriate to postindustrial circumstances and values, it is both necessary and sufficient to focus on the microsites of power. In so doing, power is resisted where it is most vulnerable on the one hand and most insidiously pervasive on the other.

The much less sanguine reading is to see these developments as a fruitless effort to make a virtue of necessity. According to this way of thinking, the shift to multiple and potentially competing agents and dimensions of emancipation amounts to a retreat from a democratic politics and from politics in general (Handler, 1992)—a retreat that has the effect of splintering the democratic left. Others might claim that critical cause lawyering is also based on misreading of current circumstances and opportunities—given the emergence of global human rights networks. Because they are insulated from resistant state structures, these networks might well be able to provide the resources and leverage that would enable cause lawyers to pursue vigorous, egalitarian democratic advocacy.

Whether one reads critical cause lawyering as an altogether appropriate step in the right direction or as a betrayal of redistributive social and economic democracy, the evidence strongly suggests that this adaptation has been more or less imposed on radical democratic cause-lawyering cadres. Surely this work provides the democratic left with material and symbolic resources insofar as it serves the immediate needs of the dispossessed and dramatizes serious racial, gender, and material inequities. What is less clear is whether it will be sufficient to superimpose a critical rationale on the potentially discouraging combination of discrete and distant gratifications of "*lost* cause" egalitarian democratic cause lawyering (Scheingold, 1998, cf. Trubek and Kransberger, 1998). No doubt some will stay the course, but can modest achievements and precarious professional circumstances sustain a critical cause-lawyering enterprise?[11]

The Correlates of Liberal Democratic Cause Lawyering

When they shift from an egalitarian agenda to a liberal agenda, cause lawyers are on much firmer and more salubrious terrain. This is the case across a wide range of political regimes, including: well-established liberal democracies where cause lawyers are struggling to enhance and protect rights; emergent democracies where rights and the rule of law are precarious; neocorporatist settings where legitimacy is associated with accommodation rather than rights; and authoritarian settings where the vindication of any right is a triumph of sorts. Some cause lawyers trim their egalitarian democratic sails to accommodate the prevailing neoliberal winds. In other cases, the cause lawyers are committed to basic liberal democratic aspirations like the rule of law, civil society, and political accountability. Either way, it turns out that cause lawyers who pursue liberal democratic goals can count, to varying degrees, on transnational, professional, and/or political support.

Thus, transnational and global networks do support vigorous and confrontational human rights advocacy, but they regularly marginalize the assertion of social and economic rights. According to Dezalay and Garth, the liberal legal advocacy associated with human rights networks is a product of the forces that gave birth to, and have sustained, the international human rights movement throughout the post–World War II period. Initially, the driving force behind this process was the affinity between human rights and anticommunism. More recently the affinity would seem to be between the rule of law and the expansion of a globalized neoliberal order. Recall that Meili's findings lend credence to this argument. He notes that cause-lawyering networks that go beyond conventional iterations of human rights and the rule of law in an effort realize social and economic rights are unable to secure external funding and must, more or less, go it alone—being marginalized professionally and politically as well as financially.

In the United States, death penalty lawyers were able through strategic compromise to enlist the American Bar Association as a political ally. Specifically, Sarat found that the support of the A.B.A. for public funding of death penalty resource centers was conditioned on refocusing from unconditional to conditional opposition to the death penalty. Rather than privileging the abolition of the death penalty and the exposure of law's violence, the death penalty lawyers shifted to establishing rules to guide, to civilize, and perhaps to curtail the imposition of law's violence. "For the A.B.A., the rejection of the death penalty takes the form of an effort to prevent the erosion of the boundaries between law's violence and its extra-legal counterpart. Fairness, due process, equal protection, values vigorously defended by the anti–death penalty bar, help solidify that boundary" (Sarat, 1998). This strategy stands in sharp contrast to the assault by some death penalty lawyers reported in the first volume who were unconditionally abolitionist (ibid.). For the abolitionists, the death penalty and its violence were the targets, not the way in which it was administered. Indeed, this moral absolute justified transgressing legality and established professional values. By returning to the much less controversial terrain of due process and the like, death penalty lawyers were thus able to conserve their dwindling supply of social capital. As Sarat puts it, they were actually able to establish a "fragile and unstable" alliance with the organized legal profession (ibid.).[12]

Boon's findings reveal much the same convergence among cause lawyering, the state, and the legal profession in the United Kingdom. The ascendance of neoliberal values under Margaret Thatcher and its subsequent consolidation in the Blair government, in effect, defunded egalitarian democratic cause lawyers working in publicly funded law centers and legal aid programs. In partial compensation, pro bono lawyering has been promoted with some quantitative success. Qualitatively speaking, however, the current circumstances tend to favor at most a kind of classic adversarial legalism, and in the United Kingdom this is particularly problematic, as Sterrett (1998) discovered in her research on immigration lawyers. She found that British courts privilege legal strategies that call upon them to adjudicate individual cases. In this way, the judges are able to steer clear of not only class actions but also rulings with implications that transcend the specifics of the case at hand.

In nascent democracies where neither the rule of law, nor cause lawyering itself, is well established, the almost irresistible attractions of a liberal-legal agenda are readily apparent. As has already been suggested, cause lawyers wishing to call upon external resources from transnational networks are likely to find that this funding is available only for an agenda compatible with neoliberal values. In addition, internal support from the local legal establishment tends to be similarly conditional, as Lev's cause lawyering research in Southeast Asia revealed (1998). In this setting, an independent judiciary and other limited objectives associated with the rule of law represent a potential point of convergence for the agents of neoliberal globalization, local political and business elites, and the legal profession itself.

White discovered this same convergence in Ghana, but she underscores the down side of privileging neoliberalism. Women's rights lawyers were induced to pursue the same neoliberal goals, which were initially attractive only to the economic development lawyers working within the Ghanaian state.

> More recently, as part of their campaign for "good governance," foreign funders
> have encouraged the women's rights lawyers to put aside substantive priorities

altogether, and take up the formal proceduralist agenda of providing "access to legal services" for all Ghanaian women. Like access to health care, this service might be offered on a "cash and carry" basis, so long as access was even-handed for those who were willing to pay.

She concludes that insofar as "the Ghanaian legal landscape is embedded in wider global dynamics, it should not be surprising that these two groups of Ghanaian cause lawyers function as unknowing agents of this global agenda."

Hajjar, drawing on the work of Keck and Sikkink (1998), makes a much stronger case for the democratic potential of human rights discourse, practices, and networks and finds some support for the expansive opportunities of human rights cause lawyering in her research on Israel-Palestine.[13] In effect, Hajjar traces the trajectory of human rights lawyering on behalf of Palestinians from efforts to use law as a shield to efforts to use it as a sword. Thus, she calls attention to the work of the advocacy organization, Al-Haq, that deployed human rights discourse to challenge the Israeli occupation and more generally "the Israeli state's narrative of legitimacy." Her analysis suggests that in autocratic settings a transformative campaign can be constructed on a human rights foundation. However, what are we to make of a loss of vigor among human rights lawyers on both sides of the Israel-Palestine divide after the peace accords? Among Palestinians, human rights were subordinated to the imperatives of the emerging Palestinian state, while in Israel the peace process itself seems to take precedence over human rights. The extent to which Hajjar provides an exception to the minimalist agenda ordinarily associated with human rights cause lawyering would thus seem to remain an open question.

Only in neocorporatist democratic settings is cause lawyering on behalf of the rule of law and individual rights not the line of least resistance. There, the available research reveals strong incentives for cause lawyers to curtail such aspirations. Consider, to begin with, the Israeli example where what might be unthinkable in the United States—the movement of civil rights activists back and forth between ACRI and the justice ministry (Dotan)—is deemed normal and natural. Consider also the ANC activists who found their way into the postapartheid South African state (Klug). In both of these instances, cause lawyers were prepared to subordinate rights to the needs of the collectivity. In Israel, Dotan's research reveals a trade-off between the rights of suspected "terrorists" and the security of the state. Similarly, in South Africa, according to Klug, the long-term stability of the state—in terms of the political support of white landholders—took precedence over commitments made by the ANC prior to coming to power to distribute land to landless agricultural workers.

There is, moreover, reason to believe that these were more than idiosyncratic retreats in the name of state security. In Israel, the general discomfort with aggressive adversarial legalism is demonstrated in Morag-Levine's findings. She discovered that the efforts by U.S.-backed and-trained environmental lawyers to engage in adversarial legalism were on balance distrusted—and not only or primarily because of their American origins. More important seems to have been the broadly based hostility to an abstract and aggressive legal rights campaign deemed out of touch with Israeli political values and practices. Note also that at least in Israel and South Africa, the decision to work in close proximity to the state is not so much a strategic calculation as a voluntary act of ideological identification with the aspirations of the state.[14]

The plight of neoliberal democratic cause lawyering in a neocorporatist state is revealed by research on cause lawyers in Osaka and Kyoto, Japan (Miyazawa, 1996, unpublished). These lawyers tend to think of themselves as critics of the prevailing neocorporatist political culture, but the neocorporatist institutions and political culture of Japan force them into a path of accommodation and compromise. In other words, unlike the Israeli and South African situations, accommodation is imposed upon Japanese cause lawyers rather than freely chosen by them.

The upshot of all this is that in both Israel and Japan[15] a third form of cause lawyering seems to be developing. The somewhat surprising hallmark of democratic cause lawyering in neocorporatist states is its tendency toward politicization (see also Kidder and Miyazawa, 1993). Rather like their enviromentalist counterparts in Israel, Japanese cause lawyers are persuaded, *much to their consternation*, that adversarial legalism is ineffective. Certainly in Japan, although not necessarily in Israel, cause lawyers believe that the most that they can get from the judges are suggestions that their claims have some merit and that *something* really should be done—although probably not by the judiciary. Accordingly, one of the strongly held beliefs among Japanese cause lawyers is that even the most modest results are possible only when it can be demonstrated outside the courtroom that their claims find resonance in the polity. Thus, Japanese cause lawyers regularly, if reluctantly, take on the onerous chore of organizing plaintiffs and helping them to orchestrate campaigns to raise public consciousness and in this way get the attention of the government. The net result is, however, a minimalist agenda rooted in accommodation and compromise and, thus, is unwelcome to neoliberal and egalitarian cause lawyers alike.

Conclusions

The principal finding of this essay is that, in an age of sweeping globalization and creeping democratization, just as in the past, cause lawyering is very much a creature of, and a contributor to, legal-liberal forms of democracy. In other words, the evidence on cause lawyering tends to reinforce the broader record of a liberal-legal homology. This homology can be traced to state structures, to the culture of the legal profession, and to the interaction between them.[16] In other settings cause lawyering is a more precarious enterprise although often able, nevertheless, to make a meaningful contribution to democratic values.

One of the more intriguing findings of recent cause-lawyering research is the role of cause lawyers under conditions of neocorporatist democracy. Consider, for example, the Israeli state with its neocorporatist tendencies, a racialized inflection of citizenship, and a longstanding life-and-death conflict with the Palestinian-Arab *other*. In this setting it makes good sense for the Israeli *insiders* to practice collaborative cause lawyering in close proximity to the state. After all, it works for them—not only because they have access and influence but also because their objectives are shaped by their sense of solidarity with the state. Conversely, Israeli Arabs, Bedouins, and Palestinians (each to varying degrees) accept neither the corporatist compact from which they tend to be excluded nor the state imperatives derived from that compact. Still, rule-of-law institutions are in place and there are cause lawyers who are willing to operate from beyond the corporatist compact; the influence of transnational human rights is felt; and basic rights are, thus, not out of reach (Hajjar).

In autocratic and/or in dangerously unstable polities, on the other hand, even the pursuit of minimal rights puts a cause lawyer's career and physical well-being in serious jeopardy. Indeed, this volume honors the memory of a Sri Lankan cause lawyer, Neelam Tiruchelvam, who was a martyr to rule-of-law values and to human rights. Certainly, there are many states, present-day China to name just one, where to claim basic human rights is ipso facto deemed a confrontational and hostile *political* act. Thus, even the most modest imaginable forms of cause lawyering are not tolerated. Predictably, we know much less about whether cause lawyering can exist under these conditions, much less what it can accomplish. The record of Apartheid South Africa suggests that cause lawyering, even in fundamentally hostile settings, can make meaningful contributions (Abel, 1995). Insofar as such states are seeking to play a role in the global political economy, there is pressure on them to accept the rudiments of liberal democracy including the rule of law and civil society. To that degree, there is space and potential for cause lawyering in concert, perhaps, with transnational human rights. In short, it is in the bleakest setting where synergy is to be found between globalization and democratic cause lawyering and also where the aspirations of liberal democratic cause lawyering are genuinely transformative.

Inevitably, this leads back to liberal democratic cause lawyering and to the interdependencies that link it to the rule of law and to other liberal democratic institutions. Where adversarial legalism and democratic pluralism are well established, there may be substantial tolerance for legal confrontation and at times receptivity to egalitarian and redistributive cause-lawyering projects. And even if this advocacy is not immediately and directly successful, it may contribute to a redefinition of the discursive terrain and ultimately to egalitarian transformation (McCann, 1994). However, this is inherently unstable terrain for cause lawyers. Cause lawyers who are closely and unequivocally identified with transformative egalitarian goals and social movements put in jeopardy the discursive cover that insulates the legal profession, or is seen to insulate the profession, from partisan scrutiny and from the threat of an unregulated market for legal services.[17] Accordingly, once the political winds shift, cause lawyers are likely to find themselves deprived of the social capital otherwise available to them as legal professionals.

Conversely, insofar as the ambitions of cause lawyers are confined to the rule of law, an independent judiciary, due process, and basic rights, they effectively align themselves with both the professional mainstream and the incentives and institutions of globalization. By thus confining themselves to generally accepted *legal* terrain and/or by pursuing incremental goals *politically* in a spirit of give and take, cause lawyers can often curtail the professional, and perhaps even the political costs, of cause lawyering. At the same time, they can make important contributions to the maintenance and even to the extension of democratic values. They do so by founding their democratic advocacy on a combination of supportive structures and allies: an independent judiciary committed to due process and basic rights; an alliance with mainstream professionals; and the incentives and institutions of globalization. In other words, there are both legal and political routes to a relatively safe harbor for liberal democratic cause lawyers.

Notes

1. It is important to acknowledge that neither this essay nor the cause-lawyering volumes from which is derived incorporate so-called right-wing cause lawyering—whether that of economic conservatives, associated with organizations like the Manhattan Institute and the Pacific Legal Foundation, or that of social conservatives, associated, for example, with the religious right. The legal work of these conservative groups presents intriguing opportunities for anyone interested in cause lawyering and, indeed, in the relationship between cause lawyering and democracy. There is, however, regrettably little research so far on the relatively recent phenomenon of right-wing cause lawyering. This is not surprising given the extensive historical record of left-liberal cause lawyering as well the longtime hostility of conservatives to the kind of judicial activism that has been intrinsic to cause lawyering. In other words, because the theory and practice of cause lawyering have been forged in the caldron of liberal-left politics, it is both appropriate and inevitable to similarly confine the stocktaking of this essay. Right-wing cause lawyering, however, remains inviting, indeed compelling, terrain for theorizing and for empirical research on cause lawyering in general and on the relationship between cause lawyering and the democratic project in particular.

2. Henceforth references to research in this volume will be indicated solely with the name(s) of the author(s).

3. Action in these several venues may be coordinated with one another or go forward separately. Thus, political strategies, *while not precluding litigation*, are more likely to entail lobbying, social-movement mobilization, direct action (or support of direct action), and so forth. It is also the case that political cause lawyering can be pragmatic (McCann and Silverstein, 1998) as well as ideological (Scheingold, 1998).

4. Certainly in the United States, the so-called Washington lawyer is included within the professional elite. On the genealogy of this development, see Auerbach, 1976. For accounts of this kind of legal practice, see Goulden, 1971, and Green, 1978. The point is not that these lawyers are cause lawyers, although some of them either are cause lawyers or at least do

some cause lawyering. They are, however, unequivocally political in terms of where and how they practice, and in spite, or perhaps because, of this they are honored professionally.

5. One can also think of ideological distance and proximity, but this dimension is not so much descriptive as explanatory and will thus be taken up below. In other words, ideological affinities and antipathies are often at the root of decisions about distance and proximity.

6. As Shamir sees it, New Deal lawyers who took on a representational role *within* the state settled into a moderation that took the critical edge off of their original "realist" project. "With the growing reliance of the state on their services, and their own growing involvement with the ongoing affairs of the administration, the realists became trapped in a representational position. In this new capacity, the radical elements of their critical discourse were cast aside by a rational discourse that legitimized their new role as state experts.... Representation functions, in other words, pull experts—whether intellectual or technocrats—away from the emancipatory and hermeneutic potential of a critical agenda and push it toward using knowledge as an instrumental currency" (Shamir, 1995: 174).

7. In their essay in this volume, Dezalay and Garth adapt an earlier analysis of the legal profession (1996), based on Bordieu's concept of the "legal field," to cause lawyering.

8. The complexity, contingency, and ambiguity that hovers over the concept of cause lawyering and the construction of cause-lawyering practice in a personal injury firm is poignantly conveyed in Haar's *A Civil Action* (1995).

9. It is important to acknowledge that the essays in this volume do not, for the most part, provide the full range of biographical data that Dezalay and Garth believe to be essential to a full legal-field inquiry. Moreover, in this analysis more weight is probably given to nonmaterial incentives than they might believe is appropriate. Nonetheless, the basic insights of their work are at the heart of this effort to explain the patterns of variation that have been identified above.

10. In contrast to Fitzpatrick, Shamir and Ziv argue that covert strategies are best employed in concert with strategies that call upon the "majestic constitutive form of law." The implication of Fitzpatrick's analysis is that invoking the law's "relational" capacities is an alternative, perhaps a mutually exclusive alternative to, invoking the law's "surpassing" capacities.

11. Note that there are also likely to be life-cycle forces at work. It is much easier for the young and unattached to thumb their noses at material rewards. Family responsibilities tend to divert even the most committed and idealistic cause lawyers into more settled and remunerative career paths (Scheingold, 1998).

12. In this instance, scaled-down aspirations were pursued via the classic mode of adversarial legalism. Then there is the critical and arguably apolitical approach that adopts a self-consciously small-scale agenda—pursuing discrete and personalized goals while eschewing what Halliday and Karpik (1997) refer to as politics writ large and what others have called grand political narratives (Trubek and Kransberger, 1998; Scheingold, 1998).

13. She notes that Keck and Sikkink (1998) distinguish so-called first-generation rights (civil and political) from second-generation rights (redressing social and economic inequalities). However, Hajjar's own analysis does not provide any evidence of cause-lawyering advocacy on behalf of second-generation human rights.

14. This is not to say that adversarial legalism, rights activism, and, for that matter, egalitarian democratic cause lawyering are not to be found in Israel and South Africa. Instead, the point is that in these two states neoliberal democratic cause lawyering is not the privileged route to accruing social capital—nor is it the moderate option for democratic cause lawyers.

15. We have no comparable information on South Africa.

16. Painting on a broader canvas, Halliday and Karpik (1997) make much the same point about the legal profession more generally. While they and their contributors demonstrate that law, lawyers, and liberalism are inextricably entangled with one another, the synergistic relationship that the two editors attribute to liberalism and the legal professions, broadly conceived, raises questions that need to be answered (Scheingold, 1999). However, research on cause lawyering indicates how and why at least that segment of the legal profession, a segment that is much in evidence around the world does have mutually constitutive relationships with liberal-democratic regimes—albeit relationships that reflect variation among these regimes.

17. These problems are compounded for cause lawyers who represent the socially constructed *other*—especially when this *other* is in an extralegal and/or pariah status. Among the examples are cause lawyers in Israel representing dispossessed Bedouins (Shamir and Chinsky, 1998) or practicing before Israeli military courts (Bisharat, 1998, and Hajjar, 1997), as well as capital punishment and immigration lawyers in the United States (Sarat, 1998, and Coutin, this volume). Roughly the same point could be made from a different political perspective about cause lawyers who might choose to represent white Afrikaners in post-apartheid South Africa or the interests of a displaced bourgeoisie in Cuba.

References

Abel, Richard L. (1995). *Politics by Other Means: Law in the Struggle Against Apartheid, 1980–1994.* New York: Routledge.
Auerbach, Jerold S. (1976). *Unequal Justice: Lawyers and Social Change in Modern America.* New York: Oxford University Press.
Bisharat, George (1998). "Attorneys for the People, Attorneys for the Land: The Emergence of Cause Lawyering in the Israeli-Occupied Territories," in *Cause Lawyering: Political Commitments and Professional Responsibilities*, ed. Austin Sarat and Stuart Scheingold, 453–86. New York: Oxford University Press.
Dezalay, Yves, and Bryant G. Garth (1996). *Dealing in Virtue: International Commercial Arbitration and the Construction of a Transnational Legal Order.* Chicago: University of Chicago Press.
Fitzpatrick, Peter (1992). "Law as Resistance," in *The Critical Lawyers' Handbook,* ed. Ian Grigg-Spall and Paddy Ireland, 44–48. London: Pluto Press.
Goulden, Joseph (1971). *The Superlawyers: The Small and Powerful World of the Great Washington Law Firms.* New York: Weybright and Talley.
Green, Mark (1978). *The Other Government: The Unseen Power of Washington Lawyers.* New York: Norton.
Grigg-Spall, Ian, and Paddy Ireland, eds. (1992). *The Critical Lawyers' Handbook.* London: Pluto Press.
Haar, Jonathan (1995). *A Civil Action.* New York: Random House.
Hajjar, Lisa (1997). "Cause Lawyering in Transnational Perspective: National Conflict and Human Rights in Israel/Palestine." 31:2 *Law and Society Review*, 473–504.
Halliday, Terrence C. (1999). "Politics and Civic Professionalism: Legal Elites and Cause Lawyers." 24:4 *Law and Social Inquiry* (Fall), 1013–60.
Halliday, Terrence C., and Lucien Karpik, eds. (1997). *Lawyers and the Rise of Western Liberalism: Europe and North America from the Eighteenth to Twentieth Centuries.* New York: Oxford University Press.

Handler, Joel (1992). "Postmodernism, Protest, and the New Social Movements," 26:4 *Law and Society Review*, 697–731.

Keck, Margaret, and Kathryn Sikkink (1998). *Activists Without Borders: Transnational Advocacy Networks in International Politics*. Ithaca, N.Y.: Cornell University Press.

Kidder, Robert, and Setsuo Miyazawa (1993). "Long-Term Strategies in Japanese Environmental Litigation," 18:4 *Law and Social Inquiry*, 605–27.

Lev, Daniel (1998), "Lawyers' Causes in Indonesia and Malaysia," in *Cause Lawyering: Political Commitments and Professional Responsibilities*, ed. Austin Sarat and Stuart Scheingold, 431–52. New York: Oxford University Press.

Luban, David (1988). *Lawyers and Justice: An Ethical Study*. Princeton, N.J.: Princeton University Press.

McCann, Michael W. (1994). *Rights at Work: Pay Equity Reform and the Politics of Legal Mobilization*. Chicago: University of Chicago Press.

McCann, Michael, and Helena Silverstein (1998). "Rethinking Law's 'Allurements': A Relational Analysis of Social Movement Lawyers in the United States," in *Cause Lawyering: Political Commitments and Professional Responsibilities*, ed. Austin Sarat and Stuart Scheingold, 261–92. New York: Oxford University Press.

Menkel-Meadow, Carrie (1998). "The Causes of Cause Lawyering: Toward an Understanding of the Motivation and Commitment of Social Justice Lawyers," in *Cause Lawyering: Political Commitments and Professional Responsibilities*, ed. Austin Sarat and Stuart Scheingold, 31–68. New York: Oxford University Press.

Michalowski, Raymond (1998). "All or Nothing: An Inquiry into the (Im)Possibility of Cause Lawyering under Cuban Socialism," in *Cause Lawyering: Political Commitments and Professional Responsibilities*, ed. Austin Sarat and Stuart Scheingold, 523–45. New York: Oxford University Press.

Miyazawa, Setsuo (1996). "Cause Lawyering by a Cartelized Legal Profession: Profiles in Cause Lawyering in Japan." Unpublished paper.

Olson, Susan M. (1984). *Clients and Lawyers: Securing Rights for Disabled Persons*. Westport, Conn.: Greenwood Press.

Sarat, Austin (1998). "Between (the Presence of) Violence and (the Possibility of) Justice: Lawyering Against Capital Punishment," in *Cause Lawyering: Political Commitments and Professional Responsibilities*, ed. Austin Sarat and Stuart Scheingold, 317–46. New York: Oxford University Press.

Sarat, Austin, and Stuart Scheingold (1998). "Cause Lawyering and the Reproduction of Professional Authority: An Introduction," in *Cause Lawyering: Political Commitments and Professional Responsibilities*, ed. Austin Sarat and Stuart Scheingold, 431–52. New York: Oxford University Press.

Scheingold, Stuart A. (1999). "Taking Weber Seriously: Lawyers, Politics, and the Liberal State," 24:4 *Law and Social Inquiry* (Fall), 1061–81.

———. (1988). "Radical Lawyers and Socialist Ideals," 15:1 *Journal of Law and Society* (Spring), 122–38.

———. (1998). "The Struggle to Politicize Legal Practice: Left-Activist Lawyering in Seattle," in *Cause Lawyering: Political Commitments and Professional Responsibilities*, ed. Austin Sarat and Stuart Scheingold, 431–52. New York: Oxford University Press.

Scheingold Stuart A., and Anne Bloom, (1998). "Transgressive Cause Lawyering: Practice Sites and the Politicization of the Professional," 5: 2/3 *International Journal of the Legal Profession*, 209–53.

Shamir, Ronen (1995). *Managing Legal Uncertainty: Elite Lawyers in the New Deal*. Durham, N.C.: Duke University Press.

Shamir, Ronen, and Sara Chinsky (1998). "Destruction of Houses and Construction of a Cause: Lawyers and Bedouins in Israeli Courts," in *Cause Lawyering: Political Commitments and Professional Responsibilities*, ed. Austin Sarat and Stuart Scheingold, 227–57. New York: Oxford University Press.

Silverstein, Helena (1996). *Unleashing Rights: Law, Meaning, and the Animal Rights Movement*. Ann Arbor: University of Michigan Press.

Simon, William (1978) "The Ideology of Advocacy," 1978 *Wisconsin Law Review*, 30–144.

Sterrett, Susan (1998). "Caring about Individual Cases: Immigration Lawyering in Britain," In *Cause Lawyering: Political Commitments and Professional Responsibilities*, ed. Austin Sarat and Stuart Scheingold, 293–316. New York: Oxford University Press.

Thomson, Alan (1992) "Critical Approaches to Law: Who Needs Legal Theory?" Foreword to *The Critical Lawyers' Handbook*, ed. Ian Grigg-Spall and Paddy Ireland, 2–10. London: Pluto Press.

Trubek, Louise, and M. Elizabeth Kransberger (1998). "Critical Lawyers: Social Justice and the Structures of Private Practice," in *Cause Lawyering: Political Commitments and Professional Responsibilities*, ed. Austin Sarat and Stuart Scheingold, 201–26. New York: Oxford University Press.

Index

ABC settlement, 132–33
Abel, Richard, 265, 267
Abolition, of capital punishment, 20, 191–94, 204, 397. *See also* Capital punishment
Abortion, 202–3, 245
Abrams, Elliot, 367
Absolute right, to file transnational lawsuits, 96–97
Academy of Human Rights, 315
Access to Justice Act, 159
Access to Justice Bill, 164, 165–66
ACRI (Association for Civil Rights in Israel), 21, 85–86, 246–52, 257, 289–98, 388
ADA (Americans with Disabilities Act), 20–21, 211–43, 388; campaign, representing persons with disabilities during, 221–23; case study, 214–16
ADAPT, 228
Advice Services Alliance, 154
Advisory Commission on Land Allocation, 269
Advisory Committee on Education and Conduct, 159
Affirmative action, 271
African Americans, 196. *See also* Racism
African Growth and Opportunity Act, 50, 51
Ah hoc contacts, 313–14
AIDS, 53, 230. *See also* HIV
AJUP (Institute for Popular Legal Support), 313, 315
Al Muhajiroun (Muslim group), 172
Aladjem, Terry, 188
Alfonsin, Raul, 368
Al-Haq, 83–85, 87, 398
Alienation, 300, 394
Allende, Isabelle, 358–59, 361
Alternative lawyers, 308, 317, 323, 325–27
Altruism, 391, 392, 393

American Baptist Churches v. Thorburgh, 121, 139 n.17
American Bar Association (ABA), 20, 162, 190–91, 193–205, 396–97
American Civil Liberties Union (ACLU), 85, 257, 334, 365
American Institute of Architects (AIA), 234
American Natural Resources Defense Council, 24
Americas Watch, 316, 365, 370
Amicus briefs, 107–8
Amnesty International, 79, 316, 358–60, 366, 373 n.7, 373 n.10
ANC (African National Congress), 264–76, 390, 398
An-Na'im, Abdullahi, 74
Anti-Terrorism and Effective Death Penalty Act, 19, 130, 193–94, 198
Apartheid, 22, 264–68, 355, 386, 400
Arava desert, 342
Archimedes, 192
Arévalo, Juana Martinez, 123–28, 134
Argentina, 314, 316–17, 320–21, 359, 365, 368
Armistice boundary (1949 Green Line), 79, 81, 82, 85, 86
Ashanti, 57
Association for Civil Rights, 21, 388
Association of Katsir, 293
Association of Salvadorans in Los Angeles (ASOSAL), 121–23
Asylum, 120, 122, 124–28, 133. *See also* Immigration
Atlantic Breeze Hotel, 50
Atomization, 300
Authoritarianism, 8, 222

Baez, Joan, 360
Baka el Garbiya, 292–94
Barak, Aharon, 294, 343
Bar Association of the City of New York, 357

Bar Council, 154
Barristers, 146–47, 152–53
Beck, Ulrich, 212, 289, 300
Bedouins, 110, 256, 392–93, 403 n.17
Bell, Peter, 363
Benvenuto, Jaime, 312
Bernstein, Robert, 365, 376 n.27
BIA (Board of Immigration Appeals), 131
Biculturalism, 136
Bifocal organizations, 24
Bilionis, Louis, 194–95, 206 n.10
Bill of Rights, in South Africa, 276, 278
Bindman, Geoffrey, 151, 153, 167–68, 179 n.50
Bindman and Partners, 148–49, 151–53, 168
Binswanger, Hans, 274
Bird, Kai, 361
Birnberg, Benedict, 165
Blackmun, Harry, 191–94
Block contracting, 168
Bloom, Anne, 17, 96–116, 145–46, 148
Boateng, Paul, 161, 162
Boon, Andrew, 18–20, 143–85, 397
Bosnia, 91
Botchwey, Kwesi, 46–47
Boulos, Jawad, 88
Bourdieu, Pierre, 187, 355
Brazil, 308, 318–20, 326, 359, 362, 368–70
Brazilian Landless Peasant Movement, 308
Bretton Woods institutions, 274
Britain, 40–51, 59. *See also* United Kingdom
British Aerospace, 162–63
Buckley, William, 360
Budlender, Geoff, 272, 279–80
Buergenthal, Thomas, 362
Bundy, MacGeorge, 360–61
Burkhalter, Holly, 87
Bush, George Herbert Walker, 161, 215
Business in the Community (organization), 162
Butler, Richard, 171

Cab rank rule, 152–54
Callins v. Collins, 191, 194
CALS (Centre for Applied Legal Studies), 272
Calvert Cliffs case, 339, 343
Canada, 272–73
Capacity, crisis of, 187–88

Cape Coast, 38, 39–40
Cape Town, 267
Capital, symbolic, 187, 189, 193, 201, 204–5
Capitalism, 5–10, 12, 37; authoritarian, 8; and cause lawyering in the United Kingdom, 143–44, 150, 155–56; corporate, 5–7, 9–10, 14; turbo, 6–7, 9
Capital punishment, 19–20, 185–210, 395; moratorium on, 190–91, 194–204, 390; and neoliberalism, 19–20, 188, 190–91, 204; politics of, from legality to efficacy in, 190–94; and symbolic capital, 187, 189, 193, 201, 204–5; in the United Kingdom, 171–72
Capozzi, David, 240 n.3
CARECEN (Central American Resource Center), 120–23
Carmel Beach Towers, 345–47, 350
Carmichael, William, 363
Carrió, Alejandro, 313
Cash-and-carry systems, 43–44, 45
Castro, Fidel, 389
Catholic Action for Street Children, 66 n.3
Catholic Church, 66 n.3, 358–59
Cause(s): case and, conflict between, 321–22; notion of, 68. *See also* Cause lawyering
Cause lawyering: and the Americans with Disabilities Act, 20–21, 211–43, 388; and capital punishment, 19–20, 185–210; and the cause-lawyer label, 59–60; Congress as a forum for, 211–43; conventional lawyers and, distinction between, 13, 68; egalitarian democratic, correlates of, 394–96; forms and limits of, explaining, 391–399; and Ghana, 15–16, 21, 35–67; and immigration, 117–39; and Israel/Palestine, 16–18, 21–24, 68–95, 244–65; and land claims advocacy, 21–22, 264–86; in Latin America, 23–25; legislative, 20–21, 211–43; liberal democratic, correlates of, 397–99; networks, transnational, 23–24, 307–33; new political economy of, 165–75; as occurring on the margins of the law, 119–22; and personal injury litigation, 96–116; politics of, 107–9; possibilities of, 3–34; and the rights of foreign workers, 17, 96–116; sites of, 148–49; strategic questions confronting, 384–85; subpolitics as a locus for, 22, 289, 300–301

CCD (Consortium of Citizens with Disabilities), 221–24, 226–35
CED (community economic development), 299
Center for Disease Control, 232
Center for Justice in International Law, 321
Center for Rights and Society, 313, 319
Center for the Study of Law and Society, 315
Central Europe, 8
Change-oriented lawyers, 308
Chapman, Vicki, 149–50, 163–64
Charlas, 128–32
Charter of Rights, 273
Chaskalson, Arthur, 265
Chaskalson, Matthew, 276
Chavez, Roberto, 97
Cheah, Pheng, 27 n.11, 28 n.14
Childbirth, 37, 45
Child Poverty Action Group, 150
Children's rights, 307
Chile, 312–14, 317–19, 321, 324, 354–81
Chilean Bar Association, 319
China, 400
Chinski, Sara, 107, 110, 115, 322
Christiansen, Robert, 274, 275
CIA (Central Intelligence Agency), 361
CIDES (Center for Rights and Society), 313, 319
Civic professionalism, 204, 258
Civil rights, 246–47, 251; and the Americans with Disabilities Act, 215, 220–22; and environmental cause lawyering, in Israel, 340; movement, in the United States, 214, 220–22, 360, 365. *See also* Civil Rights Act
Civil Rights Act, 220, 232, 240 n.52
Claassens, Aninka, 272
Clients, redefinition of, 214–15, 217, 223–24, 227–31
Clifford Chance and Collyer-Bristow (firm), 171
Clinton, Bill, 50, 132, 206 n.2, 371
CLOs (Cause Lawyering Organizations), 334–41, 345, 349–50
Codesa, 272, 273
CODEUCA (Commission for Human Rights in Central America), 312, 315, 320
Cohen, Haim, 84–85

Cohen, Stanley, 69
Cold War, 25, 72, 356, 360–66, 371–72
Collective action frame, 336–37, 339
Colonialism, 12, 39–41, 53, 72, 81
Columbia, 312–13, 316, 327
Committee for the Protection of Natural Resources, 316
Communism, 81, 396
Communitarians, 288
Community Legal Service, 159, 163, 165, 173
Community Mothers, 327
Conditional fees, 165–67, 177 n.16
Conference on International Human Rights, 27 n.12
Congress (United States), 190, 203; ADA (Americans with Disabilities Act), 20–21, 211–43, 388; Anti-Terrorism and Effective Death Penalty Act, 19, 130, 193–94, 198; Civil Rights Act, 220, 232; Freedom of Information Act, 121; IIRIRA (Illegal Immigration Reform and Immigrant Responsibility Act), 133, 136, 137 n.3, 138 n.14; Individuals with Disabilities Educational Act, 237; members of, relationships with, 231–35
Congress on Racial Equality, 361
Consensus, politics of, 337
Conservative Party (Britain), 156–58, 173
Constitution (Germany), 278
Constitution (South Africa), 264–86
Constitution (United States), 191–92, 194
Constitutional Committee (ANC), 269–70, 271
Constitutional Court, 265–66
Constitutional Principle II (CPII), 279
Consumer Association, 157
Consumer law, 307, 314
Conveyancing, 157
Cooper, Lee, 203
Co-optation, 235–37
Copelon, Rhonda, 74
Cosmopolitanism, 163, 177 n.24
Costa Rica, 17, 96–116, 312, 315, 320, 392
Council of Europe, 362
Courtis, Christian, 318
Courts and Legal Services Act, 157
Coutin, Susan B., 18, 117–39
Cover, Robert, 207 n.11
Cox, Sebastian, 319, 321

Criminal Defence Service, 159–60
Crisis-oriented contacts, 313–14
Cross, Catherine, 272
Cuba, 389
Currency, 48

Davis, Uri, 293–90
Day, Martin, 153
DBCP (dibromochoropropane), 97–98
Death penalty, 19–20, 185–210, 395; moratorium on, 190–91, 194–204, 390; politics of, from legality to efficacy in, 190–94; and neoliberalism, 19–20, 188, 190–91, 204; and symbolic capital, 187, 189, 193, 201, 204–5; in the United Kingdom, 171–72
Death Penalty Post-Conviction Center, 195
Debt, foreign, 43, 50
Decency, standards of, 192
Decentralization, 44
Declaration of Principles, 89
Decolonization, 72
Deference, politics of, 337
De Klerk, F. W., 268–69, 272–74
Democratization, 4–10, 25, 71, 399–401; and cause lawyering, mutually constitutive relationship between, 25; Congress as a symbol of, 212; as a contested concept, 9; and crises of legitimacy, 112–13; expectations of entitlements under, 18; and the forms and limits of cause lawyering, 391, 394–99; and Ghana, 50–51, 62; and Israel/Palestine, 267, 269, 271; and land claims advocacy, 267, 269, 271; and Latin America, 309, 313, 323, 329–30; minimalist, 394; and Reagan, 368; restricted visions of, 9–10; Scheingold on, 382–405; third-wave, 8; and the United Kingdom, 143–44, 173; and the universalistic language of human rights, 12
Department of Land Affairs, 268
Deportation, 123, 125–27, 135–36. *See also* Immigration
Dezalay, Yves, 15, 35, 315, 316
Diasporas, 117
Dibb Lupton Alsop, 172
Diego Portables University, 312, 324
Disability rights, 20–21, 211–43, 388, 390

Disney, 54
Doggett, Lloyd, 99–100, 103, 108, 113
Dolny, Helena, 268
Donnelly, Jack, 73
Dotan, Yoav, 21, 244–65
Dow Chemical Company and Shell Oil Company v. Domingo Castro Alfaro et al., 96–116
Drinan, Robert, 361
Du Bois, W. E. B., 40
Due Process, 19, 78, 192, 193, 205
Dumm, Thomas, 206 n.6
Dutch colonialism, 39–41

Eastern Europe, 8
East Timor, 91
EC (European Community), 173
Eco-Advocate, 348–49
Economic Recovery Programme, 41
Ecuador, 313, 316, 319
Education, 122, 126, 321; in Ghana, 43–45, 63; in Israel/Palestine, 258, 301; in the United Kingdom, 158
Effectiveness, crises of, 188
Egalitarianism, 9, 25, 400
EIS regulations, 342–43
E-LAW (Environmental Law Alliance Worldwide), 344
El Beit, 290–91, 293
Elections, participation in, 9, 122. *See also* Democratization
Elite lawyers, 144
El Rescate, 120–23
El Salvador, 18, 118–139
Emergency laws, 84
Emerging Africa initiative, 45–46, 53
Empowerment, 12, 37; and land segregation, 288, 296, 297; postmodern conceptions of, 23
England, 18, 146–48, 152, 168–69, 354. *See also* United Kingdom
Entrepreneurs, 51, 58
Environmental Defense Fund, 316
Environmental issues, 49, 53; in Israel/Palestine, 334–53, 398–99; and in Latin America, 307, 310, 314–16, 318, 328; in the United States, 339
Epistemic communities, 311–12
Equal protection, 192, 205
Esquivel, Adolfo Pérez, 320, 323

Ethics, 217–20, 297, 386. *See also* Morality
European Court of Human Rights, 171, 362
Ex-parte mode, 217

Factory Offices, and Shops Act, 49
Fahum, Walid, 82
Falk, Richard, 73
Famine, 41
Farm workers, 17, 96–116
Federation of Independent Advice Centres, 154
Feldblum, Chai, 211, 223, 239 n.19
FIDA (Federacion Internacional de Abogadas), 55–57, 59, 63
Fitzpatrick, Peter, 395
FMLN, 120
Ford Foundation, 314, 338, 360–64, 370–71
Foreign: debt, 43, 50; workers, rights of, 17, 96–116
Foreign Policy Establishment, 360
FORJA (Institute for Juridical Formation), 319, 321
Forum non conveniens, doctrine of, 98–100, 102–6
Foucault, Michel, 189
Foundation for the Environment and Natural Resources in Argentina, 316
Fourth Geneva Convention, 76–77, 83, 86, 91
Franchising, 168
Fraser, Donald, 361
Freedom Charter, 268
Freedom of Information Act, 121
Free Representation Unit, 168
Free-trade zones, 47–48, 51–55. *See also* Trade
Free Zone Act, 47–48, 52
Friends of the Earth, 316
FRU (Free Representation Unit), 148
Fundamentalism, 158
Fundo Publico, 313
Furman v. Georgia, 191, 192, 204

Gacey, John, 191
GAJOP (Legal Assistance Group for Popular Organization), 312, 315
Galli, Beatriz, 321
Garces, Juan, 69
Gardner, James, 375 n.21
Garreton, Roberto, 370

Garth, Bryant G., 15, 24–25, 35, 315–16, 354–81, 396
Garzón, Balthusar, 69
Gaza, 69–70, 75–76, 79–83, 85, 235–65
Gaza Bar Association, 90
Gaza Center for Rights and Law, 85, 91
GDP (gross domestic product), 42, 63
Gehry, Frank, 51
Gender, 36–38, 63–65. *See also* Women's rights
Germany, 90, 271, 278
Ghana, 15–16, 21, 35–67, 397–98; Economic Recovery Programme in, 41; Great Decline in, 41–42, 45, 48–49; and Nkrumah, 39, 40–41, 44, 48, 50–51, 62; short vignettes of, 38–57
Ghanaian Customs Service, 48
Ghanaian Trade Union Congress, 52
Ghana School of Law, 50, 52, 57, 58
Globalization: and the blurring of institutional lines, 256–68; counterhegomonic potential of, 64; and democratization, Scheingold on, 382–405; and environmental cause lawyering, 335, 341–42, and Ghana, 15–16, 21, 35–67; and immigration, 117–39; and Israel/Palestine, 16–18, 21–24, 68–95, 244–68, 335, 341–42; and land claims advocacy, 264–86; and Latin America, 309–33; and the market for legal services, 155–60; which occurs "below" the state, 118; and personal injury litigation, 96–116; and the possibilities of cause lawyering, 3–34; and the United Kingdom, 143–85
Glorious Revolution, 156
Goldberg, Arthur, 365
Gold Coast, 40–41
Gonzalez, Felipe, 324
Great Decline, in Ghana, 41–42, 45, 48–49
Green Line (1949 armistice boundary), 79, 81, 82, 85, 86
Greenpeace, 316, 344
Gregg v. Georgia, 191
GSS (General Security Services), 86
Guatemala, 120, 129

Habeas corpus, 19, 194
Hadera, 294–96
Haifa Chemicals, 344, 345, 347
Haifa District Court, 342

Hajjar, Lisa, 16–17, 68–95, 249, 398
Halliday, Terrence C., 3, 172–73, 187–88, 204, 315, 319, 335
Handler, Joel F., 213, 339
Hanoi, 41
Harris, Robert Alton, 188–89
Harvard Magazine, 52
Harvard University, 46–47
Hass, Peter M., 311
HCJ (Israeli High Court of Justice), 245–46, 250–54, 257
HCJD (Israeli High Court of Justice Department), 246–52, 257
Health care: in Ghana, 37, 42–49, 53, 59, 63; in Israel/Palestine, 301
Hebrew University, 80
Hegemony, 11, 74; counter-, of globalization, 64; of foreign capital, 60; and the notion of cause, 68
Held, David, 50
Helsinki Accords, 365–66, 377 n.29
Heritage Foundation, 364, 375 n.23
Herrera v. Collins, 195
Heshin, Justice, 343
Hiltermann, Joost, 85
HIV, 44, 53, 229–32
Hobson's choice, 25
Hope for Africa Bill, 49–50
House of Lords, 160, 164
Hoyer, Steny, 211, 225, 234
Humanism, 192
Human rights: "brain drain," 368–71; discourse, creation of, in the decades following World War II, 72; global language of, 11–12, 244–65; investing in, as an alternative political strategy, 354–81; norms, and the possibilities for advocacy, 14; as one of the most prominent and common causes, 69; transformation of, into an international movement, 11, 69
Human Rights Act, 173
Human Rights Watch, 87, 363–68
Humphrey, Hubert, 361

ICESCR (International Covenant on Economic, Social and Cultural Rights), 327, 327
ICJ (International Commission of Jurists), 84, 85, 359, 361, 362
Ideology, 250, 253, 257, 287; of advocacy, 386; and capital punishment, 187; and the forms and limits of cause lawyering, 391; of public service, 163
IDF (Israel Defense Forces), 79, 81, 247, 249
IIRIRA (Illegal Immigration Reform and Immigrant Responsibility Act), 133, 136, 137 n.3, 138 n.14
Illegal aliens, 118–39
ILO (International Labor Organization), 52, 54, 327
ILSA (Latin American Institute for Alternative Law), 312, 314–15, 317, 319–20, 327
Immigration, 117–39, 258, 387; categories, deconstruction of, 130; and charlas, 128–32; and political advocacy, 132–35
Imperialism: cultural, 11; retro-, 53
Import quotas, 53. *See also* Trade
Indian Claims Commission, 285 n.13
Indigenous persons, rights of, 285 n.13, 307
Individual(s): notions of, broad acceptance of, 11; state paradigms, 20. *See also* Individualization
Individualization, 161, 192, 300–301. *See also* Individuals
Individuals with Disabilities Educational Act, 237
Industrialization, 55
Inflation, 62, 156
INS (U.S. Immigration and Naturalization Service), 121, 122, 131–33, 135, 138 n.7
Institute for International Development (Harvard University), 46–47
Instrumentalism, 151
Inter-American Commission on Human Rights, 316, 354, 370
Inter-American Foundation, 363
International Covenant on Economic, Social and Cultural Rights, 317
International Human Rights Law Group, 363
Internationalism, 81
International Monetary Fund (IMF), 5, 15, 41–42, 49, 61
Intifada (Palestinian uprising), 86–89, 246–47
Ireland, 146–47, 150
Iron Fist, 86
Israel, 16–18, 21–24, 68–95, 289–304, 398–400; Carmel Beach Towers case in, 345–47, 350; environmental cause lawyering in, 24, 334–53; and the Green Line, 79,

81, 82, 85, 86; High Court of, 80, 84, 92; and the Katsir case, 22–23, 289–98, 300–301; patterns of cooperation between state and civil rights lawyers in, 244–65; Supreme Court of, 245, 256–57, 296–97, 298, 301–2, 341, 343–44, 346; Trans-Israel Highway case, 342–48
Israeli-Palestinian Declaration of Principles, 71
Israel Land Authority, 294
IUED (Israel Union for Environmental Defense), 24, 336, 337–50

Jabarin, Taufiq, 292–97
Jackson, Jesse, Jr., 50
Jamaica Council for Human Rights, 170
Japan, 160, 399
Javaid, Makbool, 172
Jewish Agency, 292–93, 294, 297, 302
Jews, 21, 23, 78–83. *See also* Israel; Jewish Agency
Judicial Committee of the Privy Council, 169
Justice Department, 135

Kaadan, Adel, 292–302
Kaadan, Iman, 292–94, 298–302
Karpik, Lucien, 315, 319, 335
Kasena Nankana district (Ghana), 42–43, 45
Katsir, 22–23, 289–98, 300–301
Keck, Margaret E., 23, 163–64, 309–11, 325–28, 335, 363
Kempton Park, 276
Kennedy, Edward, 225, 232
Kenya, 172
Khan, Imran, 153–54, 172, 275
Khor, Martin, 274
Kirkpatrick, Jeane, 365
Kishon River, 344
Klug, Heinz, 21–22, 264–86
Kosovo, 91
Kumasai, battle of, 40
Kuttab, Jonathan, 84, 90

Labor: law, 48–49, 54, 307; unions, 52–53, 287
Labour Court, 265
Labour Party, 158, 161, 175
LAG (Legal Action Group), 149, 154–55, 163–64, 165
Laissez-faire policy, 7, 43

Land: claims advocacy, in South Africa, 21–22, 264–86, 298, 393; segregation, in Israel/Palestine, 22–23, 287–304, 388, 395
Land Acts, 271
Land Affairs, 265
Landau, Moshe, 80, 86–87
Landau Commission, 86–87
Land Claims Court, 277
Land Commission (African National Congress), 268–69, 270–75
Land Manifesto, 270
Langer, Felicia, 78–81, 90
Language, of human rights, 11–12, 244–65
LAPC (Land and Agricultural Policy Centre), 274
Latin America, 23–25, 47, 307–33. *See also specific countries*
Latin American Future, 316
Law Centre Federation, 154
Law and Development movement, 314
Law and order rhetoric, 19, 188
Law Society, 153–54, 157, 164, 168–69, 173
Lawrence Inquiry, 153–54
Lawyer, The, 153
Lawyers Committee for Human Rights, 363
Legal Resources Centre, 265, 267, 279
Legislative cause lawyering, 20–21, 211–43
Legitimacy, 118, 290, 309, 330; and the Americans with Disabilities Act, 235–37; of Amnesty International, 360; and capital punishment, 187–91, 203; crises of, 112–13, 187–88, 203; gaining, through the exchange of power for law, 355; and personal injury litigation, 112–13; of property rights, 271
Leigh Day and Company, 148–49, 150–51, 153, 166
Leninism, 8
Liberal humanism, 192
Liberalism: advanced, 9; and capital punishment, 197; and environmental cause lawyering, 335; procedural, 322; social rights, 323
Liberty and Justice (organization), 154
Liberty Pro Bono Panel, 169–71
Life expectancy, 46
London, 144, 153. *See also* United Kingdom
London Panel, 170, 172
Lonely Planet, 40–42
Long, Soraya, 320
Loyalty, decline of, 6–7

LSM (Law in the Service of Man/Al-Haq), 83–85, 87, 398
Luttwak, Edward, 6, 26 n.4
Lynch, Dennis, 319

MacArthur Foundation, 359
McCann, Michael, 322–23, 336, 352
McCloy, John, 373 n.11
McVeigh, Timothy, 191
Mahamid, Fat'hi, 293–98, 300–301
Malaysia, 274
Mandela, Nelson, 90, 265, 277, 279
Mandela Institute for Political Prisoners, 90
Manhattan Institute, 401 n.1
Mansfield, Michael, 153–54, 176 n.10
Manufacturing sector, 6, 50, 54–55
Marginalization, 167–68, 272, 394
Martinez, Maria Elba, 314
Marx, Karl, 8, 40
Marxist-Leninism, 8
Materialism, 161
Matzpen, 81
Mauritius, 47, 52–53
Mbabane, 274
Mediterranean Sea, 344
Meili, Stephen, 23–25, 307–33, 390, 394, 396
Mendoza v. Contico, 104
Menkel-Meadow, Carrie, 326–27, 391
Mexican-American Legal Defense and Education Fund, 361
Mexican Center for Environmental Rights, 316
Mexican Center for Human Rights, 311–21
Mexican Foundation for Environmental Education, 316
Mexican Foundation for Environmental Protection, 316
Mexico, 54, 104, 311–21, 326, 359, 368
Michalowski, Raymond, 389
Middein, Freih Abu, 90
Middle class, politics, subpolitics as, 300–301
Migration, 18, 118–39
Ministry of Trade and Industry, 52
Mitchell, Irwin, 150, 151, 166
Modderdam settlement, 267
Model Rules, 219–20, 223–24
Morag-Levine, Noga, 24, 334–53

Morality, 14, 25, 369; and the Americans with Disabilities Act, 216–20; and cause lawyering in the United Kingdom, 151; role, 216–20. *See also* Ethics
Mortality rates, 42, 46, 63
Muhassen, Sabri, 296

NAACP (National Association for the Advancement of Colored People), 334, 361
NACARA (Nicaraguan Adjustment and Central American Relief Act), 133, 136
NAFTA (North American Free Trade Area), 5, 117
Nathan Cummings Foundation, 338, 351 n.15
National Association of Democratic Lawyers, 266
National Conference on Affirmative Action, 271
National Conference on Land Policy, 279
National Consumer Council, 154
National Council on the Handicapped, 225
National Environmental Protection Act (NEPA), 342, 343
National Federation of Independent Businesses, 233
Nationalism: and Ghana, 51; and Israel/Palestine, 16, 82, 86, 88
National Lawyers Guild, 111
National Organization on Disability, 237
National Party, 277
National Plan for Coastlines, 346
National Wildlife Federation, 316
Nation-states, 3, 23. *See also* State
Naturalization, 122
Navarro, Oscar, 123–28, 132
Neier, Aryeh, 365, 367, 376 n.35
Nelson, Rosmary, 176 n.9
Neocolonialism, 7
Neoimperialism, 7
Neoliberalism, 6–9, 397, 399; and capital punishment, 19–20, 188, 190–91, 204; and globalization, 14–15; and the new international economic order, 18–19
NEPA (National Environmental Protection Act), 342, 343
Network of NGOs for Environmental Rights, 316
Neutrality: and cause lawyering in the United Kingdom, 147, 149–50, 152–54;

and political action, 149–50; and
transgressiveness, 152–54
New Deal, 390
New Israel Fund, 338, 340
Newman, Frank, 362
New York Times, The, 358–59, 367
Nixon, Richard M., 361, 362
Njobe, Bongiwe, 268
Nkrumah, Kwame, 39–41, 44, 48, 50–51, 62
Nonaccountability, 216–20
Normative sphere, 160–64
NRDC (Natural Resource Defense Council), 336

Occupied Territories, 235–65. *See also* Israel
Occupier's Law (Shehadeh), 85
Open-door trade policy, 58. *See also* Trade
Opoku-Agyemang, Kwado, 38–39
O'Quinn, John, 102–3
Orchard, Steve, 167
Organization of American States, 359
Oslo Accords, 17
Other, concept of, 385
Oxfam International, 316

PA (Palestinian Authority), 71, 89–92
Pacific Legal Foundation, 401 n.1
"Palace wars," 25
Palestine Center for Human Rights (PHCR), 91
Palestine Liberation Organization, 82, 86, 88–89
Palestinian(s), 16–17, 21, 68–95, 244–65, 398, 400; and the Palestinian National Movement, 79; uprising of (*Intifada*), 86–89, 246–47. *See also* Israel
Paradigms, 215, 271
Partisanship, 216–20
PCHR (Palestine Center for Human Rights), 91
Peace Committee, 358–59, 373 n.5
Peace Now, 302 n.4
Personal injury litigation, 19, 96–116; aftermath of, 103–4; in the United Kingdom, 149–51; and *forum non conveniens*, doctrine of, 98–100, 102–3, 105–6; and legislative reversals, 101–3; and the politics of cause lawyering, 107–9; in the United Kingdom, 149–51

Peru, 314, 316–17
Peruvian Society for Environmental Rights, 316
Pesticides, 17, 96–116
Pinochet, Augusto, 69, 73, 91, 152, 354, 358, 362, 365, 368–70
Piovesan, Flavia, 320
PLO (Palestine Liberation Organization), 82, 86, 88–89
Pluralism, 7, 24, 25; in Ghana, 51; in Israel, 335, 337, 350
Poder Ciudadano, 370
Poetry, 38–39
Portugal, 40
Posner, Michael, 27 n.27, 367
Possible, imagination of the, 12
Post-Conviction Defender Organizations, 198
Postmodernism, 61, 288
Poverty law, 318
Pragmatism, 35
Pressburger, Miguel, 313
Proceduralism, 158
Property rights, 21–22, 264–86
Psychological person, notion of, 288
Public Committee Against Torture, 87
Public Fund, 316
Putnam, Robert, 50

Rabbani, Mouin, 84
Racism: and capital punishment, 188, 196; in the United Kingdom, 172. *See also* African Americans
Random House, 365
Rationalization, 193
Rawlings, Jerry, 41–42
Reagan, Ronald, 156, 364–68, 371
Refugees, and immigration, 118–39
Rehabilitation Act, 233
Rehnquist, William, 189, 195
Restitution of Land Claims Act, 277
Retributivism, 188
Revisionism, 193
Riego, Chrstian, 312, 315, 317–19
Rio Frio, 97
Rodriguez-Olivera v. Salant Corporation, 104
Romera, Amanda, 312–13, 320–21, 327
Rose, Nikolas, 6
Rosenberg, Gerald, 336
RRP (Rural Restructuring Program), 275

Rueschemeyer, Dietrich, 8–9
Rule of law, 4, 8, 322–25, 327, 386–87; and the forms and limits of cause lawyering, 396; in Ghana, 55–56; institutions, strengthening of, 26; and Israel/Palestine, 21, 78–80, 84, 252–53, 400
Rule of Law in the Territories Adminstered by Israel, The (Shehadeh and Kuttab), 84–85
Russell, David, 267
Rwanda, 73

Sachs, Albie, 273
Sachs, Jeffrey, 46–47
Santos, Boaventura de Sousa, 64, 163
Sarat, Austin, 3–34, 186–210, 385–86, 389–90, 395
Sassen, Saskia, 36
Sayyad, Ahmed, 90
Scenic Hudson case, 339
Scheingold, Stuart, 3–34, 145–46, 147, 148, 382–405
Scotland, 146–47
Self-determination, 75–77
SERPAL (Latin American Peace and Justice Service), 315, 320–21
Shamir, Ronen, 10, 22–23, 107, 110, 115, 287–304, 322, 387–88, 393–94
Shehadeh, Raja, 84, 89, 90
Shell Oil Company, 96–97. *See also Dow Chemical Company and Shell Oil Company v. Domingo Castro Alfaro et al.*
Siegel, Charles, 105–7
Sikkink, Kathryn, 23, 163–64, 309–11, 325–28, 335, 363
Silbey, Susan, 5
Simons, Bernard, 169
Simons Muirhead and Burton, 169
Singapore, 46, 54
SLAPP (Strategic Lawsuits Against Public Participation), 346
Slavery, 38–39, 45–46
Smith, Roger, 164
SMOs (Social Movement Organizations), 334
Socialism, 51, 358
Sociological person, notion of, 288
Solicitors, 146–47, 169
Solicitors' Pro Bono Group, 169
Sourani, Raji, 85

South Africa, 18, 21–22, 264–86, 386, 398–99; ANC (African National Congress), 264–76, 390, 398; and banking institutions, 274–75; Women's Budget Initiative in, 65
South African Agricultural Union, 277–78
South African Law Commission, 270
Southern Christian Leadership Conference, 361
Southwest Council of La Raza, 361
Sovereignty, 16, 75–76
Soyinka, Wole, 45, 38
Spain, 354
SPNI (Society for the Protection of Nature), 338
Sri Lanka, 400
Standard Fruit Company, 98
State: boundaries of, 155–56, 215; and cause lawyering in the United Kingdom, 155–56, 172–73; decentering, 299–300; distance from, 389–91; as an ensemble of trust strategies, 173; ideal liberal, conceptions of, 322–25; investments in symbolic capital, 187; proximity to, 389–91; transformation, and human rights, 10, 11–12
Sterrett, Susan, 397
Subjectivity, reconstruction of, 6
Subpolitics, as a locus for cause lawyering, 22, 289, 300–301
Swaziland, 274
Symbolic capital, 187, 189, 193, 201, 204–5

Tal, Alon, 338, 340, 347–49
Tanzania, 172
Tariffs, 58
Taxation: and the boundaries of the state, 156; in Ghana, 43, 48, 53, 55, 58; in South Africa, 271; and turbo-capitalism, 6; in the United Kingdom, 156, 158
Team, use of the term, 224–25
Technology transfer, 54, 55
Terrorism, 69, 78–80, 88, 91–92
Texas, 17, 96–116
Texas Trial Lawyers Association (TTLA), 102, 104
Thatcher, Margaret, 18, 19, 156, 173, 394, 397
Theme Committee, 278
Third-World Network, 274
Thomson, Alan, 390

Tocqueville, Alexis de, 288
Torture, 87, 92
Trade: free, 47–48, 51–55; and Ghana, 42, 47–49, 51, 58; and immigration, 117; incentives, 48, 49; liberalization, 42, 47–48
Transgressiveness, 145–46, 148–49, 151–54
Trans-Israel Highway, 342–48
Trans Resources, Inc., 344
Trinidad, 170
Trotskyists, 81
Trust strategies, the state as an ensemble of, 173
Truth, speaking, to power, 271
Truth and Reconciliation Commission, 265
Tsemel, Leah, 80–81, 87, 90
Tunisia, 86

Ulster, 150
Um-El-Fahem, 289
Underdevelopment, 63–64
Unemployment, 156
United Kingdom, 18, 143–85, 397. *See also specific countries*
United Nations: Charter, 362; Committee on Human Rights, 315–16; Decade of Women, 72; Development Program (UNDP), 42–44, 46; and Zaire, 370
United States Information Agency (USIA), 57
Universal Declaration of Human Rights, 289, 326, 361–62
Universalism, 72, 81
University of Buenos Aires, 318
University of California at Berkeley, 362
University of Diego Portales, 370
University of Natal, 266
Urban Foundation, 273–74
Urban League, 361

Vicariate for Solidarity, 356, 358, 361–64, 370, 371
Vienna Conference on Human Rights, 11
Vietnam War, 360, 361, 365
Viva Rio, 369–70
Vivenco, Jose, 370

Voice of America, 342, 351 n.9
Voter registration, 122

Wales, 146–48, 152, 168–69. *See also* United Kingdom
Wallace, George, 188
War crimes, 73
War on Poverty, 360
Washington Office on Latin America, 316
Wealth tax, 271. *See also* Taxation
Welfare state, 6, 9; in the United Kingdom, 156–58; in the United States, 364–65
West Bank, 69–70, 75–84, 235–65
West Bank and the Rule of Law, The (Shehadeh and Kuttab), 84
White, Lucie, 15–16, 35–67
Wilson, Richard, 11
With My Own Eyes (Langer), 78–80
Women's Budget Initiative, 65
Women's rights, 15–16, 35–67, 307, 314
Workers rights, 17, 19, 96–116; aftermath of, 103–4; in the United Kingdom, 149–51; and *forum non conveniens*, doctrine of, 98–100, 102–3, 105–6; and legislative reversals, 101–3; and the politics of cause lawyering, 107–9; in the United Kingdom, 149–51
World Bank, 5, 22, 42, 61, 274–75, 278, 360
World Trade Center, 276, 286 n.21
World Trade Organization, 5
World War II, 72, 74, 147, 156, 396; expansion of the welfare budget after, 156; wealth tax adopted after, 271
Wright, P., 223

Yarkon River, 348
Yediot Aharonot, 345
YMCA, 131
Yugoslavia, 73

Zaire, 370
Zalaquett, Jose, 358, 359, 370
Zambia, 268
Zionism, 289, 338
Ziv, Neta, 20–23, 211–43, 287–304, 387–90
Zurich Financial Services, 163

www.ingramcontent.com/pod-product-compliance
Ingram Content Group UK Ltd.
Pitfield, Milton Keynes, MK11 3LW, UK
UKHW041952230426
12048UKWH00008B/283